q 95
44

Inset map (Jerusalem region):

Ai
Aiath
Michmash
Beeroth (Berea)
Bethel
Geba
Ramah
Azmaveth
Anathoth
Adasa
Hazor
Mizpah
Capharsalama
Gibeon
Chephirah
Meronoth
Kiriath-jearim
Elasa
Jerusalem
Ananiah

10 Miles
10 Kilometres

**Main map labels:**

AMMON

Philadelphia (Rabbah)
(Araq el-Emir)
Jazer
Gadara
Heshbon
Samaga
Medeba
Libba
Dabaloth
Machaerus
R. Arnon
(Araq el-Emir)

NABATAEANS

MOAB

Jericho
Doka
Senaah
Beth-giglal (Gilgal)
Khirbet Qumran
'Ain Feshkha

Lake Asphalt-itis (Dead Sea)

RIVER
Alexandrium
(Abu Dudu)

Shiloh
Tephon (Tappuah)
Rathamin (Ramathaim)
Timnath
Neballat
Hadid
Lod (Lydda)
Modein
Gath (Gittaim)
Beth-horon
Gazara (Gezer)
Kiriath-jearim
Emmaus
Beerzeth (Berzetho)
Baal-hazor
Bethel
Geba
Cophna
Beeroth
Mizpah
Gibeon
Anathoth

JUDAH (JUDEA)

Jerusalem
Beth-haccherem
Netophah
Beth-basi
Tekoa
Engedi
Masada

Bethlehem
Beth-zechariah
Adullam
Beth-zaith
Nebo
Beth-zur
Hebron (Kiriath-arba)

Zorah
Zanoah
Jarmuth
Azekah
Harim
Keilah
Elam
Adoraim

Ekron
Marisa
Lachish
Eglon
Gerar
Ziklag
En-rimmon
Hormah

Kedron
Jamnia (Jabneel)
Ashdod (Azotus)
Ashkelon (Ascalon)
Gaza
Anthedon
Raphia

IDUMEA

Jektabzeel
Moladah
Beer-sheba
Jeshua
Hazar-shual

LAND OF THE PHILISTINES

Aphek (Peqai)
Ono
Joppa

32°
36° 30'
36°
35° 30'
35°
34° 30'
31° 30'
31°

5
6
7
V
W
X
Y

THE APOCRYPHA

EXPANDED EDITION

REVISED STANDARD VERSION

Daniel R. OTTESON

THE OXFORD ANNOTATED APOCRYPHA

THE
APOCRYPHA

OF THE OLD TESTAMENT
REVISED STANDARD VERSION

EXPANDED EDITION CONTAINING
THE THIRD AND FOURTH BOOKS
OF THE MACCABEES AND PSALM 151

Translated from the Greek and Latin Languages
Being the Version Set Forth A.D. 1611, Revised A.D. 1894
Compared with the Most Ancient Authorities
And Revised A.D. 1957
Introductions, Comments, Cross References, Chronological Tables of Rulers, and Index

EDITED BY
BRUCE M. METZGER

NEW YORK   OXFORD UNIVERSITY PRESS
1977

TABLE OF CONTENTS

For further information concerning the history and significance of the Old Testament Apocrypha, reference may be made to Bruce M. Metzger, *An Introduction to the Apocrypha* (New York: Oxford University Press, 1957). For extensive introductions to and commentaries on apocryphal and pseudepigraphical books, the most comprehensive work in English is the two volumes edited by R. H. Charles, *The Apocrypha and Pseudepigrapha of the Old Testament* (Oxford: at the Clarendon Press, 1913).

THE EDITOR'S PREFACE

THIS ANNOTATED EDITION of the books of the Apocrypha (like THE NEW OXFORD ANNOTATED BIBLE) is intended to serve both the general reader and the student of biblical literature. Besides containing the several books or parts of books that have been customarily reckoned as the Apocrypha, or the Deuterocanonical writings (see pp. xii and xiii below), the present edition includes three other texts that are highly regarded by Eastern Orthodox Churches, namely, 3 and 4 Maccabees and Psalm 151. It supplies the following helps:

1. A general introduction presents information concerning the meanings and usage of the word "apocrypha," the types of literature represented in apocryphal books, divergent attitudes in the Christian Church toward the apocrypha, and the pervasive influence of the Apocrypha.

2. Each of the books of the Apocrypha has an introduction dealing with aspects of its composition, date, and contents.

3. Each chapter is provided with annotations which explain literary, historical, geographical, and religious matters in the text. In addition to the comments there are selected cross references to other passages of the Apocrypha and the Bible which shed light upon the verse under consideration. The words in bold-face type at the beginning of each section of the annotations serve as an outline of the subject matter.

4. The tables of rulers during the inter-testamental period provide a chronological framework for the history of the period between the Old and the New Testaments.

5. An index to the chief annotations directs attention to comments on important persons, places, and ideas in the Apocrypha.

The following persons contributed to the OXFORD ANNOTATED APOCRYPHA:

The introductions and annotations for individual books of the Apocrypha were written by Walter J. Harrelson, The Divinity School, Vanderbilt University, Nashville, Tennessee (1 Esdras); Robert C. Dentan, Emeritus, General Theological Seminary, New York City (Tobit, Judith); Floyd V. Filson, Emeritus, McCormick Theological Seminary, Chicago, Illinois (Additions to Esther, Wisdom of Solomon); Herbert G. May, Emeritus, Graduate School of Theology, Oberlin College, Oberlin, Ohio (Baruch, Letter of Jeremiah); Sherman E. Johnson, Emeritus, Church Divinity School of the Pacific, Berkeley, California (1, 2, and 4 Maccabees); and Demetrios J. Constantelos, Stockton State College, Pomona, New Jersey (3 Maccabees). The editor is responsible for the introductions and annotations for the remaining books of the Apocrypha, as well as for

[vii]

the general introduction, the chronological tables, and the chart of titles given to books associated with Ezra and Nehemiah.

It remains to be mentioned that the translation of the three additional texts included in this expanded edition of the Apocrypha (3 and 4 Maccabees and Psalm 151) was prepared by a subcommittee of the Revised Standard Version Bible Committee, comprised of Demetrios J. Constantelos, Robert A. Kraft, Sherman E. Johnson, Allen P. Wikgren, and Bruce M. Metzger, who also served as chairman of the subcommittee.

The editor expresses his gratitude to those named above, as well as to Father Eugene H. Maly, Mt. St. Mary's Seminary of the West, Norwood, Ohio, and to the late Luther A. Weigle, Sterling Professor of Religious Education and Dean of the Divinity School, Emeritus, Yale University, New Haven, Connecticut, for their willingness to read the introductions and annotations and for their judicious counsel concerning several features of this annotated edition of the Apocrypha. May its varied helps prove useful in bringing about a wider appreciation of the literature that forms a bridge between the Old and New Testaments.

Princeton Theological Seminary　　　　　　　　　　BRUCE M. METZGER
Princeton, New Jersey

PREFACE TO THE APOCRYPHA

IN RESPONSE to the request of the General Convention of the Protestant Episcopal Church, October, 1952, the Division of Christian Education of the National Council of the Churches of Christ in the U.S.A. organized a committee of scholars to undertake revision of the English translation of the Apocrypha; and its publication was authorized by the General Board, NCCCUSA, December 12, 1952. The scholars accepting this assignment were Millar Burrows, Winkley Professor of Biblical Theology, Yale University; Henry J. Cadbury, Hollis Professor of Divinity, Harvard University; Clarence T. Craig, Dean and Professor of New Testament, Drew Theological Seminary; Floyd V. Filson, Dean and Professor of New Testament Literature and History, McCormick Theological Seminary; Frederick C. Grant, Professor of Biblical Theology, Union Theological Seminary; Bruce M. Metzger, Professor of New Testament, Princeton Theological Seminary; Robert H. Pfeiffer, Hancock Professor of Hebrew and other Oriental Languages, Harvard University; Allen P. Wikgren, Professor of New Testament, University of Chicago; and Luther A. Weigle, Sterling Professor of Religious Education and Dean of the Divinity School, Emeritus, Yale University, who was appointed chairman of the Committee. A great loss was sustained in the death, August 20, 1953, of Dean Craig. In 1954, J. Carter Swaim, Professor of New Testament at Western Theological Seminary, Pittsburgh, became Executive Director, Department of the English Bible, in the Division of Christian Education, NCCCUSA, and was added to the membership of the Committee. Roy G. Ross, General Secretary of the National Council of the Churches of Christ in the U.S.A., and Paul C. Payne, Chairman, and Gerald E. Knoff, Executive Secretary, of its Division of Christian Education, have been members of the Committee ex officio.

The work has involved the preparation and circulation of mimeographed drafts of translation, the discussion and resolution of all disputed points in face-to-face conference, the circulation of new drafts embodying the decisions reached in conference, and a final review of each book in the light of written agenda proposed by the members of the Committee and of the Advisory Board made up of representatives appointed by denominations which accepted the invitation to review the drafts. This procedure is similar to that followed by the Committee which prepared the Revised Standard Version of the Bible, containing the Old and New Testaments; and, in general, similar principles of translation have been followed.

The Apocrypha here translated are those books and portions of books which appear in the Latin Vulgate, either as part of the Old Testament or as an appendix, but are not in the Hebrew Bible. With the exception of 2 Esdras these books appear in the Greek version of the Old Testament which is known as the Septuagint, but they are not included in the Hebrew Canon of Holy Scripture.

Because of their inclusion in the Latin Vulgate, the Church throughout the medieval period looked upon these books as belonging to the Scriptures, though not unaware of their lack of canonical status among the Jews. In 1546, the Council of Trent decreed that the Canon of the Old Testament includes them (except the Prayer of Manasseh and

[ix]

1 and 2 Esdras), and condemned any one who "does not accept these entire books, with all their parts, as they have customarily been read in the Catholic Church and are found in the ancient editions of the Latin Vulgate, as sacred and canonical."

In Luther's German translation of the Bible (1534) the Apocrypha stand between the Old Testament and the New Testament, with the title: "Apocrypha, that is, books which are not held equal to the sacred Scriptures, and nevertheless are useful and good to read." Coverdale's English translation of the Bible (1535) gave them the same position, with the title: "Apocrypha. The books and treatises which among the fathers of old are not reckoned to be of like authority with the other books of the Bible, neither are they found in the Canon of the Hebrew."

The Apocrypha had a place in all the sixteenth century English translations of the Bible, and in the King James Version (1611). The Thirty-nine Articles of the Church of England say concerning the Apocrypha: "And the other books (as Jerome saith) the Church doth read for example of life, and instruction of manners; but yet doth it not apply them to establish any doctrine." The Puritans opposed every use of them that would suggest that they possessed any authority; and the Westminster Confession (1648) declares: "The books commonly called Apocrypha, not being of divine inspiration, are no part of the Canon of Scripture; and therefore are of no authority in the Church of God, nor to be otherwise approved, or made use of, than other human writings."

The basic Greek text of the books of the Apocrypha from which the present translation was made is the edition of the Septuagint prepared by Alfred Rahlfs, published by the Württemberg Bible Society, Stuttgart, 1935. This text is based mainly upon the Codex Vaticanus (4th century A.D.), the Codex Sinaiticus (4th century), and the Codex Alexandrinus (5th century). For the book of Tobit the Greek text found in the codices Vaticanus and Alexandrinus was followed; and for the Additions to Daniel (namely, Susanna, the Prayer of Azariah and the Song of the Three Young Men, and Bel and the Dragon) the translators used the Greek version of Theodotion. In both these cases the Committee's procedure was in accord with general usage.

The basic text followed in the case of 2 Esdras is the Old Latin version edited by Robert L. Bensly. This was supplemented by consulting the Latin text edited by Bruno Violet, as well as the several Oriental versions of 2 Esdras, namely, the Syriac, Ethiopic, Arabic (two forms, referred to as Arabic 1 and Arabic 2), Armenian, and Georgian versions. In addition, account was taken of a few verses of the fifteenth chapter of 2 Esdras which have been preserved in Greek (Oxyrhynchus Papyrus number 1010).

In the translation of Sirach, constant reference was made to the medieval Hebrew fragments of a large part of this book, which were discovered at the end of the nineteenth century. Throughout the work of translating the books of the Apocrypha consideration was given to variant readings, including those in the *apparatus criticus* of Rahlfs as well as those in other editions of the Septuagint or of single books of the Apocrypha. Likewise, a search was made for all portions of the Apocrypha preserved in the Greek papyri from Egypt, and the text of these fragments was collated with that of Rahlfs.

The quarrels over the authority of the Apocrypha are now largely matters of the past. A generation that has witnessed the discovery of the Dead Sea Scrolls will probably agree with the statement by Professor Frank C. Porter, in Hastings' Dictionary of the Bible (1901), that "modern historical interest, on the other hand, is putting the Apocrypha in their true place as significant documents of a most important era in religious history."

—1957

INTRODUCTION TO THE APOCRYPHA

1. Meanings and usage of the word "apocrypha."
2. Kinds of literature in the Apocrypha.
3. Divergent attitudes in the Christian Church toward the Apocrypha.
4. The pervasive influence of the Apocrypha.
5. Other apocryphal and pseudepigraphical literature.

1. Meanings and usage of the word "apocrypha."

The word "apocrypha" is used in a variety of ways that can be confusing to the general reader. Confusion arises partly from the ambiguity of the ancient usage of the word, and partly from the modern application of the term to different groups of books. Etymologically the word means "things that are hidden," but why it was chosen to describe certain books is not clear. Some have suggested that the books were "hidden" or withdrawn from common use because they were deemed to contain mysterious or esoteric lore, too profound to be communicated to any except the initiated (compare 2 Esd.14.45–46). Others have suggested that the term was employed by those who held that such books deserved to be "hidden" because they were spurious or heretical. Thus it appears that in antiquity the term had an honorable significance as well as a derogatory one, depending upon the point of view of those who made use of the word.

According to traditional usage "Apocrypha" has been the designation applied to the fifteen books, or portions of books, listed below. (In many earlier editions of the Apocrypha, the Letter of Jeremiah is incorporated as the final chapter of the Book of Baruch; hence in these editions there are fourteen books.)

The First Book of Esdras
The Second Book of Esdras
Tobit
Judith
The Additions to the Book of Esther
The Wisdom of Solomon
Ecclesiasticus, or the Wisdom of Jesus the Son of Sirach
Baruch
The Letter of Jeremiah
The Prayer of Azariah and the Song of the Three Young Men
Susanna

[xi]

    Bel and the Dragon
    The Prayer of Manasseh
    The First Book of the Maccabees
    The Second Book of the Maccabees

In addition, the present expanded edition includes these three texts which are of special interest to Eastern Orthodox readers (see p. xiii):

    The Third Book of the Maccabees
    The Fourth Book of the Maccabees
    Psalm 151

None of these books is included in the Hebrew canon of holy Scripture. All of them, however, with the exception of 2 Esdras, are present in copies of the Greek version of the Old Testament known as the Septuagint. The Old Latin translations of the Old Testament, made from the Septuagint, also include them, along with 2 Esdras. As a consequence, many of the early Church Fathers quoted most of these books as authoritative Scripture (see sect. 3 below).

At the end of the fourth century Pope Damasus commissioned Jerome, the most learned biblical scholar of his day, to prepare a standard Latin version of the Scriptures (the Latin Vulgate). In the Old Testament Jerome followed the Hebrew canon and by means of prefaces called the reader's attention to the separate category of the apocryphal books. Subsequent copyists of the Latin Bible, however, were not always careful to transmit Jerome's prefaces, and during the medieval period the Western Church generally regarded these books as part of the holy Scriptures. In 1546 the Council of Trent decreed that the canon of the Old Testament includes them (except the Prayer of Manasseh and 1 and 2 Esdras). Subsequent editions of the Latin Vulgate text, officially approved by the Roman Catholic Church, contain these books incorporated within the sequence of the Old Testament books. Thus Tobit and Judith stand after Nehemiah; the Wisdom of Solomon and Ecclesiasticus stand after the Song of Solomon; Baruch (with the Letter of Jeremiah as chapter 6) stands after Lamentations; and 1 and 2 Maccabees conclude the books of the Old Testament. An appendix after the New Testament contains the Prayer of Manasseh and 1 and 2 Esdras, without implying canonical status.

Editions of the Bible prepared by Protestants have followed the Hebrew canon. The disputed books have generally been placed in a separate section, usually bound between the Old and New Testaments, but occasionally placed after the close of the New Testament.

Modern Roman Catholic scholars commonly employ a distinction introduced by Sixtus of Sienna in 1566 to designate the two groups of books. The terms "protocanonical" and "deuterocanonical" are used to signify respectively those books of Scripture that were received by the entire Church from the beginning as inspired, and those whose inspiration came to be recognized later, after the matter had been disputed by certain Fathers and local churches. Thus Roman Catholics accept as fully canonical those books and parts of books which Protestants call the Apocrypha (except the Prayer of Manasseh and 1 and 2 Esdras, which both groups regard as apocryphal). In short, as a popular Roman Catholic Catechism puts it, "*Deuterocanonical* does not mean *Apocryphal*, but simply 'later added to the canon.' "

The Eastern Orthodox Churches recognize several other books as authoritative. Editions of the Old Testament approved by the Holy Synod of the Greek Orthodox Church contain, besides the Deuterocanonical books, 1 Esdras, Psalm 151, the Prayer of Manasseh, and 3 Maccabees, while 4 Maccabees stands in an appendix. Slavonic Bibles approved by the Russian Orthodox Church contain, besides the Deuterocanonical books, 1 and 2 Esdras (called 2 and 3 Esdras), Psalm 151, and 3 Maccabees.

Besides the books that are included in the present edition, many other Jewish and Jewish-Christian works have survived from the period between about 200 B.C. to about A.D. 200. Since most of these profess to have been written by ancient worthies of Israel, who lived long before the books were actually composed, they are generally called "pseudepigrapha" (for a description of several of the more noteworthy pseudepigrapha, see sect. 5 below).

2. Kinds of literature in the Apocrypha.

The books of the Apocrypha represent several different literary genres, including the historical, novelistic, didactic, devotional, epistolary, and apocalyptic types. Though several of the books combine material belonging to more than one of these genres, most of the books can be classified as predominantly of one type or another. Thus 1 Esdras, 1 Maccabees, and, in a certain sense, 2 Maccabees belong to the genre of historical writing. Second Maccabees, which is characterized by bombastic rhetoric, fiery arguments, exaggerated numbers, and superabundant use of invectives against the enemies of Jewish orthodoxy, falls more precisely into the category, then so popular in the Hellenistic world, known as "pathetic history"—a type of literature that uses all possible means to strike the imagination and move the emotions of the reader.

Ostensibly historical but actually quite imaginative are the books of Tobit, Judith, Susanna, and Bel and the Dragon, which may be called moralistic novels. In fact, the last two are noteworthy as ancient examples of the detective story.

Of a serious and didactic nature are the two treatises on wisdom, the Wisdom of Solomon and Ecclesiasticus, or the Wisdom of Jesus the Son of Sirach. The latter shows particularly close connections with the style and content of the Old Testament book of Proverbs, from which it is a natural development.

The Prayer of Manasseh takes its place with devotional literature of a relatively high order. The psalmody of the Prayer of Azariah and the Song of the Three Young Men is of a decidedly liturgical cast.

The Old Testament contains no books that are in the form of a letter, but twenty-one of the twenty-seven books of the New Testament are in epistolary form. The Letter of Jeremiah, which dates from inter-testamental times, may have provided later writers with an example of how this literary form could be used for religious purposes, a form which offers the possibility of combining profound theological content with a direct personal approach to the reader.

Finally, 2 Esdras, a book which purports to reveal the future, is a specimen of that type of literature called apocalyptic. An apocalypse is literally "an unveiling." Like the last six chapters of Daniel in the Old Testament and the book of Revelation in the New Testament, which also are apocalypses, 2 Esdras includes many symbols involving mysterious numbers, strange beasts, and the disclosure of hitherto hidden truths through angelic visitants.

Despite the diversities of literary form, most of which are parallel to, or developments from, similar genres in the Old Testament, the attentive reader of the Apocrypha will be struck by the absence of the prophetic element. From first to last the apocryphal books bear testimony to the assertion of the Jewish historian Josephus (*Against Apion*, i.8), that "the exact succession of the prophets" had been broken after the close of the Hebrew canon of the Old Testament. Sometimes there is a direct confession that the gift of prophecy had departed (1 Macc.9.27); at other times a hope is expressed that it might one day return (1 Macc.4.46; 14.41). When a writer imitates the prophetic character, as in the book of Baruch, he repeats with slight modifications the language of the older prophets. But the introductory phrase, "Thus says the LORD," which occurs so frequently in the Old Testament, is conspicuous by its absence from the books of the Apocrypha.

3. Divergent attitudes in the Christian Church toward the Apocrypha.

Ecclesiastical opinions concerning the nature and worth of the books of the Apocrypha have varied with age and place.

None of the authors of the books of the New Testament makes a direct quotation from any of the fifteen books of the Apocrypha, although frequent quotations occur from most of the thirty-nine books of the Hebrew canon of the Old Testament. On the other hand, several New Testament writers make occasional allusions to one or more apocryphal books. For example, what seem to be literary echoes from the Wisdom of Solomon are present in Paul's Letter to the Romans (compare Rom.1.20–29 with Wis.13.5,8; 14.24,27; and Rom.9.20–23 with Wis.12.12,20; 15.7) and in his correspondence with the Corinthians (compare 2 Cor.5.1,4 with Wis.9.15). The short Letter of James, a typical bit of "wisdom literature" in the New Testament, contains allusions not only to the Old Testament book of Proverbs but to gnomic sayings in Sirach as well (compare Jas.1.19 with Sir.5.11; and Jas.1.13 with Sir.15.11–12).

During the early Christian centuries most Greek and Latin Church Fathers, such as Irenaeus, Tertullian, Clement of Alexandria, and Cyprian (none of whom knew any Hebrew), quoted passages from the Apocrypha as "Scripture," "divine Scripture," "inspired," and the like. In this period only an occasional Father made an effort to learn the limits of the Palestinian Jewish canon (as

Melito of Sardis) or to distinguish between the Hebrew text of Daniel and the addition of the story of Susanna in the Greek version (as Africanus).

In the fourth century many Greek Fathers (including Eusebius, Athanasius, Cyril of Jerusalem, Gregory of Nazianzus, Amphilochius, and Epiphanius) came to recognize a distinction between the books in the Hebrew canon and the rest, though the latter were still customarily cited as Scripture. During the following centuries usage fluctuated in the East, but at the important Synod of Jerusalem in 1672 the books of Wisdom, Judith, Tobit, Bel and the Dragon, Susanna, Maccabees, and Ecclesiasticus were expressly designated as canonical.

In the Latin Church, on the other hand, though opinion has not been unanimous, a generally high regard for the books of the Apocrypha has prevailed. More than one local synodical council (e.g. Hippo, A.D. 393, and Carthage, 397 and 419) justified and authorized their use as Scripture. The so-called *Decretum Gelasianum,* a Latin document handed down most frequently under the name of Pope Gelasius (A.D. 492–496), but in some manuscripts as the work of Damasus (366–384) or Hormisdas (514–523), contains, among other material, lists of the books to be read as divine Scripture and of books to be avoided as apocryphal. The former list, which is not present in all the manuscripts, includes among the biblical books Tobit, Judith, Wisdom, Ecclesiasticus, and 1 and 2 Maccabees. Irrespective of the problem of its authorship (many scholars today believe it to be the work of a cleric who lived in south Gaul), the list without doubt reflects the views of the Roman Church at the beginning of the sixth century.

There were, however, occasional voices raised to question the legitimacy of regarding the disputed books as Scripture. At the close of the fourth century, Jerome spoke out decidedly for the Hebrew canon, declaring unreservedly that books which were outside that canon should be classed as apocryphal. When he prepared his celebrated revision of the Latin Bible, the Vulgate, he scrupulously separated the apocryphal Additions to Daniel and Esther, marking them with prefatory notes as absent from the original Hebrew. But, as was remarked above, subsequent scribes were not always careful to transmit Jerome's explanatory material, and during the Middle Ages most readers of the Latin Bible made no distinction between the two classes of books. It is noteworthy, however, that throughout these centuries more than one highly respected ecclesiastical writer (such as Gregory the Great, Walafrid Strabo, Hugh of St. Victor, Hugh of St. Cher, and Nicholas of Lyra), being influenced by the great authority of Jerome, raised theoretical doubts about the disputed books.

Toward the close of the fourteenth century John Wyclif ("the father of English prose") and his disciples, Nicholas of Hereford and John Purvey, produced the first English version of the Bible. This translation, having been rendered from the Latin Vulgate, included all of the disputed books, with the exception of 2 Esdras. In the Prologue to the Old Testament, however, a distinction is made between the books of the Hebrew canon, which are thereupon enumerated, and the others which, the writer says, "shal be set among apocrifa, that is, with outen autorite of bileue." In the case of the books of Esther and Daniel, the translators included a rendering of Jerome's notes calling the reader's attention to the additions.

In the controversies that arose at the time of the Reformation, Protestant leaders soon recognized the need to distinguish between books that were authoritative for the establishment of doctrine and those that were not. Thus, disputes over the doctrines of Purgatory and of the efficacy of prayers and Masses for the dead inevitably involved discussion concerning the authority of 2 Maccabees, which contains what was held to be scriptural warrant for them (12.43–45).

The first extensive discussion of the canon from the Protestant point of view was a treatise in Latin, *De Canonicis Scripturis Libellus*, published at Wittenberg in 1520 by Andreas Bodenstein, who is commonly known as Carlstadt, the name of his birthplace. Besides distinguishing the canonical books of the Hebrew Old Testament from the books of the Apocrypha, Carlstadt classified the latter into two divisions. Of one group, containing Wisdom, Ecclesiasticus, Judith, Tobit, and 1 and 2 Maccabees, he says, "These are Apocrypha, that is, are outside the Hebrew canon; yet they are holy writings" (sect. 114). In explaining his view of the status and worth of such books as Tobit, Wisdom, and Ecclesiasticus, he writes:

> What they contain is not to be despised at once; still it is not right that a Christian should relieve, much less slake, his thirst with them. . . . Before all things the best books must be read, that is, those which are canonical beyond all controversy; afterwards, if one has the time, it is allowed to peruse the controverted books, provided that you have the set purpose of comparing and collating the non-canonical books with those which are truly canonical (sect. 118).

The second group of apocryphal books, namely 1 and 2 Esdras, Baruch, Prayer of Manasseh, and the Additions to Daniel, Carlstadt declared to be filled with ridiculous puerilities worthy of the censor's ban, and therefore to be contemptuously discarded.

The first Bible in a modern vernacular to segregate the apocryphal books from the others was the Dutch Bible published by Jacob van Liesveldt in 1526 at Antwerp. After Malachi there follows a section embodying the Apocrypha, which is entitled, "The books which are not in the canon, that is to say, which one does not find among the Jews in the Hebrew."

The first edition of the Swiss-German Bible, prepared by ministers of the Church in Zurich, was published in six volumes (Zurich, 1527–29), the fifth of which contains the Apocrypha. The title page of this volume states, "These are the books which are not reckoned as biblical by the ancients, nor are found among the Hebrews." A one-volume edition of the Zurich Bible, which appeared in 1530, contains the apocryphal books grouped together after the New Testament. In commenting on the attitude of Protestants respecting the dis-

puted books, Œcolampadius, perhaps on the whole the best representative of
the Swiss Reformers, declared in a formal statement issued in 1530: "We do not
despise Judith, Tobit, Ecclesiasticus, Baruch, the last two books of Esdras, the
three books of Maccabees, the Additions to Daniel; but we do not allow them
divine authority with the others."

In reaction to Protestant criticism of the disputed books, on April 8, 1546,
the Council of Trent gave what is regarded by Roman Catholics as the first
infallible and effectually promulgated declaration on the canon of the holy
Scriptures. After enumerating the books, which in the Old Testament include
Tobit, Judith, Wisdom, Ecclesiasticus, Baruch, and the two books of Maccabees,
the decree pronounces an anathema upon any one who "does not accept as
sacred and canonical the aforesaid books in their entirety and with all their
parts, as they have been accustomed to be read in the Catholic Church and as
they are contained in the old Latin Vulgate Edition" (trans. by Father H. J.
Schroeder). The reference to "books in their entirety and with all their parts" is
intended to cover the Letter of Jeremiah as chapter 6 of Baruch, the Additions
to Esther, and the chapters in Daniel concerning the Song of the Three
Young Men, Susanna, and Bel and the Dragon. It is noteworthy, however,
that the Prayer of Manasseh and 1 and 2 Esdras, though included in some
manuscripts of the Latin Vulgate, were denied canonical status by the Council.
In the official edition of the Vulgate, published in 1592, these three are printed
as an appendix after the New Testament, "lest they should perish altogether."

In England, though Protestants were unanimous in declaring that the apocryphal books were not to be used to establish any doctrine, differences arose as
to the proper use and place of non-canonical books. The milder view prevailed
in the Church of England, and the lectionary attached to the Book of Common
Prayer, from 1549 onward, has always contained prescribed lessons from the
Apocrypha. In reply to those who urged the discontinuance of reading lessons
from apocryphal books, as being inconsistent with the sufficiency of Scripture,
the bishops at the Savoy Conference, held in 1661, replied that the same objection could be raised against the preaching of sermons, and that it was much to
be desired that all sermons should give as useful instruction as did the chapters
selected from the Apocrypha.

A more strict point of view was taken by the Puritans, who felt uneasy that
there should be any books included within the covers of the Bible besides those
which they regarded as authoritative. In time this aversion to associating
merely human books with those acknowledged as the only sacred and canonical
ones found a natural expression in the publication of editions of the Bible from
which the section devoted to the Apocrypha was omitted. The earliest copies of
the English Bible which excluded the Apocrypha are certain Geneva Bibles
printed in 1599 mainly in the Low Countries. The omission of the sheets containing the Apocrypha was presumably due to those responsible for binding the
copies, for the titles of the apocryphal books occur in the table of contents at
the beginning of the edition.

It would seem that the practice of issuing copies of the Bible without the Apocrypha continued, for in 1615 George Abbot, Archbishop of Canterbury, who had been one of the translators of the King James Version of 1611, directed public notices to be given that no Bibles were to be bound up and sold without the Apocrypha on pain of a whole year's imprisonment. Despite the severe penalty, however, not a few printings of the King James Version appeared in London and Cambridge without the Apocrypha; copies lacking the disputed books are dated 1616, 1618, 1620, 1622, 1626, 1627, 1629, 1630, and 1633. Like the copies of the Geneva Bible of 1599, these seem to have been the work of publishers who wished to satisfy a growing demand for less bulky and less expensive editions of the Bible.

During subsequent centuries the editions of Bibles that lacked the books of the Apocrypha came to outnumber by far those that included them, and soon it became difficult to obtain ordinary editions of the King James Version containing the Apocrypha.

4. The pervasive influence of the Apocrypha.

Most readers will probably be surprised to learn how pervasive the influence of the Apocrypha has been over the centuries. Not only have these books inspired homilies, meditations, and liturgical forms, but poets, dramatists, composers, and artists have drawn freely upon them for subject matter. Common proverbs and familiar names are derived from their pages. Even the discovery of the New World was due in part to the influence of a passage in 2 Esdras upon Christopher Columbus. In what follows the reader will find a representative selection of such examples, most of them chosen from the editor's book, *An Introduction to the Apocrypha*, and arranged under the headings of (*a*) English Literature, (*b*) Music, (*c*) Art, and (*d*) Miscellaneous.

(*a*) English Literature. Sometime during the ninth or the tenth century an unknown poet, using the West-Saxon dialect, turned the story of Judith into an Old English epic of twelve cantos, transforming at the same time the heroine into a Christian. It is thought that the poem was written to celebrate the prowess of Æthelflæd, "The Lady of the Mercians," who, like the indomitable Judith, delivered her people from the fury of invaders, the heathen Northmen.

During the fourteenth and fifteenth centuries a poem called "The Pistill [i.e. Epistle] of Swete Susan" circulated in Scotland. Written in stanzas of thirteen lines and characterized by an unusual combination of alliteration and rhyme, the ancient apocryphal story was adorned with many imaginative details by the author, thought to have been a certain Huchown (Hugh) of Ayrshire in western Scotland.

How conversant Shakespeare was with the contents of the Bible is a question which, like many another concerning the bard of Avon, has been keenly debated. In any case, it is a fact that two of the poet's daughters bore the names of two of the chief heroines of the Apocrypha—Susanna and Judith—and, what is of greater significance, allusions to about eighty passages from eleven books of the Apocrypha have been identified in his plays.

Noteworthy among American writers who have drawn upon the Apocrypha for themes as well as subject matter is Henry Wadsworth Longfellow. His *New England Tragedies* contains references to 1 and 2 Maccabees, and the chief episodes of the courageous Maccabean uprising are included in his poetic dramatization, *Judas Maccabaeus*.

(*b*) Music. More than one hymn writer has drawn inspiration, as well as, in some cases, the words themselves, from the Apocrypha. For example, the exalted hymn of thanksgiving, "Nun danket alle Gott," written by Pastor Martin Rinkart about 1636 when the devastating Thirty Years War was nearing its end, is dependent upon Luther's translation of Sir.50.22–24. Two stanzas of the hymn, as translated by Catherine Winkworth, will show the amount of borrowing (here printed in italics):

Now thank we all our God	O may this bounteous God
With heart and hands and voices,	*Through all our life be near us,*
Who wondrous things hath done,	*With ever joyful hearts*
In whom His world rejoices;	*And blessed peace to cheer us;*
Who, from our mother's arms,	*And keep us in His grace,*
Hath blessed us on our way	And guide us when perplexed,
With countless gifts of love,	*And free us from all ills*
And still is ours today.	In this world and the next.

Strange though it may seem, ideas included in the Christmas hymn, "It Came upon the Midnight Clear," are traceable to the Old Testament Apocrypha. In the New Testament accounts of the Nativity, nothing is said of the exact time of Jesus' birth. The subsequent identification of the hour of his birth as midnight is doubtless due to the influence of a remarkable passage in the Wisdom of Solomon. At an early century in the Christian era the imagination of more than one Church Father was caught by pseudo-Solomon's vivid reference to the time when God's "all-powerful word [the Logos] leaped from heaven, from the royal throne," namely when "night in its swift course was now half gone" (Wis.18.14–15). Despite the context of the passage, which speaks of the destruction of the first-born Egyptians at the time of the Exodus, the words were interpreted as referring to the Incarnation of the eternal Word of God, Jesus Christ. Thus by a curious, not to say ironical, twist of fortune, a passage which tells of a stern warrior with a sharp sword filling a doomed land with death has had a share in fixing popular traditions concerning the time and circumstances of the birth of the Prince of Peace.

The influence of the Apocrypha can also be traced in many an anthem, cantata, oratorio, and opera. Handel's oratorios *Susanna* and *Judas Maccabaeus*, as well as his *Alexander Balus*, an historical sequel to the latter, will occur at once to music lovers. At an early date in operatic history the stirring story of

Judith was found to lend itself admirably to dramatic presentation. Italian and German operas on this theme were written by Andrea Salvadori, Marco da Gangliano, Martin Opitz, and Joachim Beccau. In the nineteenth century the noted Russian pianist and composer, Anton Rubenstein, published *The Maccabees*, an opera of monumental proportions, the libretto of which was written by one of his collaborators, Dr. H. S. von Mosenthal.

(*c*) Art. During the Renaissance and later, many painters chose subjects from the books of the Apocrypha. Almost every large gallery in Europe and America has one or more works of the old masters depicting Judith, Tobit, or Susanna, who were the three most popular subjects from the Apocrypha.

Besides paintings, down through the ages artists in almost every other medium have chosen themes from the Apocrypha. Were space available here for an inventory, examples could be cited from such divergent types of *objets d'art* as mosaics, frescoes, gems, ivories, sarcophagi, enameled plaques, terra cottas, stained glass, manuscript illumination, sculpture, and tapestries.

(*d*) Miscellaneous. The influence of the Apocrypha in everyday life can be observed in the currency of such names as Edna, Susanna (or one of its many derivatives, such as Susan, Suzanne, and Sue), Judith (or Judy), Raphael, and Tobias (or Toby).

The word "macabre," according to the opinion of several lexicographers, may be derived ultimately from "Maccabee," alluding to the grisly and gruesome tortures inflicted upon the Jewish martyrs.

Some of the most common expressions and proverbs have come from the Apocrypha. The sententious sayings, "A good name endures for ever" and "You can't touch pitch without being defiled," are derived from Sir.41.13 and 13.1. The noble affirmation in 1 Esd.4.41, "Great is Truth, and mighty above all things" (King James Version), or its Latin form, *Magna est veritas, et praevalet*, has been used frequently as a motto or maxim in a wide variety of contexts.

A passage from the Apocrypha encouraged Christopher Columbus in the enterprise that resulted in his discovery of the New World. To be sure, the verse in 2 Esdras is an erroneous comment upon the Genesis narrative of creation, and Columbus was mistaken in attributing its authority to the "prophet Ezra" of the Old Testament, but—for all that—it played a significant part in pushing back the earth's horizons, both figuratively and literally. The words of 2 Esd.6.42 concerning God's work of creation ("On the third day thou didst command the waters to be gathered together in the seventh part of the earth; six parts thou didst dry up and keep so that some of them might be planted and cultivated and be of service before thee") led Columbus to reason that, if only one-seventh of the earth's surface is covered with water, the ocean between the west coast of Europe and the east coast of Asia could be no great width and might be navigated in a few days with a fair wind. It was partly by quoting this verse from what was regarded as an authoritative book that Columbus managed to persuade Ferdinand and Isabella of Spain to provide the necessary financial support for his voyage.

5. Other apocryphal and pseudepigraphical literature.

Besides the fifteen books or parts of books which are traditionally called the Apocrypha, there are many other Jewish or Jewish-Christian works, dating from the centuries immediately before and after the beginning of the Christian era, which for a time were popular among certain groups of Jews and in early Eastern Churches. It is customary to classify these writings as Palestinian pseudepigrapha (those composed in Hebrew or Aramaic) and Alexandrian pseudepigrapha (those composed in Greek). Of the scores of such documents which are known to have circulated more or less widely, the following have been chosen as representative examples. (For a definition of pseudepigrapha, see p. xiii.)

(*a*) Palestinian pseudepigrapha. The Book of Jubilees is a legendary expansion of Gen.1.1–Ex.12.47, written in Hebrew not long before 100 B.C. by an unknown author of nationalist and rigoristic outlook, who deplored contemporary laxity. It attempts to show that the Mosaic law, with its prescriptions about feasts, the Sabbath offerings, abstinence from blood and from fornication (which for the writer includes intermarriage with Gentiles), was promulgated in patriarchal times, and indeed existed eternally with God in heaven. Events recorded in Genesis are dated exactly (but fictitiously) according to the jubilee (every forty-nine years) and its subdivisions. The book has been transmitted in its entirety in an Ethiopic translation, and portions of the text survive in Greek, Latin, and Syriac versions. At about the middle of the present century five fragmentary manuscripts of Jubilees, written in a good style of Hebrew, were discovered at Qumran by the Dead Sea. These manuscripts, which preserve portions of fifteen of the fifty chapters of the book, show that the Latin and Ethiopic versions are faithful translations of the original.

In addition to the 150 psalms comprising the Book of Psalms in the Hebrew Bible, during the intertestamental period other psalms were composed in Hebrew and in other languages. One of these, which celebrates the prowess of young David in slaying Goliath, is appended (as Ps. 151) to the Psalter in Greek manuscripts. Part of this psalm came to be incorporated in the Ethiopian coronation ritual.

The Psalms of Solomon is a collection of eighteen songs of generally exalted sentiments, composed in Hebrew during the last century B.C. They are extant today in Greek and Syriac. The author, who is usually thought to reflect Pharisaic polemic against Sadducean dominance in the religious ceremonial of his day, looked forward to the time when the Messiah would reign as king at Jerusalem. According to an extended description of the coming Messiah (chs. 17–18), he is to be sinless, strong through the spirit of holiness, gaining his wisdom from God, shepherding the flock of the Lord with fidelity and righteousness, and conquering the entire heathen world without warfare, "by the word of his mouth."

The book of Enoch, also called 1 Enoch or Ethiopic Enoch, is a heterogeneous collection of apocalypses and other material written by several authors in Aramaic (or Hebrew) during the last two centuries B.C. It embodies a series of revelations, of which Enoch is the professed recipient, on such matters as the origin of evil, the angels and their destinies, the nature of Gehenna and Paradise, and the pre-existent Messiah. Interspersed throughout the lengthy and rambling work are sections which have been called "the book of celestial physics." These sections, which are one of the curiosities of ancient pseudo-scientific literature, set forth contemporary speculations concerning such meteorological and astronomical phenomena as lightning, hail, snow, the twelve winds, the heavenly luminaries, and the like. The entire work is preserved in an Ethiopic translation, which includes what have been thought to be Christian interpolations in chs. 37–71, where the Messiah is called the Son of Man. Portions of the book are extant in Greek and Latin; recently eight manuscripts of part of the work (but not chs. 37–71) have turned up in Aramaic at Qumran. It is of interest that a quotation from the book of Enoch (1.9) occurs in the New Testament letter of Jude (vv. 14–15).

(b) Alexandrian pseudepigrapha. Third Maccabees is a religious novel written in Greek by an Alexandrian Jew sometime between 100 B.C. and A.D. 70. The title is a misnomer, for the book has nothing to do with the Maccabees. With many legendary embellishments the author recounts three stories of conflict between Ptolemy IV (221–203 B.C.) and the Jews of Egypt. The most dramatic section describes how the Jews were herded into the hippodrome near Alexandria, to be trampled under the feet of intoxicated elephants. After the king's purpose had been several times providentially delayed, it was finally foiled by a vision of angels which turned the elephants upon the persecutors.

Fourth Maccabees is a Greek philosophical treatise addressed to Jews on the supremacy of devout reason over the passions of body and soul. In the form of a Stoic diatribe, or popular address, the author begins with a philosophical exposition of his theme, which he then illustrates with examples drawn from 2 Maccabees. He describes at length the gruesome tortures that tested the fortitude of Eleazar, the seven brothers, and their mother, all of whom preferred death to committing apostasy. The book was probably written by a Hellenistic Jew of Alexandria at some time later than 2 Maccabees and before A.D. 70.

From what has been said above the reader will be able to form some opinion of the importance of apocryphal and pseudepigraphical literature, both for its own sake as well as for the information it supplies concerning the development of Jewish life and thought just prior to the beginning of the Christian era. The stirring political fortunes of the Jews in the time of the Maccabees; the rise of what has been called normative Judaism, and the emergence of the sects of the Pharisees and the Sadducees; the lush growth of popular belief in the activities of angels and demons, and the use of apotropaic magic to avert the malevolent influence of the latter; the growing preoccupation concerning original sin and its relation to the "evil inclination" present in every person; the blossoming of apocalyptic hopes relating to the coming Messiah, the resurrection of the body, and the vindication of the righteous—all these and many other topics receive welcome light from the books of the Apocrypha.

THE BOOKS OF THE APOCRYPHA

*The abbreviations for the books of the Bible are
those used in* THE NEW OXFORD ANNOTATED BIBLE.

MISCELLANEOUS ABBREVIATIONS

Ant.	Josephus, *Antiquities of the Jews*
Arab	Arabic
Arm	Armenian
Arrian	Flavius Arrianus (Greek historian, 2nd cent. A.D.)
Ch., chs.	Chapter, chapters
Cn	Correction; made where the text has suffered in transmission and the versions provide no satisfactory restoration, but where the Standard Bible Committee agrees with the judgment of competent scholars as to the most probable restoration of the original text.
e.g.	for example

Abbreviations

Ethiop	Ethiopic
Georg	Georgian
Enoch	The Book of Enoch (see pp. xxi–xxii)
Gk	Greek
Heb	Hebrew
Her	Herodotus (Greek historian, 5th cent. B.C.)
i.e.	that is
Josephus	Flavius Josephus (Jewish historian, about A.D. 37 to about 100)
Lat	Latin
lit.	literally
LXX	Septuagint
Ms(s)	Manuscript(s)
n.	note
Polyb	Polybius (Greek historian, 2nd cent. B.C.)
Syr	Syriac
Vg	Vulgate
v., vv.	Verse, verses

OTHER EXPLANATIONS

In the annotations italics are used to designate the words which are quoted verbatim from the text of the Apocrypha. In the notes belonging to the Revised Standard Version (designated by italic letters and standing at the foot of the second column of the text of the Apocrypha) alternative renderings or readings are printed in italics.

THE FIRST BOOK OF

ESDRAS

The book which is known in the Apocrypha as 1 Esdras is called 3 Esdras in the Latin Vulgate Bible, where it is now placed (since the Council of Trent) in an appendix after the New Testament. None of the other apocryphal books is so intimately connected with the Old Testament. Beginning somewhat abruptly with a description of the great passover held by King Josiah in Jerusalem (about 621 B.C.), the book reproduces the substance of 2 Chr.35.1–36.23, the whole of Ezra, and Neh.7.38–8.12, breaking off in the middle of a sentence after an account of Ezra's reforms (about 398 B.C.). There are numerous minor discrepancies between the apocryphal and canonical accounts, including a rearrangement of the materials; and the story of the three young men in the court of Darius (3.1–5.6) has no parallel in the Old Testament.

The origin of the book is a matter of dispute. It is not a translation of the Masoretic Hebrew text of the Old Testament, though it may represent some other Hebrew or Aramaic original. The book is quite independent of the Septuagint Greek version of the canonical Ezra-Nehemiah. The Jewish historian Josephus followed 1 Esdras rather than the Septuagint as his authority for the history of the period.

The purpose of the unknown author was to emphasize the contribution of Josiah, Zerubbabel, and Ezra to the reform of Israelite worship. The book was written after Daniel (about 165 B.C.) and before Josephus wrote his *Antiquities of the Jewish People* (A.D. 93–94). A date late in the second century B.C. is probable.

JOSIAH KEPT THE PASSOVER TO HIS Lord in Jerusalem; he killed the passover lamb on the fourteenth day of the first month, [2]having placed the priests according to their divisions, arrayed in their garments, in the temple of the Lord. [3]And he told the Levites, the temple servants of Israel, that they should sanctify themselves to the Lord and put the holy ark of the Lord in the house which Solomon the king, the son of David, had built; [4]and he said, "You need no longer carry it upon your shoulders. Now worship the Lord your God and serve his people Israel; and prepare yourselves by your families and kindred, [5]in accordance with the directions of David king of Israel and the magnificence of Solomon his son. Stand in order in the temple according to the grouping of the fathers' houses of you Levites, who minister before your brethren the people of Israel, [6]and kill the passover lamb and prepare the sacrifices for your brethren, and keep the passover according to the commandment of the Lord which was given to Moses."

7 And Josiah gave to the people who were present thirty thousand lambs and kids, and three thousand calves; these were given from the king's possessions, as he promised, to the people and the priests and Levites. [8]And Hilkiah, Zechariah, and Jehiel,[a] the chief officers of the temple, gave to the priests for the passover two thousand six hundred sheep and three hundred calves. [9]And Jeconiah and Shemaiah and Nethanel his brother, and Hashabiah and Ochiel and Joram, captains over thousands, gave the Levites for the passover five thousand sheep and seven hundred calves.

10 And this is what took place. The priests and the Levites, properly arrayed and having the unleavened

a Gk *Esyelus*

1.1–33: Josiah's passover; his effort to intercept the Egyptians at Megiddo, and his death (2 Chr.35.1–27). According to 2 Kg.23.21–23 the passover celebration concluded Josiah's religious reform, the account of which is omitted in 1 Esdras. **7–9:** The list of offerings

[1]

bread, stood according to kindred [11]and the grouping of the fathers' houses, before the people, to make the offering to the Lord as it is written in the book of Moses; this they did in the morning. [12]They roasted the passover lamb with fire, as required; and they boiled the sacrifices in brass pots and caldrons, with a pleasing odor, [13]and carried them to all the people. Afterward they prepared the passover for themselves and for their brethren the priests, the sons of Aaron, [14]because the priests were offering the fat until night; so the Levites prepared it for themselves and for their brethren the priests, the sons of Aaron. [15]And the temple singers, the sons of Asaph, were in their place according to the arrangement made by David, and also Asaph, Zechariah, and Eddinus, who represented the king. [16]The gatekeepers were at each gate; no one needed to depart from his duties, for their brethren the Levites prepared the passover for them.

17 So the things that had to do with the sacrifices to the Lord were accomplished that day: the passover was kept [18]and the sacrifices were offered on the altar of the Lord, according to the command of King Josiah. [19]And the people of Israel who were present at that time kept the passover and the feast of unleavened bread seven days. [20]No passover like it had been kept in Israel since the times of Samuel the prophet; [21]none of the kings of Israel had kept such a passover as was kept by Josiah and the priests and the Levites and the men of Judah and all of Israel who were dwelling in Jerusalem. [22]In the eighteenth year of the reign of Josiah this passover was kept. [23]And the deeds of Josiah were upright in the sight of

his Lord, for his heart was full of godliness. [24]The events of his reign have been recorded in the past, concerning those who sinned and acted wickedly toward the Lord beyond any other people or kingdom, and how they grieved the Lord[b] deeply, so that the words of the Lord rose up against Israel.

25 After all these acts of Josiah, it happened that Pharaoh, king of Egypt, went to make war at Carchemish on the Euphrates, and Josiah went out against him. [26]And the king of Egypt sent word to him saying, "What have we to do with each other, king of Judea? [27]I was not sent against you by the Lord God, for my war is at the Euphrates. And now the Lord is with me! The Lord is with me, urging me on! Stand aside, and do not oppose the Lord."

28 But Josiah did not turn back to his chariot, but tried to fight with him, and did not heed the words of Jeremiah the prophet from the mouth of the Lord. [29]He joined battle with him in the plain of Megiddo, and the commanders came down against King Josiah. [30]And the king said to his servants, "Take me away from the battle, for I am very weak." And immediately his servants took him out of the line of battle. [31]And he got into his second chariot; and after he was brought back to Jerusalem he died, and was buried in the tomb of his fathers. [32]And in all Judea they mourned for Josiah. Jeremiah the prophet lamented for Josiah, and the principal men, with the women,[c] have made lamentation for him to this day; it was ordained that this should always be done throughout the whole nation of Israel. [33]These things are written in the book of the histories

b Gk *him*   c Or *their wives*

---

differs slightly from that in 2 Chr.35.7–9. **15:** *Zechariah* and *Eddinus* appear in 2 Chr.35.15 as Heman and Jeduthun. **17–33:** 1 Esdras follows the account in 2 Chr.35.16–27 faithfully, apart from the omission of the Pharaoh's name, Josiah's disguising himself, and his being struck by an arrow.

of the kings of Judea; and every one of the acts of Josiah, and his splendor, and his understanding of the law of the Lord, and the things that he had done before and these that are now told, are recorded in the book of the kings of Israel and Judah.

34 And the men of the nation took Jeconiah the son of Josiah, who was twenty-three years old, and made him king in succession to Josiah his father. ³⁵And he reigned three months in Judah and Jerusalem. Then the king of Egypt deposed him from reigning in Jerusalem, ³⁶and fined the nation a hundred talents of silver and a talent of gold. ³⁷And the king of Egypt made Jehoiakim his brother king of Judea and Jerusalem. ³⁸Jehoiakim put the nobles in prison, and seized his brother Zarius and brought him up out of Egypt.

39 Jehoiakim was twenty-five years old when he began to reign in Judea and Jerusalem, and he did what was evil in the sight of the Lord. ⁴⁰And Nebuchadnezzar king of Babylon came up against him, and bound him with a chain of brass and took him away to Babylon. ⁴¹Nebuchadnezzar also took some of the holy vessels of the Lord, and carried them away, and stored them in his temple in Babylon. ⁴²But the things that are reported about Jehoiakim*ᵈ* and his uncleanness and impiety are written in the chronicles of the kings.

43 Jehoiachin*ᵉ* his son became king in his stead; when he was made king he was eighteen years old, ⁴⁴and he reigned three months and ten days

in Jerusalem. He did what was evil in the sight of the Lord. ⁴⁵So after a year Nebuchadnezzar sent and removed him to Babylon, with the holy vessels of the Lord, ⁴⁶and made Zedekiah king of Judea and Jerusalem.

Zedekiah was twenty-one years old, and he reigned eleven years. ⁴⁷He also did what was evil in the sight of the Lord, and did not heed the words that were spoken by Jeremiah the prophet from the mouth of the Lord. ⁴⁸And though King Nebuchadnezzar had made him swear by the name of the Lord, he broke his oath and rebelled; and he stiffened his neck and hardened his heart and transgressed the laws of the Lord, the God of Israel. ⁴⁹Even the leaders of the people and of the priests committed many acts of sacrilege and lawlessness beyond all the unclean deeds of all the nations, and polluted the temple of the Lord which had been hallowed in Jerusalem. ⁵⁰So the God of their fathers sent by his messenger to call them back, because he would have spared them and his dwelling place. ⁵¹But they mocked his messengers, and whenever the Lord spoke, they scoffed at his prophets, ⁵²until in his anger against his people because of their ungodly acts he gave command to bring against them the kings of the Chaldeans. ⁵³These slew their young men with the sword around their holy temple, and did not spare young man or virgin, old

d Gk *him*
e Gk *Jehoiakim*

1.34–58: The last kings of Judah; Jerusalem's fall to the Babylonians (2 Chr.36.1–21). **34:** The expression *men of the nation* corresponds to the "people of the land" of 2 Chr.36.1; in pre-exilic times these were conservative landowners who often came to the support of reforming kings or who themselves instituted reforms (2 Kg.12.18,20; 21.24; 23.30). *Jeconiah*, also called Jehoahaz (2 Kg.23.30–31; 2 Chr.36.1–2) and Shallum (Jer.22.11). **38:** The author has misunderstood 2 Chr.36.4. Neco of Egypt removed Jehoahaz from the throne and installed Josiah's elder son Eliakim as king, changing his name to Jehoiakim. Jehoahaz was taken to Egypt where presumably he died (Jer.22.10–12). 1 Esdras has *Jehoiakim* bring up his brother *Zarius* from Egypt; the name *Zarius* is apparently an orthographic corruption (through confusion of the Hebrew letters *d* and *r*) of Zedekiah, who was a brother of Jehoiakim (2 Kg.24.17). **39:** 1 Esdras omits the length of Jehoiakim's reign, which was eleven years (2 Chr.36.5). **43:** 1 Esdras mistakenly man or child, for he gave them all into their hands. ⁵⁴And all the holy vessels of the Lord, great and small, and the treasure chests of the Lord, and the royal stores, they took and carried away to Babylon. ⁵⁵And they burned the house of the Lord and broke down the walls of Jerusalem and burned their towers with fire, ⁵⁶and utterly destroyed all its glorious things. The survivors he led away to Babylon with the sword, ⁵⁷and they were servants to him and to his sons until the Persians began to reign, in fulfilment of the word of the Lord by the mouth of Jeremiah: ⁵⁸"Until the land has enjoyed its sabbaths, it shall keep sabbath all the time of its desolation until the completion of seventy years."

2 In the first year of Cyrus as king of the Persians, that the word of the Lord by the mouth of Jeremiah might be accomplished, ²the Lord stirred up the spirit of Cyrus king of the Persians, and he made a proclamation throughout all his kingdom and also put it in writing:

3 "Thus says Cyrus king of the Persians: The Lord of Israel, the Lord Most High, has made me king of the world, ⁴and he has commanded me to build him a house at Jerusalem, which is in Judea. ⁵If any one of you, therefore, is of his people, may his Lord be with him, and let him go up to Jerusalem, which is in Judea, and build the house of the Lord of Israel—he is the Lord who dwells in Jerusalem, ⁶and let each man, wherever he may live, be helped by the men of his place with gold and silver, ⁷with gifts, and with horses and cattle, besides the other things added as votive offerings for the temple of the Lord which is in Jerusalem."

8 Then arose the heads of families of the tribes of Judah and Benjamin, and the priests and the Levites, and all whose spirit the Lord had stirred to go up to build the house in Jerusalem for the Lord; ⁹and their neighbors helped them with everything, with silver and gold, with horses and cattle, and with a very great number of votive offerings from many whose hearts were stirred.

10 Cyrus the king also brought out the holy vessels of the Lord which Nebuchadnezzar had carried away from Jerusalem and stored in his temple of idols. ¹¹When Cyrus king of the Persians brought these out, he gave them to Mithridates his treasurer, ¹²and by him they were given to Sheshbazzar*ᶠ* the governor of Judea. ¹³The number of these was: a thousand gold cups, a thousand silver cups, twenty-nine silver censers, thirty gold bowls, two thousand four hundred and ten silver bowls, and a thousand other vessels. ¹⁴All the vessels were handed over, gold and silver, five thousand four hundred and sixty-nine, ¹⁵and they were carried back by Sheshbazzar*ᶠ* with the returning exiles from Babylon to Jerusalem.

ᶠ Gk Sanabassarus

---

gives Jehoiakim (see note *e*) as the name of that king's son and successor, rather than Jehoiachin; but the king's age at the beginning of his reign is correctly given (*eighteen years;* not eight, as in 2 Chr.36.9). **58:** To *keep sabbath* means that the land is to continue in a state of "sabbath" rest (i.e., to lie untended as in the seventh or sabbatical years) until the exiles return (Jer.25.11–12; 29.10; compare Lev.25.1–7; 26.27–39).

2.1–15: Cyrus of Persia permits the exiles to return (Ezra 1.1–11). The text is virtually identical with that in Ezra, although the inventory of the sacred vessels appears to be better preserved in 1 Esdras than in Ezra. **1:** *First year of Cyrus,* i.e. 538 B.C.

2.16–30: Opposition to the rebuilding of the temple and the city walls (Ezra 4.7–24). A misplaced account of opposition to rebuilding the walls of Jerusalem in the time of Artaxerxes I (464–423 B.C.). Cyrus was succeeded by Cambyses (529–521), who was followed by Darius I (521–485). Josephus (*Antiq.* XI. ii.1–3) substitutes Cambyses for Artaxerxes, thus providing the correct sequence of Persian kings. The original location of the passage was probably between

16 But in the time of Artaxerxes king of the Persians, Bishlam, Mithridates, Tabeel, Rehum, Beltethmus, Shimshai the scribe, and the rest of their associates, living in Samaria and other places, wrote him the following letter, against those who were living in Judea and Jerusalem:
17 "To King Artaxerxes our lord, Your servants Rehum the recorder and Shimshai the scribe and the other judges of their council in Coelesyria and Phoenicia: ¹⁸Now be it known to our lord the king that the Jews who came up from you to us have gone to Jerusalem and are building that rebellious and wicked city, repairing its market places and walls and laying the foundations for a temple. ¹⁹Now if this city is built and the walls finished, they will not only refuse to pay tribute but will even resist kings. ²⁰And since the building of the temple is now going on, we think it best not to neglect such a matter, ²¹but to speak to our lord the king, in order that, if it seems good to you, search may be made in the records of your fathers. ²²You will find in the chronicles what has been written about them, and will learn that this city was rebellious, troubling both kings and other cities, ²³and that the Jews were rebels and kept setting up blockades in it from of old. That is why this city was laid waste. ²⁴Therefore we now make known to you, O lord and king, that if this city is built and its

walls finished, you will no longer have access to Coelesyria and Phoenicia."
25 Then the king, in reply to Rehum the recorder and Beltethmus and Shimshai the scribe and the others associated with them and living in Samaria and Syria and Phoenicia, wrote as follows:
26 "I have read the letter which you sent me. So I ordered search to be made, and it has been found that this city from of old has fought against kings, ²⁷and that the men in it were given to rebellion and war, and that mighty and cruel kings ruled in Jerusalem and exacted tribute from Coelesyria and Phoenicia. ²⁸Therefore I have now issued orders to prevent these men from building the city and to take care that nothing more be done ²⁹and that such wicked proceedings go no further to the annoyance of kings."
30 Then, when the letter from King Artaxerxes was read, Rehum and Shimshai the scribe and their associates went in haste to Jerusalem, with horsemen and a multitude in battle array, and began to hinder the builders. And the building of the temple in Jerusalem ceased until the second year of the reign of Darius king of the Persians.

3 Now King Darius gave a great banquet for all that were under him and all that were born in his house and all the nobles of Media and Persia ²and all the satraps and

Ezra ch. 10 and Neh. ch. 1. **16:** The name *Beltethmus* is a Greek transliteration of the Aramaic title of the office held by *Rehum;* the same mistake occurs in v. 25. **17:** The persons named are officials of the Persian province called "Beyond the River" (Ezra 4.10), which included the lands of Syria, Phoenicia, and Palestine. *Rehum* is designated "the commander" in Ezra 4.8f.; the translation *recorder* is supported by Josephus. **20:** The account differs considerably from that in Ezra 4.14, which contains no reference to the rebuilding of the *temple* at this point (compare Ezra 4.24, however, where work on the *temple* is said to have stopped). **25:** *Rehum* the governor is again identified as the *recorder* rather than as the commander of Persian forces in Samaria (Ezra 4.17). As in v. 16 the name *Beltethmus* is a transliteration of the Aramaic title of *Rehum* and is not the name of a third addressee. **30:** An erroneous reference (as also in Ezra 4.24) to the halting of work on the *temple*.
3.1–5.6: The three young bodyguards in the court of Darius. This famous story, found only in 1 Esdras among the several works attributed to Ezra, provides sufficient reason for the preservation of the book throughout the centuries. The story probably originated outside the Jewish

generals and governors that were under him in the hundred and twenty-seven satrapies from India to Ethiopia. ³They ate and drank, and when they were satisfied they departed; and Darius the king went to his bedroom, and went to sleep, and then awoke.

4 Then the three young men of the bodyguard, who kept guard over the person of the king, said to one another, ⁵"Let each of us state what one thing is strongest; and to him whose statement seems wisest, Darius the king will give rich gifts and great honors of victory. ⁶He shall be clothed in purple, and drink from gold cups, and sleep on a gold bed, and have a chariot with gold bridles, and a turban of fine linen, and a necklace about his neck; ⁷and because of his wisdom he shall sit next to Darius and shall be called kinsman of Darius."

8 Then each wrote his own statement, and they sealed them and put them under the pillow of Darius the king, ⁹and said, "When the king wakes, they will give him the writing; and to the one whose statement the king and the three nobles of Persia judge to be wisest the victory shall be given according to what is written." ¹⁰The first wrote, "Wine is strongest." ¹¹The second wrote, "The king is strongest." ¹²The third wrote, "Women are strongest, but truth is victor over all things."

13 When the king awoke, they took the writing and gave it to him, and he read it. ¹⁴Then he sent and summoned all the nobles of Persia and Media and the satraps and generals and governors and prefects, ¹⁵and he took his seat in the council chamber, and the writing was read in their presence. ¹⁶And he said, "Call the young men, and they shall explain their statements." So they were summoned, and came in. ¹⁷And they said to them, "Explain to us what you have written."

Then the first, who had spoken of the strength of wine, began and said: ¹⁸"Gentlemen, how is wine the strongest? It leads astray the minds of all who drink it. ¹⁹It makes equal the mind of the king and the orphan, of the slave and the free, of the poor and the rich. ²⁰It turns every thought to feasting and mirth, and forgets all sorrow and debt. ²¹It makes all hearts feel rich, forgets kings and satraps, and makes every one talk in millions.ᵍ ²²When men drink they forget to be friendly with friends and brothers, and before long they draw their swords. ²³And when they recover from the wine, they do not remember what they have done. ²⁴Gentlemen, is not wine the strongest, since it forces men to do these things?" When he had said this, he stopped speaking.

g Gk *talents*

---

community as a popular tale praising the relative strength of wine, kings, and women (the original order was perhaps kings, wine, and women). The praise of the strength of truth (4.33–41; compare 3.12) was added later in the transmission of the story, perhaps by a Greek-speaking editor (this part of the story has close parallels to Greek thought and literature). The author of 1 Esdras, adopting the story, needed only to identify the third youth with Zerubbabel (4.13) and to add a sequel to the tale, relating how Darius rewarded Zerubbabel by supporting the rebuilding of Jerusalem and its temple (4.42–5.6). The version of the story found in Josephus (*Antiq.* XI. iii.2–9) differs from the one given here in several particulars.

3.1–17a: The contest planned. 1–3: Apparently Darius' banquet was held at Susa, though the location is not explicitly mentioned. **2:** During Darius' reign (521–485 B.C.) there were actually only about twenty provinces (*satrapies*); this number was increased during Seleucid times (after 312 B.C.), and the total *one hundred twenty-seven* became conventional in later literature (Est.1.1; Josephus, *Antiq.* XI. iii.2). **4–12:** The three bodyguards decide upon a form of entertainment for the king that would bring riches and honor to one of them. According to Josephus (*Antiq.* XI. iii.2) it was the king who proposed the contest. **13–17a:** The entire court is assembled to hear the guardsmen defend their respective answers; such a scene is entirely consonant with court practices in the ancient world.

3.17b–24: In praise of the strength of wine. *Wine* is the great leveler in society; it takes away man's capacity for discernment and remembrance, overpowering king and commoner alike.

4 Then the second, who had spoken of the strength of the king, began to speak: ²"Gentlemen, are not men strongest, who rule over land and sea and all that is in them? ³But the king is stronger; he is their lord and master, and whatever he says to them they obey. ⁴If he tells them to make war on one another, they do it; and if he sends them out against the enemy, they go, and conquer mountains, walls, and towers. ⁵They kill and are killed, and do not disobey the king's command; if they win the victory, they bring everything to the king—whatever spoil they take and everything else. ⁶Likewise those who do not serve in the army or make war but till the soil, whenever they sow, reap the harvest and bring some to the king; and they compel one another to pay taxes to the king. ⁷And yet he is only one man! If he tells them to kill, they kill; if he tells them to release, they release; ⁸if he tells them to attack, they attack; if he tells them to lay waste, they lay waste; if he tells them to build, they build; ⁹if he tells them to cut down, they cut down; if he tells them to plant, they plant. ¹⁰All his people and his armies obey him. Moreover, he reclines, he eats and drinks and sleeps, ¹¹but they keep watch around him and no one may go away to attend to his own affairs, nor do they disobey him. ¹²Gentlemen, why is not the king the strongest, since he is to be obeyed in this fashion?" And he stopped speaking.

13 Then the third, that is Zerubbabel, who had spoken of women and truth, began to speak: ¹⁴"Gentlemen, is not the king great, and are not men many, and is not wine strong? Who then is their master, or who is their lord? Is it not women? ¹⁵Women gave birth to the king and to every people that rules over sea and land. ¹⁶From women they came; and women brought up the very men who plant the vineyards from which comes wine. ¹⁷Women make men's clothes; they bring men glory; men cannot exist without women. ¹⁸If men gather gold and silver or any other beautiful thing, and then see a woman lovely in appearance and beauty, ¹⁹they let all those things go, and gape at her, and with open mouths stare at her, and all prefer her to gold or silver or any other beautiful thing. ²⁰A man leaves his own father, who brought him up, and his own country, and cleaves to his wife. ²¹With his wife he ends his days, with no thought of his father or his mother or his country. ²²Hence you must realize that women rule over you!

"Do you not labor and toil, and bring everything and give it to women? ²³A man takes his sword, and goes out to travel and rob and steal and to sail the sea and rivers; ²⁴he faces lions, and he walks in darkness, and when he steals and robs and plunders, he brings it back to the woman he loves. ²⁵A man loves his wife more than his father or his mother. ²⁶Many men have lost their minds because of women, and have become slaves because of them. ²⁷Many have perished, or stumbled, or sinned, because of women. ²⁸And now do you not believe me?

"Is not the king great in his power? Do not all lands fear to touch him? ²⁹Yet I have seen him with Apame, the king's concubine, the daughter of the illustrious Bartacus; she would sit at the king's right hand ³⁰and take the crown from the king's head and put it on her own, and slap the king with her left hand. ³¹At this the king

---

4.1–12: In praise of the strength of kings. The arbitrary power of oriental kings here portrayed is quite true to the actual situation in the ancient world. No polemic against kingship need be seen in the passage.
4.13–32: In praise of the strength of women. The third youth, identified for the first time as *Zerubbabel* (v. 13), depicts the strength of *women*, who give birth to kings, who receive from men the treasures won in warfare and heroic deeds, who can humiliate their masters, including kings, and yet are sought after and fawned upon by those whom they humiliate. **29:** The king's concubine *Apame*, daughter of Bartacus, cannot be identified.

would gaze at her with mouth agape. If she smiles at him, he laughs; if she loses her temper with him, he flatters her, that she may be reconciled to him. [32]Gentlemen, why are not women strong, since they do such things?"

33 Then the king and the nobles looked at one another; and he began to speak about truth: [34]"Gentlemen, are not women strong? The earth is vast, and heaven is high, and the sun is swift in its course, for it makes the circuit of the heavens and returns to its place in one day. [35]Is he not great who does these things? But truth is great, and stronger than all things. [36]The whole earth calls upon truth, and heaven blesses her. All God's[h] works quake and tremble, and with him there is nothing unrighteous. [37]Wine is unrighteous, the king is unrighteous, women are unrighteous, all the sons of men are unrighteous, all their works are unrighteous, and all such things. There is no truth in them and in their unrighteousness they will perish. [38]But truth endures and is strong for ever, and lives and prevails for ever and ever. [39]With her there is no partiality or preference, but she does what is righteous instead of anything that is unrighteous or wicked. All men approve her deeds, [40]and there is nothing unrighteous in her judgment. To her belongs the strength and the kingship and the power and the majesty of all the ages. Blessed be the God of

truth!" [41]He ceased speaking; then all the people shouted, and said, "Great is truth, and strongest of all!"

42 Then the king said to him, "Ask what you wish, even beyond what is written, and we will give it to you, for you have been found to be the wisest. And you shall sit next to me, and be called my kinsman." [43]Then he said to the king, "Remember the vow which you made to build Jerusalem, in the day when you became king, [44]and to send back all the vessels that were taken from Jerusalem, which Cyrus set apart when he began[i] to destroy Babylon, and vowed to send them back there. [45]You also vowed to build the temple, which the Edomites burned when Judea was laid waste by the Chaldeans. [46]And now, O lord the king, this is what I ask and request of you, and this befits your greatness. I pray therefore that you fulfil the vow whose fulfilment you vowed to the King of heaven with your own lips."

47 Then Darius the king rose, and kissed him, and wrote letters for him to all the treasurers and governors and generals and satraps, that they should give escort to him and all who were going up with him to build Jerusalem. [48]And he wrote letters to all the governors in Coelesyria and Phoenicia and to those in Lebanon, to bring cedar

h Gk *All the works*
i Cn: Gk *vowed*

4.33–41: In praise of the strength of truth. The strength of *truth*, an addition to the original story probably made prior to the story's adaptation to the Jewish author's purpose, is portrayed in imagery akin to the depiction of truth in Greek literature. The Jewish adapter of the story may have modified the original somewhat to make truth more nearly akin to Hebraic ideas of truth (firmness, reliability). The closing references to truth suggest that it is virtually equivalent to the will of God: "Blessed be the God of truth!" (v. 40). The audience responds (v. 41) with the declaration, "Great is truth, and strongest of all!" The Latin proverb *magna est veritas et praevalet* ("Great is truth, and it prevails") is the most famous line from the Vulgate text of 1 Esdras.
4.42–57: Zerubbabel's reward. Darius authorizes Zerubbabel to return to Jerusalem and rebuild the temple, with generous support from the Persian treasury. **43:** The historically improbable vow of Darius to rebuild Jerusalem and its temple upon his accession to the kingship is not otherwise attested; indeed, the author has already recounted Cyrus' proclamation authorizing the return of the exiles and the restoration of the temple vessels (2.1–15). **45:** *The Edomites* are credited with having burned the temple, contrary to 1.55 (see Ob.11–14). **48–57:** Darius magnificently supports the program outlined by Zerubbabel. The historical background

timber from Lebanon to Jerusalem, and to help him build the city. ⁴⁹And he wrote for all the Jews who were going up from his kingdom to Judea, in the interest of their freedom, that no officer or satrap or governor or treasurer should forcibly enter their doors; ⁵⁰that all the country which they would occupy should be theirs without tribute; that the Idumeans should give up the villages of the Jews which they held; ⁵¹that twenty talents a year should be given for the building of the temple until it was completed, ⁵²and an additional ten talents a year for burnt offerings to be offered on the altar every day, in accordance with the commandment to make seventeen offerings; ⁵³and that all who came from Babylonia to build the city should have their freedom, they and their children and all the priests who came. ⁵⁴He wrote also concerning their support and the priests' garments in whichʲ they were to minister. ⁵⁵He wrote that the support for the Levites should be provided until the day when the temple should be finished and Jerusalem built. ⁵⁶He wrote that land and wages should be provided for all who guarded the city. ⁵⁷And he sent back from Babylon all the vessels which Cyrus had set apart; everything that Cyrus had ordered to be done, he also commanded to be done and to be sent to Jerusalem.

58 When the young man went out, he lifted up his face to heaven toward Jerusalem, and praised the King of heaven, saying, ⁵⁹"From thee is the

victory; from thee is wisdom; and thine is the glory. I am thy servant. ⁶⁰Blessed art thou, who hast given me wisdom; I give thee thanks, O Lord of our fathers."

61 So he took the letters, and went to Babylon and told this to all his brethren. ⁶²And they praised the God of their fathers, because he had given them release and permission ⁶³to go up and build Jerusalem and the temple which is called by his name; and they feasted, with music and rejoicing, for seven days.

5 After this the heads of fathers' houses were chosen to go up, according to their tribes, with their wives and sons and daughters, and their menservants and maidservants, and their cattle. ²And Darius sent with them a thousand horsemen to take them back to Jerusalem in safety, with the music of drums and flutes; ³and all their brethren were making merry. And he made them go up with them.

4 These are the names of the men who went up, according to their fathers' houses in the tribes, over their groups: ⁵the priests, the sons of Phinehas, son of Aaron; Jeshua the son of Jozadak, son of Seraiah, and Joakim the son of Zerubbabel, son of Shealtiel, of the house of David, of the lineage of Phares, of the tribe of Judah, ⁶who spoke wise words before Darius the king of the Persians, in the second year of his reign, in the month of Nisan, the first month.

7 These are the men of Judea who

ʲ Gk *in what priestly garments*

---

is reflected more accurately in the decree issued by Darius after the governor of Samaria had complained about the rebuilding of the temple (Ezra 6.1–13; 1 Esd.6.23–34). The decree of Cyrus allowing the exiles to return and restore the temple and its cult (2.1–15) is no doubt historical, and Darius confirmed this decree (6.23–34); but Zerubbabel's return was hardly supported by Darius in the manner here portrayed.

4.58–60: Zerubbabel's prayer. The language of this prayer is similar to a prayer of Daniel (Dan.2.20–23) and may be dependent upon it.

4.61–5.6: Preparations for the return. Zerubbabel journeys (perhaps from Susa) to Babylon and there recruits leaders for the returning exiles (5.4–6). The list of the leaders is hopelessly confused. *Jeshua* (5.5) is clearly the leading priest, and *Zerubbabel* is the hero of the story, not his son *Joakim*. In Neh.12.10,26, Joakim appears as the son of Jeshua; 1 Chr.3.17–24 gives a different genealogy for Zerubbabel (where he is said to be a grandson of Jehoiachin).

5.7–46: A list of the returning exiles (Ezra 2.1–70 and Neh.7.6–73a). The list in 1 Esdras

[9]

came up out of their sojourn in captivity, whom Nebuchadnezzar king of Babylon had carried away to Babylon [8]and who returned to Jerusalem and the rest of Judea, each to his own town. They came with Zerubbabel and Jeshua, Nehemiah, Seraiah, Resaiah, Bigvai,[k] Mordecai, Bilshan,[l] Mispar,[m] Reeliah, Rehum, and Baanah, their leaders.

9 The number of the men of the nation and their leaders: the sons of Parosh, two thousand one hundred and seventy-two. The sons of Shephatiah, four hundred and seventy-two. [10]The sons of Arah, seven hundred and fifty-six. [11]The sons of Pahathmoab, of the sons of Jeshua and Joab, two thousand eight hundred and twelve. [12]The sons of Elam, one thousand two hundred and fifty-four. The sons of Zattu, nine hundred and forty-five. The sons of Chorbe, seven hundred and five. The sons of Bani, six hundred and forty-eight. [13]The sons of Bebai, six hundred and twenty-three. The sons of Azgad, one thousand three hundred and twenty-two. [14]The sons of Adonikam, six hundred and sixty-seven. The sons of Bigvai, two thousand and sixty-six. The sons of Adin, four hundred and fifty-four. [15]The sons of Ater, namely of Hezekiah, ninety-two. The sons of Kilan and Azetas, sixty-seven. The sons of Azaru, four hundred and thirty-two. [16]The sons of Annias, one hundred and one. The sons of Arom. The sons of Bezai, three hundred and twenty-three. The sons of Jorah,[n] one hundred and twelve. [17]The sons of Baiterus, three thousand and five. The sons of Bethlehem,[o] one hundred and twenty-three. [18]The men of Netophah, fifty-five. The men of Anathoth, one hundred and fifty-eight. The men of Bethasmoth, forty-two. [19]The men of Kiriatharim, twenty-five. The men of Chephirah and Beeroth, seven hundred

and forty-three. [20]The Chadiasans and Ammidians, four hundred and twenty-two. The men of Ramah[p] and Geba, six hundred and twenty-one. [21]The men of Michmas,[q] one hundred and twenty-two. The men of Bethel,[r] fifty-two. The sons of Magbish,[s] one hundred and fifty-six. [22]The sons of the other Elam[t] and Ono, seven hundred and twenty-five. The sons of Jericho, three hundred and forty-five. [23]The sons of Senaah, three thousand three hundred and thirty.

24 The priests: the sons of Jedaiah the son of Jeshua, of the sons of Anasib, nine hundred and seventy-two. The sons of Immer, one thousand and fifty-two. [25]The sons of Pashhur, one thousand two hundred and forty-seven. The sons of Harim, one thousand and seventeen.

26 The Levites: the sons of Jeshua and Kadmiel and Bannas and Sudias, seventy-four. [27]The temple singers: the sons of Asaph, one hundred and twenty-eight. [28]The gatekeepers: the sons of Shallum, the sons of Ater, the sons of Talmon, the sons of Akkub, the sons of Hatita, the sons of Shobai, in all one hundred and thirty-nine.

29 The temple servants: the sons of Ziha,[u] the sons of Hasupha, the sons of Tabbaoth, the sons of Keros, the sons of Siaha,[v] the sons of Padon, the sons of Lebanah, the sons of Hagabah, [30]the sons of Akkub, the sons of Uthai, the sons of Ketab, the sons of Hagab, the sons of Shamlai,[w] the sons of Hana, the sons of Cathua, the sons of Gahar,[x] [31]the sons of Reaiah,[y] the sons of Rezin,[z] the sons of Nekoda,[a] the sons of Chezib, the sons of Gazzam,[b] the sons of Uzza, the sons of

k Gk *Eneneus*   l Gk *Beelsarus*
m Gk *Aspharasus*   n Gk *Arsiphurith*
o Gk *Bethlomon*   p Gk *Kirama*
q Gk *Macalon*   r Gk *Betolio*
s Gk *Niphis*   t Gk *Calamolalus*
u Gk *Esau*   v Gk *Sua*
w Gk *Subai*   x Gk *Geddur*   y Gk *Jairus*
z Gk *Daisan*   a Gk *Noeba*   b Gk *Gazera*

---

differs from that in Ezra at many points, both as to names and numbers. The totals, however, are almost identical. The numbers of the priests and Levites are almost identical in the three lists, an indication that priestly and Levitical genealogies were more carefully preserved than the other lists. **24–25:** Only four divisions of priests are given, while in 1 Chr. ch. 24 twenty-four

Paseah,[c] the sons of Hasrah, the sons of Besai,[d] the sons of Asnah, the sons of the Meunites,[e] the sons of Nephisim, the sons of Bakbuk,[f] the sons of Hakupha, the sons of Asur, the sons of Pharakim, the sons of Bazluth, [32]the sons of Mehida, the sons of Cutha, the sons of Charea, the sons of Barkos, the sons of Sisera,[g] the sons of Temah, the sons of Neziah, the sons of Hatipha.

33 The sons of Solomon's servants: the sons of Hassophereth,[h] the sons of Peruda, the sons of Jaalah, the sons of Lozon, the sons of Giddel,[i] the sons of Shephatiah, [34]the sons of Hattil,[j] the sons of Pochereth-hazzebaim, the sons of Sarothie, the sons of Masiah, the sons of Gas, the sons of Addus, the sons of Subas, the sons of Apherra, the sons of Barodis, the sons of Shaphat, the sons of Ami.[k]

35 All the temple servants and the sons of Solomon's servants were three hundred and seventy-two.

36 The following are those who came up from Telmelah[l] and Telharsha, under the leadership of Cherub, Addan, and Immer, [37]though they could not prove by their fathers' houses or lineage that they belonged to Israel: the sons of Delaiah the son of Tobiah, the sons of Nekoda, six hundred and fifty-two.

38 Of the priests the following had assumed the priesthood but were not found registered: the sons of Habaiah, the sons of Hakkoz, the sons of Jaddus who had married Agia, one of the daughters of Barzillai, and was called by his name. [39]And when the genealogy of these men was sought in the register and was not found, they were excluded

from serving as priests. [40]And Nehemiah and Attharias[m] told them not to share in the holy things until a high priest should appear wearing Urim and Thummim.[n]

41 All those of Israel, twelve or more years of age, besides menservants and maidservants, were forty-two thousand three hundred and sixty; [42]their menservants and maidservants were seven thousand three hundred and thirty-seven; there were two hundred and forty-five musicians and singers. [43]There were four hundred and thirty-five camels, and seven thousand and thirty-six horses, two hundred and forty-five mules, and five thousand five hundred and twenty-five asses.

44 Some of the heads of families, when they came to the temple of God which is in Jerusalem, vowed that they would erect the house on its site, to the best of their ability, [45]and that they would give to the sacred treasury for the work a thousand minas of gold, five thousand minas of silver, and one hundred priests' garments.

46 The priests, the Levites, and some of the people[o] settled in Jerusalem and its vicinity; and the temple singers, the gatekeepers, and all Israel in their towns.

47 When the seventh month came, and the sons of Israel were each in his own home, they gathered as one man in the square before the first gate toward the east. [48]Then Jeshua the son of Jozadak, with his fellow priests, and Zerubbabel the son of Shealtiel,

c Gk Phinoe   d Gk Basthai   e Gk Maani
f Gk Acub or Acuph or Acum   g Gk Serar
h Gk Assaphioth   i Gk Isdael
j Gk Agia   k Gk Allon   l Gk Thermeleth
m Or the governor   n Gk Manifestation and Truth
o Or those who were of the people

---

divisions appear. **40**: The name *Nehemiah* is not found in the lists in Ezra and Nehemiah; "the governor" (see note *m*) orders the community to await the appearance of a high priest before participating in the holy things. The name is an addition to the text, arising from the circumstance that Nehemiah served as governor of Judah under appointment by Artaxerxes I (Neh.5.14). *Urim and Thummim* are the sacred lots used by the priests to receive oracular decisions (Ex.28.30; Lev.8.8; Dt.33.8; 1 Sam.14.41). **41**: The total exceeds the sum of the several groups listed, it being assumed that others were present who are not specifically mentioned in the list.

5.47–73: Work on the temple commences and is interrupted (Ezra 3.1–4.5; compare Josephus, *Antiq.* XI. iv.1–3). This section is confused because the building of the temple is placed both in with his kinsmen, took their places and prepared the altar of the God of Israel, ⁴⁹to offer burnt offerings upon it, in accordance with the directions in the book of Moses the man of God. ⁵⁰And some joined them from the other peoples of the land. And they erected the altar in its place, for all the peoples of the land were hostile to them and were stronger than they; and they offered sacrifices at the proper times and burnt offerings to the Lord morning and evening. ⁵¹They kept the feast of booths, as it is commanded in the law, and offered the proper sacrifices every day, ⁵²and thereafter the continual offerings and sacrifices on sabbaths and at new moons and at all the consecrated feasts. ⁵³And all who had made any vow to God began to offer sacrifices to God, from the new moon of the seventh month, though the temple of God was not yet built. ⁵⁴And they gave money to the masons and the carpenters, and food and drink ⁵⁵and carts*ᵖ* to the Sidonians and the Tyrians, to bring cedar logs from Lebanon and convey them in rafts to the harbor of Joppa, according to the decree which they had in writing from Cyrus king of the Persians.

56 In the second year after their coming to the temple of God in Jerusalem, in the second month, Zerubbabel the son of Shealtiel and Jeshua the son of Jozadak made a beginning, together with their brethren and the Levitical priests and all who had come to Jerusalem from the captivity; ⁵⁷and

they laid the foundation of the temple of God on the new moon of the second month in the second year after they came to Judea and Jerusalem. ⁵⁸And they appointed the Levites who were twenty or more years of age to have charge of the work of the Lord. And Jeshua arose, and his sons and brethren and Kadmiel his brother and the sons of Jeshua Emadabun and the sons of Joda son of Iliadun, with their sons and brethren, all the Levites, as one man pressing forward the work on the house of God.

So the builders built the temple of the Lord. ⁵⁹And the priests stood arrayed in their garments, with musical instruments and trumpets, and the Levites, the sons of Asaph, with cymbals, ⁶⁰praising the Lord and blessing him, according to the directions of David king of Israel; ⁶¹and they sang hymns, giving thanks to the Lord, because his goodness and his glory are for ever upon all Israel. ⁶²And all the people sounded trumpets and shouted with a great shout, praising the Lord for the erection of the house of the Lord. ⁶³Some of the Levitical priests and heads of fathers' houses, old men who had seen the former house, came to the building of this one with outcries and loud weeping, ⁶⁴while many came with trumpets and a joyful noise, ⁶⁵so that the people could not hear the trumpets because of the weeping of the people.

For the multitude sounded the trum-

p The Greek text is uncertain at this point

---

the reign of Cyrus (538–529 B.C.) and that of Darius (521–485 B.C.). A first return of exiles under Sheshbazzar and a second return under Zerubbabel and Jeshua have been merged. The true sequence of events is that Sheshbazzar returned to Judah shortly after 538 B.C., restored the sacrificial altar, resumed the cultic services, and laid the foundation of the temple. The work was halted until the return of additional exiles under Zerubbabel and Jeshua; when the work was resumed, opposition from Samaria, the capital of the province to which Judah belonged, quickly developed. Haggai and Zechariah encouraged the community to complete the temple, and work was begun once more; the temple was finally dedicated in 516 B.C. 47–55: It is highly doubtful that Zerubbabel and Jeshua were involved in the initial work under Sheshbazzar; the events recorded here belong to the period of rebuilding begun in the second year of Darius, not Cyrus. 51: The *feast of booths* is observed for one week beginning on the fifteenth day of the seventh month (Lev.23.39). 54: Minted *money* was in use in the Persian period. 56: Apparently the *second year* of Cyrus is intended, but the second year of Darius is the correct date. 59–65: The author erroneously speaks of the temple's being built at this time; the ceremony described

pets loudly, so that the sound was
heard afar; ⁶⁶and when the enemies of
the tribe of Judah and Benjamin heard
it, they came to find out what the sound
of the trumpets meant. ⁶⁷And they
learned that those who had returned
from captivity were building the temple
for the Lord God of Israel. ⁶⁸So they
approached Zerubbabel and Jeshua
and the heads of the fathers' houses
and said to them, "We will build with
you. ⁶⁹For we obey your Lord just as
you do, and we have been sacrificing
to him ever since the days of Esarhaddon*q* king of the Assyrians, who
brought us here." ⁷⁰But Zerubbabel
and Jeshua and the heads of the fathers'
houses in Israel said to them, "You
have nothing to do with us in building
the house for the Lord our God, ⁷¹for
we alone will build it for the Lord of
Israel, as Cyrus the king of the Persians
has commanded us." ⁷²But the peoples
of the land pressed hard*r* upon those in
Judea, cut off their supplies, and hindered their building; ⁷³and by plots and
demagoguery and uprisings they pre-
vented the completion of the building
as long as King Cyrus lived. And they
were kept from building for two years,
until the reign of Darius.

6 Now in the second year of the
reign of Darius, the prophets
Haggai and Zechariah the son of Iddo
prophesied to the Jews who were in
Judea and Jerusalem; they prophesied
to them in the name of the Lord God
of Israel. ²Then Zerubbabel the son of
Shealtiel and Jeshua the son of Jozadak
arose and began to build the house of
the Lord which is in Jerusalem, with
the help of the prophets of the Lord
who were with them.

3 At the same time Sisinnes the
governor of Syria and Phoenicia and
Sathrabuzanes and their associates
came to them and said, ⁴"By whose
order are you building this house and
this roof and finishing all the other
things? And who are the builders
that are finishing these things?" ⁵Yet
the elders of the Jews were dealt with
kindly, for the providence of the Lord
was over the captives; ⁶and they were
not prevented from building until
word could be sent to Darius concerning them and a report made.

7 A copy of the letter which Sisinnes the governor of Syria and Phoenicia, and Sathrabuzanes, and their
associates the local rulers in Syria
and Phoenicia, wrote and sent to
Darius:

8 "To King Darius, greeting. Let
it be fully known to our lord the king
that, when we went to the country of
Judea and entered the city of Jerusalem, we found the elders of the Jews,
who had been in captivity, ⁹building in
the city of Jerusalem a great new house
for the Lord, of hewn stone, with costly
timber laid in the walls. ¹⁰These operations are going on rapidly, and the
work is prospering in their hands and
being completed with all splendor and
care. ¹¹Then we asked these elders, 'At
whose command are you building this
house and laying the foundations of
this structure?' ¹²And in order that
we might inform you in writing who
the leaders are, we questioned them
and asked them for a list of the names
of those who are at their head. ¹³They
answered us, 'We are the servants of
the Lord who created the heaven and

q Gk *Asbasareth*
r The Greek text is uncertain at this point

---

in Ezra 3.10–13 occurred when the foundation of the temple was laid. **66–73:** Enemies interrupt
the work; they hear the sound of celebration, a detail not found in Ezra. **69:** Instead of *Esarhaddon,* Josephus (*Antiq.* XI. iv.3) reads Shalmaneser (as in 2 Kg. ch. 17). **73:** The *two years* from
the reign of Cyrus to that of Darius (compare 2.30) is a mistake; Ezra lacks this detail, although
in Ezra 4.24 the cessation of work until the time of Darius introduces a similar confusion.
 6.1–7.15: The temple completed (Ezra 4.24–6.22). Haggai and Zechariah encourage the
resumption of work on the temple and succeed in gaining support for Zerubbabel and Jeshua
(= Joshua; compare Hag.1.1–4; 2.1–4; Zech.4.9; 6.15). **6.3:** *Sisinnes* is Tattenai, governor of
the province "Beyond the River"; *Sathrabuzanes* is Shetherbozenai (Ezra 5.3). **14:** *A king of*

the earth. [14]And the house was built many years ago by a king of Israel who was great and strong, and it was finished. [15]But when our fathers sinned against the Lord of Israel who is in heaven, and provoked him, he gave them over into the hands of Nebuchadnezzar king of Babylon, king of the Chaldeans; [16]and they pulled down the house, and burned it, and carried the people away captive to Babylon. [17]But in the first year that Cyrus reigned over the country of Babylonia, King Cyrus wrote that this house should be rebuilt. [18]And the holy vessels of gold and of silver, which Nebuchadnezzar had taken out of the house in Jerusalem and stored in his own temple, these Cyrus the king took out again from the temple in Babylon, and they were delivered to Zerubbabel and Sheshbazzar[s] the governor [19]with the command that he should take all these vessels back and put them in the temple at Jerusalem, and that this temple of the Lord should be rebuilt on its site. [20]Then this Sheshbazzar,[s] after coming here, laid the foundations of the house of the Lord which is in Jerusalem, and although it has been in process of construction from that time until now, it has not yet reached completion.' [21]Now therefore, if it seems wise, O king, let search be made in the royal archives of our lord[t] the king that are in Babylon; [22]and if it is found that the building of the house of the Lord in Jerusalem was done with the consent of King Cyrus, and if it is approved by our lord the king, let him send us directions concerning these things."

23 Then King Darius commanded that search be made in the royal archives that were deposited in Babylon. And in Ecbatana, the fortress which is in the country of Media, a scroll[u] was found in which this was recorded: [24]"In the first year of the reign of Cyrus, King Cyrus ordered the building of the house of the Lord in Jerusalem, where they sacrifice with perpetual fire; [25]its height to be sixty cubits and its breadth sixty cubits, with three courses of hewn stone and one course of new native timber; the cost to be paid from the treasury of Cyrus the king; [26]and that the holy vessels of the house of the Lord, both of gold and of silver, which Nebuchadnezzar took out of the house in Jerusalem and carried away to Babylon, should be restored to the house in Jerusalem, to be placed where they had been."

27 So Darius[v] commanded Sisinnes the governor of Syria and Phoenicia, and Sathrabuzanes, and their associates, and those who were appointed as local rulers in Syria and Phoenicia, to keep away from the place, and to permit Zerubbabel, the servant of the Lord and governor of Judea, and the elders of the Jews to build this house of the Lord on its site. [28]"And I command that it be built completely, and that full effort be made to help the men who have returned from the captivity of Judea, until the house of the Lord is finished; [29]and that out of the tribute of Coelesyria and Phoenicia a portion be scrupulously given to these men, that is, to Zerubbabel the governor, for sacrifices to the Lord, for bulls and rams and lambs, [30]and likewise wheat and salt and wine and oil, regularly every year, without quibbling, for daily use as the priests in Jerusalem may indicate, [31]in order that libations may be made to the Most High God for the king and his children, and prayers be offered for their life."

32 And he commanded that if any should transgress or nullify any of the things herein written,[w] a beam should

s Gk *Sanabassarus*
t Other authorities read *of Cyrus*
u Other authorities read *passage*   v Gk *he*
w Other authorities read *stated above* or *added in writing*

Israel, namely Solomon. **18:** *Zerubbabel* is an addition; only Sheshbazzar is mentioned in Ezra 5.14 and in Josephus (*Antiq.* XI. iv.4). **23:** *Ecbatana* was the summer residence of Darius. **32:** Ezra 6.11 prescribes that violators of the decree be impaled and their house be made a be taken out of his house and he should be hanged upon it, and his property should be forfeited to the king.

33 "Therefore may the Lord, whose name is there called upon, destroy every king and nation that shall stretch out their hands to hinder or damage that house of the Lord in Jerusalem.

34 "I, King Darius, have decreed that it be done with all diligence as here prescribed."

7 Then Sisinnes the governor of Coelesyria and Phoenicia, and Sathrabuzanes, and their associates, following the orders of King Darius, ²supervised the holy work with very great care, assisting the elders of the Jews and the chief officers of the temple. ³And the holy work prospered, while the prophets Haggai and Zechariah prophesied; ⁴and they completed it by the command of the Lord God of Israel. So with the consent of Cyrus and Darius and Artaxerxes, kings of the Persians, ⁵the holy house was finished by the twenty-third day of the month of Adar, in the sixth year of King Darius. ⁶And the people of Israel, the priests, the Levites, and the rest of those from the captivity who joined them, did according to what was written in the book of Moses. ⁷They offered at the dedication of the temple of the Lord one hundred bulls, two hundred rams, four hundred lambs, ⁸and twelve he-goats for the sin of all Israel, according to the number of the twelve leaders of the tribes of Israel; ⁹and the priests and the Levites stood arrayed in their garments, according to kindred, for the services of the Lord God of Israel in accordance with the book of Moses; and the gatekeepers were at each gate.

10 The people of Israel who came from the captivity kept the passover on the fourteenth day of the first month, after the priests and the Levites were purified together. ¹¹Not all of the returned captives were purified, but the Levites were all purified together,ˣ ¹²and they sacrificed the passover lamb for all the returned captives and for their brethren the priests and for themselves. ¹³And the people of Israel who came from the captivity ate it, all those who had separated themselves from the abominations of the peoples of the land and sought the Lord. ¹⁴And they kept the feast of unleavened bread seven days, rejoicing before the Lord, ¹⁵because he had changed the will of the king of the Assyrians concerning them, to strengthen their hands for the service of the Lord God of Israel.

8 After these things, when Artaxerxes the king of the Persians was reigning, Ezra came, the son of Seraiah, son of Azariah, son of Hilkiah, son of Shallum, ²son of Zadok, son of Ahitub, son of Amariah, son of Uzzi, son of Bukki, son of Abishua, son of Phineas, son of Eleazar, son of Aaron the chief priest. ³This Ezra came up from Babylon as a scribe skilled in the law of Moses, which was given by the God of Israel; ⁴and the king showed him honor, for he found favor before the kingʸ in all his requests. ⁵There came up with him to Jerusalem some of the people of Israel and some of the priests

x The Greek text of this verse is uncertain   y Gk him

---

dunghill (2 Kg.10.27; Dan.2.5). **7.4:** *Artaxerxes* (see 8.1–9.36 n.) is erroneously named here (as also in Ezra 6.14); the name is omitted by Josephus because of the anachronism. **5:** The date intended is February-March, 516 B.C. **7–8:** Compare the account of the dedication of the first temple (1 Kg.8.5,63). **9:** Compare Ezra 6.18. **13:** Contrary to Ezra 6.21 the account here seems to suggest that only the returned exiles participated in the passover. **15:** The expression *king of the Assyrians* may be used because the Persian empire comprised the former empire of Assyria. Josephus refers to the Persian king (*Antiq.* XI. iv.8).

8.1–9.55: The history of Ezra (Ezra 7.1–10.44 and Neh.7.73–8.12). Ezra, whose name appears as author or central personality in 1 Esdras, is first introduced at this point in the document.

8.1–9.36: Ezra leads a group of exiles from Babylonia. The author ignores the work of Nehemiah (Neh. chs. 1–7), as Sirach ignores the work of Ezra (Sir.49.13). It is probable that and Levites and temple singers and gatekeepers and temple servants, [6]in the seventh year of the reign of Artaxerxes, in the fifth month (this was the king's seventh year); for they left Babylon on the new moon of the first month and arrived in Jerusalem on the new moon of the fifth month, by the prosperous journey which the Lord gave them.[z] [7]For Ezra possessed great knowledge, so that he omitted nothing from the law of the Lord or the commandments, but taught all Israel all the ordinances and judgments.

8 The following is a copy of the written commission from Artaxerxes the king which was delivered to Ezra the priest and reader of the law of the Lord:

9 "King Artaxerxes to Ezra the priest and reader of the law of the Lord, greeting. [10]In accordance with my gracious decision, I have given orders that those of the Jewish nation and of the priests and Levites and others in our realm, who freely choose to do so, may go with you to Jerusalem. [11]Let as many as are so disposed, therefore, depart with you as I and the seven friends who are my counselors have decided, [12]in order to look into matters in Judea and Jerusalem, in accordance with what is in the law of the Lord, [13]and to carry to Jerusalem the gifts for the Lord of Israel which I and my friends have vowed, and to collect for the Lord in Jerusalem all the gold and silver that may be found in the country of Babylonia, [14]together with what is given by the nation for the temple of their Lord which is in Jerusalem, both gold and silver for bulls and rams and lambs and

what goes with them, [15]so as to offer sacrifices upon the altar of their Lord which is in Jerusalem. [16]And whatever you and your brethren are minded to do with the gold and silver, perform it in accordance with the will of your God; [17]and deliver the holy vessels of the Lord which are given you for the use of the temple of your God which is in Jerusalem. [18]And whatever else occurs to you as necessary for the temple of your God, you may provide out of the royal treasury.

19 "And I, Artaxerxes the king, have commanded the treasurers of Syria and Phoenicia that whatever Ezra the priest and reader of the law of the Most High God sends for, they shall take care to give him, [20]up to a hundred talents of silver, and likewise up to a hundred cors of wheat, a hundred baths of wine, and salt in abundance. [21]Let all things prescribed in the law of God be scrupulously fulfilled for the Most High God, so that wrath may not come upon the kingdom of the king and his sons. [22]You are also informed that no tribute or any other tax is to be laid on any of the priests or Levites or temple singers or gatekeepers or temple servants or persons employed in this temple, and that no one has authority to impose any tax upon them.

23 "And you, Ezra, according to the wisdom of God, appoint judges and justices to judge all those who know the law of your God, throughout all Syria and Phoenicia; and those who do not know it you shall teach. [24]And all who transgress the law of your God or the law of the kingdom shall be strictly punished, whether by death or

z Other authorities add *for him* or *upon him*

Ezra came to Judea under Artaxerxes II (404–358 B.C.) rather than under Artaxerxes I (464–423 B.C.).

8.1–7: Ezra identified. 1–2: The genealogy is briefer than that in Ezra 7.1–5. **6:** *The seventh year* of Artaxerxes II was 398 or 397 B.C. (If Ezra came in the seventh year of Artaxerxes I, the date would be 458 or 457 B.C.). **7:** Ezra comes specifically as a teacher of *the law of the Lord.*

8.8–24: The letter of Artaxerxes to Ezra (Ezra 7.12–26). **11:** *The seven friends* or counselors of the king are referred to in Est.1.14 and Herodotus, *Hist.* III. 84. **20:** The *talent* was 75.5 U.S. pounds; the *cor* 6.5 bushels; and the *bath* about 6 gallons. **22:** Temple personnel are exempt from all taxes. **23–24:** Ezra is given authority to appoint judges throughout the entire province in order to maintain the Jewish law.

[16]

some other punishment, either fine or imprisonment."

25 Blessed be the Lord alone, who put this into the heart of the king, to glorify his house which is in Jerusalem, 26and who honored me in the sight of the king and his counselors and all his friends and nobles. 27I was encouraged by the help of the Lord my God, and I gathered men from Israel to go up with me.

28 These are the principal men, according to their fathers' houses and their groups, who went up with me from Babylon, in the reign of Artaxerxes the king: 29Of the sons of Phineas, Gershom. Of the sons of Ithamar, Gamael. Of the sons of David, Hattush the son of Shecaniah. 30Of the sons of Parosh, Zechariah, and with him a hundred and fifty men enrolled. 31Of the sons of Pahathmoab, Eliehoenai the son of Zerahiah, and with him two hundred men. 32Of the sons of Zattu, Shecaniah the son of Jahaziel, and with him three hundred men. Of the sons of Adin, Obed the son of Jonathan, and with him two hundred and fifty men. 33Of the sons of Elam, Jeshaiah the son of Gotholiah, and with him seventy men. 34Of the sons of Shephatiah, Zeraiah the son of Michael, and with him seventy men. 35Of the sons of Joab, Obadiah the son of Jehiel, and with him two hundred and twelve men. 36Of the sons of Bani, Shelomith the son of Josiphiah, and with him a hundred and sixty men. 37Of the sons of Bebai, Zechariah the son of Bebai, and with him twenty-eight men. 38Of the sons of Azgad, Johanan the son of Hakkatan, and with him a hundred and ten men. 39Of the sons of Adonikam, the last ones, their names being Eliphelet, Jeuel, and Shemaiah, and with them seventy men.

40Of the sons of Bigvai, Uthai the son of Istalcurus, and with him seventy men.

41 I assembled them at the river called Theras, and we encamped there three days, and I inspected them. 42When I found there none of the sons of the priests or of the Levites, 43I sent word to Eliezar, Iduel, Maasmas, 44Elnathan, Shemaiah, Jarib, Nathan, Elnathan, Zechariah, and Meshullam, who were leaders and men of understanding; 45and I told them to go to Iddo, who was the leading man at the place of the treasury, 46and ordered them to tell Iddo and his brethren and the treasurers at that place to send us men to serve as priests in the house of our Lord. 47And by the mighty hand of our Lord they brought us competent men of the sons of Mahli the son of Levi, son of Israel, namely Sherebiah*a* with his sons and kinsmen, eighteen; 48also Hashabiah and Annunus and Jeshaiah his brother, of the sons of Hananiah, and their sons, twenty men; 49and of the temple servants, whom David and the leaders had given for the service of the Levites, two hundred and twenty temple servants; the list of all their names was reported.

50 There I proclaimed a fast for the young men before our Lord, to seek from him a prosperous journey for ourselves and for our children and the cattle that were with us. 51For I was ashamed to ask the king for foot soldiers and horsemen and an escort to keep us safe from our adversaries; 52for we had said to the king, "The power of our Lord will be with those who seek him, and will support them in every way." 53And again we prayed to our Lord about these things, and we found him very merciful.

54 Then I set apart twelve of the

a Gk *Asebebias*

8.25–60: Ezra leads the exiles to Jerusalem (Ezra 7.27–8.30). **28–40**: The list of those who returned differs in a few particulars from that found in Ezra 8.1–14. **41**: *The river . . . Theras* (Ahava in Ezra 8.21) is probably a tributary of the Euphrates. **42–49**: Because neither priests nor Levites were among the group first assembled by Ezra, special measures had to be taken to secure the required number of both. **50**: Fasting prior to an important undertaking was common leaders of the priests, Sherebiah and Hashabiah, and ten of their kinsmen with them; ⁵⁵and I weighed out to them the silver and the gold and the holy vessels of the house of our Lord, which the king himself and his counselors and the nobles and all Israel had given. ⁵⁶I weighed and gave to them six hundred and fifty talents of silver, and silver vessels worth a hundred talents, and a hundred talents of gold, ⁵⁷and twenty golden bowls, and twelve bronze vessels of fine bronze that glittered like gold. ⁵⁸And I said to them, "You are holy to the Lord, and the vessels are holy, and the silver and the gold are vowed to the Lord, the Lord of our fathers. ⁵⁹Be watchful and on guard until you deliver them to the leaders of the priests and the Levites, and to the heads of the fathers' houses of Israel, in Jerusalem, in the chambers of the house of our Lord." ⁶⁰So the priests and the Levites who took the silver and the gold and the vessels which had been in Jerusalem carried them to the temple of the Lord.

61 We departed from the river Theras on the twelfth day of the first month; and we arrived in Jerusalem by the mighty hand of our Lord which was upon us; he delivered us from every enemy on the way, and so we came to Jerusalem. ⁶²When we had been there three days, the silver and the gold were weighed and delivered in the house of our Lord to Meremoth the priest, son of Uriah; ⁶³and with him was Eleazar the son of Phinehas,

and with them were Jozabad the son of Jeshua and Moeth the son of Binnui,[b] the Levites. ⁶⁴The whole was counted and weighed, and the weight of everything was recorded at that very time. ⁶⁵And those who had come back from captivity offered sacrifices to the Lord, the God of Israel, twelve bulls for all Israel, ninety-six rams, ⁶⁶seventy-two lambs, and as a thank offering twelve he-goats—all as a sacrifice to the Lord. ⁶⁷And they delivered the king's orders to the royal stewards and to the governors of Coelesyria and Phoenicia; and these officials[c] honored the people and the temple of the Lord.

68 After these things had been done, the principal men came to me and said, ⁶⁹"The people of Israel and the leaders and the priests and the Levites have not put away from themselves the alien peoples of the land and their pollutions, the Canaanites, the Hittites, the Perizzites, the Jebusites, the Moabites, the Egyptians, and the Edomites. ⁷⁰For they and their sons have married the daughters of these people,[d] and the holy race has been mixed with the alien peoples of the land; and from the beginning of this matter the leaders and the nobles have been sharing in this iniquity."

71 As soon as I heard these things, I rent my garments and my holy mantle, and pulled out hair from my head and beard, and sat down in anxiety and grief. ⁷²And all who were ever moved

b Gk *Sabannus*
c Gk *they*
d Gk *their daughters*

(2 Chr.20.3; Est.4.16; Jer.36.9). **58:** *Holy* objects could be entrusted only to those who were *holy* themselves.

8.61–67: Arrival in Jerusalem (Ezra 8.31–36). The treasures are placed in the temple storehouses (*chambers*, v. 59), sacrifices are offered to God, and the king's orders delivered to the provincial officers; the latter have no choice but to obey.

8.68–9.36: Mixed marriages in Judah (Ezra 9.1–10.44). No sooner does Ezra arrive than he is presented with evidence that the community has been corrupted by mixed marriages. The older legislation had warned against marriage with the population of Canaan upon entrance into the land (Dt.7.3) but had not expressly forbidden mixed marriages. Strong warnings had been issued, however, against Israel's adopting the abominable practices of the surrounding nations (Lev.18.24–30). During the exile Israel had been able to survive only on the basis of maintaining a relatively high level of racial integrity. The strict separation carried out by Ezra is therefore understandable; in the exile standards were probably higher on this issue than they were in Judah. (Nehemiah also faced the same problem; Neh.10.28–30; 13.3, 23–30).

at*ᵉ* the word of the Lord of Israel gathered round me, as I mourned over this iniquity, and I sat grief-stricken until the evening sacrifice. ⁷³Then I rose from my fast, with my garments and my holy mantle rent, and kneeling down and stretching forth my hands to the Lord ⁷⁴I said,

"O Lord, I am ashamed and confounded before thy face. ⁷⁵For our sins have risen higher than our heads, and our mistakes have mounted up to heaven ⁷⁶from the times of our fathers, and we are in great sin to this day. ⁷⁷And because of our sins and the sins of our fathers we with our brethren and our kings and our priests were given over to the kings of the earth, to the sword and captivity and plundering, in shame until this day. ⁷⁸And now in some measure mercy has come to us from thee, O Lord, to leave to us a root and a name in thy holy place, ⁷⁹and to uncover a light for us in the house of the Lord our God, and to give us food in the time of our servitude. ⁸⁰Even in our bondage we were not forsaken by our Lord, but he brought us into favor with the kings of the Persians, so that they have given us food ⁸¹and glorified the temple of our Lord, and raised Zion from desolation, to give us a stronghold in Judea and Jerusalem.

82 "And now, O Lord, what shall we say, when we have these things? For we have transgressed thy commandments, which thou didst give by thy servants the prophets, saying, ⁸³'The land which you are entering to take possession of it is a land polluted with the pollution of the aliens of the land, and they have filled it with their uncleanness. ⁸⁴Therefore do not give your daughters in marriage to their sons, and do not take their daughters for your sons; ⁸⁵and do not seek ever to have peace with them, in order that

you may be strong and eat the good things of the land and leave it for an inheritance to your children for ever.' ⁸⁶And all that has happened to us has come about because of our evil deeds and our great sins. For thou, O Lord, didst lift the burden of our sins ⁸⁷and give us such a root as this; but we turned back again to transgress thy law by mixing with the uncleanness of the peoples of the land. ⁸⁸Wast thou not angry enough with us to destroy us without leaving a root or seed or name? ⁸⁹O Lord of Israel, thou art true; for we are left as a root this day. ⁹⁰Behold, we are now before thee in our iniquities; for we can no longer stand in thy presence because of these things."

91 While Ezra was praying and making his confession, weeping and lying upon the ground before the temple, there gathered about him a very great throng from Jerusalem, men and women and youths; for there was great weeping among the multitude. ⁹²Then Shecaniah the son of Jehiel, one of the men of Israel, called out, and said to Ezra, "We have sinned against the Lord, and have married foreign women from the peoples of the land; but even now there is hope for Israel. ⁹³Let us take an oath to the Lord about this, that we will put away all our foreign wives, with their children, ⁹⁴as seems good to you and to all who obey the law of the Lord. ⁹⁵Arise*ᶠ* and take action, for it is your task, and we are with you to take strong measures." ⁹⁶Then Ezra arose and had the leaders of the priests and Levites of all Israel take oath that they would do this. And they took the oath.

9 Then Ezra rose and went from the court of the temple to the chamber

e Or *zealous for*
f Other authorities read *as seems good to you." And all who obeyed the law of the Lord rose and said to Ezra, "Arise*

8.74–90: Ezra's prayer (Ezra 9.6–15). Ezra speaks for the entire community, acknowledging the sin of all and the justice of their punishment by God. **82–85:** The prophetic books contain no such statement; the author may have in mind Lev.18.19–30.
　　8.91–9.36: The people repent and dismiss their foreign wives (Ezra 10.1–44). **9.4:** *The ruling*

of Jehohanan the son of Eliashib, ²and spent the night there; and he did not eat bread or drink water, for he was mourning over the great iniquities of the multitude. ³And a proclamatiòn was made throughout Judea and Jerusalem to all who had returned from the captivity that they should assemble at Jerusalem, ⁴and that if any did not meet there within two or three days, in accordance with the decision of the ruling elders, their cattle should be seized for sacrifice and the men themselvesᵍ expelled from the multitude of those who had returned from the captivity.

5 Then the men of the tribe of Judah and Benjamin assembled at Jerusalem within three days; this was the ninth month, on the twentieth day of the month. ⁶And all the multitude sat in the open square before the temple, shivering because of the bad weather that prevailed. ⁷Then Ezra rose and said to them, "You have broken the law and married foreign women, and so have increased the sin of Israel. ⁸Now then make confession and give glory to the Lord the God of our fathers, ⁹and do his will; separate yourselves from the peoples of the land and from your foreign wives." ¹⁰Then all the multitude shouted and said with a loud voice, "We will do as you have said. ¹¹But the multitude is great and it is winter, and we are not able to stand in the open air. This is not a work we can do in one day or two, for we have sinned too much in these things. ¹²So let the leaders of the multitude stay, and let all those in our settlements who have foreign wives come at the time appointed, ¹³with the elders and judges of each place, until we are freed from the wrath of the Lord over this matter."

¹⁴Jonathan the son of Asahel and Jahzeiah the son of Tikvahʰ undertook the matter on these terms, and Meshullam and Levi and Shabbethai served with them as judges. ¹⁵And those who had returned from the captivity acted in accordance with all this.

16 Ezra the priest chose for himself the leading men of their fathers' houses, all of them by name; and on the new moon of the tenth month they began their sessions to investigate the matter. ¹⁷And the cases of the men who had foreign wives were brought to an end by the new moon of the first month.

18 Of the priests those who were brought in and found to have foreign wives were: ¹⁹of the sons of Jeshua the son of Jozadak and his brethren, Maaseiah, Eliezar, Jarib, and Jodan. ²⁰They pledged themselves to put away their wives, and to give rams in expiation of their error. ²¹Of the sons of Immer: Hanani and Zebadiah and Maaseiah and Shemaiah and Jehiel and Azariah. ²²Of the sons of Pashhur: Elioenai, Maaseiah, Ishmael, and Nathanael, and Gedaliah, and Elasah.ⁱ

23 And of the Levites: Jozabad and Shimei and Kelaiah, who was Kelita, and Pethahiah and Judah and Jonah. ²⁴Of the temple singers: Eliashib and Zaccur.ʲ ²⁵Of the gatekeepers: Shallum and Telem.ᵏ

26 Of Israel: of the sons of Parosh: Ramiah, Izziah, Malchijah, Mijamin, and Eleazar, and Asibias, and Benaiah. ²⁷Of the sons of Elam: Mattaniah and

g Gk he himself   h Gk Thocanus
i Gk Salthas or Saloas
j Gk Bacchurus
k Gk Tolbanes

---

elders issue orders for the entire community to assemble within two or three days; Ezra is the religious, not the political, authority in the land. **7**: *The law,* i.e. Dt.7.3. **8**: To *give glory to the Lord* is to acknowledge themselves to be in the wrong (compare Jos.7.19). **11–13**: Because of the severe winter weather, it is agreed that the separation should take place in the local districts, and the multitude is dismissed. **16–17**: Three months are required to settle the cases, from the first of the *tenth month* (Tebet = December-January) to the first of the *first month* (Nisan = March-April). **18–36**: The list of those who put away foreign wives, including priests, Levites, and the laity. The list was probably preserved in the temple archives. **20**: An offering of a ram as a guilt offering (Ezra 10.19) was made *in expiation* of the sin. **22**: *Gedaliah,* Greek "Ocidelos" (the parallel in Ezra 10.22 reads "Jozabad"; compare Ezra 10.18).

Zechariah, Jehiel[l] and Abdi, and Jeremoth and Elijah. [28]Of the sons of Zattu:[m] Elioenai,[n] Eliashib, Othoniah, Jeremoth, and Zabad and Zerdaiah. [29]Of the sons of Bebai: Jehohanan and Hananiah and Zabbai and Emathis. [30]Of the sons of Bani:[o] Meshullam,[p] Malluch,[q] Adaiah, Jashub, and Sheal and Jeremoth. [31]Of the sons of Addi: Naathus and Moossias, Laccunus and Naidus, and Bescaspasmys and Sesthel, and Belnuus and Manasseas. [32]Of the sons of Annan: Elionas and Asaias and Melchias and Sabbaias and Simon Chosamaeus. [33]Of the sons of Hashum: Mattenai and Mattattah and Zabad and Eliphelet and Manasseh and Shimei. [34]Of the sons of Bani: Jeremai, Maadai,[r] Amram,[s] Joel, Mamdai and Bedeiah and Vaniah, Carabasion and Eliashib and Machnadebai,[t] Eliasis, Binnui, Elialis, Shimei, Shelemiah, Nethaniah. Of the sons of Ezora: Shashai, Azarel, Azael, Shemaiah,[u] Amariah,[v] Joseph. [35]Of the sons of Nebo:[w] Mattithiah,[x] Zabad, Iddo, Joel, Benaiah. [36]All these had married foreign women, and they put them away with their children.

37 The priests and the Levites and the men of Israel settled in Jerusalem and in the country. On the new moon of the seventh month, when the sons of Israel were in their settlements, [38]the whole multitude gathered with one accord into the open square before the east gate of the temple; [39]and they told Ezra the chief priest and reader to bring the law of Moses which had been given by the Lord God of Israel. [40]So Ezra the chief priest brought the law, for all the multitude, men and women, and all

the priests to hear the law, on the new moon of the seventh month. [41]And he read aloud in the open square before the gate of the temple from early morning until midday, in the presence of both men and women; and all the multitude gave attention to the law. [42]Ezra the priest and reader of the law stood on the wooden platform which had been prepared; [43]and beside him stood Mattathiah, Shema, Anaiah,[y] Azariah, Uriah, Hezekiah, and Baalsamus on his right hand, [44]and on his left Pedaiah, Mishael, Malchijah, Lothasubus, Nabariah, and Zechariah. [45]Then Ezra took up the book of the law in the sight of the multitude, for he had the place of honor in the presence of all. [46]And when he opened the law, they all stood erect. And Ezra blessed the Lord God Most High, the God of hosts, the Almighty; [47]and all the multitude answered, "Amen." And they lifted up their hands, and fell to the ground and worshiped the Lord. [48]Jeshua and Anniuth and Sherebiah, Jamin,[z] Akkub, Shabbethai, Hodiah, Maaseiah[a] and Kelita, Azariah and Jozabad, Hanan, Pelaiah, the Levites, taught the law of the Lord,[b] at the same time explaining what was read.

49 Then Attharates[c] said to Ezra the chief priest and reader, and to the

l Gk *Jezrielus*   m Gk *Zamoth*
n Gk *Eliadas*   o Gk *Mani*
p Gk *Olamus*   q Gk *Mamuchus*
r Gk *Momdius*   s Gk *Maerus*
t Gk *Mamnitanemus*
u Gk *Samatus*   v Gk *Zambris*
w Gk *Nooma*   x Gk *Mazitias*
y Gk *Ananias*   z Gk *Jadinus*
a Gk *Maiannas*
b Other authorities add *and read the law of the Lord to the multitude*
c Or *the governor*

9.37–55: Ezra's public reading of the law (Neh.7.73–8.12). **37:** *The new moon* or first day *of the seventh month* was a day of holy convocation (Lev.23.23–24; Num.29.1), the day of the New Year. **39:** Ezra is not identified elsewhere as the *chief priest* (in Neh.8.2 he is called the priest). *The law of Moses* is either the present Pentateuch or (more probably) the major legal portions of it. **42:** The *platform* erected for Ezra probably continued the tradition whereby kings would appear before the people to reaffirm the covenant law on the festal occasion at the turn of the year (compare 2 Chr.20.5; 23.13; 29.4). **48:** The Levites explained the law to the people, perhaps translating it (or its difficult portions) into Aramaic for those who may not have been familiar with Hebrew. **49:** *Attharates* is a corruption of *tirshatha*, "governor," in Neh.8.9. 1 Esdras does not intend to indicate that Nehemiah, whom some have identified with Attharates the governor, was a participant in the festivity (in Neh.8.9 the name of Nehemiah is

Levites who were teaching the multitude, and to all, [50]"This day is holy to the Lord"—now they were all weeping as they heard the law—[51]"so go your way, eat the fat and drink the sweet, and send portions to those who have none; [52]for the day is holy to the Lord; and do not be sorrowful, for the Lord will exalt you." [53]And the Levites commanded all the people, saying,

"This day is holy; do not be sorrowful." [54]Then they all went their way, to eat and drink and enjoy themselves, and to give portions to those who had none, and to make great rejoicing; [55]because they were inspired by the words which they had been taught. And they came together.[d]

d The Greek text ends abruptly: compare Nehemiah 8.13

---

an intrusion). **50–55**: The people are to rejoice even though the words of the law cause them to recognize their sin. **55**: The book ends abruptly; originally it may have continued with the story of the great celebration of the feast of booths (Neh.8.13–18). This would have been a fitting conclusion to the work, since it begins with the account of Josiah's great passover celebration.

THE SECOND BOOK OF

ESDRAS

The book commonly known as 2 Esdras differs from the other fourteen books of the Apocrypha in being an apocalypse (for the characteristics of apocalyptic literature, see p. xii above). The main part of 2 Esdras is a series of seven revelations (3.1–5.20; 5.21–6.34; 6.35–9.25; 9.38–10.59; 11.1–12.51; 13.1–58; 14.1–48), in which the seer is instructed by the angel Uriel concerning some of the great mysteries of the moral world.

The problems concerning the composition and transmission of 2 Esdras are extremely complicated. The author of the central portion (chs. 3–14) was an unknown Palestinian Jew who probably wrote in Hebrew or Aramaic near the close of the first century A.D. Subsequently his book was translated into Greek. About the middle of the next century an unknown Christian editor added in Greek an introductory section, which now comprises chs. 1–2. Nearly a century later another unknown Christian appended chs. 15–16, also in Greek.

The Semitic original and almost all of the Greek text have been lost (only 15.57–59 survives on a scrap of Greek papyrus). Before the text of the central section (chs. 3–14) perished, however, translations were made into several other languages, namely Syriac, Coptic, Ethiopic, Arabic (two independent versions), Armenian, and Georgian. In the West the entire book (chs. 1–16) circulated in several Old Latin versions. A later form of the Latin text is printed, since the Council of Trent, as an appendix to the New Testament in the Roman Catholic Vulgate Bible, where it is called the Fourth Book of Esdras.

The purpose of the original author of 2 Esdras was not only to denounce the wickedness of Rome (under the image of "Babylon") and to lament the sorrows that had befallen Jerusalem, but to wrestle with one of the most perplexing of all religious questions, the problem of theodicy, that is the reconciliation of God's justice, wisdom, power, and goodness with the many evils that beset mankind. In spite of the essentially pessimistic outlook of the book, the seer's strong religious faith enabled him to rise above the fires of adversity to high spiritual levels. His agonizing is both honorable and pathetic as he seeks "to justify the ways of God to man."

THE SECOND BOOK OF THE PROPHET Ezra the son of Seraiah, son of Azariah, son of Hilkiah, son of Shallum, son of Zadok, son of Ahitub, ²son of Ahijah, son of Phinehas, son of Eli, son of Amariah, son of Azariah, son of Meraioth, son of Arna, son of Uzzi, son of Borith, son of Abishua, son of Phinehas, son of Eleazar, ³son of Aaron, of the tribe of Levi, who was a captive in the country of the Medes in the reign of Artaxerxes, king of the Persians.

4 The word of the Lord came to me, saying, ⁵"Go and declare to my people their evil deeds, and to their children the iniquities which they have committed against me, so that they may tell their children's children ⁶that the sins of their parents have increased in them, for they have forgotten me and have offered sacrifices to strange gods. ⁷Was it not I who brought them out of the land of Egypt, out of the house of bondage? But they have angered me and despised my counsels. ⁸Pull out the hair of your head and hurl all evils upon them, for they have not obeyed my law—they are a rebellious people. ⁹How long shall I endure them, on

---

1.1–2.48: Ezra is commanded to reprove the Jewish people. 1.1–3: The genealogy of Ezra, who is of priestly descent (compare the somewhat different genealogies in Ezra 7.1–5 and 1 Esd.8.1–2). **3:** *Artaxerxes* II, reigned 404–358 B.C.

1.4–11: Ezra receives a prophetic call. 4: The expression, *the word of the Lord came . . .*, so typical of prophetic authorization, is absent from the canonical book of Ezra. **5:** Is.58.1. **8:** The command to *pull out his hair* is to be connected with Ezra's denunciation (*hurl all evils*) of his

[23]

whom I have bestowed such great benefits? ¹⁰For their sake I have overthrown many kings; I struck down Pharaoh with his servants, and all his army. ¹¹I have destroyed all nations before them, and scattered in the east the people of two provinces, Tyre and Sidon; I have slain all their enemies.

12 "But speak to them and say, Thus says the Lord: ¹³Surely it was I who brought you through the sea, and made safe highways for you where there was no road; I gave you Moses as leader and Aaron as priest; ¹⁴I provided light for you from a pillar of fire, and did great wonders among you. Yet you have forgotten me, says the Lord.

15 "Thus says the Lord Almighty: The quails were a sign to you; I gave you camps for your protection, and in them you complained. ¹⁶You have not exulted in my name at the destruction of your enemies, but to this day you still complain. ¹⁷Where are the benefits which I bestowed on you? When you were hungry and thirsty in the wilderness, did you not cry out to me, ¹⁸saying, 'Why hast thou led us into this wilderness to kill us? It would have been better for us to serve the Egyptians than to die in this wilderness.' ¹⁹I pitied your groanings and gave you manna for food; you ate the bread of angels. ²⁰When you were thirsty, did I not cleave the rock so that waters flowed in abundance? Because of the heat I covered you with the leaves of trees. ²¹I divided fertile lands among you; I drove out the Canaanites, the Perizzites, and the Philistines before you. What more can I do for you? says the Lord. ²²Thus says the Lord Almighty: When you were in the wilderness, at the bitter stream, thirsty and blaspheming my name, ²³I did not send fire upon you for your blasphemies, but threw a tree into the water and made the stream sweet.

24 "What shall I do to you, O Jacob? You would not obey me, O Judah. I will turn to other nations and will give them my name, that they may keep my statutes. ²⁵Because you have forsaken me, I also will forsake you. When you beg mercy of me, I will show you no mercy. ²⁶When you call upon me, I will not listen to you; for you have defiled your hands with blood, and your feet are swift to commit murder. ²⁷It is not as though you had forsaken me; you have forsaken yourselves, says the Lord.

28 "Thus says the Lord Almighty: Have I not entreated you as a father entreats his sons or a mother her daughters or a nurse her children, ²⁹that you should be my people and I should be your God, and that you should be my sons and I should be your father? ³⁰I gathered you as a hen gathers her brood under her wings. But now, what shall I do to you? I will cast you out from my presence. ³¹When you offer oblations to me, I will turn my face from you; for I have rejected your feast days, and new moons, and circumcisions of the flesh. ³²I sent to you my servants the prophets, but you have taken and slain them and torn their bodies in pieces; their blood I will require of you, says the Lord.

33 "Thus says the Lord Almighty: Your house is desolate; I will drive you out as the wind drives straw; ³⁴and your sons will have no children, be-

---

people. **10:** Ex.14.28. **11:** The author is confused; *Tyre and Sidon*, which were cities, not *provinces*, lay to the west of the land of the Medes (v. 3).
    1.12–23: Summary of God's mercies to Israel. 13: Ex.14.29. **14:** Ex.13.21. **15:** Ex.16.13; Ps.105.40. **17–18:** Num.14.3. **19:** *The bread of angels*, Ps. 78.25; Wis.16.20. **20:** Num.20.11; Wis.11.4. **22–23:** Ex.15.22–25.
    1.24–32: The casting-off of Israel. 26: Is.1.15; 59.7. **29:** Jer.24.7; Heb.8.10. **30:** The similarity with Mt.23.37 and Lk.13.34 suggests that the author of this part of 2 Esdras was a Jewish Christian. **32:** Compare Mt. 23.34–35.
    1.33–40: God will give Israel's houses to another people. 35–36: Gentile Christians are meant

cause with you they have neglected my commandment and have done what is evil in my sight. ³⁵I will give your houses to a people that will come, who without having heard me will believe. Those to whom I have shown no signs will do what I have commanded. ³⁶They have seen no prophets, yet will recall their former state.ᵃ ³⁷I call to witness the gratitude of the people that is to come, whose children rejoice with gladness; though they do not see me with bodily eyes, yet with the spirit they will believe the things I have said.

38 "And now, father, look with pride and see the people coming from the east; ³⁹to them I will give as leaders Abraham, Isaac, and Jacob and Hosea and Amos and Micah and Joel and Obadiah and Jonah ⁴⁰and Nahum and Habakkuk, Zephaniah, Haggai, Zechariah and Malachi, who is also called the messenger of the Lord.

2 "Thus says the Lord: I brought this people out of bondage, and I gave them commandments through my servants the prophets; but they would not listen to them, and made my counsels void. ²The mother who bore them says to them, 'Go, my children, because I am a widow and forsaken. ³I brought you up with gladness; but with mourning and sorrow I have lost you, because you have sinned before the Lord God and have done what is evil in my sight. ⁴But now what can I do for you? For I am a widow and forsaken. Go, my children, and ask for mercy from the Lord.' ⁵I call upon you, father, as a witness in addition to the mother of the children, because they would not

keep my covenant, ⁶that you may bring confusion upon them and bring their mother to ruin, so that they may have no offspring. ⁷Let them be scattered among the nations, let their names be blotted out from the earth, because they have despised my covenant.

8 "Woe to you, Assyria, who conceal the unrighteous in your midst! O wicked nation, remember what I did to Sodom and Gomorrah, ⁹whose land lies in lumps of pitch and heaps of ashes. So will I do to those who have not listened to me, says the Lord Almighty."

10 Thus says the Lord to Ezra: "Tell my people that I will give them the kingdom of Jerusalem, which I was going to give to Israel. ¹¹Moreover, I will take back to myself their glory, and will give to these others the everlasting habitations, which I had prepared for Israel.ᵇ ¹²The tree of life shall give them fragrant perfume, and they shall neither toil nor become weary. ¹³Ask and you will receive; pray that your days may be few, that they may be shortened. The kingdom is already prepared for you; watch! ¹⁴Call, O call heaven and earth to witness, for I left out evil and created good, because I live, says the Lord.

15 "Mother, embrace your sons; bring them up with gladness, as does the dove; establish their feet, because I have chosen you, says the Lord. ¹⁶And I will raise up the dead from their places, and will bring them out from their tombs, because I recognize

a Other authorities read *their iniquities*
b Lat *those*

(compare Rom.10.14–20). **37:** *With bodily eyes,* Jn.20.29. **38:** God is represented as addressing Ezra as *father* of the nation. **39–40:** The three patriarchs and the twelve minor prophets, arranged in the order of the Septuagint.

　　2.1–9: The Lord's anger against Israel. 2: *The mother who bore them,* Jerusalem (Is.54.1; Gal.4.26–27). *Go . . . ,* Bar.4.19. **3:** *I* Bar.4.11. **5:** The writer addresses Ezra as *father.* **6:** *To ruin,* in the fall of Jerusalem, A.D. 70. **8:** By the name *Assyria,* Israel's ancient foe, the author refers cryptically to Rome. *Sodom and Gomorrah,* Gen.19.24.

　　2.10–14: Israel's habitation to be given to others. 10: *My people,* i.e. the Christians (compare Hos.2.23). **11:** *Everlasting habitations,* Lk.16.9. **12:** Rev.2.7; 22.2,14. **13:** Mt.7.7–8; Lk.11.9–10; Mt.25.34.

　　2.15–32: Exhortation to good works. 15: *Mother,* probably a reference to the church.

my name in them. ¹⁷Do not fear, mother of the sons, for I have chosen you, says the Lord. ¹⁸I will send you help, my servants Isaiah and Jeremiah. According to their counsel I have consecrated and prepared for you twelve trees loaded with various fruits, ¹⁹and the same number of springs flowing with milk and honey, and seven mighty mountains on which roses and lilies grow; by these I will fill your children with joy. ²⁰Guard the rights of the widow, secure justice for the fatherless, give to the needy, defend the orphan, clothe the naked, ²¹care for the injured and the weak, do not ridicule a lame man, protect the maimed, and let the blind man have a vision of my splendor. ²²Protect the old and the young within your walls; ²³when you find any who are dead, commit them to the grave and mark it,ᶜ and I will give you the first place in my resurrection. ²⁴Pause and be quiet, my people, because your rest will come. ²⁵Good nurse, nourish your sons, and strengthen their feet. ²⁶Not one of the servants whom I have given you will perish, for I will require them from among your number. ²⁷Do not be anxious, for when the day of tribulation and anguish comes, others shall weep and be sorrowful, but you shall rejoice and have abundance. ²⁸The nations shall envy you but they shall not be able to do anything against you, says the Lord. ²⁹My hands will cover you, that your sons may not see Gehenna. ³⁰Rejoice, O mother, with your sons, because I will deliver you, says the Lord. ³¹Remember your sons that sleep, because I will bring them out of the hiding places of the earth, and will show mercy to them; for I am merciful, says the Lord Almighty. ³²Embrace your children until I come,

and proclaim mercy to them; because my springs run over, and my grace will not fail."

33 I, Ezra, received a command from the Lord on Mount Horeb to go to Israel. When I came to them they rejected me and refused the Lord's commandment. ³⁴Therefore I say to you, O nations that hear and understand, "Await your shepherd; he will give you everlasting rest, because he who will come at the end of the age is close at hand. ³⁵Be ready for the rewards of the kingdom, because the eternal light will shine upon you for evermore. ³⁶Flee from the shadow of this age, receive the joy of your glory; I publicly call on my Savior to witness.ᵈ ³⁷Receive what the Lord has entrusted to you and be joyful, giving thanks to him who has called you to heavenly kingdoms. ³⁸Rise and stand, and see at the feast of the Lord the number of those who have been sealed. ³⁹Those who have departed from the shadow of this age have received glorious garments from the Lord. ⁴⁰Take again your full number, O Zion, and conclude the list of your people who are clothed in white, who have fulfilled the law of the Lord. ⁴¹The number of your children, whom you desired, is full; beseech the Lord's power that your people, who have been called from the beginning, may be made holy."

42 I, Ezra, saw on Mount Zion a great multitude, which I could not number, and they all were praising the Lord with songs. ⁴³In their midst was a young man of great stature, taller than any of the others, and on the head of each of them he placed a crown, but he was more exalted than they. And I

c Or *seal it; or mark them and commit them to the grave*
d Other authorities read *I testify that my Savior has been commissioned by the Lord*

18: *Twelve trees,* Rev.22.2. **19:** *Milk and honey,* Dt.31.20. **23:** *Find any . . . dead,* compare Tob.1.17–19. **26:** Jn.17.12. **29:** *Gehenna,* place of torment.
2.33–41: Rejected by Israel, Ezra turns to the Gentiles. 33: *On Mount Horeb,* like a second Moses (Ex.3.1; 2 Chr.5.10). **35:** *The eternal light,* Is.60.20; Rev.21.23; 22.5. **40:** *Zion,* Heb. 12.22–23. *Clothed in white,* Rev.3.4; 6.11; 7.14. **41:** *The number . . . is full,* see 4.36–37 n.; Rev. 6.11. *Called,* Rom.8.29–30.
2.42–48: Ezra's vision of a great multitude. 42: Rev.7.9. **43:** *A young man,* compare v. 47 and Enoch 46.1.

was held spellbound. ⁴⁴Then I asked an angel, "Who are these, my lord?" ⁴⁵He answered and said to me, "These are they who have put off mortal clothing and have put on the immortal, and they have confessed the name of God; now they are being crowned, and receive palms." ⁴⁶Then I said to the angel, "Who is that young man who places crowns on them and puts palms in their hands?" ⁴⁷He answered and said to me, "He is the Son of God, whom they confessed in the world." So I began to praise those who had stood valiantly for the name of the Lord. ⁴⁸Then the angel said to me, "Go, tell my people how great and many are the wonders of the Lord God which you have seen."

3 In the thirtieth year after the destruction of our city, I Salathiel, who am also called Ezra, was in Babylon. I was troubled as I lay on my bed, and my thoughts welled up in my heart, ²because I saw the desolation of Zion and the wealth of those who lived in Babylon. ³My spirit was greatly agitated, and I began to speak anxious words to the Most High, and said, ⁴"O sovereign Lord, didst thou not speak at the beginning when thou didst form the earth—and that without help—and didst command the dust*e* ⁵and it gave*f* thee Adam, a lifeless body? Yet he was the workmanship of thy hands, and thou didst breathe into him the breath of life, and he was made alive in thy presence. ⁶And thou didst lead him into the garden which thy right hand had planted before the earth appeared. ⁷And thou didst lay upon

him one commandment of thine; but he transgressed it, and immediately thou didst appoint death for him and for his descendants. From him there sprang nations and tribes, peoples and clans, without number. ⁸And every nation walked after its own will and did ungodly things before thee and scorned thee, and thou didst not hinder them. ⁹But again, in its time thou didst bring the flood upon the inhabitants of the world and destroy them. ¹⁰And the same fate befell them: as death came upon Adam, so the flood upon them. ¹¹But thou didst leave one of them, Noah with his household, and all the righteous who have descended from him.

12 "When those who dwelt on earth began to multiply, they produced children and peoples and many nations, and again they began to be more ungodly than were their ancestors. ¹³And when they were committing iniquity before thee, thou didst choose for thyself one of them, whose name was Abraham; ¹⁴and thou didst love him, and to him only didst thou reveal the end of the times, secretly by night. ¹⁵Thou didst make with him an everlasting covenant, and promise him that thou wouldst never forsake his descendants; and thou gavest to him Isaac, and to Isaac thou gavest Jacob and Esau. ¹⁶And thou didst set apart Jacob for thyself, but Esau thou didst reject; and Jacob became a great multitude. ¹⁷And when thou didst lead his descendants out of Egypt, thou didst bring them to Mount Sinai. ¹⁸Thou

e Syr Ethiop
f Syr

3.1–5.20: The first vision. 3.1–3: Introduction. 1: *The thirtieth year after the destruction* of Jerusalem by Nebuchadnezzar in 587/6 B.C. (2 Kg.25.1ff.) would be 557/6 B.C. The date specified may imply that the author was writing about A.D.100 (i.e. thirty years after the fall of Jerusalem in A.D.70). *Salathiel* is the Greek form of Shealtiel (Ezra 3.2; 5.2; Neh.12.1). The words *who am also called Ezra* are an anachronistic gloss; Ezra lived a century later.

3.4–36: The author raises perplexing questions. Whence comes sin with its consequent misery? How can Israel's continuing affliction be reconciled with God's justice? 4–5: The creation of Adam. 6–8: Adam's sin brings death on all mankind. 7: The words *immediately thou didst appoint death* imply that Adam was not originally intended to be mortal (compare Wis.1.13–14; 2.23–24). 8: Gen.6.12. 9–11: The flood (Gen.6.11ff.). 12–16: The choice of Abraham (Gen. 12.1; 17.5). 14: *By night*, Gen.15.5,12,17. 17–19: The Exodus and the giving of the law. 18:

didst bend down the heavens and shake[g] the earth, and move the world, and make the depths to tremble, and trouble the times. [19]And thy glory passed through the four gates of fire and earthquake and wind and ice, to give the law to the descendants of Jacob, and thy commandment to the posterity of Israel.

20 "Yet thou didst not take away from them their evil heart, so that thy law might bring forth fruit in them. [21]For the first Adam, burdened with an evil heart, transgressed and was overcome, as were also all who were descended from him. [22]Thus the disease became permanent; the law was in the people's heart along with the evil root, but what was good departed, and the evil remained. [23]So the times passed and the years were completed, and thou didst raise up for thyself a servant, named David. [24]And thou didst command him to build a city for thy name, and in it to offer thee oblations from what is thine. [25]This was done for many years; but the inhabitants of the city transgressed, [26]in everything doing as Adam and all his descendants had done, for they also had the evil heart. [27]So thou didst deliver the city into the hands of thy enemies.

28 "Then I said in my heart, Are the deeds of those who inhabit Babylon any better? Is that why she has gained dominion over Zion? [29]For when I came here I saw ungodly deeds without number, and my soul has seen many sinners during these thirty years.[h] And my heart failed me, [30]for I have seen how thou dost endure those who sin, and hast spared those who act wickedly, and hast destroyed thy people, and hast preserved thy enemies, [31]and hast not shown to any one how thy way may be comprehended.[i] Are the deeds of Babylon better than those of Zion? [32]Or has another nation known thee besides Israel? Or what tribes have so believed thy covenants as these tribes of Jacob? [33]Yet their reward has not appeared and their labor has borne no fruit. For I have traveled widely among the nations and have seen that they abound in wealth, though they are unmindful of thy commandments. [34]Now therefore weigh in a balance our iniquities and those of the inhabitants of the world; and so it will be found which way the turn of the scale will incline. [35]When have the inhabitants of the earth not sinned in thy sight? Or what nation has kept thy commandments so well? [36]Thou mayest indeed find individual men who have kept thy commandments, but nations thou wilt not find."

4 Then the angel that had been sent to me, whose name was Uriel, answered [2]and said to me, "Your understanding has utterly failed regarding this world, and do you think you can comprehend the way of the Most High?" [3]Then I said, "Yes, my lord." And he replied to me, "I have been sent to show you three ways, and to put before you three problems. [4]If you can solve one of them for me, I also will show you the way you desire to see, and will teach you why the heart is evil."

5 I said, "Speak on, my lord." And he said to me, "Go, weigh for me the weight of fire, or measure for

g Syr Ethiop Arab 1 Georg: Lat *didst set fast*
h Ethiop Arab 1 Arm: Lat Syr *in this thirtieth year*
i Syr: Lat *how this way should be forsaken*

Compare Ex.19.16–18; Ps. 68.7–8. **20–27:** The tendency to sin is universal and permanent. **20:** *Evil heart*, the evil *yeser* (see Sir.15.14 n.). **28–36:** The deeds of Babylon compared with those of Israel. **28:** *Babylon*, i.e. Rome (Rev.14.8). **29:** *Came here*, to Rome. The first *thirty years* of the Babylonian exile are meant. **30:** Here the author expresses the essence of the problem. **34:** For God's balance, compare Job 31.6; Ps. 62.9; Pr.16.2; Dan.5.27; Enoch 41.1; 61.8. **36:** *Individual men* among the Gentiles.
4.1–5.19: The reply: God's ways are beyond human comprehension.
4.1–12: The limitations of the human mind (Wis.9.16). **1:** The name *Uriel* in Hebrew means "the fire of God." According to Enoch 20.2 Uriel is a watcher over the world and over Tartarus, the lowest part of hell (compare 2 Pet.2.4 marg.).

me a measure[j] of wind, or call back for me the day that is past."

6 I answered and said, "Who of those that have been born can do this, that you ask me concerning these things?"

7 And he said to me, "If I had asked you, 'How many dwellings are in the heart of the sea, or how many streams are at the source of the deep, or how many streams are above the firmament, or which are the exits of hell, or which are the entrances[k] of paradise?' [8]perhaps you would have said to me, 'I never went down into the deep, nor as yet into hell, neither did I ever ascend into heaven.' [9]But now I have asked you only about fire and wind and the day, things through which you have passed and without which you cannot exist,[l] and you have given me no answer about them!" [10]And he said to me, "You cannot understand the things with which you have grown up; [11]how then can your mind comprehend the way of the Most High? And how can one who is already worn out[m] by the corrupt world understand incorruption?"[n] When I heard this, I fell on my face[o] [12]and said to him, "It would be better for us not to be here than to come here and live in ungodliness, and to suffer and not understand why."

13 He answered me and said, "I went into a forest of trees of the plain, and they made a plan [14]and said, 'Come, let us go and make war against the sea, that it may recede before us, and that we may make for ourselves more forests.' [15]And in like manner the waves of the sea also made a plan and said, 'Come, let us go up and subdue the forest of the plain so that there also we may gain more territory for ourselves.' [16]But the plan of the forest was in vain, for the fire came and consumed it; [17]likewise also the plan of the waves of the sea, for the sand stood firm and stopped them. [18]If now you

were a judge between them, which would you undertake to justify, and which to condemn?"

19 I answered and said, "Each has made a foolish plan, for the land is assigned to the forest, and to the sea is assigned a place to carry its waves."

20 He answered me and said, "You have judged rightly, but why have you not judged so in your own case? [21]For as the land is assigned to the forest and the sea to its waves, so also those who dwell upon earth can understand only what is on the earth, and he who is above the heavens can understand what is above the height of the heavens."

22 Then I answered and said, "I beseech you, my lord, why[p] have I been endowed with the power of understanding? [23]For I did not wish to inquire about the ways above, but about those things which we daily experience: why Israel has been given over to the Gentiles as a reproach; why the people whom you loved has been given over to godless tribes, and the law of our fathers has been made of no effect and the written covenants no longer exist; [24]and why we pass from the world like locusts, and our life is like a mist,[q] and we are not worthy to obtain mercy. [25]But what will he do for his name, by which we are called? It is about these things that I have asked."

26 He answered me and said, "If you are alive, you will see, and if you live long,[r] you will often marvel, because the age is hastening swiftly to its end. [27]For it will not be able to bring the things that have been promised to the righteous in their appointed times, because this age is full of sadness

j Syr Ethiop Arab Georg: Lat *a blast*
k Syr Compare Ethiop Arab 2 Arm: Latin omits *of hell, or which are the entrances*
l Other Latin manuscripts read *from which you cannot be separated*
m The text here is uncertain
n Syr Ethiop *the way of the incorruptible?*
o Syr Ethiop Arab 1: Latin is corrupt
p Syr Ethiop Arm: Latin is corrupt
q Syr Ethiop Arab Georg: Lat *a trembling*
r Syr: Lat *live*

4.13–21: **Parable of the conflict between the forest and the sea. 21:** Is.55.8–9; Jn.3.31; 1 Cor. 2.14.
4.22–32: **Additional questions. 26–32:** The angel answers that the new age, soon to dawn,

and infirmities. [28]For the evil about which[s] you ask me has been sown, but the harvest of it has not yet come. [29]If therefore that which has been sown is not reaped, and if the place where the evil has been sown does not pass away, the field where the good has been sown will not come. [30]For a grain of evil seed was sown in Adam's heart from the beginning, and how much ungodliness it has produced until now, and will produce until the time of threshing comes! [31]Consider now for yourself how much fruit of ungodliness a grain of evil seed has produced. [32]When heads of grain without number are sown, how great a threshing floor they will fill!"

33 Then I answered and said, "How long[t] and when will these things be? Why are our years few and evil?" [34]He answered me and said, "You do not hasten faster than the Most High, for your haste is for yourself,[u] but the Highest hastens on behalf of many. [35]Did not the souls of the righteous in their chambers ask about these matters, saying, 'How long are we to remain here?[v] And when will come the harvest of our reward?' [36]And Jeremiel the archangel answered them and said, 'When the number of those like yourselves is completed;[w] for he has weighed the age in the balance, [37]and measured the times by measure, and numbered the times by number; and he will not move or arouse them until that measure is fulfilled.' "

38 Then I answered and said, "O sovereign Lord, but all of us also are full of ungodliness. [39]And it is perhaps on account of us that the time of threshing is delayed for the righteous— on account of the sins of those who dwell on earth."

40 He answered me and said, "Go and ask a woman who is with child if, when her nine months have been completed, her womb can keep the child within her any longer."

41 And I said, "No, lord, it cannot." And he said to me, "In Hades the chambers of the souls are like the womb. [42]For just as a woman who is in travail makes haste to escape the pangs of birth, so also do these places hasten to give back those things that were committed to them from the beginning. [43]Then the things that you desire to see will be disclosed to you."

44 I answered and said, "If I have found favor in your sight, and if it is possible, and if I am worthy, [45]show me this also: whether more time is to come than has passed, or whether for us the greater part has gone by. [46]For I know what has gone by, but I do not know what is to come."

47 And he said to me, "Stand at my right side, and I will show you the interpretation of a parable."

48 So I stood and looked, and behold, a flaming furnace passed by before me, and when the flame had gone by I looked, and behold, the smoke remained. [49]And after this a cloud full of water passed before me and poured down a heavy and violent rain, and when the rainstorm had

---

s Syr Ethiop: Latin is uncertain
t Syr Ethiop: Latin is uncertain
u Syr Ethiop Arab Arm: the Latin is corrupt
v Syr Ethiop Arab 2 Georg: Lat *How long do I hope thus?*
w Syr Ethiop Arab 2: Lat *number of seeds is completed for you*

---

will solve all problems; but first the evil which is sown must be reaped. **30:** *A grain of evil seed*, the evil *yeṣer* (see Sir.15.14 n.).

4.33–43: The seer asks when the new age will come; he is told that first the predetermined number of the righteous must be completed. **35:** *The righteous*, i.e. the righteous dead. *Chambers*, literally "storehouses" or "garners"; according to rabbinical teaching the souls of the righteous dead are beneath the throne of God (compare Rev.6.9f.). **36:** *Jeremiel*, probably the same as Remiel, the seventh of seven archangels mentioned in Enoch 20.1–8. *Completed*, 2.41; Rev.6.11. **36–37:** *Weighed ... measured ... numbered*, God has determined the times and periods of history (see Sir.36.8 n.). **41:** *Chambers*, see v. 35 n.

4.44–50: The seer asks what proportion of time remains; he is told by a parable that the end is near.

passed, drops remained in the cloud.

50 And he said to me, "Consider it for yourself; for as the rain is more than the drops, and the fire is greater than the smoke, so the quantity that passed was far greater; but drops and smoke remained."

51 Then I prayed and said, "Do you think that I shall live until those days? Or who will be alive in those days?"

52 He answered me and said, "Concerning the signs about which you ask me, I can tell you in part; but I was not sent to tell you concerning your life, for I do not know.

5 "Now concerning the signs: behold, the days are coming when those who dwell on earth shall be seized with great terror,*x* and the way of truth shall be hidden, and the land shall be barren of faith. ²And unrighteousness shall be increased beyond what you yourself see, and beyond what you heard of formerly. ³And the land which you now see ruling shall be waste and untrodden,*y* and men shall see it as desolate. ⁴But if the Most High grants that you live, you shall see it thrown into confusion after the third period;*z*

and the sun shall suddenly shine
    forth at night,
    and the moon during the day.
⁵Blood shall drip from wood,
    and the stone shall utter its voice;
the peoples shall be troubled,
    and the stars shall fall.*a*
⁶And one shall reign whom those who dwell on earth do not expect, and the birds shall fly away together; ⁷and the sea of Sodom shall cast up fish; and

one whom the many do not know shall make his voice heard by night, and all shall hear his voice.*b* ⁸There shall be chaos also in many places, and fire shall often break out, and the wild beasts shall roam beyond their haunts, and menstruous women shall bring forth monsters. ⁹And salt waters shall be found in the sweet, and all friends shall conquer one another; then shall reason hide itself, and wisdom shall withdraw into its chamber, ¹⁰and it shall be sought by many but shall not be found, and unrighteousness and unrestraint shall increase on earth. ¹¹And one country shall ask its neighbor, 'Has righteousness, or any one who does right, passed through you?' And it will answer, 'No.' ¹²And at that time men shall hope but not obtain; they shall labor but their ways shall not prosper. ¹³These are the signs which I am permitted to tell you, and if you pray again, and weep as you do now, and fast for seven days, you shall hear yet greater things than these."

14 Then I awoke, and my body shuddered violently, and my soul was so troubled that it fainted. ¹⁵But the angel who had come and talked with me held me and strengthened me and set me on my feet.

16 Now on the second night Phaltiel, a chief of the people, came to me and said, "Where have you been? And

x Syr: Ethiop *confusion*: Latin is uncertain
y Syr: Latin is corrupt
z Literally *after the third*; Ethiop *after three months*; Arm *after the third vision*; Georg *after the third day*
a Ethiop Compare Syr and Arab: Latin is uncertain
b Cn: Lat *fish*; *and it shall make its voice heard by night, which the many have not known, but all shall hear its voice.*

4.51–5.13: **The seer asks whether the end will come during his own lifetime;** he is given a description of the signs which will precede the end (compare Mt.24.4–31; Mk.13.5–27; Lk.21.8–28). **5.2:** Mt.24.12. **3:** *The land which you now see ruling,* i.e. the Roman Empire. **4:** The reference to *the third period* is cryptic (compare 14.11–13). **5:** *The stone shall utter its voice,* Hab.2.11; Lk.19.40. **6:** *The birds,* foreseeing impending disasters, *shall fly away.* **7:** *The sea of Sodom,* i.e. the Dead Sea. **8a:** Syriac, "a fissure shall arise over wide regions" (compare Zech.14.4). *Shall often break out,* or "shall burst forth for a long period." **10–11:** Is.59.14–15. **13:** For the author, fasting prepared one to receive a divine revelation; he refers to three fasts each of seven days (5.20; 6.35; 12.51).

5.14–19: **Conclusion of the vision. 14:** *Then I awoke,* from the dream-vision. *My soul . . . fainted,* Pss. 84.2; 107.5; Jon.2.7; compare Is.6.5; Dan.10.17b. **16:** *Phaltiel,* the historical reference is uncertain; compare Paltiel in Num.34.26; 2 Sam.3.15.

why is your face sad? ¹⁷Or do you not know that Israel has been entrusted to you in the land of their exile? ¹⁸Rise therefore and eat some bread, so that you may not forsake us, like a shepherd who leaves his flock in the power of cruel wolves."

19 Then I said to him, "Depart from me and do not come near me for seven days, and then you may come to me."

He heard what I said and left me. ²⁰So I fasted seven days, mourning and weeping, as Uriel the angel had commanded me.

21 And after seven days the thoughts of my heart were very grievous to me again. ²²Then my soul recovered the spirit of understanding, and I began once more to speak words in the presence of the Most High. ²³And I said, "O sovereign Lord, from every forest of the earth and from all its trees thou hast chosen one vine, ²⁴and from all the lands of the world thou hast chosen for thyself one region,^c and from all the flowers of the world thou hast chosen for thyself one lily, ²⁵and from all the depths of the sea thou hast filled for thyself one river, and from all the cities that have been built thou hast consecrated Zion for thyself, ²⁶and from all the birds that have been created thou hast named for thyself one dove, and from all the flocks that have been made thou hast provided for thyself one sheep, ²⁷and from all the multitude of peoples thou hast gotten for thyself one people; and to this people, whom thou hast loved, thou hast given the law which is approved by all. ²⁸And now, O Lord, why hast thou given over the one to the many, and dishonored^d the one root beyond the others, and scattered thine only one among the

many? ²⁹And those who opposed thy promises have trodden down those who believed thy covenants. ³⁰If thou dost really hate thy people, they should be punished at thy own hands."

31 When I had spoken these words, the angel who had come to me on a previous night was sent to me, ³²and he said to me, "Listen to me, and I will instruct you; pay attention to me, and I will tell you more."

33 And I said, "Speak, my lord." And he said to me, "Are you greatly disturbed in mind over Israel?^e Or do you love him more than his Maker does?"

34 And I said, "No, my lord, but because of my grief I have spoken; for every hour I suffer agonies of heart, while I strive to understand the way of the Most High and to search out part of his judgment."

35 And he said to me, "You cannot." And I said, "Why not, my lord? Why then was I born? Or why did not my mother's womb become my grave, that I might not see the travail of Jacob and the exhaustion of the people of Israel?"

36 He said to me, "Count up for me those who have not yet come, and gather for me the scattered raindrops, and make the withered flowers bloom again for me; ³⁷open for me the closed chambers, and bring forth for me the winds shut up in them, or show me the picture of a voice; and then I will explain to you the travail that you ask to understand."^f

38 And I said, "O sovereign Lord, who is able to know these things except he whose dwelling is not with men? ³⁹As for me, I am without wis-

c Ethiop: Lat *pit*
d Syr Ethiop Arab: Lat *prepared*
e Or *You are greatly distracted in mind over Israel.*
f Lat *see*

5.21–6.34: The second vision. 5.21–30: The seer reiterates his complaints of divine inequity in dealing with Israel. 23–28: Most of the figures representing Israel have been drawn from the Old Testament: the *vine* (v. 23), Ps. 80.8–15; the *lily* (v. 24), S. of S.2.2 (interpreted allegorically); Hos.14.5; the *river* (v. 25), Is.8.6; the city of *Zion* (v. 25), Ps. 132.13; the *dove* (v. 26), Ps.74.19; the *sheep* (v. 26), Ps. 79.13; Is.53.7; the *root* (v. 28), Enoch 93.8, compare Rom.11.17–18. **33:** It is unthinkable that man should love Israel more than God their *Maker does* (8.47). **35:** Job 3.11; 10.18–19. **36–40:** If the seer cannot understand the things of earth, how can he dom, and how can I speak concerning the things which thou hast asked me?"

40 He said to me, "Just as you cannot do one of the things that were mentioned, so you cannot discover my judgment, or the goal of the love that I have promised my people."

41 And I said, "Yet behold, O Lord, thou dost have charge of those who are alive at the end, but what will those do who were before us, or we, or those who come after us?"

42 He said to me, "I shall liken my judgment to a circle;^{g} just as for those who are last there is no slowness, so for those who are first there is no haste."

43 Then I answered and said, "Couldst thou not have created at one time those who have been and those who are and those who will be, that thou mightest show thy judgment the sooner?"

44 He replied to me and said, "The creation cannot make more haste than the Creator, neither can the world hold at one time those who have been created in it."

45 And I said, "How hast thou said to thy servant that thou^h wilt certainly give life at one time to thy creation? If therefore all creatures will live at one time^i and the creation will sustain them, it might even now be able to support all of them present at one time."

46 He said to me, "Ask a woman's womb, and say to it, 'If you bear ten^j children, why one after another?' Request it therefore to produce ten at one time."

47 I said, "Of course it cannot, but only each in its own time."

48 He said to me, "Even so have I

given the womb of the earth to those who from time to time are sown in it. ^{49}For as an infant does not bring forth, and a woman who has become old does not bring forth any longer, so have I organized the world which I created."

50 Then I inquired and said, "Since thou hast now given me the opportunity, let me speak before thee. Is our mother, of whom thou hast told me, still young? Or is she now approaching old age?"

51 He replied to me, "Ask a woman who bears children, and she will tell you. ^{52}Say to her, 'Why are those whom you have borne recently not like those whom you bore before, but smaller in stature?' ^{53}And she herself will answer you, 'Those born in the strength of youth are different from those born during the time of old age, when the womb is failing.' ^{54}Therefore you also should consider that you and your contemporaries are smaller in stature than those who were before you, ^{55}and those who come after you will be smaller than you, as born of a creation which already is aging and passing the strength of youth."

56 And I said, "O Lord, I beseech thee, if I have found favor in thy sight, show thy servant through whom thou dost visit thy creation."

6 And he said to me, "At the beginning of the circle of the earth,^{k}

g Or crown
h Syr Ethiop Arab 1: Latin text is uncertain
i Latin omits If . . . one time
j Syr Ethiop Arab 2 Arm: Latin text is corrupt
k The text is uncertain: compare Syr The beginning by the hand of man, but the end by my own hands. For as before the land of the world existed there, and before: Ethiop At first by the Son of Man, and afterwards myself. For before the earth and the lands were created, and before

expect to fathom the judgments and purpose of God? **40:** *My . . . I,* the angel speaks in God's name.

5.41–55: The place of successive generations in the divine plan for the world. The seer inquires about the status of those who have died before the messianic age shall begin (v. 41); he is told, in effect, that the last shall be as the first, and the first as the last (v. 42). He inquires why all generations of men could not have lived at the same time, namely at the beginning of the messianic age (v. 43); the reply is that generations must follow one another (vv. 44–49). *Mother* earth has become old and the last generations are inferior to the early ones (vv. 50–55). **52:** *Smaller in stature,* compare Gen.6.4 (the Nephilim, "giants"); Num.13.33.

5.56–6.6: The end of the age. As God alone created the world (without an intermediate agency), so he will bring about its end by himself alone (7.39–44).

before the portals of the world were in place, and before the assembled winds blew, [2]and before the rumblings of thunder sounded, and before the flashes of lightning shone, and before the foundations of paradise were laid, [3]and before the beautiful flowers were seen, and before the powers of movement[l] were established, and before the innumerable hosts of angels were gathered together, [4]and before the heights of the air were lifted up, and before the measures of the firmaments were named, and before the footstool of Zion was established, [5]and before the present years were reckoned; and before the imaginations of those who now sin were estranged, and before those who stored up treasures of faith were sealed—[6]then I planned these things, and they were made through me and not through another, just as the end shall come through me and not through another."

7 And I answered and said, "What will be the dividing of the times? Or when will be the end of the first age and the beginning of the age that follows?"

8 He said to me, "From Abraham to Isaac,[m] because from him were born Jacob and Esau, for Jacob's hand held Esau's heel from the beginning. [9]For Esau is the end of this age, and Jacob is the beginning of the age that follows. [10]For the beginning of a man is his hand, and the end of a man is his heel;[n] between the heel and the hand seek for nothing else, Ezra!"

11 I answered and said, "O sovereign Lord, if I have found favor in thy sight, [12]show thy servant the end of thy signs which thou didst show me in part on a previous night."

13 He answered and said to me, "Rise to your feet and you will hear a full, resounding voice. [14]And if the place where you are standing is greatly shaken [15]while the voice is speaking, do not be terrified; because the word concerns the end, and the foundations of the earth will understand [16]that the speech concerns them. They will tremble and be shaken, for they know that their end must be changed."

17 When I heard this, I rose to my feet and listened, and behold, a voice was speaking, and its sound was like the sound of many waters. [18]And it said, "Behold, the days are coming, and it shall be that when I draw near to visit the inhabitants of the earth, [19]and when I require from the doers of iniquity the penalty of their iniquity, and when the humiliation of Zion is complete, [20]and when the seal is placed upon the age which is about to pass away, then I will show these signs: the books shall be opened before the firmament, and all shall see it together. [21]Infants a year old shall speak with their voices, and women with child shall give birth to premature children at three or four months, and these shall live and dance. [22]Sown places shall suddenly appear unsown, and full storehouses shall suddenly be found to be empty; [23]and the trumpet shall sound aloud, and when all hear it, they shall suddenly be terrified. [24]At that time friends shall make war on friends like enemies, and the earth and those who inhabit it shall be terrified, and the springs of the fountains shall stand still, so that for three hours they shall not flow.

25 "And it shall be that whoever

l Or *earthquake*
m Other authorities read *Abraham*
n Syr: Latin is defective here

6.7–10: The dividing of the times. In allegorical language the seer is told that the present corrupt age (symbolized by *Esau*) will be followed immediately, without a break, by the glorious age to come (symbolized by *Jacob*).
6.11–28: The signs of the end of the age. 12: *Thou didst show me in part,* 4.51–5.13. **17:** *I rose to my feet,* presumably the author had previously been lying down, experiencing a dream-vision. *Many waters,* Rev.1.15; 14.2; 19.6. **20:** *The books shall be opened,* i.e. the celestial books in which are written the deeds of men (Dan.7.10; 12.1; Mal.3.16; Rev.20.12; compare Ex.32.32; Ps. 69.28; Lk.10.20; Heb.12.23). **23:** *The trumpet,* 1 Cor.15.52; 1 Thess.4.16. **26:** *The men who*

remains after all that I have foretold to you shall himself be saved and shall see my salvation and the end of my world. ²⁶And they shall see the men who were taken up, who from their birth have not tasted death; and the heart of the earth'sᵒ inhabitants shall be changed and converted to a different spirit. ²⁷For evil shall be blotted out, and deceit shall be quenched; ²⁸faithfulness shall flourish, and corruption shall be overcome, and the truth, which has been so long without fruit, shall be revealed."

29 While he spoke to me, behold, little by little the place where I was standing began to rock to and fro.ᵖ ³⁰And he said to me, "I have come to show you these things this night.ᑫ ³¹If therefore you will pray again and fast again for seven days, I will again declare to you greater things than these,ʳ ³²because your voice has surely been heard before the Most High; for the Mighty One has seen your uprightness and has also observed the purity which you have maintained from your youth. ³³Therefore he sent me to show you all these things, and to say to you: 'Believe and do not be afraid! ³⁴Do not be quick to think vain thoughts concerning the former times, lest you be hasty concerning the last times.' "

35 Now after this I wept again and fasted seven days as before, in order to complete the three weeks as I had been told. ³⁶And on the eighth night my heart was troubled within me again, and I began to speak in the presence of the Most High. ³⁷For my spirit was greatly aroused, and my soul was in distress.

38 I said, "O Lord, thou didst speak at the beginning of creation, and didst say on the first day, 'Let heaven and earth be made,' and thy word accomplished the work. ³⁹And then the Spirit was hovering, and darkness and silence embraced everything; the sound of man's voice was not yet there.ˢ ⁴⁰Then thou didst command that a ray of light be brought forth from thy treasuries, so that thy works might then appear.

41 "Again, on the second day, thou didst create the spirit of the firmament, and didst command him to divide and separate the waters, that one part might move upward and the other part remain beneath.

42 "On the third day thou didst command the waters to be gathered together in the seventh part of the earth; six parts thou didst dry up and keep so that some of them might be planted and cultivated and be of service before thee. ⁴³For thy word went forth, and at once the work was done. ⁴⁴For immediately fruit came forth in endless abundance and of varied appeal to the taste; and flowers of inimitable color; and odors of inexpressible fragrance. These were made on the third day.

45 "On the fourth day thou didst command the brightness of the sun, the light of the moon, and the arrangement of the stars to come into being; ⁴⁶and thou didst command them to serve man, who was about to be formed.

47 "On the fifth day thou didst command the seventh part, where the

o Syr Compare Ethiop Arab 1 Arm: Latin omits *earth's*
p Syr Ethiop Compare Arab Arm: Latin is corrupt
q Syr Compare Ethiop: Latin is corrupt
r Syr Ethiop Arab 1 Arm: Latin adds *by day*
s Syr Ethiop: Lat *was not yet from thee*

---

were taken up, such as Enoch (Gen.5.24; Sir.44.16) and Elijah (2 Kg.2.11–12); compare also 14.9. *Shall be . . . converted*, by the preaching of Elijah (Mal.4.6).

6.29–34: Conclusion of the vision. 34: The seer is cautioned against being oversolicitous.

6.35–9.25: The third vision. 6.35–37: Introduction. 35: *I . . . fasted seven days*, see 5.13 n. *The three weeks* (compare Dan.10.2–3), so far only two fasts of seven days have been mentioned (here and at 5.20); presumably the author is thinking also of another fast prior to the first vision (3.1–5.20), not mentioned in the present form of the book.

6.38–59: The seer recounts God's work in creation. If the world was created for Israel (v. 55), why has the nation not possessed its inheritance? **38–54:** Gen. ch. 1. **38:** *Thy word accomplished the work*, Ps. 33.6; Heb.11.3; 2 Pet.3.5. **40:** God's *treasuries* are in heaven. **41:** *The spirit of the* water had been gathered together, to bring forth living creatures, birds, and fishes; and so it was done. [48]The dumb and lifeless water produced living creatures, as it was commanded,[t] that therefore the nations might declare thy wondrous works.

49 "Then thou didst keep in existence two living creatures;[u] the name of one thou didst call Behemoth and the name of the other Leviathan. [50]And thou didst separate one from the other, for the seventh part where the water had been gathered together could not hold them both. [51]And thou didst give Behemoth one of the parts which had been dried up on the third day, to live in it, where there are a thousand mountains; [52]but to Leviathan thou didst give the seventh part, the watery part; and thou hast kept them to be eaten by whom thou wilt, and when thou wilt.

53 "On the sixth day thou didst command the earth to bring forth before thee cattle, beasts, and creeping things; [54]and over these thou didst place Adam, as ruler over all the works which thou hadst made; and from him we have all come, the people whom thou hast chosen.

55 "All this I have spoken before thee, O Lord, because thou hast said that it was for us that thou didst create this world.[v] [56]As for the other nations which have descended from Adam, thou hast said that they are nothing, and that they are like spittle, and thou hast compared their abundance to a drop from a bucket. [57]And now, O Lord, behold, these nations, which are reputed as nothing, domineer over us and devour us. [58]But we thy people, whom thou hast called thy first-born,

only begotten, zealous for thee,[w] and most dear, have been given into their hands. [59]If the world has indeed been created for us, why do we not possess our world as an inheritance? How long will this be so?"

7 When I had finished speaking these words, the angel who had been sent to me on the former nights was sent to me again, [2]and he said to me, "Rise, Ezra, and listen to the words that I have come to speak to you."

3 I said, "Speak, my lord." And he said to me, "There is a sea set in a wide expanse so that it is broad[x] and vast, [4]but it has an entrance set in a narrow place, so that it is like a river. [5]If any one, then, wishes to reach the sea, to look at it or to navigate it, how can he come to the broad part unless he passes through the narrow part? [6]Another example: There is a city built and set on a plain, and it is full of all good things; [7]but the entrance to it is narrow and set in a precipitous place, so that there is fire on the right hand and deep water on the left; [8]and there is only one path lying between them, that is, between the fire and the water, so that only one man can walk upon that path. [9]If now that city is given to a man for an inheritance, how will the heir receive his inheritance unless he passes through the danger set before him?"

10 I said, "He cannot, lord." And he said to me, "So also is Israel's portion. [11]For I made the world for their sake, and when Adam transgressed my statutes, what had been made was

t The text of this verse is uncertain
u Syr Ethiop: Lat *two souls*
v Syr Ethiop Arab 2: Lat *the first-born world* Compare Arab 1 *first world*
w The meaning of the Latin text is obscure
x Syr Compare Ethiop Arab 1: Lat *deep*

---

firmament is an angel (compare the angel with power over fire, Rev.14.18, and the angel of water, Rev.16.5). **46**: Ps. 8.6–8. **49–52**: *Behemoth* and *Leviathan* are two primeval monsters (compare Job 7.12; 26.12–13; Ps.74.12–15; 89.10–11; Is.30.7; 51.9–10). **55**: The idea that the world was created for the sake of Israel (7.11) is not found in the Old Testament, but was deduced by Jewish rabbis from such passages as Ex.4.22; Dt.10.15; 14.2. **56**: *A drop from a bucket*, Is.40.15.
7.1–25: The angel instructs the seer. The wickedness of this world makes the path to the next world narrow and dangerous. **1**: *The former nights*, at the beginning of each vision. **11**: Though *the world* was created for Israel's *sake*, that inheritance was spoiled *when Adam transgressed* (compare Rom.5.18–20). **12 and 13**: *The entrances*, Ethiopic, "the ways," i.e. the paths of life

judged. [12]And so the entrances of this world were made narrow and sorrowful and toilsome; they are few and evil, full of dangers and involved in great hardships. [13]But the entrances of the greater world are broad and safe, and really yield the fruit of immortality. [14]Therefore unless the living pass through the difficult and vain experiences, they can never receive those things that have been reserved for them. [15]But now why are you disturbed, seeing that you are to perish? And why are you moved, seeing that you are mortal? [16]And why have you not considered in your mind what is to come, rather than what is now present?"

17 Then I answered and said, "O sovereign Lord, behold, thou hast ordained in thy law that the righteous shall inherit these things, but that the ungodly shall perish. [18]The righteous therefore can endure difficult circumstances while hoping for easier ones; but those who have done wickedly have suffered the difficult circumstances and will not see the easier ones."

19 And he said to me, "You are not a better judge than God, or wiser than the Most High! [20]Let many perish who are now living, rather than that the law of God which is set before them be disregarded! [21]For God strictly commanded those who came into the world, when they came, what they should do to live, and what they should observe to avoid punishment. [22]Nevertheless they were not obedient, and spoke against him;

they devised for themselves vain thoughts,

[23]and proposed to themselves
wicked frauds;
they even declared that the Most
High does not exist,
and they ignored his ways!
[24]They scorned his law,
and denied his covenants;
they have been unfaithful to his
statutes,
and have not performed his works.

25 "Therefore, Ezra, empty things are for the empty, and full things are for the full. [26]For behold, the time will come, when the signs which I have foretold to you will come to pass, that the city which now is not seen shall appear,[y] and the land which now is hidden shall be disclosed. [27]And every one who has been delivered from the evils that I have foretold shall see my wonders. [28]For my son the Messiah[z] shall be revealed with those who are with him, and those who remain shall rejoice four hundred years. [29]And after these years my son the Messiah shall die, and all who draw human breath. [30]And the world shall be turned back to primeval silence for seven days, as it was at the first beginnings; so that no one shall be left. [31]And after seven days the world, which is not yet awake, shall be roused, and that which is corruptible shall perish. [32]And the earth shall give up those who are asleep in it, and the dust those who dwell silently in it; and the chambers shall give up the souls which have been committed to them. [33]And the Most High shall be

y Arm: Lat Syr *that the bride shall appear, even the city appearing*
z Syr Arab 1: Ethiop *my Messiah;* Arab 2 *the Messiah;* Arm *the Messiah of God;* Lat *my son Jesus*

here on earth, and in the world of immortality. **13:** *The greater world,* Syriac, "the future world." **14:** *Things ... reserved for them,* 1 Cor.2.9. **15–16:** The seer should not brood over difficulties and death; though inevitable, they are but preliminary to something better (2 Cor. 4.18). **17–18:** The seer inquires whether the future bliss is only for the righteous Jews, or for all the Jews. **19–25:** The angel replies that those who disregard the Mosaic law will be punished. **25:** Mt.13.12.

7.26–44: The messianic kingdom and the end of the world. 26: *The signs ... foretold,* 6.20–24. *The city,* the heavenly Jerusalem. *The land,* the heavenly paradise. **28:** *Those who remain,* after the tribulations that will precede the inauguration of the messianic kingdom. *Four hundred years,* so the Latin and Arabic 1; Syriac, "thirty years"; Arabic 2, "one thousand years"; Ethiopic and Armenian omit. **31:** *The world ... not yet awake,* i.e. the world to come. **32:** Dan.12.2. *Chambers,* see 4.35 n. **33:** *Judgment,* Syriac adds, "and then comes the end." *Away,* revealed upon the seat of judgment, and compassion shall pass away, and patience shall be withdrawn;*a* 34but only judgment shall remain, truth shall stand, and faithfulness shall grow strong. 35And recompense shall follow, and the reward shall be manifested; righteous deeds shall awake, and unrighteous deeds shall not sleep.*b* [36]Then the pit*c* of torment shall appear, and opposite it shall be the place of rest; and the furnace of hell*d* shall be disclosed, and opposite it the paradise of delight. [37]Then the Most High will say to the nations that have been raised from the dead, 'Look now, and understand whom you have denied, whom you have not served, whose commandments you have despised! [38]Look on this side and on that; here are delight and rest, and there are fire and torments!' Thus he will*e* speak to them on the day of judgment—[39]a day that has no sun or moon or stars, [40]or cloud or thunder or lightning or wind or water or air, or darkness or evening or morning, [41]or summer or spring or heat or winter*f* or frost or cold or hail or rain or dew, [42]or noon or night, or dawn or shining or brightness or light, but only the splendor of the glory of the Most High, by which all shall see what has been determined for them. [43]For it will last for about a week of years. [44]This is my judgment and its prescribed order; and to you alone have I shown these things."

[45] I answered and said, "O sovereign Lord, I said then and I say now:*g* Blessed are those who are alive and keep thy commandments! [46]But what of those for whom I prayed? For who among the living is there that has not sinned, or who among men that has not transgressed thy covenant? [47]And now I see that the world to come will bring delight to few, but torments to many. [48]For an evil heart has grown up in us, which has alienated us from God,*h* and has brought us into corruption and the ways of death, and has shown us the paths of perdition and removed us far from life—and that not just a few of us but almost all who have been created!"

[49] He answered me and said, "Listen to me, Ezra,*i* and I will instruct you, and will admonish you yet again. [50]For this reason the Most High has made not one world but two. [51]For whereas you have said that the righteous are not many but few, while the ungodly abound, hear the explanation for this.

[52] "If you have just a few precious stones, will you add to them lead and clay?"*j*

[53] I said, "Lord, how could that be?"

[54] And he said to me, "Not only

a Lat *gather together*
b The passage from verse [36] to verse [105], formerly missing, has been restored to the text
c Syr Ethiop: Lat *place*
d Lat *gehenna*
e Syr Ethiop Arab 1: Lat *thou shalt*
f Or *storm*
g Syr: Lat *And I answered, "I said then, O Lord, and I say now:*
h Cn: Lat Syr Ethiop *from these*
i Syr Arab 1 Georg: Lat Ethiop omit *Ezra*
j Arab 1: Lat Syr Ethiop are corrupt

Syriac adds, "and pity shall be far off." The final judgment will be conducted in strict accord with justice and truth. **34:** *Grow strong*, i.e. triumph. **35:** *Righteous deeds shall awake*, acts of charity hitherto concealed shall be disclosed (compare Mt.25.35–46). **[36–105]:** These verses are lacking from the standard editions of the Latin Vulgate and from the King James version. They are present in the Syriac, Ethiopic, Arabic, and Armenian versions, and in two Latin manuscripts. The section was probably deliberately cut out of an ancestor of most extant Latin manuscripts because of dogmatic reasons, for the passage contains an emphatic denial of the value of prayers for the dead (v. [105]). **[36]:** *Pit*, Rev.9.2. *Opposite*, Lk.16.23–24. **[37]:** Mt. 25.31ff. **[39–43]:** Description of the day of judgment. **[42]:** *Only* the uncreated light *of the Most High* will serve to illuminate the judgment scene (compare Is.60.19–20; Rev.21.23). **[43]:** *A week of years*, seven years.

7.[45–61]: The small number of the saved (contrast Lk.13.23–30). **[48]:** *An evil heart*, see 3.20 n. **[49]:** 5.32. **[52]:** The question implies that the number of the elect cannot be increased by adding base elements.

that, but ask the earth and she will tell you; defer to her, and she will declare it to you. [55]Say to her, 'You produce gold and silver and brass, and also iron and lead and clay; [56]but silver is more abundant than gold, and brass than silver, and iron than brass, and lead than iron, and clay than lead.' [57]Judge therefore which things are precious and desirable, those that are abundant or those that are rare?"

[58] I said, "O sovereign Lord, what is plentiful is of less worth, for what is more rare is more precious."

[59] He answered me and said, "Weigh within yourself*k* what you have thought, for he who has what is hard to get rejoices more than he who has what is plentiful. [60]So also will be the judgment*l* which I have promised; for I will rejoice over the few who shall be saved, because it is they who have made my glory to prevail now, and through them my name has now been honored. [61]And I will not grieve over the multitude of those who perish; for it is they who are now like a mist, and are similar to a flame and smoke—they are set on fire and burn hotly, and are extinguished."

[62] I replied and said, "O earth, what have you brought forth, if the mind is made out of the dust like the other created things! [63]For it would have been better if the dust itself had not been born, so that the mind might not have been made from it. [64]But now the mind grows with us, and therefore we are tormented, because we perish and know it. [65]Let the human race lament, but let the beasts of the field be glad; let all who have been born lament, but let the four-footed beasts and the flocks rejoice! [66]For it is much better with them than with us; for they do not look for a judgment, nor do they know of any torment or salvation promised to them after death. [67]For what does it profit us that we shall be preserved alive but cruelly tormented? [68]For all who have been born are involved in iniquities, and are full of sins and burdened with transgressions. [69]And if we were not to come into judgment after death, perhaps it would have been better for us."

[70] He answered me and said, "When the Most High made the world and Adam and all who have come from him, he first prepared the judgment and the things that pertain to the judgment. [71]And now understand from your own words, for you have said that the mind grows with us. [72]For this reason, therefore, those who dwell on earth shall be tormented, because though they had understanding they committed iniquity, and though they received the commandments they did not keep them, and though they obtained the law they dealt unfaithfully with what they received. [73]What, then, will they have to say in the judgment, or how will they answer in the last times? [74]For how long the time is that the Most High has been patient with those who inhabit the world, and not for their sake, but because of the times which he has foreordained!"

[75] I answered and said, "If I have found favor in thy sight, O Lord, show this also to thy servant: whether after death, as soon as every one of us yields up his soul, we shall be kept in rest until those times come when thou wilt renew the creation, or whether we shall be tormented at once?"

[76] He answered me and said, "I will show you that also, but do not be associated with those who have shown scorn, nor number yourself among those who are tormented. [77]For you

k Syr Ethiop Arab 1: Latin is corrupt here
l Syr Arab 1: Lat *creation*

7.[62–74]: The seer's lament over the human race. [63]: 4.12. [64]: The possession of reasoning powers intensifies sufferings. [67]: The author identifies himself with sinners (contrast 6.32–34). [70]: *Things that pertain to the judgment*, according to rabbinical teaching, before the beginning of the world God created Paradise and Gehenna.

7.[75–101]: The state of the departed after death and before the judgment. [77]: *A treasure of* have a treasure of works laid up with the Most High; but it will not be shown to you until the last times. [78]Now, concerning death, the teaching is: When the decisive decree has gone forth from the Most High that a man shall die, as the spirit leaves the body to return again to him who gave it, first of all it adores the glory of the Most High. [79]And if it is one of those who have shown scorn and have not kept the way of the Most High, and who have despised his law, and who have hated those who fear God—[80]such spirits shall not enter into habitations, but shall immediately wander about in torments, ever grieving and sad, in seven ways. [81]The first way, because they have scorned the law of the Most High. [82]The second way, because they cannot now make a good repentance that they may live. [83]The third way, they shall see the reward laid up for those who have trusted the covenants of the Most High. [84]The fourth way, they shall consider the torment laid up for themselves in the last days. [85]The fifth way, they shall see how the habitations of the others are guarded by angels in profound quiet. [86]The sixth way, they shall see how some of them will pass over*m* into torments. [87]The seventh way, which is worse*n* than all the ways that have been mentioned, because they shall utterly waste away in confusion and be consumed with shame,*o* and shall wither with fear at seeing the glory of the Most High before whom they sinned while they were alive, and before whom they are to be judged in the last times.

[88] "Now this is the order of those who have kept the ways of the Most High, when they shall be separated from their mortal body.*p* [89]During the time that they lived in it,*q* they laboriously served the Most High, and withstood danger every hour, that they might keep the law of the Lawgiver perfectly. [90]Therefore this is the teaching concerning them: [91]First of all, they shall see with great joy the glory of him who receives them, for they shall have rest in seven orders. [92]The first order, because they have striven with great effort to overcome the evil thought which was formed with them, that it might not lead them astray from life into death. [93]The second order, because they see the perplexity in which the souls of the ungodly wander, and the punishment that awaits them. [94]The third order, they see the witness which he who formed them bears concerning them, that while they were alive they kept the law which was given them in trust. [95]The fourth order, they understand the rest which they now enjoy, being gathered into their chambers and guarded by angels in profound quiet, and the glory which awaits them in the last days. [96]The fifth order, they rejoice that they have now escaped what is corruptible, and shall inherit what is to come; and besides they see the straits and toil*r* from which they have been delivered, and the spacious liberty which they are to receive and enjoy in immortality. [97]The sixth order, when it is shown to them how their face is to shine like the sun, and how they are to be made like the light of the stars, being incorruptible from then on. [98]The seventh order, which is greater than all that have been mentioned, because they shall rejoice with

m Cn: the text of this verse is corrupt
n Lat *greater*
o Syr Ethiop: Latin is corrupt
p Literally *the corruptible vessel*
q Syr Ethiop: Latin is corrupt
r Syr Ethiop: Lat *fulness*

---

works, 8.33,36. *Will not be shown*, see v. 35 n. [78]: Ec.12.7. The first act of the departed spirit (whether righteous or wicked) is to adore God. [80–87]: Seven kinds of torment for the wicked. [80]: *Habitations*, Lk.16.9; elsewhere called "chambers," see 4.35 n. [83]: Compare Lk.16.23. [85]: *The others*, i.e. the righteous. [88–99]: Seven kinds of joyous rest for the righteous. The author implies that the *mortal body* has been merely a prison-house for the spirit (contrast 1 Cor.15.53; 2 Cor.5.2–4). [92]: *The evil thought*, the evil *yeṣer* (see Sir.15.14 n.). [95]: *Chambers*, see 4.35 n. *In the last days*, better, "at their latter end." [97]: *Shine*, v. [125]; Dan.12.3;

boldness, and shall be confident without confusion, and shall be glad without fear, for they hasten to behold the face of him whom they served in life and from whom they are to receive their reward when glorified. [99]This is the order of the souls of the righteous, as henceforth is announced;[s] and the aforesaid are the ways of torment which those who would not give heed shall suffer hereafter."

[100] I answered and said, "Will time therefore be given to the souls, after they have been separated from the bodies, to see what you have described to me?"

[101] He said to me, "They shall have freedom for seven days, so that during these seven days they may see the things of which you have been told, and afterwards they shall be gathered in their habitations."

[102] I answered and said, "If I have found favor in thy sight, show further to me, thy servant, whether on the day of judgment the righteous will be able to intercede for the ungodly or to entreat the Most High for them, [103]fathers for sons or sons for parents, brothers for brothers, relatives for their kinsmen, or friends[t] for those who are most dear."

[104] He answered me and said, "Since you have found favor in my sight, I will show you this also. The day of judgment is decisive[u] and displays to all the seal of truth. Just as now a father does not send his son, or a son his father, or a master his servant, or a friend his dearest friend, to be ill[v] or sleep or eat or be healed in his stead, [105]so no one shall ever pray for another on that day, neither shall any one lay a burden on another;[w] for then every one shall bear his own righteousness or unrighteousness."

36 [106] I answered and said, "How then do we find that first Abraham prayed for the people of Sodom, and Moses for our fathers who sinned in the desert, 37[107]and Joshua after him for Israel in the days of Achan, 38[108]and Samuel in the days of Saul,[x] and David for the plague, and Solomon for those in the sanctuary, 39[109]and Elijah for those who received the rain, and for the one who was dead, that he might live, 40[110]and Hezekiah for the people in the days of Sennacherib, and many others prayed for many? 41[111]If therefore the righteous have prayed for the ungodly now, when corruption has increased and unrighteousness has multiplied, why will it not be so then as well?"

42 [112] He answered me and said, "This present world is not the end; the full glory does not[y] abide in it;[z] therefore those who were strong prayed for the weak. 43[113]But the day of judgment will be the end of this age and the beginning[a] of the immortal age to come, in which corruption has passed away, 44[114]sinful indulgence has come to an end, unbelief has been cut off, and righteousness has increased and truth has appeared. 45[115]Therefore no one will then be able to have mercy on him who has been condemned in the judgment, or to harm[b] him who is victorious."

46 [116] I answered and said, "This is my first and last word, that it would

s Syr: Latin is corrupt here
t Syr Ethiop Arab 1: Lat *kinsmen for their nearest, friends* (literally *the confident*) *for their dearest*
u Lat *bold*
v Syr Ethiop Arm: Lat *understand*
w Syr: Latin omits *on that . . . another*
x Syr Ethiop Arab 1: Latin omits *in the days of Saul*
y Latin omits *not*
z Or *the glory does not continuously abide in it*
a Latin omits *the beginning*
b Syr Ethiop: Lat *overwhelm*

Mt.13.43. [98]: *To behold the face* of God (Mt.5.8; Heb.12.14; 1 Jn.3.2; Rev.22.4). *Reward,* 1 Cor.3.14; Rev.22.12. [101]: *Habitations,* see v. [80] n.

7.[102–115]: **No intercession for the wicked on the day of judgment** (compare Dt.24.16; Jer. 31.30). [106]: Gen.18.23; Ex.32.11. [107]: Jos.7.6–7. [108]: *Samuel,* 1 Sam.7.9; 12.23. *David,* 2 Sam.24.17. *Solomon,* 1 Kg.8.22–23,30. [109]: 1 Kg.18.42,45; 17.20–21. [110]: 2 Kg.19.15–19. [112–115]: During the present order intercession *for the weak* is possible, but the day of judgment means the closing of all accounts on the basis of strict justice (see v. 33 n.).

7.[116–131]: **The seer laments the fate of the mass of humanity.** [116]: *My first . . . word,* 3.5ff.

have been better if the earth had not produced Adam, or else, when it had produced him, had restrained him from sinning. 47[117]For what good is it to all that they live in sorrow now and expect punishment after death? 48[118]O Adam, what have you done? For though it was you who sinned, the fall was not yours alone, but ours also who are your descendants. 49[119]For what good is it to us, if an eternal age has been promised to us, but we have done deeds that bring death? 50[120]And what good is it that an everlasting hope has been promised us, but we have miserably failed? 51[121]Or that safe and healthful habitations have been reserved for us, but we have lived wickedly? 52[122]Or that the glory of the Most High will defend those who have led a pure life, but we have walked in the most wicked ways? 53[123]Or that a paradise shall be revealed, whose fruit remains unspoiled and in which are abundance and healing, but we shall not enter it, 54[124]because we have lived in unseemly places? 55[125]Or that the faces of those who practiced self-control shall shine more than the stars, but our faces shall be blacker than darkness? 56[126]For while we lived and committed iniquity we did not consider what we should suffer after death."

57 [127] He answered and said, "This is the meaning of the contest which every man who is born on earth shall wage, 58[128]that if he is defeated he shall suffer what you have said, but if he is victorious he shall receive what I have said.*c* 59[129]For this is the way of which Moses, while he was alive, spoke to the people, saying, 'Choose for yourself life, that you may live!' 60[130]But they did not believe him, or the proph-

ets after him, or even myself who have spoken to them. 61[131]Therefore there shall not be*d* grief at their destruction, so much as joy over those to whom salvation is assured."

62 [132] I answered and said, "I know, O Lord, that the Most High is now called merciful, because he has mercy on those who have not yet come into the world; 63[133]and gracious, because he is gracious to those who turn in repentance to his law; 64[134]and patient, because he shows patience toward those who have sinned, since they are his own works; 65[135]and bountiful, because he would rather give than take away;*e* 66[136]and abundant in compassion, because he makes his compassions abound more and more to those now living and to those who are gone and to those yet to come, 67[137]for if he did not make them abound, the world with those who inhabit it would not have life; 68[138]and he is called giver, because if he did not give out of his goodness so that those who have committed iniquities might be relieved of them, not one ten-thousandth of mankind could have life; 69[139]and judge, because if he did not pardon those who were created by his word and blot out the multitude of their sins,*f* 70[140]there would probably be left only very few of the innumerable multitude."

8 He answered me and said, "The Most High made this world for the sake of many, but the world to come for the sake of few. 2But I will tell you a parable, Ezra. Just as, when you ask the earth, it will tell you that it provides very much clay from which earthen-

c Syr Ethiop Arab 1: Lat I say
d Syr: Lat was not
e Or is ready to give according to requests
f Lat contempts

---

[118]: 4.30–31. [123]: *Fruit*, compare Ezek.47.12; Rev.22.2. [125]: *Shine more than the stars*, Dan.12.3; compare Mt.13.43. *Darkness*, Mt.8.12; 22.13; Jude 13. [127–129]: Man is responsible for his choices (Dt.30.19).

7.[132]–8.3: The seer acknowledges (and implicitly appeals to) God's mercy. Will a merciful God permit so many to perish? He is told that nothing can alter their doom, for *many have been created, but few shall be saved* (8.3). [132–139]: For the sevenfold attributes of God, compare Ex.34.6–7. [132]: *O Lord*, better, "sir." [135]: Acts 20.35. [138]: *Life*, i.e. eternal life. 8.2: *A parable*, an analogous illustration (as in 7.[54–57]). 3: Mt.22.14.

ware is made, but only a little dust from which gold comes; so is the course of the present world. ³Many have been created, but few shall be saved."

4 I answered and said, "Then drink your fill of understanding, O my soul, and drink wisdom, O my heart!ᵍ ⁵For not of your own will did you come into the world,ʰ and against your will you depart, for you have been given only a short time to live. ⁶O Lord who art over us, grant to thy servant that we may pray before thee, and give us seed for our heart and cultivation of our understanding so that fruit may be produced, by which every mortal who bears the likenessⁱ of a human being may be able to live. ⁷For thou alone dost exist, and we are a work of thy hands, as thou hast declared. ⁸And because thou dost give life to the body which is now fashioned in the womb, and dost furnish it with members, what thou hast created is preserved in fire and water, and for nine months the wombʲ which thou hast formed endures thy creation which has been created in it. ⁹But that which keeps and that which is kept shall both be kept by thy keeping.ᵏ And when the womb gives up again what has been created in it, ¹⁰thou hast commanded that from the members themselves (that is, from the breasts) milk should be supplied which is the fruit of the breasts, ¹¹so that what has been fashioned may be nourished for a time; and afterwards thou wilt guide him in thy mercy. ¹²Thou hast brought him up in thy righteousness, and instructed him in thy law,

and reproved him in thy wisdom. ¹³Thou wilt take away his life, for he is thy creation; and thou wilt make him live, for he is thy work. ¹⁴If then thou wilt suddenly and quicklyˡ destroy him who with so great labor was fashioned by thy command, to what purpose was he made? ¹⁵And now I will speak out: About all mankind thou knowest best; but I will speak about thy people, for whom I am grieved, ¹⁶and about thy inheritance, for whom I lament, and about Israel, for whom I am sad, and about the seed of Jacob, for whom I am troubled. ¹⁷Therefore I will pray before thee for myself and for them, for I see the failings of us who dwell in the land, ¹⁸andᵐ I have heard of the swiftness of the judgment that is to come. ¹⁹Therefore hear my voice, and understand my words, and I will speak before thee."

The beginning of the words of Ezra's prayer, before he was taken up. He said: ²⁰"O Lord who inhabitest eternity,ⁿ whose eyes are exaltedᵒ and whose upper chambers are in the air, ²¹whose throne is beyond measure and whose glory is beyond comprehension, before whom the hosts of angels stand trembling ²²and at whose command they are changed to wind and fire,ᵖ whose word is sure and whose utterances are certain, whose ordinance is strong and whose com-

g Syr: Lat *let it feed on what it understands*
h Syr: Latin is corrupt here   i Syr: Lat *place*
j Literally *what thou hast formed*
k Syr: Latin is corrupt here
l Syr: Lat *shalt with a light command*
m Literally *but*   n Or *abidest for ever*
o Another Latin text reads *whose are the highest heavens*
p Syr: Lat *they whose service takes the form of wind and fire*

8.4–36: The seer implores God to show mercy upon his creation. 4–19a: Why should God wonderfully fashion and sustain all mankind, only to destroy the great majority? **4–5:** The pre-existence of the soul is implied here (Wis.8.19). **7:** Is.44.6; 45.11; 60.21. **14:** *Was fashioned by thy command*, Ps.139.14–15. **15–16:** The seer leaves the fate of *mankind* in God's hands, and speaks particularly about Israel, God's *inheritance* (Ps.28.9). **19b–36:** A beautiful and liturgically structured prayer (invocation to God, whose attributes are recalled, vv. 20–23; petitions, interspersed with confession and intercessions, vv. 24–35; concluding ascription of praise, v. 36). This prayer also occurs separately, with the title "Confessio Esdrae," in the section of canticles and hymns contained in many manuscripts of the Latin Vulgate Bible. This circumstance accounts for the presence (in v. 19b) of a superscription in the third person. **19b:** The words, *before he was taken up*, indicate that the belief was current that Ezra, like Enoch and Elijah, was translated to heaven without dying. **22:** *Wind and fire*, Ps.104.4; Heb.1.7.

mand is terrible, [23]whose look dries up the depths and whose indignation makes the mountains melt away, and whose truth is established for ever[q]— [24]hear, O Lord, the prayer of thy servant, and give ear to the petition of thy creature; attend to my words. [25]For as long as I live I will speak, and as long as I have understanding I will answer. [26]O look not upon the sins of thy people, but at those who have served thee in truth. [27]Regard not the endeavors of those who act wickedly, but the endeavors of those who have kept thy covenants amid afflictions. [28]Think not on those who have lived wickedly in thy sight; but remember those who have willingly acknowledged that thou art to be feared. [29]Let it not be thy will to destroy those who have had the ways of cattle; but regard those who have gloriously taught thy law.[r] [30]Be not angry with those who are deemed worse than beasts; but love those who have always put their trust in thy glory. [31]For we and our fathers have passed our lives in ways that bring death;[s] but thou, because of us sinners, art called merciful. [32]For if thou hast desired to have pity on us, who have no works of righteousness, then thou wilt be called merciful. [33]For the righteous, who have many works laid up with thee, shall receive their reward in consequence of their own deeds. [34]But what is man, that thou art angry with him; or what is a corruptible race, that thou art so bitter against it? [35]For in truth there is no one among those who have been born who has not acted wickedly, and among those who have

existed[t] there is no one who has not transgressed. [36]For in this, O Lord, thy righteousness and goodness will be declared, when thou art merciful to those who have no store of good works."

37 He answered me and said, "Some things you have spoken rightly, and it will come to pass according to your words. [38]For indeed I will not concern myself about the fashioning of those who have sinned, or about their death, their judgment, or their destruction; [39]but I will rejoice over the creation of the righteous, over their pilgrimage also, and their salvation, and their receiving their reward. [40]As I have spoken, therefore, so it shall be.

41 "For just as the farmer sows many seeds upon the ground and plants a multitude of seedlings, and yet not all that have been sown will come up[u] in due season, and not all that were planted will take root; so also those who have been sown in the world will not all be saved."

42 I answered and said, "If I have found favor before thee, let me speak.[v] [43]For if the farmer's seed does not come up, because it has not received thy rain in due season, or if it has been ruined by too much rain, it perishes.[w] [44]But man, who has been formed by thy hands and is called thy own image because he is made like thee, and for whose sake thou hast formed all things—hast thou also made him like the

q Arab 2: other authorities read *bears witness*
r Syr *have received the brightness of thy law*
s Syr Ethiop: the Latin text is uncertain
t Syr: the Latin text is corrupt
u Syr Ethiop *will live;* Lat *will be saved*
v Cn: Compare Syr Arab 1 Arm Georg: the Latin is corrupt

23: *Dries up*, Is.50.2; 51.10. *Mountains melt*, Mic.1.4; Sir.16.18–19. **32:** Rom.3.19–26. **33:** 7.[77].

8.37–40: The divine reply to the seer's prayer: God will rejoice in the righteous and forget the sinners (the central petition of the prayer—mercy on the wicked—is ignored). **39:** *Their pilgrimage,* i.e. their return home to God (compare 2 Cor.5.6–8). **40:** Instead of *I have spoken,* the reading of the Ethiopic, "you have spoken," is to be preferred in view of v. 37 and the irony of the divine reply: "it is to be as you have *spoken,* but not as you had intended" (in vv. 26–36 the seer prayed God to ignore the wicked and their doings and pay attention to the righteous only; this, the Almighty replies, he will do, but in the sense of being unconcerned about the *destruction* of the wicked, v. 38).

8.41–45: Mankind is like the farmer's seed; only a few individuals will escape destruction. **45:** An anguished entreaty: *spare thy people,* Jl.2.17.

farmer's seed? ⁴⁵No, O Lord*ˣ* who art over us! But spare thy people and have mercy on thy inheritance, for thou hast mercy on thy own creation."

46 He answered me and said, "Things that are present are for those who live now, and things that are future are for those who will live hereafter. ⁴⁷For you come far short of being able to love my creation more than I love it. But you have often compared yourself*ʸ* to the unrighteous. Never do so! ⁴⁸But even in this respect you will be praiseworthy before the Most High, ⁴⁹because you have humbled yourself, as is becoming for you, and have not deemed yourself to be among the righteous in order to receive*ᶻ* the greatest glory. ⁵⁰For many miseries will affect those who inhabit the world in the last times, because they have walked in great pride. ⁵¹But think of your own case, and inquire concerning the glory of those who are like yourself, ⁵²because it is for you that paradise is opened, the tree of life is planted, the age to come is prepared, plenty is provided, a city is built, rest is appointed,*ᵃ* goodness is established and wisdom perfected beforehand. ⁵³The root of evil is sealed up from you, illness is banished from you, and death*ᵇ* is hidden; hell has fled and corruption has been forgotten;*ᶜ* ⁵⁴sorrows have passed away, and in the end the treasure of immortality is made manifest. ⁵⁵Therefore do not ask any more questions about the multitude of those who perish. ⁵⁶For they also received freedom, but they despised the Most High, and were contemptuous of his law, and forsook his ways. ⁵⁷Moreover

they have even trampled upon his righteous ones, ⁵⁸and said in their hearts that there is no God—though knowing full well that they must die. ⁵⁹For just as the things which I have predicted await*ᵈ* you, so the thirst and torment which are prepared await them. For the Most High did not intend that men should be destroyed; ⁶⁰but they themselves who were created have defiled the name of him who made them, and have been ungrateful to him who prepared life for them. ⁶¹Therefore my judgment is now drawing near; ⁶²I have not shown this to all men, but only to you and a few like you."

Then I answered and said, ⁶³"Behold, O Lord, thou hast now shown me a multitude of the signs which thou wilt do in the last times, but thou hast not shown me when thou wilt do them."

9 He answered me and said, "Measure carefully in your mind, and when you see that a certain part of the predicted signs are past, ²then you will know that it is the very time when the Most High is about to visit the world which he has made. ³So when there shall appear in the world earthquakes, tumult of peoples, intrigues of nations, wavering of leaders, confusion of princes, ⁴then you will know that it was of these that the Most High spoke from the days that were of old, from the beginning. ⁵For just as with everything that has occurred in the world,

x Ethiop Arab Compare Syr: Latin omits *O Lord*
y Syr Ethiop: Lat *brought yourself near*
z Or *righteous; so that you will receive*
a Syr: Lat *allowed*
b Syr Ethiop Arm: Latin omits *death*
c Syr: Lat *Hades and corruption have fled into oblivion,* or *corruption has fled into Hades to be forgotten*
d Syr: Lat *will receive*

8.46–62: The final divine reply: The seer is assured that his lot is with the blessed, and is advised to think no more about sinners, who deserve their doom because they have *despised the Most High* (v. 56). **46–47:** The seer's objection (v. 44) is invalid, for the simile of the seeds suits the *present* corruptible order; *the future* has standards of its own. Moreover, God's love for his *creation* far exceeds man's love (see 5.33 n.). **48:** *In this respect*, i.e. the seer's humility (compare Lk.18.13–14). **52:** The future joys of heaven are already in existence and may be contemplated now (1 Pet.1.4). *Tree of life*, 7.[123]; Rev.2.7; 22.2. **53:** *Hell* is personified (as in Rev.6.8). **56:** *Freedom*, i.e. free will. **58:** Ps.14.1; 53.1. **59:** *The things . . . predicted*, in vv. 52–54. *Thirst*, in the fire of hell (Lk.16.24). *The Most High did not intend* man's destruction (Mt.18.14; 1 Tim.2.4). **62:** *A few like you*, i.e. prophets (apocalyptists) like the seer.
8.63–9.13: The end, and the signs which will precede it (4.51–5.13; 6.11–24). **8.63:** *When*, 4.33;

the beginning is evident,[e] and the end
manifest; [6]so also are the times of the
Most High: the beginnings are manifest in wonders and mighty works, and
the end in requital[f] and in signs. [7]And
it shall be that every one who will be
saved and will be able to escape on
account of his works, or on account of
the faith by which he has believed,
[8]will survive the dangers that have been
predicted, and will see my salvation in
my land and within my borders, which
I have sanctified for myself from the
beginning. [9]Then those who have now
abused my ways shall be amazed, and
those who have rejected them with
contempt shall dwell in torments. [10]For
as many as did not acknowledge me
in their lifetime, although they received
my benefits, [11]and as many as scorned
my law while they still had freedom,
and did not understand but despised
it[g] while an opportunity of repentance
was still open to them, [12]these must in
torment acknowledge it[h] after death.
[13]Therefore, do not continue to be
curious as to how the ungodly will be
punished; but inquire how the righteous will be saved, those to whom the
age belongs and for whose sake the age
was made."[i]

[14]I answered and said, [15]"I said
before, and I say now, and will say it
again: there are more who perish than
those who will be saved, [16]as a wave is
greater than a drop of water."

[17]He answered me and said, "As
is the field, so is the seed; and as are
the flowers, so are the colors; and as
is the work, so is the product; and as
is the farmer, so is the threshing floor.
[18]For there was a time in this age when
I was preparing for those who now

exist, before the world was made for
them to dwell in, and no one opposed
me then, for no one existed; [19]but now
those who have been created in this
world which is supplied both with an
unfailing table and an inexhaustible
pasture,[j] have become corrupt in their
ways. [20]So I considered my world, and
behold, it was lost, and my earth, and
behold, it was in peril because of the
devices of those who[k] had come into
it. [21]And I saw and spared some[l] with
great difficulty, and saved for myself
one grape out of a cluster, and one
plant out of a great forest.[m] [22]So let
the multitude perish which has been
born in vain, but let my grape and my
plant be saved, because with much
labor I have perfected them. [23]But if
you will let seven days more pass—do
not fast during them, however; [24]but
go into a field of flowers where no
house has been built, and eat only of
the flowers of the field, and taste no
meat and drink no wine, but eat only
flowers, [25]and pray to the Most High
continually—then I will come and talk
with you."

26 So I went, as he directed me, into
the field which is called Ardat;[n] and
there I sat among the flowers and ate
of the plants of the field, and the
nourishment they afforded satisfied
me. [27]And after seven days, as I lay
on the grass, my heart was troubled
again as it was before. [28]And my
mouth was opened, and I began to

e Syr: Ethiop *in the word*: Latin is corrupt
f Syr: Lat Ethiop *in effects*
g Or *me*   h Or *me*
i Syr: Lat *saved, and whose is the age and for whose sake the age was made and when*   j Cn: Lat *law*
k Cn: Lat *devices which*   l Lat *them*
m Syr Ethiop Arab 1: Lat *tribe*
n Syr Ethiop *Arpad*: Arm *Ardab*

contrast Acts 1.7. **9.3:** The messianic woes on earth. **9–12:** The state of the wicked immediately after death. **11:** Opportunity of repentance (Wis.12.10,20; Heb.12.17). **12:** *Acknowledge*, their earlier opportunity of repentance; or the word may be translated "be brought to know."

9.14–25: Recapitulation: The seer again deplores the fate of the wicked, and the small number of the saved is explained a last time. **19:** Restore "law" (see note *j*) to the text: the meaning is that despite God's gracious provision of earthly sustenance and divine law, men *have become corrupt.* **21–22:** The preservation of a small remnant is the result of God's grace. **24:** Likewise Daniel and his companions ate only vegetables (Dan.1.8–16; compare 2 Macc.5.27).

9.26–10.59: The fourth vision. 9.26–28: Introduction. **26:** *Ardat*, an unknown location, probably of symbolical or mystic significance.

speak before the Most High, and said, ²⁹"O Lord, thou didst show thyself among us, to our fathers in the wilderness when they came out from Egypt and when they came into the untrodden and unfruitful wilderness; ³⁰and thou didst say, 'Hear me, O Israel, and give heed to my words, O descendants of Jacob. ³¹For behold, I sow my law in you, and it shall bring forth fruit in you, and you shall be glorified through it for ever.' ³²But though our fathers received the law, they did not keep it, and did not observe the statutes; yet the fruit of the law did not perish—for it could not, because it was thine. ³³Yet those who received it perished, because they did not keep what had been sown in them. ³⁴And behold, it is the rule that, when the ground has received seed, or the sea a ship, or any dish food or drink, and when it happens that what was sown or what was launched or what was put in is destroyed, ³⁵they are destroyed, but the things that held them remain; yet with us it has not been so. ³⁶For we who have received the law and sinned will perish, as well as our heart which received it; ³⁷the law, however, does not perish but remains in its glory."

38 When I said these things in my heart, I lifted up my eyes*ᵒ* and saw a woman on my right, and behold, she was mourning and weeping with a loud voice, and was deeply grieved at heart, and her clothes were rent, and there were ashes on her head. ³⁹Then I dismissed the thoughts with which I had been engaged, and turned to her ⁴⁰and said to her, "Why are you weeping, and why are you grieved at heart?"

41 And she said to me, "Let me alone, my lord, that I may weep for myself and continue to mourn, for I am greatly embittered in spirit and deeply afflicted."

42 And I said to her, "What has happened to you? Tell me."

43 And she said to me, "Your servant was barren and had no child, though I lived with my husband thirty years. ⁴⁴And every hour and every day during those thirty years I besought the Most High, night and day. ⁴⁵And after thirty years God heard your handmaid, and looked upon my low estate, and considered my distress, and gave me a son. And I rejoiced greatly over him, I and my husband and all my neighbors;*ᵖ* and we gave great glory to the Mighty One. ⁴⁶And I brought him up with much care. ⁴⁷So when he grew up and I came to take a wife for him, I set a day for the marriage feast.

10 "But it happened that when my son entered his wedding chamber, he fell down and died. ²Then we all put out the lamps, and all my neighbors*�q* attempted to console me; and I remained quiet until evening of the second day. ³But when they all had stopped consoling me, that I might be quiet, I got up in the night and fled, and came to this field, as you see. ⁴And now I intend not to return to the city, but to stay here, and I will neither eat nor drink, but without ceasing mourn and fast until I die."

5 Then I broke off the reflections with which I was still engaged, and answered her in anger and said, ⁶"You most foolish of women, do you not see our mourning, and what has happened to us? ⁷For Zion, the mother of us all, is in deep grief and great affliction. ⁸It is most appropriate to mourn now, because we are all

o Syr Arab Arm: Lat *I looked about me with my eyes*
p Literally *all my fellow citizens*
q Literally *all my fellow citizens*

9.29–37: **The abiding glory of the Mosaic law,** contrasted with Israel. **29:** Ex.19.9; 24.10; Dt.4.12.

9.38–10.24: **The seer speaks with a disconsolate woman. 38:** *Ashes on her head,* a sign of mourning. **47:** It was customary for the father to arrange for the wedding (see Sir.7.25 n.). **10.2:** *Lamps,* because weddings took place at night. **2:** *I remained quiet,* shows the depth of her grief, for ordinarily there was loud lamentation. **7:** *Zion, the mother of us all,* Gal.4.26.

mourning, and to be sorrowful, because we are all sorrowing; you are sorrowing for one son, but we, the whole world, for our mother.[r] [9]Now ask the earth, and she will tell you that it is she who ought to mourn over so many who have come into being upon her. [10]And from the beginning all have been born of her, and others will come; and behold, almost all go to perdition, and a multitude of them are destined for destruction. [11]Who then ought to mourn the more, she[s] who lost so great a multitude, or you who are grieving for one? [12]But if you say to me, 'My lamentation is not like the earth's, for I have lost the fruit of my womb, which I brought forth in pain and bore in sorrow; [13]but it is with the earth according to the way of the earth—the multitude that is now in it goes as it came'; [14]then I say to you, 'As you brought forth in sorrow, so the earth also has from the beginning given her fruit, that is, man, to him who made her.' [15]Now, therefore, keep your sorrow to yourself, and bear bravely the troubles that have come upon you. [16]For if you acknowledge the decree of God to be just, you will receive your son back in due time, and will be praised among women. [17]Therefore go into the city to your husband."

18 She said to me, "I will not do so; I will not go into the city, but I will die here."

19 So I spoke again to her, and said, [20]"Do not say that, but let yourself be persuaded because of the troubles of Zion, and be consoled because of the sorrow of Jerusalem. [21]For you see that our sanctuary has been laid •waste, our altar thrown down, our temple destroyed; [22]our harp has been laid low, our song has been silenced, and our rejoicing has been ended; the light of our lampstand has been put out, the ark of our covenant has been plundered, our holy things have been polluted, and the name by which we are called has been profaned; our free men[t] have suffered abuse, our priests have been burned to death, our Levites have gone into captivity, our virgins have been defiled, and our wives have been ravished; our righteous men have been carried off, our little ones have been cast out, our young men have been enslaved and our strong men made powerless. [23]And, what is more than all, the seal of Zion—for she has now lost the seal of her glory, and has been given over into the hands of those that hate us. [24]Therefore shake off your great sadness and lay aside your many sorrows, so that the Mighty One may be merciful to you again, and the Most High may give you rest, a relief from your troubles."

25 While I was talking to her, behold, her face suddenly shone exceedingly, and her countenance flashed like lightning, so that I was too frightened to approach her, and my heart was terrified. While[u] I was wondering what this meant, [26]behold, she suddenly uttered a loud and fearful cry, so that the earth shook at the sound. [27]And I looked, and behold, the woman was no longer visible to me, but there was an established city,[v] and a place of huge foundations showed itself. Then I was afraid, and cried with a loud voice and said, [28]"Where is the angel Uriel,

r Compare Syr: Latin is corrupt
s Syr
t Or *children*
u Syr Ethiop Arab 1: Latin omits *I was too ... terrified. While*
v Syr Ethiop Arab: Lat *a city was being built*

16: To *acknowledge* the justice of God's *decree* is equivalent to pious submission to his will. *You will receive your son back in due time*, i.e. in the birth of another son, after returning to her husband (v. 17). **21–23**: A pathetic account of the utter ruin of Israel. **22**: *Harp* symbolizes the service of praise. The extinction of the perpetually burning *lamp* marked the cessation of temple services. *Our holy things* are enumerated in 1 Macc.4.49–51. *The name* Israel was bestowed by God (Gen.32.28). **23**: *The seal* of a nation is symbolic of its independence.

10.25–28: A vision of the heavenly Jerusalem. 27: *An established city*, Heb.11.10; Rev.21.9–21. **28**: *At first*, 4.1.

who came to me at first? For it was he who brought me into this overpowering bewilderment; my end has become corruption, and my prayer a reproach."

29 As I was speaking these words, behold, the angel who had come to me at first came to me, and he looked upon me; [30]and behold, I lay there like a corpse and I was deprived of my understanding. Then he grasped my right hand and strengthened me and set me on my feet, and said to me, [31]"What is the matter with you? And why are you troubled? And why are your understanding and the thoughts of your mind troubled?"

32 I said, "Because you have forsaken me! I did as you directed, and went out into the field, and behold, I saw, and still see, what I am unable to explain."

33 He said to me, "Stand up like a man, and I will instruct you."

34 I said, "Speak, my lord; only do not forsake me, lest I die before my time.[w] [35]For I have seen what I did not know, and I have heard what I do not understand. [36]Or is my mind deceived, and my soul dreaming? [37]Now therefore I entreat you to give your servant an explanation of this bewildering vision."

38 He answered me and said, "Listen to me and I will inform you, and tell you about the things which you fear, for the Most High has revealed many secrets to you. [39]For he has seen your righteous conduct, that you have sorrowed continually for your people, and mourned greatly over Zion. [40]This therefore is the meaning of the vision. [41]The woman who appeared to you a little while ago, whom you saw mourning and began to console—[42]but you do not now see the form of a woman,

but an established city[x] has appeared to you—[43]and as for her telling you about the misfortune of her son, this is the interpretation: [44]This woman whom you saw, whom you now behold as an established city, is Zion.[y] [45]And as for her telling you that she was barren for thirty years, it is because there were three thousand[y] years in the world before any offering was offered in it.[z] [46]And after three thousand[y] years Solomon built the city, and offered offerings; then it was that the barren woman bore a son. [47]And as for her telling you that she brought him up with much care, that was the period of residence in Jerusalem. [48]And as for her saying to you, 'When my son entered his wedding chamber he died,' and that misfortune had overtaken her,[a] that was the destruction which befell Jerusalem. [49]And behold, you saw her likeness, how she mourned for her son, and you began to console her for what had happened.[b] [50]For now the Most High, seeing that you are sincerely grieved and profoundly distressed for her, has shown you the brilliance of her glory, and the loveliness of her beauty. [51]Therefore I told you to remain in the field where no house had been built, [52]for I knew that the Most High would reveal these things to you. [53]Therefore I told you to go into the field where there was no foundation of any building, [54]for no work of man's building could endure in a place where the city of the Most High was to be revealed.

55 "Therefore do not be afraid, and do not let your heart be terrified; but go in and see the splendor and vastness

w Syr Ethiop Arab: Lat *die to no purpose*
x Syr Ethiop Arab: Lat *a city to be built*
y Syr Ethiop Arab Arm: Latin is corrupt
z Cn: Lat Syr Arab Arm *her*   a Or *him*
b Most Latin manuscripts and Arab 2 add *these were the things to be opened to you*

10.29–59: Interpretation of the vision. 30: *Like a corpse*, Rev.1.17; compare Dan.8.18; 10.9. **32:** *And still see*, the vision is still before the seer's eyes. *Unable to explain*, compare 2 Cor.12.3–4 (also of an ecstatic experience). **33:** *Stand up*, 5.15; 6.13,17. **44:** *Zion*, i.e. the heavenly Jerusalem. **45:** *In it*, in the world. **46:** *A son*, i.e. the earthly Jerusalem. **49:** The *likeness*, or model, of the earthly city is the heavenly Zion, who *mourned for her son* (the ruined earthly Jerusalem). For the idea of a heavenly counterpart or model, compare Ex.25.9,40; Heb.8.5. **55–56:** 1 Cor.

of the building, as far as it is possible for your eyes to see it, ⁵⁶and afterward you will hear as much as your ears can hear. ⁵⁷For you are more blessed than many, and you have been called before the Most High, as but few have been. ⁵⁸But tomorrow night you shall remain here, ⁵⁹and the Most High will show you in those dream visions what the Most High will do to those who dwell on earth in the last days."

So I slept that night and the following one, as he had commanded me.

|| On the second night I had a dream, and behold, there came up from the sea an eagle that had twelve feathered wings and three heads. ²And I looked, and behold, he spread his wings over*c* all the earth, and all the winds of heaven blew upon him, and the clouds were gathered about him.*d* ³And I looked, and out of his wings there grew opposing wings; but they became little, puny wings. ⁴But his heads were at rest; the middle head was larger than the other heads, but it also was at rest with them. ⁵And I looked, and behold, the eagle flew with his wings, to reign over the earth and over those who dwell in it. ⁶And I saw how all things under heaven were subjected to him, and no one spoke against him, not even one creature that was on the earth. ⁷And I looked, and behold, the eagle rose upon his talons, and uttered a cry to his wings, saying, ⁸"Do not all watch at the same time; let each sleep in his own place, and watch in his turn; ⁹but let the heads be reserved for the last."

10 And I looked, and behold, the voice did not come from his heads, but from the midst of his body. ¹¹And I counted his opposing wings, and

behold, there were eight of them. ¹²And I looked, and behold, on the right side one wing arose, and it reigned over all the earth. ¹³And while it was reigning it came to its end and disappeared, so that its place was not seen. Then the next wing arose and reigned, and it continued to reign a long time. ¹⁴And while it was reigning its end came also, so that it disappeared like the first. ¹⁵And behold, a voice sounded, saying to it, ¹⁶"Hear me, you who have ruled the earth all this time; I announce this to you before you disappear. ¹⁷After you no one shall rule as long as you, or even half as long."

18 Then the third wing raised itself up, and held the rule like the former ones, and it also disappeared. ¹⁹And so it went with all the wings; they wielded power one after another and then were never seen again. ²⁰And I looked, and behold, in due course the wings that followed*e* also rose up on the right*f* side, in order to rule. There were some of them that ruled, yet disappeared suddenly; ²¹and others of them rose up, but did not hold the rule.

22 And after this I looked, and behold, the twelve wings and the two little wings disappeared; ²³and nothing remained on the eagle's body except the three heads that were at rest and six little wings. ²⁴And I looked, and behold, two little wings separated from the six and remained under the head that was on the right side; but four remained in their place. ²⁵And I looked, and behold, these little wings*g* planned to set themselves up and hold

c Arab 2 Arm: Lat Syr *in*
d Syr Compare Ethiop Arab: Latin omits *the clouds* and *about him*
e Syr Arab 2 *the little wings*
f Some Ethiopic manuscripts read *left*
g Syr: Lat *underwings*

2.9; 2 Cor.12.4. *Go in and see*, the city is conceived as still standing before Ezra. **57**: *You have been called before the Most High*, Arabic 1, "your name is known [or recognized] before the Most High," i.e. God has singled you out for honor (Is.45.3–4).

11.1–12.51: **The fifth vision (the eagle vision)**. **11.1**: *From the sea*, Dan.7.3; Rev.13.1. *An eagle*, symbol of the Roman Empire. **2**: *Spread his wings*, asserted his dominion. *The winds*, 13.2; Dan.7.2. **3**: *Opposing wings*, symbolizing usurpers who revolted against the Roman emperors. *But they became little*, i.e. they were subdued. **4**: *Were at rest*, i.e. were not troubled by the opposing wings. **13**: *It came to its end*, i.e. the ruler perished.

the rule. ²⁶And I looked, and behold, one was set up, but suddenly disappeared; ²⁷a second also, and this disappeared more quickly than the first. ²⁸And I looked, and behold, the two that remained were planning between themselves to reign together; ²⁹and while they were planning, behold, one of the heads that were at rest (the one which was in the middle) awoke; for it was greater than the other two heads. ³⁰And I saw how it allied the two heads with itself, ³¹and behold, the head turned with those that were with it, and it devoured the two little wings*ʰ* which were planning to reign. ³²Moreover this head gained control of the whole earth, and with much oppression dominated its inhabitants; and it had greater power over the world than all the wings that had gone before.

33 And after this I looked, and behold, the middle head also suddenly disappeared, just as the wings had done. ³⁴But the two heads remained, which also ruled over the earth and its inhabitants. ³⁵And I looked, and behold, the head on the right side devoured the one on the left.

36 Then I heard a voice saying to me, "Look before you and consider what you see." ³⁷And I looked, and behold, a creature like a lion was aroused out of the forest, roaring; and I heard how he uttered a man's voice to the eagle, and spoke, saying, ³⁸"Listen and I will speak to you. The Most High says to you, ³⁹'Are you not the one that remains of the four beasts which I had made to reign in my world, so that the end of my times might come through them? ⁴⁰You, the fourth that has come, have conquered all the beasts that have gone before; and you have held sway over the world with much terror, and over all the earth with grievous oppression; and for so long you have dwelt on the earth with deceit.*ⁱ* ⁴¹And you have judged the earth, but not with truth; ⁴²for you have afflicted the meek and injured the peaceable; you have hated those who tell the truth, and have loved liars; you have destroyed the dwellings of those who brought forth fruit, and have laid low the walls of those who did you no harm. ⁴³And so your insolence has come up before the Most High, and your pride to the Mighty One. ⁴⁴And the Most High has looked upon his times, and behold, they are ended, and his ages are completed! ⁴⁵Therefore you will surely disappear, you eagle, and your terrifying wings, and your most evil little wings, and your malicious heads, and your most evil talons, and your whole worthless body, ⁴⁶so that the whole earth, freed from your violence, may be refreshed and relieved, and may hope for the judgment and mercy of him who made it.'"

12 While the lion was saying these words to the eagle, I looked, ²and behold, the remaining head disappeared. And the two wings that had gone over to it arose*ʲ* and set themselves up to reign, and their reign was brief and full of tumult. ³And I looked, and behold, they also disappeared, and the whole body of the eagle was burned, and the earth was exceedingly terrified.

Then I awoke in great perplexity of mind and great fear, and I said to my spirit, ⁴"Behold, you have brought this upon me, because you search out the ways of the Most High. ⁵Behold, I am still weary in mind and very weak in my spirit, and not even a little strength is left in me, because of the great fear with which I have been terrified this night. ⁶Therefore I will now beseech the Most High that he may strengthen me to the end."

h Syr: Lat *underwings*
i Syr Arab Arm: Lat Ethiop *The fourth came, however, and conquered . . . and held sway . . . and for so long dwelt*
j Ethiop: Latin omits *arose*

36: *Look before you,* the seer is alerted to the special importance of what follows. **43:** Dan.5.20.
   12.3b–39: The interpretation of the vision. 3b–9: The seer awakes and asks for an interpretation of the vision. **11:** *The fourth kingdom* in Daniel's vision (Dan.7.7) symbolized the Greek or

7 And I said, "O sovereign Lord, if I have found favor in thy sight, and if I have been accounted righteous before thee beyond many others, and if my prayer has indeed come up before thy face, [8]strengthen me and show me, thy servant, the interpretation and meaning of this terrifying vision, that thou mayest fully comfort my soul. [9]For thou hast judged me worthy to be shown the end of the times and the last events of the times."

10 He said to me, "This is the interpretation of this vision which you have seen: [11]The eagle which you saw coming up from the sea is the fourth kingdom which appeared in a vision to your brother Daniel. [12]But it was not explained to him as I now explain or have explained it to you. [13]Behold, the days are coming when a kingdom shall arise on earth, and it shall be more terrifying than all the kingdoms that have been before it. [14]And twelve kings shall reign in it, one after another. [15]But the second that is to reign shall hold sway for a longer time than any other of the twelve. [16]This is the interpretation of the twelve wings which you saw. [17]As for your hearing a voice that spoke, coming not from the eagle's[k] heads but from the midst of his body, this is the interpretation: [18]In the midst of[l] the time of that kingdom great struggles shall arise, and it shall be in danger of falling; nevertheless it shall not fall then, but shall regain its former power.[m] [19]As for your seeing eight little wings[n] clinging to his wings, this is the interpretation: [20]Eight kings shall arise in it, whose times shall be short and their years swift; [21]and two of them shall perish when the middle of its time draws near; and four shall

be kept for the time when its end approaches; but two shall be kept until the end. [22]As for your seeing three heads at rest, this is the interpretation: [23]In its last days the Most High will raise up three kings,[o] and they[p] shall renew many things in it, and shall rule the earth [24]and its inhabitants more oppressively than all who were before them; therefore they are called the heads of the eagle. [25]For it is they who shall sum up his wickedness and perform his last actions. [26]As for your seeing that the large head disappeared, one of the kings[q] shall die in his bed, but in agonies. [27]But as for the two who remained, the sword shall devour them. [28]For the sword of one shall devour him who was with him; but he also shall fall by the sword in the last days. [29]As for your seeing two little wings[r] passing over to[s] the head which was on the right side, [30]this is the interpretation: It is these whom the Most High has kept for the eagle's[t] end; this was the reign which was brief and full of tumult, as you have seen.

31 "And as for the lion whom you saw rousing up out of the forest and roaring and speaking to the eagle and reproving him for his unrighteousness, and as for all his words that you have heard, [32]this is the Messiah[u] whom the Most High has kept until the end of days, who will arise from the posterity of David, and will come and speak to

k Lat *his*
l Syr Arm: Lat *After*
m Ethiop Arab 1 Arm: Lat Syr *beginning*
n Syr: Lat *underwings*
o Syr Ethiop Arab Arm: Lat *kingdoms*
p Syr Ethiop Arm: Lat *he*
q Lat *them*
r Arab 1: Lat *underwings*
s Syr Ethiop: Latin omits *to*
t Lat *his*
u Literally *anointed one*

Macedonian Empire; here, however, it is reinterpreted (compare v. 12) to refer to the Roman Empire (see 11.1 n.). **13:** *The days are coming,* the seer is represented as prophesying during the exile. **17:** 11.10; compare 11.15. **18:** There is nothing in the vision which corresponds to what is said in this verse. The author probably refers to *the time of great struggles* for power which followed the death of Nero A.D. 68. **19:** *Little wings,* 11.3,11. *Clinging to his wings,* Armenian, "sprouting out around his great wings." **20:** *In it,* within the Roman Empire. **21:** *Its time,* the time of the kingdom. *Its end,* the end of the kingdom. **23:** *Its last days,* the last days of the kingdom. **23–24:** 11.30–32. **28:** *But . . . days,* there is nothing corresponding to this in the vision. **30:** *As you have seen,* v. 3. **31:** *The lion,* 11.37ff. **32:** *Whom the Most High has kept until the end* them;[v] he will denounce them for their ungodliness and for their wickedness, and will cast up before them their contemptuous dealings. [33]For first he will set them living before his judgment seat, and when he has reproved them, then he will destroy them. [34]But he will deliver in mercy the remnant of my people, those who have been saved throughout my borders, and he will make them joyful until the end comes, the day of judgment, of which I spoke to you at the beginning. [35]This is the dream that you saw, and this is its interpretation. [36]And you alone were worthy to learn this secret of the Most High. [37]Therefore write all these things that you have seen in a book, and put it in a hidden place; [38]and you shall teach them to the wise among your people, whose hearts you know are able to comprehend and keep these secrets. [39]But wait here seven days more, so that you may be shown whatever it pleases the Most High to show you." Then he left me.

40 When all the people heard that the seven days were past and I had not returned to the city, they all gathered together, from the least to the greatest, and came to me and spoke to me, saying, [41]"How have we offended you, and what harm have we done you, that you have forsaken us and sit in this place? [42]For of all the prophets you alone are left to us, like a cluster of grapes from the vintage, and like a lamp in a dark place, and like a haven for a ship saved from a storm. [43]Are not the evils which have befallen us sufficient? [44]Therefore if you forsake us, how much better it would have been for us if we also had been consumed in the burning of Zion! [45]For we are no

better than those who died there." And they wept with a loud voice.

Then I answered them and said, [46]"Take courage, O Israel; and do not be sorrowful, O house of Jacob; [47]for the Most High has you in remembrance, and the Mighty One has not forgotten you in your struggle. [48]As for me, I have neither forsaken you nor withdrawn from you; but I have come to this place to pray on account of the desolation of Zion, and to seek mercy on account of the humiliation of our[w] sanctuary. [49]Now go, every one of you to his house, and after these days I will come to you." [50]So the people went into the city, as I told them to do. [51]But I sat in the field seven days, as the angel[x] had commanded me; and I ate only of the flowers of the field, and my food was of plants during those days.

13 After seven days I dreamed a dream in the night; [2]and behold, a wind arose from the sea and stirred up all its waves. [3]And I looked, and behold, this wind made something like the figure of a man come up out of the heart of the sea. And I looked, and behold,[y] that man flew[z] with the clouds of heaven; and wherever he turned his face to look, everything under his gaze trembled, [4]and whenever his voice issued from his mouth, all who heard his voice melted as wax melts[a] when it feels the fire.

5 After this I looked, and behold, an innumerable multitude of men were gathered together from the four winds

v Syr: Latin omits *of days . . . and speak*
w Syr Ethiop: Lat *your*
x Literally *he*
y Syr: Latin omits *this wind . . . and behold*
z Syr Ethiop Arab Arm: Lat *grew strong*
a Syr: Lat *burned as the earth rests*

---

of days, the pre-existent Messiah in heaven (Dan.7.13–14; Enoch 48.6; 62.7). *He will denounce them*, 13.37. **34:** *He will make them joyful*, 7.28. **35:** *The dream*, 11.1. **37:** The seer is bidden to compose an esoteric book. **37–38:** To *put the book in a hidden place* suggests that it is an apocryphal book, which only the elect (*the wise*) can *comprehend*. **39:** *He*, the angel Uriel (see 4.1 n.).

12.40–51: The seer comforts those who were grieved because of his absence. 40: *The seven days*, 9.23,27. **42:** *A lamp*, 2 Pet.1.19. **49:** *These days*, v. 39. **51:** 9.24–26.

13.1–58: The sixth vision (the man from the sea). 3: *Something like the figure of a man*, the Messiah (Dan.7.13); compare v. 32 "my Son," i.e. the Son of God. *Flew with the clouds*, Is.19.1;

of heaven to make war against the man who came up out of the sea. ⁶And I looked, and behold, he carved out for himself a great mountain, and flew up upon it. ⁷And I tried to see the region or place from which the mountain was carved, but I could not.

8 After this I looked, and behold, all who had gathered together against him, to wage war with him, were much afraid, yet dared to fight. ⁹And behold, when he saw the onrush of the approaching multitude, he neither lifted his hand nor held a spear or any weapon of war; ¹⁰but I saw only how he sent forth from his mouth as it were a stream of fire, and from his lips a flaming breath, and from his tongue he shot forth a storm of sparks.ᵇ ¹¹All these were mingled together, the stream of fire and the flaming breath and the great storm, and fell on the onrushing multitude which was prepared to fight, and burned them all up, so that suddenly nothing was seen of the innumerable multitude but only the dust of ashes and the smell of smoke. When I saw it, I was amazed.

12 After this I saw the same man come down from the mountain and call to him another multitude which was peaceable. ¹³Then many peopleᶜ came to him, some of whom were joyful and some sorrowful; some of them were bound, and some were bringing others as offerings.

Then in great fear I awoke; and I besought the Most High, and said, ¹⁴"From the beginning thou hast shown thy servant these wonders, and hast deemed me worthy to have my prayer heard by thee; ¹⁵now show me also the interpretation of this dream. ¹⁶For as I consider it in my mind, alas for

those who will be left in those days! And still more, alas for those who are not left! ¹⁷For those who are not left will be sad, ¹⁸because they understand what is reserved for the last days, but cannot attain it. ¹⁹But alas for those also who are left, and for that very reason! For they shall see great dangers and much distress, as these dreams show. ²⁰Yet it is betterᵈ to come into these things,ᵉ though incurring peril, than to pass from the world like a cloud, and not to see what shall happen in the last days."

He answered me and said, ²¹"I will tell you the interpretation of the vision, and I will also explain to you the things which you have mentioned. ²²As for what you said about those who are left, this is the interpretation: ²³He who brings the peril at that time will himself protect those who fall into peril, who have works and have faith in the Almighty. ²⁴Understand therefore that those who are left are more blessed than those who have died. ²⁵This is the interpretation of the vision: As for your seeing a man come up from the heart of the sea, ²⁶this is he whom the Most High has been keeping for many ages, who will himself deliver his creation; and he will direct those who are left. ²⁷And as for your seeing wind and fire and a storm coming out of his mouth, ²⁸and as for his not holding a spear or weapon of war, yet destroying the onrushing multitude which came to conquer him, this is the interpretation: ²⁹Behold, the days are coming when the Most High will deliver those who are on the earth. ³⁰And bewilderment of

b Compare Syr: Latin is corrupt
c Lat Syr Arab 2 literally *the faces of many people*
d Ethiop Compare Arab 2: Lat *easier*
e Syr: Lat *this*

Dan.7.13; Rev.1.7. **4:** *As wax melts*, Mic.1.4; Jdt.16.15. **6:** *Carved out*, Dan.2.45. **10:** Is.11.4. **13a:** *Some . . . were bound*, Jews who came from captivity. *Others as offerings*, Is.66.20.

13.13b–20: The seer prays that God will interpret the vision to him. 14: *From the beginning*, when the seer first began to have the visions. *My prayer*, 9.25ff. **19:** *For that very reason*, better, "for this reason—" (the reason follows).

13.21–56: The interpretation of the vision. 21: *Things . . . mentioned*, in vv. 16–20. **22:** *Left*, Syriac and Arabic 1 add, "and of those who do not survive." **23:** *He who brings the peril*, the Messiah, whose advent is preceded by the messianic woes. **26:** *He whom the Most High has been keeping for many ages*, the pre-existent heavenly Messiah (v. 52; 12.32). **27–28:** Vv. 9–11.

mind shall come over those who dwell on the earth. ³¹And they shall plan to make war against one another, city against city, place against place, people against people, and kingdom against kingdom. ³²And when these things come to pass and the signs occur which I showed you before, then my Son will be revealed, whom you saw as a man coming up from the sea.ᶠ ³³And when all the nations hear his voice, every man shall leave his own land and the warfare that they have against one another; ³⁴and an innumerable multitude shall be gathered together, as you saw, desiring to come and conquer him. ³⁵But he will stand on the top of Mount Zion. ³⁶And Zion will come and be made manifest to all people, prepared and built, as you saw the mountain carved out without hands. ³⁷And he, my Son, will reprove the assembled nations for their ungodliness (this was symbolized by the storm), ³⁸and will reproach them to their face with their evil thoughts and the torments with which they are to be tortured (which were symbolized by the flames), and will destroy them without effort by the lawᵍ (which was symbolized by the fire). ³⁹And as for your seeing him gather to himself another multitude that was peaceable, ⁴⁰these are the ten tribes which were led away from their own land into captivity in the days of King Hoshea, whom Shalmaneser the king of the Assyrians led captive; he took them across the river, and they were taken into another land. ⁴¹But they formed this plan for themselves, that they would leave the multitude of the nations and go to a more distant region, where mankind had never lived, ⁴²that there at least they might keep their statutes which they had

not kept in their own land. ⁴³And they went in by the narrow passages of the Euphrates river. ⁴⁴For at that time the Most High performed signs for them, and stopped the channels of the river until they had passed over. ⁴⁵Through that region there was a long way to go, a journey of a year and a half; and that country is called Arzareth.ʰ

46 "Then they dwelt there until the last times; and now, when they are about to come again, ⁴⁷the Most High will stopⁱ the channels of the river again, so that they may be able to pass over. Therefore you saw the multitude gathered together in peace. ⁴⁸But those who are left of your people, who are found within my holy borders, shall be saved.ʲ ⁴⁹Therefore when he destroys the multitude of the nations that are gathered together, he will defend the people who remain. ⁵⁰And then he will show them very many wonders."

51 I said, "O sovereign Lord, explain this to me: Why did I see the man coming up from the heart of the sea?"

52 He said to me, "Just as no one can explore or know what is in the depths of the sea, so no one on earth can see my Son or those who are with him, except in the time of his day.ᵏ ⁵³This is the interpretation of the dream which you saw. And you alone have been enlightened about this, ⁵⁴because you have forsaken your own ways and have applied yourself to mine, and have searched out my law; ⁵⁵for you have devoted your life to wisdom, and called

f Syr and most Latin manuscripts omit *from the sea*
g Syr: Lat *and the law*
h That is *Another Land*
i Syr: Lat *stops*
j Syr: Latin omits *shall be saved*
k Syr: Ethiop *except when his time and his day have come.* Latin omits *his*

31: Is.19.2; Mt.24.7. **32**: *Then my son will be revealed,* 7.28; Mt.24.30; Mk.13.26. **34**: Rev.16.16; 19.19. **36**: *Zion,* the heavenly Jerusalem (7.26; Rev.21.2, 9f.). *Without hands,* Dan.2.34,45. **37**: 12.32. **40**: 2 Kg.17.1–6. *The ten tribes,* the Northern Kingdom. *The river,* the Euphrates. **44**: *Stopped . . . the river,* Jos.3.14–16. **45**: *Arzareth,* Hebrew for "Another Land" (see note *h*; compare Dt.29.28). **47**: *Will stop . . . the river,* Is.11.15–16. |**49**: *The people that remain,* presumably Israel, including the ten tribes who have returned to Palestine (v. 48). **50**: *Then,* in the messianic age. **52**: *Those . . . with him,* perhaps angels (Mt.24.31; 25.31). *Except . . . day,* until the day on which the Messiah appears.

understanding your mother. [56]Therefore I have shown you this, for there is a reward laid up with the Most High. And after three more days I will tell you other things, and explain weighty and wondrous matters to you."

57 Then I arose and walked in the field, giving great glory and praise to the Most High because of his wonders, which he did from time to time, [58]and because he governs the times and whatever things come to pass in their seasons. And I stayed there three days.

14 On the third day, while I was sitting under an oak, behold, a voice came out of a bush opposite me and said, "Ezra, Ezra." [2]And I said, "Here I am, Lord," and I rose to my feet. [3]Then he said to me, "I revealed myself in a bush and spoke to Moses, when my people were in bondage in Egypt; [4]and I sent him and led[l] my people out of Egypt; and I led him up on Mount Sinai, where I kept him with me many days; [5]and I told him many wondrous things, and showed him the secrets of the times and declared to him[m] the end of the times. Then I commanded him, saying, [6]'These words you shall publish openly, and these you shall keep secret.' [7]And now I say to you: [8]Lay up in your heart the signs that I have shown you, the dreams that you have seen, and the interpretations that you have heard; [9]for you shall be taken up from among men, and henceforth you shall live with my Son and with those who are like you, until the times are ended. [10]For the age has lost its youth, and the times begin to grow old. [11]For the age is divided into twelve parts, and nine[n] of its parts have already passed, [12]as well as half of the tenth part; so two of its parts remain, besides half of the tenth part.[o]

[13]Now therefore, set your house in order, and reprove your people; comfort the lowly among them, and instruct those that are wise.[p] And now renounce the life that is corruptible, [14]and put away from you mortal thoughts; cast away from you the burdens of man, and divest yourself now of your weak nature, [15]and lay to one side the thoughts that are most grievous to you, and hasten to escape from these times. [16]For evils worse than those which you have now seen happen shall be done hereafter. [17]For the weaker the world becomes through old age, the more shall evils be multiplied among[q] its inhabitants. [18]For truth shall go farther away, and falsehood shall come near. For the eagle[r] which you saw in the vision is already hastening to come."

19 Then I answered and said, "Let me speak in thy presence, Lord.[s] [20]For behold, I will go, as thou hast commanded me, and I will reprove the people who are now living; but who will warn those who will be born hereafter? For the world lies in darkness, and its inhabitants are without light. [21]For thy law has been burned, and so no one knows the things which have been done or will be done by thee. [22]If then I have found favor before thee, send the Holy Spirit into me, and I will write everything that has happened in the world from the beginning, the things which were written in thy law, that men may be able to find the path, and that those who wish to live in the last days may live."

l Other authorities read *he led*
m Syr Ethiop Arab Arm: Latin omits *declared to him*
n Cn: Lat Ethiop *ten*
o Syr omits verses 11, 12: Ethiop *For the world is divided into ten parts, and has come to the tenth, and half of the tenth remains. Now ...*
p Latin omits *and ... wise*
q Literally *upon*
r Syr Ethiop Arab Arm: Latin is corrupt
s Most Latin manuscripts omit *Let me speak*

14.1–48: The seventh vision (the legend of Ezra and the holy Scriptures). 1–18: God speaks to Ezra. 1: *A bush*, compare Ex.3.4. 4: *Many days*, forty days (Ex.34.28). 9: *My son*, the preexistent heavenly Messiah (7.28; 13.32,52). 10: 5.50–55. 13: *House*, of Israel. 14: 2 Cor.5.4. 16: Mt.24.8. 18: *The eagle*, ch. 11.

14.19–26: Ezra's prayer for inspiration to restore the holy Scriptures. 20: *Without light*, without the light of God's law (Ps.19.8b). 21: 4.23. 22: *The Holy Spirit* will guide Ezra in

23 He answered me and said, "Go and gather the people, and tell them not to seek you for forty days. ²⁴But prepare for yourself many writing tablets, and take with you Sarea, Dabria, Selemia, Ethanus, and Asiel— these five, because they are trained to write rapidly; ²⁵and you shall come here, and I will light in your heart the lamp of understanding, which shall not be put out until what you are about to write is finished. ²⁶And when you have finished, some things you shall make public, and some you shall deliver in secret to the wise; tomorrow at this hour you shall begin to write."

27 Then I went as he commanded me, and I gathered all the people together, and said, ²⁸"Hear these words, O Israel. ²⁹At first our fathers dwelt as aliens in Egypt, and they were delivered from there, ³⁰and received the law of life, which they did not keep, which you also have transgressed after them. ³¹Then land was given to you for a possession in the land of Zion; but you and your fathers committed iniquity and did not keep the ways which the Most High commanded you. ³²And because he is a righteous judge, in due time he took from you what he had given. ³³And now you are here, and your brethren are farther in the interior.ᵗ ³⁴If you, then, will rule over your minds and discipline your hearts, you shall be kept alive, and after death you shall obtain mercy. ³⁵For after death the judgment will come, when we shall live again; and then the names of the righteous will become manifest, and the deeds of the ungodly will be disclosed. ³⁶But let no one come to me now, and let no one seek me for forty days."

37 So I took the five men, as he commanded me, and we proceeded to the field, and remained there. ³⁸And on the next day, behold, a voice called me, saying, "Ezra, open your mouth and drink what I give you to drink." ³⁹Then I opened my mouth, and behold, a full cup was offered to me; it was full of something like water, but its color was like fire. ⁴⁰And I took it and drank; and when I had drunk it, my heart poured forth understanding, and wisdom increased in my breast, for my spirit retained its memory; ⁴¹and my mouth was opened, and was no longer closed. ⁴²And the Most High gave understanding to the five men, and by turns they wrote what was dictated, in characters which they did not know.ᵘ They sat forty days, and wrote during the daytime, and ate their bread at night. ⁴³As for me, I spoke in the daytime and was not silent at night. ⁴⁴So during the forty days ninety-fourᵛ books were written. ⁴⁵And when the forty days were ended, the Most High spoke to me, saying, "Make public the twenty-fourʷ books that you wrote first and let the worthy and the unworthy read them; ⁴⁶but keep

t Syr Ethiop Arm: Lat *are among you*
u Syr Compare Ethiop Arab 2 Arm: Latin is corrupt
v Syr Ethiop Arab 1 Arm: Latin is corrupt
w Syr Arab 1: Latin omits *twenty-four*

rewriting the law, which has been burned (v. 21). **23**: *Forty days*, Ex.24.18; 34.28; Dt.9.9,18. **24**: *Many*, compare v. 44. **26**: *Some things . . . make public*, namely, the rewritten books of the Old Testament. *Some . . . deliver in secret*, namely, the apocalypses (see 12.37–38 n.).

14.27–36: The last words of Ezra. 29: *Aliens*, Gen.47.4. **30**: *The law*, which, if observed, would confer *life*. **33**: *Farther*, 13.45. **34**: *Kept alive*, i.e. spiritually alive. **36**: *Forty days*, v. 23.

14.37–48: The restoration of the holy Scriptures. 37: *The five men*, v. 24. **39**: *A full cup* of inspiration, containing the fire of the Spirit (v. 22). **41**: *Was opened*, in fluent speech. **42**: *In characters which they did not know*, in a new Hebrew script, the (modern) square characters. **45**: *The twenty-four books* of the Hebrew canon comprise the five books of the Law (Gen., Ex., Lev., Num., Dt.), eight books of the Prophets (the former prophets, Jos., Jg., 1 and 2 Sam. [as one book], 1 and 2 Kg. [as one book]; the latter prophets, Is., Jer., Ezek., and the Twelve [counted as one book]), and eleven books of the Writings (Ps., Pr., Job, S. of S., Ru., Lam., Ec., Est., Dan., Ezra-Neh. [as one book], 1 and 2 Chr. [as one book]). **46**: *The seventy* are esoteric, apocalyptic books (see 12.37–38 n.).

the seventy that were written last, in order to give them to the wise among your people. [47]For in them is the spring of understanding, the fountain of wisdom, and the river of knowledge." [48]And I did so.[x]

15[y] The Lord says, "Behold, speak in the ears of my people the words of the prophecy which I will put in your mouth, [2]and cause them to be written on paper; for they are trustworthy and true. [3]Do not fear the plots against you, and do not be troubled by the unbelief of those who oppose you. [4]For every unbeliever shall die in his unbelief."

5 "Behold," says the Lord, "I bring evils upon the world, the sword and famine and death and destruction. [6]For iniquity has spread throughout every land, and their harmful deeds have reached their limit. [7]Therefore," says the Lord, [8]"I will be silent no longer concerning their ungodly deeds which they impiously commit, neither will I tolerate their wicked practices. Behold, innocent and righteous blood cries out to me, and the souls of the righteous cry out continually. [9]I will surely avenge them," says the Lord, "and will receive to myself all the innocent blood from among them. [10]Behold, my people is led like a flock to the slaughter; I will not allow them to live any longer in the land of Egypt, [11]but I will bring them out with a mighty hand and with an uplifted arm, and will smite Egypt with plagues, as before, and will destroy all its land."

12 Let Egypt mourn, and its foundations, for the plague of chastisement and punishment that the Lord will bring upon it. [13]Let the farmers that till the ground mourn, because their seed shall fail and their trees shall be ruined by blight and hail and by a terrible tempest. [14]Alas for the world and for those who live in it! [15]For the sword and misery draw near them, and nation shall rise up to fight against nation, with swords in their hands. [16]For there shall be unrest among men; growing strong against one another, they shall in their might have no respect for their king or the chief of their leaders. [17]For a man will desire to go into a city, and shall not be able. [18]For because of their pride the cities shall be in confusion, the houses shall be destroyed, and people shall be afraid. [19]A man shall have no pity upon his neighbors, but shall make an assault upon their houses with the sword, and plunder their goods, because of hunger for bread and because of great tribulation.

20 "Behold," says God, "I call together all the kings of the earth to fear me, from the rising sun and from the south, from the east and from Lebanon; to turn and repay what they have given them. [21]Just as they have done to my elect until this day, so I will do, and will repay into their bosom." Thus says the Lord God: [22]"My right hand will not spare the sinners, and my sword will not cease from those who shed innocent blood on the earth." [23]And a fire will go forth from his wrath, and will consume the foundations of the earth, and the sinners, like straw that is kindled. [24]"Woe to those

x Syr adds *in the seventh year of the sixth week, five thousand years and three months and twelve days after creation.*
At that time Ezra was caught up, and taken to the place of those who are like him, after he had written all these things. And he was called the Scribe of the knowledge of the Most High for ever and ever. Ethiop Arab 1 Arm have a similar ending
y Chapters 15 and 16 (except 15:57–59 which has been found in Greek) are extant only in Latin

---

15.1–16.78: An appendix. 15.1–4: The certainty of this prophecy. **1:** *Which I will put in your mouth,* Is.51.16; Jer.1.9.
    15.5–11: God will take vengeance upon the wicked. 9: *All the innocent blood,* i.e. all the souls of the righteous (compare Rev.6.10; 19.2). **10:** Ps.44.22; Is.53.7. **11:** *Will smite Egypt . . . as before,* perhaps an allusion to the occurrence during the reign of Gallienus (A.D. 260–268) of a terrible famine, followed by a plague, which killed two-thirds of the population of Alexandria.
    15.12–27: The signs of the end. 15: *Nation . . . against nation,* Mt.24.7; Mk.13.8; Lk.21.10. **18:** Lk.21.26.

who sin and do not observe my commandments," says the Lord; [25]"I will not spare them. Depart, you faithless children! Do not pollute my sanctuary." [26]For the Lord knows all who transgress against him; therefore he will hand them over to death and slaughter. [27]For now calamities have come upon the whole earth, and you shall remain in them; for God will not deliver you, because you have sinned against him.

28 Behold, a terrifying sight, appearing from the east! [29]The nations of the dragons of Arabia shall come out with many chariots, and from the day that they set out, their hissing shall spread over the earth, so that all who hear them fear and tremble. [30]Also the Carmonians, raging in wrath, shall go forth like wild boars of the forest, and with great power they shall come, and engage them in battle, and shall devastate a portion of the land of the Assyrians with their teeth. [31]And then the dragons, remembering their origin, shall become still stronger; and if they combine in great power and turn to pursue them, [32]then these shall be disorganized and silenced by their power, and shall turn and flee. [33]And from the land of the Assyrians an enemy in ambush shall beset them and destroy one of them, and fear and trembling shall come upon their army, and indecision upon their kings.

34 Behold, clouds from the east, and from the north to the south; and their appearance is very threatening, full of wrath and storm. [35]They shall dash against one another and shall pour out a heavy tempest upon the earth, and their own tempest; and there shall be blood from the sword as high as a horse's belly [36]and a man's thigh and a camel's hock. [37]And there

shall be fear and great trembling upon the earth; and those who see that wrath shall be horror-stricken, and they shall be seized with trembling. [38]And, after that, heavy storm clouds shall be stirred up from the south, and from the north, and another part from the west. [39]And the winds from the east shall prevail over the cloud that was[z] raised in wrath, and shall dispel it; and the tempest that was to cause destruction by the east wind shall be driven violently toward the south and west. [40]And great and mighty clouds, full of wrath and tempest, shall rise, to destroy all the earth and its inhabitants, and shall pour out upon every high and lofty place[a] a terrible tempest, [41]fire and hail and flying swords and floods of water, that all the fields and all the streams may be filled with the abundance of those waters. [42]And they shall destroy cities and walls, mountains and hills, trees of the forests, and grass of the meadows, and their grain. [43]And they shall go on steadily to Babylon, and shall destroy her. [44]They shall come to her and surround her; they shall pour out the tempest and all its wrath upon her; then the dust and smoke shall go up to heaven, and all who are about her shall wail over her. [45]And those who survive shall serve those who have destroyed her.

46 And you, Asia, who share in the glamour of Babylon and the glory of her person—[47]woe to you, miserable wretch! For you have made yourself like her; you have decked out your daughters in harlotry to please and glory in your lovers, who have always lusted after you. [48]You have imitated that hateful harlot in all her deeds and devices; therefore God says, [49]"I

z Literally *that he*
a Or *eminent person*

15.28–63: A vision of warfare. This section is thought to reflect events of the third century A.D., including the attack of King Sapor I of Persia (A.D. 240–273) upon the Roman province of Syria. 30: *The Carmonians*, from Carmania (Kirman), the southern province of the Parthian empire. *Like wild boars*, Ps.80.13. 35: *As high as . . .*, Rev.14.20. 43: *Babylon*, i.e. Rome. 47–48: Rev.14.8; 17.4–5. 49: Rev.18.7–8.

will send evils upon you, widowhood, poverty, famine, sword, and pestilence, to lay waste your houses and bring you to destruction and death. [50]And the glory of your power shall wither like a flower, when the heat rises that is sent upon you. [51]You shall be weakened like a wretched woman who is beaten and wounded, so that you cannot receive your mighty lovers. [52]Would I have dealt with you so violently," says the Lord, [53]"if you had not always killed my chosen people, exulting and clapping your hands and talking about their death when you were drunk? [54]Trick out the beauty of your face! [55]The reward of a harlot is in your bosom, therefore you shall receive your recompense. [56]As you will do to my chosen people," says the Lord, "so God will do to you, and will hand you over to adversities. [57]Your children shall die of hunger, and you shall fall by the sword, and your cities shall be wiped out, and all your people who are in the open country shall fall by the sword. [58]And those who are in the mountains and highlands[b] shall perish of hunger, and they shall eat their own flesh in hunger for bread and drink their own blood in thirst for water. [59]Unhappy above all others, you shall come and suffer fresh afflictions. [60]And as they pass they shall wreck the hateful[c] city, and shall destroy a part of your land and abolish a portion of your glory, as they return from devastated Babylon. [61]And you shall be broken down by them like stubble, and they shall be like fire to you. [62]And they shall devour you and your cities, your land and your mountains; they shall burn with fire all your forests and your fruitful trees. [63]They shall carry your children away captive, and shall plunder your wealth, and abolish the glory of your countenance."

16 Woe to you, Babylon and Asia! Woe to you, Egypt and Syria!

[2]Gird yourselves with sackcloth and haircloth, and wail for your children, and lament for them; for your destruction is at hand. [3]The sword has been sent upon you, and who is there to turn it back? [4]A fire has been sent upon you, and who is there to quench it? [5]Calamities have been sent upon you, and who is there to drive them away? [6]Can one drive off a hungry lion in the forest, or quench a fire in the stubble, when once it has begun to burn? [7]Can one turn back an arrow shot by a strong archer? [8]The Lord God sends calamities, and who will drive them away? [9]Fire will go forth from his wrath, and who is there to quench it? [10]He will flash lightning, and who will not be afraid? He will thunder, and who will not be terrified? [11]The Lord will threaten, and who will not be utterly shattered at his presence? [12]The earth and its foundations quake, the sea is churned up from the depths, and its waves and the fish also shall be troubled at the presence of the Lord and before the glory of his power. [13]For his right hand that bends the bow is strong, and his arrows that he shoots are sharp and will not miss when they begin to be shot to the ends of the world. [14]Behold, calamities are sent forth and shall not return until they come over the earth. [15]The fire is kindled, and shall not be put out until it consumes the foundations of the earth. [16]Just as an arrow shot by a mighty archer does not return, so the calamities that are sent upon the earth shall not return. [17]Alas for me! Alas for me! Who will deliver me in those days?

18 The beginning of sorrows, when there shall be much lamentation; the beginning of famine, when many shall perish; the beginning of wars, when the powers shall be terrified; the beginning of calamities, when all shall

b Gk: Latin omits *and highlands*
c Another reading is *idle* or *unprofitable*

16.1–34: Denunciation of Babylon, Asia, Egypt, and Syria. 1: *Babylon,* i.e. Rome. **2:** *Sackcloth and haircloth,* signs of mourning. **12:** Ps.18.15. **15:** *Until it consumes . . . the earth,* an tremble. What shall they do in these circumstances, when the calamities come? [19]Behold, famine and plague, tribulation and anguish are sent as scourges for the correction of men. [20]Yet for all this they will not turn from their iniquities, nor be always mindful of the scourges. [21]Behold, provisions will be so cheap upon earth that men will imagine that peace is assured for them, and then the calamities shall spring up on the earth—the sword, famine, and great confusion. [22]For many of those who live on the earth shall perish by famine; and those who survive the famine shall die by the sword. [23]And the dead shall be cast out like dung, and there shall be no one to console them; for the earth shall be left desolate, and its cities shall be demolished. [24]No one shall be left to cultivate the earth or to sow it. [25]The trees shall bear fruit, and who will gather it? [26]The grapes shall ripen, and who will tread them? For in all places there shall be great solitude; [27]one man will long to see another, or even to hear his voice. [28]For out of a city, ten shall be left; and out of the field, two who have hidden themselves in thick groves and clefts in the rocks. [29]As in an olive orchard three or four olives may be left on every tree, [30]or as when a vineyard is gathered some clusters may be left by those who search carefully through the vineyard, [31]so in those days three or four shall be left by those who search their houses with the sword. [32]And the earth shall be left desolate, and its fields shall be for briers, and its roads and all its paths shall bring forth thorns, because no sheep will go along them. [33]Virgins shall mourn because they have no bridegrooms; women shall mourn because they have no husbands; their daughters shall mourn, because they have no helpers. [34]Their bridegrooms shall be killed in war, and their husbands shall perish of famine.

35 Listen now to these things, and understand them, O servants of the Lord. [36]Behold the word of the Lord, receive it; do not disbelieve what the Lord says.[d] [37]Behold, the calamities draw near, and are not delayed. [38]Just as a woman with child, in the ninth month, when the time of her delivery draws near, has great pains about her womb for two or three hours beforehand, and when the child comes forth from the womb, there will not be a moment's delay, [39]so the calamities will not delay in coming forth upon the earth, and the world will groan, and pains will seize it on every side.

40 "Hear my words, O my people; prepare for battle, and in the midst of the calamities be like strangers on the earth. [41]Let him that sells be like one who will flee; let him that buys be like one who will lose; [42]let him that does business be like one who will not make a profit; and let him that builds a house be like one who will not live in it; [43]let him that sows be like one who will not reap; so also him that prunes the vines, like one who will not gather the grapes; [44]them that marry, like those who will have no children; and them that do not marry, like those who are widowed. [45]Because those who labor, labor in vain; [46]for strangers shall gather their fruits, and plunder their goods, and overthrow their houses, and take their children captive; for in captivity and famine they will beget their children. [47]Those who conduct business, do it only to be plundered; the more they adorn their cities, their houses and possessions, and their persons, [48]the more angry I will be with them for their sins," says the Lord. [49]Just as a respectable and virtuous woman abhors a harlot, [50]so righteousness shall abhor iniquity, when she decks herself out, and shall accuse her to her face, when he comes who will defend him who searches out every sin on earth.

d Cn: Lat *do not believe the gods of whom the Lord speaks*

---

apocalyptic idea from Persian eschatology (compare 2 Pet.3.10). **29:** Is.17.6. **16.35–50: God's people are warned of impending disasters. 38:** 4.40. **41:** 1 Cor.7.29–31.

51 Therefore do not be like her or her works. ⁵²For behold, just a little while, and iniquity will be removed from the earth, and righteousness will reign over us. ⁵³Let no sinner say that he has not sinned; for God*ᵉ* will burn coals of fire on the head of him who says, "I have not sinned before God and his glory." ⁵⁴Behold, the Lord knows all the works of men, their imaginations and their thoughts and their hearts. ⁵⁵He said, "Let the earth be made," and it was made; "Let the heaven be made," and it was made. ⁵⁶At his word the stars were fixed, and he knows the number of the stars. ⁵⁷It is he who searches the deep and its treasures, who has measured the sea and its contents; ⁵⁸who has enclosed the sea in the midst of the waters, and by his word has suspended the earth over the water; ⁵⁹who has spread out the heaven like an arch, and founded it upon the waters; ⁶⁰who has put springs of water in the desert, and pools on the tops of the mountains, to send rivers from the heights to water the earth; ⁶¹who formed man, and put a heart in the midst of his body, and gave him breath and life and understanding ⁶²and the spirit of Almighty God; who made all things and searches out hidden things in hidden places. ⁶³Surely he knows your imaginations and what you think in your hearts! Woe to those who sin and want to hide their sins! ⁶⁴Because the Lord will strictly examine all their works, and will make a public spectacle of all of you. ⁶⁵And when your sins come out before men, you shall be put to shame; and your own iniquities shall stand as your accusers in that day. ⁶⁶What will you do? Or

how will you hide your sins before God and his angels? ⁶⁷Behold, God is the judge, fear him! Cease from your sins, and forget your iniquities, never to commit them again; so God will lead you forth and deliver you from all tribulation.

68 For behold, the burning wrath of a great multitude is kindled over you, and they shall carry off some of you and shall feed you what was sacrificed to idols. ⁶⁹And those who consent to eat shall be held in*ᶠ* derision and contempt, and be trodden under foot. ⁷⁰For in many places*ᵍ* and in neighboring cities there shall be a great insurrection against those who fear the Lord. ⁷¹They shall be like mad men, sparing no one, but plundering and destroying those who continue to fear the Lord. ⁷²For they shall destroy and plunder their goods, and drive them out of their houses. ⁷³Then the tested quality of my elect shall be manifest, as gold that is tested by fire.

74 "Hear, my elect," says the Lord. "Behold, the days of tribulation are at hand, and I will deliver you from them. ⁷⁵Do not fear or doubt, for God is your guide. ⁷⁶You who keep my commandments and precepts," says the Lord God, "do not let your sins pull you down, or your iniquities prevail over you." ⁷⁷Woe to those who are choked by their sins and overwhelmed by their iniquities, as a field is choked with underbrush and its path*ʰ* overwhelmed with thorns, so that no one can pass through! ⁷⁸It is shut off and given up to be consumed by fire.

e Literally *he*
f Literally *consent to them shall be for these in*
g The Latin is uncertain
h Another reading is *seed*

16.51–67: The impossibility of hiding sin from God.
16.68–78: Though persecuted, God's elect will be delivered. 73: Zech.13.9; 1 Pet.1.7.

TOBIT

A fascinating amalgam of *Arabian Nights* romance, kindly Jewish piety, and sound moral teaching, Tobit is one of the most popular of the books of the Apocrypha. Originally composed in Hebrew or Aramaic, probably sometime during the second century B.C., its author is unknown, as is also the place where he wrote it, although Jerusalem, Antioch, and Alexandria have all been suggested as possibilities.

Besides the intrinsic interest of the tale, which is compounded in large part of themes derived from ancient folklore, the book's principal value lies in the picture it gives of Jewish culture and religious life in an age not too remote, either in time or temper, from that of the New Testament.

The ostensible setting of the story is the Assyrian capital, Nineveh, where the people of Northern Israel had been taken captive in the latter part of the eighth century B.C. (2 Kg.17.1-6). There, it is said, dwelt the pious Tobit, who, despite his many charitable deeds, became blind and poor (chs. 1-2). But God heard his prayer, as well as the prayer of demon-haunted Sarah in faraway Media, and sent the angel Raphael to save them both (ch. 3). When Tobit commissioned his son Tobias to collect a deposit of money he had made long before in Media, the angel accompanied him and revealed magic formulas which would heal his father's blindness and exorcise Sarah's demon-lover, Asmodeus (chs. 4-6). Tobias successfully completed his mission and married Sarah (chs. 7-14).

The book exists in numerous recensions and versions which differ considerably from one another in matters of detail.

THE BOOK OF THE ACTS*a* OF TOBIT the son of Tobiel, son of Ananiel, son of Aduel, son of Gabael, of the descendants of Asiel and the tribe of Naphtali, ²who in the days of Shalmaneser,*b* king of the Assyrians, was taken into captivity from Thisbe, which is to the south of Kedesh Naphtali in Galilee above Asher.

3 I, Tobit, walked in the ways of truth and righteousness all the days of my life, and I performed many acts of charity to my brethren and countrymen who went with me into the land of the Assyrians, to Nineveh. ⁴Now when I was in my own country, in the land of Israel, while I was still a young man, the whole tribe of Naphtali my forefather deserted the house of Jerusalem. This was the place which had been chosen from among all the tribes of Israel, where all the tribes should sacrifice and where the temple of the dwelling of the Most High was consecrated and established for all generations for ever.

5 All the tribes that joined in apostasy used to sacrifice to the calf*c* Baal, and so did the house of Naphtali my forefather. ⁶But I alone went often to Jerusalem for the feasts, as it is ordained for all Israel by an everlasting decree. Taking the first fruits and the tithes of my produce and the first shearings, I would give these to the priests, the sons of Aaron, at the altar. ⁷Of all my produce I would give a tenth to the sons of Levi who ministered at Jerusalem; a second tenth I would sell,

a Gk *words*
b Gk *Enemessarus*
c Other authorities read *heifer*

1.1–2: Title. **2:** *Shalmaneser* (or rather Sargon; see v. 15 n.) took Samaria, the capital of Israel, in 722 B.C. and transported a large part of the population to Assyria (2 Kg.17.1-6). *Thisbe* is unidentified. *Kedesh Naphtali*, 2 Kg.15.29. *Asher* is probably Hazor.

1.3–3.6: Tobit's own account of his virtuous life and unhappy fate.

1.3–22: Tobit's piety brings him into conflict with the king. **3:** *Nineveh* was the capital of Assyria. **4:** Since the rebellion of the northern tribes against Jerusalem (1 Kg.12.19-20) occurred about 922 B.C., Tobit could not have been *still a young man*, or even born, when it happened. Such chronological, and other historical, difficulties make it clear that the story is fiction (compare v. 15 n., 6.1 n., 9.2 n., 14.15 n.). **5:** *Calf*, 1 Kg.12.28-29. **6-8:** During the apostasy, Tobit alone remains loyal to the divinely-appointed temple in Jerusalem. **6:** *An everlasting decree*, Dt.12.11, and I would go and spend the proceeds each year at Jerusalem; [8]the third tenth I would give to those to whom it was my duty, as Deborah my father's mother had commanded me, for I was left an orphan by my father. [9]When I became a man I married Anna, a member of our family, and by her I became the father of Tobias.

10 Now when I was carried away captive to Nineveh, all my brethren and my relatives ate the food of the Gentiles; [11]but I kept myself from eating it, [12]because I remembered God with all my heart. [13]Then the Most High gave me favor and good appearance in the sight of Shalmaneser,[b] and I was his buyer of provisions. [14]So I used to go into Media, and once at Rages in Media I left ten talents of silver in trust with Gabael, the brother of Gabrias. [15]But when Shalmaneser[b] died, Sennacherib his son reigned in his place; and under him the highways were unsafe, so that I could no longer go into Media.

16 In the days of Shalmaneser[b] I performed many acts of charity to my brethren. [17]I would give my bread to the hungry and my clothing to the naked; and if I saw any one of my people dead and thrown out behind the wall of Nineveh, I would bury him. [18]And if Sennacherib the king put to death any who came fleeing from Judea, I buried them secretly. For in his anger he put many to death. When the bodies were sought by the king, they were not found. [19]Then one of

the men of Nineveh went and informed the king about me, that I was burying them; so I hid myself. When I learned that I was being searched for, to be put to death, I left home in fear. [20]Then all my property was confiscated and nothing was left to me except my wife Anna and my son Tobias.

21 But not fifty[d] days passed before two of Sennacherib's[e] sons killed him, and they fled to the mountains of Ararat. Then Esarhaddon,[f] his son, reigned in his place; and he appointed Ahikar, the son of my brother Anael, over all the accounts of his kingdom and over the entire administration. [22]Ahikar interceded for me, and I returned to Nineveh. Now Ahikar was cupbearer, keeper of the signet, and in charge of administration of the accounts, for Esarhaddon[f] had appointed him second to himself.[g] He was my nephew.

2 When I arrived home and my wife Anna and my son Tobias were restored to me, at the feast of Pentecost, which is the sacred festival of the seven weeks, a good dinner was prepared for me and I sat down to eat. [2]Upon seeing the abundance of food I said to my son, "Go and bring whatever poor man of our brethren you may find who is mindful of the Lord, and I will wait for you." [3]But he came back and said, "Father, one of our people has been strangled and thrown into the market

b Gk *Enemessarus*
d Other authorities read *fifty-five*
e Gk *his*   *f* Gk *Sacherdonus*
g Or *a second time*

13–14. **10–12:** Even in captivity among Gentiles Tobit refuses to violate the dietary laws. **14:** *Media* is the northern part of modern Iran, east of Assyria. *Rages* was an important city whose ruins are located about five miles southeast of modern Teheran. *Ten talents*, at least $10,000. **15–20:** Tobit arouses Sennacherib's wrath and flees the country. **15:** *Shalmaneser* actually died before the fall of Samaria, which was taken by Sargon. *Sennacherib* succeeded his father Sargon in 705 B.C. **17:** It was for the Jews a great calamity that a dead body should lie unburied. **21–22:** Under a new king, *Esarhaddon* (681–669 B.C.), Tobit is able to return. **21:** *Ahikar* was a legendary ancient wise man whose story survives in several oriental languages. An Aramaic version of his adventures, dating from the fifth century B.C., was found among the Jewish papyri at Elephantine in upper Egypt (see also 14.10 n.). **2.1–14:** Another act of charity results in Tobit's blindness and impoverishment. **1:** *Pentecost . . . seven weeks*, approximately, after Passover (Lev.23.15–21; Dt.16.9–11). **2:** Generosity toward the poor is one of the virtues taught by this book (4.7–11,16). **3:** *Strangled*, presumably executed (compare 1.18). Leaving the body unburied was intended as additional punishment, so place." [4]So before I tasted anything I sprang up and removed the body[h] to a place of shelter until sunset. [5]And when I returned I washed myself and ate my food in sorrow. [6]Then I remembered the prophecy of Amos, how he said,

"Your feasts shall be turned into mourning,
and all your festivities into lamentation."

And I wept.

7 When the sun had set I went and dug a grave and buried the body.[h] [8]And my neighbors laughed at me and said, "He is no longer afraid that he will be put to death for doing this; he once ran away, and here he is burying the dead again!" [9]On the same night I returned from burying him, and because I was defiled I slept by the wall of the courtyard, and my face was uncovered. [10]I did not know that there were sparrows on the wall and their fresh droppings fell into my open eyes and white films formed on my eyes. I went to physicians, but they did not help me. Ahikar, however, took care of me until he[i] went to Elymais.

11 Then my wife Anna earned money at women's work. [12]She used to send the product to the owners. Once when they paid her wages, they also gave her a kid; [13]and when she returned to me it began to bleat. So I said to her, "Where did you get the kid? It is not stolen, is it? Return it to the owners; for it is not right to eat what is stolen." [14]And she said, "It was given to me as a gift in addition to my wages." But I did not believe her, and told her to return it to the owners; and I blushed for her. Then she replied to me, "Where are your charities and your righteous deeds? You seem to know everything!"

3 Then in my grief I wept, and I prayed in anguish, saying, [2]"Righteous art thou, O Lord; all thy deeds and all thy ways are mercy and truth, and thou dost render true and righteous judgment for ever. [3]Remember me and look favorably upon me; do not punish me for my sins and for my unwitting offenses and those which my fathers committed before thee. [4]For they disobeyed thy commandments, and thou gavest us over to plunder, captivity, and death; thou madest us a byword of reproach in all the nations among which we have been dispersed. [5]And now thy many judgments are true in exacting penalty from me for my sins and those of my fathers, because we did not keep thy commandments. For we did not walk in truth before thee. [6]And now deal with me according to thy pleasure; command my spirit to be taken up, that I may depart and become dust. For it is better for me to die than to live, because I have heard false reproaches, and great is the sorrow within me. Command that I now be released from my distress to go to the eternal abode; do not turn thy face away from me."

7 On the same day, at Ecbatana in Media, it also happened that Sarah, the daughter of Raguel, was reproached by her father's maids, [8]because she had been given to seven husbands, and the evil demon Asmodeus had slain each of them before he had been with her as his wife. So the maids[j] said to her, "Do you not know that you strangle your husbands? You already have had seven and have had no benefit from[k] any of them. [9]Why do you beat us? If they are dead, go with them! May we never see a son or daughter of yours!"

h Gk *him*   *i* Other authorities read *I*   *j* Gk *they*
k Other authorities read *have not borne the name of*

Tobit's act of charity was an act of defiance toward the king. **5**: *Washed myself*, ceremonially, after touching a corpse (Num.19.11–13). **9**: *Defiled*, from handling the corpse. **10**: *Elymais*, a city, or possibly a region, in Persia (1 Macc.6.1).

3.1–6: Tobit's prayer.

3.7–17: God hears the prayer of Tobit, and also of Sarah, plagued by a demon-lover. From this point on the story is told in the third person. **7–10**: Sarah contemplates suicide. **7**: *Ecbatana*,

10 When she heard these things she was deeply grieved, even to the thought of hanging herself. But she said, "I am the only child of my father; if I do this, it will be a disgrace to him, and I shall bring his old age down in sorrow to the grave."[*l*] [11]So she prayed by her window and said, "Blessed art thou, O Lord my God, and blessed is thy holy and honored name for ever. May all thy works praise thee for ever. [12]And now, O Lord, I have turned my eyes and my face toward thee. [13]Command that I be released from the earth and that I hear reproach no more. [14]Thou knowest, O Lord, that I am innocent of any sin with man, [15]and that I did not stain my name or the name of my father in the land of my captivity. I am my father's only child, and he has no child to be his heir, no near kinsman or kinsman's[*m*] son for whom I should keep myself as wife. Already seven husbands of mine are dead. Why should I live? But if it be not pleasing to thee to take my life, command that respect be shown to me and pity be taken upon me, and that I hear reproach no more."

16 The prayer of both was heard in the presence of the glory of the great God. [17]And Raphael[*n*] was sent to heal the two of them: to scale away the white films from Tobit's eyes; to give Sarah the daughter of Raguel in marriage to Tobias the son of Tobit, and to bind Asmodeus the evil demon, because Tobias was entitled to possess her. At that very moment Tobit returned and entered his house and Sarah the daughter of Raguel came down from her upper room.

4 On that day Tobit remembered the money which he had left in trust with Gabael at Rages in Media, and he said to himself: [2]"I have asked for death. Why do I not call my son Tobias so that I may explain to him about the money[*o*] before I die?" [3]So he called him and said, "My son, when I die, bury me, and do not neglect your mother. Honor her all the days of your life; do what is pleasing to her, and do not grieve her. [4]Remember, my son, that she faced many dangers for you while you were yet unborn. When she dies, bury her beside me in the same grave.

5 "Remember the Lord our God all your days, my son, and refuse to sin or to transgress his commandments. Live uprightly all the days of your life, and do not walk in the ways of wrongdoing. [6]For if you do what is true, your ways will prosper through your deeds. [7]Give alms from your possessions to all who live uprightly, and do not let your eye begrudge the gift when you make it. Do not turn your face away from any poor man, and the face of God will not be turned away from you. [8]If you have many possessions, make your gift from them in proportion; if few, do not be afraid to give according to the little you have. [9]So you will be laying up a good treasure for yourself against the day of necessity. [10]For charity delivers from death and keeps you from entering the darkness; [11]and for all who practice it charity is an excellent offering in the presence of the Most High.

12 "Beware, my son, of all immo-

l Gk *to Hades*   *m* Gk *his*
n Other authorities read *the great Raphael. And he*
o Other authorities omit *about the money*

capital of Media, in Persia. **8:** The name *Asmodeus* means "destroyer." **11–15:** Sarah's prayer. **11:** *Blessed art thou* is the traditional beginning of a Jewish prayer (compare 8.5, 15 and see Jdt.13.17 n.). **16–17:** The angel Raphael is sent in ánswer to both the prayers. **17:** The name *Raphael* means "God heals." *Entitled to possess her*, 6.11. The phrase *at that very moment* is a dramatic device which heightens the interest of the story.
4.1–21: Preparing to send his son for the trust-money, Tobit imparts his philosophy of life. **1:** *The money . . . at Rages*, 1.14. **5–19:** This section of general ethical counsel epitomizes the moral teaching of the book. There are many close parallels with other books of wisdom, such as Proverbs and Sirach. **6:** Morality guarantees prosperity; a dogma of orthodox Hebrew wisdom (Ps.1.1–3, Pr.10.27–30). **7–11:** The value of almsgiving; the emphasis is typical of the period (12.8–9; 14.10–11; Sir.3.30; 35.2; Mt.6.2–4). **12–13:** One should marry within his own

[66]

rality. First of all take a wife from among the descendants of your fathers and do not marry a foreign woman, who is not of your father's tribe; for we are the sons of the prophets. Remember, my son, that Noah, Abraham, Isaac, and Jacob, our fathers of old, all took wives from among their brethren. They were blessed in their children, and their posterity will inherit the land. ¹³So now, my son, love your brethren, and in your heart do not disdain your brethren and the sons and daughters of your people by refusing to take a wife for yourself from among them. For in pride there is ruin and great confusion; and in shiftlessness there is loss and great want, because shiftlessness is the mother of famine. ¹⁴Do not hold over till the next day the wages of any man who works for you, but pay him at once; and if you serve God you will receive payment.

"Watch yourself, my son, in everything you do, and be disciplined in all your conduct. ¹⁵And what you hate, do not do to any one. Do not drink wine to excess or let drunkenness go with you on your way. ¹⁶Give of your bread to the hungry, and of your clothing to the naked. Give all your surplus to charity, and do not let your eye begrudge the gift when you make it. ¹⁷Place your bread on the grave of the righteous, but give none to sinners. ¹⁸Seek advice from every wise man, and do not despise any useful counsel. ¹⁹Bless the Lord God on every occasion; ask him that your ways may be made straight and that all your paths and plans may prosper. For none of the nations has understanding; but the Lord himself gives all good things, and

according to his will he humbles whomever he wishes.

"So, my son, remember my commands, and do not let them be blotted out of your mind. ²⁰And now let me explain to you about the ten talents of silver which I left in trust with Gabael the son of Gabrias at Rages in Media. ²¹Do not be afraid, my son, because we have become poor. You have great wealth if you fear God and refrain from every sin and do what is pleasing in his sight."

5 Then Tobias answered him, "Father, I will do everything that you have commanded me; ²but how can I obtain the money when I do not know the man?" ³Then Tobit gave him the receipt, and said to him, "Find a man to go with you and I will pay him wages as long as I live; and go and get the money." ⁴So he went to look for a man; and he found Raphael, who was an angel, ⁵but Tobias^p did not know it. Tobias^p said to him, "Can you go with me to Rages in Media? Are you acquainted with that region?" ⁶The angel replied, "I will go with you; I am familiar with the way, and I have stayed with our brother Gabael." ⁷Then Tobias said to him, "Wait for me, and I shall tell my father." ⁸And he said to him, "Go, and do not delay." So he went in and said to his father, "I have found some one to go with me." He said, "Call him to me, so that I may learn to what tribe he belongs, and whether he is a reliable man to go with you."

9 So Tobias^p invited him in; he entered and they greeted each other. ¹⁰Then Tobit said to him, "My

p Gk *he*

family group; this is a keynote of the book (1.9; 3.15; 6.11–12). **13:** *Pride*, Pr.16.18. *Shiftlessness*, Pr.19.15; Sir.22.1–2. **14:** Lev.19.13. **15:** *What you hate, do not do*, the Golden Rule (Mt.7.12) in negative form, which was enunciated also by the great Jewish teacher, Hillel (flourished in the time of Herod the Great, 37–4 B.C.). *Wine*, Pr.23.29–35; Sir.31.29–31. **16:** Compare vv. 7–11. **17:** Placing food on graves was a pagan practice, forbidden in the Old Testament (Dt.26.14) and deprecated by many Jews (compare Sir.30.18). Some interpret the verse as a reference to the meals provided the mourners at funerals (compare Jer.16.7; Ezek.24.17). **19:** A sound moral life needs to be sustained by prayer.
5.1–21: Raphael, in the disguise of Azarias, is employed as Tobias' guide. **5:** *Tobias did not know it*, as frequently in folklore, where angels (or gods) traveling in disguise are a favorite

brother, to what tribe and family do you belong? Tell me." [11]But he answered, "Are you looking for a tribe and a family or for a man whom you will pay to go with your son?" And Tobit said to him, "I should like to know, my brother, your people and your name." [12]He replied, "I am Azarias the son of the great Ananias, one of your relatives." [13]Then Tobit said to him, "You are welcome, my brother. Do not be angry with me because I tried to learn your tribe and family. You are a relative of mine, of a good and noble lineage. For I used to know Ananias and Jathan, the sons of the great Shemaiah, when we went together to Jerusalem to worship and offered the first-born of our flocks and the tithes of our produce. They did not go astray in the error of our brethren. My brother, you come of good stock. [14]But tell me, what wages am I to pay you—a drachma a day, and expenses for yourself as for my son? [15]And besides, I will add to your wages if you both return safe and sound." So they agreed to these terms.

16 Then he said to Tobias, "Get ready for the journey, and good success to you both." So his son made the preparations for the journey. And his father said to him, "Go with this man; God who dwells in heaven will prosper your way, and may his angel attend you." So they both went out and departed, and the young man's dog was with them.

17 But Anna,[q] his mother, began to weep, and said to Tobit, "Why have you sent our child away? Is he not the staff of our hands as he goes in and out before us? [18]Do not add money to money, but consider it rubbish as com-pared to our child. [19]For the life that is given to us by the Lord is enough for us." [20]And Tobit said to her, "Do not worry, my sister; he will return safe and sound, and your eyes will see him. [21]For a good angel will go with him; his journey will be successful, and he will come back safe and sound." So she stopped weeping.

6 Now as they proceeded on their way they came at evening to the Tigris river and camped there. [2]Then the young man went down to wash himself. A fish leaped up from the river and would have swallowed the young man; [3]and the angel said to him, "Catch the fish." So the young man seized the fish and threw it up on the land. [4]Then the angel said to him, "Cut open the fish and take the heart and liver and gall and put them away safely." [5]So the young man did as the angel told him; and they roasted and ate the fish.

And they both continued on their way until they came near to Ecbatana. [6]Then the young man said to the angel, "Brother Azarias, of what use is the liver and heart and gall of the fish?" [7]He replied, "As for the heart and the liver, if a demon or evil spirit gives trouble to any one, you make a smoke from these before the man or woman, and that person will never be troubled again. [8]And as for the gall, anoint with it a man who has white films in his eyes, and he will be cured."

9 When they approached Ecbatana,[r] [10]the angel said to the young man, "Brother, today we shall stay with Raguel. He is your relative, and he has

q Other authorities omit *Anna*
r Other authorities read *Rages*

---

theme (compare Gen. ch. 18; Heb.13.2). **12**: In Hebrew *Azarias* means "God helps." **14**: A *drachma* was the normal day's wage for an artisan, about sixteen cents. **16**: The *dog* is a surprising feature of the story, but plays no special role (see 11.4 n.). **21**: Pleasing irony; Tobit does not know that Raphael is the *good angel*.

6.1–8: On the journey, Raphael instructs Tobias in obtaining magical medicines from a man-eating fish. **1**: *The Tigris* is actually west of Nineveh, so they would not have crossed it going to Persia (see 1.4 n.). **6–8**: Belief in the healing properties of the fish's organs is typical of folklore.

6.9–17: Raphael prepares Tobias to seek the hand of Sarah. **12**: *According to the law of Moses,* an only daughter named Sarah. I will suggest that she be given to you in marriage, [11]because you are entitled to her and to her inheritance, for you are her only eligible kinsman. [12]The girl is also beautiful and sensible. Now listen to my plan. I will speak to her father, and as soon as we return from Rages we will celebrate the marriage. For I know that Raguel, according to the law of Moses, cannot give her to another man without incurring the penalty of death, because you rather than any other man are entitled to the inheritance."

13 Then the young man said to the angel, "Brother Azarias, I have heard that the girl has been given to seven husbands and that each died in the bridal chamber. [14]Now I am the only son my father has, and I am afraid that if I go in I will die as those before me did, for a demon is in love with her, and he harms no one except those who approach her. So now I fear that I may die and bring the lives of my father and mother to the grave in sorrow on my account. And they have no other son to bury them."

15 But the angel said to him, "Do you not remember the words with which your father commanded you to take a wife from among your own people? Now listen to me, brother, for she will become your wife; and do not worry about the demon, for this very night she will be given to you in marriage. [16]When you enter the bridal chamber, you shall take live ashes of incense and lay upon them some of the heart and liver of the fish so as to make a smoke. [17]Then the demon will smell it and flee away, and will never again return. And when you approach her, rise up, both of you, and cry out to the

merciful God, and he will save you and have mercy on you. Do not be afraid, for she was destined for you from eternity. You will save her, and she will go with you, and I suppose that you will have children by her." When Tobias heard these things, he fell in love with her and yearned deeply for her.

7 When they reached Ecbatana and arrived at the house of Raguel, Sarah met them and greeted them. They returned her greeting, and she brought them into the house. [2]Then Raguel said to his wife Edna, "How much the young man resembles my cousin Tobit!" [3]And Raguel asked them, "Where are you from, brethren?" They answered him, "We belong to the sons of Naphtali, who are captives in Nineveh." [4]So he said to them, "Do you know our brother Tobit?" And they said, "Yes, we do." And he asked them, "Is he in good health?" [5]They replied, "He is alive and in good health." And Tobias said, "He is my father." [6]Then Raguel sprang up and kissed him and wept. [7]And he blessed him and exclaimed, "Son of that good and noble man!" When he heard that Tobit had lost his sight, he was stricken with grief and wept. [8]And his wife Edna and his daughter Sarah wept. They received them very warmly; and they killed a ram from the flock and set large servings of food before them.

Then Tobias said to Raphael, "Brother Azarias, speak of those things which you talked about on the journey, and let the matter be settled." [9]So he communicated the proposal to Raguel. And Raguel said to Tobias, "Eat, drink, and be merry; [10]for it is your right to take my child. But let me

---

presumably Num.36.6–8, although there is no mention of a death penalty. **14:** *To bury them*, one of the chief concerns of this book (see 1.17 n.; 4.3–4; 14.10). **17:** *Cry out . . . to God*, magic is not enough, prayer is necessary too. *From eternity*, "marriages are made in heaven" (compare Gen.24.14).

7.1–8a: Tobias and Raphael arrive at the home of Sarah's father. 1: *Ecbatana*, 3.7. The following conversation implies that Sarah and her family had not previously been aware of Tobias' existence. **4–5:** The Syriac and Latin Vulgate omit the conversation about Tobit's health, probably on account of his blindness.

explain the true situation to you. ¹¹I have given my daughter to seven husbands, and when each came to her he died in the night. But for the present be merry." And Tobias said, "I will eat nothing here until you make a binding agreement with me." ¹²So Raguel said, "Take her right now, in accordance with the law. You are her relative, and she is yours. The merciful God will guide you both for the best." ¹³Then he called his daughter Sarah, and taking her by the hand he gave her to Tobias to be his wife, saying, "Here she is; take her according to the law of Moses, and take her with you to your father." And he blessed them. ¹⁴Next he called his wife Edna, and took a scroll and wrote out the contract; and they set their seals to it. ¹⁵Then they began to eat.

16 And Raguel called his wife Edna and said to her, "Sister, make up the other room, and take her into it." ¹⁷So she did as he said, and took her there; and the girl*ˢ* began to weep. But the mother*ˢ* comforted her daughter in her tears, and said to her, ¹⁸"Be brave, my child; the Lord of heaven and earth grant you joy*ᵗ* in place of this sorrow of yours. Be brave, my daughter."

8 When they had finished eating, they escorted Tobias in to her. ²As he went he remembered the words of Raphael, and he took the live ashes of incense and put the heart and liver of the fish upon them and made a smoke. ³And when the demon smelled the odor he fled to the remotest parts of Egypt, and the angel bound him. ⁴When the door was shut and the two were alone, Tobias got up from the bed and said, "Sister, get up, and let us pray that the Lord may have mercy upon us." ⁵And Tobias began to pray,

"Blessed art thou, O God of our fathers,
and blessed be thy holy and glorious name for ever.
Let the heavens and all thy creatures bless thee.
⁶Thou madest Adam and gavest him Eve his wife
as a helper and support.
From them the race of mankind has sprung.
Thou didst say, 'It is not good that the man should be alone;
let us make a helper for him like himself.'
⁷And now, O Lord, I am not taking this sister of mine because of lust, but with sincerity. Grant that I may find mercy and may grow old together with her." ⁸And she said with him, "Amen." ⁹Then they both went to sleep for the night.

But Raguel arose and went and dug a grave, ¹⁰with the thought, "Perhaps he too will die." ¹¹Then Raguel went into his house ¹²and said to his wife Edna, "Send one of the maids to see whether he is alive; and if he is not, let us bury him without any one knowing about it." ¹³So the maid opened the door and went in, and found them both asleep. ¹⁴And she came out and told them that he was alive. ¹⁵Then Raguel blessed God and said,

"Blessed art thou, O God, with every pure and holy blessing.
Let thy saints and all thy creatures bless thee;
let all thy angels and thy chosen people bless thee for ever.

---

s Gk *she*
t Other authorities read *favor*

7.8b–18: Tobias proposes and the wedding takes place. 13: *Taking her by the hand*, like a modern father "giving away the bride," he marries her to Tobias. **14:** Signing *the contract* was the only other ceremony required.

8.1–9a: On the wedding night, Tobias routs the demon. 3: *Egypt* was the traditional home of magic and witchcraft (compare Ex.7.11). **4:** See 6.17 n. **5–8:** Tobias and Sarah join in prayer before consummating the marriage. **5:** *Blessed art thou*, see 3.11 n.

8.9b–21: Raguel's fears are happily disappointed and he provides an extended wedding feast. 9b: *Dug a grave*, because he did not, of course, know that Tobias was provided with an effective means to drive away the demon. **19:** For joy Raguel doubles the usual length of a wedding

[16] Blessed art thou, because thou hast made me glad.
It has not happened to me as I expected;
but thou hast treated us according to thy great mercy.
[17] Blessed art thou, because thou hast had compassion on two only children.
Show them mercy, O Lord;
and bring their lives to fulfilment in health and happiness and mercy."

[18] Then he ordered his servants to fill in the grave.

19 After this he gave a wedding feast for them which lasted fourteen days. [20] And before the days of the feast were over, Raguel declared by oath to Tobias*u* that he should not leave until the fourteen days of the wedding feast were ended, [21] that then he should take half of Raguel's*v* property and return in safety to his father, and that the rest would be his "when my wife and I die."

9 Then Tobias called Raphael and said to him, [2] "Brother Azarias, take a servant and two camels with you and go to Gabael at Rages in Media and get the money for me; and bring him to the wedding feast. [3] For Raguel has sworn that I should not leave; [4] but my father is counting the days, and if I delay long he will be greatly distressed." [5] So Raphael made the journey and stayed over night with Gabael. He gave him the receipt, and Gabael*w* brought out the money bags with their seals intact and gave them to them. [6] In the morning they both got up early

and came to the wedding feast. And Gabael blessed Tobias and his wife.*x*

10 Now his father Tobit was counting each day, and when the days for the journey had expired and they did not arrive, [2] he said, "Is it possible that he has been detained?*y* Or is it possible that Gabael has died and there is no one to give him the money?" [3] And he was greatly distressed. [4] And his wife said to him, "The lad has perished; his long delay proves it." Then she began to mourn for him, and said, [5] "Am I not distressed, my child, that I let you go, you who are the light of my eyes?" [6] But Tobit said to her, "Be still and stop worrying; he is well." [7] And she answered him, "Be still and stop deceiving me; my child has perished." And she went out every day to the road by which they had left; she ate nothing in the daytime, and throughout the nights she never stopped mourning for her son Tobias, until the fourteen days of the wedding feast had expired which Raguel had sworn that he should spend there.

At that time Tobias said to Raguel, "Send me back, for my father and mother have given up hope of ever seeing me again." [8] But his father-in-law said to him, "Stay with me, and I will send messengers to your father, and they will inform him how things are with you." [9] Tobias replied, "No, send me back to my father." [10] So Raguel arose and gave him his wife

u Gk *him*   *v* Gk *his*   *w* Gk *he*
x Cn: Gk *And Tobias blessed his wife*
y One Gk Ms Lat: Gk *they are put to shame* or *they are disappointed*

---

feast (11.19; Jg.14.12). The oath complicates Tobias' affairs and makes necessary Raphael's solitary mission in the next chapter.

9.1–6: Raphael goes to Rages and obtains the money from Gabael. 2: From Ecbatana to *Rages* was a journey which, according to the ancient historian Arrian (*Anabasis*, III. 19–20), took Alexander's army eleven days of forced marches; the author evidently supposed it to be much shorter (see 1.4 n.). **3:** *Has sworn*, 8.20. **4:** Tobias' tender concern for his father is typical of the spirit of the book. The son's unwillingness to prolong his visit is thoroughly justified by the touching description of his parent's uneasiness in 10.1–7.

10.1–7a: Tobias' father and mother grow anxious at their son's absence. 1: In *counting each day*, Tobit had naturally made no allowance for a two-week wedding celebration. **4:** *The lad has perished*, the mother's feminine tendency to suspect the worst and her husband's courageous attempts to console her illustrate the author's fine sensitivity to human feeling.

Sarah and half of his property in slaves, cattle, and money. ¹¹And when he had blessed them he sent them away, saying, "The God of heaven will prosper you, my children, before I die." ¹²He said also to his daughter, "Honor your father-in-law and your mother-in-law; they are now your parents. Let me hear a good report of you." And he kissed her. And Edna said to Tobias, "The Lord of heaven bring you back safely, dear brother, and grant me to see your children by my daughter Sarah, that I may rejoice before the Lord. See, I am entrusting my daughter to you; do nothing to grieve her."

11 After this Tobias went on his way, praising God because he had made his journey a success. And he blessed Raguel and his wife Edna.

So he continued on his way until they came near to Nineveh. ²Then Raphael said to Tobias, "Are you not aware, brother, of how you left your father? ³Let us run ahead of your wife and prepare the house. ⁴And take the gall of the fish with you." So they went their way, and the dog went along behind them.

5 Now Anna sat looking intently down the road for her son. ⁶And she caught sight of him coming, and said to his father, "Behold, your son is coming, and so is the man who went with him!"

7 Raphael said, "I know, Tobias, that your father will open his eyes. ⁸You therefore must anoint his eyes with the gall; and when they smart he will rub them, and will cause the white films to fall away, and he will see you."

9 Then Anna ran to meet them, and embraced her son, and said to him, "I have seen you, my child; now I am ready to die." And they both wept. ¹⁰Tobit started toward the door, and stumbled. But his son ran to him ¹¹and took hold of his father, and he sprinkled the gall upon his father's eyes, saying, "Be of good cheer, father." ¹²And when his eyes began to smart he rubbed them, ¹³and the white films scaled off from the corners of his eyes. ¹⁴Then he saw his son and embraced him, and he wept and said, "Blessed art thou, O God, and blessed is thy name for ever, and blessed are all thy holy angels. ¹⁵For thou hast afflicted me, but thou hast had mercy upon me; here I see my son Tobias!" And his son went in rejoicing, and he reported to his father the great things that had happened to him in Media.

16 Then Tobit went out to meet his daughter-in-law at the gate of Nineveh, rejoicing and praising God. Those who saw him as he went were amazed because he could see. ¹⁷And Tobit gave thanks before them that God had been merciful to him. When Tobit came near to Sarah his daughter-in-law, he blessed her, saying, "Welcome, daughter! Blessed is God who has brought you to us, and blessed are your father and your mother." So there was rejoicing among all his brethren in Nineveh. ¹⁸Ahikar and his nephew Nadab*ᶻ* came, ¹⁹and Tobias' marriage was celebrated for seven days with great festivity.

12 Tobit then called his son Tobias and said to him, "My son, see to the wages of the man who went with you; and he must also be given more." ²He replied, "Father, it would do me

z Other authorities read *Nasbas*

10.7b–12: Tobias and Sarah start for home. 11: *The God of heaven* was a favorite name for Israel's God in the Persian period and later (Jdt.5.8; Ezra 1.2).

11.1–15: Tobias and Raphael precede Sarah into the city and heal Tobit's blindness. 4: *The dog* appears again for the first time since 5.16; perhaps his presence in the story is a survival from an older folk tale, in which he had a real function. **14:** *Blessed art thou*, see 3.11 n.

11.16–19: Tobit meets his daughter-in-law and celebrates the marriage. 18: *Ahikar . . . Nadab*, see 14.10 n. **19:** *Seven days*, apparently the normal period of a wedding celebration (see 8.19 n.).

12.1–22: Raphael, being offered his wages, gives good advice and discloses his true identity. 1–5: Tobias generously wishes to reward Raphael far beyond the amount agreed upon (5.14).

no harm to give him half of what I have brought back. ³For he has led me back to you safely, he cured my wife, he obtained the money for me, and he also healed you." ⁴The old man said, "He deserves it." ⁵So he called the angel and said to him, "Take half of all that you two have brought back."

6 Then the angel*ᵃ* called the two of them privately and said to them: "Praise God and give thanks to him; exalt him and give thanks to him in the presence of all the living for what he has done for you. It is good to praise God and to exalt his name, worthily declaring the works of God. Do not be slow to give him thanks. ⁷It is good to guard the secret of a king, but gloriously to reveal the works of God. Do good, and evil will not overtake you. ⁸Prayer is good when accompanied by fasting, almsgiving, and righteousness. A little with righteousness is better than much with wrongdoing. It is better to give alms than to treasure up gold. ⁹For almsgiving delivers from death, and it will purge away every sin. Those who perform deeds of charity and of righteousness will have fulness of life; ¹⁰but those who commit sin are the enemies of their own lives.

11 "I will not conceal anything from you. I have said, 'It is good to guard the secret of a king, but gloriously to reveal the works of God.' ¹²And so, when you and your daughter-in-law Sarah prayed, I brought a reminder of your prayer before the Holy One; and when you buried the dead, I was like-wise present with you. ¹³When you did not hesitate to rise and leave your dinner in order to go and lay out the dead, your good deed was not hidden from me, but I was with you. ¹⁴So now God sent me to heal you and your daughter-in-law Sarah. ¹⁵I am Raphael, one of the seven holy angels who present the prayers of the saints and enter into the presence of the glory of the Holy One."

16 They were both alarmed; and they fell upon their faces, for they were afraid. ¹⁷But he said to them, "Do not be afraid; you will be safe. But praise God for ever. ¹⁸For I did not come as a favor on my part, but by the will of our God. Therefore praise him for ever. ¹⁹All these days I merely appeared to you and did not eat or drink, but you were seeing a vision. ²⁰And now give thanks to God, for I am ascending to him who sent me. Write in a book everything that has happened." ²¹Then they stood up; but they saw him no more. ²²So they confessed the great and wonderful works of God, and acknowledged that the angel of the Lord had appeared to them.

13 Then Tobit wrote a prayer of rejoicing, and said:
"Blessed is God who lives for ever,
    and blessed is his kingdom.
²For he afflicts, and he shows mercy;
    he leads down to Hades, and
      brings up again,
    and there is no one who can
      escape his hand.

a Gk *he*

6–10: In the style of a Jewish teacher of wisdom, Raphael delivers a brief exhortation on the good life, similar to that of Tobit in ch. 4. **8:** *Prayer . . . fasting, almsgiving, and righteousness* ("piety") are mentioned together also in Mt.6.1–18 (on almsgiving, compare 4.7–11 and see Sir.3.30 n.). **11:** V. 7. **12–15:** Raphael reveals himself as an angelic intercessor who brings the prayers of men into the presence of God. From v. 15 we learn that there are six others. "Uriel" is named in 2 Esd.4.1; "Gabriel" and "Michael," respectively, in Dan.9.21 and 10.13. The growth of angelology was characteristic of the Judaism of the period; this was partly due to an increasing sense of God's transcendence and partly, perhaps, to Persian influences. **17:** *Do not be afraid*, compare Mt.28.5,10.

    13.1–18: Tobit's hymn of praise. Some scholars believe that chs. 13 and 14 were added to the book much later in order to give substance to the words of 12.22a and to round out the account of Tobit's life. The hymn contains numerous echoes of Old Testament passages and has no particular appropriateness to Tobit's personal situation. **1–6:** Exhortation to the exiles. **2:**

³Acknowledge him before the nations,
  O sons of Israel;
  for he has scattered us among
    them.
⁴Make his greatness known there,
  and exalt him in the presence of
    all the living;
  because he is our Lord and God,
    he is our Father for ever.
⁵He will afflict us for our iniquities;
  and again he will show mercy,
  and will gather us from all the
    nations
    among whom you^b have been
      scattered.
⁶If you turn to him with all your heart
  and with all your soul,
  to do what is true before him,
  then he will turn to you
  and will not hide his face from
    you.
But see what he will do with you;
  give thanks to him with your
    full voice.
Praise the Lord of righteousness,
  and exalt the King of the ages.
I give him thanks in the land of my
    captivity,
  and I show his power and majesty
    to a nation of sinners.
Turn back, you sinners, and do
    right before him;
  who knows if he will accept you
    and have mercy on you?
⁷I exalt my God;
  my soul exalts the King of heaven,
  and will rejoice in his majesty.
⁸Let all men speak,
  and give him thanks in
    Jerusalem.
⁹O Jerusalem, the holy city,
  he will afflict you for the deeds
    of your sons,
  but again he will show mercy to
    the sons of the righteous.
¹⁰Give thanks worthily to the Lord,
  and praise the King of the ages,
  that his tent may be raised for
    you again with joy.

May he cheer those within you who
    are captives,
  and love those within you who
    are distressed,
  to all generations for ever.
¹¹Many nations will come from afar
    to the name of the Lord God,
  bearing gifts in their hands, gifts
    for the King of heaven.
Generations of generations will give
    you joyful praise.
¹²Cursed are all who hate you;
  blessed for ever will be all who
    love you.
¹³Rejoice and be glad for the sons of
    the righteous;
  for they will be gathered together,
  and will praise the Lord of the
    righteous.
¹⁴How blessed are those who love
    you!
  They will rejoice in your peace.
Blessed are those who grieved over
    all your afflictions;
  for they will rejoice for you upon
    seeing all your glory,
  and they will be made glad for
    ever.
¹⁵Let my soul praise God the great
    King.
¹⁶For Jerusalem will be built with
    sapphires and emeralds,
  her^c walls with precious stones,
  and her towers and battlements
    with pure gold.
¹⁷The streets of Jerusalem will be
    paved^d with beryl and ruby and
    stones of Ophir;
¹⁸ all her lanes will cry 'Hallelujah!'
    and will give praise,
  saying, 'Blessed is God, who has
    exalted you for ever.' "

14 Here Tobit ended his words of
praise. ²He was fifty-eight years
old when he lost his sight, and after
eight years he regained it. He gave

b Other authorities read *we*
c Gk *your*
d Or *inlaid*

---

1 Sam.2.6–8; Lk.1.52–53. **4:** *Our Father*, Is.63.16; 64.8; Sir.23.1,4; Mt.6.9. **7:** The psalmist
offers his own praise. **8–18:** God's favor to Jerusalem. **10:** *Tent*, temple. **16–18:** That *Jerusalem
will be built* with precious stones is an echo of Is.54.11–12 (compare Rev.21.18–21).

alms, and he continued to fear the Lord God and to praise him. ³When he had grown very old he called his son and grandsons, and said to him, "My son, take your sons; behold, I have grown old and am about to depart this life. ⁴Go to Media, my son, for I fully believe what Jonah the prophet said about Nineveh, that it will be overthrown. But in Media there will be peace for a time. Our brethren will be scattered over the earth from the good land, and Jerusalem will be desolate. The house of God in it will be burned down and will be in ruins for a time. ⁵But God will again have mercy on them, and bring them back into their land; and they will rebuild the house of God,ᵉ though it will not be like the former one until the times of the age are completed. After this they will return from the places of their captivity, and will rebuild Jerusalem in splendor. And the house of God will be rebuilt there with a glorious building for all generations for ever, just as the prophets said of it. ⁶Then all the Gentiles will turn to fear the Lord God in truth, and will bury their idols. ⁷All the Gentiles will praise the Lord, and his people will give thanks to God, and the Lord will exalt his people. And all who love the Lord God in truth and righteousness will rejoice, showing mercy to our brethren.

8 "So now, my son, leave Nineveh, because what the prophet Jonah said will surely happen. ⁹But keep the law and the commandments, and be merciful and just, so that it may be well with you. ¹⁰Bury me properly, and your mother with me. And do not live in Nineveh any longer. See, my son, what Nadabᶠ did to Ahikar who had reared him, how he brought him from light into darkness, and with what he repaid him. But Ahikar was saved, and the other received repayment as he himself went down into the darkness. Ahikarᵍ gave alms and escaped the deathtrap which Nadabʰ had set for him; but Nadabᶠ fell into the trap and perished. ¹¹So now, my children, consider what almsgiving accomplishes and how righteousness delivers." As he said this he died in his bed. He was a hundred and fifty-eight years old; and Tobiasʰ gave him a magnificent funeral. ¹²And when Anna died he buried her with his father.

Then Tobias returned with his wife and his sons to Ecbatana, to Raguel his father-in-law. ¹³He grew old with honor, and he gave his father-in-law and mother-in-law magnificent funerals. He inherited their property and that of his father Tobit. ¹⁴He died in Ecbatana of Media at the age of a hundred and twenty-seven years. ¹⁵But before he died he heard of the destruction of Nineveh, which Nebuchadnezzar and Ahasuerus had captured. Before his death he rejoiced over Nineveh.

e Gk *house*
f Other authorities read *Aman*
g Other authorities read *Manasses*
h Gk *he*

14.1–12: Tobit's final counsel, and death. 3–8: He advises his son to leave Nineveh, which is to be destroyed, and predicts the future course of Israel's history. **4:** *What Jonah the prophet said,* Jon.3.4 (Jonah's prophecy, however, was not fulfilled, Jon.3.10). **6:** That *the Gentiles will turn* to Judaism was a characteristic belief of the post-exilic age (e.g. Zech.8.20–23). **10:** *Bury me properly,* see 6.14 n. *Nadab* (also Nasbas or Nadin) is the villain of the *Ahikar* story (see 1.21 n.). *Gave alms,* 4.7–11. **15:** *Nebuchadnezzar . . . Ahasuerus,* i.e. Xerxes (Est.1.1). Both names are anachronistic; Nineveh's conquerors were Nabopolassar and Cyaxares (see 1.4 n.).

JUDITH

Rising slowly to a climax of unforgettable horror, the plot of Judith is a masterpiece of ancient Jewish narrative art. Although obviously a work of fiction, the atmosphere of the tale is entirely realistic, untouched by the aura of the marvelous which envelops such books as Jonah and Tobit. This is not to say that it is irreligious, but that its religion is of a national, legal, and practical type which tends to equate piety with patriotism and to encourage the belief that God helps those who help themselves. In mood and theme the book is closely akin to the book of Esther in the canonical Old Testament, but the character of its heroine is far more positive than Esther's. Judith observes the Mosaic law with scrupulous devotion; she does not, like Esther, demur when duty calls; the impulse to save her people is her own, and the grim stratagem which brings deliverance is of her own devising.

The first part of the book (chs. 1–7) describes at somewhat wearisome length how Nebuchadnezzar's general, Holofernes, invaded the west and at length laid siege to the Jewish town of Bethulia, hoping to starve it into submission. Judith, a beautiful and pious widow, is introduced in ch. 8, and the rest of the story relates how she beguiled Holofernes into entertaining her in his tent, where, when he had become thoroughly drunk, she decapitated him.

The story was probably written in Hebrew during the latter part of the second century B.C. It has been transmitted to us today in three slightly different Greek versions, two Latin versions, a Syriac version, as well as several later Hebrew recensions. The stirring narrative has inspired numerous works of painting, sculpture, and literature, notably an Anglo-Saxon epic of which extensive fragments survive.

N THE TWELFTH YEAR OF THE REIGN of Nebuchadnezzar, who ruled over the Assyrians in the great city of Nineveh, in the days of Arphaxad, who ruled over the Medes in Ecbatana—²he is the king who built walls about Ecbatana with hewn stones three cubits thick and six cubits long; he made the walls seventy cubits high and fifty cubits wide; ³at the gates he built towers a hundred cubits high and sixty cubits wide at the foundations; ⁴and he made its gates, which were seventy cubits high and forty cubits wide, so that his armies could march out in force and his infantry form their ranks—⁵it was in those days that King Nebuchadnezzar made war against King Arphaxad in the great plain which is on the borders of Ragae. ⁶He was joined by all the people of the hill country and all those who lived along the Euphrates and the Tigris and the Hydaspes and in the plain where Arioch ruled the Elymaeans. Many nations joined the forces of the Chaldeans.

7 Then Nebuchadnezzar king of the Assyrians sent to all who lived in Persia and to all who lived in the west, those who lived in Cilicia and Damascus and Lebanon and Antilebanon and

1.1–6: Nebuchadnezzar declares war on Arphaxad, king of Media. 1: *Nebuchadnezzar* (605 [or 604]–562 B.C.) was second ruler over the Neo-Babylonian Empire (not *over the Assyrians*). It was he who destroyed Jerusalem in 587–86 B.C. and carried the Jews off into their Babylonian Exile (2 Kg.24.1–25.26). The author of the book of Judith, in complete disregard of history, represents him as flourishing after the Exile (4.3; 5.19). Some scholars believe that the historical confusion of the book, of which this is but one example, is deliberate, intended to stamp the work unmistakably as fiction. *Arphaxad* is unknown. *The Medes* inhabited the northern part of modern Iran and had their capital at *Ecbatana* (Tob.3.7). 5: *Ragae*, called Rages in Tob.1.14 (see note there). 6: *Euphrates . . . Tigris*, the principal rivers of Mesopotamia (modern Iraq). *Hydaspes*, a river in India, but here evidently placed in Mesopotamia. *Arioch*, unknown. *Elymaeans*, Elamites. *Chaldeans*, the Neo-Babylonians (see v. 1 n.).

1.7–11: The Persians and the western nations refuse Nebuchadnezzar's plea for help. 7–10: The nations enumerated correspond to modern Syria, Lebanon, Palestine, and Egypt. 7: *Persia*, the south of modern Iran.

all who lived along the seacoast, ⁸and those among the nations of Carmel and Gilead, and Upper Galilee and the great Plain of Esdraelon, ⁹and all who were in Samaria and its surrounding towns, and beyond the Jordan as far as Jerusalem and Bethany and Chelous and Kadesh and the river of Egypt, and Tahpanhes and Raamses and the whole land of Goshen, ¹⁰even beyond Tanis and Memphis, and all who lived in Egypt as far as the borders of Ethiopia. ¹¹But all who lived in the whole region disregarded the orders of Nebuchadnezzar king of the Assyrians, and refused to join him in the war; for they were not afraid of him, but looked upon him as only one man,ᵃ and they sent back his messengers empty-handed and shamefaced.

12 Then Nebuchadnezzar was very angry with this whole region, and swore by his throne and kingdom that he would surely take revenge on the whole territory of Cilicia and Damascus and Syria, that he would kill them by the sword, and also all the inhabitants of the land of Moab, and the people of Ammon, and all Judea, and every one in Egypt, as far as the coasts of the two seas. ¹³In the seventeenth year he led his forces against King Arphaxad, and defeated him in battle, and overthrew the whole army of Arphaxad, and all his cavalry and all his chariots. ¹⁴Thus he took possession of his cities, and came to Ecbatana, captured its towers, plundered its markets, and turned its beauty into shame. ¹⁵He captured Arphaxad in the mountains of Ragae and struck him down with hunting spears; and he utterly destroyed him, to this day. ¹⁶Then he returned with them to Nineveh, he and all his com-

bined forces, a vast body of troops; and there he and his forces rested and feasted for one hundred and twenty days.

2 In the eighteenth year, on the twenty-second day of the first month, there was talk in the palace of Nebuchadnezzar king of the Assyrians about carrying out his revenge on the whole region, just as he had said. ²He called together all his officers and all his nobles and set forth to them his secret plan and recounted fully, with his own lips, all the wickedness of the region;ᵇ ³and it was decided that every one who had not obeyed his command should be destroyed. ⁴When he had finished setting forth his plan, Nebuchadnezzar king of the Assyrians called Holofernes, the chief general of his army, second only to himself, and said to him,

5 "Thus says the Great King, the lord of the whole earth: When you leave my presence, take with you men confident in their strength, to the number of one hundred and twenty thousand foot soldiers and twelve thousand cavalry. ⁶Go and attack the whole west country, because they disobeyed my orders. ⁷Tell them to prepare earth and water, for I am coming against them in my anger, and will cover the whole face of the earth with the feet of my armies, and will hand them over to be plundered by my troops,ᶜ ⁸till their wounded shall fill their valleys, and every brook and river shall be filled with their dead, and overflow; ⁹and I will lead them away captive to the ends of the whole earth. ¹⁰You shall go and seize all their terri-

ᵃ Or *a man*
ᵇ The meaning of the Greek of the last clause of this verse is uncertain   ᶜ Gk *them*

1.12–16: Angry at the western nations, Nebuchadnezzar defeats Arphaxad without their assistance. 12: *The two seas*, presumably the Red and the Mediterranean.
2.1–13: Nebuchadnezzar orders Holofernes to lead a punitive expedition against the West. 4: Next to Judith, *Holofernes* is the principal character of the book. So far as is known, Nebuchadnezzar had no such general, but the name is found in classical authors of a much later period. His career may have been suggested by memories of a Persian general of similar name who was a leader in the expedition which invaded the West under Artaxerxes III about 350 B.C. (Diodorus Siculus, *Hist.* xxxi. 19; see 12.11 n.). 7: *Earth and water* were characteristic signs of submission demanded by Persian (not Assyrian or Babylonian) kings (Herodotus, *Hist.* vi. 48).

tory for me in advance. They will yield themselves to you, and you shall hold them for me till the day of their punishment. ¹¹But if they refuse, your eye shall not spare and you shall hand them over to slaughter and plunder throughout your whole region. ¹²For as I live, and by the power of my kingdom, what I have spoken my hand will execute. ¹³And you—take care not to transgress any of your sovereign's commands, but be sure to carry them out just as I have ordered you; and do not delay about it."

14 So Holofernes left the presence of his master, and called together all the commanders, generals, and officers of the Assyrian army, ¹⁵and mustered the picked troops by divisions as his lord had ordered him to do, one hundred and twenty thousand of them, together with twelve thousand archers on horseback, ¹⁶and he organized them as a great army is marshaled for a campaign. ¹⁷He collected a vast number of camels and asses and mules for transport, and innumerable sheep and oxen and goats for provision; ¹⁸also plenty of food for every man, and a huge amount of gold and silver from the royal palace. ¹⁹So he set out with his whole army, to go ahead of King Nebuchadnezzar and to cover the whole face of the earth to the west with their chariots and horsemen and picked troops of infantry. ²⁰Along with them went a mixed crowd like a swarm of locusts, like the dust of the earth—a multitude that could not be counted.

21 They marched for three days from Nineveh to the plain of Bectileth, and camped opposite Bectileth near the mountain which is to the north of Upper Cilicia. ²²From there Holofernes*ᵈ* took his whole army, his infantry, cavalry, and chariots, and went up into the hill country ²³and ravaged Put and Lud, and plundered all the people of Rassis and the Ishmaelites who lived along the desert, south of the country of the Chelleans. ²⁴Then he followed*ᵉ* the Euphrates and passed through Mesopotamia and destroyed all the hilltop cities along the brook Abron, as far as the sea. ²⁵He also seized the territory of Cilicia, and killed every one who resisted him, and came to the southern borders of Japheth, fronting toward Arabia. ²⁶He surrounded all the Midianites, and burned their tents and plundered their sheepfolds. ²⁷Then he went down into the plain of Damascus during the wheat harvest, and burned all their fields and destroyed their flocks and herds and sacked their cities and ravaged their lands and put to death all their young men with the edge of the sword.

28 So fear and terror of him fell upon all the people who lived along the seacoast, at Sidon and Tyre, and those who lived in Sur and Ocina and all who lived in Jamnia. Those who lived in Azotus and Ascalon feared him exceedingly.

3 So they sent messengers to sue for peace, and said, ²"Behold, we the servants of Nebuchadnezzar, the Great King, lie prostrate before you. Do with us whatever you will. ³Behold, our buildings, and all our land, and all

d Gk *he*   *e* Or *crossed*

2.14–27: Holofernes brings an enormous army to Damascus. 21: The *three days* march is impossible, since *Nineveh*, the capital of Assyria, is at least three hundred miles from *Bectileth* (an unidentified site), which is described as *north of Upper Cilicia*. Cilicia is in southeastern Asia Minor. **23:** *Put and Lud*, probably in Asia Minor. *Rassis*, unknown. *Ishmaelites*, Arabs (Gen. 16.11–12). *Chelleans*, unknown. **24:** The geography here is confused. *Abron*, unknown. The natural line of march would be directly south from Cilicia to Damascus. **26:** *Midianites*, archaic for Arabs (Jg.6.1–6). **27:** *Damascus*, the ancient and beautiful capital of Syria, was noted for its fertile surroundings.

2.28–3.8: Through fear the people of the seacoast submit voluntarily. 2.28: *Sidon and Tyre*, on the Phoenician coast, west of Damascus. *Sur and Ocina*, unknown. *Jamnia*, just north of *Azotus* (Ashdod) *and Ascalon* (Ashkelon), important Philistine cities in southwest Palestine.

our wheat fields, and our flocks and herds, and all our sheepfolds with their tents, lie before you; do with them whatever you please. ⁴Our cities also and their inhabitants are your slaves; come and deal with them in any way that seems good to you."

5 The men came to Holofernes and told him all this. ⁶Then he went down to the seacoast with his army and stationed garrisons in the hilltop cities and took picked men from them as his allies. ⁷And these people and all in the country round about welcomed him with garlands and dances and tambourines. ⁸And he demolished all their shrines*f* and cut down their sacred groves; for it had been given to him to destroy all the gods of the land, so that all nations should worship Nebuchadnezzar only, and all their tongues and tribes should call upon him as god.

9 Then he came to the edge of Esdraelon, near Dothan, fronting the great ridge of Judea; ¹⁰here he camped between Geba and Scythopolis, and remained for a whole month in order to assemble all the supplies for his army.

4 By this time the people of Israel living in Judea heard of everything that Holofernes, the general of Nebuchadnezzar the king of the Assyrians, had done to the nations, and how he had plundered and destroyed all their temples; ²they were therefore very greatly terrified at his approach, and were alarmed both for Jerusalem and for the temple of the Lord their God. ³For they had only recently returned from the captivity, and all the people of Judea were newly gathered together, and the sacred vessels and the altar and the temple had been consecrated after their profanation. ⁴So they sent to every district of Samaria, and to Kona and Beth-horon and Belmain and Jericho and to Choba and Aesora and the valley of Salem, ⁵and immediately seized all the high hilltops and fortified the villages on them and stored up food in preparation for war—since their fields had recently been harvested. ⁶And Joakim, the high priest, who was in Jerusalem at that time, wrote to the people of Bethulia and Betomesthaim, which faces Esdraelon opposite the plain near Dothan, ⁷ordering them to seize the passes up into the hills, since by them Judea could be invaded, and it was easy to stop any who tried to enter, for the approach was narrow, only wide enough for two men at the most.

8 So the Israelites did as Joakim the high priest and the senate of the whole people of Israel, in session at Jerusalem, had given order. ⁹And every man of Israel cried out to God with great

f Syr: Gk *borders*

3.8: Holofernes seems here to go beyond his original commission, which was merely punitive; now he seeks to impose religious unity by forcing all men to worship Nebuchadnezzar alone. The language is suggested directly by such passages as Dan. chs. 3 and 6, and indirectly by the persecutions of Antiochus Epiphanes as related in 1 Macc.1.10–2.26 and 2 Macc. chs. 6–7. Holofernes' invasion thus becomes a threat to Israel's religious integrity as well as her national security. 3.9–4.15: When Holofernes reaches the soil of Palestine, the Jews prepare to resist. 3.9: *Esdraelon* is the great plain which cuts across Palestine just north of Mt. Carmel. *Dothan* is a short distance south of the plain. *Scythopolis* is identical with Beth-shan, located at the junction of Esdraelon and the Jordan Valley. 4.3: The statement that *they had only recently returned from the captivity* is flagrantly anachronistic, since it was Nebuchadnezzar who had begun the captivity (compare 1.1 n.), and the return took place nearly fifty years later under the Persian Empire, which had succeeded the Babylonian (Ezra 1.1–3). 4: The inclusion of *Samaria* is quite unrealistic, since the people of Judea (v. 1) and the Samaritans were separate and increasingly hostile communities in the post-exilic era. 6: The name of the high priest, *Joakim*, is no doubt derived from Neh.12.26. The identification of *Bethulia*, the center of the story's action, is one of the major puzzles of the book; the most probable suggestion is that it is a pseudonym for Shechem (see 6.11 n.; 7.18 n.; and 10.10 n.). 8: *Senate*, an anachronism of the author (see 1.1 n. and 1 Macc.12.6 n.).

fervor, and they humbled themselves with much fasting. ¹⁰They and their wives and their children and their cattle and every resident alien and hired laborer and purchased slave—they all girded themselves with sackcloth. ¹¹And all the men and women of Israel, and their children, living at Jerusalem, prostrated themselves before the temple and put ashes on their heads and spread out their sackcloth before the Lord. ¹²They even surrounded the altar with sackcloth and cried out in unison, praying earnestly to the God of Israel not to give up their infants as prey and their wives as booty, and the cities they had inherited to be destroyed, and the sanctuary to be profaned and desecrated to the malicious joy of the Gentiles. ¹³So the Lord heard their prayers and looked upon their affliction; for the people fasted many days throughout Judea and in Jerusalem before the sanctuary of the Lord Almighty. ¹⁴And Joakim the high priest and all the priests who stood before the Lord and ministered to the Lord, with their loins girded with sackcloth, offered the continual burnt offerings and the vows and freewill offerings of the people. ¹⁵With ashes upon their turbans, they cried out to the Lord with all their might to look with favor upon the whole house of Israel.

5 When Holofernes, the general of the Assyrian army, heard that the people of Israel had prepared for war and had closed the passes in the hills and had fortified all the high hilltops and set up barricades in the plains, ²he was very angry. So he called together all the princes of Moab and the commanders of Ammon and all the governors of the coastland, ³and said to them, "Tell me, you Canaanites, what people is this that lives in the hill country? What cities do they inhabit? How large is their army, and in what does their power or strength consist? Who rules over them as king, leading their army? ⁴And why have they alone, of all who live in the west, refused to come out and meet me?"

5 Then Achior, the leader of all the Ammonites, said to him, "Let my lord now hear a word from the mouth of your servant, and I will tell you the truth about this people that dwells in the nearby mountain district. No falsehood shall come from your servant's mouth. ⁶This people is descended from the Chaldeans. ⁷At one time they lived in Mesopotamia, because they would not follow the gods of their fathers who were in Chaldea. ⁸For they had left the ways of their ancestors, and they worshiped the God of heaven, the God they had come to know; hence they drove them out from the presence of their gods; and they fled to Mesopotamia, and lived there for a long time. ⁹Then their God commanded them to leave the place where they were living and go to the land of Canaan. There they settled, and prospered, with much gold and silver and very many cattle. ¹⁰When a famine spread over Canaan they went down to Egypt and lived there as long as they had food; and

---

14: *The continual burnt offerings* were the prescribed daily sacrifices (Ex.29.38–42); the *freewill offerings* were presented voluntarily as occasion required (Lev.22.18–30).

5.1–24: Holofernes is advised by Achior that the Jews are invincible as long as they keep God's law. **2**: *Moab* was the region directly east of the Dead Sea, while *Ammon* lay north and east of it. Both nations were traditional enemies of the Jews (Jg.3.12–30; 2 Sam.10–12; 2 Kg.3.4–27; 24.2). **3**: The circumstance that Israel inhabited the rugged *hill country* had often helped her to preserve her independence in the past. **5–21**: To explain the character of the Jews, Achior summarizes their entire history from Abraham to the return from exile. **6–9**: The migration of Abraham and the prosperity of his descendants (Gen.11.27–37.1). **6**: *Chaldeans*, Abraham came from Ur of the Chaldees (Gen.11.27–31). **7**: *Mesopotamia* here is the region in the north around Haran (Gen.11.31). Late Jewish tradition ascribed the migration of Abraham's family to a desire to escape the influence of polytheism. **8**: *The God of heaven* was a favorite name for Israel's God during the Persian period and later (Tob.10.11; Ezra 1.2). **10–13**: The descent into there they became a great multitude—so great that they could not be counted. ¹¹So the king of Egypt became hostile to them; he took advantage of them and set them to making bricks, and humbled them and made slaves of them. ¹²Then they cried out to their God, and he afflicted the whole land of Egypt with incurable plagues; and so the Egyptians drove them out of their sight. ¹³Then God dried up the Red Sea before them, ¹⁴and he led them by the way of Sinai and Kadesh-barnea, and drove out all the people of the wilderness. ¹⁵So they lived in the land of the Amorites, and by their might destroyed all the inhabitants of Heshbon; and crossing over the Jordan they took possession of all the hill country. ¹⁶And they drove out before them the Canaanites and the Perizzites and the Jebusites and the Shechemites and all the Gergesites, and lived there a long time. ¹⁷As long as they did not sin against their God they prospered, for the God who hates iniquity is with them. ¹⁸But when they departed from the way which he had appointed for them, they were utterly defeated in many battles and were led away captive to a foreign country; the temple of their God was razed to the ground, and their cities were captured by their enemies. ¹⁹But now they have returned to their God, and have come back from the places to which they were scattered, and have occupied Jerusalem, where their sanctuary is, and have settled in the hill country, because it was uninhabited. ²⁰Now therefore, my master and lord, if there is any unwitting error in this people and they sin against their God and we find out their offense, then we will go up and defeat them. ²¹But if there is no transgression in their nation, then

let my lord pass them by; for their Lord will defend them, and their God will protect them, and we shall be put to shame before the whole world."

22 When Achior had finished saying this, all the men standing around the tent began to complain; Holofernes' officers and all the men from the seacoast and from Moab insisted that he must be put to death. ²³"For," they said, "we will not be afraid of the Israelites; they are a people with no strength or power for making war. ²⁴Therefore let us go up, Lord Holofernes, and they will be devoured by your vast army."

6 When the disturbance made by the men outside the council died down, Holofernes, the commander of the Assyrian army, said to Achior and all the Moabites in the presence of all the foreign contingents:

2 "And who are you, Achior, and you hirelings of Ephraim, to prophesy among us as you have done today and tell us not to make war against the people of Israel because their God will defend them? Who is God except Nebuchadnezzar? ³He will send his forces and will destroy them from the face of the earth, and their God will not deliver them—we the king's*ᶠ* servants will destroy them as one man. They cannot resist the might of our cavalry. ⁴We will burn them up,*ᵍ* and their mountains will be drunk with their blood, and their fields will be full of their dead. They*ʰ* cannot withstand us, but will utterly perish. So says King Nebuchadnezzar, the lord of the whole earth. For he has spoken; none of his words shall be in vain.

f Gk *his*
g Other authorities add *with it*
h Gk *The track of their feet*

Egypt and the Exodus (Gen.37.2–Ex.18.27). **14**: *Sinai*, Ex.19.1–Num.10.10. *Kadesh-barnea*, Num.20.1. **15–16**: The conquests in Transjordan and Canaan (Num.20.14–Jos.11.23). **15**: *Amorites . . . Heshbon*, Num.21.21–32. **17**: *They prospered*, the philosophy of Deuteronomy (28.1–14). **18**: The exile (see 1.1 n.). **19**: The return from exile (Ezra chs. 1–3); see 4.3 n. **22–24**: Holofernes' other advisers oppose the view of Achior.

6.1–21: For his presumption, Achior is handed over to the Jews to perish with them in the fall of Bethulia. **1–9**: Holofernes' denunciation of Achior. **2**: By calling Achior and his Ammonite

5 "But you, Achior, you Ammonite hireling, who have said these words on the day of your iniquity, you shall not see my face again from this day until I take revenge on this race that came out of Egypt. ⁶Then the sword of my army and the spear*ⁱ* of my servants shall pierce your sides, and you shall fall among their wounded, when I return. ⁷Now my slaves are going to take you back into the hill country and put you in one of the cities beside the passes, ⁸and you will not die until you perish along with them. ⁹If you really hope in your heart that they will not be taken, do not look downcast! I have spoken and none of my words shall fail."

10 Then Holofernes ordered his slaves, who waited on him in his tent, to seize Achior and take him to Bethulia and hand him over to the men of Israel. ¹¹So the slaves took him and led him out of the camp into the plain, and from the plain they went up into the hill country and came to the springs below Bethulia. ¹²When the men of the city saw them,*ʲ* they caught up their weapons and ran out of the city to the top of the hill, and all the slingers kept them from coming up by casting stones at them. ¹³However, they got under the shelter of the hill and they bound Achior and left him lying at the foot of the hill, and returned to their master.

14 Then the men of Israel came down from their city and found him; and they untied him and brought him into Bethulia and placed him before the magistrates of their city, ¹⁵who in those days were Uzziah the son of Micah, of the tribe of Simeon, and Chabris the son of Gothoniel, and Charmis the son of Melchiel. ¹⁶They

called together all the elders of the city, and all their young men and their women ran to the assembly; and they set Achior in the midst of all their people, and Uzziah asked him what had happened. ¹⁷He answered and told them what had taken place at the council of Holofernes, and all that he had said in the presence of the Assyrian leaders, and all that Holofernes had said so boastfully against the house of Israel. ¹⁸Then the people fell down and worshiped God, and cried out to him, and said,

19 "O Lord God of heaven, behold their arrogance, and have pity on the humiliation of our people, and look this day upon the faces of those who are consecrated to thee."

20 Then they consoled Achior, and praised him greatly. ²¹And Uzziah took him from the assembly to his own house and gave a banquet for the elders; and all that night they called on the God of Israel for help.

7 The next day Holofernes ordered his whole army, and all the allies who had joined him, to break camp and move against Bethulia, and to seize the passes up into the hill country and make war on the Israelites. ²So all their warriors moved their camp that day; their force of men of war was one hundred and seventy thousand infantry and twelve thousand cavalry, together with the baggage and the foot soldiers handling it, a very great multitude. ³They encamped in the valley near Bethulia, beside the spring, and they spread out in breadth over Dothan as far as Balbaim and in length from Bethulia to Cyamon, which faces Esdraelon.

i Lat Syr: Gk *people*
j Other authorities add *on the top of the hill*

---

friends *hirelings of Ephraim* (i.e. Israel), Holofernes may intend to say that Achior has been corrupted by Jewish money. **10–13:** Achior is left bound in sight of the men of Bethulia. **11:** With whatever place the mysterious Bethulia may be identified (see 4.6 n.), it is clearly pictured as a city on a hill *with springs* below it. **14–21:** The Jews bring Achior inside the city, which then hears the story of Holofernes' arrogance.

7.1–7: Holofernes and his allies advance to Bethulia and survey the situation. **1–3:** The line of march is south from Esdraelon. **3:** *Beside the spring*, see 6.11 n. *Dothan*, see 3.9 n. *Balbaim* and *Cyamon* are unknown. *Esdraelon*, see 3.9 n.

4 When the Israelites saw their vast numbers they were greatly terrified, and every one said to his neighbor, "These men will now lick up the face of the whole land; neither the high mountains nor the valleys nor the hills will bear their weight." ⁵Then each man took up his weapons, and when they had kindled fires on their towers they remained on guard all that night.

6 On the second day Holofernes led out all his cavalry in full view of the Israelites in Bethulia, ⁷and examined the approaches to the city, and visited the springs that supplied their water, and seized them and set guards of soldiers over them, and then returned to his army.

8 Then all the chieftains of the people of Esau and all the leaders of the Moabites and the commanders of the coastland came to him and said, ⁹"Let our lord hear a word, lest his army be defeated. ¹⁰For these people, the Israelites, do not rely on their spears but on the height of the mountains where they live, for it is not easy to reach the tops of their mountains. ¹¹Therefore, my lord, do not fight against them in battle array, and not a man of your army will fall. ¹²Remain in your camp, and keep all the men in your forces with you; only let your servants take possession of the spring of water that flows from the foot of the mountain—¹³for this is where all the people of Bethulia get their water. So thirst will destroy them, and they will give up their city. We and our people will go up to the tops of the nearby mountains and camp there to keep watch that not a man gets out of the city. ¹⁴They and their wives and children will waste away with famine, and before the sword reaches them they will be strewn about in the streets where they live. ¹⁵So you will pay them back with evil, because they rebelled and did not receive you peaceably."

16 These words pleased Holofernes and all his servants, and he gave orders to do as they had said. ¹⁷So the army of the Ammonites moved forward, together with five thousand Assyrians, and they encamped in the valley and seized the water supply and the springs of the Israelites. ¹⁸And the sons of Esau and the sons of Ammon went up and encamped in the hill country opposite Dothan; and they sent some of their men toward the south and the east, toward Acraba, which is near Chusi beside the brook Mochmur. The rest of the Assyrian army encamped in the plain, and covered the whole face of the land, and their tents and supply trains spread out in great number, and they formed a vast multitude.

19 The people of Israel cried out to the Lord their God, for their courage failed, because all their enemies had surrounded them and there was no way of escape from them. ²⁰The whole Assyrian army, their infantry, chariots, and cavalry, surrounded them for thirty-four days, until all the vessels of water belonging to every inhabitant of Bethulia were empty; ²¹their cisterns were going dry, and they did not have enough water to drink their fill for a single day, because it was measured out to them to drink. ²²Their children lost heart, and the women and young men fainted from thirst and fell down in the streets of the city and in the passages through the gates; there was no strength left in them any longer.

23 Then all the people, the young men, the women, and the children,

---

7.8–18: They cut off the city's water supply by seizing the springs. **8:** *Esau* means Edom, southeast of the Dead Sea. These people have not previously been mentioned, but were also traditional enemies of the Jews (see e.g. Ob.18). **18:** The localities of *Acraba* and *Chusi* and the valley of *Mochmur* have all been identified with sites in the neighborhood of Shechem (see 4.6 n.).

7.19–28: Driven to desperation, the citizens of Bethulia urge their leaders to capitulate. **23:** *Uzziah,* 6.15.

gathered about Uzziah and the rulers of the city and cried out with a loud voice, and said before all the elders, ²⁴"God be judge between you and us! For you have done us a great injury in not making peace with the Assyrians. ²⁵For now we have no one to help us; God has sold us into their hands, to strew us on the ground before them with thirst and utter destruction. ²⁶Now call them in and surrender the whole city to the army of Holofernes and to all his forces, to be plundered. ²⁷For it would be better for us to be captured by them;ᵏ for we will be slaves, but our lives will be spared, and we shall not witness the death of our babes before our eyes, or see our wives and children draw their last breath. ²⁸We call to witness against you heaven and earth and our God, the Lord of our fathers, who punishes us according to our sins and the sins of our fathers. Let him not do this day the things which we have described!"

29 Then great and general lamentation arose throughout the assembly, and they cried out to the Lord God with a loud voice. ³⁰And Uzziah said to them, "Have courage, my brothers! Let us hold out for five more days; by that time the Lord our God will restore to us his mercy, for he will not forsake us utterly. ³¹But if these days pass by, and no help comes for us, I will do what you say."

32 Then he dismissed the people to their various posts, and they went up on the walls and towers of their city. The women and children he sent home. And they were greatly depressed in the city.

8 At that time Judith heard about these things: she was the daughter of Merari the son of Ox, son of Joseph, son of Oziel, son of Elkiah, son of Ananias, son of Gideon, son of Raphaim, son of Ahitub, son of Elijah, son of Hilkiah, son of Fliab, son of Nathanael, son of Salamiel, son of Sarasadai, son of Israel. ²Her husband Manasseh, who belonged to her tribe and family, had died during the barley harvest. ³For as he stood overseeing the men who were binding sheaves in the field, he was overcome by the burning heat, and took to his bed and died in Bethulia his city. So they buried him with his fathers in the field between Dothan and Balamon. ⁴Judith had lived at home as a widow for three years and four months. ⁵She set up a tent for herself on the roof of her house, and girded sackcloth about her loins and wore the garments of her widowhood. ⁶She fasted all the days of her widowhood, except the day before the sabbath and the sabbath itself, the day before the new moon and the day of the new moon, and the feasts and days of rejoicing of the house of Israel. ⁷She was beautiful in appearance, and had a very lovely face; and her husband Manasseh had left her gold and silver, and men and women slaves, and cattle, and fields; and she maintained this estate. ⁸No one spoke ill of her, for she feared God with great devotion.

9 When Judith heard the wicked words spoken by the people against the ruler, because they were faint for lack of water, and when she heard all that Uzziah said to them, and how he promised them under oath to surrender the city to the Assyrians after five days, ¹⁰she sent her maid, who was in charge of all she possessed, to summonˡ Chabris and Charmis, the elders

k Other authorities add *than to die of thirst*
l Some authorities add *Uzziah and* (See verses 28 and 35)

7.29–32: Uzziah advises a delay of five days.

8.1–8: The character of Judith. 1: The name *Judith* means "Jewess." Her ancestors cannot be identified: some of the names are unparalleled in the Old Testament. **2–3:** Her husband had died of sunstroke (compare 2 Kg.4.18–20). **6:** The rigorous piety which is her outstanding quality is of the rabbinical or Pharisaical type. She omits fasting only on days when it is forbidden. **7:** Beauty and wealth are normal elements in the character of a romantic heroine.

8.9–27: Judith presents sound theological arguments against Uzziah's proposal. 12: Note the of her city. [11]They came to her, and she said to them,

"Listen to me, rulers of the people of Bethulia! What you have said to the people today is not right; you have even sworn and pronounced this oath between God and you, promising to surrender the city to our enemies unless the Lord turns and helps us within so many days. [12]Who are you, that have put God to the test this day, and are setting yourselves up in the place of[m] God among the sons of men? [13]You are putting the Lord Almighty to the test—but you will never know anything! [14]You cannot plumb the depths of the human heart, nor find out what a man is thinking; how do you expect to search out God, who made all these things, and find out his mind or comprehend his thought? No, my brethren, do not provoke the Lord our God to anger. [15]For if he does not choose to help us within these five days, he has power to protect us within any time he pleases, or even to destroy us in the presence of our enemies. [16]Do not try to bind the purposes of the Lord our God; for God is not like man, to be threatened, nor like a human being, to be won over by pleading. [17]Therefore, while we wait for his deliverance, let us call upon him to help us, and he will hear our voice, if it pleases him.

18 "For never in our generation, nor in these present days, has there been any tribe or family or people or city of ours which worshiped gods made with hands, as was done in days gone by— [19]and that was why our fathers were handed over to the sword, and to be plundered, and so they suffered a great catastrophe before our enemies. [20]But we know no other god but him, and therefore we hope that he will not disdain us or any of our nation. [21]For if

we are captured all Judea will be captured and our sanctuary will be plundered; and he will exact of us[n] the penalty for its desecration. [22]And the slaughter of our brethren and the captivity of the land and the desolation of our inheritance—all this he will bring upon our heads among the Gentiles, wherever we serve as slaves; and we shall be an offense and a reproach in the eyes of those who acquire us. [23]For our slavery will not bring us into favor, but the Lord our God will turn it to dishonor.

24 "Now therefore, brethren, let us set an example to our brethren, for their lives depend upon us, and the sanctuary and the temple and the altar rest upon us. [25]In spite of everything let us give thanks to the Lord our God, who is putting us to the test as he did our forefathers. [26]Remember what he did with Abraham, and how he tested Isaac, and what happened to Jacob in Mesopotamia in Syria, while he was keeping the sheep of Laban, his mother's brother. [27]For he has not tried us with fire, as he did them, to search their hearts, nor has he taken revenge upon us; but the Lord scourges those who draw near to him, in order to admonish them."

28 Then Uzziah said to her, "All that you have said has been spoken out of a true heart, and there is no one who can deny your words. [29]Today is not the first time your wisdom has been shown, but from the beginning of your life all the people have recognized your understanding, for your heart's disposition is right. [30]But the people were very thirsty, and they compelled us to do for them what we have promised, and made us take an oath which we cannot break. [31]So pray for us, since

m Or *above*
n Gk *our blood*

---

neat balance of her antitheses: it is not for us to *put God to the test* (Dt.6.16); he is (v. 25) putting us to the test. **16:** *God is not like man*, Num.23.19; 1 Sam.15.29. **18:** The people are safe because they have been entirely loyal to God (compare 5.21). Judith's optimistic judgment of her contemporaries stands in sharp contrast to the attitude of the great prophets, but is similar to that of Ps.44.17–18. **27:** Their present sufferings are not punitive, but educative.

8.28–35: Answering Uzziah's plea, she personally pledges to deliver the city. 30–31: The vow, you are a devout woman, and the Lord will send us rain to fill our cisterns and we will no longer be faint."

32 Judith said to them, "Listen to me. I am about to do a thing which will go down through all generations of our descendants. ³³Stand at the city gate tonight, and I will go out with my maid; and within the days after which you have promised to surrender the city to our enemies, the Lord will deliver Israel by my hand. ³⁴Only, do not try to find out what I plan; for I will not tell you until I have finished what I am about to do."

35 Uzziah and the rulers said to her, "Go in peace, and may the Lord God go before you, to take revenge upon our enemies." ³⁶So they returned from the tent and went to their posts.

9 Then Judith fell upon her face, and put ashes on her head, and uncovered the sackcloth she was wearing; and at the very time when that evening's incense was being offered in the house of God in Jerusalem, Judith cried out to the Lord with a loud voice, and said,

2 "O Lord God of my father Simeon, to whom thou gavest a sword to take revenge on the strangers who had loosed the girdle° of a virgin to defile her, and uncovered her thigh to put her to shame, and polluted her womb to disgrace her; for thou hast said, 'It shall not be done'—yet they did it. ³So thou gavest up their rulers to be slain, and their bed, which was ashamed of the deceit they had practiced, to be stained with blood, and thou didst strike down slaves along with princes, and princes on their thrones; ⁴and thou gavest their wives for a prey and their daughters to captivity, and all their

booty to be divided among thy beloved sons, who were zealous for thee, and abhorred the pollution of their blood, and called on thee for help—O God, my God, hear me also, a widow.

5 "For thou hast done these things and those that went before and those that followed; thou hast designed the things that are now, and those that are to come. Yea, the things thou didst intend came to pass, ⁶and the things thou didst will presented themselves and said, 'Lo, we are here'; for all thy ways are prepared in advance, and thy judgment is with foreknowledge.

7 "Behold now, the Assyrians are increased in their might; they are exalted, with their horses and riders; they glory in the strength of their foot soldiers; they trust in shield and spear, in bow and sling, and know not that thou art the Lord who crushest wars; the Lord is thy name. ⁸Break their strength by thy might, and bring down their power in thy anger; for they intend to defile thy sanctuary, and to pollute the tabernacle where thy glorious name rests, and to cast down the horn of thy altar with the sword. ⁹Behold their pride, and send thy wrath upon their heads; give to me, a widow, the strength to do what I plan. ¹⁰By the deceit of my lips strike down the slave with the prince and the prince with his servant; crush their arrogance by the hand of a woman.

11 "For thy power depends not upon numbers, nor thy might upon men of strength; for thou art God of the lowly, helper of the oppressed, upholder of the weak, protector of the forlorn, savior of those without hope. ¹²Hear,

o Cn: Gk *womb*

though wrong, as Judith said, had been made and its consequences could be avoided only by an act of God. **33:** Judith promises that God will act through her.

9.1–14: Judith's prayer. 1: *Evening's incense*, Ex.30.8; Ps.141.2. It may have become customary to offer prayer regularly at this time of day. **2:** *My father Simeon*, the patriarch, son of Jacob, who, with Levi, avenged their sister Dinah (Gen.34.25–26). **4:** God's special care for the *widow* was an article of Israel's faith (Dt.10.18; Ps.146.9). **5–6:** God's absolute foreknowledge and control of history, both past and future (Is.44.6–8). **10:** The author of the book apparently feels no moral inconsistency in having Judith pray for divine help in practicing *deceit* (see v. 13 n.). That an enemy should be destroyed *by the hand of a woman* would be not only remarkable, but particularly ignominious (Jg.9.54). **11:** *Thy power depends not upon*

O hear me, God of my father, God of the inheritance of Israel, Lord of heaven and earth, Creator of the waters, King of all thy creation, hear my prayer! [13]Make my deceitful words to be their wound and stripe, for they have planned cruel things against thy covenant, and against thy consecrated house, and against the top of Zion, and against the house possessed by thy children. [14]And cause thy whole nation and every tribe to know and understand that thou art God, the God of all power and might, and that there is no other who protects the people of Israel but thou alone!"

10 When Judith[p] had ceased crying out to the God of Israel, and had ended all these words, [2]she rose from where she lay prostrate and called her maid and went down into the house where she lived on sabbaths and on her feast days; [3]and she removed the sackcloth which she had been wearing, and took off her widow's garments, and bathed her body with water, and anointed herself with precious ointment, and combed her hair and put on a tiara, and arrayed herself in her gayest apparel, which she used to wear while her husband Manasseh was living. [4]And she put sandals on her feet, and put on her anklets and bracelets and rings, and her earrings and all her ornaments, and made herself very beautiful, to entice the eyes of all men who might see her. [5]And she gave her maid a bottle of wine and a flask of oil, and

filled a bag with parched grain and a cake of dried fruit and fine bread; and she wrapped up all her vessels and gave them to her to carry.

6 Then they went out to the city gate of Bethulia, and found Uzziah standing there with the elders of the city, Chabris and Charmis. [7]When they saw her, and noted how her face was altered and her clothing changed, they greatly admired her beauty, and said to her, [8]"May the God of our fathers grant you favor and fulfil your plans, that the people of Israel may glory and Jerusalem may be exalted." And she worshiped God.

9 Then she said to them, "Order the gate of the city to be opened for me, and I will go out and accomplish the things about which you spoke with me." So they ordered the young men to open the gate for her, as she had said. [10]When they had done this, Judith went out, she and her maid with her; and the men of the city watched her until she had gone down the mountain and passed through the valley and they could no longer see her.

11 The women[q] went straight on through the valley; and an Assyrian patrol met her [12]and took her into custody, and asked her, "To what people do you belong, and where are you coming from, and where are you going?" She replied, "I am a daughter of the Hebrews, but I am fleeing from them, for they are about to be handed over to you to be devoured. [13]I am on

p Gk *she*   q Gk *They*

numbers, Jg.7.2; 1 Sam.14.6. **12:** *King of all thy creation*, a favorite late Jewish title for God. **13:** This prayer for God's blessing on a lie has been frequently criticized as a serious, and basic, moral blemish in the book. While Judith's conduct may, in the abstract, seem indefensible, it has often been imitated by both Jews and Christians in similar circumstances of crisis; the moral question is complex and the practical solution sometimes agonizing.

10.1–5: Judith beautifies herself. 2: *Went down into the house*, from the roof where she apparently lived (presumably in a tent) except on the sabbath and festivals. **4:** The Latin version states that God gave her a supernatural beauty because her motive in adorning herself was virtuous, not lustful. **5:** *Vessels*, for cooking her food in accordance with the Jewish dietary laws.

10.6–10: She leaves the city with the elders' blessing. 8: *She worshiped God*, prayer and acts of piety accompany every one of her decisive acts. **10:** *Down the mountain . . . through the valley*, the geographical location of Bethulia, on the mountain with the "Assyrian" camp at the entrance of the valley leading up to it, could hardly be described more clearly.

10.11–23: Arriving at the enemy lines, she is brought into Holofernes' presence. 13: *I will* my way to the presence of Holofernes the commander of your army, to give him a true report; and I will show him a way by which he can go and capture all the hill country without losing one of his men, captured or slain."

14 When the men heard her words, and observed her face—she was in their eyes marvelously beautiful—they said to her, ¹⁵"You have saved your life by hurrying down to the presence of our lord. Go at once to his tent; some of us will escort you and hand you over to him. ¹⁶And when you stand before him, do not be afraid in your heart, but tell him just what you have said, and he will treat you well."

17 They chose from their number a hundred men to accompany her and her maid, and they brought them to the tent of Holofernes. ¹⁸There was great excitement in the whole camp, for her arrival was reported from tent to tent, and they came and stood around her as she waited outside the tent of Holofernes while they told him about her. ¹⁹And they marveled at her beauty, and admired the Israelites, judging them by her, and every one said to his neighbor, "Who can despise these people, who have women like this among them? Surely not a man of them had better be left alive, for if we let them go they will be able to ensnare the whole world!"

20 Then Holofernes' companions and all his servants came out and led her into the tent. ²¹Holofernes was resting on his bed, under a canopy which was woven with purple and gold and emeralds and precious stones. ²²When they told him of her he came forward to the front of the tent, with silver lamps carried before him. ²³And when Judith came into the presence of Holofernes^r and his servants, they all marveled at the beauty of her face; and she prostrated herself and made obeisance to him, and his slaves raised her up.

|| Then Holofernes said to her, "Take courage, woman, and do not be afraid in your heart, for I have never hurt any one who chose to serve Nebuchadnezzar, the king of all the earth. ²And even now, if your people who live in the hill country had not slighted me, I would never have lifted my spear against them; but they have brought all this on themselves. ³And now tell me why you have fled from them and have come over to us—since you have come to safety. ⁴Have courage; you will live, tonight and from now on. No one will hurt you, but all will treat you well, as they do the servants of my lord King Nebuchadnezzar."

5 Judith replied to him, "Accept the words of your servant, and let your maidservant speak in your presence, and I will tell nothing false to my lord this night. ⁶And if you follow out the words of your maidservant, God will accomplish something through you, and my lord will not fail to achieve his purposes. ⁷Nebuchadnezzar the king of the whole earth lives, and as his power endures, who has sent you to direct every living soul, not only do men serve him because of you, but also the beasts of the field and the cattle and the birds of the air will live by your power under Nebuchadnezzar and all his house. ⁸For we have heard of your wisdom and skill, and it is reported

r Gk *him*

---

show him a way. The first of her "deceitful words" (see 9.13 n.). **21:** The *canopy* was some kind of decorated mosquito net. The Anglo-Saxon poem of Judith describes it thus: "There was hung|All golden a fair fly-net round the bed|Of the folk-leader, that the baleful one,|The chief of warriors, might look through on each|Child of the brave who came therein, and none|Might look on him . . . ."

11.1–4: Holofernes graciously receives her.

11.5–23: Judith's explanation of her flight commends her to the general and his advisers. **6:** The idea that God can work through heathen kings and their armies is fairly common in the Old Testament (Is.10.5; 44.28; Jer.25.9). **7:** This verse is as obscure in the Greek as in the English.

throughout the whole world that you are the one good man in the whole kingdom, thoroughly informed and marvelous in military strategy.

9 "Now as for the things Achior said in your council, we have heard his words, for the men of Bethulia spared him and he told them all he had said to you. ¹⁰Therefore, my lord and master, do not disregard what he said, but keep it in your mind, for it is true: our nation cannot be punished, nor can the sword prevail against them, unless they sin against their God.

11 "And now, in order that my lord may not be defeated and his purpose frustrated, death will fall upon them, for a sin has overtaken them by which they are about to provoke their God to anger when they do what is wrong. ¹²Since their food supply is exhausted and their water has almost given out, they have planned to kill their cattle and have determined to use all that God by his laws has forbidden them to eat. ¹³They have decided to consume the first fruits of the grain and the tithes of the wine and oil, which they had consecrated and set aside for the priests who minister in the presence of our God at Jerusalem—although it is not lawful for any of the people so much as to touch these things with their hands. ¹⁴They have sent men to Jerusalem, because even the people living there have been doing this, to bring back to them permission from the senate. ¹⁵When the word reaches them and they proceed to do this, on that very day they will be handed over to you to be destroyed.

16 "Therefore, when I, your servant, learned all this, I fled from them; and God has sent me to accomplish with you things that will astonish the whole world, as many as shall hear about them. ¹⁷For your servant is religious, and serves the God of heaven day and night; therefore, my lord, I will remain with you, and every night your servant will go out into the valley, and I will pray to God and he will tell me when they have committed their sins. ¹⁸And I will come and tell you, and then you shall go out with your whole army, and not one of them will withstand you. ¹⁹Then I will lead you through the middle of Judea, till you come to Jerusalem; and I will set your throneˢ in the midst of it; and you will lead them like sheep that have no shepherd, and not a dog will so much as open its mouth to growl at you. For this has been told me, by my foreknowledge; it was announced to me, and I was sent to tell you."

20 Her words pleased Holofernes and all his servants, and they marveled at her wisdom and said, ²¹"There is not such a woman from one end of the earth to the other, either for beauty of face or wisdom of speech!" ²²And Holofernes said to her, "God has done well to send you before the people, to lend strength to our hands and to bring destruction upon those who have slighted my lord. ²³You are not only beautiful in appearance, but wise in speech; and if you do as you have said, your God shall be my God, and you shall live in the house of King Nebuchadnezzar and be renowned throughout the whole world."

12 Then he commanded them to bring her in where his silver dishes were kept, and ordered them to set a table for her with some of his own food and to serve her with his own wine. ²But Judith said, "I cannot eat

ˢ Or *chariot*

9: *The things Achior said*, compare 5.5–21. **11–15:** She declares that the imminent fall of Bethulia is due to the circumstance that its citizens are about to appropriate to common use food which the Mosaic law assigned to God and the temple. **13:** *First fruits*, Ex.23.19. *Tithes*, Lev.27.30. **14:** *Senate*, the Sanhedrin, the supreme religious authority of later Judaism. **17:** *God of heaven*, see 5.8 n. By telling him that *every night* she *will go out into the valley* Judith is preparing a ruse for her eventual escape (13.10). The Anglo-Saxon poem, no doubt for moral reasons, omits this element in the story.

12.1–9: For three days Judith remains and establishes a pattern of conduct. 2: Once again it, lest it be an offense; but I will be provided from the things I have brought with me." ³Holofernes said to her, "If your supply runs out, where can we get more like it for you? For none of your people is here with us." ⁴Judith replied, "As your soul lives, my lord, your servant will not use up the things I have with me before the Lord carries out by my hand what he has determined to do."

5 Then the servants of Holofernes brought her into the tent, and she slept until midnight. Along toward the morning watch she arose ⁶and sent to Holofernes and said, "Let my lord now command that your servant be permitted to go out and pray." ⁷So Holofernes commanded his guards not to hinder her. And she remained in the camp for three days, and went out each night to the valley of Bethulia, and bathed at the spring in the camp.ᵗ ⁸When she came up from the spring she prayed the Lord God of Israel to direct her way for the raising up of her people. ⁹So she returned clean and stayed in the tent until she ate her food toward evening.

10 On the fourth day Holofernes held a banquet for his slaves only, and did not invite any of his officers. ¹¹And he said to Bagoas, the eunuch who had charge of all his personal affairs, "Go now and persuade the Hebrew woman who is in your care to join us and eat and drink with us. ¹²For it will be a disgrace if we let such a woman go without enjoying her company, for if

we do not embrace her she will laugh at us." ¹³So Bagoas went out from the presence of Holofernes, and approached her and said, "This beautiful maidservant will please come to my lord and be honored in his presence, and drink wine and be merry with us, and become today like one of the daughters of the Assyrians who serve in the house of Nebuchadnezzar." ¹⁴And Judith said, "Who am I, to refuse my lord? Surely whatever pleases him I will do at once, and it will be a joy to me until the day of my death!" ¹⁵So she got up and arrayed herself in all her woman's finery, and her maid went and spread on the ground for her before Holofernes the soft fleeces which she had received from Bagoas for her daily use, so that she might recline on them when she ate.

16 Then Judith came in and lay down, and Holofernes' heart was ravished with her and he was moved with great desire to possess her; for he had been waiting for an opportunity to deceive her, ever since the day he first saw her. ¹⁷So Holofernes said to her, "Drink now, and be merry with us!" ¹⁸Judith said, "I will drink now, my lord, because my life means more to me today than in all the days since I was born." ¹⁹Then she took and ate and drank before him what her maid had prepared. ²⁰And Holofernes was greatly pleased with her, and drank a great quantity of wine, much more than he had ever drunk in any one day since he was born.

ᵗ Other authorities omit *in the camp*

the narrative stresses Judith's meticulous observance of the Jewish dietary laws, even in the presence of the Gentiles. Her behavior contrasts markedly with that of Esther (Est.2.20; compare Dan.1.8). **6–7**: Since she had gone out every night, her departure after Holofernes' assassination would occasion no surprise. **8**: Her prayer was genuine enough, but not for the purpose previously announced (11.17).

12.10–20: Judith invited to Holofernes' banquet. 11: *Bagoas* is a well-known Persian name, spelled "Bigvai" in Ezra 2.2 and the Elephantine papyri. Diodorus Siculus (*Hist.* XVI. 47) mentions an officer Bagoas in the army of Artaxerxes III (see 2.4 n.). In oriental kingdoms the officer in charge of the women was normally a *eunuch;* eunuchs often attained also to positions of considerable responsibility in the state (Dan.1.3; Acts 8.27). **14**: Judith pretends to be pleased by his obviously dishonorable intentions toward her. Her real thoughts are paraphrased in the Anglo-Saxon poem as follows: ". . . the Saviour's handmaid then|Gloried, intently mindful how she might|Take from the hateful one most easily|His life. . . ."

13 When evening came, his slaves quickly withdrew, and Bagoas closed the tent from outside and shut out the attendants from his master's presence; and they went to bed, for they all were weary because the banquet had lasted long. ²So Judith was left alone in the tent, with Holofernes stretched out on his bed, for he was overcome with wine.

3 Now Judith had told her maid to stand outside the bedchamber and to wait for her to come out, as she did every day; for she said she would be going out for her prayers. And she had said the same thing to Bagoas. ⁴So every one went out, and no one, either small or great, was left in the bedchamber. Then Judith, standing beside his bed, said in her heart, "O Lord God of all might, look in this hour upon the work of my hands for the exaltation of Jerusalem. ⁵For now is the time to help thy inheritance, and to carry out my undertaking for the destruction of the enemies who have risen up against us."

6 She went up to the post at the end of the bed, above Holofernes' head, and took down his sword that hung there. ⁷She came close to his bed and took hold of the hair of his head, and said, "Give me strength this day, O Lord God of Israel!" ⁸And she struck his neck twice with all her might, and severed his head from his body. ⁹Then she tumbled his body off the bed and pulled down the canopy from the posts; after a moment she went out, and gave Holofernes' head to her maid, ¹⁰who placed it in her food bag.

Then the two of them went out together, as they were accustomed to go for prayer; and they passed through the camp and circled around the valley and went up the mountain to Bethulia and came to its gates. ¹¹Judith called out from afar to the watchmen at the gates, "Open, open the gate! God, our God, is still with us, to show his power in Israel, and his strength against our enemies, even as he has done this day!"

12 When the men of her city heard her voice, they hurried down to the city gate and called together the elders of the city. ¹³They all ran together, both small and great, for it was unbelievable that she had returned; they opened the gate and admitted them, and they kindled a fire for light, and gathered around them. ¹⁴Then she said to them with a loud voice, "Praise God, O praise him! Praise God, who has not withdrawn his mercy from the house of Israel, but has destroyed our enemies by my hand this very night!"

15 Then she took the head out of the bag and showed it to them, and said, "See, here is the head of Holofernes, the commander of the Assyrian army, and here is the canopy beneath which he lay in his drunken stupor. The Lord has struck him down by the hand of a woman. ¹⁶As the Lord lives, who has protected me in the way I went, it was my face that tricked him to his destruction, and yet he committed no act of sin with me, to defile and shame me."

17 All the people were greatly astonished, and bowed down and worshiped God, and said with one accord, "Blessed art thou, our God, who hast brought into contempt this day the enemies of thy people."

18 And Uzziah said to her, "O

13.1–10a: Judith beheads Holofernes. 4–7: Judith's prayer before she decapitates the enemy of her people is both the most dramatic and most horrifying moment of the story. In the Anglo-Saxon version, the prayer becomes an invocation of the Holy Trinity. **9:** *Pulled down the canopy* (10.21) and carried it off as a trophy (v. 15). **10a:** Even the bag in which she brought her food (10.5) is now seen to have been part of a well-laid plan.

13.10b–20: She escapes and returns to her own people. 10b: Her established habit of leaving the camp each night for prayer (11.17; 12.7) permits her an easy escape. **17:** *Blessed art thou, our God*, is the most common formula of late Jewish prayers (see Tob.3.11 n.). **18:** Uzziah's words are reminiscent of those spoken concerning Jael under similar circumstances (Jg.5.24); also of Melchizedek's greeting to Abraham (Gen.14.19–20).

daughter, you are blessed by the Most High God above all women on earth; and blessed be the Lord God, who created the heavens and the earth, who has guided you to strike the head of the leader of our enemies. ¹⁹Your hope will never depart from the hearts of men, as they remember the power of God. ²⁰May God grant this to be a perpetual honor to you, and may he visit you with blessings, because you did not spare your own life when our nation was brought low, but have avenged our ruin, walking in the straight path before our God." And all the people said, "So be it, so be it!"

14 Then Judith said to them, "Listen to me, my brethren, and take this head and hang it upon the parapet of your wall. ²And as soon as morning comes and the sun rises, let every valiant man take his weapons and go out of the city, and set a captain over them, as if you were going down to the plain against the Assyrian outpost; only do not go down. ³Then they will seize their arms and go into the camp and rouse the officers of the Assyrian army; and they will rush into the tent of Holofernes, and will not find him. Then fear will come over them, and they will flee before you, ⁴and you and all who live within the borders of Israel shall pursue them and cut them down as they flee. ⁵But before you do all this, bring Achior the Ammonite to me, and let him see and recognize the man who despised the house of Israel and sent him to us as if to his death."

6 So they summoned Achior from the house of Uzziah. And when he came and saw the head of Holofernes in the hand of one of the men at the gathering of the people, he fell down on his face and his spirit failed him. ⁷And when they raised him up he fell at Judith's feet, and knelt before her, and said, "Blessed are you in every tent of Judah! In every nation those who hear your name will be alarmed. ⁸Now tell me what you have done during these days."

Then Judith described to him in the presence of the people all that she had done, from the day she left until the moment of her speaking to them. ⁹And when she had finished, the people raised a great shout and made a joyful noise in their city. ¹⁰And when Achior saw all that the God of Israel had done, he believed firmly in God, and was circumcised, and joined the house of Israel, remaining so to this day.

11 As soon as it was dawn they hung the head of Holofernes on the wall, and every man took his weapons, and they went out in companies to the passes in the mountains. ¹²And when the Assyrians saw them they sent word to their commanders, and they went to the generals and the captains and to all their officers. ¹³So they came to Holofernes' tent and said to the steward in charge of all his personal affairs, "Wake up our lord, for the slaves have been so bold as to come down against us to give battle, in order to be destroyed completely."

14 So Bagoas went in and knocked at the door of the tent, for he supposed that he was sleeping with Judith. ¹⁵But when no one answered, he opened it and went into the bedchamber and found him thrown down on the platform dead, with his head cut off and missing. ¹⁶And he cried out with a

---

14.1–10: Achior identifies the head of Holofernes and is converted to Judaism. 1–4: Judith suggests tactics which will put the enemy to flight with minimum effort by the Jewish forces. In the Latin version, v. 5 is omitted and vv. 6–7, more logically, precede vv. 1–4. 5: *Achior*, the Ammonite leader whom Holofernes had left to be destroyed with the Jews (5.5–6.21). The full irony of the situation is evident when one remembers that Achior had been told he would see that face again only on the day of Holofernes' vengeance (6.5). 10: The author seems to have forgotten that the conversion of an Ammonite to Judaism is strictly forbidden by the law (Dt.23.3).
14.11–19: The enemy discovers Holofernes' death. 11–13: As Judith had planned, the threatening movements of the Jews lead to the discovery of Holofernes' body.

loud voice and wept and groaned and shouted, and rent his garments. ¹⁷Then he went to the tent where Judith had stayed, and when he did not find her he rushed out to the people and shouted, ¹⁸"The slaves have tricked us! One Hebrew woman has brought disgrace upon the house of King Nebuchadnezzar! For look, here is Holofernes lying on the ground, and his head is not on him!"

19 When the leaders of the Assyrian army heard this, they rent their tunics and were greatly dismayed, and their loud cries and shouts arose in the midst of the camp.

15 When the men in the tents heard it, they were amazed at what had happened. ²Fear and trembling came over them, so that they did not wait for one another, but with one impulse all rushed out and fled by every path across the plain and through the hill country. ³Those who had camped in the hills around Bethulia also took to flight. Then the men of Israel, every one that was a soldier, rushed out upon them. ⁴And Uzziah sent men to Betomasthaim and Bebai and Choba and Kola, and to all the frontiers of Israel, to tell what had taken place and to urge all to rush out upon their enemies to destroy them. ⁵And when the Israelites heard it, with one accord they fell upon the enemy,ᵘ and cut them down as far as Choba. Those in Jerusalem and all the hill country also came, for they were told what had happened in the camp of the enemy; and those in Gilead and in Galilee outflanked them with great slaughter, even

beyond Damascus and its borders. ⁶The rest of the people of Bethulia fell upon the Assyrian camp and plundered it, and were greatly enriched. ⁷And the Israelites, when they returned from the slaughter, took possession of what remained, and the villages and towns in the hill country and in the plain got a great amount of booty, for there was a vast quantity of it.

8 Then Joakim the high priest, and the senate of the people of Israel who lived at Jerusalem, came to witness the good things which the Lord had done for Israel, and to see Judith and to greet her. ⁹And when they met her they all blessed her with one accord and said to her, "You are the exaltation of Jerusalem, you are the great glory of Israel, you are the great pride of our nation! ¹⁰You have done all this singlehanded; you have done great good to Israel, and God is well pleased with it. May the Almighty Lord bless you for ever!" And all the people said, "So be it!"

11 So all the people plundered the camp for thirty days. They gave Judith the tent of Holofernes and all his silver dishes and his beds and his bowls and all his furniture; and she took them and loaded her mule and hitched up her carts and piled the things on them.

12 Then all the women of Israel gathered to see her, and blessed her, and some of them performed a dance for her; and she took branches in her hands and gave them to the women who were with her; ¹³and they crowned

ᵘ Gk them

15.1–7: The Assyrians, fleeing in panic, are slaughtered and despoiled by the Jews. **3**: *Those who had camped in the hills* were the Edomites and Ammonites (7.18). **4**: As with so many place names in this book, *Betomasthaim and Bebai and Choba and Kola* have never been satisfactorily identified. **5**: *Gilead*, which was situated in the northern part of Transjordan, and *Galilee*, in the north of Palestine proper, lay on either flank of the enemy's northeastward flight through *Damascus* and back toward Assyria.

15.8–13: Judith is led in triumph to Jerusalem. **11**: The *thirty days* of plundering is obviously unrealistic. While the people apparently intend that Judith herself shall have Holofernes' treasure, she accepts the gifts only with the intention of dedicating them to God (16.19). **12**: *A dance*, compare 1 Sam.18.6; Ps.149.3–9. *Branches*, Ps.118.27; 1 Macc.13.51; 2 Macc.10.7. **13**: The reference to *olive wreaths* seems to indicate a late date for the book, for the custom is Greek, not Jewish. The destination of the procession is the temple in Jerusalem (16.18).

themselves with olive wreaths, she and those who were with her; and she went before all the people in the dance, leading all the women, while all the men of Israel followed, bearing their arms and wearing garlands and with songs on their lips.

16 Then Judith began this thanksgiving before all Israel, and all the people loudly sang this song of praise. ²And Judith said,

Begin a song to my God with
   tambourines,
   sing to my Lord with cymbals.
Raise to him a new psalm;ᵛ
   exalt him, and call upon his
   name.
³For God is the Lord who crushes
   wars;
   for he has delivered me out of
   the hands of my pursuers,
   and brought me into his camp,
   in the midst of the people.

⁴The Assyrian came down from the
   mountains of the north;
   he came with myriads of his
   warriors;
   their multitude blocked up the
   valleys,
   their cavalry covered the hills.
⁵He boasted that he would burn up
   my territory,
   and kill my young men with the
   sword,
   and dash my infants to the
   ground
   and seize my children as prey,
   and take my virgins as booty.

⁶But the Lord Almighty has foiled
   them
   by the hand of a woman.
⁷For their mighty one did not fall
   by the hands of the young
   men,

nor did the sons of the Titans
   smite him,
   nor did tall giants set upon him;
   but Judith the daughter of Merari
   undid him
   with the beauty of her
   countenance.

⁸For she took off her widow's
   mourning
   to exalt the oppressed in Israel.
She anointed her face with ointment
   and fastened her hair with a
   tiara
   and put on a linen gown to
   deceive him.
⁹Her sandal ravished his eyes,
   her beauty captivated his mind,
   and the sword severed his
   neck.
¹⁰The Persians trembled at her
   boldness,
   the Medes were daunted at her
   daring.

¹¹Then my oppressed people shouted
   for joy;
   my weak people shoutedʷ and
   the enemyˣ trembled;
   they lifted up their voices, and the
   enemyˣ were turned back.
¹²The sons of maidservants have
   pierced them through;
   they were wounded like the
   children of fugitives,
   they perished before the army of
   my Lord.

¹³I will sing to my God a new song:
O Lord, thou art great and
   glorious,
   wonderful in strength, invincible.

v Other authorities read *a psalm and praise*
w Other authorities read *feared*
x Gk *they*

16.1–17: Judith's thanksgiving psalm. In the book of Tobit (ch. 13) a prayer composed by Tobit occupies a similar position at the end of the story. It is Israel, personified as a woman, who sings the hymn; Judith herself is referred to only in the third person (v. 7). 2–3: A call to praise (compare Ex.15.21; Jg.5.2). 2: The phrase "a new" psalm (compare v. 13) is a cliché drawn from the Psalter (e.g. Pss.96.1; 98.1). 4–12: Description of the victory. 7: *Sons of the Titans* is Greek; perhaps the original had "sons of Rephaim" (compare Dt.3.11). 13–16: A general hymn of praise. 13: *I will sing . . . a new song*, Ps.144.9. The hymn begins in the next

¹⁴Let all thy creatures serve thee,
for thou didst speak, and they
were made.
Thou didst send forth thy Spirit,ʸ
and it formed them;
there is none that can resist thy
voice.
¹⁵For the mountains shall be shaken
to their foundations with the
waters;
at thy presence the rocks shall
melt like wax,
but to those who fear thee
thou wilt continue to show
mercy.
¹⁶For every sacrifice as a fragrant
offering is a small thing,
and all fat for burnt offerings to
thee is a very little thing,
but he who fears the Lord shall be
great for ever.

¹⁷Woe to the nations that rise up
against my people!
The Lord Almighty will take
vengeance on them in the day
of judgment;
fire and worms he will give to their
flesh;
they shall weep in pain for ever.

18 When they arrived at Jerusalem
they worshiped God. As soon as the
people were purified, they offered
their burnt offerings, their freewill
offerings, and their gifts. ¹⁹Judith
also dedicated to God all the vessels
of Holofernes, which the people had
given her; and the canopy which she
took for herself from his bedchamber
she gave as a votive offering to the
Lord. ²⁰So the people continued feasting in Jerusalem before the sanctuary
for three months, and Judith remained
with them.
21 After this every one returned
home to his own inheritance, and
Judith went to Bethulia, and remained
on her estate, and was honored in her
time throughout the whole country.
²²Many desired to marry her, but she
remained a widow all the days of her
life after Manasseh her husband died
and was gathered to his people. ²³She
became more and more famous, and
grew old in her husband's house, until
she was one hundred and five years old.
She set her maid free. She died in
Bethulia, and they buried her in the
cave of her husband Manasseh, ²⁴and
the house of Israel mourned for her
seven days. Before she died she distributed her property to all those who
were next of kin to her husband
Manasseh, and to her own nearest
kindred. ²⁵And no one ever again
spread terror among the people of
Israel in the days of Judith, or for a
long time after her death.

y Or *breath*

---

line. 14: Pss.33.6; †04.30. 16: *Every sacrifice . . . is a small thing;* to compare sacrifice un-
favorably with moral obedience ("to fear the Lord") is a commonplace of Old Testament religion, especially in later times (1 Sam.15.22; Pss.40.6–8; 50.8–15; 51.16–17; Hos.6.6; compare
Sir.34.18–19). 17: Concluding anathema on Israel's enemies (compare Jg.5.31). *Fire and
worms,* Is.66.24; Sir.7.17. As in Dan.12.2, the punishment of the wicked is eternal.
   16.18–20: A victory celebration in Jerusalem. 20: *Three months,* Syriac, "a month of days."
   16.21–25: Judith remains a widow and dies at a ripe old age. 24: She *distributed her property,*
according to the Mosaic law (Num.27.11).

THE ADDITIONS TO THE BOOK OF

ESTHER

Translated in the order of the Greek version of Esther but with the chapter and verse numbers of the King James Version

After the book of Esther had been translated from Hebrew into Greek, six Additions totaling 107 verses were incorporated at various points in the narrative. These supplementary sections were also included in the Old Latin translation, which was based on the Greek. In the fourth century A.D. Jerome, when making the Latin Vulgate Bible, removed all of the Additions and placed them at the end of the book of Esther. Rearranged in their proper chronological order, and with chapter and verse numbering which reflects Jerome's order, the six Additions are: 11.2–12.6, Mordecai saves the king's life; 13.1–7, The king's letter ordering the massacre of the Jews; 13.8–14, The prayers of Mordecai and Esther; 15.1–16, Esther risks her life to appeal to the king; 16.1–24, The king's second letter, denouncing Haman and directing his subjects to help the Jews; 10.4–11.1, Mordecai's dream interpreted and the book of Esther attested as genuine.

Some of the Additions were probably introduced by Lysimachus, an Alexandrian Jew who lived at Jerusalem and who translated the canonical book of Esther about 114 B.C. (11.1). Other Additions appear to have been inserted several years later, either by Lysimachus or by another person.

The purpose of the Additions is partly to make the story more vivid but chiefly to supply a religious element that is lacking in the canonical book of Esther, which never mentions God or religious practices. The Additions make frequent reference to God, emphasize his choice of Abraham and Israel, and give prominence to prayer. They occasionally contradict the canonical book of Esther, and have little or no historical value.

---

11 ²IN THE SECOND YEAR OF THE reign of Artaxerxes the Great, on the first day of Nisan, Mordecai the son of Jair, son of Shimei, son of Kish, of the tribe of Benjamin, had a dream. ³He was a Jew, dwelling in the city of Susa, a great man, serving in the court of the king. ⁴He was one of the captives whom Nebuchadnezzar king of Babylon had brought from Jerusalem with Jeconiah king of Judea. And this was his dream:

5 Behold, noise*a* and confusion, thunders and earthquake, tumult upon the earth! ⁶And behold, two great dragons came forward, both ready to fight, and they roared terribly. ⁷And at their roaring every nation prepared for war, to fight against the nation of the righteous. ⁸And behold, a day of darkness and gloom, tribulation and distress, affliction and great tumult upon the earth! ⁹And the whole righteous nation was troubled; they feared the evils that threatened them, and were ready to perish. ¹⁰Then they cried to God; and from their cry, as though from a tiny spring, there came a great river, with abundant water; ¹¹light came, and the sun rose, and the lowly were exalted and consumed those held in honor.

12 Mordecai saw in this dream what

a Or voices

11.2–12: Mordecai's dream of impending conflict between two *dragons* (Mordecai and Haman; compare 10.7) pictures how the *righteous nation* Israel, threatened with annihilation, is delivered by God. **2:** *Artaxerxes* is Xerxes I (486 [or 485]–465 B.C.). His *second year* was 485 [or 484] B.C. **4:** This verse dates Mordecai's captivity in 597 B.C. (2 Kg.24.15); v. 2 dates his dream 112 years later. **7:** *Nation of the righteous*, that is, the Jews. **10:** The expressions *tiny spring* and *great river* refer to Esther (10.6). **12:** Mordecai knows that the *dream* forecasts God's action, but does not yet grasp the interpretation given in 10.6–12.

God had determined to do, and after he awoke he had it on his mind and sought all day to understand it in every detail.

12 Now Mordecai took his rest in the courtyard with Gabatha and Tharra, the two eunuchs of the king who kept watch in the courtyard. ²He overheard their conversation and inquired into their purposes, and learned that they were preparing to lay hands upon Artaxerxes the king; and he informed the king concerning them. ³Then the king examined the two eunuchs, and when they confessed they were led to execution. ⁴The king made a permanent record of these things, and Mordecai wrote an account of them. ⁵And the king ordered Mordecai to serve in the court and rewarded him for these things. ⁶But Haman, the son of Hammedatha, a Bougaean, was in great honor with the king, and he sought to injure Mordecai and his people because of the two eunuchs of the king.

*Esther 1.1–3.13 follows
here in the Greek*

13 This is a copy of the letter: "The Great King, Artaxerxes, to the rulers of the hundred and twenty-seven provinces from India to Ethiopia and to the governors under them, writes thus:

2 "Having become ruler of many nations and master of the whole world, not elated with presumption of authority but always acting reasonably and with kindness, I have determined to settle the lives of my subjects in lasting tranquillity and, in order to make my kingdom peaceable and open to travel throughout all its extent, to re-establish the peace which all men desire.

3 "When I asked my counselors how this might be accomplished, Haman, who excels among us in sound judgment, and is distinguished for his unchanging good will and steadfast fidelity, and has attained the second place in the kingdom, ⁴pointed out to us that among all the nations in the world there is scattered a certain hostile people, who have laws contrary to those of every nation and continually disregard the ordinances of the kings, so that the unifying of the kingdom which we honorably intend cannot be brought about. ⁵We understand that this people, and it alone, stands constantly in opposition to all men, perversely following a strange manner of life and laws, and is ill-disposed to our government, doing all the harm they can so that our kingdom may not attain stability.

6 "Therefore we have decreed that those indicated to you in the letters of Haman, who is in charge of affairs and is our second father, shall all, with their wives and children, be utterly destroyed by the sword of their enemies, without pity or mercy, on the fourteenth day of the twelfth month, Adar, of this present year, ⁷so that those who have long been and are now hostile may in one day go down in violence to Hades, and leave our government completely secure and untroubled hereafter."

12.1–6: Mordecai saves the king's life when two eunuchs posted to protect the king plot instead to kill him. **5:** The king rewards Mordecai (in Est.6.3, however, it is said later that "nothing has been done for him"). **6:** It is implied that Haman shared in the plot and so resented Mordecai's action. *Bougaean* represents a Greek word which in Est.3.1 translates the Hebrew word Agagite (compare 1 Sam.15.8).

13.1–7: The king's letter ordering the massacre of the Jews. This addition follows Est.3.1–13, in which Haman has induced Artaxerxes to send a letter to all provinces of his kingdom, ordering complete annihilation of *a certain hostile people*, the Jews, because they observe *a strange manner of life and laws;* they observe the Mosaic law. **6:** *Our second father* implies that Haman ranked second only to the king. *Fourteenth day*, according to 16.20 (and Est.3.13; 8.12; 9.1) it was the thirteenth day. *Adar*, February-March.

Esther 3.14–4.17 follows here in the Greek

8 Then Mordecai[b] prayed to the Lord, calling to remembrance all the works of the Lord. He said:

9 "O Lord, Lord, King who rulest over all things, for the universe is in thy power and there is no one who can oppose thee if it is thy will to save Israel. [10]For thou hast made heaven and earth and every wonderful thing under heaven, [11]and thou art Lord of all, and there is no one who can resist thee, who art the Lord. [12]Thou knowest all things; thou knowest, O Lord, that it was not in insolence or pride or for any love of glory that I did this, and refused to bow down to this proud Haman. [13]For I would have been willing to kiss the soles of his feet, to save Israel! [14]But I did this, that I might not set the glory of man above the glory of God, and I will not bow down to any one but to thee, who art my Lord; and I will not do these things in pride. [15]And now, O Lord God and King, God of Abraham, spare thy people; for the eyes of our foes are upon us[c] to annihilate us, and they desire to destroy the inheritance that has been thine from the beginning. [16]Do not neglect thy portion, which thou didst redeem for thyself out of the land of Egypt. [17]Hear my prayer, and have mercy upon thy inheritance; turn our mourning into feasting, that we may live and sing praise to thy name, O Lord; do not destroy the mouth of those who praise thee."

18 And all Israel cried out mightily, for their death was before their eyes.

14 And Esther the queen, seized with deathly anxiety, fled to the Lord; [2]she took off her splendid apparel and put on the garments of distress and mourning, and instead of costly perfumes she covered her head with ashes and dung, and she utterly humbled her body, and every part that she loved to adorn she covered with her tangled hair. [3]And she prayed to the Lord God of Israel, and said:

"O my Lord, thou only art our King; help me, who am alone and have no helper but thee, [4]for my danger is in my hand. [5]Ever since I was born I have heard in the tribe of my family that thou, O Lord, didst take Israel out of all the nations, and our fathers from among all their ancestors, for an everlasting inheritance, and that thou didst do for them all that thou didst promise. [6]And now we have sinned before thee, and thou hast given us into the hands of our enemies, [7]because we glorified their gods. Thou art righteous, O Lord! [8]And now they are not satisfied that we are in bitter slavery, but they have covenanted with their idols [9]to abolish what thy mouth has ordained and to destroy thy inheritance, to stop the mouths of those who praise thee and to quench thy altar and the glory of thy house, [10]to open the mouths of the nations for the praise of vain idols, and to magnify for ever a mortal king. [11]O Lord, do not surrender thy scepter to what has no being; and do not let them mock at our downfall; but turn their plan against themselves, and make an example of the man who began this against us. [12]Remember, O Lord;

b Gk *he*   c Gk *for they are looking upon us*

13.8–14.19: The prayers of Mordecai and Esther. The canonical book of Esther never mentions God or prayer or calls Israel God's chosen people. These prayers are added to give the book a deeply religious tone. They call God *Lord* and *King* and *Lord God of Abraham*. He is righteous, has created and rules all things, has redeemed his people Israel from Egypt, answers prayer, and can save them now. **13.12–14:** Mordecai did not *bow down* to Haman, as the king's other servants did (Est.3.2), because such homage is due only to God. **18:** All Israel echoed Mordecai's prayer.

14.1–19: Esther joins in her people's prayer for deliverance. 1–2: She discards every trace of queenly attire and elegance and prays as an unworthy member of Israel. **6–7:** Her people's captivity is due to their sinfulness and idolatry while living in Palestine (Dan.9.16); Israel does not deserve to be saved. **11:** Esther begs God not to let pagan idols, that have no real existence, make thyself known in this time of our affliction, and give me courage, O King of the gods and Master of all dominion! ¹³Put eloquent speech in my mouth before the lion, and turn his heart to hate the man who is fighting against us, so that there may be an end of him and those who agree with him. ¹⁴But save us by thy hand, and help me, who am alone and have no helper but thee, O Lord. ¹⁵Thou hast knowledge of all things; and thou knowest that I hate the splendor of the wicked and abhor the bed of the uncircumcised and of any alien. ¹⁶Thou knowest my necessity—that I abhor the sign of my proud position, which is upon my head on the days when I appear in public. I abhor it like a menstruous rag, and I do not wear it on the days when I am at leisure. ¹⁷And thy servant has not eaten at Haman's table, and I have not honored the king's feast or drunk the wine of the libations. ¹⁸Thy servant has had no joy since the day that I was brought here until now, except in thee, O Lord God of Abraham. ¹⁹O God, whose might is over all, hear the voice of the despairing, and save us from the hands of evildoers. And save me from my fear!"

15 On the third day, when she ended her prayer, she took off the garments in which she had worshiped, and arrayed herself in splendid attire. ²Then, majestically adorned, after invoking the aid of the all-seeing God and Savior, she took her two maids with her, ³leaning daintily on one, ⁴while the other followed carrying her train. ⁵She was radiant with perfect beauty, and she looked happy, as if beloved, but her heart was frozen

with fear. ⁶When she had gone through all the doors, she stood before the king. He was seated on his royal throne, clothed in the full array of his majesty, all covered with gold and precious stones. And he was most terrifying.

7 Lifting his face, flushed with splendor, he looked at her in fierce anger. And the queen faltered, and turned pale and faint, and collapsed upon the head of the maid who went before her. ⁸Then God changed the spirit of the king to gentleness, and in alarm he sprang from his throne and took her in his arms until she came to herself. And he comforted her with soothing words, and said to her, ⁹"What is it, Esther? I am your brother. Take courage; ¹⁰you shall not die, for our law applies only to the people.^d Come near."

11 Then he raised the golden scepter and touched it to her neck; ¹²and he embraced her, and said, "Speak to me." ¹³And she said to him, "I saw you, my lord, like an angel of God, and my heart was shaken with fear at your glory. ¹⁴For you are wonderful, my lord, and your countenance is full of grace." ¹⁵But as she was speaking, she fell fainting. ¹⁶And the king was agitated, and all his servants sought to comfort her.

*Esther 5.3–8.12 follows
here in the Greek*

16 The following is a copy of this letter:
"The Great King, Artaxerxes, to the rulers of the provinces from India

d The meaning of the Greek text of this clause is obscure

rule the world. **16–18:** Esther says she hates her position as queen and wife of the king, and has never *eaten at Haman's table* or *honored the king's feast* (but compare Est.2.18, as well as Est.5.5 and 7.1).

15.1–16: Esther risks her life to appeal to the king. This passage expands and exaggerates Est.5.1–2. Any one who entered the king's presence without his summons or permission was put to death, unless the king forgave the intrusion (Est.4.11). To avoid personal danger and to induce the king to reverse his decree, Esther enhanced her charm by splendid attire; then with fearful heart she entered the king's presence. The king's initial anger was changed to tender concern by her fright and fainting; she then could plead for her people.

16.1–24: The king's second letter, denouncing Haman and directing his subjects to help the to Ethiopia, one hundred and twenty-seven satrapies, and to those who are loyal to our government, greeting.

2 "The more often they are honored by the too great kindness of their benefactors, the more proud do many men become. ³They not only seek to injure our subjects, but in their inability to stand prosperity they even undertake to scheme against their own benefactors. ⁴They not only take away thankfulness from among men, but, carried away by the boasts of those who know nothing of goodness, they suppose that they will escape the evil-hating justice of God, who always sees everything. ⁵And often many of those who are set in places of authority have been made in part responsible for the shedding of innocent blood, and have been involved in irremediable calamities, by the persuasion of friends who have been entrusted with the administration of public affairs, ⁶when these men by the false trickery of their evil natures beguile the sincere good will of their sovereigns.

7 "What has been wickedly accomplished through the pestilent behavior of those who exercise authority unworthily, can be seen not so much from the more ancient records which we hand on as from investigation of matters close at hand. ⁸For the future we will take care to render our kingdom quiet and peaceable for all men, ⁹by changing our methods and always judging what comes before our eyes with more equitable consideration. ¹⁰For Haman, the son of Hammedatha, a Macedonian (really an alien to the Persian blood, and quite devoid of our kindliness), having become our guest, ¹¹so far enjoyed the good will that we have for every nation that he was called our father and was continually bowed down to by all as the person second to the royal throne. ¹²But, unable to

restrain his arrogance, he undertook to deprive us of our kingdom and our life, ¹³and with intricate craft and deceit asked for the destruction of Mordecai, our savior and perpetual benefactor, and of Esther, the blameless partner of our kingdom, together with their whole nation. ¹⁴He thought that in this way he would find us undefended and would transfer the kingdom of the Persians to the Macedonians.

15 "But we find that the Jews, who were consigned to annihilation by this thrice accursed man, are not evildoers but are governed by most righteous laws ¹⁶and are sons of the Most High, the most mighty living God, who has directed the kingdom both for us and for our fathers in the most excellent order.

17 "You will therefore do well not to put in execution the letters sent by Haman the son of Hammedatha, ¹⁸because the man himself who did these things has been hanged at the gate of Susa, with all his household. For God, who rules over all things, has speedily inflicted on him the punishment he deserved.

19 "Therefore post a copy of this letter publicly in every place, and permit the Jews to live under their own laws. ²⁰And give them reinforcements, so that on the thirteenth day of the twelfth month, Adar, on that very day they may defend themselves against those who attack them at the time of their affliction. ²¹For God, who rules over all things, has made this day to be a joy to his chosen people instead of a day of destruction for them.

22 "Therefore you shall observe this with all good cheer as a notable day among your commemorative festivals, ²³so that both now and hereafter it may mean salvation for us and the loyal Persians, but that for those who

---

Jews. 10–14: Haman, already executed (Est.7.6–10), is (falsely) called a *Macedonian* trying to overthrow Persian rule. **15–16:** The king commends the Mosaic *laws*, praises the Jews, and recognizes God's rule. All Persian subjects are commanded to ignore Haman's letter (according to 13.1–6 it was really the king's letter) and help the Jews defend themselves on the thirteenth plot against us it may be a reminder of destruction.

24 "Every city and country, without exception, which does not act accordingly, shall be destroyed in wrath with spear and fire. It shall be made not only impassable for men, but also most hateful for all time to beasts and birds."

*This is followed in the Greek
by 8.13–10.3, where the Hebrew
Esther ends. The Greek version
adds the following:*

10 ⁴And Mordecai said, "These things have come from God. ⁵For I remember the dream that I had concerning these matters, and none of them has failed to be fulfilled. ⁶The tiny spring which became a river, and there was light and the sun and abundant water—the river is Esther, whom the king married and made queen. ⁷The two dragons are Haman and myself. ⁸The nations are those that gathered to destroy the name of the Jews. ⁹And my nation, this is Israel, who cried out to God and were saved.

The Lord has saved his people; the Lord has delivered us from all these evils; God has done great signs and wonders, which have not occurred among the nations. ¹⁰For this purpose he made two lots, one for the people of God and one for all the nations. ¹¹And these two lots came to the hour and moment and day of decision before God and among all the nations. ¹²And God remembered his people and vindicated his inheritance. ¹³So they will observe these days in the month of Adar, on the fourteenth and fifteenth of that month, with an assembly and joy and gladness before God, from generation to generation for ever among his people Israel."

11 ¹In the fourth year of the reign of Ptolemy and Cleopatra, Dositheus, who said that he was a priest and a Levite,ᵉ and Ptolemy his son brought to Egyptᶠ the preceding Letter of Purim, which they said was genuine and had been translated by Lysimachus the son of Ptolemy, one of the residents of Jerusalem.

*e Or priest, and Levitas
f Cn: Gk brought in*

day of Adar, the prescribed day of annihilation. **24:** Destruction faces every place which does not defend and respect the Jews.

　　10.4–11.1: Mordecai's dream interpreted and the book of Esther attested as genuine. This passage interprets the dream of 11.5–11. The threat to Israel is here ascribed not to one man, Haman, as in the canonical Esther, but to a general anti-Semitic hostility against the Jews. **13:** As in Est.9.20–22, Israel is to celebrate this deliverance annually. **11.1:** *Fourth year,* that is 114–113 B.C. *Letter of Purim,* a reference not merely to Mordecai's letter (Est.9.20–22) but to the entire book of Esther. *Lysimachus* is a Greek name; on his work of translating the Hebrew book of Esther into Greek, see the Introduction.

THE WISDOM OF SOLOMON

The Wisdom of Solomon, which the Latin Vulgate Bible entitles simply the book of Wisdom, professes to have been written by Solomon (7.1–14 and 8.17–9.18 recall Solomon's prayer for wisdom in 1 Kg.3.6–9 and 2 Chr.1.8–10). Internal evidence, however, indicates that the book was composed in Greek by an unknown Hellenistic Jew, probably at Alexandria during the latter part of the first century B.C. He no doubt used traditional wisdom material, which perhaps included for the earlier chapters material originally written in Hebrew and then translated into Greek. Such a supposition helps to account for the fact that the word "wisdom" occurs twenty-nine times in the first ten chapters, where the concept of wisdom is personified, while in the last nine chapters the word appears only twice and with a much vaguer meaning. Whatever oral or written sources were used, however, it is probable that one man wrote the entire book.

The literary style of the book varies from poetic patches of high lyrical quality to plodding and pedestrian prose. Impersonating King Solomon, the author promises reward and immortality to the righteous and warns the wicked of judgment (chs. 1–5); praises wisdom and describes her nature and works (chs. 6–9); illustrates wisdom's guidance of God's people from Adam to Moses and recalls God's judgment on the Egyptians and Canaanites (chs. 10–12); explains the origin and folly of idolatry (chs. 13–15); and contrasts God's plagues on the Egyptians and his kindness to his people (chs. 16–19).

LOVE RIGHTEOUSNESS, YOU RULERS OF the earth,
think of the Lord with uprightness,
and seek him with sincerity of heart;
2because he is found by those who do not put him to the test,
and manifests himself to those who do not distrust him.
3For perverse thoughts separate men from God,
and when his power is tested, it convicts the foolish;
4because wisdom will not enter a deceitful soul,
nor dwell in a body enslaved to sin.
5For a holy and disciplined spirit will flee from deceit,
and will rise and depart from foolish thoughts,
and will be ashamed at the approach of unrighteousness.

6For wisdom is a kindly spirit and will not free a blasphemer from the guilt of his words;
because God is witness of his inmost feelings,
and a true observer of his heart, and a hearer of his tongue.
7Because the Spirit of the Lord has filled the world,
and that which holds all things together knows what is said;
8therefore no one who utters unrighteous things will escape notice,
and justice, when it punishes, will not pass him by.
9For inquiry will be made into the counsels of an ungodly man,
and a report of his words will come to the Lord,
to convict him of his lawless deeds;
10because a jealous ear hears all things,
and the sound of murmurings does not go unheard.
11Beware then of useless murmuring,
and keep your tongue from slander;
because no secret word is without result,*a*

a Or *will go unpunished*

1.1–5.23: Commendation of wisdom as guide to happiness and immortality. 1.1–5: *Rulers* (compare 6.1) are urged to *love righteousness* and seek God. *Wisdom* dwells only in a sincere, holy, and disciplined soul.
   1.6–11: The ungodly will not escape punishment; God knows their unrighteous thoughts, words, and deeds and will judge them. **6:** *A kindly spirit,* literally "a spirit that loves man"; wisdom's concern for man's welfare will not tolerate blasphemous or unrighteous words.

and a lying mouth destroys the soul.

¹²Do not invite death by the error of
  your life,
  nor bring on destruction by the
    works of your hands;
¹³because God did not make death,
  and he does not delight in the death
    of the living.
¹⁴For he created all things that they
    might exist,
  and the generative forces*b* of the
    world are wholesome,
  and there is no destructive poison in
    them;
  and the dominion*c* of Hades is not
    on earth.
¹⁵For righteousness is immortal.

¹⁶But ungodly men by their words and
    deeds summoned death;*d*
  considering him a friend, they pined
    away,
  and they made a covenant with
    him,
  because they are fit to belong to his
    party.

2 For they reasoned unsoundly,
  saying to themselves,
  "Short and sorrowful is our life,
  and there is no remedy when a
    man comes to his end,
  and no one has been known to
    return from Hades.
²Because we were born by mere
    chance,
  and hereafter we shall be as though
    we had never been;
  because the breath in our nostrils is
    smoke,
  and reason is a spark kindled by the
    beating of our hearts.
³When it is extinguished, the body
    will turn to ashes,
  and the spirit will dissolve like
    empty air.

⁴Our name will be forgotten in time,
  and no one will remember our
    works;
  our life will pass away like the traces
    of a cloud,
  and be scattered like mist
  that is chased by the rays of the sun
  and overcome by its heat.
⁵For our allotted time is the passing
    of a shadow,
  and there is no return from our
    death,
  because it is sealed up and no one
    turns back.

⁶"Come, therefore, let us enjoy the
    good things that exist,
  and make use of the creation to the
    full as in youth.
⁷Let us take our fill of costly wine
    and perfumes,
  and let no flower of spring pass by
    us.
⁸Let us crown ourselves with
    rosebuds before they wither.
⁹Let none of us fail to share in our
    revelry,
  everywhere let us leave signs of
    enjoyment,
  because this is our portion, and this
    our lot.
¹⁰Let us oppress the righteous poor
    man;
  let us not spare the widow
  nor regard the gray hairs of the
    aged.
¹¹But let our might be our law of
    right,
  for what is weak proves itself to be
    useless.

¹²"Let us lie in wait for the righteous
    man,
  because he is inconvenient to us
    and opposes our actions;

b Or *the creatures*   *c* Or *palace*   *d* Gk *him*

1.12–15: God has made man for immortality. 15: Righteous living leads to immortality.
  1.16–2.24: The reasoning of the materialist or sensualist. 2.1–5: The ungodly say that life is
short, birth the result of *mere chance*, life without real meaning, and physical death the end of
existence. 6–9: They encourage one another to live lives of sensual satisfaction before death
snuffs out existence. 10–20: They urge one another to oppress *righteous*, helpless folk, whose
godly words and lives reproach them, and to persecute, torture, and kill those who call *God*

he reproaches us for sins against
the law,
and accuses us of sins against our
training.
¹³He professes to have knowledge of
God,
and calls himself a child*ᵉ* of the
Lord.
¹⁴He became to us a reproof of our
thoughts;
¹⁵the very sight of him is a burden
to us,
because his manner of life is unlike
that of others,
and his ways are strange.
¹⁶We are considered by him as
something base,
and he avoids our ways as
unclean;
he calls the last end of the
righteous happy,
and boasts that God is his father.
¹⁷Let us see if his words are true,
and let us test what will happen at
the end of his life;
¹⁸for if the righteous man is God's
son, he will help him,
and will deliver him from the hand
of his adversaries.
¹⁹Let us test him with insult and
torture,
that we may find out how gentle
he is,
and make trial of his forbearance.
²⁰Let us condemn him to a shameful
death,
for, according to what he says, he
will be protected."

²¹Thus they reasoned, but they were
led astray,
for their wickedness blinded them,
²²and they did not know the secret
purposes of God,
nor hope for the wages of holiness,

nor discern the prize for blameless
souls;
²³for God created man for
incorruption,
and made him in the image of his
own eternity,*ᶠ*
²⁴but through the devil's envy death
entered the world,
and those who belong to his party
experience it.

3 But the souls of the righteous
are in the hand of God,
and no torment will ever touch
them.
²In the eyes of the foolish they
seemed to have died,
and their departure was thought to
be an affliction,
³and their going from us to be their
destruction;
but they are at peace.
⁴For though in the sight of men they
were punished,
their hope is full of immortality.
⁵Having been disciplined a little,
they will receive great good,
because God tested them and found
them worthy of himself;
⁶like gold in the furnace he tried
them,
and like a sacrificial burnt offering
he accepted them.
⁷In the time of their visitation they
will shine forth,
and will run like sparks through
the stubble.
⁸They will govern nations and rule
over peoples,
and the Lord will reign over them
for ever.
⁹Those who trust in him will
understand truth,

e Or *servant*
f Other ancient authorities read *nature*

their *father.* **21–24:** Such false reasoning arises from *wickedness* and consequent failure to
know God. God made man in his image to be immortal, but *the devil's envy* (compare 1.16)
brought *death* into *the world.*
    3.1–9: The blessed estate of the righteous. Though affliction, suffering, and the early death of
the righteous may seem to be divine punishment, after death their *souls* are forever safe and at
peace with God; they enjoy sure *immortality.* **7–9:** Their discipline and testing will be followed
by a divine *visitation;* God will vindicate them, let them share in his rule over all peoples, and
give them understanding of his ways.

and the faithful will abide with him
in love,
because grace and mercy are upon
his elect,
and he watches over his holy ones.[g]

[10]But the ungodly will be punished
as their reasoning deserves,
who disregarded the righteous
man[h]
and rebelled against the Lord;
[11]for whoever despises wisdom and
instruction is miserable.
Their hope is vain, their labors are
unprofitable,
and their works are useless.
[12]Their wives are foolish, and their
children evil;
[13]their offspring are accursed.
For blessed is the barren woman
who is undefiled,
who has not entered into a sinful
union;
she will have fruit when God
examines souls.
[14]Blessed also is the eunuch whose
hands have done no lawless
deed,
and who has not devised wicked
things against the Lord;
for special favor will be shown him
for his faithfulness,
and a place of great delight in the
temple of the Lord.
[15]For the fruit of good labors is
renowned,
and the root of understanding does
not fail.
[16]But children of adulterers will not
come to maturity,
and the offspring of an unlawful
union will perish.
[17]Even if they live long they will be
held of no account,
and finally their old age will be
without honor.

[18]If they die young, they will have
no hope
and no consolation in the day of
decision.
[19]For the end of an unrighteous
generation is grievous.

4 Better than this is childlessness
with virtue,
for in the memory of virtue[i] is
immortality,
because it is known both by God
and by men.
[2]When it is present, men imitate[j]
it,
and they long for it when it has
gone;
and throughout all time it marches
crowned in triumph,
victor in the contest for prizes that
are undefiled.
[3]But the prolific brood of the
ungodly will be of no use,
and none of their illegitimate
seedlings will strike a deep root
or take a firm hold.
[4]For even if they put forth boughs
for a while,
standing insecurely they will be
shaken by the wind,
and by the violence of the winds
they will be uprooted.
[5]The branches will be broken off
before they come to maturity,
and their fruit will be useless,
not ripe enough to eat, and good
for nothing.
[6]For children born of unlawful
unions
are witnesses of evil against their
parents when God examines
them.[k]

g The text of this line is uncertain, and it is omitted here
  by some ancient authorities. Compare 4.15
h Or *what is right*   i Gk *it*
j Other ancient authorities read *honor*
k Gk *at their examination*

3.10–4.6: The punishment of the ungodly. The ungodly will meet a sad end, because disregarding what *the righteous* could teach them *they rebelled against the Lord* (v. 10). In Israel the possession of many children and a long life were often considered proof of God's favor. But the
barren woman and the *eunuch* are also blessed by God (vv. 13–14); a virtuous life is what counts,
for it alone assures *immortality*. The wicked, even if they *live long* (v. 17) and have many children
(4.3), have *no* justified *hope* for the future; their children usually die early, are *of no account*,
and attest their parents' wickedness (3.16–18).

⁷But the righteous man, though he
die early, will be at rest.
⁸For old age is not honored for
length of time,
nor measured by number of years;
⁹but understanding is gray hair for
men,
and a blameless life is ripe old age.

¹⁰There was one who pleased God
and was loved by him,
and while living among sinners he
was taken up.
¹¹He was caught up lest evil change
his understanding
or guile deceive his soul.
¹²For the fascination of wickedness
obscures what is good,
and roving desire perverts the
innocent mind.
¹³Being perfected in a short time, he
fulfilled long years;
¹⁴for his soul was pleasing to the
Lord,
therefore he took him quickly from
the midst of wickedness.
¹⁵Yet the peoples saw and did not
understand,
nor take such a thing to heart,
that God's grace and mercy are
with his elect,
and he watches over his holy ones.

¹⁶The righteous man who has died
will condemn the ungodly who
are living,
and youth that is quickly perfected*
will condemn the prolonged old
age of the unrighteous man.
¹⁷For they will see the end of the wise
man,
and will not understand what the
Lord purposed for him,
and for what he kept him safe.

¹⁸They will see, and will have
contempt for him,
but the Lord will laugh them to
scorn.
After this they will become
dishonored corpses,
and an outrage among the dead
for ever;
¹⁹because he will dash them
speechless to the ground,
and shake them from the
foundations;
they will be left utterly dry and
barren,
and they will suffer anguish,
and the memory of them will
perish.

²⁰They will come with dread when
their sins are reckoned up,
and their lawless deeds will convict
them to their face.

5 Then the righteous man will
stand with great confidence
in the presence of those who have
afflicted him,
and those who make light of his
labors.
²When they see him, they will be
shaken with dreadful fear,
and they will be amazed at his
unexpected salvation.
³They will speak to one another in
repentance,
and in anguish of spirit they will
groan, and say,
⁴"This is the man whom we once
held in derision
and made a byword of reproach—
we fools!
We thought that his life was
madness
and that his end was without honor.

l Or *ended*

4.7–19: The blessedness of the righteous despite premature death. The righteous man who dies
young has three advantages: he *will be at rest* with God (v. 7); *a blameless life* means more than
long years; and early death ends the danger of falling into evil. **10–15:** Enoch is an example of a
good man *perfected in a short time;* he lived 365 years, several hundred years less than any
other listed in Gen. ch. 5. **14–15:** *The peoples . . . did not understand* that God was good to
Enoch in removing him *from the midst of wickedness.* The wicked, who have contempt for such
good men, will be judged by God for their sins.
    4.20–5.14: The confusion and remorse of the ungodly at the judgment. 5.3–14: The wicked who
have persecuted the righteous will repent; they will see that their lawless, godless way has done

⁵Why has he been numbered among
the sons of God?
And why is his lot among the
saints?
⁶So it was we who strayed from the
way of truth,
and the light of righteousness did
not shine on us,
and the sun did not rise upon
us.
⁷We took our fill of the paths of
lawlessness and destruction,
and we journeyed through
trackless deserts,
but the way of the Lord we have
not known.
⁸What has our arrogance profited
us?
And what good has our boasted
wealth brought us?

⁹"All those things have vanished
like a shadow,
and like a rumor that passes
by;
¹⁰like a ship that sails through the
billowy water,
and when it has passed no trace
can be found,
nor track of its keel in the waves;
¹¹or as, when a bird flies through the
air,
no evidence of its passage is found;
the light air, lashed by the beat of
its pinions
and pierced by the force of its
rushing flight,
is traversed by the movement of its
wings,
and afterward no sign of its coming
is found there;
¹²or as, when an arrow is shot at a
target,
the air, thus divided, comes
together at once,
so that no one knows its pathway.

¹³So we also, as soon as we were born,
ceased to be,
and we had no sign of virtue to
show,
but were consumed in our
wickedness."
¹⁴Because the hope of the ungodly
man is like chaff*ᵐ* carried by
the wind,
and like a light hoarfrost*ⁿ* driven
away by a storm;
it is dispersed like smoke before
the wind,
and it passes like the remembrance
of a guest who stays but a day.

¹⁵But the righteous live for ever,
and their reward is with the Lord;
the Most High takes care of them.
¹⁶Therefore they will receive a
glorious crown
and a beautiful diadem from the
hand of the Lord,
because with his right hand he will
cover them,
and with his arm he will shield
them.
¹⁷The Lord*ᵒ* will take his zeal as his
whole armor,
and will arm all creation to repel*ᵖ*
his enemies;
¹⁸he will put on righteousness as a
breastplate,
and wear impartial justice as a
helmet;
¹⁹he will take holiness as an
invincible shield,
²⁰and sharpen stern wrath for a
sword,
and creation will join with him to
fight against the madmen.
²¹Shafts of lightning will fly with
true aim,

m Or *dust*
n Other authorities read *spider's web*
o Gk *He*
p Or *punish*

---

them no good. **5**: *Sons of God*, either angels, or God's holy people. **6–7**: *Way of truth . . . way of the Lord*, the way which the righteous chose and followed. **9**: *All those things*, namely their wealth and pleasure in tormenting the righteous, give no permanent pleasure or benefit; they vanish without a trace.

    5.15–23: The future bliss of the righteous and the misery of the ungodly at the judgment. 17–23: The Lord will put on his full armor (*breastplate, helmet, shield, sword;* compare Eph.6.11–17), and with *lightning*, hail, raging waves, rushing rivers, and mighty winds will fight and overwhelm

and will leap to the target as from a
well-drawn bow of clouds,
22and hailstones full of wrath will be
hurled as from a catapult;
the water of the sea will rage
against them,
and rivers will relentlessly
overwhelm them;
23a mighty wind will rise against them,
and like a tempest it will winnow
them away.
Lawlessness will lay waste the
whole earth,
and evil-doing will overturn the
thrones of rulers.

6 Listen therefore, O kings, and
understand;
learn, O judges of the ends of the
earth.
2Give ear, you that rule over
multitudes,
and boast of many nations.
3For your dominion was given you
from the Lord,
and your sovereignty from the Most
High,
who will search out your works and
inquire into your plans.
4Because as servants of his kingdom
you did not rule rightly,
nor keep the law,
nor walk according to the purpose
of God,
5he will come upon you terribly and
swiftly,
because severe judgment falls on
those in high places.
6For the lowliest man may be
pardoned in mercy,
but mighty men will be mightily
tested.
7For the Lord of all will not stand
in awe of any one,

nor show deference to greatness;
because he himself made both small
and great,
and he takes thought for all alike.
8But a strict inquiry is in store for
the mighty.
9To you then, O monarchs, my
words are directed,
that you may learn wisdom and not
transgress.
10For they will be made holy who
observe holy things in holiness,
and those who have been taught
them will find a defense.
11Therefore set your desire on my
words;
long for them, and you will be
instructed.

12Wisdom is radiant and unfading,
and she is easily discerned by those
who love her,
and is found by those who seek her.
13She hastens to make herself known
to those who desire her.
14He who rises early to seek her will
have no difficulty,
for he will find her sitting at his
gates.
15To fix one's thought on her is
perfect understanding,
and he who is vigilant on her
account will soon be free from
care,
16because she goes about seeking
those worthy of her,
and she graciously appears to them
in their paths,
and meets them in every thought.

17The beginning of wisdom*q* is the
most sincere desire for
instruction,

q Gk *Her beginning*

the wicked. **23:** The statement that *evil-doing* overthrows *thrones* recalls 1.1 and prepares for
6.1–11.
    6.1–9.18: Commendation of wisdom as the guide of life. 6.1–11: Further admonition to rulers,
who receive their authority from God and must answer to him for lawless, godless acts; for he
treats alike lowly and *mighty, small and great* (vv. 6–7). *Monarchs* need *wisdom,* and will receive
it if they desire it (vv. 9–11).
    6.12–16: Wisdom is easily found; for she seeks out those who desire to know her, and gives
them understanding (compare Pr. ch. 8, which also refers to rulers).
    6.17–20: The steps from the love of wisdom to immortality. A sorites (a form of logic much

and concern for instruction is love
of her,
¹⁸and love of her is the keeping of her
laws,
and giving heed to her laws is
assurance of immortality,
¹⁹and immortality brings one near to
God;
²⁰so the desire for wisdom leads to a
kingdom.

²¹Therefore if you delight in thrones
and scepters, O monarchs over
the peoples,
honor wisdom, that you may reign
for ever.
²²I will tell you what wisdom is and
how she came to be,
and I will hide no secrets from
you,
but I will trace her course from the
beginning of creation,
and make the knowledge of her
clear,
and I will not pass by the truth;
²³neither will I travel in the company
of sickly envy,
for envy^r does not associate with
wisdom.
²⁴A multitude of wise men is the
salvation of the world,
and a sensible king is the stability
of his people.
²⁵Therefore be instructed by my
words, and you will profit.

7 I also am mortal, like all men,
a descendant of the first-formed
child of earth;
and in the womb of a mother I was
molded into flesh,
²within the period of ten months,
compacted with blood,

from the seed of a man and the
pleasure of marriage.
³And when I was born, I began to
breathe the common air,
and fell upon the kindred earth,
and my first sound was a cry, like
that of all.
⁴I was nursed with care in swaddling
cloths.
⁵For no king has had a different
beginning of existence;
⁶there is for all mankind one
entrance into life, and a common
departure.

⁷Therefore I prayed, and
understanding was given me;
I called upon God, and the spirit
of wisdom came to me.
⁸I preferred her to scepters and
thrones,
and I accounted wealth as nothing
in comparison with her.
⁹Neither did I liken to her any
priceless gem,
because all gold is but a little sand
in her sight,
and silver will be accounted as clay
before her.
¹⁰I loved her more than health and
beauty,
and I chose to have her rather than
light,
because her radiance never ceases.
¹¹All good things came to me along
with her,
and in her hands uncounted wealth.
¹²I rejoiced in them all, because
wisdom leads them;
but I did not know that she was
their mother.
¹³I learned without guile and I impart

r Gk *this*

---

used by the Stoics), tracing the path from desire for *wisdom* to its results in *immortality* and
fellowship with God. **20:** *A kingdom,* God's eternal kingdom, in which rulers and others who
truly desire wisdom participate.

6.21–25: A promise of instruction in the nature of wisdom. The writer speaks in the name of
Solomon. **24:** The beneficial results of wisdom: *wise men* save *the world;* rulers guided by wisdom give *stability* to their *people.*

7.1–22a: Solomon received wisdom from God. 1–10: Recognizing his need for wisdom, Solomon *prayed* for and received it, and valued it above every other gift (1 Kg.3.5–15). **11–22a:**
With the gift of wisdom Solomon received *all good things, friendship with God,* and *unerring
knowledge* of the world, the heavenly bodies, and plant and animal life.

without grudging;
I do not hide her wealth,
14for it is an unfailing treasure for
    men;
those who get it obtain friendship
    with God,
commended for the gifts that come
    from instruction.

15May God grant that I speak with
    judgment
and have thoughts worthy of what
    I have received,
for he is the guide even of wisdom
and the corrector of the wise.
16For both we and our words are in
    his hand,
as are all understanding and skill
    in crafts.
17For it is he who gave me unerring
    knowledge of what exists,
to know the structure of the world
    and the activity of the elements;
18the beginning and end and middle
    of times,
the alternations of the solstices and
    the changes of the seasons,
19the cycles of the year and the
    constellations of the stars,
20the natures of animals and the
    tempers of wild beasts,
the powers of spirits[s] and the
    reasonings of men,
the varieties of plants and the
    virtues of roots;
21I learned both what is secret and
    what is manifest,
22for wisdom, the fashioner of all
    things, taught me.

For in her there is a spirit that is
    intelligent, holy,
unique, manifold, subtle,
mobile, clear, unpolluted,
distinct, invulnerable, loving the
    good, keen,

irresistible, 23beneficent, humane,
steadfast, sure, free from anxiety,
all-powerful, overseeing all,
and penetrating through all
    spirits
that are intelligent and pure and
    most subtle.
24For wisdom is more mobile than
    any motion;
because of her pureness she pervades
    and penetrates all things.
25For she is a breath of the power of
    God,
and a pure emanation of the glory
    of the Almighty;
therefore nothing defiled gains
    entrance into her.
26For she is a reflection of eternal
    light,
a spotless mirror of the working of
    God,
and an image of his goodness.
27Though she is but one, she can do
    all things,
and while remaining in herself, she
    renews all things;
in every generation she passes into
    holy souls
and makes them friends of God,
    and prophets;
28for God loves nothing so much
    as the man who lives with
    wisdom.
29For she is more beautiful than the
    sun,
and excels every constellation of
    the stars.
Compared with the light she is
    found to be superior,
30for it is succeeded by the night,
    but against wisdom evil does not
    prevail.

8 She reaches mightily from one
    end of the earth to the other,
and she orders all things well.

s Or *winds*

7.22b–8.1: The nature and beneficial works of wisdom. 22b–23: Wisdom's twenty-one (3 × 7)
attributes. **24:** She is a pure, freely moving, and all-penetrating *spirit*. **25–26:** She emanates
from God; his *power, glory,* purity, *light,* and *goodness* are expressed through her (compare
Jn.1.1–14; Heb.1.1–3). **7.27–8.1:** She is everywhere, *orders all things well,* and *can do all things.*
Her greatest work is to enter *holy souls* and make them *friends of God, and prophets. Evil* cannot
defeat her.

²I loved her and sought her from
my youth,
and I desired to take her for my
bride,
and I became enamored of her
beauty.
³She glorifies her noble birth by
living with God,
and the Lord of all loves her.
⁴For she is an initiate in the
knowledge of God,
and an associate in his works.
⁵If riches are a desirable possession
in life,
what is richer than wisdom who
effects all things?
⁶And if understanding is effective,
who more than she is fashioner of
what exists?
⁷And if any one loves righteousness,
her labors are virtues;
for she teaches self-control and
prudence,
justice and courage;
nothing in life is more profitable
for men than these.
⁸And if any one longs for wide
experience,
she knows the things of old, and
infers the things to come;
she understands turns of speech
and the solutions of riddles;
she has foreknowledge of signs and
wonders
and of the outcome of seasons and
times.
⁹Therefore I determined to take
her to live with me,
knowing that she would give me
good counsel
and encouragement in cares and
grief.
¹⁰Because of her I shall have glory
among the multitudes
and honor in the presence of the
elders, though I am young.
¹¹I shall be found keen in judgment,
and in the sight of rulers I shall be
admired.
¹²When I am silent they will wait
for me,
and when I speak they will give
heed;
and when I speak at greater length
they will put their hands on their
mouths.
¹³Because of her I shall have
immortality,
and leave an everlasting
remembrance to those who
come after me.
¹⁴I shall govern peoples,
and nations will be subject to me;
¹⁵dread monarchs will be afraid of
me when they hear of me;
among the people I shall show
myself capable, and courageous
in war.
¹⁶When I enter my house, I shall
find rest with her,
for companionship with her has
no bitterness,
and life with her has no pain, but
gladness and joy.
¹⁷When I considered these things
inwardly,
and thought upon them in my mind,
that in kinship with wisdom there
is immortality,
¹⁸and in friendship with her, pure
delight,
and in the labors of her hands,
unfailing wealth,
and in the experience of her
company, understanding,
and renown in sharing her words,
I went about seeking how to get
her for myself.
¹⁹As a child I was by nature
well endowed,

8.2–16: Solomon desires to take wisdom as his bride. 4–6: She is *God's associate in his works*,
and his agent in making all things (Pr.8.22–30; compare Jn.1.3; Col.1.16; Heb.1.2). **7:** She
teaches self-control, prudence, justice, and *courage,* which (according to Plato and the Stoics) are
the four cardinal virtues. **8:** She knows the past and the future, and so can give good counsel.
10–16: *Because of her* Solomon receives *honor* and respect, *immortality,* a great empire, *rest*
and *joy.*
**8.17–21: Considering all the benefits conferred by wisdom, Solomon prays to God to grant her
to him. 19–20:** The Platonic view of the soul as pre-existent.

and a good soul fell to my lot;
²⁰or rather, being good, I entered an
    undefiled body.
²¹But I perceived that I would not
    possess wisdom unless God gave
    her to me—
and it was a mark of insight to
    know whose gift she was—
so I appealed to the Lord and
    besought him,
and with my whole heart I said:

9 "O God of my fathers and Lord
    of mercy,
who hast made all things by thy
    word,
²and by thy wisdom hast formed
    man,
to have dominion over the creatures
    thou hast made,
³and rule the world in holiness and
    righteousness,
and pronounce judgment in
    uprightness of soul,
⁴give me the wisdom that sits by
    thy throne,
and do not reject me from among
    thy servants.
⁵For I am thy slave and the son of
    thy maidservant,
a man who is weak and short-lived,
with little understanding of
    judgment and laws;
⁶for even if one is perfect among
    the sons of men,
yet without the wisdom that comes
    from thee he will be regarded as
    nothing.
⁷Thou hast chosen me to be king of
    thy people
and to be judge over thy sons and
    daughters.
⁸Thou hast given command to build
    a temple on thy holy mountain,
and an altar in the city of thy
    habitation,
a copy of the holy tent which thou

didst prepare from the
    beginning.
⁹With thee is wisdom, who knows
    thy works
and was present when thou didst
    make the world,
and who understands what is
    pleasing in thy sight
and what is right according to thy
    commandments.
¹⁰Send her forth from the holy
    heavens,
and from the throne of thy glory
    send her,
that she may be with me and toil,
and that I may learn what is
    pleasing to thee.
¹¹For she knows and understands all
    things,
and she will guide me wisely in my
    actions
and guard me with her glory.
¹²Then my works will be acceptable,
and I shall judge thy people justly,
and shall be worthy of the throne*ᵗ*
    of my father.
¹³For what man can learn the
    counsel of God?
Or who can discern what the Lord
    wills?
¹⁴For the reasoning of mortals is
    worthless,
and our designs are likely to fail,
¹⁵for a perishable body weighs down
    the soul,
and this earthy tent burdens the
    thoughtful*ᵘ* mind.
¹⁶We can hardly guess at what is on
    earth,
and what is at hand we find with
    labor;
but who has traced out what is in
    the heavens?
¹⁷Who has learned thy counsel,
    unless thou hast given wisdom

t Gk thrones   u Or anxious

9.1–18: Solomon's prayer for wisdom (1 Kg.3.6–9). **1–2:** God *made all things* by his *word* and
wisdom (compare Jn.1.1–3); here "word" and "wisdom" are synonyms. **6–9:** The *king* needs
wisdom to learn God's will and to know what is right. **10–12:** Only by wisdom's presence and
guidance can the king govern well. **13–15:** Man's *perishable body*, though not called evil (compare 8.20), *burdens* and *hampers* the mind. **16–17:** Man knows even earthly things imperfectly;
only through *wisdom*, also called *the holy Spirit*, can he learn heavenly things (1 Cor.2.7–12).

and sent thy holy Spirit from on
high?
[18]And thus the paths of those on
earth were set right,
and men were taught what pleases
thee,
and were saved by wisdom."

10 Wisdom[v] protected the
first-formed father of the
world, when he alone had been
created;
she delivered him from his
transgression,
[2]and gave him strength to rule all
things.
[3]But when an unrighteous man
departed from her in his anger,
he perished because in rage he slew
his brother.
[4]When the earth was flooded
because of him, wisdom again
saved it,
steering the righteous man by a
paltry piece of wood.

[5]Wisdom[w] also, when the nations
in wicked agreement had been
confounded,
recognized the righteous man and
preserved him blameless before
God,
and kept him strong in the face
of his compassion for his child.

[6]Wisdom[w] rescued a righteous man
when the ungodly were
perishing;
he escaped the fire that descended
on the Five Cities.[x]
[7]Evidence of their wickedness still
remains:
a continually smoking wasteland,
plants bearing fruit that does not
ripen,
and a pillar of salt standing as a

monument to an unbelieving
soul.
[8]For because they passed wisdom
by,
they not only were hindered from
recognizing the good,
but also left for mankind a
reminder of their folly,
so that their failures could never
go unnoticed.

[9]Wisdom rescued from troubles
those who served her.
[10]When a righteous man fled from
his brother's wrath,
she guided him on straight paths;
she showed him the kingdom of
God,
and gave him knowledge of
angels;[y]
she prospered him in his labors,
and increased the fruit of his toil.
[11]When his oppressors were covetous,
she stood by him and made him
rich.
[12]She protected him from his
enemies,
and kept him safe from those who
lay in wait for him;
in his arduous contest she gave him
the victory,
so that he might learn that godliness
is more powerful than anything.

[13]When a righteous man was sold,
wisdom[z] did not desert him,
but delivered him from sin.
She descended with him into the
dungeon,
[14]and when he was in prison she did
not leave him,
until she brought him the scepter
of a kingdom

v Gk *She*   w Gk *She*
x Or *Pentapolis*
y Or *of holy things*
z Gk *she*

18: *Wisdom* guides, teaches, and saves men. The remaining chapters of the book tell how
wisdom saved Israel and her ancestors, though references to wisdom by name almost disappear
after ch. 10.
    10.1–12.27: Historical illustrations of the power of wisdom. 10.1–11.4: From Adam to Moses.
10.1–2: Adam (Gen.1.26–5.5). **3:** Cain (Gen.4.1–16). *Perished*, spiritual death. **4:** Noah (Gen.
5.28–9.29). **5:** Abraham (Gen.11.26–25.10). *Nations*, Gen.11.1–9. **6–8:** *A righteous man*, Lot
(Gen. ch. 19). **9–12:** Jacob (Gen.25.19–49.33, especially ch. 28). **13–14:** Joseph (Gen. chs.

and authority over his masters.
Those who accused him she showed
  to be false,
and she gave him everlasting honor.

15A holy people and blameless race
wisdom*a* delivered from a nation
  of oppressors.
16She entered the soul of a servant
  of the Lord,
and withstood dread kings with
  wonders and signs.
17She gave to holy men the reward
  of their labors;
she guided them along a marvelous
  way,
and became a shelter to them by
  day,
and a starry flame through the
  night.
18She brought them over the Red Sea,
and led them through deep waters;
19but she drowned their enemies,
and cast them up from the depth
  of the sea.
20Therefore the righteous plundered
  the ungodly;
they sang hymns, O Lord, to thy
  holy name,
and praised with one accord thy
  defending hand,
21because wisdom opened the mouth
  of the dumb,
and made the tongues of babes
  speak clearly.

11 Wisdom*a* prospered their works
by the hand of a holy prophet.
2They journeyed through an
  uninhabited wilderness,
and pitched their tents in untrodden
  places.
3They withstood their enemies and
  fought off their foes.

4When they thirsted they called
  upon thee,
and water was given them out of
  flinty rock,
and slaking of thirst from hard
  stone.
5For through the very things by
  which their enemies were
  punished,
they themselves received benefit
  in their need.
6Instead of the fountain of an
  ever-flowing river,
stirred up and defiled with blood
7in rebuke for the decree to slay the
  infants,
thou gavest them abundant water
  unexpectedly,
8showing by their thirst at that time
how thou didst punish their
  enemies.
9For when they were tried, though
  they were being disciplined in
  mercy,
they learned how the ungodly were
  tormented when judged in wrath.
10For thou didst test them as a father
  does in warning,
but thou didst examine the
  ungodly*b* as a stern king does in
  condemnation.
11Whether absent or present, they
  were equally distressed,
12for a twofold grief possessed them,
and a groaning at the memory of
  what had occurred.
13For when they heard that through
  their own punishments
the righteous*c* had received benefit,
they perceived it was the
  Lord's doing.
14For though they had mockingly
  rejected him who long before

a Gk *she*   *b* Gk *those*   *c* Gk *they*

37–50). **15–21:** Through Moses wisdom delivered Israel from Egypt (Ex.1.1–15.21, especially chs. 12–15).

    11.1–12.2: The contrast between the fortunes of Israel and Egypt. 11.1–4: Wisdom guided Israel through the wilderness (Ex.15.22–17.16). **1:** *A holy prophet,* that is, Moses (Dt.18.15,18).

    11.5–14: How water was used to bless the Israelites and to punish the Egyptians. Israel's thirst was God's discipline in *mercy* (v. 9); *water* from the *rock* (vv. 4, 7) showed that God could help in every need. But the Egyptians were *judged in wrath;* the Nile was turned to *blood* (vv. 6–9). They suffered *twofold grief:* the *memory* of their own punishment and the knowledge that through it Israel had been blessed and Moses vindicated (vv. 11–14).

had been cast out and exposed,
at the end of the events they
marveled at him,
for their thirst was not like that of
the righteous.

¹⁵In return for their foolish and
wicked thoughts,
which led them astray to worship
irrational serpents and worthless
animals,
thou didst send upon them a
multitude of irrational creatures
to punish them,
¹⁶that they might learn that one is
punished by the very things by
which he sins.
¹⁷For thy all-powerful hand,
which created the world out of
formless matter,
did not lack the means to send
upon them a multitude of bears,
or bold lions,
¹⁸or newly created unknown beasts
full of rage,
or such as breathe out fiery
breath,
or belch forth a thick pall of
smoke,
or flash terrible sparks from their
eyes;
¹⁹not only could their damage
exterminate men,*d*
but the mere sight of them could
kill by fright.
²⁰Even apart from these, men*e* could
fall at a single breath
when pursued by justice
and scattered by the breath of thy
power.
But thou hast arranged all things
by measure and number and
weight.

²¹For it is always in thy power to
show great strength,
and who can withstand the might
of thy arm?
²²Because the whole world before
thee is like a speck that tips the
scales,
and like a drop of morning dew
that falls upon the ground.
²³But thou art merciful to all, for
thou canst do all things,
and thou dost overlook men's sins,
that they may repent.
²⁴For thou lovest all things that
exist,
and hast loathing for none of the
things which thou hast made,
for thou wouldst not have made
anything if thou hadst hated
it.
²⁵How would anything have endured
if thou hadst not willed it?
Or how would anything not called
forth by thee have been
preserved?
²⁶Thou sparest all things, for they
are thine, O Lord who lovest the
living.

12 For thy immortal spirit is in
all things.
²Therefore thou dost correct little
by little those who trespass,
and dost remind and warn them
of the things wherein they sin,
that they may be freed from
wickedness and put their trust
in thee, O Lord.

³Those who dwelt of old in thy holy
land
⁴thou didst hate for their detestable
practices,
their works of sorcery and unholy
rites,

d Gk *them*
e Gk *they*

11.15–20: **The plague of frogs and lice.** The wicked man is *punished by the very things by which
he sins;* the Egyptians worshiped *irrational creatures,* and were punished by frogs, flies, lice,
locusts (Ex. chs. 8 and 10). But God was merciful; he could have sent *bears, lions,* or newly
created fierce *beasts,* or killed the Egyptians by *a single breath.*

11.21–12.2: **God's universal love.** God is almighty, but he is *merciful to all,* withholding
punishment to give time to *repent.* He loves and preserves *all,* and corrects *little by little those
who trespass* in order to lead them to repentance.

12.3–11: **An example of God's patience and mercy.** He hated the pagan peoples of Canaan

⁵their merciless slaughter*ᶠ* of
  children,
and their sacrificial feasting on
  human flesh and blood.
These initiates from the midst of
  a heathen cult,*ᵍ*
⁶these parents who murder helpless
  lives,
thou didst will to destroy by the
  hands of our fathers,
⁷that the land most precious of all
  to thee
might receive a worthy colony of
  the servants*ʰ* of God.
⁸But even these thou didst spare,
  since they were but men,
and didst send wasps*ⁱ* as
  forerunners of thy army,
to destroy them little by little,
⁹though thou wast not unable to
  give the ungodly into the hands
  of the righteous in battle,
or to destroy them at one blow by
  dread wild beasts or thy stern
  word.
¹⁰But judging them little by little
  thou gavest them a chance to
  repent,
though thou wast not unaware
  that their origin*ʲ* was evil
and their wickedness inborn,
and that their way of thinking
  would never change.
¹¹For they were an accursed race
  from the beginning,
and it was not through fear of any
  one that thou didst leave them
  unpunished for their sins.

¹²For who will say, "What hast thou
  done?"
Or who will resist thy judgment?
Who will accuse thee for the
  destruction of nations which
  thou didst make?
Or who will come before thee to

plead as an advocate for
  unrighteous men?
¹³For neither is there any god
  besides thee, whose care is for
  all men,*ᵏ*
to whom thou shouldst prove that
  thou hast not judged unjustly;
¹⁴nor can any king or monarch
  confront thee about those whom
  thou hast punished.
¹⁵Thou art righteous and rulest all
  things righteously,
deeming it alien to thy power
to condemn him who does not
  deserve to be punished.
¹⁶For thy strength is the source of
  righteousness,
and thy sovereignty over all causes
  thee to spare all.
¹⁷For thou dost show thy strength
  when men doubt the
  completeness of thy power,
and dost rebuke any insolence
  among those who know it.*ˡ*
¹⁸Thou who art sovereign in strength
  dost judge with mildness,
and with great forbearance thou
  dost govern us;
for thou hast power to act whenever
  thou dost choose.

¹⁹Through such works thou hast
  taught thy people
that the righteous man must be
  kind,
and thou hast filled thy sons with
  good hope,
because thou givest repentance for
  sins.
²⁰For if thou didst punish with such
  great care and indulgence*ᵐ*

f Cn: Gk *slaughterers*
g The Greek text of this line is uncertain
h Or *children*   *i* Or *hornets*
j Or *nature*   *k* Or *all things*
l The Greek text of this line is uncertain
m Some ancient authorities omit *and indulgence;* others
  read *and entreaty*

(Ex.23.23; Dt.7.1) for their evil *practices;* but he judged them *little by little* (v. 8; compare
Ex.23.29–30), giving them *a chance to repent* (v. 10; compare 2 Esd.9.11; Heb.12.17).
  12.12–18: God's supreme power delights in benevolence. God, *sovereign,* all-powerful, is
answerable to no one; he is *righteous,* condemns no man unjustly, and judges with *mildness*
and *forbearance.* He cares *for all men* (v. 13) and rules *all things* (v. 15).
  12.19–22: God's mercy is an example to Israel. Israel may think that God has *judged* them

the enemies of thy servants[n] and
those deserving of death,
granting them time and opportunity
to give up their wickedness,
21with what strictness thou hast
judged thy sons,
to whose fathers thou gavest oaths
and covenants full of good
promises!
22So while chastening us thou
scourgest our enemies ten
thousand times more,
so that we may meditate upon thy
goodness when we judge,
and when we are judged we may
expect mercy.

23Therefore those who in folly of
life lived unrighteously
thou didst torment through their
own abominations.
24For they went far astray on the
paths of error,
accepting as gods those animals
which even their enemies[o]
despised;
they were deceived like foolish
babes.
25Therefore, as to thoughtless
children,
thou didst send thy judgment to
mock them.
26But those who have not heeded
the warning of light rebukes
will experience the deserved
judgment of God.
27For when in their suffering they
became incensed
at those creatures which they had
thought to be gods, being
punished by means of them,
they saw and recognized as the true
God him whom they had before
refused to know.

Therefore the utmost condemnation
came upon them.

13 For all men who were ignorant
of God were foolish by nature;
and they were unable from the
good things that are seen to
know him who exists,
nor did they recognize the craftsman
while paying heed to his
works;
2but they supposed that either fire
or wind or swift air,
or the circle of the stars, or
turbulent water,
or the luminaries of heaven were
the gods that rule the world.
3If through delight in the beauty
of these things men[p] assumed
them to be gods,
let them know how much better
than these is their Lord,
for the author of beauty created
them.
4And if men[p] were amazed at their
power and working,
let them perceive from them
how much more powerful is he
who formed them.
5For from the greatness and beauty
of created things
comes a corresponding perception
of their Creator.
6Yet these men are little to be
blamed,
for perhaps they go astray
while seeking God and desiring to
find him.
7For as they live among his works
they keep searching,
and they trust in what they see,
because the things that are seen
are beautiful.

n Or *children*   *o* Gk *they*   *p* Gk *they*

strictly (v. 21), but he *scourges* Israel's *enemies* far *more;* he chastens Israel in *mercy* and for
their own good.
  12.23–27: Further comments on the punishment of the Egyptians (in accord with the principle
set forth in 11.16). The Egyptians were tormented by the *animals* that they worshiped. **27:**
Though the Egyptians *recognized* Israel's God as *the true God,* they refused to let Israel go.
The utmost condemnation, i.e. the death of their first-born sons.
  **13.1–15.17: The origin and folly of idolatry. 13.1–9: Nature-worship is the least culpable form
of false worship.** *Ignorant, foolish* men, misled by the *beauty* and *power* of *created things,* thought
them *gods.* **6–7:** The author partly excuses such idolatry as arising from honest search for God.

⁸Yet again, not even they are to be
  excused;
⁹for if they had the power to know
  so much
    that they could investigate the
    world,
  how did they fail to find sooner
    the Lord of these things?

¹⁰But miserable, with their hopes set
  on dead things, are the men
  who give the name "gods" to the
    works of men's hands,
  gold and silver fashioned with
    skill,
  and likenesses of animals,
  or a useless stone, the work of an
    ancient hand.
¹¹A skilled woodcutter may saw down
  a tree easy to handle
  and skilfully strip off all its bark,
  and then with pleasing workmanship
  make a useful vessel that serves
    life's needs,
¹²and burn the castoff pieces of his
    work
  to prepare his food, and eat his fill.
¹³But a castoff piece from among
    them, useful for nothing,
  a stick crooked and full of knots,
  he takes and carves with care in his
    leisure,
  and shapes it with skill gained in
    idleness;*q*
  he forms it like the image of a man,
¹⁴or makes it like some worthless
    animal,
  giving it a coat of red paint and
    coloring its surface red
  and covering every blemish in it
    with paint;
¹⁵then he makes for it a niche that
    befits it,
  and sets it in the wall, and fastens
    it there with iron.
¹⁶So he takes thought for it, that it
  may not fall,

because he knows that it cannot
  help itself,
for it is only an image and has
  need of help.
¹⁷When he prays about possessions
  and his marriage and children,
he is not ashamed to address a
  lifeless thing.
¹⁸For health he appeals to a thing
  that is weak;
for life he prays to a thing that is
  dead;
for aid he entreats a thing that is
  utterly inexperienced;
for a prosperous journey, a thing
  that cannot take a step;
¹⁹for money-making and work and
  success with his hands
he asks strength of a thing whose
  hands have no strength.

14 Again, one preparing to sail
  and about to voyage over
  raging waves
calls upon a piece of wood more
  fragile than the ship which
  carries him.
²For it was desire for gain that
  planned that vessel,
and wisdom was the craftsman who
  built it;
³but it is thy providence, O Father,
  that steers its course,
because thou hast given it a path
  in the sea,
and a safe way through the waves,
⁴showing that thou canst save from
  every danger,
so that even if a man lacks skill, he
  may put to sea.
⁵It is thy will that the works of thy
  wisdom should not be without
  effect;
therefore men trust their lives even
  to the smallest piece of wood,
and passing through the billows on

q Other authorities read with intelligent skill

8–9: Yet it cannot be *excused;* such idolaters should have discerned *the Lord* of created things.
   13.10–19: The folly of image-worship (compare the Letter of Jeremiah). A *woodcutter* fells a
tree, makes of some knotty *castoff* piece an *image* of *man* or *animal,* and calls it his god, although
it cannot stand or act and has no life.
   14.1–7: The folly of the seafarer who trusts in a wooden image on a ship's prow. Though men

a raft they come safely to land.
⁶For even in the beginning, when
arrogant giants were perishing,
the hope of the world took refuge
on a raft,
and guided by thy hand left to the
world the seed of a new
generation.
⁷For blessed is the wood by which
righteousness comes.

⁸But the idol made with hands is
accursed, and so is he who made
it;
because he did the work, and the
perishable thing was named a
god.
⁹For equally hateful to God are the
ungodly man and his
ungodliness,
¹⁰for what was done will be punished
together with him who did it.
¹¹Therefore there will be a visitation
also upon the heathen idols,
because, though part of what God
created, they became an
abomination,
and became traps for the souls of
men
and a snare to the feet of the
foolish.

¹²For the idea of making idols was
the beginning of fornication,
and the invention of them was the
corruption of life,
¹³for neither have they existed from
the beginning
nor will they exist for ever.
¹⁴For through the vanity of men
they entered the world,
and therefore their speedy end has
been planned.
¹⁵For a father, consumed with grief
at an untimely bereavement,

made an image of his child, who
had been suddenly taken from
him;
and he now honored as a god
what was once a dead human
being,
and handed on to his dependents
secret rites and initiations.
¹⁶Then the ungodly custom, grown
strong with time, was kept as a
law,
and at the command of monarchs
graven images were worshiped.
¹⁷When men could not honor
monarchs*ʳ* in their presence,
since they lived at a distance,
they imagined their appearance
far away,
and made a visible image of the
king whom they honored,
so that by their zeal they might
flatter the absent one as though
present.
¹⁸Then the ambition of the craftsman
impelled
even those who did not know the
king to intensify their worship.
¹⁹For he, perhaps wishing to please
his ruler,
skilfully forced the likeness to take
more beautiful form,
²⁰and the multitude, attracted by the
charm of his work,
now regarded as an object of
worship the one whom shortly
before they had honored as a
man.
²¹And this became a hidden trap for
mankind,
because men, in bondage to
misfortune or to royal authority,
bestowed on objects of stone or
wood the name that ought not
to be shared.

r Gk them

planned the vessel, a safe voyage is God's doing. **6:** God saved Noah and his family in the ark
(Gen. chs. 6–8). **7:** *The wood* refers not (as some have thought) to the cross of Christ but to
Noah's ark, which carried forward God's righteous will.
    14.8–11: Idolaters will be punished. 9: Contrast 11.24–26.
    14.14–21: The origins of idolatry. A grief-stricken *father* made and *worshiped* an *image* of his
dead child (vv. 15–16). Subjects living at a distance made and worshiped images of their king
(v. 17); moreover skilled craftsmen made the image *more beautiful* than the king (vv. 18–20).
(Euhemerus, about 300 B.C., taught that all gods were deified mortals.)

22Afterward it was not enough for
    them to err about the knowledge
    of God,
but they live in great strife due to
    ignorance,
and they call such great evils
    peace.
23For whether they kill children in
    their initiations, or celebrate
    secret mysteries,
or hold frenzied revels with strange
    customs,
24they no longer keep either their
    lives or their marriages pure,
but they either treacherously kill
    one another, or grieve one
    another by adultery,
25and all is a raging riot of blood and
    murder, theft and deceit,
    corruption, faithlessness, tumult,
    perjury,
26confusion over what is good,
    forgetfulness of favors,
pollution of souls, sex perversion,
disorder in marriage, adultery, and
    debauchery.
27For the worship of idols not to be
    named
is the beginning and cause and end
    of every evil.
28For their worshipers*s* either rave
    in exultation, or prophesy lies,
or live unrighteously, or readily
    commit perjury;
29for because they trust in lifeless
    idols
they swear wicked oaths and
    expect to suffer no harm.
30But just penalties will overtake
    them on two counts:
because they thought wickedly of
    God in devoting themselves to
    idols,
and because in deceit they swore
    unrighteously through contempt
    for holiness.

31For it is not the power of the things
    by which men swear,*t*
but the just penalty for those who
    sin,
that always pursues the
    transgression of the unrighteous.

15 But thou, our God, art kind
    and true,
patient, and ruling all things*u* in
    mercy.
2For even if we sin we are thine,
    knowing thy power;
but we will not sin, because we
    know that we are accounted
    thine.
3For to know thee is complete
    righteousness,
and to know thy power is the root
    of immortality.
4For neither has the evil intent of
    human art misled us,
nor the fruitless toil of painters,
a figure stained with varied colors,
5whose appearance arouses yearning
    in fools,
so that they desire*v* the lifeless
    form of a dead image.
6Lovers of evil things and fit for
    such objects of hope*w*
are those who either make or
    desire or worship them.

7For when a potter kneads the soft
    earth
and laboriously molds each vessel
    for our service,
he fashions out of the same clay
both the vessels that serve clean uses
and those for contrary uses, making
    all in like manner;
but which shall be the use of each
    of these
the worker in clay decides.

s Gk *they*   t Or *of the oaths men swear*
u Or *ruling the universe*
v Gk *and he desires*   w Gk *such hopes*

14.22–31: The evil results of idolatry (Rom.1.24–32). Ignorance of God, *strife*, moral wrong, and perversion (v. 26), will bring sure punishment.
15.1–17: The contrast between the worshipers of the true God and idolaters. 1–5: The purifying influence of the worship of the true God on the life of Israel. **3:** *To know* God is *righteousness* and true life (compare Jn.17.3). **6–17:** The folly and wickedness of making and worshiping clay idols. For financial profit *a potter* molds from one mass of *clay* both useful *vessels* and

8With misspent toil, he forms a
    futile god from the same clay—
this man who was made of earth
    a short time before
and after a little while goes to the
    earth from which he was taken,
when he is required to return the
    soul that was lent him.
9But he is not concerned that he is
    destined to die
or that his life is brief,
but he competes with workers in
    gold and silver,
and imitates workers in copper;
and he counts it his glory that he
    molds counterfeit gods.
10His heart is ashes, his hope is
    cheaper than dirt,
and his life is of less worth than
    clay,
11because he failed to know the one
    who formed him
and inspired him with an active
    soul
and breathed into him a living
    spirit.
12But he[x] considered our existence
    an idle game,
and life a festival held for profit,
for he says one must get money
    however one can, even by base
    means.
13For this man, more than all others,
    knows that he sins
when he makes from earthy matter
    fragile vessels and graven images.

14But most foolish, and more
    miserable than an infant,
are all the enemies who oppressed
    thy people.
15For they thought that all their
    heathen idols were gods,
though these have neither the use
    of their eyes to see with,
nor nostrils with which to draw
    breath,

nor ears with which to hear,
nor fingers to feel with,
and their feet are of no use for
    walking.
16For a man made them,
and one whose spirit is borrowed
    formed them;
for no man can form a god which
    is like himself.
17He is mortal, and what he makes
    with lawless hands is dead,
for he is better than the objects he
    worships,
since[y] he has life, but they never
    have.

18The enemies of thy people[z] worship
    even the most hateful animals,
which are worse than all others,
    when judged by their lack of
    intelligence;
19and even as animals they are not
    so beautiful in appearance that
    one would desire them,
but they have escaped both the
    praise of God and his blessing.

16 Therefore those men were
    deservedly punished through
    such creatures,
and were tormented by a multitude
    of animals.
2Instead of this punishment thou
    didst show kindness to thy
    people,
and thou didst prepare quails to
    eat,
a delicacy to satisfy the desire of
    appetite;
3in order that those men, when
    they desired food,
might lose the least remnant of
    appetite[a]
because of the odious creatures
    sent to them,

x Other authorities read *they*
y Other authorities read *of which*
z Gk *They*
a Gk *loathe the necessary appetite*

---

counterfeit gods; cheap imitations of gold, silver, and copper *images.* **14–17:** The stupidity of
Israel's *enemies,* who worship useless, lifeless images.
　　15.18–19.22: The contrast between God's treatment of the Egyptians and of the Israelites
(compare 11.1–14). **16.1–4:** The Egyptians, *tormented* by the *animals* they worshiped (Ex. chs. 8
and 10), lost all appetite (v. 3); the Israelites, after brief hunger, enjoyed *quails* (Num. ch. 11).

while thy people,[b] after suffering
want a short time,
might partake of delicacies.
⁴For it was necessary that upon
those oppressors inexorable want
should come,
while to these it was merely shown
how their enemies were being
tormented.

⁵For when the terrible rage of wild
beasts came upon thy people[c]
and they were being destroyed by
the bites of writhing serpents,
thy wrath did not continue to the
end;
⁶they were troubled for a little
while as a warning,
and received a token of deliverance
to remind them of thy law's
command.
⁷For he who turned toward it was
saved, not by what he saw,
but by thee, the Savior of all.
⁸And by this also thou didst
convince our enemies
that it is thou who deliverest from
every evil.
⁹For they were killed by the bites
of locusts and flies,
and no healing was found for them,
because they deserved to be
punished by such things;
¹⁰but thy sons were not conquered
even by the teeth of venomous
serpents,
for thy mercy came to their help
and healed them.
¹¹To remind them of thy oracles
they were bitten,
and then were quickly delivered,
lest they should fall into deep
forgetfulness
and become unresponsive[d] to thy
kindness.
¹²For neither herb nor poultice cured
them,
but it was thy word, O Lord,

which heals all men.
¹³For thou hast power over life and
death;
thou dost lead men down to the
gates of Hades and back again.
¹⁴A man in his wickedness kills
another,
but he cannot bring back the
departed spirit,
nor set free the imprisoned soul.

¹⁵To escape from thy hand is
impossible;
¹⁶for the ungodly, refusing to know
thee,
were scourged by the strength of
thy arm,
pursued by unusual rains and hail
and relentless storms,
and utterly consumed by fire.
¹⁷For—most incredible of all—in
the water, which quenches all
things,
the fire had still greater effect,
for the universe defends the
righteous.
¹⁸At one time the flame was
restrained,
so that it might not consume the
creatures sent against the
ungodly,
but that seeing this they might
know
that they were being pursued by
the judgment of God;
¹⁹and at another time even in the
midst of water it burned more
intensely than fire,
to destroy the crops of the
unrighteous land.
²⁰Instead of these things thou didst
give thy people the food of
angels,
and without their toil thou didst
supply them from heaven with
bread ready to eat,

b. Gk *they*   *c* Gk *them*
d The meaning of the Greek is obscure

5–14: The Egyptians were killed by *bites of locusts and flies* (not mentioned in Exodus); Israel,
bitten by serpents (Num.21.6–9), suffered briefly as a *warning* (vv. 6,11), and were *quickly*
healed by God's *word* (vv. 11–12). God has *power over life and death* (vv. 13–14).

16.15–29: How fire from God punished the Egyptians. **20:** The food of angels is manna,

providing every pleasure and suited
to every taste.
21For thy sustenance manifested thy
sweetness toward thy children;
and the bread, ministering*e* to the
desire of the one who took it,
was changed to suit every one's
liking.
22Snow and ice withstood fire without
melting,
so that they might know that the
crops of their enemies
were being destroyed by the fire
that blazed in the hail
and flashed in the showers of
rain;
23whereas the fire,*f* in order that the
righteous might be fed,
even forgot its native power.

24For the creation, serving thee who
hast made it,
exerts itself to punish the
unrighteous,
and in kindness relaxes on behalf
of those who trust in thee.
25Therefore at that time also, changed
into all forms,
it served thy all-nourishing bounty,
according to the desire of those
who had need,*g*
26so that thy sons, whom thou didst
love, O Lord, might learn
that it is not the production of
crops that feeds man,
but that thy word preserves those
who trust in thee.
27For what was not destroyed by fire
was melted when simply warmed
by a fleeting ray of the sun,
28to make it known that one must rise
before the sun to give thee
thanks,
and must pray to thee at the
dawning of the light;
29for the hope of an ungrateful man

will melt like wintry frost,
and flow away like waste water.

17 Great are thy judgments and
hard to describe;
therefore uninstructed souls have
gone astray.
2For when lawless men supposed
that they held the holy nation
in their power,
they themselves lay as captives of
darkness and prisoners of long
night,
shut in under their roofs, exiles
from eternal providence.
3For thinking that in their secret
sins they were unobserved
behind a dark curtain of
forgetfulness,
they were scattered, terribly*h*
alarmed,
and appalled by specters.
4For not even the inner chamber
that held them protected them
from fear,
but terrifying sounds rang out
around them,
and dismal phantoms with gloomy
faces appeared.
5And no power of fire was able to
give light,
nor did the brilliant flames of the
stars
avail to illumine that hateful
night.
6Nothing was shining through to
them
except a dreadful, self-kindled
fire,
and in terror they deemed the
things which they saw
to be worse than that unseen
appearance.

e Gk *and it, ministering*
f Gk *this*
g Or *who made supplication*
h Or, with other authorities, *unobserved, they were
darkened behind a dark curtain of forgetfulness, terribly*

suited to the taste of each Israelite (vv. 20–21,25). **22–27:** The *fire* God sent executed his judgment; now he kept fire from melting *snow and ice* (a poetical expression for the manna; compare
19.21); now *a fleeting ray of the sun* melted it (Ex.16.21). **28–29:** Man should *rise* at dawn to
thank God, for God's blessing escapes the *ungrateful man* as fast as the rising sun melts *wintry
frost*.
　　　17.1–18.4: The contrast between the Egyptians and the Israelites during the plague of darkness.
God's judgment made *lawless men* (the Egyptians) terrified *captives of darkness*, unaided by

⁷The delusions of their magic art
    lay humbled,
and their boasted wisdom was
    scornfully rebuked.
⁸For those who promised to drive
    off the fears and disorders of a
    sick soul
were sick themselves with ridiculous
    fear.
⁹For even if nothing disturbing
    frightened them,
yet, scared by the passing of beasts
    and the hissing of serpents,
¹⁰they perished in trembling fear,
    refusing to look even at the air,
    though it nowhere could be
    avoided.
¹¹For wickedness is a cowardly thing,
    condemned by its own
    testimony;*i*
distressed by conscience, it has
    always exaggerated*j* the
    difficulties.
¹²For fear is nothing but surrender
    of the helps that come from
    reason;
¹³and the inner expectation of help,
    being weak,
prefers ignorance of what causes
    the torment.
¹⁴But throughout the night, which
    was really powerless,
and which beset them from the
    recesses of powerless Hades,
they all slept the same sleep,
¹⁵and now were driven by monstrous
    specters,
and now were paralyzed by their
    souls' surrender,
for sudden and unexpected fear
    overwhelmed them.
¹⁶And whoever was there fell down,
    and thus was kept shut up in a
    prison not made of iron;
¹⁷for whether he was a farmer or a
    shepherd
or a workman who toiled in the
    wilderness,
he was seized, and endured the

inescapable fate;
for with one chain of darkness they
    all were bound.
¹⁸Whether there came a whistling
    wind,
or a melodious sound of birds in
    wide-spreading branches,
or the rhythm of violently rushing
    water,
¹⁹or the harsh crash of rocks hurled
    down,
or the unseen running of leaping
    animals,
or the sound of the most savage
    roaring beasts,
or an echo thrown back from a
    hollow of the mountains,
it paralyzed them with terror.
²⁰For the whole world was illumined
    with brilliant light,
and was engaged in unhindered
    work,
²¹while over those men alone heavy
    night was spread,
an image of the darkness that was
    destined to receive them;
but still heavier than darkness
    were they to themselves.

18 But for thy holy ones there
    was very great light.
Their enemies*k* heard their voices
    but did not see their forms,
and counted them happy for not
    having suffered,
²and were thankful that thy holy
    ones,*k* though previously wronged,
    were doing them no injury;
and they begged their pardon for
    having been at variance with
    them.*l*
³Therefore thou didst provide a
    flaming pillar of fire
as a guide for thy people's*m*
    unknown journey,
and a harmless sun for their
    glorious wandering.

---

i The Greek text of this line is uncertain and probably
corrupt
j Other ancient authorities read *anticipated* *k* Gk *they*
l The meaning of the Greek of this line is uncertain
m Gk *their*

---

their *magic art* or *boasted wisdom* (Ex.10.21–23). **18.1:** *Thy holy ones,* the Israelites. **3:** *Pillar
of fire . . . a harmless sun* (Ex.13.21–22). Most details here come from the author's imagination
or from Jewish tradition.

⁴For their enemies*ⁿ* deserved to be
deprived of light and imprisoned
in darkness,
those who had kept thy sons
imprisoned,
through whom the imperishable
light of the law was to be given
to the world.

⁵When they had resolved to kill the
babes of thy holy ones,
and one child had been exposed
and rescued,
thou didst in punishment take
away a multitude of their
children;
and thou didst destroy them all
together by a mighty flood.
⁶That night was made known
beforehand to our fathers,
so that they might rejoice in sure
knowledge of the oaths in which
they trusted.
⁷The deliverance of the righteous
and the destruction of their
enemies
were expected by thy people.
⁸For by the same means by which
thou didst punish our enemies
thou didst call us to thyself and
glorify us.
⁹For in secret the holy children of
good men offered sacrifices,
and with one accord agreed to the
divine law,
that the saints would share alike
the same things,
both blessings and dangers;
and already they were singing the
praises of the fathers.*ᵒ*
¹⁰But the discordant cry of their
enemies echoed back,
and their piteous lament for their
children was spread abroad.
¹¹The slave was punished with the
same penalty as the master,
and the common man suffered the

same loss as the king;
¹²and they all together, by the one
form of death,
had corpses too many to count.
For the living were not sufficient
even to bury them,
since in one instant their most
valued children had been
destroyed.
¹³For though they had disbelieved
everything because of their
magic arts,
yet, when their first-born were
destroyed, they acknowledged
thy people to be God's son.
¹⁴For while gentle silence enveloped
all things,
and night in its swift course was
now half gone,
¹⁵thy all-powerful word leaped from
heaven, from the royal throne,
into the midst of the land that was
doomed,
a stern warrior ¹⁶carrying the sharp
sword of thy authentic command,
and stood and filled all things
with death,
and touched heaven while standing
on the earth.
¹⁷Then at once apparitions in dreadful
dreams greatly troubled them,
and unexpected fears assailed them;
¹⁸and one here and another there,
hurled down half dead,
made known why they were dying;
¹⁹for the dreams which disturbed
them forewarned them of this,
so that they might not perish
without knowing why they
suffered.

²⁰The experience of death touched
also the righteous,
and a plague came upon the
multitude in the desert,

n Gk *those men*
o Other authorities read *dangers, the fathers already leading the songs of praise*

18.5–25: The contrast between the visitation of death on the Egyptians and on the Israelites.
5: *Resolved*, Ex.1.16. *Exposed and rescued*, Ex.2.1–10. *A multitude of their children*, the Egyptian
first-born (Ex.12.29). *Didst destroy them*, Ex.14.27–28. **6:** *That night*, the first Passover. **15:**
God's *all-powerful word*, as a *stern warrior*, *leaped from heaven* and carried out God's judgment
(this recalls Rev.19.13 rather than Jn.1.1–18). **20–25:** When *a plague* struck Israel *in the desert*,

but the wrath did not long
continue.
21For a blameless man was quick to
act as their champion;
he brought forward the shield of
his ministry,
prayer and propitiation by incense;
he withstood the anger and put an
end to the disaster,
showing that he was thy servant.
22He conquered the wrath*p* not by
strength of body,
and not by force of arms,
but by his word he subdued the
punisher,
appealing to the oaths and
covenants given to our fathers.
23For when the dead had already
fallen on one another in heaps,
he intervened and held back the
wrath,
and cut off its way to the living.
24For upon his long robe the whole
world was depicted,
and the glories of the fathers were
engraved on the four rows of
stones,
and thy majesty on the diadem
upon his head.
25To these the destroyer yielded,
these he*q* feared;
for merely to test the wrath was
enough.

19 But the ungodly were assailed
to the end by pitiless anger,
for God*r* knew in advance even
their future actions,
2that, though they themselves had
permitted*s* thy people to depart
and hastily sent them forth,
they would change their minds
and pursue them.
3For while they were still busy at
mourning,
and were lamenting at the graves
of their dead,

they reached another foolish
decision,
and pursued as fugitives those
whom they had begged and
compelled to depart.
4For the fate they deserved drew
them on to this end,
and made them forget what had
happened,
in order that they might fill up the
punishment which their torments
still lacked,
5and that thy people might
experience*t* an incredible journey,
but they themselves might meet a
strange death.

6For the whole creation in its nature
was fashioned anew,
complying with thy commands,
that thy children*u* might be kept
unharmed.
7The cloud was seen overshadowing
the camp,
and dry land emerging where water
had stood before,
an unhindered way out of the Red
Sea,
and a grassy plain out of the raging
waves,
8where those protected by thy hand
passed through as one nation,
after gazing on marvelous wonders.
9For they ranged like horses,
and leaped like lambs,
praising thee, O Lord, who didst
deliver them.
10For they still recalled the events
of their sojourn,
how instead of producing animals
the earth brought forth gnats,
and instead of fish the river spewed
out vast numbers of frogs.
11Afterward they saw also a new

p Cn: Gk *multitude*   q Other authorities read *they*
r Gk *he*
s Other authorities read *had changed their minds to permit*
t Other authorities read *accomplish*   u Or *servants*

Aaron stopped the destroying angel of God from inflicting further death (Num.16.41–50).
24: From Ex. ch. 28 and Jewish tradition.
   19.1–21: God judged the Egyptians and delivered Israel at the Red Sea. 1–5: The Egyptians'
foolish decision to pursue Israel and enslave them again. **6–12:** God worked changes in nature
to deliver Israel. **7:** *Cloud*, Ex.13.21–22. *Dry land*, Ex.14.21–22. **10:** Ex. ch. 8. **11–12:** Num.

kind^v of birds,
when desire led them to ask for
luxurious food;
¹²for, to give them relief, quails came
up from the sea.

¹³The punishments did not come
upon the sinners
without prior signs in the violence
of thunder,
for they justly suffered because of
their wicked acts;
for they practiced a more bitter
hatred of strangers.
¹⁴Others had refused to receive
strangers when they came to
them,
but these made slaves of guests
who were their benefactors.
¹⁵And not only so, but punishment
of some sort will come upon the
former
for their hostile reception of the
aliens;
¹⁶but the latter, after receiving them
with festal celebrations,
afflicted with terrible sufferings
those who had already shared the
same rights.
¹⁷They were stricken also with loss
of sight—
just as were those at the door of
the righteous man—
when, surrounded by yawning
darkness,
each tried to find the way through
his own door.

¹⁸For the elements changed^w places
with one another,
as on a harp the notes vary the
nature of the rhythm,
while each note remains the same.^x
This may be clearly inferred from
the sight of what took place.
¹⁹For land animals were transformed
into water creatures,
and creatures that swim moved
over to the land.
²⁰Fire even in water retained its
normal power,
and water forgot its fire-quenching
nature.
²¹Flames, on the contrary, failed to
consume
the flesh of perishable creatures
that walked among them,
nor did they melt^y the crystalline,
easily melted kind of heavenly
food.

²²For in everything, O Lord, thou
hast exalted and glorified thy
people;
and thou hast not neglected to
help them at all times and in all
places.

v Or *production*
w Gk *changing*
x The meaning of this verse is uncertain
y Cn: Gk *nor could be melted*

---

ch. 11; compare Ex.16.13. **13–17**: The Egyptians treated *strangers* worse than did the men of
Sodom, and so deserved greater *punishment*. **14**: *Others*, men of Sodom (Gen.19.1–11). *These*,
the Egyptians. *Guests*, Israel was invited to Egypt (Gen.45.16–20). **17**: Gen.19.11; Ex.10.21–23.
18–21: In the plagues and at the Red Sea nature and *animals* changed their customary action to
effect God's redemptive purpose. **19**: *Land animals*, apparently a reference to Israel and their
cattle crossing the Red Sea. *Creatures that swim*, frogs (Ex.8.1–7). **20–21**: 16.17. *Heavenly food*,
the manna. **22**: The lesson of the preceding historical survey.

ECCLESIASTICUS, OR THE WISDOM
OF JESUS THE SON OF

SIRACH

Ecclesiasticus, or the Wisdom of Jesus the Son of Sirach, is the only book in the Apocrypha of which the name of the author is known (50.27). From internal hints we may infer that Joshua ben Sira (which is Hebrew for "Jesus the son of Sirach") was a Jewish scribe, that is, a professional teacher of the Old Testament law. The invitation in 51.23 suggests that the author conducted an academy, probably in Jerusalem, where he lectured to young men on ethical and religious subjects. About 180 B.C. this seasoned scribe and sage committed to writing the distilled wisdom that he had been accustomed to impart orally. Though the material is loosely arranged and the author almost desultory in passing from one subject to another, it appears that he intended to compose a work in two volumes (chs. 1–23 and 24–51), each of which commences with an encomium on wisdom.

Soon after 132 B.C. Ben Sira's grandson (see the Prologue) translated the original Hebrew text into Greek. About three or four centuries later a Syriac translation was made from a Hebrew text that differed considerably from that which underlies the Greek translation. Five fragmentary Hebrew manuscripts, which date from the medieval period, preserve a little more than two-thirds of the book. In the relatively few places where they overlap, these Hebrew manuscripts sometimes present quite different readings, and not infrequently a word in one manuscript is represented by a synonym in another. There is no unanimity of opinion concerning the importance of these Hebrew manuscripts; some scholars maintain that they are secondary, having been translated from an inferior form of the Greek, while others believe that they derive from Ben Sira's original Hebrew text, though embodying certain modifications adopted from the Greek and Syriac versions. In 1952 several tiny fragments of the Hebrew text, dating from about the time of Christ, were discovered in a cave near Qumran by the Dead Sea. This new evidence confirms the antiquity of the corresponding readings in the medieval Hebrew manuscripts.

In the Latin Church during the third century A.D. the book of Sirach came to be known as Ecclesiasticus, which means "The Church Book." This rather nondescript title was apparently meant to suggest that the book is the most important of the several deuterocanonical books which, though not in the Palestinian Jewish canon of the Scriptures, are accepted as inspired by the Roman Catholic Church.

Sirach is a significant link in the history of the development of ancient Jewish thought. It is the last great example of the type of wisdom literature represented in the Old Testament book of Proverbs, and the first specimen of that form of Judaism which subsequently developed into the rabbinical schools of the Pharisees and the Sadducees.

The Prologue

WHEREAS MANY GREAT TEACHings have been given to us through the law and the prophets and the others that followed them, on account of which we should praise Israel for instruction and wisdom; and since it is necessary not only that the readers themselves should acquire understanding but also that those who love learning should be able to help the outsiders by both speaking and writing, my grandfather Jesus, after devoting himself especially to the reading of the law and the prophets and the other books of our fathers, and after acquiring considerable proficiency in them, was himself also led to write something pertaining to instruction and wisdom, in order that, by becoming conversant with this also, those who love learning should make even greater progress in living according to the law.

You are urged therefore to read

with good will and attention, and to be indulgent[a] in cases where, despite our diligent labor in translating, we may seem to have rendered some phrases imperfectly. For what was originally expressed in Hebrew does not have exactly the same sense when translated into another language. Not only this work, but even the law itself, the prophecies, and the rest of the books differ not a little as originally expressed.

When I came to Egypt in the thirty-eighth year of the reign of Euergetes and stayed for some time, I found opportunity for no little instruction.[b] It seemed highly necessary that I should myself devote some pains and labor to the translation of the following book, using in that period of time great watchfulness and skill in order to complete and publish the book for those living abroad who wished to gain learning, being prepared in character to live according to the law.

‖ All wisdom comes from the
‖ Lord
   and is with him for ever.
²The sand of the sea, the drops of
      rain,
   and the days of eternity—who
      can count them?
³The height of heaven, the breadth
      of the earth,
   the abyss, and wisdom—who
      can search them out?
⁴Wisdom was created before all
      things,
   and prudent understanding from
      eternity.[c]
⁶The root of wisdom—to whom has
      it been revealed?

Her clever devices—who knows
      them?[d]
⁸There is One who is wise, greatly
      to be feared,
   sitting upon his throne.
⁹The Lord himself created wisdom;[e]
   he saw her and apportioned
      her,
   he poured her out upon all his
      works.
¹⁰She dwells with all flesh according
      to his gift,
   and he supplied her to those
      who love him.

¹¹The fear of the Lord is glory and
      exultation,
   and gladness and a crown of
      rejoicing.
¹²The fear of the Lord delights the
      heart,
   and gives gladness and joy and
      long life.
¹³With him who fears the Lord it
      will go well at the end;
   on the day of his death he will
      be blessed.

¹⁴To fear the Lord is the beginning
      of wisdom;
   she is created with the faithful
      in the womb.
¹⁵She made[f] among men an eternal
      foundation,
   and among their descendants
      she will be trusted.

a Or *Please read therefore with good will and attention, and be indulgent*
b Other authorities read *a copy affording no little instruction*
c Other authorities add as verse 5, *The source of wisdom is God's word in the highest heaven, and her ways are the eternal commandments.*
d Other authorities add as verse 7, *The knowledge of wisdom—to whom was it manifested? And her abundant experience—who has understood it?*
e Gk *her*
f Gk *made as nest*

1.1–10: The origin of wisdom. 1: The opening statement, *all wisdom comes from the Lord,* serves as a text on which the author's discourse is based (compare Pr.3.13–20). **2–3:** Illustrations of the impossibility of fathoming the depths of divine wisdom (18.5; Rom.11.33). **3:** *Height of heaven,* Ps.103.11. **8:** *Sitting upon his throne,* Ps.47.8; Is.6.1. **9:** *The Lord . . . created wisdom,* Pr.8.22–31. **10:** *All flesh,* mankind in general. *According to his gift,* i.e. in measured quantity, but *to those who love him,* i.e. to Israel, he gave wisdom unstintedly.

1.11–20: The fear of the Lord leads to obedience of the divine law. In the wisdom literature the fear of the Lord is roughly equivalent to religion and piety (Job 28.28; Ps.111.10; Pr.1.7; 9.10). **12:** *Long life,* v. 20; Pr.3.16. **15a:** Syriac, "With faithful men is she, and she has been established

¹⁶To fear the Lord is wisdom's full
measure;
she satisfies*ᵍ* men with her
fruits;
¹⁷she fills their whole house with
desirable goods,
and their storehouses with her
produce.
¹⁸The fear of the Lord is the crown
of wisdom,
making peace and perfect health
to flourish.
¹⁹He saw her and apportioned her;
he rained down knowledge and
discerning comprehension,
and he exalted the glory of those
who held her fast.
²⁰To fear the Lord is the root of
wisdom,
and her branches are long life.*ʰ*

²²Unrighteous anger cannot be
justified,
for a man's anger tips the scale
to his ruin.
²³A patient man will endure until
the right moment,
and then joy will burst forth for
him.
²⁴He will hide his words until the
right moment,
and the lips of many will tell of
his good sense.
²⁵In the treasuries of wisdom are
wise sayings,
but godliness is an abomination
to a sinner.
²⁶If you desire wisdom, keep the
commandments,
and the Lord will supply it for
you.

²⁷For the fear of the Lord is wisdom
and instruction,
and he delights in fidelity and
meekness.
²⁸Do not disobey the fear of the
Lord;
do not approach him with a
divided mind.
²⁹Be not a hypocrite in men's sight,*ⁱ*
and keep watch over your lips.
³⁰Do not exalt yourself lest you fall,
and thus bring dishonor upon
yourself.
The Lord will reveal your secrets
and cast you down in the midst
of the congregation,
because you did not come in the
fear of the Lord,
and your heart was full of deceit.

2 My son, if you come forward
to serve the Lord,
prepare yourself for temptation.*ʲ*
²Set your heart right and be
steadfast,
and do not be hasty in time of
calamity.
³Cleave to him and do not depart,
that you may be honored at the
end of your life.
⁴Accept whatever is brought upon
you,
and in changes that humble you
be patient.
⁵For gold is tested in the fire,
and acceptable men in the
furnace of humiliation.
⁶Trust in him, and he will help you;

g Gk *intoxicates*
h Other authorities add as verse 21, *The fear of the Lord
drives away sins; and where it abides, it will turn away
all anger.*
i Syr: Gk *in the mouths of men*   *j* Or *trials*

---

from eternity." **16**: *Her fruits*, Pr.8.19; 11.30. **17**: Wis.7.11. **20**: *Long life*, v. 12; Pr.4.10.
   1.22–30: **Wisdom is shown in the exercise of patience, self-control, and humility. 22**: Pr.29.22.
24: *Will hide his words*, a patient man is not hasty to speak. **26**: 19.20; Ec.12.13. **27**: Pr.15.33.
28: Obedience is the result of trust. *A divided mind*, 2.12; Jas.1.6–8; 4.8. **29**: *Hypocrite*, 32.15;
33.2. **30**: *Do not exalt yourself*, Mt.23.12. *In the . . . congregation*, 4.7; 7.7; Pr.5.14. *Full of
deceit*, 19.26.
   2.1–6: **Serving God faithfully. 1**: *My son*, the usual mode of a Jewish teacher's address to his
pupil (7.3; Pr.2.1; 3.1). *Prepare . . . for temptation*, Jas.1.2–4 and 12–15. **2**: *Do not be hasty*, i.e.
do not be impatient and fearful, but calm and self-possessed (Is.52.12; 1 Pet.4.12). **3**: *Cleave
to him*, to God (Dt.10.20). *At the end of your life*, 1.13. **4**: *Accept* divinely appointed adversities
(Job 2.10; Jas.1.2). *Be patient*, Jas.5.7–8. **5**: Pr.17.3; 27.21; Wis.3.6; Jas.1.12; 1 Pet.1.7.
6: Ps.37.3,5.

make your ways straight, and
  hope in him.

7You who fear the Lord, wait for
    his mercy;
  and turn not aside, lest you fall.
8You who fear the Lord, trust in
    him,
  and your reward will not fail;
9you who fear the Lord, hope for
    good things,
  for everlasting joy and mercy.
10Consider the ancient generations
    and see:
  who ever trusted in the Lord
    and was put to shame?
  Or who ever persevered in the fear
    of the Lord^k and was
    forsaken?
  Or who ever called upon him
    and was overlooked?
11For the Lord is compassionate and
    merciful;
  he forgives sins and saves in
    time of affliction.

12Woe to timid hearts and to slack
    hands,
  and to the sinner who walks
    along two ways!
13Woe to the faint heart, for it has
    no trust!
  Therefore it will not be sheltered.
14Woe to you who have lost your
    endurance!
  What will you do when the
    Lord punishes you?
15Those who fear the Lord will not
    disobey his words,
  and those who love him will
    keep his ways.

16Those who fear the Lord will seek
    his approval,
  and those who love him will be
    filled with the law.
17Those who fear the Lord will
    prepare their hearts,
  and will humble themselves
    before him.
18Let us fall^l into the hands of the
    Lord,
  but not into the hands of men;
  for as his majesty is,
    so also is his mercy.

3 Listen to me your father, O
    children;
  and act accordingly, that you
    may be kept in safety.
2For the Lord honored the father
    above the children,
  and he confirmed the right of
    the mother over her sons.
3Whoever honors his father atones
    for sins,
4   and whoever glorifies his mother
    is like one who lays up
    treasure.
5Whoever honors his father will be
    gladdened by his own children,
  and when he prays he will be
    heard.
6Whoever glorifies his father will
    have long life,
  and whoever obeys the Lord
    will refresh his mother;
7   he will serve his parents as his
    masters.^m
8Honor your father by word and
    deed,

k Gk *of him*   l Gk *We shall fall*
m In other authorities this line is preceded by *Whoever
fears the Lord will honor his father*,

2.7–11: **The reward of those who fear the Lord. 7**: *Wait for his mercy*, Jdt.8.17. **9**: *Everlasting
joy*, Is.35.10; 51.11; 61.7. **10**: Ps.37.25. **11**: *Compassionate and merciful*, Ex.34.6–7; Ps.103.8–9;
145.8; Jon.4.2.
    2.12–14: **A threefold woe against the unfaithful. 12**: *Timid hearts*, 22.18; Dt.20.8. *Slack hands*,
25.23; Heb.12.12. **14**: *Endurance*, compare v. 1.
    2.15–18: **Characteristics of those who fear the Lord. 15**: Jn.14.15; 15.10. **16**: *Will be filled
with the law*, will be in heart and mind saturated with the Mosaic statutes (32.15). **17**: *Will
humble themselves*, 3.18; 7.17; 18.21. **18**: 2 Sam.24.14.
    3.1–16: **Filial duty and its reward** (Ex.20.12; Dt.5.16; Eph.6.1–3). In accord with the Jewish
doctrine that the observance of the Mosaic law is meritorious, Sirach teaches that the keeping
of the commandment to honor one's parents (Ex.20.12) *atones for sins* (vv. 14–15); contrast
the teaching in Lk.17.10. **4**: *Lays up treasure*, Mt.6.20. **6**: *Will refresh*, will give rest from

that a blessing from him may
come upon you.
⁹For a father's blessing strengthens
the houses of the children,
but a mother's curse uproots
their foundations.

¹⁰Do not glorify yourself by
dishonoring your father,
for your father's dishonor is no
glory to you.
¹¹For a man's glory comes from
honoring his father,
and it is a disgrace for children
not to respect their mother.
¹²O son, help your father in his old
age,
and do not grieve him as long
as he lives;
¹³even if he is lacking in
understanding, show
forbearance;
in all your strength do not
despise him.
¹⁴For kindness to a father will not
be forgotten,
and against your sins it will be
credited to you;
¹⁵in the day of your affliction it will
be remembered in your favor;
as frost in fair weather, your sins
will melt away.
¹⁶Whoever forsakes his father is like
a blasphemer,
and whoever angers his mother
is cursed by the Lord.

¹⁷My son, perform your tasks in
meekness;
then you will be loved by those
whom God accepts.
¹⁸The greater you are, the more you
must humble yourself;
so you will find favor in the sight
of the Lord.ⁿ
²⁰For great is the might of the Lord;
he is glorified by the humble.
²¹Seek not what is too difficult for
you,
nor investigate what is beyond
your power.
²²Reflect upon what has been
assigned to you,
for you do not need what is
hidden.
²³Do not meddle in what is beyond
your tasks,
for matters too great for human
understanding have been shown
you.
²⁴For their hasty judgment has led
many astray,
and wrong opinion has caused
their thoughts to slip.ᵒ

²⁶A stubborn mind will be afflicted
at the end,
and whoever loves danger will
perish by it.
²⁷A stubborn mind will be burdened
by troubles,
and the sinner will heap sin
upon sin.
²⁸The affliction of the proud has no
healing,
for a plant of wickedness has
taken root in him.
²⁹The mind of the intelligent man
will ponder a parable,
and an attentive ear is the wise
man's desire.

n Other authorities add as verse 19, *Many are lofty and
renowned, but to the meek he reveals his secrets.*
o Other authorities add as verse 25, *If you have no eyes
you will be without light; if you lack knowledge do not
profess to have it.*

---

anxieties (Pr.29.17). **9**: Hebrew, "The blessing of a father establishes the root, but the curse of
a mother uproots the young plant." **10**: *Your father's dishonor,* i.e. the dishonor brought
upon a father by his son. **13**: Or, "Even if his mind fail, be considerate with him." **14–15**: Compare v. 3. *Will not be forgotten . . . will be credited . . . will be remembered* by God. **16**: Lev.20.9;
Dt.27.16; Pr.19.26; 30.11,17. *Forsakes,* Hebrew and Syriac, "despises."
  3.17–24: On humility. 17: Hebrew, "My son, when in prosperity walk with humility, and
you will be loved more than a giver of gifts." **18**: Mt.20.26–28; Phil.2.3–8; 1 Pet.5.5–6. **21**:
Ps.131.1; Jer.45.5; Rom.12.16. **22**: Dt.29.29. **23**: 1 Cor.2.9. **24**: Or, "their conceit has misled
many," referring perhaps to speculations of Greek philosophers.
  3.26–31: Retribution and reward. 26: Pr.28.14; Rom.2.5. **28**: *Has no healing,* i.e. adversity
works no reformation in *the proud.* **29**: Hebrew, "the ear that listens to wisdom rejoices."

³⁰Water extinguishes a blazing fire:
    so almsgiving atones for sin.
³¹Whoever requites favors gives
      thought to the future;
    at the moment of his falling he
      will find support.

4 My son, deprive not the poor
   of his living,
    and do not keep needy eyes
      waiting.
²Do not grieve the one who is
      hungry,
    nor anger a man in want.
³Do not add to the troubles of an
      angry mind,
    nor delay your gift to a beggar.
⁴Do not reject an afflicted suppliant,
    nor turn your face away from
      the poor.
⁵Do not avert your eye from the
      needy,
    nor give a man occasion to
      curse you;
⁶for if in bitterness of soul he calls
      down a curse upon you,
    his Creator will hear his
      prayer.

⁷Make yourself beloved in the
      congregation;
    bow your head low to a great
      man.
⁸Incline your ear to the poor,
    and answer him peaceably and
      gently.
⁹Deliver him who is wronged from
      the hand of the wrongdoer;
    and do not be fainthearted in
      judging a case.
¹⁰Be like a father to orphans,
    and instead of a husband to
      their mother;
    you will then be like a son of the
      Most High,

and he will love you more than
    does your mother.

¹¹Wisdom exalts her sons
    and gives help to those who
      seek her.
¹²Whoever loves her loves life,
    and those who seek her early
      will be filled with joy.
¹³Whoever holds her fast will obtain
      glory,
    and the Lord will bless the place
      she*ᵖ* enters.
¹⁴Those who serve her will minister
      to the Holy One;*�q*
    the Lord loves those who love
      her.
¹⁵He who obeys her will judge the
      nations,
    and whoever gives heed to her
      will dwell secure.
¹⁶If he has faith in her he will obtain
      her;
    and his descendants will remain
      in possession of her.
¹⁷For at first she will walk with him
      on tortuous paths,
    she will bring fear and cowardice
      upon him,
    and will torment him by her
      discipline
    until she trusts him,
    and she will test him with her
      ordinances.
¹⁸Then she will come straight
      back to him and gladden
      him,
    and will reveal her secrets to
      him.
¹⁹If he goes astray she will forsake
      him,
    and hand him over to his
      ruin.

p Or he
q Or at the holy place

30: That *almsgiving atones for sin* accords with the Jewish doctrine of the efficacy of good works (Tob.4.7–11; contrast Gal.2.16; Eph.2.9); see also 7.10 n.; 29.11 n.

    4.1–10: Duties toward the poor (7.32–36; 29.8–13; Dt.15.7–11). **1:** *Do not keep needy eyes waiting*, when they look for help. **4:** Mt.5.42. **6:** Ex.22.23; Dt.15.9; Pr.17.5. **7:** *Make yourself beloved*, by giving alms to the poor. **7:** *A great man*, Hebrew, "the ruler of the city." **10:** Job 29.16; 31.18; Ps.82.3; Is.1.17; Jas.1.27.

    4.11–19: The rewards of wisdom. 11: 6.27. **12:** Pr.3.16–17; 8.17; Wis.8.17–18. **14–15:** The disciples of wisdom are like priests and judges. **18:** *Secrets*, 39.7; Job 11.6; Dan.2.21–22.

²⁰Observe the right time, and beware
of evil;*ʳ*
and do not bring shame on
yourself.
²¹For there is a shame which brings
sin,
and there is a shame which is
glory and favor.
²²Do not show partiality, to your
own harm,
or deference, to your downfall.
²³Do not refrain from speaking at
the crucial time,*ˢ*
and do not hide your wisdom.*ᵗ*
²⁴For wisdom is known through
speech,
and education through the words
of the tongue.
²⁵Never speak against the truth,
but be mindful of your
ignorance.
²⁶Do not be ashamed to confess your
sins,
and do not try to stop the current
of a river.
²⁷Do not subject yourself to a foolish
fellow,
nor show partiality to a ruler.
²⁸Strive even to death for the truth
and the Lord God will fight for
you.

²⁹Do not be reckless in your speech,
or sluggish and remiss in your
deeds.
³⁰Do not be like a lion in your home,
nor be a faultfinder with your
servants.
³¹Let not your hand be extended to
receive,
but withdrawn when it is time
to repay.

5 Do not set your heart on your
wealth,

nor say, "I have enough."
²Do not follow your inclination and
strength,
walking according to the desires
of your heart.
³Do not say, "Who will have power
over me?"
for the Lord will surely punish
you.

⁴Do not say, "I sinned, and what
happened to me?"
for the Lord is slow to anger.
⁵Do not be so confident of
atonement
that you add sin to sin.
⁶Do not say, "His mercy is great,
he will forgive*ᵘ* the multitude of
my sins,"
for both mercy and wrath are with
him,
and his anger rests on sinners.
⁷Do not delay to turn to the Lord,
nor postpone it from day to
day;
for suddenly the wrath of the Lord
will go forth,
and at the time of punishment
you will perish.

⁸Do not depend on dishonest
wealth,
for it will not benefit you in the
day of calamity.
⁹Do not winnow with every wind,
nor follow every path:
the double-tongued sinner does
that.
¹⁰Be steadfast in your understanding,
and let your speech be consistent.

r Or an evil man
s Cn: Gk at a time of salvation
t So some Gk Mss and Heb Syr Vg: other Gk Mss omit
  and do not hide your wisdom
u Heb: Gk he (or it) will atone for

4.20–5.3: Precepts for everyday life. 22: That is, a man should not be afraid of offending another so long as he does what is right; even if it results in his *own harm*, he will have no cause for shame. 26: That is, it is as futile to hide one's sins from God as to try to stop a river from flowing. 30: *Like a lion*, wild, hasty, relentless, destructive. 31: Compare Acts 20.35. 5.1: *Enough*, Hebrew, "the power." 3: Ps.12.4.

5.4–7: Warnings against presuming on God's mercy. 4: Ec.8.11. 5: That is, do not continue sinning, *confident of* God's forgiveness. 6: God's *mercy and wrath*, 16.11–12. 7: *Postpone it*, i.e. postpone repentance.

5.8–6.1: Honesty and sincerity. 5.8: Pr.10.2; 11.4; Ezek.7.19. 9: A condemnation of time-

¹¹Be quick to hear,
   and be deliberate in answering.
¹²If you have understanding, answer
      your neighbor;
   but if not, put your hand on
      your mouth.
¹³Glory and dishonor come from
      speaking,
   and a man's tongue is his
      downfall.

¹⁴Do not be called a slanderer,
   and do not lie in ambush with
      your tongue;
 for shame comes to the thief,
   and severe condemnation to the
      double-tongued.
¹⁵In great or small matters do not
      act amiss,
 and do not become an enemy
   instead of a friend;
 for a bad name incurs shame
   and reproach:
 so fares the double-tongued
   sinner.

²Do not exalt yourself through your
   soul's counsel,
   lest your soul be torn in pieces
      like a bull.ᵛ
³You will devour your leaves and
      destroy your fruit,
   and will be left like a withered
      tree.
⁴An evil soul will destroy him who
      has it,
   and make him the laughingstock
      of his enemies.

⁵A pleasant voice multiplies friends,
   and a gracious tongue multiplies
      courtesies.
⁶Let those that are at peace with
   you be many,

but let your advisers be one in a
   thousand.
⁷When you gain a friend, gain him
      through testing,
   and do not trust him hastily.
⁸For there is a friend who is such
      at his own convenience,
   but will not stand by you in
      your day of trouble.
⁹And there is a friend who changes
      into an enemy,
   and will disclose a quarrel to
      your disgrace.
¹⁰And there is a friend who is a table
      companion,
   but will not stand by you in
      your day of trouble.
¹¹In your prosperity he will make
      himself your equal,
   and be bold with your
      servants;
¹²but if you are brought low he will
      turn against you,
   and will hide himself from your
      presence.
¹³Keep yourself far from your
      enemies,
   and be on guard toward your
      friends.

¹⁴A faithful friend is a sturdy shelter:
   he that has found one has found
      a treasure.
¹⁵There is nothing so precious as a
      faithful friend,
   and no scales can measure his
      excellence.
¹⁶A faithful friend is an elixir of
      life;
   and those who fear the Lord will
      find him.
¹⁷Whoever fears the Lord directs his
      friendship aright,

v The meaning of the Greek of this verse is obscure

---

servers, who speak according to expediency rather than truth. **11:** Jas.1.19. **12:** *Hand on . . .*
mouth, Job 21.5; 29.9; 40.4. **13:** Pr.18.21; Mt.12.37.
   6.2–4: Self-control; a warning against lustful passions. Hebrew (freely), "Be not a slave to
your passions, lest they consume your strength; they will eat up your leaves [figurative for
youth], and destroy your fruit [offspring], and leave you as a dried-up tree. For unbridled
passion destroys its possessor, and makes him the sport of his enemies."
   6.5–17: True and false friendship. 5: 20.13; Pr.15.1. **6–7:** Care in choosing friends. **8–13:**
False friendship. **9:** Pr.25.9–10. **10:** 37.5. **11b:** Hebrew (one manuscript) and Syriac, "and
when you are in adversity, he will desert you." **13:** *Friends*, i.e. false friends. **14–17:** True

for as he is, so is his neighbor also.

¹⁸My son, from your youth up choose
    instruction,
    and until you are old you will
    keep finding wisdom.
¹⁹Come to her like one who plows
    and sows,
    and wait for her good harvest.
For in her service you will toil a
    little while,
    and soon you will eat of her
    produce.
²⁰She seems very harsh to the
    uninstructed;
    a weakling will not remain with
    her.
²¹She will weigh him down like a
    heavy testing stone,
    and he will not be slow to cast
    her off.
²²For wisdom is like her name,
    and is not manifest to many.

²³Listen, my son, and accept my
    judgment;
    do not reject my counsel.
²⁴Put your feet into her fetters,
    and your neck into her collar.
²⁵Put your shoulder under her and
    carry her,
    and do not fret under her bonds.
²⁶Come to her with all your soul,
    and keep her ways with all your
    might.
²⁷Search out and seek, and she will
    become known to you;
    and when you get hold of her,
    do not let her go.
²⁸For at last you will find the rest
    she gives,
    and she will be changed into joy
    for you.

²⁹Then her fetters will become for
    you a strong protection,
    and her collar a glorious robe.
³⁰Her yoke*ʷ* is a golden ornament,
    and her bonds are a cord of blue.
³¹You will wear her like a glorious robe,
    and put her on like a crown of
    gladness.

³²If you are willing, my son, you will
    be taught,
    and if you apply yourself you
    will become clever.
³³If you love to listen you will gain
    knowledge,
    and if you incline your ear you
    will become wise.
³⁴Stand in the assembly of the elders.
    Who is wise? Cleave to him.
³⁵Be ready to listen to every*ˣ*
    narrative,
    and do not let wise proverbs
    escape you.
³⁶If you see an intelligent man, visit
    him early;
    let your foot wear out his
    doorstep.
³⁷Reflect on the statutes of the Lord,
    and meditate at all times on his
    commandments.
It is he who will give insight to*ʸ*
    your mind,
    and your desire for wisdom will
    be granted.

7 Do no evil, and evil will never
    befall you.
2   Stay away from wrong, and it
    will turn away from you.
³My son, do not sow the furrows of
    injustice,

w Heb: Gk *Upon her*
x Heb: Gk adds *divine*
y Heb: Gk *will confirm*

friends are beyond value, and are the gift of God. **17b:** That is, *his neighbor* is as dear to him
as he is to himself.
    6.18–37: The blessings of wisdom. 18: 22.6. **19:** *Wait for the harvest,* Jas.5.7–8. **22:** *Wisdom
is like her name,* Hebrew, "Discipline [*musar*] is like her name," perhaps a play on the Hebrew
participle *musar,* meaning "removed, withdrawn"; hence the path of discipline *is not manifest
to many.* **25:** *Put your shoulder under her,* wisdom is like a yoke. *Under her bonds,* Hebrew,
"at her counsels." **27:** *Do not let her go,* Pr.4.13. **28:** *Rest,* compare Mt.11.29. **30:** *A cord of
blue,* Num.15.38. **31:** *A crown of gladness,* 1.11; 15.6; Pr.4.9; 16.31. **34:** 8.9. **37:** The law
(*statutes, commandments*) is the source of wisdom. *Meditate,* Jos.1.8; Ps.1.2.
    7.1–3: The avoidance of sin. 3: Job 4.8; Pr.22.8; Gal.6.8. *Sevenfold,* 35.11.

and you will not reap a sevenfold
crop.

⁴Do not seek from the Lord the
highest office,
nor the seat of honor from the
king.
⁵Do not assert your righteousness
before the Lord,
nor display your wisdom before
the king.
⁶Do not seek to become a judge,
lest you be unable to remove
iniquity,
lest you be partial to a powerful man,
and thus put a blot on your
integrity.
⁷Do not offend against the public,
and do not disgrace yourself
among the people.

⁸Do not commit a sin twice;
even for one you will not go
unpunished.
⁹Do not say, "He will consider the
multitude of my gifts,
and when I make an offering to
the Most High God he will
accept it."
¹⁰Do not be fainthearted in your
prayer,
nor neglect to give alms.

¹¹Do not ridicule a man who is bitter
in soul,
for there is One who abases and
exalts.
¹²Do not devise^z a lie against your
brother,
nor do the like to a friend.
¹³Refuse to utter any lie,

for the habit of lying serves no
good.
¹⁴Do not prattle in the assembly of
the elders,
nor repeat yourself in your prayer.

¹⁵Do not hate toilsome labor,
or farm work, which were
created by the Most High.
¹⁶Do not count yourself among the
crowd of sinners;
remember that wrath does not
delay.
¹⁷Humble yourself greatly,
for the punishment of the
ungodly is fire and worms.^{a}

¹⁸Do not exchange a friend for money,
or a real brother for the gold of
Ophir.
¹⁹Do not deprive yourself of a wise
and good wife,
for her charm is worth more
than gold.
²⁰Do not abuse a servant who
performs his work faithfully,
or a hired laborer who devotes
himself to you.
²¹Let your soul love^b an intelligent
servant;
do not withhold from him his
freedom.

²²Do you have cattle? Look after them;
if they are profitable to you, keep
them.
²³Do you have children? Discipline
them,

z Heb: Gk *plow*
a The Hebrew text reads *for the expectation of man is worms*
b The Hebrew text reads *Love like yourself*

7.4–7: Conduct in public life. 4: Pr.25.6–7. **6:** *A judge*, Hebrew, "a ruler."
    7.8–10: A warning against presuming upon God's forgiveness without amendment of life. **10:** According to Jewish teaching, *to give alms* is the highest form of righteousness (see 3.30 n. and 29.11 n.; compare Mt.6.1).
    7.11–17: Precepts for right conduct of life. 11: *Bitter in soul*, because of poverty (4.2; Pr.17.5). *Abases and exalts*, 1 Sam.2.7; Lk.1.52–53. **14:** Mt.6.7. **15:** Pr.24.27. **16:** *Wrath*, 5.7. **17:** *Humble*, 2.17. A motive for humility is the thought that the body is destined to corruption. *Fire and worms*, Is.66.24; Jdt.16.17; Mk.9.48.
    7.18–21: Duties to a friend, a wife, and a servant. 18: *Ophir*, 1 Kg.9.28; Job 22.24; 28.16. **19:** *Do not deprive*, Hebrew, "reject not," referring to divorce (v. 26). **21:** After six years of service a Hebrew slave was entitled to *freedom* (Ex.21.2; Lev.25.39–43; Dt.15.12–15).
    7.22–25: Duties to cattle, and to children. 23: Hebrew (one manuscript) and Syriac, "Do

and make them obedient^c from
their youth.
²⁴Do you have daughters? Be
concerned for their chastity,^d
and do not show yourself too
indulgent with them.
²⁵Give a daughter in marriage; you
will have finished a great task.
But give her to a man of
understanding.

²⁶If you have a wife who pleases
you,^e do not cast her out;
but do not trust yourself to one
whom you detest.
²⁷With all your heart honor your
father,
and do not forget the birth pangs
of your mother.
²⁸Remember that through your
parents^f you were born;
and what can you give back to
them that equals their gift to
you?

²⁹With all your soul fear the Lord,
and honor his priests.
³⁰With all your might love your Maker,
and do not forsake his ministers.
³¹Fear the Lord and honor the priest,
and give him his portion, as is
commanded you:
the first fruits, the guilt offering,
the gift of the shoulders,
the sacrifice of sanctification,
and the first fruits of the holy
things.

³²Stretch forth your hand to the poor,

so that your blessing may be
complete.
³³Give graciously to all the living,
and withhold not kindness from
the dead.
³⁴Do not fail those who weep,
but mourn with those who
mourn.
³⁵Do not shrink from visiting a sick
man,
because for such deeds you will
be loved.
³⁶In all you do, remember the end
of your life,
and then you will never sin.

8 Do not contend with a powerful
man,
lest you fall into his hands.
²Do not quarrel with a rich man,
lest his resources outweigh yours;
for gold has ruined many,
and has perverted the minds of
kings.
³Do not argue with a chatterer,
nor heap wood on his fire.

⁴Do not jest with an ill-bred person,
lest your ancestors be disgraced.
⁵Do not reproach a man who is
turning away from sin;
remember that we all deserve
punishment.
⁶Do not disdain a man when he is old,
for some of us are growing old.
⁷Do not rejoice over any one's death;
remember that we all must die.

c Gk *bend their necks*   d Gk *body*
e Heb Syr omit *who pleases you*   f Gk *them*

you have sons? Correct them, and choose wives for them while they are young." **24:** 26.10–11;
42.9–11. **25:** Marriages were arranged by the father (see v. 23 n. and 36.21 n.).
   7.26–28: Duties to one's wife and parents. 26: *Do not cast her out*, see v. 19 n. **27–28:** An
expansion of Ex.20.12.
   7.29–31: Duties to God and to the priesthood. In supporting and showing honor to God's
ministers one indirectly honors God himself. **31:** *As is commanded*, Ex.29.27; Lev.7.31–34;
Num.18.8–20; Dt.18.3.
   7.32–36: Various duties: to give alms, respect the dead, comfort mourners, visit the sick:
32: Dt.14.28–29. **33b:** Hebrew, "deny not respect to the dead," by providing honorable burial
(38.16–18; Tob.1.17) and showing solicitude for their dependents. **34:** Rom.12.15. **35:** Mt.
25.36. **36:** Ec.11.9–12.7.
   8.1–19: Warnings concerning various kinds of men. 1–3: A prudent man will avoid quarreling
with the *powerful*, the *rich*, and the *chatterer*. **2:** *Lest his resources outweigh yours*, as a bribe in
perverting *the minds of kings*. **4:** *Be disgraced*, by his railing. **5–7:** Have respect for the penitent,

⁸Do not slight the discourse of the
  sages,
    but busy yourself with their
      maxims;
  because from them you will gain
    instruction
  and learn how to serve great men.
⁹Do not disregard the discourse of
  the aged,
    for they themselves learned from
      their fathers;
  because from them you will gain
    understanding
  and learn how to give an answer
    in time of need.

¹⁰Do not kindle the coals of a sinner,
  lest you be burned in his flaming
    fire.
¹¹Do not get up and leave an
  insolent fellow,
    lest he lie in ambush against
      your words.
¹²Do not lend to a man who is
  stronger than you;
    but if you do lend anything, be
      as one who has lost it.
¹³Do not give surety beyond your
  means,
    but if you give surety, be con-
      cerned as one who must pay.

¹⁴Do not go to law against a judge,
  for the decision will favor him
    because of his standing.
¹⁵Do not travel on the road with a
  foolhardy fellow,
    lest he be burdensome to you;
  for he will act as he pleases,
    and through his folly you will
      perish with him.
¹⁶Do not fight with a wrathful man,
  and do not cross the wilderness
    with him;
  because blood is as nothing in his
    sight,

and where no help is at hand,
  he will strike you down.
¹⁷Do not consult with a fool,
  for he will not be able to keep
    a secret.
¹⁸In the presence of a stranger do
  nothing that is to be kept secret,
  for you do not know what he
    will divulge.ᵍ
¹⁹Do not reveal your thoughts to
  every one,
    lest you drive away your good
      luck.ʰ

9 Do not be jealous of the wife
  of your bosom,
    and do not teach her an evil
      lesson to your own hurt.
²Do not give yourself to a woman
  so that she gains mastery over
    your strength.
³Do not go to meet a loose woman,
  lest you fall into her snares.
⁴Do not associate with a woman
  singer,
    lest you be caught in her intrigues.
⁵Do not look intently at a virgin,
  lest you stumble and incur
    penalties for her.
⁶Do not give yourself to harlots
  lest you lose your inheritance.
⁷Do not look around in the streets
  of a city,
    nor wander about in its deserted
      sections.
⁸Turn away your eyes from a shapely
  woman,
    and do not look intently at
      beauty belonging to another;
  many have been misled by a
    woman's beauty,
    and by it passion is kindled like
      a fire.
⁹Never dine with another man's wife,

g Or *it will bring forth*
h Heb: Gk *let him not return a favor to you*

the aged, and the departed. **8–9:** Learn from men of experience. **10–11:** Warnings against
associating with sinners. **12–13:** Warnings concerning lending, and giving *surety*. **14–19:**
Warnings concerning various social relationships.
  9.1–9: Warnings concerning women. 1: *Jealous*, Num.5.14–15. **2:** Pr.31.3. **3:** Pr.23.27.
5: Job 31.1; Mt.5.28. **6:** Pr.29.3; Lk.15.13. **8:** *Belonging to another* man's wife. **9:** *Into destruction* refers to the adulterer's punishment (Lev.20.10; Dt.22.22).

nor revel with her at wine;
lest your heart turn aside to her,
and in blood[i] you be plunged
into destruction.

10Forsake not an old friend,
for a new one does not compare
with him.
A new friend is like new wine;
when it has aged you will drink
it with pleasure.

11Do not envy the honors of a
sinner,
for you do not know what his
end will be.
12Do not delight in what pleases the
ungodly;
remember that they will not be
held guiltless as long as they
live.

13Keep far from a man who has the
power to kill,
and you will not be worried by
the fear of death.
But if you approach him, make no
misstep,
lest he rob you of your life.
Know that you are walking in the
midst of snares,
and that you are going about
on the city battlements.

14As much as you can, aim to know
your neighbors,
and consult with the wise.
15Let your conversation be with men
of understanding,
and let all your discussion be
about the law of the Most
High.
16Let righteous men be your dinner
companions,
and let your glorying be in the
fear of the Lord.
17A work will be praised for the skill
of the craftsmen;

so a people's leader is proved
wise by his words.
18A babbler is feared in his city,
and the man who is reckless in
speech will be hated.

10 A wise magistrate will educate
his people,
and the rule of an understanding
man will be well ordered.
2Like the magistrate of the people,
so are his officials;
and like the ruler of the city, so
are all its inhabitants.
3An undisciplined king will ruin his
people,
but a city will grow through the
understanding of its rulers.
4The government of the earth is in
the hands of the Lord,
and over it he will raise up the
right man for the time.
5The success of a man is in the
hands of the Lord,
and he confers his honor upon
the person of the scribe.[j]

6Do not be angry with your neighbor
for any injury,
and do not attempt anything by
acts of insolence.
7Arrogance is hateful before the
Lord and before men,
and injustice is outrageous to
both.
8Sovereignty passes from nation to
nation
on account of injustice and
insolence and wealth.
9How can he who is dust and ashes
be proud?
for even in life his bowels
decay.[k]
10A long illness baffles the physician;[l]
the king of today will die
tomorrow.

i Heb: Gk *by your spirit*
j Or *the official*
k Heb: Gk is obscure
l Heb Vg: Gk is uncertain

9.10–18: Precepts concerning various kinds of persons. 11: Ps.37.1; 73.3 and 17. 15b: Ps.1.2.
16b: 10.22.
10.1–5: Concerning rulers. 4: Pr.8.15–16; Wis.6.1–3. *For the* right *time.*
10.6–18: Concerning arrogance and pride, especially in rulers (Pr.16.18). 6: Lev.19.17;

¹¹For when a man is dead,
  he will inherit creeping things,
  and wild beasts, and worms.
¹²The beginning of man's pride is to
  depart from the Lord;
  his heart has forsaken his
  Maker.
¹³For the beginning of pride is sin,
  and the man who clings to it
  pours out abominations.
  Therefore the Lord brought upon
  them extraordinary afflictions,
  and destroyed them utterly.
¹⁴The Lord has cast down the thrones
  of rulers,
  and has seated the lowly in their
  place.
¹⁵The Lord has plucked up the roots
  of the nations,ᵐ
  and has planted the humble in
  their place.
¹⁶The Lord has overthrown the lands
  of the nations,
  and has destroyed them to the
  foundations of the earth.
¹⁷He has removed some of them and
  destroyed them,
  and has extinguished the memory
  of them from the earth.
¹⁸Pride was not created for men,
  nor fierce anger for those born of
  women.

¹⁹What race is worthy of honor?
  The human race.
  What race is worthy of honor?
  Those who fear the Lord.
  What race is unworthy of honor?
  The human race.
  What race is unworthy of honor?
  Those who transgress the
  commandments.
²⁰Among brothers their leader is
  worthy of honor,
  and those who fear the Lord are
  worthy of honor in his eyes.ⁿ

²²The rich, and the eminent, and the
  poor—
  their glory is the fear of the
  Lord.
²³It is not right to despise an
  intelligent poor man,
  nor is it proper to honor a sinful
  man.
²⁴The nobleman, and the judge, and
  the ruler will be honored,
  but none of them is greater than
  the man who fears the Lord.
²⁵Free men will be at the service of
  a wise servant,
  and a man of understanding will
  not grumble.

²⁶Do not make a display of your wisdom when you do your work,
  nor glorify yourself at a time
  when you are in want.
²⁷Better is a man who works and has
  an abundance of everything,
  than one who goes about
  boasting, but lacks bread.
²⁸My son, glorify yourself with
  humility,
  and ascribe to yourself honor
  according to your worth.
²⁹Who will justify the man that sins
  against himself?
  And who will honor the man
  that dishonors his own life?
³⁰A poor man is honored for his
  knowledge,
  while a rich man is honored for
  his wealth.
³¹A man honored in poverty, how
  much more in wealth!
  And a man dishonored in wealth,
  how much more in poverty!

‖ The wisdom of a humble man
‖ will lift up his head,

m Some authorities read *proud nations*
n Other authorities add as verse 21, *The fear of the Lord
is the beginning of acceptance; obduracy and pride are
the beginning of rejection.*

Mt.18.21. **11:** Job 17.14; Is.14.11. **12:** Dt.8.14. **14:** 1 Sam.2.8; Lk.1.52. **16:** Is.40.15–17;
Wis.11.21–22.
  10.19–25: True honor. **19:** Jer.9.23–24; 1 Cor.1.26–31; 2 Cor.10.17; Jas.1.9. **23:** Jas.2.1–4.
25: Pr.17.2.
  10.26–11.1: Wrong and right estimation of self. **27:** Pr.12.9. **11.1:** 39.4; compare Gen.41.40;
Dan.6.3.

and will seat him among the
great.

²Do not praise a man for his good
looks,
nor loathe a man because of his
appearance.
³The bee is small among flying
creatures,
but her product is the best of
sweet things.
⁴Do not boast about wearing fine
clothes,
nor exalt yourself in the day that
you are honored;
for the works of the Lord are
wonderful,
and his works are concealed
from men.
⁵Many kings have had to sit on the
ground,
but one who was never thought
of has worn a crown.
⁶Many rulers have been greatly
disgraced,
and illustrious men have been
handed over to others.

⁷Do not find fault before you
investigate;
first consider, and then
reprove.
⁸Do not answer before you have
heard,
nor interrupt a speaker in the
midst of his words.
⁹Do not argue about a matter which
does not concern you,
nor sit with sinners when they
judge a case.

¹⁰My son, do not busy yourself with
many matters;
if you multiply activities you will
not go unpunished,
and if you pursue you will not
overtake,

and by fleeing you will not
escape.
¹¹There is a man who works, and
toils, and presses on,
but is so much the more in want.
¹²There is another who is slow and
needs help,
who lacks strength and abounds
in poverty;
but the eyes of the Lord look upon
him for his good;
he lifts him out of his low estate
¹³and raises up his head,
so that many are amazed at him.

¹⁴Good things and bad, life and
death,
poverty and wealth, come from
the Lord.ᵒ
¹⁷The gift of the Lord endures for
those who are godly,
and what he approves will have
lasting success.
¹⁸There is a man who is rich through
his diligence and self-denial,
and this is the reward allotted to
him:
¹⁹when he says, "I have found rest,
and now I shall enjoyᵖ my
goods!"
he does not know how much time
will pass
until he leaves them to others
and dies.
²⁰Stand by your covenant�q and
attend to it,
and grow old in your work.

²¹Do not wonder at the works of a
sinner,
but trust in the Lord and keep at
your toil;

o Other authorities add as verses 15 and 16, ¹⁵*Wisdom,
understanding, and knowledge of the law come from the
Lord; affection and the ways of good works come from
him.* ¹⁶*Error and darkness were created with sinners;
evil will grow old with those who take pride in malice.*
p Gk *eat of*
q Heb *task*

11.2–9: Warnings against hasty judgments, based on *looks* (v. 2), size (v. 3), or *clothes* (v. 4);
compare 1 Sam.16.7. **6:** 1 Sam.15.28; Est.7.10. **8:** Pr.18.13. **9b:** Ps.1.1.

11.10–13: Discretion in conduct. 11: Pr.10.3; Ec.9.11. **12b:** Ps.34.15.

11.14–28: All things come from God. 14: A summary of the following section (1 Sam.2.7;
Job 1.21; Is.45.7). **19:** Lk.12.19. **21:** 9.11; Pr.3.31; 23.17. *Keep at your toil*, Hebrew and
Syriac, "abide in his light."

for it is easy in the sight of the Lord
   to enrich a poor man quickly
   and suddenly.
²²The blessing of the Lord is^r the
   reward of the godly,
   and quickly God causes his
   blessing to flourish.
²³Do not say, "What do I need,
   and what prosperity could be
   mine in the future?"
²⁴Do not say, "I have enough,
   and what calamity could
   happen to me in the future?"
²⁵In the day of prosperity, adversity
   is forgotten,
   and in the day of adversity,
   prosperity is not remembered.
²⁶For it is easy in the sight of the
   Lord
   to reward a man on the day of
   death according to his
   conduct.
²⁷The misery of an hour makes one
   forget luxury,
   and at the close of a man's life
   his deeds will be revealed.
²⁸Call no one happy before his
   death;
   a man will be known through
   his children.

²⁹Do not bring every man into your
   home,
   for many are the wiles of the
   crafty.
³⁰Like a decoy partridge in a cage,
   so is the mind of a proud man,
   and like a spy he observes your
   weakness;^s
³¹for he lies in wait, turning good
   into evil,
   and to worthy actions he will
   attach blame.
³²From a spark of fire come many
   burning coals,

and a sinner lies in wait to shed
   blood.
³³Beware of a scoundrel, for he
   devises evil,
   lest he give you a lasting
   blemish.
³⁴Receive a stranger into your home
   and he will upset you with
   commotion,
   and will estrange you from your
   family.

12 If you do a kindness, know to
   whom you do it,
   and you will be thanked for your
   good deeds.
²Do good to a godly man, and you
   will be repaid—
   if not by him, certainly by the
   Most High.
³No good will come to the man who
   persists in evil
   or to him who does not give
   alms.
⁴Give to the godly man, but do not
   help the sinner.
⁵ Do good to the humble, but do
   not give to the ungodly;
   hold back his bread, and do not
   give it to him,
   lest by means of it he subdue
   you;
   for you will receive twice as much
   evil
   for all the good which you do to
   him.
⁶For the Most High also hates
   sinners
   and will inflict punishment on
   the ungodly.^t
⁷Give to the good man, but do not
   help the sinner.

r Gk *is in*
s Heb: Gk *downfall*
t Other authorities add *and he is keeping them for the
  mighty day of their punishment*

26–27: Sirach's theology does not include a future life.   **28:** *Through his children*, Hebrew,
"by his latter end," i.e. a man's circumstances at the time of his death indicate the kind of life
he has lived.
    11.29–34: Care in choosing companions. 31: Hebrew, "The backbiter turns good to evil."
32: Pr.1.11.
    12.1–7: The need of discretion in almsgiving (Mt.7.6). **3:** Hebrew, "No good comes to him
who helps the wicked, nor is it an act of benevolence which he has done." **4–5:** Contrast
Lk.6.27–31; Gal.6.10.

⁸A friend will not be known" in
    prosperity,
  nor will an enemy be hidden in
    adversity.
⁹A man's enemies are grieved when
    he prospers,
  and in his adversity even his
    friend will separate from him.
¹⁰Never trust your enemy,
  for like the rusting of copper, so
    is his wickedness.
¹¹Even if he humbles himself and
    goes about cringing,
  watch yourself, and be on your
    guard against him;
  and you will be to him like one
    who has polished a mirror,
  and you will know that it was
    not hopelessly tarnished.
¹²Do not put him next to you,
  lest he overthrow you and take
    your place;
  do not have him sit at your right,
    lest he try to take your seat of
    honor,
  and at last you will realize the
    truth of my words,
  and be stung by what I have
    said.

¹³Who will pity a snake charmer
    bitten by a serpent,
  or any who go near wild beasts?
¹⁴So no one will pity a man who
    associates with a sinner
  and becomes involved in his sins.
¹⁵He will stay with you for a time,
  but if you falter, he will not
    stand by you.

¹⁶An enemy will speak sweetly with
    his lips,
  but in his mind he will plan to
    throw you into a pit;
  an enemy will weep with his eyes,
  but if he finds an opportunity

his thirst for blood will be
    insatiable.
¹⁷If calamity befalls you, you will
    find him there ahead of you;
  and while pretending to help
    you, he will trip you by the
    heel;
¹⁸he will shake his head, and clap
    his hands,
  and whisper much, and change
    his expression.

13 Whoever touches pitch will
    be defiled,
  and whoever associates with a
    proud man will become like
    him.
²Do not lift a weight beyond your
    strength,
  nor associate with a man
    mightier and richer than
    you.
How can the clay pot associate
    with the iron kettle?
The pot will strike against it,
    and will itself be broken.
³A rich man does wrong, and he
    even adds reproaches;
  a poor man suffers wrong, and
    he must add apologies.
⁴A rich manᵛ will exploit you if you
    can be of use to him,
  but if you are in need he will
    forsake you.
⁵If you own something, he will live
    with you;
  he will drain your resources and
    he will not care.
⁶When he needs you he will deceive
    you,
  he will smile at you and give you
    hope.
He will speak to you kindly and
    say, "What do you need?"

u Other authorities read *punished*
v Gk *He*

12.8–18: False friends (compare 6.5–17). **9a:** Hebrew, "When a man is prosperous, even his
enemy is friendly" (Pr.19.4,6). **11c,d:** As one can prevent tarnish on a metal mirror by constantly polishing it, so the dangers of false friendship can be avoided by constant watchfulness.
18: *Shake his head*, a gesture of derisive triumph (13.7; Job 16.4; Ps.22.7; Mt.27.39). *Whisper*,
secretly conspiring (Ps.41.7). *Change his expression*, openly showing his enmity.
  13.1–20: Warnings concerning associates. 1: A summary of what follows. **3:** *He must add*

⁷He will shame you with his foods,
   until he has drained you two or
      three times;
   and finally he will deride you.
Should he see you afterwards, he
      will forsake you,
   and shake his head at you.

⁸Take care not to be led astray,
   and not to be humiliated in your
      feasting.ʷ
⁹When a powerful man invites you,
      be reserved;
   and he will invite you the more
      often.
¹⁰Do not push forward, lest you be
      repulsed;
   and do not remain at a distance,
      lest you be forgotten.
¹¹Do not try to treat him as an equal,
      nor trust his abundance of words;
   for he will test you through much
      talk,
   and while he smiles he will be
      examining you.
¹²Cruel is he who does not keep
      words to himself;
   he will not hesitate to injure or
      to imprison.
¹³Keep words to yourself and be very
      watchful,
   for you are walking about with
      your own downfall.ˣ

¹⁵Every creature loves its like,
   and every person his neighbor;
¹⁶all living beings associate by species,
   and a man clings to one like
      himself.
¹⁷What fellowship has a wolf with a
      lamb?
   No more has a sinner with a
      godly man.
¹⁸What peace is there between a
      hyena and a dog?
   And what peace between a rich
      man and a poor man?
¹⁹Wild asses in the wilderness are

the prey of lions;
   likewise the poor are pastures
      for the rich.
²⁰Humility is an abomination to a
      proud man;
   likewise a poor man is an
      abomination to a rich one.

²¹When a rich man totters, he is
      steadied by friends,
   but when a humble man falls, he
      is even pushed away by friends.
²²If a rich man slips, his helpers are
      many;
   he speaks unseemly words, and
      they justify him.
If a humble man slips, they even
      reproach him;
   he speaks sensibly, and receives
      no attention.
²³When the rich man speaks all are
      silent,
   and they extol to the clouds what
      he says.
When the poor man speaks they
      say, "Who is this fellow?"
And should he stumble, they
      even push him down.

²⁴Riches are good if they are free
      from sin,
   and poverty is evil in the
      opinion of the ungodly.
²⁵A man's heart changes his
      countenance,
   either for good or for evil.ʸ
²⁶The mark of a happy heart is a
      cheerful face,
   but to devise proverbs requires
      painful thinking.

14 Blessed is the man who does
   not blunder with his lips
   and need not suffer grief for sin.
²Blessed is he whose heart does

w Other authorities read *folly*
x Other authorities add *When you hear these things in
  your sleep, wake up!* ¹⁴*During all your life love the
  Lord, and call on him for your salvation.*
y Other authorities add *and a glad heart makes a cheerful
  countenance*

---

apologies, as though it were he who committed the wrong. **7**: Compare Pr.23.1–3. *Shake his
head*, see 12.18 n. **15**: 27.9. **17**: 2 Cor.6.14. **19**: Job 24.5. **20**: Pr.29.27.
   13.21–14.2: The rich and the poor. 21–23: Pr.14.20; 19.4,7. **26a**: Pr.15.13. **26b**: Ec.12.12.
14.2: Rom.14.22; 1 Jn.3.21.

not condemn him,
and who has not given up his hope.

³Riches are not seemly for a stingy
man;
and of what use is property to
an envious man?
⁴Whoever accumulates by depriving
himself, accumulates for others;
and others will live in luxury on
his goods.
⁵If a man is mean to himself, to
whom will he be generous?
He will not enjoy his own riches.
⁶No one is meaner than the man
who is grudging to himself,
and this is the retribution for
his baseness;
⁷even if he does good, he does it
unintentionally,
and betrays his baseness in the end.
⁸Evil is the man with a grudging eye;
he averts his face and disregards
people.
⁹A greedy man's eye is not satisfied
with a portion,
and mean injustice withers the
soul.
¹⁰A stingy man's eye begrudges bread,
and it is lacking at his table.

¹¹My son, treat yourself well,
according to your means,
and present worthy offerings to
the Lord.
¹²Remember that death will not delay,
and the decree* of Hades has
not been shown to you.
¹³Do good to a friend before you die,
and reach out and give to him
as much as you can.
¹⁴Do not deprive yourself of a happy
day;
let not your share of desired
good pass by you.

¹⁵Will you not leave the fruit of your
labors to another,
and what you acquired by toil
to be divided by lot?
¹⁶Give, and take, and beguile yourself,
because in Hades one cannot
look for luxury.
¹⁷All living beings become old like a
garment,
for the decree* from of old is,
"You must surely die!"
¹⁸Like flourishing leaves on a
spreading tree
which sheds some and puts
forth others,
so are the generations of flesh and
blood:
one dies and another is born.
¹⁹Every product decays and ceases to
exist,
and the man who made it will
pass away with it.

²⁰Blessed is the man who meditates
on* wisdom
and who reasons intelligently.
²¹He who reflects in his mind on her
ways
will also ponder her secrets.
²²Pursue wisdom* like a hunter,
and lie in wait on her paths.
²³He who peers through her
windows
will also listen at her doors;
²⁴he who encamps near her house
will also fasten his tent peg to
her walls;
²⁵he will pitch his tent near her,
and will lodge in an excellent
lodging place;
²⁶he will place his children under
her shelter,
and will camp under her boughs;

z Gk *covenant*   a Gk *covenant*
b Other authorities read *dies in*   c Gk *her*

14.3–19: Envy and avarice. 4: 11.19–20; Job 27.16–17; Pr.13.22; Ec.6.2; Lk.12.16–21.
8: *Averts his face*, 4.4; Tob.4.7. **10:** Pr.23.6–7. The Hebrew and Syriac add, "A good eye
[i.e. a liberal man] causes bread to increase, and 'A dry spring sends forth water' [this appears
to be a proverb] upon his table." **11–16:** Wealth should be used wisely during life, for it must
be left behind at death. **13:** Tob.4.7; Lk.14.13. **14:** Ec.5.18. **15:** V. 4. **16:** Ec.9.10. *Hades*,
Hebrew "sheol." **17:** *Like a garment*, Ps.102.26; compare Is.40.6; Jas.1.10; 1 Pet.1.24. **18:**
Ec.1.4. **19:** Contrast Rev.14.13.
  14.20–15.10: The search for wisdom and its blessings (Pr.8.32–35). **26a:** Hebrew, "He builds

²⁷he will be sheltered by her from
the heat,
and will dwell in the midst of her
glory.

15 The man who fears the Lord
will do this,
and he who holds to the law will
obtain wisdom.ᵈ
²She will come to meet him like a
mother,
and like the wife of his youth
she will welcome him.
³She will feed him with the bread
of understanding,
and give him the water of
wisdom to drink.
⁴He will lean on her and will not
fall,
and he will rely on her and will
not be put to shame.
⁵She will exalt him above his
neighbors,
and will open his mouth in the
midst of the assembly.
⁶He will find gladness and a crown
of rejoicing,
and will acquire an everlasting
name.
⁷Foolish men will not obtain her,
and sinful men will not see
her.
⁸She is far from men of pride,
and liars will never think of
her.

⁹A hymn of praise is not fitting on
the lips of a sinner,
for it has not been sent from the
Lord.
¹⁰For a hymn of praise should be

uttered in wisdom,
and the Lord will prosper it.

¹¹Do not say, "Because of the Lord
I left the right way";
for heᵉ will not do what he hates.
¹²Do not say, "It was he who led me
astray";
for he has no need of a sinful
man.
¹³The Lord hates all abominations,
and they are not loved by those
who fear him.
¹⁴It was he who created man in the
beginning,
and he left him in the power of
his own inclination.
¹⁵If you will, you can keep the
commandments,
and to act faithfully is a matter
of your own choice.
¹⁶He has placed before you fire and
water:
stretch out your hand for
whichever you wish.
¹⁷Before a manᶠ are life and death,
and whichever he chooses will be
given to him.
¹⁸For great is the wisdom of the
Lord;
he is mighty in power and sees
everything;
¹⁹his eyes are on those who fear him,
and he knows every deed of
man.
²⁰He has not commanded any one
to be ungodly,
and he has not given any one
permission to sin.

d Gk *her*
e Heb: Gk *you*   *f* Gk *men*

---

his nest in her foliage." **15.1:** Hebrew prefixes "For," connecting 14.20–27 (telling how wisdom
must be sought) with 15.1–8 (telling how wisdom will welcome those who seek her). *The law*
is identified with wisdom (1.26; 19.20; 21.11; 24.23). **2b:** Hebrew, "Like a young bride she will
embrace him." **3:** Pr.9.2,5. **9–10:** Compare Pr.27.21b.
   15.11–20: Free will and responsibility for sin (17.1–12). **11–12:** Jas.1.13. **13b:** Hebrew,
"and he does not let them come near those who fear him." **14:** Gen.1.27. *Inclination,* the
Hebrew word *yeṣer* is a technical term, used here in a neutral sense meaning "free will."
Elsewhere *yeṣer* is sometimes used in a good sense (Is.26.3; 1 Chr.29.18); but usually it refers to
an evil tendency or inclination toward sin (Gen.6.5; 8.21; compare 2 Esd.4.30–31). In post-
biblical times the doctrine arose of a good and an evil *yeṣer* which every person possesses. **16:**
Fire and water, representing opposite extremes. *Fire* here has no eschatological significance.
17: Dt.30.19; Jer.21.8. **18–19:** Ps.33.13,18; 34.15; Heb.4.13.

16 Do not desire a multitude
of useless children,
nor rejoice in ungodly sons.
²If they multiply, do not rejoice in
them,
unless the fear of the Lord is in
them.
³Do not trust in their survival,
and do not rely on their
multitude;
for one is better than a thousand,ᵍ
and to die childless is better
than to have ungodly children.
⁴For through one man of
understanding a city will be
filled with people,
but through a tribe of lawless
men it will be made desolate.
⁵Many such things my eye has seen,
and my ear has heard things
more striking than these.

⁶In an assembly of sinners a fire will
be kindled,
and in a disobedient nation
wrath was kindled.
⁷He was not propitiated for the
ancient giants
who revolted in their might.
⁸He did not spare the neighbors of
Lot,
whom he loathed on account of
their insolence.
⁹He showed no pity for a nation
devoted to destruction,
for those destroyed in their sins;
¹⁰nor for the six hundred thousand
men on foot,
who rebelliously assembled in
their stubbornness.
¹¹Even if there is only one stiff-necked
person,
it will be a wonder if he remains
unpunished.

For mercy and wrath are with the
Lord;ʰ
he is mighty to forgive, and he
pours out wrath.
¹²As great as his mercy, so great is
also his reproof;
he judges a man according to
his deeds.
¹³The sinner will not escape with his
plunder,
and the patience of the godly
will not be frustrated.
¹⁴He will make room for every act
of mercy;
every one will receive in
accordance with his deeds.ⁱ

¹⁷Do not say, "I shall be hidden from
the Lord,
and who from on high will
remember me?
Among so many people I shall not
be known,
for what is my soul in the
boundless creation?
¹⁸Behold, heaven and the highest
heaven,
the abyss and the earth, will
tremble at his visitation.
¹⁹The mountains also and the
foundations of the earth
shake with trembling when he
looks upon them.
²⁰And no mind will reflect on this.
Who will ponder his ways?
²¹Like a tempest which no man can
see,
so most of his works are
concealed.

---

g The text of this line is uncertain
h Gk *him*
i Other authorities add ¹⁵*The Lord hardened Pharaoh so
that he did not know him; in order that his works might
be known under heaven.* ¹⁶*His mercy is manifest to the
whole of creation, and he divided his light and darkness
with a plumb line.*

16.1–5: The misfortune of having ungodly children. 3c: Hebrew and Syriac, "For better is
one who does the will [of the Lord] than a thousand [godless children]."
    16.6–23: The certainty of punishment for sin. 6: *A fire will be kindled*, 21.9; compare Num.
16.35. **7:** *Ancient giants*, Gen.6.4; Wis.14.6; Bar.3.26–28. **8:** Gen.19.14–25. **10:** 46.8; Num.
11.21. **11:** *Mercy and wrath*, 5.6. **12b:** Ps.62.12. **16b** (in note *i*): Hebrew, "and his light and his
darkness he has apportioned to the children of men." **17d:** Hebrew, "and what is my soul
among the multitudes of spirits of all the children of men?" **18–19:** A parenthetical meditation
on the supreme power of God. **20–22:** Hebrew, continuing the thought of v. 17, "In truth, he
[God] does not set his heart on me [pays no attention to me]; and as for my ways, who will

²²Who will announce his acts of
  justice?
  Or who will await them? For
    the covenant is far off."
²³This is what one devoid of
    understanding thinks;
  a senseless and misguided man
    thinks foolishly.

²⁴Listen to me, my son, and acquire
    knowledge,
  and pay close attention to my
    words.
²⁵I will impart instruction by weight,
  and declare knowledge accurately.

²⁶The works of the Lord have existed
    from the beginning by his
    creation,ʲ
  and when he made them, he
    determined their divisions.
²⁷He arranged his works in an eternal
    order,
  and their dominionᵏ for allˡ
    generations;
  they neither hunger nor grow weary,
  and they do not cease from their
    labors.
²⁸They do not crowd one another
    aside,
  and they will never disobey his
    word.
²⁹After this the Lord looked upon
    the earth,
  and filled it with his good things;
³⁰with all kinds of living beings he
    covered its surface,
  and to it they return.

17 The Lord created man out of
    earth,
  and turned him back to it again.

²He gave to menᵐ few days, a
    limited time,
  but granted them authority over
    the things upon the earth.ⁿ
³He endowed them with strength
    like his own,ᵒ
  and made them in his own image.
⁴He placed the fear of themᵖ in all
    living beings,
  and granted them dominion
    over beasts and birds.�q
⁶He made for themʳ tongue and eyes;
  he gave them ears and a mind
    for thinking.
⁷He filled them with knowledge
    and understanding,
  and showed them good and evil.
⁸He set his eye upon their hearts
  to show them the majesty of his
    works.ˢ
¹⁰And they will praise his holy name,
  to proclaim the grandeur of his
    works.
¹¹He bestowed knowledge upon them,
  and allotted to them the law of life.
¹²He established with them an eternal
    covenant,
  and showed them his judgments.
¹³Their eyes saw his glorious majesty,
  and their ears heard the glory of
    his voice.
¹⁴And he said to them, "Beware of
    all unrighteousness."ᵗ
  And he gave commandment to
    each of them concerning his
    neighbor.

j Heb: Gk *judgment*   *k* Or *elements*
l Gk *their*   *m* Gk *them*   *n* Gk *it*
o Cn: Gk *proper to them*   *p* Syr: Gk *him*
q Other authorities add ⁵*They obtained the use of the five operations of the Lord; as sixth he distributed to them the gift of mind, and as seventh reason, the interpreter of his operations.*   *r* Syr: Gk *Inclination and*
s Other authorities add ⁹*and he gave them to boast of his marvels for ever*   *t* Or *every unrighteous man*

mark them? ²¹ If I sin, no eye will see me, or if I deal untruly in all secrecy, who will know it?
²² My righteous dealing, who shall declare it? And what hope is there? For the decree is distant" (i.e. the decreed reward for righteousness is remote and uncertain). **23**: Sirach's own
view of the ideas expressed in vv. 17–22.
16.24–17.14: Divine wisdom seen in creation. 16.27–28: 43.10; Is.40.26. **29**: *After this*, compare Gen.1.20–31. **30**: *To it*, the earth (Gen.3.19; Ps.104.29). **17.1**: Gen.2.7; 3.19; Ps.146.4.
2a: Literally, "He granted them days by number, and a set time" (Gen.6.3; Ps.90.10). **3**: Gen.
1.26–27. **4**: Gen.1.28; Ps.8.6–8. **5** (in note *q*): *The five operations*, or "powers" (i.e. the five
senses). **7**: Gen.2.17. **11**: Syriac, "He set before them the covenant" (Dt.4.44). *The law of life*,
the law which gives life (45.5; Bar.4.1). **12**: *Eternal covenant*, Ex.19.16–24.18. **14**: A summary
of all the prohibitory commandments.

¹⁵Their ways are always before him,
  they will not be hid from his
  eyes.ᵘ
¹⁷He appointed a ruler for every
  nation,
  but Israel is the Lord's own
  portion.ᵛ
¹⁹All their works are as the sun
  before him,
  and his eyes are continually
  upon their ways.
²⁰Their iniquities are not hidden
  from him,
  and all their sins are before the
  Lord.ʷ
²²A man's almsgiving is like a signet
  with the Lord,ˣ
  and he will keep a person's
  kindness like the apple of his eye.
²³Afterward he will arise and requite
  them,
  and he will bring their
  recompense on their heads.
²⁴Yet to those who repent he grants
  a return,
  and he encourages those whose
  endurance is failing.

²⁵Turn to the Lord and forsake your
  sins;
  pray in his presence and lessen
  your offenses.
²⁶Return to the Most High and turn
  away from iniquity,ʸ
  and hate abominations intensely.
²⁷Who will sing praises to the Most
  High in Hades,
  as do those who are alive and
  give thanks?
²⁸From the dead, as from one who
  does not exist, thanksgiving
  has ceased;
  he who is alive and well sings
  the Lord's praises.
²⁹How great is the mercy of the Lord,
  and his forgiveness for those

who turn to him!
³⁰For all things cannot be in men,ᶻ
  since a son of man is not immortal.
³¹What is brighter than the sun? Yet
  its light fails.ᵃ
  So flesh and blood devise evil.
³²He marshals the host of the height
  of heaven;
  but all men are dust and ashes.

18 He who lives for ever created
  the whole universe;
² the Lord alone will be declared
  righteous.ᵇ
⁴To none has he given power to
  proclaim his works;
  and who can search out his
  mighty deeds?
⁵Who can measure his majestic
  power?
  And who can fully recount his
  mercies?
⁶It is not possible to diminish or
  increase them,
  nor is it possible to trace the
  wonders of the Lord.
⁷When a man has finished, he is
  just beginning,
  and when he stops, he will be
  at a loss.
⁸What is man, and of what use is
  he?
  What is his good and what is
  his evil?

u Other authorities add ¹⁶*Their ways from youth tend
toward evil, and they are unable to make for themselves
hearts of flesh in place of their stony hearts.* ¹⁷*For in
the division of the nations of the whole earth*
v Other authorities add ¹⁸*whom, being his first-born, he
brings up with discipline, and allotting to him the light of
his love, he does not neglect him.*
w Other authorities add ²¹*But the Lord, who is gracious
and knows his creatures, has neither left nor abandoned
them, but spared them.*   x Gk *him*
y Other authorities add *for he will lead you out of darkness to the light of health*
z The Greek text of this line is uncertain
a Or *suffers eclipse*
b Other authorities add *and there is no other beside him;*
³*he steers the world with the span of his hand, and all
things obey his will; for he is king of all things, by his
power separating among them the holy things from the
profane.*

17.15–24: The divine judge. 17: Dt.32.8–9. **22:** *Almsgiving,* 29.12–13. *Apple of his eye,*
Dt.32.10; Ps.17.8; Pr.7.2. **23:** *Arise,* in judgment. **24:** *A return,* to God's favor.
17.25–32: Exhortation to turn to God. 25–26: Jer.3.12. **27–28:** Ps.6.5; 115.17; Is.38.18;
Bar.2.17. **30:** Syriac, "For it is not like this in man [i.e. only God has such mercy and forgiveness (18.13)], nor is his [i.e. God's] thought like the thoughts of the children of men." **31b:**
Syriac, "So is man who has the inclination [see 15.14 n.] of flesh and blood."
18.1–14: The majesty of God. 4b: Ps.106.2. **8:** Ps.8.4. **9:** Compare Ps.90.10.

⁹The number of a man's days is
　　great if he reaches a hundred
　　years.
¹⁰Like a drop of water from the sea
　　and a grain*ᶜ* of sand
　　so are a few years in the day of
　　eternity.
¹¹Therefore the Lord is patient with
　　them
　　and pours out his mercy upon
　　them.
¹²He sees and recognizes that their
　　end will be evil;
　　therefore he grants them
　　forgiveness in abundance.
¹³The compassion of man is for his
　　neighbor,
　　but the compassion of the Lord
　　is for all living beings.
He rebukes and trains and teaches
　　them,
　　and turns them back, as a
　　shepherd his flock.
¹⁴He has compassion on those who
　　accept his discipline
　　and who are eager for his
　　judgments.

¹⁵My son, do not mix reproach with
　　your good deeds,
　　nor cause grief by your words
　　when you present a gift.
¹⁶Does not the dew assuage the
　　scorching heat?
　　So a word is better than a gift.
¹⁷Indeed, does not a word surpass a
　　good gift?
　　Both are to be found in a
　　gracious man.
¹⁸A fool is ungracious and abusive,
　　and the gift of a grudging man
　　makes the eyes dim.

¹⁹Before you speak, learn,
　　and before you fall ill, take care
　　of your health.
²⁰Before judgment, examine yourself,

and in the hour of visitation
　　you will find forgiveness.
²¹Before falling ill, humble yourself,
　　and when you are on the point
　　of sinning, turn back.
²²Let nothing hinder you from
　　paying a vow promptly,
　　and do not wait until death to
　　be released from it.
²³Before making a vow,*ᵈ* prepare
　　yourself;
　　and do not be like a man who
　　tempts the Lord.
²⁴Think of his wrath on the day of
　　death,
　　and of the moment of vengeance
　　when he turns away his face.
²⁵In the time of plenty think of the
　　time of hunger;
　　in the days of wealth think of
　　poverty and need.
²⁶From morning to evening
　　conditions change,
　　and all things move swiftly
　　before the Lord.

²⁷A wise man is cautious in
　　everything,
　　and in days of sin he guards
　　against wrongdoing.
²⁸Every intelligent man knows
　　wisdom,
　　and he praises the one who finds
　　her.
²⁹Those who understand sayings
　　become skilled themselves,
　　and pour forth apt proverbs.

³⁰Do not follow your base desires,
　　but restrain your appetites.
³¹If you allow your soul to take
　　pleasure in base desire,
　　it will make you the
　　laughingstock of your enemies.
³²Do not revel in great luxury,

c Gk *pebble*
d Or *offering a prayer*

18.15–18: The right spirit in giving alms. 15: Do not humiliate the receiver of charity (41.22).
16b: Syriac, "So a [kindly] word changes [the character of] a gift." 17a: Syriac, "For there is a
good word which is better than a gift."
18.19–29: The need of foresight. 22: Dt.23.21; Ec.5.4. 24: 7.36.
18.30–19.3: An exhortation to self-control. 33: Hebrew, "Do not be a squanderer and a

lest you become impoverished
by its expense.
33 Do not become a beggar by feasting
with borrowed money,
when you have nothing in your
purse.

19 A workman who is a drunkard
will not become rich;
he who despises small things
will fail little by little.
2 Wine and women lead intelligent
men astray,
and the man who consorts with
harlots is very reckless.
3 Decay and worms will inherit him,
and the reckless soul will be
snatched away.

4 One who trusts others too quickly
is lightminded,
and one who sins does wrong to
himself.
5 One who rejoices in wickedness[e]
will be condemned,[f]
6 and for one who hates gossip
evil is lessened.
7 Never repeat a conversation,
and you will lose nothing at
all.
8 With friend or foe do not report
it,
and unless it would be a sin for
you, do not disclose it;
9 for some one has heard you and
watched you,
and when the time comes he
will hate you.
10 Have you heard a word? Let it die
with you.
Be brave! It will not make you
burst!
11 With such a word a fool will suffer
pangs
like a woman in labor with a
child.

12 Like an arrow stuck in the flesh of
the thigh,
so is a word inside a fool.
13 Question a friend, perhaps he did
not do it;
but if he did anything, so that
he may do it no more.
14 Question a neighbor, perhaps he
did not say it;
but if he said it, so that he may
not say it again.
15 Question a friend, for often it is
slander;
so do not believe everything you
hear.
16 A person may make a slip without
intending it.
Who has never sinned with his
tongue?
17 Question your neighbor before you
threaten him;
and let the law of the Most
High take its course.[g]

20 All wisdom is the fear of the
Lord,
and in all wisdom there is the
fulfilment of the law.[h]
22 But the knowledge of wickedness
is not wisdom,
nor is there prudence where
sinners take counsel.
23 There is a cleverness which is
abominable,
but there is a fool who merely
lacks wisdom.

e Other authorities read *heart*
f Other authorities add *but he who withstands pleasures crowns his life.* 6*He who controls his tongue will live without strife,*
g Other authorities add *and do not be angry.* 18*The fear of the Lord is the beginning of acceptance, and wisdom obtains his love.* 19*The knowledge of the Lord's commandments is life-giving discipline; and those who do what is pleasing to him enjoy the fruit of the tree of immortality.*
h Other authorities add, *and the knowledge of his omnipotence.* 21*When a servant says to his master, "I will not act as you wish," even if later he does it, he angers the one who supports him.*

---

drunkard, else there will be nothing in your purse." **19.1:** *Will fail . . . little*, Hebrew, "will become altogether naked," i.e. destitute.
    19.4–12: A warning against too much talking. 7b: Syriac, "then no one will reproach you" (Pr.25.9–10). **8:** *Unless* by keeping silent *it would be a sin.* **9:** Pr.25.10.
    19.13–17: On administering reproof. 16: Jas.3.2. **17:** Lev.19.17; Mt.18.15; Lk.17.3.
    19.20–30: Wisdom and craftiness contrasted. 20: Jas.1.25. **21** (in note *h*): Mt.21.28–32. **23:** *Who merely lacks wisdom*, and is guileless.

²⁴Better is the God-fearing man who
  lacks intelligence,
    than the highly prudent man
      who transgresses the law.
²⁵There is a cleverness which is
  scrupulous but unjust,
    and there are people who distort
      kindness to gain a verdict.
²⁶There is a rascal bowed down in
  mourning,ⁱ
    but inwardly he is full of deceit.
²⁷He hides his face and pretends not
  to hear;
    but where no one notices, he
      will forestall you.
²⁸And if by lack of strength he is
  prevented from sinning,
    he will do evil when he finds an
      opportunity.
²⁹A man is known by his appearance,
  and a sensible man is known
    by his face, when you meet
      him.
³⁰A man's attire and open-mouthed
  laughter,
    and a man's manner of walking,
      show what he is.

20 There is a reproof which is
   not timely;
    and there is a man who keeps
      silent but is wise.
²How much better it is to reprove
  than to stay angry!
    And the one who confesses his
      fault will be kept from loss.ʲ
⁴Like a eunuch's desire to violate a
  maiden
    is a man who executes
      judgments by violence.
⁵There is one who by keeping silent
  is found wise,
    while another is detested for
      being too talkative.
⁶There is one who keeps silent
  because he has no answer,
    while another keeps silent

because he knows when to
  speak.
⁷A wise man will be silent until the
  right moment,
    but a braggart and fool goes
      beyond the right moment.
⁸Whoever uses too many words will
  be loathed,
    and whoever usurps the right to
      speak will be hated.

⁹There may be good fortune for a
  man in adversity,
    and a windfall may result in a
      loss.
¹⁰There is a gift that profits you
  nothing,
    and there is a gift that brings a
      double return.
¹¹There are losses because of glory,
  and there are men who have
    raised their heads from humble
      circumstances.
¹²There is a man who buys much for
  a little,
    but pays for it seven times over.
¹³The wise man makes himself
  beloved through his words,
    but the courtesies of fools are
      wasted.
¹⁴A fool's gift will profit you nothing,
  for he has many eyes instead of
    one.
¹⁵He gives little and upbraids much,
  he opens his mouth like a
    herald;
    today he lends and tomorrow he
      asks it back;
      such a one is a hateful man.
¹⁶A fool will say, "I have no friend,
  and there is no gratitude for my
    good deeds;
    those who eat my bread speak
      unkindly."

i Gk *blackness*
j Other authorities add ³*How good it is to show repentance when you are reproved, for so you will escape
   deliberate sin!*

30: Instead of *and . . . laughter*, the Syriac reads, "proclaims his deeds," i.e. his occupation.
  20.1–26: Use and abuse of the tongue. **1–8:** Proper times for speech and for silence. **2:** Syriac,
"He that reproves a sinner gets no thanks, but let him that makes confession be kept back from
hurt" (i.e. be spared humiliation). **5:** Pr.17.28. **7:** V. 20b; Ec.3.7.
  20.9–17: Paradoxes. **13:** 6.5. *Are wasted*, are thrown away. **14:** Syriac, "for he looks for
sevenfold repayment."

¹⁷How many will ridicule him, and
   how often!

¹⁸A slip on the pavement is better
   than a slip of the tongue;
   so the downfall of the wicked
   will occur speedily.
¹⁹An ungracious man is like a story
   told at the wrong time,
   which is continually on the lips
   of the ignorant.
²⁰A proverb from a fool's lips will
   be rejected,
   for he does not tell it at its
   proper time.

²¹A man may be prevented from
   sinning by his poverty,
   so when he rests he feels no
   remorse.
²²A man may lose his life through
   shame,
   or lose it because of his foolish
   look.
²³A man may for shame make
   promises to a friend,
   and needlessly make him an
   enemy.

²⁴A lie is an ugly blot on a man;
   it is continually on the lips of
   the ignorant.
²⁵A thief is preferable to a habitual
   liar,
   but the lot of both is ruin.
²⁶The disposition of a liar brings
   disgrace,
   and his shame is ever with him.

²⁷He who speaks wisely will advance
   himself,
   and a sensible man will please
   great men.

²⁸Whoever cultivates the soil will
   heap up his harvest,
   and whoever pleases great men
   will atone for injustice.
²⁹Presents and gifts blind the eyes of
   the wise;
   like a muzzle on the mouth they
   avert reproofs.
³⁰Hidden wisdom and unseen treasure,
   what advantage is there in either
   of them?
³¹Better is the man who hides his folly
   than the man who hides his
   wisdom.ᵏ

21 Have you sinned, my son?
   Do so no more,
   but pray about your former sins.
²Flee from sin as from a snake;
   for if you approach sin, it will
   bite you.
   Its teeth are lion's teeth,
   and destroy the souls of men.
³All lawlessness is like a two-edged
   sword;
   there is no healing for its wound.

⁴Terror and violence will lay waste
   riches;
   thus the house of the proud will
   be laid waste.
⁵The prayer of a poor man goes from
   his lips to the ears of God,ˡ
   and his judgment comes speedily.
⁶Whoever hates reproof walks in
   the steps of the sinner,
   but he that fears the Lord will
   repent in his heart.
⁷He who is mighty in speech is
   known from afar;

k Other authorities add ³²*Unwearied patience in seeking
the Lord is better than a masterless charioteer of one's
own life.*   l Gk *his ears*

20.18–20: Concerning inappropriate speech. 19: Syriac, "As the fat tail of a sheep [Ex.29.22],
eaten without salt, so is a word spoken out of season."
   20.21–23: Sin unintentionally avoided, and intentionally committed. 22: 4.20–21. **23:** *Make
him an enemy*, because of inability to fulfil the promises.
   20.24–26: Lying. Ps.5.6; Pr.12.22; 13.5.
   20.27–31: The reward of the wise. 27: *Will please*, Syriac, "will rule." **28:** Pr.12.11. **29:**
Presents and gifts, i.e. bribes (Dt.16.19; Pr.17.8). **30:** 41.14–15.
   21.1–10: Warnings against sin. 2–3: The characteristics of sin are subtlety, strength, and
deadliness. **5:** 35.17–19. **5b:** Syriac, "and it ascends unto the presence of the eternal Judge."
7: Syriac, "The wise man recognizes him that is before him, and discerns the sinner in a mo-

but the sensible man, when he
    slips, is aware of it.

⁸A man who builds his house with
        other people's money
    is like one who gathers stones
        for his burial mound.ᵐ
⁹An assembly of the wicked is like
        tow gathered together,
    and their end is a flame of fire.
¹⁰The way of sinners is smoothly
        paved with stones,
    but at its end is the pit of Hades.

¹¹Whoever keeps the law controls
        his thoughts,
    and wisdom is the fulfilment of
        the fear of the Lord.
¹²He who is not clever cannot be
        taught,
    but there is a cleverness which
        increases bitterness.
¹³The knowledge of a wise man will
        increase like a flood,
    and his counsel like a flowing
        spring.
¹⁴The mind of a fool is like a broken
        jar;
    it will hold no knowledge.

¹⁵When a man of understanding
        hears a wise saying,
    he will praise it and add to it;
    when a reveler hears it, he dislikes
        it
    and casts it behind his back.
¹⁶A fool's narration is like a burden
        on a journey,
    but delight will be found in the
        speech of the intelligent.
¹⁷The utterance of a sensible man
    will be sought in the assembly,
    and they will ponder his words
        in their minds.

¹⁸Like a house that has vanished, so
    is wisdom to a fool;

and the knowledge of the
        ignorant is unexamined talk.
¹⁹To a senseless man education is
        fetters on his feet,
    and like manacles on his right
        hand.
²⁰A fool raises his voice when he
        laughs,
    but a clever man smiles quietly.
²¹To a sensible man education is like
        a golden ornament,
    and like a bracelet on the right
        arm.

²²The foot of a fool rushes into a
        house,
    but a man of experience stands
        respectfully before it.
²³A boor peers into the house from
        the door,
    but a cultivated man remains
        outside.
²⁴It is ill-mannered for a man to
        listen at a door,
    and a discreet man is grieved by
        the disgrace.
²⁵The lips of strangers will speak of
        these things,ⁿ
    but the words of the prudent
        will be weighed in the balance.
²⁶The mind of fools is in their mouth,
    but the mouth of wise men is
        inᵒ their mind.
²⁷When an ungodly man curses his
        adversary,ᵖ
    he curses his own soul.
²⁸A whisperer defiles his own soul
    and is hated in his neighborhood.

22 The indolent may be compared
    to a filthy stone,
    and every one hisses at his disgrace.
²The indolent may be compared to
    the filth of dunghills;

m Other authorities read *for the winter*
n The Greek text of this line is uncertain
o Other authorities omit *in*
p Or *curses Satan*

ment." **8:** That is, he prepares for his own destruction. **9:** 16.6. **10:** *Smoothly paved*, Pr.14.12;
16.25; Mt.7.13.
    21.11–28: The contrast between the wise man and the fool. 15: *Dislikes*, Syriac, "mocks at."
18a: Syriac, "As a prison-house is wisdom to a fool." **21:** This verse should follow v. 19.
20: 19.30; Ec.7.6. **22:** Pr.25.17. **28:** 5.14; 28.13.
    22.1–18: Concerning laziness and foolishness. 1b: Syriac, "Everyone flees from the stench

any one that picks it up will
    shake it off his hand.

³It is a disgrace to be the father of
    an undisciplined son,
    and the birth of a daughter is a
    loss.
⁴A sensible daughter obtains her
    husband,
    but one who acts shamefully
    brings grief to her father.
⁵An impudent daughter disgraces
    father and husband,
    and will be despised by both.
⁶Like music in mourning is a tale
    told at the wrong time,
    but chastising and discipline are
    wisdom at all times.

⁷He who teaches a fool is like
    one who glues potsherds
    together,
    or who rouses a sleeper from
    deep slumber.
⁸He who tells a story to a fool tells
    it to a drowsy man;
    and at the end he will say,
    "What is it?"�q
¹¹Weep for the dead, for he lacks
    the light;
    and weep for the fool, for he
    lacks intelligence;
    weep less bitterly for the dead, for
    he has attained rest;
    but the life of the fool is worse
    than death.
¹²Mourning for the dead lasts seven
    days,
    but for a fool or an ungodly man
    it lasts all his life.

¹³Do not talk much with a foolish
    man,
    and do not visit an unintelligent
    man;
    guard yourself from him to escape
    trouble,
    and you will not be soiled when
    he shakes himself off;

avoid him and you will find rest,
    and you will never be wearied by
    his madness.
¹⁴What is heavier than lead?
    And what is its name except
    "Fool"?
¹⁵Sand, salt, and a piece of iron
    are easier to bear than a stupid
    man.

¹⁶A wooden beam firmly bonded
    into a building
    will not be torn loose by an
    earthquake;
    so the mind firmly fixed on a
    reasonable counsel
    will not be afraid in a crisis.
¹⁷A mind settled on an intelligent
    thought
    is like the stucco decoration on
    the wall of a colonnade.ʳ
¹⁸Fences set on a high place
    will not stand firm against the
    wind;
    so a timid heart with a fool's
    purpose
    will not stand firm against any
    fear.

¹⁹A man who pricks an eye will
    make tears fall,
    and one who pricks the heart
    makes it show feeling.
²⁰One who throws a stone at birds
    scares them away,
    and one who reviles a friend will
    break off the friendship.
²¹Even if you have drawn your sword
    against a friend,
    do not despair, for a renewal of
    friendship is possible.
²²If you have opened your mouth
    against your friend,
    do not worry, for reconciliation
    is possible;
    but as for reviling, arrogance,

q Other authorities add ⁹*Children who are brought up in
a good life, conceal the lowly birth of their parents.*
¹⁰*Children who are disdainfully and boorishly haughty
stain the nobility of their kindred.*
r Or *on a smooth wall*

---

thereof." **3–6**: 16.1–5. **4**: *Obtains*, Hebrew, "becomes a treasure to." **5**: 42.11. **6**: Pr.25.20.
7: A thankless task. **12**: *Seven days*, Gen.50.10; Jdt.16.24. **13b**: *An unintelligent man*, Syriac,
"a pig in the way" (compare v. 13d). **15**: *Sand*, Job 6.3; Pr.27.3.

disclosure of secrets, or a
    treacherous blow—
    in these cases any friend will
        flee.

²³Gain the trust of your neighbor in
        his poverty,
    that you may rejoice with him
        in his prosperity;
    stand by him in time of affliction,
    that you may share with him in
        his inheritance.^s
²⁴The vapor and smoke of the
        furnace precede the fire;
    so insults precede bloodshed.
²⁵I will not be ashamed to protect
        a friend,
    and I will not hide from him;
²⁶but if some harm should happen
        to me because of him,
    whoever hears of it will beware
        of him.

²⁷O that a guard were set over my
        mouth,
    and a seal of prudence upon my
        lips,
    that it may keep me from falling,
    so that my tongue may not
        destroy me!^t
23 O Lord, Father and Ruler
        of my life,
    do not abandon me to their
        counsel,
    and let me not fall because of
        them!
²O that whips were set over my
        thoughts,
    and the discipline of wisdom
        over my mind!^u
    That they may not spare me in my
        errors,
    and that it may not pass by my^v
        sins;
³in order that my mistakes may not
        be multiplied,
    and my sins may not abound;
    then I will not fall before my
        adversaries,

and my enemy will not rejoice
        over me.
⁴O Lord, Father and God of my life,
    do not give me haughty eyes,
⁵   and remove from me evil desire.
⁶Let neither gluttony nor lust
        overcome me,
    and do not surrender me to a
        shameless soul.

⁷Listen, my children, to instruction
        concerning speech;
    the one who observes it will
        never be caught.
⁸The sinner is overtaken through
        his lips,
    the reviler and the arrogant are
        tripped by them.
⁹Do not accustom your mouth to
        oaths,
    and do not habitually utter the
        name of the Holy One;
¹⁰for as a servant who is continually
        examined under torture
    will not lack bruises,
    so also the man who always swears
        and utters the Name
    will not be cleansed from sin.
¹¹A man who swears many oaths will
        be filled with iniquity,
    and the scourge will not leave
        his house;
    if he offends, his sin remains on
        him,
    and if he disregards it, he sins
        doubly;
    if he has sworn needlessly, he will
        not be justified,
    for his house will be filled with
        calamities.

¹²There is an utterance which is
        comparable to death;^w
    may it never be found in the
        inheritance of Jacob!

s Other authorities add *For one should not always despise
   restricted circumstances, nor admire a rich man who
   is stupid.*
t Or *Who will set a guard . . . destroy me?*
u Or *Who will set whips . . . my mind?*   v Gk *their*
w Other authorities read *clothed about with death*

22.19–26: The preservation of friendship. 25: *A friend,* Syriac adds, "who becomes poor."
22.27–23.6: A prayer for self-control. 27: Ps.141.3.
23.7–15: The proper use of the tongue (compare Jas.3.5–12). **11:** Lev.5.4. **12a:** Lev.24.15–16.

For all these errors will be far from
   the godly,
   and they will not wallow in
      sins.
¹³Do not accustom your mouth to
   lewd vulgarity,
   for it involves sinful speech.
¹⁴Remember your father and
   mother
   whenˣ you sit among great
      men;
   lest you be forgetful in their
      presence,
   and be deemed a fool on
      account of your habits;
   then you will wish that you had
      never been born,
   and you will curse the day of
      your birth.
¹⁵A man accustomed to use insulting
   words
   will never become disciplined
      all his days.

¹⁶Two sorts of men multiply sins,
   and a third incurs wrath.
The soul heated like a burning fire
   will not be quenched until it is
      consumed;
a man who commits fornication
   with his near of kinʸ
   will never cease until the fire
      burns him up.
¹⁷To a fornicator all bread tastes
   sweet;
   he will never cease until he dies.
¹⁸A man who breaks his marriage
   vows
   says to himself, "Who sees me?
Darkness surrounds me, and the
   walls hide me,
   and no one sees me. Why should
      I fear?
The Most High will not take notice
   of my sins."
¹⁹His fear is confined to the eyes of
   men,
   and he does not realize that the
      eyes of the Lord

are ten thousand times brighter
   than the sun;
they look upon all the ways of
   men,
   and perceive even the hidden
      places.
²⁰Before the universe was created, it
   was known to him;
   so it was also after it was
      finished.
²¹This man will be punished in the
   streets of the city,
   and where he least suspects it,
   he will be seized.
²²So it is with a woman who leaves
   her husband
   and provides an heir by a
      stranger.
²³For first of all, she has disobeyed
   the law of the Most High;
   second, she has committed
      an offense against her
      husband;
   and third, she has committed
      adultery through harlotry
      and brought forth children by
      another man.
²⁴She herself will be brought before
   the assembly,
   and punishment will fall on her
      children.
²⁵Her children will not take root,
   and her branches will not bear
      fruit.
²⁶She will leave her memory for a
   curse,
   and her disgrace will not be
      blotted out.
²⁷Those who survive her will
   recognize
   that nothing is better than the
      fear of the Lord,
   and nothing sweeter than to heed
      the commandments of the
      Lord.ᶻ

x Gk *for*
y Gk *in the body of his flesh*
z Other authorities add ²⁸*It is a great honor to follow*
God, and to be received by him is long life.

23.16–27: Sins of the flesh. **16**: *The fire*, of passion. **17**: *All bread*, a euphemism (Syriac,
"all flesh"). **18**: Job 24.15. **19**: 15.19; Pr.15.3. **21–22**: Lev.20.10; Dt.22.21–23. **24–25**: Dt.23.2;
Wis.3.16–19; 4.3–6.

24 Wisdom will praise herself,
and will glory in the midst
of her people.ª
²In the assembly of the Most High
she will open her mouth,
and in the presence of his host
she will glory:
³"I came forth from the mouth of
the Most High,
and covered the earth like a mist.
⁴I dwelt in high places,
and my throne was in a pillar of
cloud.
⁵Alone I have made the circuit of
the vault of heaven
and have walked in the depths
of the abyss.
⁶In the waves of the sea, in the
whole earth,
and in every people and nation
I have gotten a possession.
⁷Among all these I sought a resting
place;
I sought in whose territory I
might lodge.

⁸"Then the Creator of all things
gave me a commandment,
and the one who created me
assigned a place for my tent.
And he said, 'Make your dwelling
in Jacob,
and in Israel receive your
inheritance.'
⁹From eternity, in the beginning,
he created me,
and for eternity I shall not cease
to exist.
¹⁰In the holy tabernacle I ministered
before him,
and so I was established in Zion.
¹¹In the beloved city likewise he
gave me a resting place,
and in Jerusalem was my
dominion.
¹²So I took root in an honored people,
in the portion of the Lord, who
is their inheritance.

¹³"I grew tall like a cedar in Lebanon,
and like a cypress on the heights
of Hermon.
¹⁴I grew tall like a palm tree in
En-ge′di,ᵇ
and like rose plants in Jericho;
like a beautiful olive tree in the
field,
and like a plane tree I grew
tall.
¹⁵Like cassia and camel's thorn I
gave forth the aroma of spices,
and like choice myrrh I spread
a pleasant odor,
like galbanum, onycha, and stacte,
and like the fragrance of
frankincense in the tabernacle.
¹⁶Like a terebinth I spread out my
branches,
and my branches are glorious
and graceful.
¹⁷Like a vine I caused loveliness to
bud,
and my blossoms became
glorious and abundant
fruit.ᶜ

¹⁹"Come to me, you who desire
me,
and eat your fill of my produce.
²⁰For the remembrance of me is
sweeter than honey,
and my inheritance sweeter than
the honeycomb.
²¹Those who eat me will hunger for
more,
and those who drink me will
thirst for more.
²²Whoever obeys me will not be put
to shame,
and those who work with my
help will not sin."

²³All this is the book of the covenant
of the Most High God,
the law which Moses
commanded us

a Or *will glorify herself in the midst of the people.*
b Other authorities read *on the beaches*
c Other authorities add ¹⁸*I am the mother of beautiful love, of fear, of knowledge, and of holy hope; being eternal, I therefore am given to all my children, to those who are named by him.*

24.1–34: Praise of wisdom. 3–22: Pr.8.22–9.12. **4:** *Pillar of cloud,* Ex.33.9–10. **6:** *Have gotten a possession,* Syriac and Latin, "have ruled." **19:** Is.55.1 **20:** Ps.19.10.

as an inheritance for the
   congregations of Jacob.*d*
25It fills men with wisdom, like the
      Pishon,
   and like the Tigris at the time
      of the first fruits.
26It makes them full of understanding,
      like the Euphrates,
   and like the Jordan at harvest
      time.
27It makes instruction shine forth
      like light,
   like the Gihon at the time of
      vintage.
28Just as the first man did not know
      her perfectly,
   the last one has not fathomed
      her;
29for her thought is more abundant
      than the sea,
   and her counsel deeper than the
      great abyss.

30I went forth like a canal from a
      river
   and like a water channel into a
      garden.
31I said, "I will water my orchard
      and drench my garden
      plot";
   and lo, my canal became a
      river,
   and my river became a sea.
32I will again make instruction shine
      forth like the dawn,
   and I will make it shine afar;
33I will again pour out teaching like
      prophecy,
   and leave it to all future
      generations.
34Observe that I have not labored
      for myself alone,
   but for all who seek instruction.*e*

25 My soul takes pleasure in
      three things,

and they are beautiful in the
      sight of the Lord and of men:*f*
agreement between brothers,
      friendship between neighbors,
   and a wife and husband who
      live in harmony.
2My soul hates three kinds of
      men,
   and I am greatly offended at
      their life:
a beggar who is proud, a rich man
      who is a liar,
   and an adulterous old man who
      lacks good sense.

3You have gathered nothing in your
      youth;
   how then can you find anything
      in your old age?
4What an attractive thing is judgment
      in gray-haired men,
   and for the aged to possess good
      counsel!
5How attractive is wisdom in the
      aged,
   and understanding and counsel
      in honorable men!
6Rich experience is the crown of the
      aged,
   and their boast is the fear of the
      Lord.

7With nine thoughts I have gladdened
      my heart,
   and a tenth I shall tell with my
      tongue:
a man rejoicing in his children;
   a man who lives to see the
      downfall of his foes;
8happy is he who lives with an
      intelligent wife,

d Other authorities add 24"*Do not cease to be strong in
the Lord, cleave to him so that he may strengthen you;
the Lord Almighty alone is God, and besides him there
is no savior.*"
e Gk *it*
f Syr Vg: Gk *In three things I was beautified and I stood
in beauty before the Lord and men*

25: Gen.2.11,14.   26: Jos.3.15.   30–34: The author compares himself to an irrigation canal
leading off from the great river of wisdom.   34: 33.17.
   25.1–2: Three beautiful and three hateful things.
   25.3–6: The attractiveness of wisdom in the aged.
   25.7–11: Ten happy thoughts. 8a: Hebrew and Syriac add, "and does not plow with ox and
ass" (compare Dt.22.10).

and he who has not made a slip
with his tongue,
and he who has not served a
man inferior to himself;
⁹happy is he who has gained good
sense,
and he who speaks to attentive
listeners.
¹⁰How great is he who has gained
wisdom!
But there is no one superior to
him who fears the Lord.
¹¹The fear of the Lord surpasses
everything;
to whom shall be likened the
one who holds it fast?ᵍ

¹³Any wound, but not a wound of
the heart!
Any wickedness, but not the
wickedness of a wife!
¹⁴Any attack, but not an attack from
those who hate!
And any vengeance, but not the
vengeance of enemies!
¹⁵There is no venomʰ worse than a
snake's venom,ʰ
and no wrath worse than an
enemy's wrath.

¹⁶I would rather dwell with a lion
and a dragon
than dwell with an evil wife.
¹⁷The wickedness of a wife changes
her appearance,
and darkens her face like that of
a bear.
¹⁸Her husband takes his meals among
the neighbors,
and he cannot help sighingⁱ
bitterly.
¹⁹Any iniquity is insignificant
compared to a wife's iniquity;
may a sinner's lot befall her!
²⁰A sandy ascent for the feet of the
aged—

such is a garrulous wife for a
quiet husband.
²¹Do not be ensnared by a woman's
beauty,
and do not desire a woman for
her possessions.ʲ
²²There is wrath and impudence and
great disgrace
when a wife supports her
husband.
²³A dejected mind, a gloomy face,
and a wounded heart are caused
by an evil wife.
Drooping hands and weak knees
are caused by the wife who
does not make her husband
happy.
²⁴From a woman sin had its
beginning,
and because of her we all die.
²⁵Allow no outlet to water,
and no boldness of speech in an
evil wife.
²⁶If she does not go as you
direct,
separate her from yourself.

26 Happy is the husband of a
good wife;
the number of his days will be
doubled.
²A loyal wife rejoices her husband,
and he will complete his years
in peace.
³A good wife is a great blessing;
she will be granted among the
blessings of the man who fears
the Lord.
⁴Whether rich or poor, his heart is
glad,
and at all times his face is
cheerful.

g Other authorities add ¹²*The fear of the Lord is the
beginning of love for him, and faith is the beginning of
clinging to him.*
h Cn: Gk *head*
i Other authorities read *and listening he sighs*
j Heb Syr: Some Gk authorities read *for her beauty*

25.13–26: Wicked and virtuous women. 15: *An enemy's*, Syriac, "a woman's." **16:** Pr.21.19;
25.24. **20a:** It is tedious and wearisome. **21:** 42.12. **24:** Gen.3.6; 2 Cor.11.3; 1 Tim.2.14.
26b: Literally, "cut her off from your flesh," that is, divorce her (Dt.24.1); hitherto they had
been "one flesh" (Gen.2.24).
26.1–4: The happiness of the husband of a good wife (Pr.31.10–31). **2:** *Rejoices*, Hebrew,
"makes fat" (v.13). **3:** 36.24; Pr.12.4.

⁵Of three things my heart is afraid,
and of a fourth I am frightened:ᵏ
The slander of a city, the gathering
of a mob,
and false accusation—all these
are worse than death.
⁶There is grief of heart and sorrow
when a wife is envious of a
rival,
and a tongue-lashing makes it
known to all.
⁷An evil wife is an ox yoke which
chafes;
taking hold of her is like grasping
a scorpion.
⁸There is great anger when a wife
is drunken;
she will not hide her shame.
⁹A wife's harlotry shows in her
lustful eyes,
and she is known by her eyelids.
¹⁰Keep strict watch over a headstrong
daughter,
lest, when she finds liberty, she
use it to her hurt.
¹¹Be on guard against her impudent
eye,
and do not wonder if she sins
against you.
¹²As a thirsty wayfarer opens his
mouth
and drinks from any water near
him,
so will she sit in front of every post
and open her quiver to the arrow.

¹³A wife's charm delights her husband,
and her skill puts fat on his bones.
¹⁴A silent wife is a gift of the Lord,
and there is nothing so precious
as a disciplined soul.
¹⁵A modest wife adds charm to charm,
and no balance can weigh the
value of a chaste soul.
¹⁶Like the sun rising in the heights
of the Lord,
so is the beauty of a good wife in
her well-ordered home.

¹⁷Like the shining lamp on the holy
lampstand,
so is a beautiful face on a stately
figure.
¹⁸Like pillars of gold on a base of
silver,
so are beautiful feet with a
steadfast heart.ˡ

²⁸At two things my heart is grieved,
and because of a third anger
comes over me:
a warrior in want through poverty,
and intelligent men who are
treated contemptuously;
a man who turns back from
righteousness to sin—
the Lord will prepare him for the
sword!

²⁹A merchant can hardly keep from
wrongdoing,
and a tradesman will not be
declared innocent of sin.

27 Many have committed sin
for a trifle,ᵐ
and whoever seeks to get rich
will avert his eyes.
²As a stake is driven firmly into a
fissure between stones,

k The Greek of this line is uncertain
l Other authorities add verses 19–27:
¹⁹*My son, keep sound the bloom of your youth,*
    and do not give your strength to strangers.
²⁰*Seek a fertile field within the whole plain,*
    and sow it with your own seed, trusting in your fine
    stock.
²¹*So your offspring will survive*
    and, having confidence in their good descent, will grow
    great.
²²*A harlot is regarded as spittle,*
    and a married woman as a tower of death to her
    lovers.
²³*A godless wife is given as a portion to a lawless man,*
    but a pious wife is given to the man who fears the Lord.
²⁴*A shameless woman constantly acts disgracefully,*
    but a modest daughter will even be embarrassed before
    her husband.
²⁵*A headstrong wife is regarded as a dog,*
    but one who has a sense of shame will fear the Lord.
²⁶*A wife honoring her husband will seem wise to all,*
    but if she dishonors him in her pride she will be known
    to all as ungodly.
Happy is the husband of a good wife;
    for the number of his years will be doubled.
²⁷*A loud-voiced and garrulous wife is regarded as a war*
    trumpet for putting the enemy to flight,
    and every person like this lives in the anarchy of war.
m One ancient authority reads *gain*

26.5–12: A wicked wife. 10: 42.11.
26.13–18: A good wife. 18: *With ... heart,* other witnesses read, "upon firm heels."
26.28–27.3: Miscellaneous observations. 26.28: *A warrior,* Syriac, "a wealthy man." 27.1:
Pr.28.21.

so sin is wedged in between
　selling and buying.
³If a man is not steadfast and zealous
　in the fear of the Lord,
　his house will be quickly
　　overthrown.

⁴When a sieve is shaken, the refuse
　remains;
　so a man's filth remains in his
　　thoughts.
⁵The kiln tests the potter's vessels;
　so the test of a man is in his
　　reasoning.
⁶The fruit discloses the cultivation
　of a tree;
　so the expression of a thought
　　discloses the cultivation of a
　　man's mind.
⁷Do not praise a man before you
　hear him reason,
　for this is the test of men.

⁸If you pursue justice, you will
　attain it
　and wear it as a glorious robe.
⁹Birds flock with their kind;
　so truth returns to those who
　　practice it.
¹⁰A lion lies in wait for prey;
　so does sin for the workers of
　　iniquity.

¹¹The talk of the godly man is
　always wise,
　but the fool changes like the
　　moon.
¹²Ámong stupid people watch for a
　chance to leave,
　but among thoughtful people
　　stay on.
¹³The talk of fools is offensive,
　and their laughter is wantonly
　　sinful.
¹⁴The talk of men given to swearing
　makes one's hair stand on end,

and their quarrels make a man
　stop his ears.
¹⁵The strife of the proud leads to
　bloodshed,
　and their abuse is grievous to
　　hear.

¹⁶Whoever betrays secrets destroys
　confidence,
　and he will never find a
　　congenial friend.
¹⁷Love your friend and keep faith
　with him;
　but if you betray his secrets, do
　　not run after him.
¹⁸For as a man destroys his enemy,
　so you have destroyed the
　　friendship of your neighbor.
¹⁹And as you allow a bird to escape
　from your hand,
　so you have let your neighbor
　　go, and will not catch him
　　again.
²⁰Do not go after him, for he is too
　far off,
　and has escaped like a gazelle
　　from a snare.
²¹For a wound may be bandaged,
　and there is reconciliation after
　　abuse,
　but whoever has betrayed secrets is
　　without hope.

²²Whoever winks his eye plans evil
　deeds,
　and no one can keep him from
　　them.
²³In your presence his mouth is all
　sweetness,
　and he admires your words;
　but later he will twist his speech
　　and with your own words he
　　will give offense.
²⁴I have hated many things, but none
　to be compared to him;
　even the Lord will hate him.

27.4–7: Tests in life. **6:** Mt.7.17.
27.8–10: Reward and retribution.
27.11–15: Kinds of talk.
27.16–21: Against disclosing secrets (Pr.20.19; 25.9). **18:** *Enemy*, Syriac, "inheritance."
21: *Without hope*, of reconciliation (22.22).
27.22–24: Hypocrisy. **22:** *Winks*, with insincerity (Ps.35.19; Pr.6.13; 10.10).

²⁵Whoever throws a stone straight
　　up throws it on his own head;
　and a treacherous blow opens up
　　wounds.
²⁶He who digs a pit will fall into it,
　and he who sets a snare will be
　　caught in it.
²⁷If a man does evil, it will roll back
　　upon him,
　and he will not know where it
　　came from.
²⁸Mockery and abuse issue from the
　　proud man,ⁿ
　but vengeance lies in wait for
　　him like a lion.
²⁹Those who rejoice in the fall of the
　　godly will be caught in a
　　snare,
　and pain will consume them
　　before their death.

³⁰Anger and wrath, these also are
　　abominations,
　and the sinful man will possess
　　them.

28 He that takes vengeance will
　　suffer vengeance from the
　　Lord,
　and he will firmly establishᵒ his
　　sins.
²Forgive your neighbor the wrong
　　he has done,
　and then your sins will be
　　pardoned when you pray.
³Does a man harbor anger against
　　another,
　and yet seek for healing from
　　the Lord?
⁴Does he have no mercy toward a
　　man like himself,
　and yet pray for his own sins?
⁵If he himself, being flesh, maintains
　　wrath,
　who will make expiation for his
　　sins?
⁶Remember the end of your life, and
　　cease from enmity,

remember destruction and death,
　and be true to the
　　commandments.
⁷Remember the commandments,
　and do not be angry with your
　　neighbor;
　remember the covenant of the
　　Most High, and overlook
　　ignorance.

⁸Refrain from strife, and you will
　　lessen sins;
　for a man given to anger will
　　kindle strife,
⁹and a sinful man will disturb
　　friends
　and inject enmity among those
　　who are at peace.
¹⁰In proportion to the fuel for the
　　fire, so will be the burning,
　and in proportion to the
　　obstinacy of strife will be
　　the burning;ᵖ
　in proportion to the strength of the
　　man will be his anger,
　and in proportion to his wealth
　　he will heighten his wrath.
¹¹A hasty quarrel kindles fire,
　and urgent strife sheds blood.
¹²If you blow on a spark, it will glow;
　if you spit on it, it will be put out;
　and both come out of your mouth.

¹³Curse the whisperer and deceiver,
　for he has destroyed many who
　　were at peace.
¹⁴Slander�q has shaken many,
　and scattered them from nation
　　to nation,
　and destroyed strong cities,
　and overturned the houses of
　　great men.
¹⁵Slanderq has driven away
　　courageous women,

n Other authorities read *proud men*
o Other authorities read *closely observe*
p Other authorities place this line at the end of the verse,
　or omit it
q Gk *a third tongue*

27.25–29: Retribution (Ps.7.14–16; 9.15–16; Pr.26.27; Ec.10.8).
　　27.30–28.7: Vengeance. **1:** Dt.32.35; Rom.12.19. **2:** Mt.6.14; Mk.11.25. **3:** Mt.18.23–35.
4: Mt.5.7. **6:** 7.36.
　　28.8–12: Strife and quarrels. **8:** Pr.15.18. **10:** Pr.26.20–21; Jas.3.5. **12:** Pr.15.1.
　　28.13–26: Slander and an evil tongue (51.2–6; Jas.3.5–12). **15:** *Has driven away*, from their

and deprived them of the fruit
of their toil.
¹⁶Whoever pays heed to slander^r
will not find rest,
nor will he settle down in peace.
¹⁷The blow of a whip raises a welt,
but a blow of the tongue crushes
the bones.
¹⁸Many have fallen by the edge of
the sword,
but not so many as have fallen
because of the tongue.
¹⁹Happy is the man who is protected
from it,
who has not been exposed to its
anger,
who has not borne its yoke,
and has not been bound with its
fetters;
²⁰for its yoke is a yoke of iron,
and its fetters are fetters of
bronze;
²¹its death is an evil death,
and Hades is preferable to it.
²²It will not be master over the
godly,
and they will not be burned in its
flame.
²³Those who forsake the Lord will
fall into its power;
it will burn among them and
will not be put out.
It will be sent out against them like
a lion;
like a leopard it will mangle
them.
²⁴See that you fence in your property
with thorns,
lock up your silver and gold,
²⁵make balances and scales for your
words,
and make a door and a bolt for
your mouth.
²⁶Beware lest you err with your
tongue,^s
lest you fall before him who lies
in wait.

29 He that shows mercy will
lend to his neighbor,

and he that strengthens him with
his hand keeps the
commandments.
²Lend to your neighbor in the time
of his need;
and in turn, repay your neighbor
promptly.
³Confirm your word and keep faith
with him,
and on every occasion you will
find what you need.
⁴Many persons regard a loan as a
windfall,
and cause trouble to those who
help them.
⁵A man will kiss another's hands
until he gets a loan,
and will lower his voice in
speaking of his neighbor's
money;
but at the time for repayment he
will delay,
and will pay in words of
unconcern,
and will find fault with the
time.
⁶If the lender^t exerts pressure, he
will hardly get back half,
and will regard that as a
windfall.
If he does not, the borrower^u has
robbed him of his money,
and he has needlessly made him
his enemy;
he will repay him with curses and
reproaches,
and instead of glory will repay
him with dishonor.
⁷Because of such wickedness,
therefore,^v many have refused
to lend;
they have been afraid of being
defrauded needlessly.

⁸Nevertheless, be patient with a
man in humble circumstances,

r Gk *it*
s Gk *with it*
t Gk *he*
u Gk *he*
v Other authorities read *It is not because of wickedness
that*

---

homes. **16:** The statement refers primarily to the husband. **17:** Pr.25.15. **25b:** 22.27; Ps.141.3.
29.1–13: Concerning loans (Ex.22.25; Lev.25.36; Mt.5.42; Lk.6.35). **2:** Pr.19.17. **4:** 8.12.

and do not make him wait for your alms.

⁹Help a poor man for the commandment's sake, and because of his need do not send him away empty.

¹⁰Lose your silver for the sake of a brother or a friend, and do not let it rust under a stone and be lost.

¹¹Lay up your treasure according to the commandments of the Most High, and it will profit you more than gold.

¹²Store up almsgiving in your treasury, and it will rescue you from all affliction;

¹³more than a mighty shield and more than a heavy spear, it will fight on your behalf against your enemy.

¹⁴A good man will be surety for his neighbor, but a man who has lost his sense of shame will fail him.

¹⁵Do not forget all the kindness of your surety, for he has given his life for you.

¹⁶A sinner will overthrow the prosperity of his surety,

¹⁷ and one who does not feel grateful will abandon his rescuer.

¹⁸Being surety has ruined many men who were prosperous, and has shaken them like a wave of the sea; it has driven men of power into exile, and they have wandered among foreign nations.

¹⁹The sinner who has fallen into suretyship and pursues gain will fall into lawsuits.

²⁰Assist your neighbor according to your ability, but take heed to yourself lest you fall.

²¹The essentials for life are water and bread and clothing and a house to cover one's nakedness.

²²Better is the life of a poor man under the shelter of his roof than sumptuous food in another man's house.

²³Be content with little or much.ʷ

²⁴It is a miserable life to go from house to house, and where you are a stranger you may not open your mouth;

²⁵you will play the host and provide drink without being thanked, and besides this you will hear bitter words:

²⁶"Come here, stranger, prepare the table, and if you have anything at hand, let me have it to eat."

²⁷"Give place, stranger, to an honored person; my brother has come to stay with me; I need my house."

²⁸These things are hard to bear for a man who has feeling: scolding about lodgingˣ and the reproach of the moneylender.

30 He who loves his son will whip him often, in order that he may rejoice at the way he turns out.

²He who disciplines his son will profit by him, and will boast of him among acquaintances.

w Other authorities add *and you will not hear reproach for your sojourning.*
x Or *from the household,* or (Syr) *from the host*

10: *Rust,* Mt.6.19; Jas.5.3. 11: Syriac, "Lay up for yourself a treasure of righteousness [i.e. through almsgiving] and love, and it shall profit you more than all that you have" (see 3.30 n. and compare Mt.19.21; Lk.12.33).

29.14–20: **Concerning suretyship. 14:** Contrast Pr.6.1–5; 17.18. **20:** 8.13.

29.21–28: **On contentment and hospitality. 21:** 39.26. **23:** Phil.4.11; 1 Tim.6.8; Heb.13.5. **28:** Syriac adds, "Give very freely to the poor, and feed him from that which is at hand; if he is

³He who teaches his son will make
　　his enemies envious,
　and will glory in him in the
　　presence of friends.
⁴The^y father may die, and yet he
　　is not dead,
　for he has left behind him one
　　like himself;
⁵while alive he saw and rejoiced,
　and when he died he was not
　　grieved;
⁶he has left behind him an avenger
　　against his enemies,
　and one to repay the kindness
　　of his friends.

⁷He who spoils his son will bind up
　　his wounds,
　and his feelings will be troubled
　　at every cry.
⁸A horse that is untamed turns out
　　to be stubborn,
　and a son unrestrained turns out
　　to be wilful.
⁹Pamper a child, and he will frighten
　　you;
　play with him, and he will give
　　you grief.
¹⁰Do not laugh with him, lest you
　　have sorrow with him,
　and in the end you will gnash
　　your teeth.
¹¹Give him no authority in his
　　youth,
　and do not ignore his errors.
¹²Bow down his neck in his
　　youth,^z
　and beat his sides while he is
　　young,
　lest he become stubborn and
　　disobey you,
　and you have sorrow of soul
　　from him.^a
¹³Discipline your son and take pains
　　with him,

　　that you may not be offended by
　　　his shamelessness.

¹⁴Better off is a poor man who is well
　　and strong in constitution
　than a rich man who is severely
　　afflicted in body.
¹⁵Health and soundness are better
　　than all gold,
　and a robust body than countless
　　riches.
¹⁶There is no wealth better than
　　health of body,
　and there is no gladness above
　　joy of heart.
¹⁷Death is better than a miserable
　　life,
　and eternal rest^b than chronic
　　sickness.

¹⁸Good things poured out upon a
　　mouth that is closed
　are like offerings of food placed
　　upon a grave.
¹⁹Of what use to an idol is an
　　offering of fruit?
　For it can neither eat nor smell.
　So is he who is afflicted by the
　　Lord;
²⁰he sees with his eyes and groans,
　like a eunuch who embraces a
　　maiden and groans.

²¹Do not give yourself over to sorrow,
　and do not afflict yourself
　　deliberately.
²²Gladness of heart is the life of man,
　and the rejoicing of a man is
　　length of days.
²³Delight your soul and comfort your
　　heart,
　and remove sorrow far from you,

y Gk *His*
z Other authorities omit this line and the preceding line
a Other authorities omit this line
b Some authorities omit *eternal rest*

---

naked, clothe him; thus you will be lending unto God, and he will repay you sevenfold" (compare Is.58.7; Mt.25.35–36).
　　30.1–13: On bringing up children. 1: Pr.13.24; 23.13–14; 29.15. **2:** Pr.29.17. **11:** 7.23. **13:**
Take pains with him, Hebrew, "make his yoke heavy."
　　30.14–20: Concerning health. 18: Tob.4.17. **19:** Let.Jer.27–28; Bel 3 (compare Ps.115.5–7).
20: *Groans,* with regret.
　　30.21–25: Gladness of heart (Ec.11.9–10). **21:** 38.20; Pr.12.25. **22:** 15.13; 17.22. **23:** 38.18–
19.

for sorrow has destroyed many,
and there is no profit in it.
24 Jealousy and anger shorten life,
and anxiety brings on old age
too soon.
25 A man of cheerful and good heart
will give heed to the food he
eats.

31 Wakefulness over wealth
wastes away one's flesh,
and anxiety about it removes
sleep.
2 Wakeful anxiety prevents slumber,
and a severe illness carries off
sleep.*c*
3 The rich man toils as his wealth
accumulates,
and when he rests he fills himself
with his dainties.
4 The poor man toils as his livelihood
diminishes,
and when he rests he becomes
needy.

5 He who loves gold will not be
justified,
and he who pursues money will
be led astray*d* by it.
6 Many have come to ruin because
of gold,
and their destruction has met
them face to face.
7 It is a stumbling block to those
who are devoted to it,
and every fool will be taken
captive by it.
8 Blessed is the rich man who is
found blameless,
and who does not go after gold.
9 Who is he? And we will call him
blessed,
for he has done wonderful things
among his people.
10 Who has been tested by it and
been found perfect?
Let it be for him a ground for
boasting.

Who has had the power to
transgress and did not
transgress,
and to do evil and did not do it?
11 His prosperity will be established,
and the assembly will relate his
acts of charity.

12 Are you seated at the table of a
great man?*e*
Do not be greedy*f* at it,
and do not say, "There is
certainly much upon it!"
13 Remember that a greedy*g* eye is
a bad thing.
What has been created more
greedy*g* than the eye?
Therefore it sheds tears from
every face.
14 Do not reach out your hand for
everything you see,
and do not crowd your neighbor*h*
at the dish.
15 Judge your neighbor's feelings by
your own,
and in every matter be
thoughtful.
16 Eat like a human being what is set
before you,
and do not chew greedily, lest
you be hated.
17 Be the first to stop eating, for the
sake of good manners,
and do not be insatiable, lest
you give offense.
18 If you are seated among many
persons,
do not reach out your hand
before they do.

19 How ample a little is for a well-
disciplined man!
He does not breathe heavily
upon his bed.

c Other authorities read *sleep carries off a severe illness*
d Heb Syr: Gk *will be filled*
e Heb Syr: Gk *at a great table*
f Gk *open your throat*
g Gk *evil*   *h* Gk *him*

31.1–11: The right attitude toward wealth. 1: 1 Tim.6.9–10. **4:** The opposite of v. 3 (compare
11.11).
31.12–30: Temperance in food and drink. 12: Pr.23.1–3. **15b:** Hebrew, "and keep in mind
your own dislikes." **16:** *Like a human being*, and not like an animal. **17:** 37.29.

²⁰Healthy sleep depends on moderate
    eating;
  he rises early, and feels fit.ⁱ
The distress of sleeplessness and
    of nausea
  and colic are with the glutton.
²¹If you are overstuffed with food,
    get up in the middle of the
    meal, and you will have relief.
²²Listen to me, my son, and do not
    disregard me,
  and in the end you will appreciate
    my words.
In all your work be industrious,
  and no sickness will overtake you.

²³Men will praise the one who is
    liberal with food,
  and their testimony to his
    excellence is trustworthy.
²⁴The city will complain of the one
    who is niggardly with food,
  and their testimony to his
    niggardliness is accurate.

²⁵Do not aim to be valiant over wine,
  for wine has destroyed many.
²⁶Fire and water proveʲ the temper
    of steel,
  so wine tests hearts in the strife
    of the proud.
²⁷Wine is like life to men,
  if you drink it in moderation.
What is life to a man who is
    without wine?
  It has been created to make men
    glad.
²⁸Wine drunk in season and
    temperately
  is rejoicing of heart and gladness
    of soul.
²⁹Wine drunk to excess is bitterness
    of soul,
  with provocation and stumbling.
³⁰Drunkenness increases the anger
    of a fool to his injury,
  reducing his strength and adding
    wounds.

³¹Do not reprove your neighbor at
    a banquet of wine,
  and do not despise him in his
    merrymaking;
speak no word of reproach to him,
  and do not afflict him by making
    demands of him.

32 If they make you master of
    the feast, do not exalt
    yourself;
  be among them as one of
    them;
take good care of them and then
    be seated;
2   when you have fulfilled your
    duties, take your place,
that you may be merry on their
    account
  and receive a wreath for your
    excellent leadership.

³Speak, you who are older, for it is
    fitting that you should,
  but with accurate knowledge,
  and do not interrupt the
    music.
⁴Where there is entertainment, do
    not pour out talk;
  do not display your cleverness
    out of season.
⁵A ruby seal in a setting of gold
  is a concert of music at a
    banquet of wine.
⁶A seal of emerald in a rich setting
    of gold
  is the melody of music with
    good wine.

⁷Speak, young man, if there is need
    of you,
  but no more than twice, and
    only if asked.
⁸Speak concisely, say much in few
    words;
  be as one who knows and yet
    holds his tongue.

i Gk *his soul is with him*
j Gk *The furnace by dipping proves*

22: *Be industrious*, Hebrew, "be moderate," which suits the context better. 23: Pr.22.9. 25: Is.5.22. 27: Ps.104.15; Pr.31.6–7.
    31.31–32.13: **Etiquette at a banquet. 2:** *A wreath*, Syriac, "honor." 7–9: Advice for younger guests.

⁹Among the great do not act as
their equal;
and when another is speaking,
do not babble.

¹⁰Lightning speeds before the
thunder,
and approval precedes a modest
man.
¹¹Leave in good time and do not be
the last;
go home quickly and do not
linger.
¹²Amuse yourself there, and do what
you have in mind,
but do not sin through proud
speech.
¹³And for these things bless him who
made you
and satisfies you with his good
gifts.

¹⁴He who fears the Lord will accept
his discipline,
and those who rise early to seek
him*ᵏ* will find favor.
¹⁵He who seeks the law will be filled
with it,
but the hypocrite will stumble
at it.
¹⁶Those who fear the Lord will form
true judgments,
and like a light they will kindle
righteous deeds.
¹⁷A sinful man will shun reproof,
and will find a decision according
to his liking.

¹⁸A man of judgment will not
overlook an idea,
and an insolent*ˡ* and proud
man will not cower in
fear.*ᵐ*
¹⁹Do nothing without deliberation;
and when you have acted, do not
regret it.

²⁰Do not go on a path full of
hazards,
and do not stumble over stony
ground.
²¹Do not be overconfident on a
smooth*ⁿ* way,
²²   and give good heed to your
paths.*ᵒ*
²³Guard*ᵖ* yourself in every act,
for this is the keeping of the
commandments.

²⁴He who believes the law gives heed
to the commandments,
and he who trusts the Lord will
not suffer loss.

33 No evil will befall the man
who fears the Lord,
but in trial he will deliver him
again and again.
²A wise man will not hate the law,
but he who is hypocritical about
it is like a boat in a storm.
³A man of understanding will trust
in the law;
for him the law is as dependable
as an inquiry by means of
Urim.

⁴Prepare what to say, and thus you
will be heard;
bind together your instruction,
and make your answer.
⁵The heart of a fool is like a cart
wheel,
and his thoughts like a turning
axle.
⁶A stallion is like a mocking
friend;
he neighs under every one who
sits on him.

k Other authorities omit *to seek him*
l Heb: Gk *alien*
m The meaning of this line is uncertain. Other authorities
add the phrases *and after acting, with him, without
deliberation*
n Or *an unexplored*
o Syr Vg: Gk *and beware of your children*
p Heb Syr: Gk *Trust*

32.14–33.6: The God-fearing man contrasted with the sinner. 32.14: 18.14; Job 5.17; Heb.
12.5–7. **17:** *A decision*, i.e. an interpretation (of the law). **20b:** Hebrew and Syriac, "Do not
trip over the same obstacle twice." **24a:** Hebrew and Syriac, "He who observes the law preserves himself" (Pr.19.16). **33.1:** Pr.12.21; 1 Pet.3.13. **2:** Hebrew, "He that hates the law is not
wise, and is tossed about like a boat in a storm." **3:** *Urim*, 45.10; Ex.28.30; Num.27.21; 1 Sam.
14.41–42.

⁷Why is any day better than
    another,
  when all the daylight in the
    year is from the sun?
⁸By the Lord's decision they were
    distinguished,
  and he appointed the different
    seasons and feasts;
⁹some of them he exalted and
    hallowed,
  and some of them he made
    ordinary days.
¹⁰All men are from the ground,
  and Adam was created of the
    dust.
¹¹In the fulness of his knowledge
    the Lord distinguished them
  and appointed their different
    ways;
¹²some of them he blessed and
    exalted,
  and some of them he made
    holy and brought near to
    himself;
  but some of them he cursed and
    brought low,
  and he turned them out of their
    place.
¹³As clay in the hand of the potter—
  for all his ways are as he
    pleases—
so men are in the hand of him
  who made them,
  to give them as he decides.

¹⁴Good is the opposite of evil,
  and life the opposite of death;
  so the sinner is the opposite of
    the godly.
¹⁵Look upon all the works of the
    Most High;
  they likewise are in pairs, one
    the opposite of the other.

¹⁶I was the last on watch;

I was like one who gleans after
    the grape-gatherers;
by the blessing of the Lord I
    excelled,
  and like a grape-gatherer I filled
    my wine press.
¹⁷Consider that I have not labored
    for myself alone,
  but for all who seek instruction.
¹⁸Hear me, you who are great among
    the people,
  and you leaders of the
    congregation, hearken.

¹⁹To son or wife, to brother or
    friend,
  do not give power over yourself,
    as long as you live;
  and do not give your property to
    another,
  lest you change your mind and
    must ask for it.
²⁰While you are still alive and have
    breath in you,
  do not let any one take your
    place.
²¹For it is better that your children
    should ask from you
  than that you should look to the
    hand of your sons.
²²Excel in all that you do;
  bring no stain upon your honor.
²³At the time when you end the days
    of your life,
  in the hour of death, distribute
    your inheritance.

²⁴Fodder and a stick and burdens
    for an ass;
  bread and discipline and work
    for a servant.
²⁵Set your slave to work, and you
    will find rest;
  leave his hands idle, and he will
    seek liberty.

33.7–15: Divinely ordained diversities in nature. 10: Gen.2.7; Job 10.9. **11:** *Ways,* destinies.
12: *Blessed,* Gen.9.1; 12.2. *Made holy,* ordained to the priesthood (Num.16.5,10; Ezek.40.46;
42.13; 45.4). *Cursed,* Gen.9.25. **13:** Is.29.16; 45.9; 64.8; Jer.18.4,6; Wis.15.7–8; Rom.9.21.
15: 42.24 (compare Ec.3.2–8).
    33.16–18: The author's qualifications as a teacher (24.30–34). **17:** 24.34; Wis.6.1–2.
    33.19–23: On preserving one's financial independence.
    33.24–31: On the treatment of slaves (7.20–21). The rights of slaves were defined in the

²⁶Yoke and thong will bow the neck,
and for a wicked servant there
are racks and tortures.
²⁷Put him to work, that he may not
be idle,
for idleness teaches much evil.
²⁸Set him to work, as is fitting for
him,
and if he does not obey, make
his fetters heavy.
²⁹Do not act immoderately toward
anybody,
and do nothing without
discretion.

³⁰If you have a servant, let him be
as yourself,
because you have bought him
with blood.
³¹If you have a servant, treat him as
a brother,
for as your own soul you will
need him.
If you ill-treat him, and he leaves
and runs away,
which way will you go to seek
him?

34 A man of no understanding
has vain and false hopes,
and dreams give wings to fools.
²As one who catches at a shadow
and pursues the wind,
so is he who gives heed to
dreams.
³The vision of dreams is this against
that,
the likeness of a face confronting
a face.
⁴From an unclean thing what will
be made clean?
And from something false what
will be true?
⁵Divinations and omens and dreams
are folly,

and like a woman in travail the
mind has fancies.
⁶Unless they are sent from the Most
High as a visitation,
do not give your mind to them.
⁷For dreams have deceived many,
and those who put their hope in
them have failed.
⁸Without such deceptions the law
will be fulfilled,
and wisdom is made perfect in
truthful lips.

⁹An educated*q* man knows many
things,
and one with much experience
will speak with understanding.
¹⁰He that is inexperienced knows
few things,
but he that has traveled acquires
much cleverness.
¹¹I have seen many things in my
travels,
and I understand more than I
can express.
¹²I have often been in danger of
death,
but have escaped because of
these experiences.

¹³The spirit of those who fear the
Lord will live,
for their hope is in him who
saves them.
¹⁴He who fears the Lord will not be
timid,
nor play the coward, for he is
his hope.
¹⁵Blessed is the soul of the man who
fears the Lord!
To whom does he look? And
who is his support?
¹⁶The eyes of the Lord are upon
those who love him,

q Other authorities read A traveled

Mosaic law (Ex.21.2–6,20–21,26–27; Lev.25.46; Dt.15.12–18). **30 and 31:** Syriac, "If you have (only) one servant. . . ."

34.1–8: The vanity of dreams and omens (Dt.13.2–5; 18.9–14; Ec.5.7; Jer.29.8). **3a:** Syriac, "A dream of the night is like a mirror," i.e. the image in each is insubstantial. **4:** Job 14.4. **6:** Allowance is made for God-given dreams (Gen.37.5ff.; Jg.7.13ff.; Job 33.15–18).

34.9–12: Experience as a teacher.

34.13–17: The blessedness of those who fear God. 14: Ps.112.6–7; Pr.3.23–26; 28.1. **16:** *Eyes,* Ps.33.18; 34.15. *Shelter,* Ps.61.2–4; 91.1–4; Is.25.4.

a mighty protection and strong
　　support,
a shelter from the hot wind and a
　　shade from noonday sun,
a guard against stumbling and
　　a defense against falling.
17He lifts up the soul and gives light
　　to the eyes;
he grants healing, life, and
　　blessing.

18If one sacrifices from what has
　　been wrongfully obtained, the
　　offering is blemished;*r*
the gifts*s* of the lawless are not
　　acceptable.
19The Most High is not pleased
　　with the offerings of the
　　ungodly;
and he is not propitiated for sins
　　by a multitude of sacrifices.
20Like one who kills a son before his
　　father's eyes
is the man who offers a sacrifice
　　from the property of the poor.
21The bread of the needy is the life
　　of the poor;
whoever deprives them of it is
　　a man of blood.
22To take away a neighbor's living
　　is to murder him;
to deprive an employee of his
　　wages is to shed blood.

23When one builds and another
　　tears down,
what do they gain but toil?
24When one prays and another
　　curses,
to whose voice will the Lord
　　listen?
25If a man washes after touching a
　　dead body, and touches it
　　again,
what has he gained by his
　　washing?
26So if a man fasts for his sins,

and goes again and does the
　　same things,
who will listen to his prayer?
And what has he gained by
　　humbling himself?

35 He who keeps the law makes
　　many offerings;
he who heeds the commandments
　　sacrifices a peace offering.
2He who returns a kindness offers
　　fine flour,
and he who gives alms sacrifices
　　a thank offering.
3To keep from wickedness is pleasing
　　to the Lord,
and to forsake unrighteousness
　　is atonement.
4Do not appear before the Lord
　　empty-handed,
5　for all these things are to be
　　done because of the
　　commandment.
6The offering of a righteous man
　　anoints the altar,
and its pleasing odor rises before
　　the Most High.
7The sacrifice of a righteous man is
　　acceptable,
and the memory of it will not
　　be forgotten.
8Glorify the Lord generously,
and do not stint the first fruits
　　of your hands.
9With every gift show a cheerful
　　face,
and dedicate your tithe with
　　gladness.
10Give to the Most High as he has
　　given,
and as generously as your hand
　　has found.
11For the Lord is the one who
　　repays,
and he will repay you sevenfold.

r Other authorities read *is made in mockery*
s Other authorities read *mockeries*

34.18–26: Unacceptable sacrifices (1 Sam.15.22; Ps.51.16–19; Pr.15.8; 21.3; Hos.6.6; Am.
5.21–24; Mt.23.23). **21:** Lev.19.13; Dt.24.14–15; Tob.4.14. **25:** Num.19.11–13; 2 Pet.2.22.
　　35.1–11: Acceptable sacrifices (Is.1.11–18; Mic.6.6–8; Mk.12.33). **1:** *Peace offering,* Lev.3.1–
17. **2:** *Fine flour,* Lev.2.1–16. *Thank offering,* Lev.7.12. **3:** Dan.4.27. **4:** Ex.23.15; Dt.16.16. **8:**
7.31; Pr.3.9; 22.9. **9:** 2 Cor.9.7. **10:** Tob.4.8. **11:** Pr.19.17; 2 Cor.9.8.

¹²Do not offer him a bribe, for he
  will not accept it;
  and do not trust to an
    unrighteous sacrifice;
for the Lord is the judge,
  and with him is no partiality.
¹³He will not show partiality in the
    case of a poor man;
  and he will listen to the prayer
    of one who is wronged.
¹⁴He will not ignore the supplication
    of the fatherless,
  nor the widow when she pours
    out her story.
¹⁵Do not the tears of the widow run
    down her cheek
  as she cries out against him
    who has caused them to
    fall?
¹⁶He whose service is pleasing to the
    Lord will be accepted,
  and his prayer will reach to the
    clouds.
¹⁷The prayer of the humble pierces
    the clouds,
  and he will not be consoled until
    it reaches the Lord;ᵗ
he will not desist until the Most
    High visits him,
  and does justice for the righteous,
    and executes judgment.
¹⁸And the Lord will not delay,
  neither will he be patient with
    them,
till he crushes the loins of the
    unmerciful
  and repays vengeance on the
    nations;
till he takes away the multitude of
    the insolent,
  and breaks the scepters of the
    unrighteous;
¹⁹till he repays man according to his
    deeds,

and the works of men according
    to their devices;
till he judges the case of his people
  and makes them rejoice in his
    mercy.
²⁰Mercy is as welcome when he
    afflicts them
  as clouds of rain in the time of
    drought.

36 Have mercy upon us, O
    Lord, the God of all, and
    look upon us,
² and cause the fear of thee to fall
    upon all the nations.
³Lift up thy hand against foreign
    nations
  and let them see thy might.
⁴As in us thou hast been sanctified
    before them,
  so in them be thou magnified
    before us;
⁵and let them know thee, as we
    have known
  that there is no God but thee,
    O Lord.
⁶Show signs anew, and work further
    wonders;
  make thy hand and thy right
    arm glorious.
⁷Rouse thy anger and pour out thy
    wrath;
  destroy the adversary and wipe
    out the enemy.
⁸Hasten the day, and remember the
    appointed time,ᵘ
  and let people recount thy
    mighty deeds.
⁹Let him who survives be consumed
    in the fiery wrath,
  and may those who harm thy
    people meet destruction.

t Or *until the Lord draws near*
u Other authorities read *remember thy oath*

35.12–20: God's mercy and justice. 12: *Unrighteous sacrifice*, Hebrew and Syriac, "sacrifice
of violence (or extortion)," i.e. derived from unjust dealing (34.20). *No partiality*, Dt.10.17;
Job 34.19; Wis.6.7; Acts 10.34; Gal.2.6. **14–15:** Ex.22.22. **18:** *Will not delay*, in executing
judgment (2 Pet.3.9). Here and in vv. 19–20 the author has in mind the pagan oppressors of
God's chosen people.
  36.1–17: A prayer for the deliverance and restoration of Israel. 2–3: Ps.79.6; Is.19.16; Jer.
10.25. **4:** Ezek.20.41; 28.25. **5:** 1 Kg.8.43,60. **7:** Ps.79.6. **8a:** Hebrew and Syriac, "Hasten the
end" (of the present age). **8b:** Hebrew and Syriac, "For who may say to thee, 'What doest
thou?'" i.e. God has *appointed* the *time* of the coming of the Messianic era (see 2 Esd.4.36–37 n.;

¹⁰Crush the heads of the rulers of
the enemy,
who say, "There is no one but
ourselves."
¹¹Gather all the tribes of Jacob,
and give[v] them their inheritance,
as at the beginning.
¹²Have mercy, O Lord, upon the
people called by thy name,
upon Israel, whom thou hast
likened to a[w] first-born son.
¹³Have pity on the city of thy
sanctuary,[x]
Jerusalem, the place of thy
rest.
¹⁴Fill Zion with the celebration of
thy wondrous deeds,
and thy temple[y] with thy
glory.
¹⁵Bear witness to those whom thou
didst create in the beginning,
and fulfil the prophecies spoken
in thy name.
¹⁶Reward those who wait for thee,
and let thy prophets be found
trustworthy.
¹⁷Hearken, O Lord, to the prayer of
thy servants,
according to the blessing of
Aaron for thy people,
and all who are on the earth will
know
that thou art the Lord, the God
of the ages.

¹⁸The stomach will take any food,
yet one food is better than
another.
¹⁹As the palate tastes the kinds of
game,
so an intelligent mind detects
false words.
²⁰A perverse mind will cause grief,
but a man of experience will pay
him back.
²¹A woman will accept any man,
but one daughter is better than
another.
²²A woman's beauty gladdens the
countenance,
and surpasses every human
desire.
²³If kindness and humility mark her
speech,
her husband is not like other
men.
²⁴He who acquires a wife gets his
best possession,[z]
a helper fit for him and a pillar
of support.[a]
²⁵Where there is no fence, the
property will be plundered;
and where there is no wife, a
man will wander about and
sigh.
²⁶For who will trust a nimble
robber
that skips from city to city?
So who will trust a man that has
no home,
and lodges wherever night finds
him?

37 Every friend will say, "I too
am a friend";
but some friends are friends
only in name.
²Is it not a grief to the death
when a companion and friend
turns to enmity?
³O evil imagination, why were you
formed
to cover the land with deceit?
⁴Some companions rejoice in the
happiness of a friend,
but in time of trouble are
against him.

v Other authorities read *I gave*
w Other authorities read *hast named thy*
x Or *on thy holy city*
y Heb Syr: Gk Vg *people*
z Heb: Gk *enters upon a possession*
a Heb: Gk *rest*

Acts 1.7–8). **11:** Jer.31.10. **12:** Dan.9.18–19. **13:** Ps.132.14. **17:** *The blessing of Aaron for thy people*, Num.6.23–26; Hebrew and Syriac, "thy good favor toward thy people." *The God of the ages*, the eternal God (Gen.21.33; Is.40.28).
    36.18–26: Concerning discrimination (vv. 18–20, in general; vv. 21–26, in choosing a wife). **19:** Job 12.11; 34.3. **21a:** *Will accept*, because the marriage was arranged by her father (see 7.25 n.). **24:** *A helper fit for him*, Gen.2.18. **26:** *Home*, literally "nest."
    37.1–6: False friends (6.7–13). **3:** *Evil imagination*, the evil *yeṣer* (see 15.14 n.). **4:** *Happi-*

⁵Some companions help a friend
  for their stomachs' sake,
  and in the face of battle take up
    the shield.
⁶Do not forget a friend in your heart,
  and be not unmindful of him in
    your wealth.

⁷Every counselor praises counsel,
  but some give counsel in their
    own interest.
⁸Be wary of a counselor,
  and learn first what is his
    interest—
  for he will take thought for
    himself—
  lest he cast the lot against you
⁹   and tell you, "Your way is
    good,"
  and then stand aloof to see what
    will happen to you.
¹⁰Do not consult with one who looks
    at you suspiciously;
  hide your counsel from those
    who are jealous of you.
¹¹Do not consult with a woman
    about her rival
  or with a coward about war,
  with a merchant about barter
  or with a buyer about selling,
  with a grudging man about
    gratitude
  or with a merciless man about
    kindness,
  with an idler about any work
  or with a man hired for a year
    about completing his work,
  with a lazy servant about a big
    task—
  pay no attention to these in any
    matter of counsel.
¹²But stay constantly with a godly
    man
  whom you know to be a keeper
    of the commandments,
  whose soul is in accord with your
    soul,

and who will sorrow with you if
  you fail.
¹³And establish the counsel of your
  own heart,
  for no one is more faithful to
  you than it is.
¹⁴For a man's soul sometimes keeps
  him better informed
  than seven watchmen sitting
  high on a watchtower.
¹⁵And besides all this pray to the
  Most High
  that he may direct your way in
  truth.

¹⁶Reason is the beginning of every
  work,
  and counsel precedes every
  undertaking.
¹⁷As a clue to changes of heart
¹⁸   four turns of fortune appear,
  good and evil, life and death;
  and it is the tongue that
  continually rules them.
¹⁹A man may be shrewd and the
  teacher of many,
  and yet be unprofitable to
  himself.
²⁰A man skilled in words may be
  hated;
  he will be destitute of all
  food,
²¹for grace was not given him by the
  Lord,
  since he is lacking in all wisdom.
²²A man may be wise to his own
  advantage,
  and the fruits of his
  understanding may be
  trustworthy on his lips.
²³A wise man will instruct his own
  people,
  and the fruits of his
  understanding will be
  trustworthy.
²⁴A wise man will have praise heaped
  upon him,

---

ness, arising from feasting (see v. 5). **6:** *In your heart,* Hebrew, "in war." *In your wealth,* Hebrew, "when you take the spoil."

   37.7–15: Concerning counselors. 14: *Watchmen,* probably astrologers are meant.

   37.16–26: True and false wisdom. 17–18: Hebrew, "The roots of the heart's counsels send out four branches." **18:** Pr.18.21. **21:** *Grace,* graciousness.

and all who see him will call him
   happy.
²⁵The life of a man is numbered by
   days,
but the days of Israel are
   without number.
²⁶He who is wise among his people
   will inherit confidence,*b*
and his name will live for ever.

²⁷My son, test your soul while you
   live;
see what is bad for it and do not
   give it that.
²⁸For not everything is good for
   every one,
and not every person enjoys
   everything.
²⁹Do not have an insatiable appetite
   for any luxury,
and do not give yourself up to
   food;
³⁰for overeating brings sickness,
   and gluttony leads to nausea.
³¹Many have died of gluttony,
   but he who is careful to avoid
   it prolongs his life.

38 Honor the physician with
the honor due him,*c* according to your need of him,
for the Lord created him;
²for healing comes from the Most
   High,
and he will receive a gift from
   the king.
³The skill of the physician lifts up
   his head,
and in the presence of great
   men he is admired.
⁴The Lord created medicines from
   the earth,
and a sensible man will not
   despise them.

⁵Was not water made sweet with a
   tree
in order that his*d* power might
   be known?
⁶And he gave skill to men
   that he*e* might be glorified in
   his marvelous works.
⁷By them he heals and takes away
   pain;
⁸ the pharmacist makes of them
   a compound.
His works will never be finished;
   and from him health*f* is upon
   the face of the earth.

⁹My son, when you are sick do not
   be negligent,
but pray to the Lord, and he
   will heal you.
¹⁰Give up your faults and direct your
   hands aright,
and cleanse your heart from all
   sin.
¹¹Offer a sweet-smelling sacrifice,
   and a memorial portion of
   fine flour,
and pour oil on your offering,
   as much as you can afford.*g*
¹²And give the physician his place,
   for the Lord created him;
let him not leave you, for there
   is need of him.
¹³There is a time when success lies
   in the hands of physicians,*h*
¹⁴ for they too will pray to the Lord
   that he should grant them success
   in diagnosis*i*
and in healing, for the sake of
   preserving life.
¹⁵He who sins before his Maker,

b Other authorities read *honor*
c Other authorities omit *with the honor due him*
d Or *its*   *e* Or *they*   *f* Or *peace*
g Heb: Vulgate omits *as much as you can afford;* Greek
is obscure
h Gk *in their hands*   *i* Heb: Gk *rest*

25: *Is numbered by days,* i.e. is of limited duration, contrasted with the nation of *Israel* (39.9;
44.13–14; 2 Macc. 14.15).
   37.27–31: Temperance (31.16–22).
   38.1–15: Concerning physicians. 1: *Created him,* i.e. established his profession. **5:** Ex.15.23–
25. **8:** *His works,* God's works. **9–14:** In sickness turn first to God, by prayer, repentance, and
sacrifice (contrast 2 Chr.16.12); then call the physician. **12:** *Created,* see v. 1 n. **15:** Severe
illness, according to Jewish ideas, is divine judgment for sin (Job 5.17–18; 1 Cor.11.30). The
Hebrew text, however, reads, "He who sins before his Maker will behave himself proudly before
the physician."

may he fall into the care[j] of a
    physician.

[16]My son, let your tears fall for the
    dead,
    and as one who is suffering
        grievously begin the lament.
Lay out his body with the honor
    due him,
    and do not neglect his burial.
[17]Let your weeping be bitter and
    your wailing fervent;
    observe the mourning according
        to his merit,
for one day, or two, to avoid
    criticism;
    then be comforted for your
        sorrow.
[18]For sorrow results in death,
    and sorrow of heart saps one's
        strength.
[19]In calamity sorrow continues,
    and the life of the poor man
        weighs down his heart.
[20]Do not give your heart to
    sorrow;
    drive it away, remembering the
        end of life.
[21]Do not forget, there is no coming
    back;
    you do the dead[k] no good, and
        you injure yourself.
[22]"Remember my doom, for yours is
    like it:
    yesterday it was mine, and
        today it is yours."
[23]When the dead is at rest, let his
    remembrance cease,
    and be comforted for him when
        his spirit has departed.

[24]The wisdom of the scribe depends
    on the opportunity of
        leisure;
    and he who has little business
        may become wise.
[25]How can he become wise who
    handles the plow,

and who glories in the shaft of
    a goad,
who drives oxen and is occupied
    with their work,
    and whose talk is about[l] bulls?
[26]He sets his heart on plowing
    furrows,
    and he is careful about fodder
        for the heifers.
[27]So too is every craftsman and
    master workman
    who labors by night as well as
        by day;
those who cut the signets of
    seals,
    each is diligent in making a
        great variety;
he sets his heart on painting a
    lifelike image,
    and he is careful to finish his
        work.
[28]So too is the smith sitting by the
    anvil,
    intent upon his handiwork in
        iron;
the breath of the fire melts his
    flesh,
    and he wastes away in[m] the heat
        of the furnace;
he inclines his ear to the sound of
    the hammer,[n]
    and his eyes are on the pattern
        of the object.
He sets his heart on finishing his
    handiwork,
    and he is careful to complete its
        decoration.
[29]So too is the potter sitting at his
    work
    and turning the wheel with his
        feet;
he is always deeply concerned over
    his work,
    and all his output is by
        number.
[30]He moulds the clay with his arm

j Gk *hands*   k Gk *him*   l Or *among*
m Cn Compare Syr: Gk *contends with*
n Cn: Gk *the sound of the hammer renews his ear*

38.16–23: On mourning for the dead (22.11–12). **16d:** Hebrew, "and do not hide yourself
when he has become a corpse." **18:** *Death*, Hebrew "harm." **22:** Lugubrious counsel from the
dead man. **23:** 2 Sam.12.20.
    38.24–39.11: Various craftsmen contrasted with the scribe, a student of divine wisdom.

and makes it pliable with his
　feet;
he sets his heart to finish the
　glazing,
　and he is careful to clean the
　furnace.

³¹All these rely upon their hands,
　and each is skilful in his own
　work.
³²Without them a city cannot be
　established,
　and men can neither sojourn nor
　live there.
³³Yet they are not sought out for
　the council of the people,
　nor do they attain eminence in
　the public assembly.
They do not sit in the judge's
　seat,
　nor do they understand the
　sentence of judgment;
they cannot expound discipline or
　judgment,
　and they are not found using
　proverbs.
³⁴But they keep stable the fabric of
　the world,
　and their prayer is in the practice
　of their trade.

39 On the other hand he who
　devotes himself
to the study of the law of the
　Most High
will seek out the wisdom of all the
　ancients,
and will be concerned with
　prophecies;
²he will preserve the discourse of
　notable men
　and penetrate the subtleties of
　parables;
³he will seek out the hidden meanings
　of proverbs
　and be at home with the
　obscurities of parables.

⁴He will serve among great men
　and appear before rulers;
he will travel through the lands of
　foreign nations,
　for he tests the good and the evil
　among men.
⁵He will set his heart to rise early
　to seek the Lord who made
　him,
　and will make supplication
　before the Most High;
he will open his mouth in
　prayer
　and make supplication for his
　sins.

⁶If the great Lord is willing,
　he will be filled with the spirit
　of understanding;
he will pour forth words⁰ of
　wisdom
　and give thanks to the Lord in
　prayer.
⁷He will direct his counsel and
　knowledge aright,
　and meditate on his secrets.
⁸He will reveal instruction in his
　teaching,
　and will glory in the law of the
　Lord's covenant.
⁹Many will praise his under-
　standing,
　and it will never be blotted
　out;
his memory will not disappear,
　and his name will live through
　all generations.
¹⁰Nations will declare his wisdom,
　and the congregation will
　proclaim his praise;
¹¹if he lives long, he will leave a
　name greater than a
　thousand,
　and if he goes to rest, it is
　enough*ᵖ* for him.

o Other authorities read *his words*
p Cn: the meaning of the Greek is uncertain

38.32: Craftsmen are necessary for the well-being of the social structure. **39.1:** The threefold division of the Hebrew canon: the law, wisdom (= the writings), and the prophets (given third place here in deference to wisdom; compare the Prologue to Sirach and see 2 Esd.14.45 n.). **2–3:** These verses refer to the oral traditions of the sages. *He will preserve*, in his memory (Pr.4.21; 22.17–18). **4:** *Will travel*, 51.13. **6:** Jas.4.15. **9:** *It*, Syriac, "his name." **11:** *It*, i.e. his name, which survives him and keeps him in remembrance.

¹²I have yet more to say, which I
have thought upon,
and I am filled, like the moon
at the full.
¹³Listen to me, O you holy sons,
and bud like a rose growing by
a stream of water;
¹⁴send forth fragrance like
frankincense,
and put forth blossoms like a lily.
Scatter the fragrance, and sing a
hymn of praise;
bless the Lord for all his works;
¹⁵ascribe majesty to his name
and give thanks to him with
praise,
with songs on your lips, and with
lyres;
and this you shall say in
thanksgiving:
¹⁶"All things are the works of the
Lord, for they are very good,
and whatever he commands will
be done in his time."

¹⁷No one can say, "What is this?"
"Why is that?"
for in God's*�q* time all things
will be sought after.
At his word the waters stood in a
heap,
and the reservoirs of water at
the word of his mouth.
¹⁸At his command whatever pleases
him is done,
and none can limit his saving
power.
¹⁹The works of all flesh are before him,
and nothing can be hid from his
eyes.
²⁰From everlasting to everlasting he
beholds them,
and nothing is marvelous to him.
²¹No one can say, "What is this?"
"Why is that?"
for everything has been created
for its use.

²²His blessing covers the dry land
like a river,
and drenches it like a flood.
²³The nations will incur his wrath,
just as he turns fresh water into
salt.
²⁴To the holy his ways are straight,
just as they are obstacles to the
wicked.
²⁵From the beginning good things
were created for good people,
just as evil things for sinners.
²⁶Basic to all the needs of man's
life
are water and fire and iron and
salt
and wheat flour and milk and
honey,
the blood of the grape, and oil
and clothing.
²⁷All these are for good to the
godly,
just as they turn into evils for
sinners.

²⁸There are winds that have been
created for vengeance,
and in their anger they scourge
heavily;
in the time of consummation they
will pour out their strength
and calm the anger of their
Maker.
²⁹Fire and hail and famine and
pestilence,
all these have been created for
vengeance;
³⁰the teeth of wild beasts, and
scorpions and vipers,
and the sword that punishes the
ungodly with destruction;
³¹they will rejoice in his commands,
and be made ready on earth for
their service,
and when their times come they
will not transgress his word.

q Gk *his*

39.12–35: In praise of God the creator. 12–15: Introduction to Sirach's eulogy. **15:** *In thanks-giving*, Hebrew, "with a shout." **16:** Gen.1.31; 1 Tim.4.4. **17a:** Rom.9.20. **17c:** Ps.33.6–7; 147.15,18. **18:** Ps.135.6. **19:** 16.17–19; Heb.4.13. **22:** *A river*, the Nile is meant. *A flood*, the Euphrates is meant. **23b:** Ps.107.33. **24:** Hos.14.9. **25b:** 40.10. **26:** 29.21. **29:** 40.9; Ex.9.23. **30:** Dt.32.24; Wis.16.5. **31:** *They*, the previously mentioned instruments appointed

³²Therefore from the beginning I
    have been convinced,
  and have thought this out and
    left it in writing:
³³The works of the Lord are all
    good,
  and he will supply every need in
    its hour.
³⁴And no one can say, "This is worse
    than that,"
  for all things will prove good in
    their season.
³⁵So now sing praise with all your
    heart and voice,
  and bless the name of the Lord.

40 Much labor was created for
    every man,
  and a heavy yoke is upon the
    sons of Adam,
from the day they come forth from
    their mother's womb
  till the day they return to^r the
    mother of all.
²Their perplexities and fear of
    heart—
  their anxious thought is the day
    of death,
³from the man who sits on a
    splendid throne
  to the one who is humbled in
    dust and ashes,
⁴from the man who wears purple
    and a crown
  to the one who is clothed in
    burlap;
⁵there is anger and envy and trouble
    and unrest,
  and fear of death, and fury and
    strife.
And when one rests upon his bed,
  his sleep at night confuses his
    mind.
⁶He gets little or no rest,
  and afterward in his sleep, as
    though he were on watch,

he is troubled by the visions of his
    mind
  like one who has escaped from
    the battle-front;
⁷at the moment of his rescue he
    wakes up,
  and wonders that his fear came
    to nothing.
⁸With all flesh, both man and beast,
  and upon sinners seven times
    more,
⁹are death and bloodshed and strife
    and sword,
  calamities, famine and affliction
    and plague.
¹⁰All these were created for the
    wicked,
  and on their account the flood
    came.
¹¹All things that are from the earth
    turn back to the earth,
  and what is from the waters
    returns to the sea.

¹²All bribery and injustice will be
    blotted out,
  but good faith will stand for
    ever.
¹³The wealth of the unjust will dry
    up like a torrent,
  and crash like a loud clap of
    thunder in a rain.
¹⁴A generous man will be made glad;
  likewise transgressors will
    utterly fail.
¹⁵The children of the ungodly will
    not put forth many branches;
  they are unhealthy roots upon
    sheer rock.
¹⁶The reeds by any water or river bank
  will be plucked up before any
    grass.
¹⁷Kindness is like a garden of
    blessings,
  and almsgiving endures for ever.

r Other authorities read *are buried in*

---

to execute God's wrath. **33a:** V. 16. **34:** *In their season*, compare Ec.3.1–8. **35:** Ps.145.21.
  40.1–11: The miseries of mankind. 1: Gen.3.19; Job 7.1–2; 14.1; Ec.1.3; 2.23. **4:** *Purple*,
Hebrew, "a turban," which was worn by the high priest (Ex.28.37). **8:** *Seven times*, 35.11.
11b: Hebrew and Syriac, "and what is from above (returns) on high" (Ec.12.7).
  40.12–17: Injustice will be blotted out. 17: *Almsgiving*, see 7.10 n. The verse in Hebrew reads,
"But kindness shall never be moved, and righteousness abides forever."

¹⁸Life is sweet for the self-reliant and
the worker,ˢ
but he who finds treasure is
better off than both.
¹⁹Children and the building of a
city establish a man's name,
but a blameless wife is accounted
better than both.
²⁰Wine and music gladden the
heart,
but the love of wisdom is better
than both.
²¹The flute and the harp make
pleasant melody,
but a pleasant voice is better
than both.
²²The eye desires grace and
beauty,
but the green shoots of grain
more than both.
²³A friend or a companion never
meets one amiss,
but a wife with her husband is
better than both.
²⁴Brothers and help are for a time
of trouble,
but almsgiving rescues better
than both.
²⁵Gold and silver make the foot
stand sure,
but good counsel is esteemed
more than both.
²⁶Riches and strength lift up the
heart,
but the fear of the Lord is
better than both.
There is no loss in the fear of the
Lord,
and with it there is no need to
seek for help.
²⁷The fear of the Lord is like a
garden of blessing,
and covers a manᵗ better than
any glory.

²⁸My son, do not lead the life of a
beggar;

it is better to die than to
beg.
²⁹When a man looks to the table of
another,
his existence cannot be
considered as life.
He pollutes himself with another
man's food,
but a man who is intelligent and
well instructed guards against
that.
³⁰In the mouth of the shameless
begging is sweet,
but in his stomach a fire is
kindled.

41 O death, how bitter is the
reminder of you
to one who lives at peace among
his possessions,
to a man without distractions, who
is prosperous in everything,
and who still has the vigor to
enjoy his food!
²O death, how welcome is your
sentence
to one who is in need and is
failing in strength,
very old and distracted over
everything;
to one who is contrary, and has
lost his patience!
³Do not fear the sentence of
death;
remember your former days and
the end of life;
this is the decree from the Lord
for all flesh,
⁴ and how can you reject the
good pleasure of the Most
High?
Whether life is for ten or a hundred
or a thousand years,
there is no inquiry about it in
Hades.

s Cn: Gk *self-reliant worker*
t Gk *him*

40.18–27: The joys of life. **23b:** *A wife with her husband,* Hebrew, "a prudent wife." **27a:**
V. 17a.
40.28–30: A beggar's life is no life at all (29.24).
41.1–42.14: A series of contrasts. **41.1–7:** *Death*—bitter to some, welcome to others. **3–4:**
38.20–23. **3b:** Hebrew, "Remember that the former and the latter (share it) with you."

⁵The children of sinners are
abominable children,
and they frequent the haunts of
the ungodly.
⁶The inheritance of the children of
sinners will perish,
and on their posterity will be a
perpetual reproach.
⁷Children will blame an ungodly
father,
for they suffer reproach because
of him.
⁸Woe to you, ungodly men,
who have forsaken the law of the
Most High God!
⁹When you are born, you are born
to a curse;
and when you die, a curse is your
lot.
¹⁰Whatever is from the dust returns
to dust;
so the ungodly go from curse to
destruction.

¹¹The mourning of men is about their
bodies,
but the evil name of sinners will
be blotted out.
¹²Have regard for your name, since
it will remain for you
longer than a thousand great
stores of gold.
¹³The days of a good life are
numbered,
but a good name endures for ever.

¹⁴My children, observe instruction
and be at peace;
hidden wisdom and unseen treasure,
what advantage is there in either
of them?
¹⁵Better is the man who hides his
folly
than the man who hides his
wisdom.
¹⁶Therefore show respect for my
words:
For it is not good to retain every
kind of shame,

and not everything is confidently
esteemed by every one.

¹⁷Be ashamed of immorality, before
your father or mother;
and of a lie, before a prince or a
ruler;
¹⁸of a transgression, before a judge
or magistrate;
and of iniquity, before a
congregation or the people;
of unjust dealing, before your
partner or friend;
¹⁹   and of theft, in the place where
you live.
Be ashamed before the truth of
God and his covenant.
Be ashamed of selfish behavior
at meals,ᵘ
of surliness in receiving and giving,
²⁰   and of silence, before those who
greet you;
of looking at a woman who is a
harlot,
²¹   and of rejecting the appeal of a
kinsman;
of taking away some one's portion
or gift,
and of gazing at another man's
wife;
²²of meddling with his maidservant—
and do not approach her bed;
of abusive words, before friends—
and do not upbraid after making
a gift;
²³of repeating and telling what you
hear,
and of revealing secrets.
Then you will show proper shame,
and will find favor with every
man.

42 Of the following things do
not be ashamed,
and do not let partiality lead
you to sin:
²of the law of the Most High and
his covenant,

ᵘ Gk *of fixing the elbow on the bread*

5–13: A contrast between the memorials left by the ungodly and the just. **10:** 40.11. **12:** Pr.22.1.
41.14–42.14: True and false shame. 41.14–16: Introductory section. **17–23:** Things to be
ashamed of. **21:** Pr.6.29; Mt.5.28. **22:** 18.15. **23:** 27.16. **42.1–8:** Things of which one must

and of rendering judgment to
acquit the ungodly;
³of keeping accounts with a partner
or with traveling companions,
and of dividing the inheritance
of friends;
⁴of accuracy with scales and
weights,
and of acquiring much or little;
⁵of profit from dealing with
merchants,
and of much discipline of
children,
and of whipping a wicked
servant severely.ᵛ
⁶Where there is an evil wife, a seal
is a good thing;
and where there are many hands,
lock things up.
⁷Whatever you deal out, let it be
by number and weight,
and make a record of all that you
give out or take in.
⁸Do not be ashamed to instruct the
stupid or foolish
or the aged man who quarrels
with the young.
Then you will be truly instructed,
and will be approved before all
men.

⁹A daughter keeps her father secretly
wakeful,
and worry over her robs him of
sleep;
when she is young, lest she do not
marry,
or if married, lest she be hated;
¹⁰while a virgin, lest she be defiled
or become pregnant in her
father's house;
or having a husband, lest she prove
unfaithful,
or, though married, lest she be
barren.

¹¹Keep strict watch over a headstrong
daughter,
lest she make you a laughingstock
to your enemies,
a byword in the city and notoriousʷ
among the people,
and put you to shame before the
great multitude.

¹²Do not look upon any one for
beauty,
and do not sit in the midst of
women;
¹³for from garments comes the moth,
and from a woman comes
woman's wickedness.
¹⁴Better is the wickedness of a man
than a woman who does
good;
and it is a woman who brings
shame and disgrace.

¹⁵I will now call to mind the works
of the Lord,
and will declare what I have
seen.
By the words of the Lord his works
are done.
¹⁶The sun looks down on everything
with its light,
and the work of the Lord is full
of his glory.
¹⁷The Lord has not enabled his holy
ones
to recount all his marvelous
works,
which the Lord the Almighty has
established
that the universe may stand firm
in his glory.
¹⁸He searches out the abyss, and the
hearts of men,ˣ
and considers their crafty devices.

v Gk *making the side of a wicked servant bleed*
w Gk *called out*
x Gk *and the heart*

---

not be ashamed. **1**: Lev.19.15; Dt.1.17; Pr.24.23. **5c**: 33.26–29. **6**: *Many hands*, in the household.

42.9–11: A father's concern for his daughter (7.24–25; 26.10–12).

42.12–14: Concerning women (9.1–9). **12**: 25.21. Hebrew, "Let her not parade her charms
before men, or spend her time conversing with married women."

42.15–43.33: In praise of God, the Creator.

42.15–25: The omnipotence and omniscience of God. 17: *Holy ones*, the angels; Sirach means
that even the angels lack sufficient power to declare all the wonders of his mighty works.

For the Most High knows all that
   may be known,
and he looks into the signs[y] of
   the age.
[19]He declares what has been and
   what is to be,
and he reveals the tracks of
   hidden things.
[20]No thought escapes him,
   and not one word is hidden from
   him.
[21]He has ordained the splendors of
   his wisdom,
and he is from everlasting and to
   everlasting.
Nothing can be added or taken
   away,
and he needs no one to be his
   counselor.
[22]How greatly to be desired are all
   his works,
and how sparkling they are to
   see![z]
[23]All these things live and remain
   for ever
for every need, and are all
   obedient.
[24]All things are twofold, one opposite
   the other,
and he has made nothing
   incomplete.
[25]One confirms the good things of
   the other,
and who can have enough of
   beholding his glory?

43 The pride of the heavenly
   heights is the clear
   firmament,
the appearance of heaven in a
   spectacle of glory.
[2]The sun, when it appears, making
   proclamation as it goes
   forth,
is a marvelous instrument, the
   work of the Most High.
[3]At noon it parches the land;

and who can withstand its
   burning heat?
[4]A man tending[a] a furnace works
   in burning heat,
but the sun burns the mountains
   three times as much;
it breathes out fiery vapors,
   and with bright beams it blinds
   the eyes.
[5]Great is the Lord who made it;
   and at his command it hastens
   on its course.

[6]He made the moon also, to serve
   in its season[b]
to mark the times and to be an
   everlasting sign.
[7]From the moon comes the sign for
   feast days,
a light that wanes when it has
   reached the full.
[8]The month is named for the moon,
   increasing marvelously in its
   phases,
an instrument of the hosts on
   high
shining forth in the firmament
   of heaven.

[9]The glory of the stars is the beauty
   of heaven,
a gleaming array in the heights
   of the Lord.
[10]At the command of the Holy One
   they stand as ordered,
   they never relax in their
   watches.
[11]Look upon the rainbow, and
   praise him who made it,
exceedingly beautiful in its
   brightness.
[12]It encircles the heaven with its
   glorious arc;
   the hands of the Most High
   have stretched it out.

y Gk *sign*   z The Greek of this line is uncertain
a Other authorities read *blowing*
b The Greek text of this line is uncertain

20: Ps.139.4; Is.29.15. 21: *His counselor*, Hebrew, "his instructor" (see Is.40.13–14). 24: 33.15.
   43.1–5: The splendor of the firmament and the sun. 1: Ex.24.10. 2: Ps.19.1–5.
   43.6–8: The splendor of the moon. 6: Gen.1.16. The Hebrews followed a lunar calendar.
   43.9–12: The glory of the stars and the rainbow. 10: *They stand* like sentinels on high. 11–12:
50.7; Gen.9.13; Ezek.1.28.

13By his command he sends the
driving snow
and speeds the lightnings of his
judgment.
14Therefore the storehouses are
opened,
and the clouds fly forth like
birds.
15In his majesty he amasses the
clouds,
and the hailstones are broken in
pieces.
16At his appearing the mountains
are shaken;
at his will the south wind blows.
17The voice of his thunder rebukes
the earth;
so do the tempest from the
north and the whirlwind.
He scatters the snow like birds
flying down,
and its descent is like locusts
alighting.
18The eye marvels at the beauty of
its whiteness,
and the mind is amazed at its
falling.
19He pours the hoarfrost upon the
earth like salt,
and when it freezes, it becomes
pointed thorns.
20The cold north wind blows,
and ice freezes over the water;
it rests upon every pool of water,
and the water puts it on like a
breastplate.
21He consumes the mountains and
burns up the wilderness,
and withers the tender grass like
fire.
22A mist quickly heals all things;
when the dew appears, it
refreshes from the heat.
23By his counsel he stilled the great
deep

and planted islands in it.
24Those who sail the sea tell of its
dangers,
and we marvel at what we hear.
25For in it are strange and marvelous
works,
all kinds of living things, and
huge creatures of the sea.
26Because of him his messenger finds
the way,
and by his word all things hold
together.

27Though we speak much we cannot
reach the end,
and the sum of our words is:
"He is the all."
28Where shall we find strength to
praise him?
For he is greater than all his
works.
29Terrible is the Lord and very
great,
and marvelous is his power.
30When you praise the Lord, exalt
him as much as you can;
for he will surpass even that.
When you exalt him, put forth all
your strength,
and do not grow weary, for you
cannot praise him enough.
31Who has seen him and can describe
him?
Or who can extol him as he is?
32Many things greater than these lie
hidden,
for we have seen but few of his
works.
33For the Lord has made all things,
and to the godly he has granted
wisdom.

44 Let us now praise famous
men,
and our fathers in their
generations.

43.13–26: Marvels of nature. 13: *Snow,* Hebrew, "lightning." **14:** Job 38.22; Jer.51.16.
20: *Blows,* Hebrew, "he causes to blow." **23:** Ps.104.25–26. **26b:** Col.1.17.
   43.27–33: God is greater than all his works. 27: *He is the all,* not to be taken in a pantheistic
sense. **28a:** Hebrew, "Let us praise him the more, since we cannot fathom (him)" (Job 11.7;
Ps.145.3).
   44.1–50.24: In praise of famous men. 44.1–15: Introduction. **1:** *Famous men,* Hebrew and
Syriac, "men of piety." *Generations,* i.e. historical sequence.

²The Lord apportioned to them^c
  great glory,
  his majesty from the beginning.
³There were those who ruled in
    their kingdoms,
  and were men renowned for
    their power,
  giving counsel by their
    understanding,
  and proclaiming prophecies;
⁴leaders of the people in their
    deliberations
  and in understanding of
    learning for the people,
  wise in their words of instruction;
⁵those who composed musical tunes,
  and set forth verses in writing;
⁶rich men furnished with resources,
  living peaceably in their
    habitations—
⁷all these were honored in their
    generations,
  and were the glory of their times.
⁸There are some of them who have
    left a name,
  so that men declare their praise.
⁹And there are some who have no
    memorial,
  who have perished as though
    they had not lived;
  they have become as though they
    had not been born,
  and so have their children after
    them.
¹⁰But these were men of mercy,
  whose righteous deeds have not
    been forgotten;
¹¹their prosperity will remain with
    their descendants,
  and their inheritance to their
    children's children.^d
¹²Their descendants stand by the
    covenants;
  their children also, for their sake.
¹³Their posterity will continue for ever,
  and their glory will not be
    blotted out.
¹⁴Their bodies were buried in peace,

and their name lives to all
    generations.
¹⁵Peoples will declare their wisdom,
  and the congregation proclaims
    their praise.

¹⁶Enoch pleased the Lord, and was
    taken up;
  he was an example of repentance
    to all generations.

¹⁷Noah was found perfect and
    righteous;
  in the time of wrath he was
    taken in exchange;
  therefore a remnant was left to the
    earth
  when the flood came.
¹⁸Everlasting covenants were made
    with him
  that all flesh should not be
    blotted out by a flood.

¹⁹Abraham was the great father of
    a multitude of nations,
  and no one has been found like
    him in glory;
²⁰he kept the law of the Most High,
  and was taken into covenant
    with him;
  he established the covenant in his
    flesh,
  and when he was tested he was
    found faithful.
²¹Therefore the Lord^e assured him
    by an oath
  that the nations would be blessed
    through his posterity;
  that he would multiply him like
    the dust of the earth,
  and exalt his posterity like the
    stars,
  and cause them to inherit from
    sea to sea
  and from the River to the ends
    of the earth.

c Heb: Gk *created*
d Heb Compare Vg Syr: The Greek of this verse is
uncertain   e Gk *he*

44.16–18: Enoch and Noah. 16: 49.14; Gen.5.24; Heb.11.5. **17a:** Gen.6.9; Heb.11.7. **18:**
Gen.8.20–22; 9.12–17.
  44.19–23: Abraham, Isaac, and Jacob. 19: *Father*, Gen.17.4; Mt.3.9. **20:** *Kept the law*,
Gen.26.5. *In his flesh*, Gen.17.10–14. *Tested*, Gen.22.1–14; 1 Macc.2.52; Heb.11.17. **21:** Gen.

²²To Isaac also he gave the same
    assurance
    for the sake of Abraham his
    father.

²³The blessing of all men and the
    covenant
    he made to rest upon the head
    of Jacob;
he acknowledged him with his
    blessings,
    and gave him his inheritance;ᶠ
he determined his portions,
    and distributed them among
    twelve tribes.

45 From his descendants the
    Lordᵍ brought forth a man
    of mercy,
who found favor in the sight of
    all flesh
and was beloved by God and man,
    Moses, whose memory is blessed.
²He made him equal in glory to the
    holy ones,
    and made him great in the fears
    of his enemies.
³By his words he caused signs to
    cease;
    the Lordᵍ glorified him in the
    presence of kings.
He gave him commands for his
    people,
    and showed him part of his glory.
⁴He sanctified him through
    faithfulness and meekness;
    he chose him out of all mankind.
⁵He made him hear his voice,
    and led him into the thick
    darkness,
and gave him the commandments
    face to face,
    the law of life and knowledge,
to teach Jacob the covenant,
    and Israel his judgments.

⁶He exalted Aaron, the brother of
    Moses,ʰ

a holy man like him, of the tribe
    of Levi.
⁷He made an everlasting covenant
    with him,
    and gave him the priesthood of
    the people.
He blessed him with splendid
    vestments,
    and put a glorious robe upon
    him.
⁸He clothed him with superb
    perfection,
    and strengthened him with the
    symbols of authority,
    the linen breeches, the long robe,
    and the ephod.
⁹And he encircled him with
    pomegranates,
    with very many golden bells
    round about,
to send forth a sound as he walked,
    to make their ringing heard in
    the temple
    as a reminder to the sons of his
    people;
¹⁰with a holy garment, of gold and blue
    and purple, the work of an
    embroiderer;
    with the oracle of judgment, Urim
    and Thummim;
¹¹   with twisted scarlet, the work
    of a craftsman;
    with precious stones engraved like
    signets,
    in a setting of gold, the work of
    a jeweler,
    for a reminder, in engraved letters,
    according to the number of the
    tribes of Israel;
¹²with a gold crown upon his turban,
    inscribed like a signet with
    "Holiness,"
    a distinction to be prized, the work
    of an expert,
    the delight of the eyes, richly
    adorned.

ᶠ Heb: Gk *by inheritance*
ᵍ Gk *he*   ʰ Gk *him*

22.16–18; Gal.3.8. *River*, the Euphrates. **22**: Gen.17.19; 26.3–5. **23**: Gen.27.28; 28.14.
45.1–5: Moses. **1**: Ex.11.3. **2**: *Holy ones*, the angels. **3**: Ex.7–10. *Part*, Ex.33.18–23. **4**: *Meekness*. Num.12.3. **5**: Ex.20.21; 24.18; Dt.6.1–2.
45.6–22: Aaron. **6**: Ex.4.14. **7**: Ex.28.1–4. **8–13**: Ex. ch. 28. **10**: *Urim*, see 33.3 n.

¹³Before his time there never were
  such beautiful things.
  No outsider ever put them on,
but only his sons
  and his descendants perpetually.
¹⁴His sacrifices shall be wholly burned
  twice every day continually.
¹⁵Moses ordained him,
  and anointed him with holy
    oil;
  it was an everlasting covenant for
    him
  and for his descendants all the
    days of heaven,
  to minister to the Lord*ⁱ* and serve
    as priest
  and bless his people in his
    name.
¹⁶He chose him out of all the living
  to offer sacrifice to the Lord,
  incense and a pleasing odor as a
    memorial portion,
  to make atonement for the
    people.*ʲ*
¹⁷In his commandments he gave him
  authority in statutes and*ᵏ*
    judgments,
  to teach Jacob the testimonies,
  and to enlighten Israel with his
    law.
¹⁸Outsiders conspired against him,
  and envied him in the wilderness,
  Dathan and Abiram and their men
  and the company of Korah, in
    wrath and anger.
¹⁹The Lord saw it and was not
    pleased,
  and in the wrath of his anger
    they were destroyed;
  he wrought wonders against them
  to consume them in flaming
    fire.
²⁰He added glory to Aaron
  and gave him a heritage;
  he allotted to him the first of the
    first fruits,
  he prepared bread of first fruits
    in abundance;

²¹for they eat the sacrifices to the
    Lord,
  which he gave to him and his
    descendants.
²²But in the land of the people he
    has no inheritance,
  and he has no portion among
    the people;
  for the Lord*ˡ* himself is his*ᵐ*
    portion and inheritance.

²³Phinehas the son of Eleazar is the
    third in glory,
  for he was zealous in the fear of
    the Lord,
  and stood fast, when the people
    turned away,
  in the ready goodness of his soul,
  and made atonement for Israel.
²⁴Therefore a covenant of peace was
    established with him,
  that he should be leader of the
    sanctuary and of his people,
  that he and his descendants should
    have
  the dignity of the priesthood for
    ever.
²⁵A covenant was also established
    with David,
  the son of Jesse, of the tribe of
    Judah:
  the heritage of the king is from
    son to son only;
  so the heritage of Aaron is for
    his descendants.
²⁶May the Lord*ⁿ* grant you wisdom
    in your heart
  to judge his people in
    righteousness,
  so that their prosperity may not
    vanish,
  and that their glory may endure
    throughout their generations.*ᵒ*

i Gk *him*
j Other authorities read *thy people*
k Heb: Gk *in covenants of*
l Gk *he*
m Other authorities read *your*
n Gk *he*
o The Greek of this line is obscure

14: Num.28.3–4. **15:** Lev. ch. 8. *Bless*, Num. 6.23–27. **18:** Num. ch. 16. *Outsiders*, as in
v. 13, those who were not of the family of Aaron. **22:** Num.18.20; Dt.12.12.
  45.23–26: Phinehas (Num.25.10–13; Ps.106.30; 1 Macc.2.54). **25:** 2 Sam.7.12. **26:** *You* . . .
your, the reference is to Simon, son of Onias (see 50.1 n.), and his successors.

46 Joshua the son of Nun was
mighty in war,
and was the successor of Moses
in prophesying.
He became, in accordance with his
name,
a great savior of God's*p* elect,
to take vengeance on the enemies
that rose against them,
so that he might give Israel its
inheritance.
²How glorious he was when he lifted
his hands
and stretched out his sword
against the cities!
³Who before him ever stood so firm?
For he waged the wars of the
Lord.
⁴Was not the sun held back by his
hand?
And did not one day become as
long as two?
⁵He called upon the Most High,
the Mighty One,
when enemies pressed him on
every side,
⁶and the great Lord answered him
with hailstones of mighty power.
He hurled down war upon that
nation,
and at the descent of Beth-horon*q*
he destroyed those who resisted,
so that the nations might know
his armament,
that he was fighting in the sight
of the Lord;
for he wholly followed the
Mighty One.
⁷And in the days of Moses he did
a loyal deed,
he and Caleb the son of
Jephunneh:
they withstood the congregation,*r*
restrained the people from sin,
and stilled their wicked
murmuring.

⁸And these two alone were preserved
out of six hundred thousand
people on foot,
to bring them into their inheritance,
into a land flowing with milk
and honey.
⁹And the Lord gave Caleb strength,
which remained with him to
old age,
so that he went up to the hill
country,
and his children obtained it for
an inheritance;
¹⁰so that all the sons of Israel might see
that it is good to follow the Lord.

¹¹The judges also, with their
respective names,
those whose hearts did not fall
into idolatry
and who did not turn away from
the Lord—
may their memory be blessed!
¹²May their bones revive from where
they lie,
and may the name of those who
have been honored
live again in their sons!

¹³Samuel, beloved by his Lord,
a prophet of the Lord, established
the kingdom
and anointed rulers over his
people.
¹⁴By the law of the Lord he judged
the congregation,
and the Lord watched over
Jacob.
¹⁵By his faithfulness he was proved
to be a prophet,
and by his words he became
known as a trustworthy seer.
¹⁶He called upon the Lord, the
Mighty One,

p Gk *his*
q Compare Joshua 10.11: Greek lacks *of Beth-horon*
r Other authorities read *the enemy*

46.1–10: Joshua and Caleb. 1: *His name* means "Jehovah is salvation." **2–8:** Jos. chs. 6–11. **4:** Jos.10.12–14. **6:** Jos.10.11. **7:** Num.14.6–10; 1 Macc.2.55–56. **8:** Num.11.21; 14.38; 26.65. **9:** Jos.14.6–11.
46.11–12: The judges. 12: *Bones revive* (49.10), the meaning is to be interpreted in the light of the last line of the verse.
46.13–20: Samuel. 13: *Anointed rulers*, 1 Sam.10.1; 16.13. **15:** 1 Sam.3.19–20. **16–18:** 1 Sam. 7.9–11. **19:** 1 Sam.12.3. **20:** 1 Sam.28.18–19.

when his enemies pressed him on
every side,
and he offered in sacrifice a
sucking lamb.
¹⁷Then the Lord thundered from
heaven,
and made his voice heard with
a mighty sound;
¹⁸and he wiped out the leaders of the
people of Tyre
and all the rulers of the Philistines.
¹⁹Before the time of his eternal sleep,
Samuel^s called men to witness
before the Lord and his
anointed:
"I have not taken any one's
property,
not so much as a pair of shoes."
And no man accused him.
²⁰Even after he had fallen asleep he
prophesied
and revealed to the king his
death,
and lifted up his voice out of the
earth in prophecy,
to blot out the wickedness of
the people.

47 And after him Nathan rose
up
to prophesy in the days of David.
²As the fat is selected from the
peace offering,
so David was selected from the
sons of Israel.
³He played with lions as with young
goats,
and with bears as with lambs of
the flock.
⁴In his youth did he not kill a giant,
and take away reproach from
the people,
when he lifted his hand with a
stone in the sling
and struck down the boasting of
Goliath?
⁵For he appealed to the Lord, the
Most High,

and he gave him strength in his
right hand
to slay a man mighty in war,
to exalt the power^t of his people.
⁶So they glorified him for his ten
thousands,
and praised him for the blessings
of the Lord,
when the glorious diadem was
bestowed upon him.
⁷For he wiped out his enemies on
every side,
and annihilated his adversaries
the Philistines;
he crushed their power^t even
to this day.
⁸In all that he did he gave thanks
to the Holy One, the Most High,
with ascriptions of glory;
he sang praise with all his heart,
and he loved his Maker.
⁹He placed singers before the altar,
to make sweet melody with their
voices.
¹⁰He gave beauty to the feasts,
and arranged their times
throughout the year,^u
while they praised God's^v holy
name,
and the sanctuary resounded
from early morning.
¹¹The Lord took away his sins,
and exalted his power^w for ever;
he gave him the covenant of kings
and a throne of glory in Israel.

¹²After him rose up a wise son
who fared amply^x because of him;
¹³Solomon reigned in days of peace,
and God gave him rest on every
side,
that he might build a house for
his name
and prepare a sanctuary to stand
for ever.
¹⁴How wise you became in your youth!

s Gk *he*   t Gk *horn*
u Gk *to completion*   v Gk *his*
w Gk *horn*   x Gk *lived in a broad place*

47.1–11: David. 1: 2 Sam.7.2–3; 12.1; 1 Chr.17.1. **2:** *The fat*, the portion reserved for sacrifice (Lev.3.3–5). **3:** 1 Sam.17.34. **4:** 1 Sam.17.49–51. **6:** 1 Sam.18.7. **7:** 2 Sam.5.7; 8.1. **9:** 1 Chr.16.4. **11:** 2 Sam.12.13.
47.12–22: Solomon. 13–17: 1 Kg.4.21–32. **14:** Compare the address to Elijah in 48.4–11.

You overflowed like a river with
understanding.
¹⁵Your soul covered the earth,
and you filled it with parables
and riddles.
¹⁶Your name reached to far-off
islands,
and you were loved for your
peace.
¹⁷For your songs and proverbs and
parables,
and for your interpretations, the
countries marveled at you.
¹⁸In the name of the Lord God,
who is called the God of Israel,
you gathered gold like tin
and amassed silver like lead.
¹⁹But you laid your loins beside
women,
and through your body you were
brought into subjection.
²⁰You put a stain upon your honor,
and defiled your posterity,
so that you brought wrath upon
your children
and they were grieved*ʸ* at your
folly,
²¹so that the sovereignty was divided
and a disobedient kingdom arose
out of Ephraim.
²²But the Lord will never give up
his mercy,
nor cause any of his works to
perish;
he will never blot out the
descendants of his chosen one,
nor destroy the posterity of him
who loved him;
so he gave a remnant to Jacob,
and to David a root of his stock.

²³Solomon rested with his fathers,
and left behind him one of his
sons,
ample in*ᶻ* folly and lacking in
understanding,

Rehoboam, whose policy caused
the people to revolt.
Also Jeroboam the son of Nebat,
who caused Israel to sin
and gave to Ephraim a sinful
way.
²⁴Their sins became exceedingly many,
so as to remove them from their
land.
²⁵For they sought out every sort of
wickedness,
till vengeance came upon them.

48 Then the prophet Elijah
arose like a fire,
and his word burned like a torch.
²He brought a famine upon them,
and by his zeal he made them
few in number.
³By the word of the Lord he shut
up the heavens,
and also three times brought
down fire.
⁴How glorious you were, O Elijah,
in your wondrous deeds!
And who has the right to boast
which you have?
⁵You who raised a corpse from
death
and from Hades, by the word
of the Most High;
⁶who brought kings down to
destruction,
and famous men from their beds;
⁷who heard rebuke at Sinai
and judgments of vengeance at
Horeb;
⁸who anointed kings to inflict
retribution,
and prophets to succeed you.*ᵃ*
⁹You who were taken up by a
whirlwind of fire,
in a chariot with horses of fire;

y Other authorities read *I was grieved*
z Heb (with a play on the name Rehoboam) Syr: Gk
the people's
a Heb: Gk *him*

18: 1 Kg.10.21,27. 19: 1 Kg.11.1. 21: 1 Kg.12.15–20. 22: 2 Sam.7.15; Ps.89.33. *Nor . . . perish*,
Hebrew, "He will let none of his words fall to the ground."
    47.23–25: Solomon's successors. 23: *Rehoboam*, 1 Kg.11.43; 12.10–14. *Jeroboam*, 1 Kg.12.28–
30. **24:** 2 Kg.17.6,18.
    48.1–11: Elijah. 1: 1 Kg.17.1. *Torch*, Hebrew, "furnace." **2:** Jas.5.17. **3:** 1 Kg.18.38; 2 Kg.
1.10–12. **5:** 1 Kg.17.21–22. **6:** 2 Kg.1.16. **7:** 1 Kg.19.8. **8:** 1 Kg.19.15–16. **9:** 2 Kg.2.11. **10:**
Mal. 4.5–6.

¹⁰you who are ready*ᵇ* at the
   appointed time, it is written,
to calm the wrath of God before
   it breaks out in fury,
to turn the heart of the father to
   the son,
and to restore the tribes of
   Jacob.
¹¹Blessed are those who saw you,
   and those who have been
   adorned*ᶜ* in love;
   for we also shall surely live.*ᵈ*

¹²It was Elijah who was covered by
   the whirlwind,
and Elisha was filled with his
   spirit;
in all his days he did not tremble
   before any ruler,
and no one brought him into
   subjection.
¹³Nothing was too hard for him,
   and when he was dead his body
   prophesied.
¹⁴As in his life he did wonders,
   so in death his deeds were
   marvelous.

¹⁵For all this the people did not
   repent,
and they did not forsake their
   sins,
till they were carried away captive
   from their land
and were scattered over all the
   earth;
the people were left very few in
   number,
but with rulers from the house
   of David.
¹⁶Some of them did what was
   pleasing to God,*ᵉ*
but others multiplied sins.

¹⁷Hezekiah fortified his city,
   and brought water into the
   midst of it;

he tunneled the sheer rock with iron
   and built pools for water.
¹⁸In his days Sennacherib came up,
   and sent the Rabshakeh;*ᶠ*
he lifted up his hand against
   Zion
and made great boasts in his
   arrogance.
¹⁹Then their hearts were shaken and
   their hands trembled,
and they were in anguish, like
   women in travail.
²⁰But they called upon the Lord who
   is merciful,
spreading forth their hands
   toward him;
and the Holy One quickly heard
   them from heaven,
and delivered them by the hand
   of Isaiah.
²¹The Lord*ᵍ* smote the camp of the
   Assyrians,
and his angel wiped them
   out.
²²For Hezekiah did what was
   pleasing to the Lord,
and he held strongly to the ways
   of David his father,
which Isaiah the prophet
   commanded,
who was great and faithful in
   his vision.
²³In his days the sun went backward,
   and he lengthened the life of
   the king.
²⁴By the spirit of might he saw the
   last things,
and comforted those who
   mourned in Zion.
²⁵He revealed what was to occur to
   the end of time,
and the hidden things before
   they came to pass.

b Heb: Gk *are for reproofs*
c Other authorities read *who have died*
d The text and meaning of this verse are uncertain
e Gk lacks *to God*
f Other authorities add *and departed*
g Gk *he*

48.12–16: Elisha and subsequent generations. 12: 2 Kg.2.9,13. **13:** 2 Kg.13.20–21. **15:** 2 Kg.
18.11–12.
   48.17–25: Hezekiah and Isaiah. 17: 2 Kg.20.20. **18:** 2 Kg.18.13,17; Is.36.1. *Made . . .
boasts,* Hebrew and Syriac, "blasphemed God." **20:** 2 Kg.19.15–20. **21:** 2 Kg.19.35; Is.37.36;
1 Macc.7.41. **22:** 2 Kg.18.3. **23:** 2 Kg.20.10–11; Is.38.8. **24–25:** Is.40.1; 42.9.

49 The memory of Josiah is like
a blending of incense
prepared by the art of the
perfumer;
it is sweet as honey to every
mouth,
and like music at a banquet of
wine.
²He was led aright in converting
the people,
and took away the abominations
of iniquity.
³He set his heart upon the Lord;
in the days of wicked men he
strengthened godliness.

⁴Except David and Hezekiah and
Josiah
they all sinned greatly,
for they forsook the law of the
Most High;
the kings of Judah came to an
end;
⁵for they gave their power to others,
and their glory to a foreign
nation,
⁶who set fire to the chosen city of
the sanctuary,
and made her streets desolate,
according to the word^h of
Jeremiah.
⁷For they had afflicted him;
yet he had been consecrated in
the womb as prophet,
to pluck up and afflict and destroy,
and likewise to build and to
plant.

⁸It was Ezekiel who saw the vision
of glory
which God^i showed him above
the chariot of the cherubim.
⁹For God^i remembered his enemies
with storm,
and did good to those who
directed their ways aright.^j

¹⁰May the bones of the twelve
prophets
revive from where they lie,
for they comforted the people of
Jacob
and delivered them with
confident hope.

¹¹How shall we magnify Zerubbabel?
He was like a signet on the right
hand,
¹²   and so was Jeshua the son of
Jozadak;
in their days they built the house
and raised a temple^k holy to
the Lord,
prepared for everlasting glory.
¹³The memory of Nehemiah also is
lasting;
he raised for us the walls that
had fallen,
and set up the gates and bars
and rebuilt our ruined houses.

¹⁴No one like Enoch has been
created on earth,
for he was taken up from the
earth.
¹⁵And no man like Joseph^l has been
born,
and his bones are cared for.
¹⁶Shem and Seth were honored
among men,
and Adam above every living
being in the creation.

50 The leader of his brethren
and the pride of his
people^m
was Simon the high priest, son
of Onias,
who in his life repaired the house,

h Gk *by the hand*   i Gk *he*
j The text and meaning of this verse are uncertain
k Other authorities read *people*
l Heb Syr: Greek adds *the leader of his brothers, the support of the people*
m Heb Syr: Greek lacks this line. Compare 49.15

49.1–3: Josiah (2 Kg.22.1). **2a:** Hebrew, "For he was grieved over our backslidings" (2 Kg.
22.11–13). **3:** 2 Kg.23.3,25.
   49.4–10: The last kings and the last prophets. 5–7: 2 Chr.36.17–19. *Jeremiah*, Jer.1.5–10; 39.8.
8–9: Ezek.1.3–15; 13.11; 38.9,16,22. **10:** *Bones*, see 46.12 n.
   49.11–16: Zerubbabel, Jeshua, Nehemiah, and others. 11: Ezra 3.2; Hag.2.23. **12:** Ezra 3.2;
Hag.1.12; 2.2; Zech.3.1. **13:** Neh.7.1. **14:** 44.16. **15:** Gen.39.1ff.; 50.25–26. **16:** Gen.5.3,32.
   50.1–24: Simon, son of Onias (see 45.26 n.). **1:** Simon II was high priest about 219–196 B.C.

and in his time fortified the
temple.
²He laid the foundations for the
high double walls,ⁿ
the high retaining walls for the
temple enclosure.
³In his days a cistern for water was
quarried out,ᵒ
a reservoir like the sea in
circumference.
⁴He considered how to save his
people from ruin,
and fortified the city to
withstand a siege.
⁵How glorious he was when the
people gathered round him
as he came out of the inner
sanctuary!ᵖ
⁶Like the morning star among the
clouds,
like the moon when it is full;
⁷like the sun shining upon the
temple of the Most High,
and like the rainbow gleaming
in glorious clouds;
⁸like roses in the days of the first
fruits,
like lilies by a spring of water,
like a green shoot on Lebanon�q
on a summer day;
⁹like fire and incense in the censer,
like a vessel of hammered gold
adorned with all kinds of
precious stones;
¹⁰like an olive tree putting forth its
fruit,
and like a cypress towering in
the clouds.
¹¹When he put on his glorious robe
and clothed himself with superb
perfection
and went up to the holy altar,
he made the court of the
sanctuary glorious.
¹²And when he received the portions
from the hands of the priests,
as he stood by the hearth of the
altar
with a garland of brethren around
him,

he was like a young cedar on
Lebanon;
and they surrounded him like the
trunks of palm trees,
¹³ all the sons of Aaron in their
splendor
with the Lord's offering in their
hands,
before the whole congregation
of Israel.
¹⁴Finishing the service at the altars,
and arranging the offering to the
Most High, the Almighty,
¹⁵he reached out his hand to the cup
and poured a libation of the
blood of the grape;
he poured it out at the foot of the
altar,
a pleasing odor to the Most
High, the King of all.
¹⁶Then the sons of Aaron shouted,
they sounded the trumpets of
hammered work,
they made a great noise to be heard
for remembrance before the
Most High.
¹⁷Then all the people together made
haste
and fell to the ground upon their
faces
to worship their Lord,
the Almighty, God Most High.
¹⁸And the singers praised him with
their voices
in sweet and full-toned melody.ʳ
¹⁹And the people besought the Lord
Most High
in prayer before him who is
merciful,
till the order of worship of the
Lord was ended;
so they completed his service.
²⁰Then Simonˢ came down, and
lifted up his hands
over the whole congregation of
the sons of Israel,

n The meaning of this phrase is obscure
o Cn Compare Heb: Gk *was diminished*
p Gk *the house of the veil*
q Or *a sprig of frankincense*
r Other authorities read *in sweet melody throughout the house*   s Gk *he*

(Josephus, *Antiquities*, xii.iv.10). *Onias* is the Greek form of Johanan. *The house*, of God. **16:** *Trumpets*, Num.10.2; 31.6. **20:** *The blessing*, namely Num.6.24–27. *His name*, only the high

to pronounce the blessing of the
Lord with his lips,
and to glory in his name;
[21]and they bowed down in worship
a second time,
to receive the blessing from the
Most High.

[22]And now bless the God of all,
who in every way does great things;
who exalts our days from birth,
and deals with us according to
his mercy.
[23]May he give us[t] gladness of heart,
and grant that peace may be in
our days in Israel,
as in the days of old.
[24]May he entrust to us his mercy!
And let him deliver us in our[u] days!

[25]With two nations my soul is vexed,
and the third is no nation:
[26]Those who live on Mount Seir,[v]
and the Philistines,
and the foolish people that dwell
in Shechem.

[27]Instruction in understanding and
knowledge
I have written in this book,
Jesus the son of Sirach, son of
Eleazar, of Jerusalem,[w]
who out of his heart poured
forth wisdom.
[28]Blessed is he who concerns himself
with these things,
and he who lays them to heart
will become wise.
[29]For if he does them, he will be
strong for all things,
for the light of the Lord is his path.

51 I will give thanks to thee, O
Lord and King,

and will praise thee as God my
Savior.
I give thanks to thy name,
[2] for thou hast been my protector
and helper
and hast delivered my body from
destruction
and from the snare of a
slanderous tongue,
from lips that utter lies.
Before those who stood by
thou wast my helper, [3]and didst
deliver me,
in the greatness of thy mercy
and of thy name,
from the gnashings of teeth about
to devour me,[x]
from the hand of those who
sought my life,
from the many afflictions that I
endured,
[4]from choking fire on every side
and from the midst of fire which
I did not kindle,
[5]from the depths of the belly of Hades,
from an unclean tongue and
lying words—
[6] the slander of an unrighteous
tongue to the king.
My soul drew near to death,
and my life was very near to
Hades beneath.
[7]They surrounded me on every side,
and there was no one to help me;
I looked for the assistance of men,
and there was none.
[8]Then I remembered thy mercy, O
Lord,
and thy work from of old,
that thou dost deliver those who
wait for thee

t Other authorities read *you*
u Other authorities read *his*
v Heb Vg: Gk *on the mountain of Samaria*
w The text of this line is uncertain
x Cn Compare Vg: Gk *when I was about to be devoured*

priest (and only once a year, on the Day of Atonement), could utter the ineffable name "Yahweh." **22–24:** Doxology. **24:** Hebrew, "May his love abide upon Simon, and may he keep in him the covenant of Phinehas; may one never be cut off from him; and as for his offspring, (may it be) as the days of heaven."

    50.25–26: A fragment. **26:** *Those . . . on Mount Seir*, Edomites. *People . . . in Shechem*, Samaritans.

    50.27–29: The author's epilogue.

    51.1–30: Appendix. **1–12:** A hymn of thanksgiving for deliverance. **10a:** Hebrew, "Yea, I exalted Jehovah (saying), 'Thou art my Father [Ps.89.26], for thou art the Mighty One of my

and dost save them from the
hand of their enemies.
⁹And I sent up my supplication
from the earth,
and prayed for deliverance from
death.
¹⁰I appealed to the Lord, the Father
of my lord,
not to forsake me in the days
of affliction,
at the time when there is no
help against the proud.
¹¹I will praise thy name continually,
and will sing praise with
thanksgiving.
My prayer was heard,
¹²   for thou didst save me from
destruction
and rescue me from an evil plight.
Therefore I will give thanks to
thee and praise thee,
and I will bless the name of the
Lord.

¹³While I was still young, before I
went on my travels,
I sought wisdom openly in my
prayer.
¹⁴Before the temple I asked for her,
and I will search for her to the last.
¹⁵From blossom toʸ ripening grape
my heart delighted in her;
my foot entered upon the straight
path;
from my youth I followed her steps.
¹⁶I inclined my ear a little and
received her,
and I found for myself much
instruction.
¹⁷I made progress therein;
to him who gives me wisdom I
will give glory.
¹⁸For I resolved to live according to
wisdom,ᶻ
and I was zealous for the good;
and I shall never be put to shame.
¹⁹My soul grappled with wisdom,ᶻ

and in my conduct I was strict;ᵃ
I spread out my hands to the
heavens,
and lamented my ignorance of her.
²⁰I directed my soul to her,
and through purification I
found her.
I gained understandingᵇ with her
from the first,
therefore I will not be forsaken.
²¹My heart was stirred to seek her,
therefore I have gained a good
possession.
²²The Lord gave me a tongue as my
reward,
and I will praise him with it.

²³Draw near to me, you who are
untaught,
and lodge in my school.
²⁴Why do you say you are lacking
in these things,ᶜ
and why are your souls very
thirsty?
²⁵I opened my mouth and said,
Get these thingsᵈ for yourselves
without money.
²⁶Put your neck under the yoke,
and let your souls receive
instruction;
it is to be found close by.
²⁷See with your eyes that I have
labored little
and found for myself much rest.
²⁸Get instruction with a large sum
of silver,
and you will gain by it much gold.
²⁹May your soul rejoice in his mercy,
and may you not be put to
shame when you praise him.
³⁰Do your work before the appointed
time,
and in God'sᵉ time he will give
you your reward.

y Other authorities read *As from*   *z* Gk *her*
a The Greek text of this line is uncertain   *b* Gk *heart*
c Cn Compare Heb Syr: The Greek text of this line is
uncertain
d Greek lacks *these things*   *e* Gk *his*

---

salvation.' " **13–30:** A concluding poem (serving the purpose of a modern preface) in which the
author tells how he acquired wisdom and sought to impart it to others. The poem (like Ps.25 and
Pr.31.10–31) is an acrostic; the verses begin with the successive letters of the Hebrew alpha-
bet. **13:** *Travels,* 34.11; 39.4. **22:** *Tongue,* eloquence. **26:** *The yoke,* of wisdom (compare
Mt.11.29–30). **30:** *Your work,* of learning wisdom.

BARUCH

The book which goes under the name of Baruch purports to have been written during the Babylonian captivity by Baruch, the companion and secretary of the prophet Jeremiah (Jer. 32.12; 36.4), and sent to Jerusalem to be read on feast days as a confession of sins (1.14). The first part, which is in prose, comprises an introduction (1.1–14) and a confession of Israel's guilt (1.15–3.8). The second part is made up of two poems, one lauding wisdom as God's special gift to Israel (3.9–4.4) and the other dealing with the themes of comfort and restoration (4.5–5.9). Diverse authorship of the two parts is indicated by differing viewpoints, literary forms, and diction. For example, God is spoken of in quite different ways in the two parts; the word "Lord" appears forty-nine times in the first part but not once in the second part, where it is replaced by the word "God." Furthermore, only in the second part does one find the expressions "the Everlasting," "everlasting Savior," and "the Holy One."

That the book was written originally in Hebrew is suggested by the decidedly Hebraic cast of many sentences. In fact, the Greek text, particularly in the first part, is often incomprehensible without re-translating it back into Hebrew. Today the book is extant in Greek, from which a number of other ancient versions were made, including two in Latin, two in Syriac, and others in Coptic, Armenian, Ethiopic, and Arabic.

The date at which the several component parts of the book were brought together is disputed. According to a widely held opinion its final redaction took place sometime between about 150 and 60 B.C.

THESE ARE THE WORDS OF THE BOOK which Baruch the son of Neraiah, son of Mahseiah, son of Zedekiah, son of Hasadiah, son of Hilkiah, wrote in Babylon, ²in the fifth year, on the seventh day of the month, at the time when the Chaldeans took Jerusalem and burned it with fire. ³And Baruch read the words of this book in the hearing of Jeconiah the son of Jehoiakim, king of Judah, and in the hearing of all the people who came to hear the book, ⁴and in the hearing of the mighty men and the princes, and in the hearing of the elders, and in the hearing of all the people, small and great, all who dwelt in Babylon by the river Sud.

5 Then they wept, and fasted, and prayed before the Lord; ⁶and they collected money, each giving what he could; ⁷and they sent it to Jerusalem to Jehoiakim the high priest,ᵃ the son of Hilkiah, son of Shallum, and to the priests, and to all the people who were present with him in Jerusalem. ⁸At the same time, on the tenth day of Sivan, Baruchᵇ took the vessels of the house of the Lord, which had been carried away from the temple, to return them to the land of Judah—the silver vessels which Zedekiah the son of Josiah, king of Judah, had made, ⁹after Nebuchadnezzar king of Babylon had carried away from Jerusalem Jeconiah and the princes and the prisoners and the mighty men and the people of the land, and brought them to Babylon.

10 And they said: "Herewith we send you money; so buy with the money burnt offerings and sin offerings and incense, and prepare a cereal offering, and offer them upon the altar of the Lord our God; ¹¹and pray for the life

a Gk the priest   b Gk he

1.1–14: Historical introduction. 1–2: Authorship and date. **1:** *Baruch,* Jeremiah's secretary (Jer.36.4). **2:** *Fifth year,* after the fall of Jerusalem in 587/6 B.C. **3–4:** The book is read before the exiles. **3:** *Jeconiah,* also called Jehoiachin (2 Kg.24.15; Jer.24.1). **4:** *Sud,* unknown. **5–14:** A gift of money, the temple vessels, and the book are sent to Jerusalem. **5:** The word *Lord* occurs only in the first part of the book (1.1–3.8). **7:** *Jehoiakim the high priest,* otherwise unknown. **8:** *Sivan,* the third month (May-June). For the return of gold and *silver vessels,* see Ezra 1.7–11. **9:** Jer.24.1. **11:** Jer.29.7. *Belshazzar* was actually the son of Nabonidus. *Like the days of heaven,* without end (Dt.11.21).

[198]

of Nebuchadnezzar king of Babylon, and for the life of Belshazzar his son, that their days on earth may be like the days of heaven. ¹²And the Lord will give us strength, and he will give light to our eyes, and we shall live under the protection*c* of Nebuchadnezzar king of Babylon, and under the protection*c* of Belshazzar his son, and we shall serve them many days and find favor in their sight. ¹³And pray for us to the Lord our God, for we have sinned against the Lord our God, and to this day the anger of the Lord and his wrath have not turned away from us. ¹⁴And you shall read this book which we are sending you, to make your confession in the house of the Lord on the days of the feasts and at appointed seasons.

15 "And you shall say: 'Righteousness belongs to the Lord our God, but confusion of face, as at this day, to us, to the men of Judah, to the inhabitants of Jerusalem, ¹⁶and to our kings and our princes and our priests and our prophets and our fathers, ¹⁷because we have sinned before the Lord, ¹⁸and have disobeyed him, and have not heeded the voice of the Lord our God, to walk in the statutes of the Lord which he set before us. ¹⁹From the day when the Lord brought our fathers out of the land of Egypt until today, we have been disobedient to the Lord our God, and we have been negligent, in not heeding his voice. ²⁰So to this day there have clung to us the calamities and the curse which the Lord declared through Moses his servant at the time when he brought our fathers out of the land of Egypt to give to us a land flowing with milk and honey. ²¹We did not heed the voice of the Lord our God in all the words of the prophets whom he sent to us, but we each followed the intent of his own wicked heart by

serving other gods and doing what is evil in the sight of the Lord our God.

2 " 'So the Lord confirmed his word, which he spoke against us, and against our judges who judged Israel, and against our kings and against our princes and against the men of Israel and Judah. ²Under the whole heaven there has not been done the like of what he has done in Jerusalem, in accordance with what is written in the law of Moses, ³that we should eat, one the flesh of his son and another the flesh of his daughter. ⁴And he gave them into subjection to all the kingdoms around us, to be a reproach and a desolation among all the surrounding peoples, where the Lord has scattered them. ⁵They were brought low and not raised up, because we sinned against the Lord our God, in not heeding his voice.

6 " 'Righteousness belongs to the Lord our God, but confusion of face to us and our fathers, as at this day. ⁷All those calamities with which the Lord threatened us have come upon us. ⁸Yet we have not entreated the favor of the Lord by turning away, each of us, from the thoughts of his wicked heart. ⁹And the Lord has kept the calamities ready, and the Lord has brought them upon us, for the Lord is righteous in all his works which he has commanded us to do. ¹⁰Yet we have not obeyed his voice, to walk in the statutes of the Lord which he set before us.

11 " 'And now, O Lord God of Israel, who didst bring thy people out of the land of Egypt with a mighty hand and with signs and wonders and with great power and outstretched arm, and hast made thee a name, as at this day, ¹²we have sinned, we have been ungodly, we have done wrong, O Lord our

c Gk *in the shadow*

1.15–3.8: **Confession of sin,** for the Jerusalem community (1.15–2.5), and for the exiles (2.6–3.8); compare 1.15 and 2.6. **1.15–2.5:** Disobedience brought the judgment of exile. **1.15–18:** Based on Dan.9.7–10. **15:** Ezra 9.7. **20:** Dt. ch. 28; Jer.11.3–5. **21:** Jer.7.25–26; Dan.9.5. **2.1–2:** Dan.9.12–13. **3:** Lev.26.29; Dt.28.53; Jer.19.9; Lam.4.10. **5:** Dt.28.13. **2.6–10:** Confession of guilt. **8:** Dan.9.13. **9:** Dan.9.14. **11–26:** Supplication and confession. **11–14:** Dan.

God, against all thy ordinances. ¹³Let thy anger turn away from us, for we are left, few in number, among the nations where thou hast scattered us. ¹⁴Hear, O Lord, our prayer and our supplication, and for thy own sake deliver us, and grant us favor in the sight of those who have carried us into exile; ¹⁵that all the earth may know that thou art the Lord our God, for Israel and his descendants are called by thy name. ¹⁶O Lord, look down from thy holy habitation, and consider us. Incline thy ear, O Lord, and hear; ¹⁷open thy eyes, O Lord, and see; for the dead who are in Hades, whose spirit has been taken from their bodies, will not ascribe glory or justice to the Lord, ¹⁸but the person that is greatly distressed,*ᵈ* that goes about bent over and feeble, and the eyes that are failing, and the person that hungers, will ascribe to thee glory and righteousness, O Lord. ¹⁹For it is not because of any righteous deeds of our fathers or our kings that we bring before thee our prayer for mercy, O Lord our God. ²⁰For thou hast sent thy anger and thy wrath upon us, as thou didst declare by thy servants the prophets, saying: ²¹"Thus says the Lord: Bend your shoulders and serve the king of Babylon, and you will remain in the land which I gave to your fathers. ²²But if you will not obey the voice of the Lord and will not serve the king of Babylon, ²³I will make to cease from the cities of Judah and from the region about Jerusalem the voice of mirth and the voice of gladness, the voice of the bridegroom and the voice of the bride, and the whole land will be a desolation without inhabitants."

24 "'But we did not obey thy voice, to serve the king of Babylon; and thou hast confirmed thy words, which thou didst speak by thy servants the prophets, that the bones of our kings and the bones of our fathers would be brought out of their graves;*ᵉ* ²⁵and behold, they have been cast out to the heat of day and the frost of night. They perished in great misery, by famine and sword and pestilence. ²⁶And the house which is called by thy name thou hast made as it is today, because of the wickedness of the house of Israel and the house of Judah.

27 " 'Yet thou hast dealt with us, O Lord our God, in all thy kindness and in all thy great compassion, ²⁸as thou didst speak by thy servant Moses on the day when thou didst command him to write thy law in the presence of the people of Israel, saying, ²⁹"If you will not obey my voice, this very great multitude will surely turn into a small number among the nations, where I will scatter them. ³⁰For I know that they will not obey me, for they are a stiffnecked people. But in the land of their exile they will come to themselves, ³¹and they will know that I am the Lord their God. I will give them a heart that obeys and ears that hear; ³²and they will praise me in the land of their exile, and will remember my name, ³³and will turn from their stubbornness and their wicked deeds; for they will remember the ways of their fathers, who sinned before the Lord. ³⁴I will bring them again into the land which I swore to give to their fathers, to Abraham and to Isaac and to Jacob, and they will rule over it; and I will increase them, and they will not be diminished. ³⁵I will make an everlasting covenant with them to be their God and they shall be my people; and I will never again remove my people Israel from the land which I have given them."

3 " 'O Lord Almighty, God of Israel, the soul in anguish and the

ᵈ The meaning of the Greek is uncertain
ᵉ Gk *their place*

9.15–17. **13:** Dt.4.27; Jer.42.2. **16:** Dt.26.15. **17:** Pss.6.5; 30.9; Is.38.18; Sir.17.27–28. *Hades, Sheol.* **21:** Jer.27.11–12. **23:** Jer.7.34. **25:** Jer.36.30. **26:** Jer.7.14. **27–35:** Repentance and restoration under an everlasting covenant. **28–29:** Dt.28.58,62. **30:** 1 Kg.8.47. **31:** Jer.24.7. **33:** Dt.9.6. **34:** Lev.26.42; Dt.6.10; Jer.32.37. **35:** Jer.32.38–40; Ezek.36.26–29; Am.9.15. **3.1–8:** Impassioned plea of repentant exiles ("though penitent we are still in exile!").

wearied spirit cry out to thee. ²Hear, O Lord, and have mercy, for we have sinned before thee. ³For thou art enthroned for ever, and we are perishing for ever. ⁴O Lord Almighty, God of Israel, hear now the prayer of the dead of Israel and of the sons of those who sinned before thee, who did not heed the voice of the Lord their God, so that calamities have clung to us. ⁵Remember not the iniquities of our fathers, but in this crisis remember thy power and thy name. ⁶For thou art the Lord our God, and thee, O Lord, will we praise. ⁷For thou hast put the fear of thee in our hearts in order that we should call upon thy name; and we will praise thee in our exile, for we have put away from our hearts all the iniquity of our fathers who sinned before thee. ⁸Behold, we are today in our exile where thou hast scattered us, to be reproached and cursed and punished for all the iniquities of our fathers who forsook the Lord our God.' "

⁹Hear the commandments of life, O Israel;
  give ear, and learn wisdom!
¹⁰Why is it, O Israel, why is it that
    you are in the land of your enemies,
  that you are growing old in a foreign country,
  that you are defiled with the dead,
¹¹ that you are counted among those in Hades?
¹²You have forsaken the fountain of wisdom.
¹³If you had walked in the way of God,
  you would be dwelling in peace for ever.
¹⁴Learn where there is wisdom,

  where there is strength,
  where there is understanding,
that you may at the same time discern
  where there is length of days, and life,
  where there is light for the eyes, and peace.

¹⁵Who has found her place?
  And who has entered her storehouses?
¹⁶Where are the princes of the nations,
  and those who rule over the beasts on the earth;
¹⁷those who have sport with the birds of the air,
  and who hoard up silver and gold,
in which men trust,
  and there is no end to their getting;
¹⁸those who scheme to get silver, and are anxious,
  whose labors are beyond measure?
¹⁹They have vanished and gone down to Hades,
  and others have arisen in their place.

²⁰Young men have seen the light of day,
  and have dwelt upon the earth;
but they have not learned the way to knowledge,
  nor understood her paths,
  nor laid hold of her.
²¹Their sons have strayed far from her*f* way.
²²She has not been heard of in Canaan,
  nor seen in Teman;

f Other authorities read *their*

4: *The dead of Israel*, the Israelites in exile (v. 11; Is.59.10b; Lam.3.6). 7: Jer.32.40b. 8: The fathers' sins (2.33; 3.4–5) are visited on the sons (Lam.5.7).
  3.9–4.4: **Wisdom, found by God, was given to Israel and is the law.** 3.9–14: Introduction to the poem. 10: *Growing old*, the exile has been long (contrast 1.2). 11: Pss.28.1; 88.4. 12: Pr.18.4; Jer.2.13. 14: Pr.3.16; 8.14. 15–28: The rulers of the world and the mighty have not found wisdom. 15: Job 28.12. 16b–17a: Jer.27.6; Dan.2.38; Jdt.11.7. 22: *Canaan*, Ezek.28.3–5 associates Tyre (in Canaan) with wisdom. *Teman*, in Edom, was reputed for its wisdom (Jer.49.7;

²³the sons of Hagar, who seek for
      understanding on the earth,
   the merchants of Merran and
      Teman,
   the story-tellers and the seekers
      for understanding,
   have not learned the way to
      wisdom,
   nor given thought to her paths.

²⁴O Israel, how great is the house
      of God!
   And how vast the territory that
      he possesses!
²⁵It is great and has no bounds;
   it is high and immeasurable.
²⁶The giants were born there, who
      were famous of old,
   great in stature, expert in war.
²⁷God did not choose them,
   nor give them the way to
      knowledge;
²⁸so they perished because they had
      no wisdom,
   they perished through their
      folly.

²⁹Who has gone up into heaven,
      and taken her,
   and brought her down from the
      clouds?
³⁰Who has gone over the sea, and
      found her,
   and will buy her for pure gold?
³¹No one knows the way to her,
   or is concerned about the path
      to her.
³²But he who knows all things knows
      her,
   he found her by his
      understanding.
He who prepared the earth for all
      time
   filled it with four-footed
      creatures;

³³he who sends forth the light, and
      it goes,
   called it, and it obeyed him in
      fear;
³⁴the stars shone in their watches,
      and were glad;
   he called them, and they said,
      "Here we are!"
   They shone with gladness for
      him who made them.
³⁵This is our God;
   no other can be compared to
      him!
³⁶He found the whole way to
      knowledge,
   and gave her to Jacob his
      servant
   and to Israel whom he loved.
³⁷Afterward she appeared upon earth
   and lived among men.

4 She is the book of the
   commandments of God,
   and the law that endures for
      ever.
All who hold her fast will live,
   and those who forsake her will
      die.
²Turn, O Jacob, and take her;
   walk toward the shining of her
      light.
³Do not give your glory to another,
   or your advantages to an alien
      people.
⁴Happy are we, O Israel,
   for we know what is pleasing to
      God.

⁵Take courage, my people,
   O memorial of Israel!
⁶It was not for destruction
   that you were sold to the nations,
   but you were handed over to your
      enemies
   because you angered God.

Ob.8–9). **23**: *Merran*, probably a corruption which arose in the Hebrew text for "Midian," a son of Keturah (Gen.25.2). **24**: *House of God*, the created world. **26**: Gen.6.4; Wis.14.6; compare the book of Enoch 7.1–6. **29–37**: God found wisdom and gave her to Israel (Sir.24.1–12). **29–30**: Dt.30.12–13; Job 28.13–14. **32–34**: Job 28.23–26; Pr.8.22–31. **33**: *Light*, Gen.1.3. **34**: *Stars . . . were glad*, Job 38.7. **37**: Many church fathers took this as an allusion to the Incarnation. **4.1–3**: Wisdom is *the law* (the Torah). **1**: Sir.24.23. **2**: Is.60.3.
  4.5–5.9: Poem of comfort and restoration. 4.5–20: Israel provoked God, and Zion now mourns for her captive children. **5**: *Take courage, my people* (compare vv. 21,27,30), inspired

⁷For you provoked him who made
  you,
  by sacrificing to demons and
    not to God.
⁸You forgot the everlasting God,
  who brought you up,
  and you grieved Jerusalem, who
    reared you.
⁹For she saw the wrath that came
    upon you from God,
  and she said:
"Hearken, you neighbors of Zion,
  God has brought great sorrow
    upon me;
¹⁰for I have seen the captivity of my
    sons and daughters,
  which the Everlasting brought
    upon them.
¹¹With joy I nurtured them,
  but I sent them away with
    weeping and sorrow.
¹²Let no one rejoice over me, a widow
    and bereaved of many;
  I was left desolate because of the
    sins of my children,
  because they turned away from
    the law of God.
¹³They had no regard for his statutes;
  they did not walk in the ways
    of God's commandments,
  ·nor tread the paths of discipline
    in his righteousness.
¹⁴Let the neighbors of Zion come;
  remember the capture of my
    sons and daughters,
  which the Everlasting brought
    upon them.
¹⁵For he brought against them a
    nation from afar,
  a shameless nation, of a strange
    language,
  who had no respect for an old man,
    and had no pity for a child.
¹⁶They led away the widow's
    beloved sons,
  and bereaved the lonely woman
    of her daughters.

¹⁷"But I, how can I help you?
¹⁸For he who brought these calamities
    upon you
  will deliver you from the hand
    of your enemies.
¹⁹Go, my children, go;
  for I have been left desolate.
²⁰I have taken off the robe of peace
  and put on the sackcloth of my
    supplication;
  I will cry to the Everlasting all
    my days.

²¹"Take courage, my children, cry
    to God,
  and he will deliver you from the
    power and hand of the enemy.
²²For I have put my hope in the
    Everlasting to save you,
  and joy has come to me from
    the Holy One,
  because of the mercy which soon
    will come to you
  from your everlasting Savior.ᵍ
²³For I sent you out with sorrow and
    weeping,
  but God will give you back to
    me with joy and gladness for
    ever.
²⁴For as the neighbors of Zion have
    now seen your capture,
  so they soon will see your
    salvation by God,
  which will come to you with great
    glory
  and with the splendor of the
    Everlasting.
²⁵My children, endure with patience
    the wrath that has come upon
    you from God.
  Your enemy has overtaken you,
  but you will soon see their
    destruction
  and will tread upon their necks.
²⁶My tender sons have traveled
    rough roads;

g Or *from the Everlasting, your Savior*

---

by Is.40.1. **7:** *Demons*, Dt.32.16–17; Ps.106.37; 1 Cor.10.20. **9b–16:** Jerusalem speaks to her
neighbors (i.e. neighboring cities). **12:** *Widow*, Lam.1.1. **15:** Dt.28.49–50; Jer.6.15. **17–29:**
Jerusalem encourages her exiled children. **17–18:** Only God can help. **20:** *Robe of peace*, garment worn in time of prosperity. *Sackcloth of my supplication*, garment worn by a suppliant.
23: Ps.126.6; Jer.31.12–13. **24:** Is.60.1–3. **25:** *The wrath* is only temporary (Is.54.7–8).

they were taken away like a
flock carried off by the enemy.

27"Take courage, my children, and
cry to God,
for you will be remembered by
him who brought this upon you.
28For just as you purposed to go
astray from God,
return with tenfold zeal to seek
him.
29For he who brought these calamities
upon you
will bring you everlasting joy
with your salvation."

30Take courage, O Jerusalem,
for he who named you will
comfort you.
31Wretched will be those who
afflicted you
and rejoiced at your fall.
32Wretched will be the cities which
your children served as slaves;
wretched will be the city which
received your sons.
33For just as she rejoiced at your fall
and was glad for your ruin,
so she will be grieved at her own
desolation.
34And I will take away her pride in
her great population,
and her insolence will be turned
to grief.
35For fire will come upon her from
the Everlasting for many days,
and for a long time she will be
inhabited by demons.

36Look toward the east, O Jerusalem,
and see the joy that is coming
to you from God!
37Behold, your sons are coming,
whom you sent away;
they are coming, gathered from
east and west,
at the word of the Holy One,
rejoicing in the glory of God.

5 Take off the garment of your sorrow and affliction, O Jerusalem,
and put on for ever the beauty
of the glory from God.
2Put on the robe of the righteousness
from God;
put on your head the diadem of
the glory of the Everlasting.
3For God will show your splendor
everywhere under heaven.
4For your name will for ever be
called by God,
"Peace of righteousness and
glory of godliness."

5Arise, O Jerusalem, stand upon the
height
and look toward the east,
and see your children gathered
from west and east,
at the word of the Holy One,
rejoicing that God has
remembered them.
6For they went forth from you on
foot,
led away by their enemies;
but God will bring them back to you,
carried in glory, as on a royal
throne.
7For God has ordered that every
high mountain and the
everlasting hills be made low
and the valleys filled up, to
make level ground,
so that Israel may walk safely in
the glory of God.
8The woods and every fragrant tree
have shaded Israel at God's
command.
9For God will lead Israel with joy,
in the light of his glory,
with the mercy and righteousness
that come from him.

4.30–5.9: Jerusalem encouraged with promises concerning the destruction of her enemy and
the return of her children. **30:** *He who named you*, see 5.4 n. **31–35:** Contrast the attitude
toward Babylon in 1.11–12. **35:** *Fire*, Jer.51.58. *Demons*, Is.13.21. **36:** Is.40.9–11. **37:** Is.43.5.
5.1–9: Glorification of Jerusalem and return of the exiles. **1–2:** Is.61.3,10. **4:** Is.60.14;
62.4; Jer.33.16; Ezek.48.35. *Peace of righteousness*, Is.32.17. **5:** Is.49.18; 60.4. **6:** Is.49.22;
66.20. **7:** Is.42.16–17.

THE LETTER OF JEREMIAH

The so-called Letter of Jeremiah, which professes to be a copy of a letter sent by Jeremiah in 597 B.C. to those Jews who were about to be taken as captives to Babylon (v. 1), is an earnest though rambling discourse against the folly of idolatry. It can be characterized as an impassioned sermon on Jer.10.11, a verse (in Aramaic) which provides the exiled Jews with a response when invited to participate in the worship of idols: "Thus shall you say to them: 'The gods who did not make the heavens and the earth shall perish from the earth and from under the heavens.'" Elaborating upon this text, the author draws upon Jer.10.3–9,14 and Ps.115.4–8 (compare also Is.40.18–20; 41.6–7) for a variety of arguments to prove the utter impotence, whether for good or ill, of gods of wood and silver and gold. The style of the tractate is florid and declamatory, with no logical connection in the sequence of its statements. In a mechanical way the author divides his homily into sections by a refrain repeated with slight variations, insisting that "this shows that they are no gods" (vv. 16, 23, 29b, 40a, 44b, 52, 56b, 65, 69).

On the basis of linguistic and historical considerations most scholars date the Letter of Jeremiah in the Hellenistic period. The seven generations of exile mentioned in v. 3, at forty years for a generation, would imply a date 280 years after the exile in 597, that is 317 B.C. Others think that the Letter is still later, dating it in the Maccabean period. The original language was most probably Hebrew (see, for example, v. 72 n.), though some think that it was written in either Aramaic or Greek. The oldest manuscript remains of the book is a tiny fragment of Greek papyrus containing several words from vv. 43–44; it was discovered in Cave VII at Qumran by the Dead Sea, and is thought to date from about 100 B.C.

The Letter stands at different places in various manuscripts and versions. It appears as a separate book between Lamentations and Ezekiel in two ancient Greek manuscripts of the Old Testament (the fourth century codex Vaticanus and the fifth century codex Alexandrinus), in the Syriac Hexaplar manuscript at Milan, and in the Arabic version. In other Greek and Syriac manuscripts, as well as the Latin version, it is attached to the apocryphal book of Baruch, and consequently many English translations include it as the final (sixth) chapter of that book. Since, however, the Letter is an independent composition and has nothing to do with Baruch, the Revised Standard Version prints it as a separate book.

---

6 [h] A COPY OF A LETTER WHICH JEREMIAH sent to those who were to be taken to Babylon as captives by the king of the Babylonians, to give them the message which God had commanded him.

2 Because of the sins which you have committed before God, you will be taken to Babylon as captives by Nebuchadnezzar, king of the Babylonians. ³Therefore when you have come to Babylon you will remain there for many years, for a long time, up to seven generations; after that I will bring you away from there in peace. ⁴Now in Babylon you will see gods made of silver and gold and wood, which are carried on men's shoulders and inspire fear in the heathen. ⁵So take care not to become at all like the foreigners or to let fear for these gods[i] possess you, when you see the multitude before and behind them worshiping them. ⁶But say in your heart, "It is thou, O Lord, whom we must worship." ⁷For my angel is with you, and he is watching your lives.

h The King James Version prints *The Epistle of Jeremy* as Chapter 6 of the book of Baruch, and the chapter and verse numbers are here retained
i Gk *for them*

6.1–7: Historical introduction. 1: The exile of 597 B.C. (2 Kg.24.10–17). *Letter*, according to Jer.29.1 a letter is sent to Babylon. *King of the Babylonians*, but "king of Babylon" in the book of Jeremiah (Jer.20.4; 21.2; etc.). **2:** Jer.16.10. **3:** *Seven generations*, contrast seventy years in Jer.29.10, forty years in Ezek.4.6, seventy weeks of years in Dan.9.24. **4:** *Silver and gold*, overlaid on wood (v. 55; Is.40.19; Jer.10.3–4). *Carried on men's shoulders*, perhaps an allusion to the Babylonian New Year procession, or a reflection of Is.46.7; Jer.10.5. **5:** *Like the foreigners*, Jer.10.2. **7:** *My angel*, Ex.23.23; 32.34.

8 Their tongues are smoothed by the craftsman, and they themselves are overlaid with gold and silver; but they are false and cannot speak. [9]People[j] take gold and make crowns for the heads of their gods, as they would for a girl who loves ornaments; [10]and sometimes the priests secretly take gold and silver from their gods and spend it upon themselves, [11]and even give some of it to the harlots in the brothel. They deck their gods[k] out with garments like men—these gods of silver and gold and wood, [12]which cannot save themselves from rust and corrosion. When they have been dressed in purple robes, [13]their faces are wiped because of the dust from the temple, which is thick upon them. [14]Like a local ruler the god[l] holds a scepter, though unable to destroy any one who offends it. [15]It has a dagger in its right hand, and has an axe; but it cannot save itself from war and robbers. [16]Therefore they evidently are not gods; so do not fear them.

17 For just as one's dish is useless when it is broken, so are the gods of the heathen,[m] when they have been set up in the temples. Their eyes are full of the dust raised by the feet of those who enter. [18]And just as the gates are shut on every side upon a man who has offended a king, as though he were sentenced to death, so the priests make their temples secure with doors and locks and bars, in order that they may not be plundered by robbers. [19]They light lamps, even more than they light for themselves, though their gods[n] can

see none of them. [20]They are[o] just like a beam of the temple, but men say their hearts have melted, when worms from the earth devour them and their robes. They do not notice [21]when their faces have been blackened by the smoke of the temple. [22]Bats, swallows, and birds light on their bodies and heads; and so do cats. [23]From this you will know that they are not gods; so do not fear them.

24 As for the gold which they wear for beauty—they will not shine unless some one wipes off the rust; for even when they were being cast, they had no feeling. [25]They are bought at any cost, but there is no breath in them. [26]Having no feet, they are carried on men's shoulders, revealing to mankind their worthlessness. [27]And those who serve them are ashamed because through them these gods[n] are made to stand, lest they fall to the ground. If any one sets one of them upright, it cannot move of itself; and if it is tipped over, it cannot straighten itself; but gifts are placed before them just as before the dead. [28]The priests sell the sacrifices that are offered to these gods[p] and use the money; and likewise their wives preserve some with salt, but give none to the poor or helpless. [29]Sacrifices to them may be touched by women in menstruation or at childbirth. Since you know by these things that they are not gods, do not fear them.

j Gk *They*
k Gk *them*
l Gk *he*
m Gk *of them*
n Gk *they*
o Gk *It is*
p Gk *to them*

8–73: Condemnation of idolatry. 8–16: Idols are decked out like people. 8: *Craftsman,* Is. 40.20. **11:** *Harlots,* probably cult prostitutes. *In the brothel,* alternate translation, "on the roof." **12:** *Purple robes,* Jer.10.9. **14:** *Scepter,* Est.5.2. *Destroy,* put to death. **15:** *Dagger,* the Hebrew word behind the Greek could also mean "sword." Archaeologists have found representations of deities bearing scepters, swords, daggers, and battle-axes.

17–23: Uselessness and helplessness of idols. 17: *Dish . . . broken,* Jer.19.11; 22.28. **18:** *Gates* of the palace or doors of courtyard prison (Jer.32.2). **19:** Ps.115.5. *Lamps* have been found in excavated temples. **22:** This is the earliest Jewish reference to *cats,* which were first domesticated in Egypt.

24–29: Idols are unable to feel or move. 25: *Any cost,* great cost. *No breath,* Ps.135.17; Jer.10.14; Hab.2.19. **26:** Is.46.7. **27:** *Cannot move,* Is.46.7; Jer.10.4. *Gifts* for *the dead,* Ps. 106.28; Sir.30.18–19. **29:** Lev.12.1–8.

30 For why should they be called gods? Women serve meals for gods of silver and gold and wood; [31]and in their temples the priests sit with their clothes rent, their heads and beards shaved, and their heads uncovered. [32]They howl and shout before their gods as some do at a funeral feast for a man who has died. [33]The priests take some of the clothing of their gods[q] to clothe their wives and children. [34]Whether one does evil to them or good, they will not be able to repay it. They cannot set up a king or depose one. [35]Likewise they are not able to give either wealth or money; if one makes a vow to them and does not keep it, they will not require it. [36]They cannot save a man from death or rescue the weak from the strong. [37]They cannot restore sight to a blind man; they cannot rescue a man who is in distress. [38]They cannot take pity on a widow or do good to an orphan. [39]These things that are made of wood and overlaid with gold and silver are like stones from the mountain, and those who serve them will be put to shame. [40]Why then must any one think that they are gods, or call them gods?

Besides, even the Chaldeans themselves dishonor them; [41]for when they see a dumb man, who cannot speak, they bring him and pray Bel[r] that the man may speak, as though Bel[s] were able to understand. [42]Yet they themselves cannot perceive this and abandon them, for they have no sense. [43]And the women, with cords about them, sit along the passageways, burning bran

for incense; and when one of them is led off by one of the passers-by and is lain with, she derides the woman next to her, because she was not as attractive as herself and her cord was not broken. [44]Whatever is done for them is false. Why then must any one think that they are gods, or call them gods?

45 They are made by carpenters and goldsmiths; they can be nothing but what the craftsmen wish them to be. [46]The men that make them will certainly not live very long themselves; how then can the things that are made by them be gods? [47]They have left only lies and reproach for those who come after. [48]For when war or calamity comes upon them, the priests consult together as to where they can hide themselves and their gods.[t] [49]How then can one fail to see that these are not gods, for they cannot save themselves from war or calamity? [50]Since they are made of wood and overlaid with gold and silver, it will afterward be known that they are false. [51]It will be manifest to all the nations and kings that they are not gods but the work of men's hands, and that there is no work of God in them. [52]Who then can fail to know that they are not gods?[u]

53 For they cannot set up a king over a country or give rain to men. [54]They cannot judge their own cause or deliver one who is wronged, for they have no power; they are like crows between heaven and earth. [55]When fire breaks out in a temple of wooden

q Gk *them*
r Or *they bring Bel and pray*
s Gk *he*
t Gk *them*
u The Greek text of this verse is uncertain

30–40a: Idols cannot repay good or evil, or help mankind. 30: *Women*, there were only male ministrants in the Jewish temple. **31–32:** Ritual lamentations for dying gods (such as Tammuz, Ezek.8.14; compare Lev.21.5,10; Ezek.24.17). **34b:** Job 12.18; Dan.2.21. **35b:** Dt.23.21. **36:** On the contrary, the Lord can do this (Dt.32.39; Ps.49.15). **37:** Ps.146.8. **38:** Dt.10.18; Ps. 146.9; Jer.7.6. **39:** Hab.2.19.

40b–44: The Chaldeans dishonor their own idols. 41: *Bel*, Marduk (Is.46.1). **43:** A similar Babylonian practice is described by Herodotus (*Hist.* i. 199), according to which cult prostitutes sat among roped-off passageways.

45–52: Idols are but the work of man's hands. 45: Ps.115.4; Is.40.19; Jer.10.9. **47:** Idolaters bequeath lies and reproach, not real gods, to posterity. **50:** *Afterward*, when the veneer has been exposed for what it is. *False*, a fraud.

53–56: The impotence of idols. 53: V. 34b. *Give rain*, Dt.11.14; 28.12; Ps.147.8.

gods overlaid with gold or silver, their priests will flee and escape, but the gods[v] will be burnt in two like beams. [56]Besides, they can offer no resistance to a king or any enemies. Why then must any one admit or think that they are gods?

57 Gods made of wood and overlaid with silver and gold are not able to save themselves from thieves and robbers. [58]Strong men will strip them of their gold and silver and of the robes they wear, and go off with this booty, and they will not be able to help themselves. [59]So it is better to be a king who shows his courage, or a household utensil that serves its owner's need, than to be these false gods; better even the door of a house that protects its contents, than these false gods; better also a wooden pillar in a palace, than these false gods.

60 For sun and moon and stars, shining and sent forth for service, are obedient. [61]So also the lightning, when it flashes, is widely seen; and the wind likewise blows in every land. [62]When God commands the clouds to go over the whole world, they carry out his command. [63]And the fire sent from above to consume mountains and woods does what it is ordered. But these idols[w] are not to be compared with them in appearance or power. [64]Therefore one must not think that they are gods nor call them gods, for they are not able either to decide a case or to do good to men. [65]Since you know then that they are not gods, do not fear them.

66 For they can neither curse nor bless kings; [67]they cannot show signs in the heavens and[x] among the nations, or shine like the sun or give light like the moon. [68]The wild beasts are better than they are, for they can flee to cover and help themselves. [69]So we have no evidence whatever that they are gods; therefore do not fear them.

70 Like a scarecrow in a cucumber bed, that guards nothing, so are their gods of wood, overlaid with gold and silver. [71]In the same way, their gods of wood, overlaid with gold and silver, are like a thorn bush in a garden, on which every bird sits; or like a dead body cast out in the darkness. [72]By the purple and linen[y] that rot upon them you will know that they are not gods; and they will finally themselves be consumed, and be a reproach in the land. [73]Better therefore is a just man who has no idols, for he will be far from reproach.

v Gk *they*   w Gk *these things*
x Other ancient authorities omit *and*
y Cn: Gk *marble*, Syr *silk*

57–65: Idols are helpless, useless, and not to be compared with celestial phenomena. 60: Gen.1.14–18. **61–62:** Job 38.24–27; Ps.97.4. **63:** *Fire*, lightning. **64:** *Decide a case*, the true God does this (Ex.18.19; Ps.43.1).

66–69: The helplessness of idols. 67: *Signs*, portents (Jer.10.2; Jl.2.30; Mt.16.1).

70–73: Idols are compared with a scarecrow, thorn bush, and corpse. 70: *Scarecrow*, Jer.10.5. **71:** *Thorn bush*, an ordinary, useless shrub (compare Jg.9.14–15). **72:** The Greek text (*marble*, see note y) is a misinterpretation of the Hebrew word *shesh*, which means both "linen" and "marble" ("alabaster"). **73:** The conclusion of the matter.

SONG OF THE THREE YOUNG MEN

Additions to Daniel, inserted between 3.23 and 3.24

The ancient Greek and Latin versions of the book of Daniel contain a number of additions which are not present in the original Hebrew and Aramaic text. Besides many minor accretions throughout the book there are three lengthy Additions, now included among the Apocrypha as separate books under the respective titles: The Prayer of Azariah and the Song of the Three Young Men; Susanna; Bel and the Dragon.

The date when these Additions were composed is probably sometime in the second or first century B.C. Whether they were written originally in Hebrew, Aramaic, or Greek has been debated by scholars. Of the three Additions the Prayer of Azariah and the Song of the Three Young Men has the best claim to have been composed in Hebrew.

According to the book of Daniel, three Jewish captives in Babylon, named Shadrach, Meshach, and Abednego, refused to worship the golden image which Nebuchadnezzar had set up. By way of punishment for their refusal they were bound and thrown into the burning fiery furnace (Dan.3.23). Then follows the interpolation, which has three sections: vv. 1–22, the prayer of Azariah (Azariah is his Hebrew name; Abednego, his pagan name; see Dan.1.7); vv. 23–27, details about the furnace; vv. 28–68, the song of the three. This song is in two parts: the first is a liturgy addressed to God (vv. 29–34), and the second is a series of exhortations addressed to all creatures, animate and inanimate, to praise the Lord (vv. 35–68). Both parts of the song possess a certain solemnity and majestic rhythm owing to the presence of a regularly recurring refrain, which may have been used as the response of the congregation. The unknown hymnwriter derived much of his inspiration from the antiphonal liturgies in Pss. 136 and 148.

AND THEY WALKED ABOUT IN THE midst of the flames, singing hymns to God and blessing the Lord. ²Then Azariah stood and offered this prayer; in the midst of the fire he opened his mouth and said:
³"Blessed art thou, O Lord, God of our fathers, and worthy of praise;
and thy name is glorified for ever.
⁴For thou art just in all that thou hast done to us,
and all thy works are true and thy ways right,
and all thy judgments are truth.
⁵Thou hast executed true judgments in all that thou hast brought upon us
and upon Jerusalem, the holy city of our fathers,
for in truth and justice thou hast brought all this upon us because of our sins.
⁶For we have sinfully and lawlessly departed from thee,
and have sinned in all things and have not obeyed thy commandments;
⁷we have not observed them or done them,
as thou hast commanded us that it might go well with us.
⁸So all that thou hast brought upon us,
and all that thou hast done to us,
thou hast done in true judgment.
⁹Thou hast given us into the hands of lawless enemies, most hateful rebels,
and to an unjust king, the most wicked in all the world.
¹⁰And now we cannot open our mouths;

1–22: **The prayer of Azariah.** 1: *They*, the three men mentioned in Dan.3.23. 3: 1 Chr. 29.10,20. 4: Neh.9.33; Rev.16.7; 19.2. 6–7: Is.59.12–13; Dan.9.5–8; Bar.1.17–18. 8–10:

shame and disgrace have befallen
thy servants and worshipers.
¹¹For thy name's sake do not give us
up utterly,
and do not break thy covenant,
¹² and do not withdraw thy mercy
from us,
for the sake of Abraham thy beloved
and for the sake of Isaac thy
servant
and Israel thy holy one,
¹³to whom thou didst promise
to make their descendants as
many as the stars of heaven
and as the sand on the shore of
the sea.
¹⁴For we, O Lord, have become
fewer than any nation,
and are brought low this day in all
the world because of our sins.
¹⁵And at this time there is no prince,
or prophet, or leader,
no burnt offering, or sacrifice, or
oblation, or incense,
no place to make an offering
before thee or to find mercy.
¹⁶Yet with a contrite heart and a
humble spirit may we be
accepted,
as though it were with burnt
offerings of rams and bulls,
and with tens of thousands of
fat lambs;
¹⁷ such may our sacrifice be in thy
sight this day,
and may we wholly follow thee,
for there will be no shame for
those who trust in thee.
¹⁸And now with all our heart we
follow thee,
we fear thee and seek thy face.
¹⁹Do not put us to shame,
but deal with us in thy forbearance
and in thy abundant mercy.
²⁰Deliver us in accordance with thy
marvelous works,

and give glory to thy name, O
Lord!
Let all who do harm to thy servants
be put to shame;
²¹ let them be disgraced and
deprived of all power and
dominion,
and let their strength be broken.
²²Let them know that thou art the
Lord, the only God,
glorious over the whole world."

23 Now the king's servants who
threw them in did not cease feeding
the furnace fires with naphtha, pitch,
tow, and brush. ²⁴And the flame
streamed out above the furnace forty-
nine cubits, ²⁵and it broke through and
burned those of the Chaldeans whom
it caught about the furnace. ²⁶But the
angel of the Lord came down into the
furnace to be with Azariah and his
companions, and drove the fiery flame
out of the furnace, ²⁷and made the
midst of the furnace like a moist
whistling wind, so that the fire did not
touch them at all or hurt or trouble
them.
28 Then the three, as with one
mouth, praised and glorified and
blessed God in the furnace, saying:
²⁹"Blessed art thou, O Lord, God of
our fathers,
and to be praised and highly
exalted for ever;
³⁰And blessed is thy glorious, holy
name
and to be highly praised and
highly exalted for ever;
³¹Blessed art thou in the temple of
thy holy glory
and to be extolled and highly
glorified for ever.
³²Blessed art thou, who sittest upon
cherubim and lookest upon
the deeps,

Lev.26.14,38; Dt.28.15,63–64. **12:** *Abraham thy beloved,* 2 Chr.20.7; Is.41.8; Jas.2.23. **13:**
Gen.15.5; 22.17. **14:** Dt.28.63; Jer.42.2; Bar.2.13. **15:** Lam.2.9; Hos.3.4; 2 Esd.10.21–22.
16: Ps.51.16–17; Hos.6.6. **19:** Ps.25.3. **21:** Ps.35.26. **22:** Ps.83.18.
  23–27: The continued stoking of the furnace, and the descent of the angel of the Lord. 23:
Naphtha, a natural petroleum.
  28–69: Song of the three young men. 32–37: Ps.148. **35:** Pss.103.22; 145.10.

and to be praised and highly
exalted for ever.
33 Blessed art thou upon the throne
of thy kingdom
and to be extolled and highly
exalted for ever.
34 Blessed art thou in the firmament
of heaven
and to be sung and glorified for
ever.

35 "Bless the Lord, all works of the
Lord,
sing praise to him and highly
exalt him for ever.
36 Bless the Lord, you heavens,
sing praise to him and highly
exalt him for ever.
37 Bless the Lord, you angels of the
Lord,
sing praise to him and highly
exalt him for ever.
38 Bless the Lord, all waters above
the heaven,
sing praise to him and highly
exalt him for ever.
39 Bless the Lord, all powers,
sing praise to him and highly
exalt him for ever.
40 Bless the Lord, sun and moon,
sing praise to him and highly
exalt him for ever.
41 Bless the Lord, stars of heaven,
sing praise to him and highly
exalt him for ever.
42 Bless the Lord, all rain and
dew,
sing praise to him and highly
exalt him for ever.
43 Bless the Lord, all winds,
sing praise to him and highly
exalt him for ever.
44 Bless the Lord, fire and heat,
sing praise to him and highly
exalt him for ever.
45 Bless the Lord, winter cold and
summer heat,
sing praise to him and highly
exalt him for ever.
46 Bless the Lord, dews and snows,

sing praise to him and highly
exalt him for ever.
47 Bless the Lord, nights and days,
sing praise to him and highly
exalt him for ever.
48 Bless the Lord, light and darkness,
sing praise to him and highly
exalt him for ever.
49 Bless the Lord, ice and cold,
sing praise to him and highly
exalt him for ever.
50 Bless the Lord, frosts and snows,
sing praise to him and highly
exalt him for ever.
51 Bless the Lord, lightnings and
clouds,
sing praise to him and highly
exalt him for ever.
52 Let the earth bless the Lord;
let it sing praise to him and
highly exalt him for ever.
53 Bless the Lord, mountains and
hills,
sing praise to him and highly
exalt him for ever.
54 Bless the Lord, all things that
grow on the earth,
sing praise to him and highly
exalt him for ever.
55 Bless the Lord, you springs,
sing praise to him and highly
exalt him for ever.
56 Bless the Lord, seas and rivers,
sing praise to him and highly
exalt him for ever.
57 Bless the Lord, you whales and all
creatures that move in the
waters,
sing praise to him and highly
exalt him for ever.
58 Bless the Lord, all birds of the air,
sing praise to him and highly
exalt him for ever.
59 Bless the Lord, all beasts and
cattle,
sing praise to him and highly
exalt him for ever.
60 Bless the Lord, you sons of men,
sing praise to him and highly
exalt him for ever.

37: Pss.103.20; 148.2. 38: Ps.148.4. 39: *All powers*, i.e. with heavenly bodies or angels.
40: Ps.148.3. 44: Ps.148.8. 53: Ps.148.9. 58–59: Ps.148.10.

⁶¹Bless the Lord, O Israel,
   sing praise to him and highly
   exalt him for ever.
⁶²Bless the Lord, you priests of the
   Lord,
   sing praise to him and highly
   exalt him for ever.
⁶³Bless the Lord, you servants of the
   Lord,
   sing praise to him and highly
   exalt him for ever.
⁶⁴Bless the Lord, spirits and souls of
   the righteous,
   sing praise to him and highly
   exalt him for ever.
⁶⁵Bless the Lord, you who are holy
   and humble in heart,
   sing praise to him and highly
   exalt him for ever.

⁶⁶Bless the Lord, Hananiah, Azariah,
   and Mishael,
   sing praise to him and highly
   exalt him for ever;
   for he has rescued us from Hades
   and saved us from the hand
   of death,
   and delivered us from the midst
   of the burning fiery furnace;
   from the midst of the fire he has
   delivered us.
⁶⁷Give thanks to the Lord, for he is
   good,
   for his mercy endures for ever.
⁶⁸Bless him, all who worship the
   Lord, the God of gods,
   sing praise to him and give
   thanks to him,
   for his mercy endures for ever."

61–62: Ps.135.19. **63:** Ps.134.1. **65:** *Holy and humble in heart*, Pss.18.25,27; 86.1–2; Zeph.2.3.
67–68: Pss.106.1; 136.1–2.

SUSANNA

Of the cycle of traditions concerning Daniel which were added to the book of Daniel when it was translated into Greek the story of Susanna is undoubtedly the gem. One of the finest short stories in world literature, it is based on the familiar motif of the triumph of virtue over villainy, the narrow escape from death of an innocent victim. While inculcating lessons of morality and trust in God, the story is a model of artistic fiction. Plot, surprise, struggle, and unfolding character are present in just the right proportion, and the whole is told succinctly and pungently.

In Hebrew the name Susanna means "a lily" and the name Daniel means "God has judged." Both are obviously appropriate names for the heroine and hero in a story that tells how Susanna was cleared of a false charge of adultery through the timely intervention of a sagacious and brave youth.

The position of this addition in the book of Daniel varies in the manuscripts. In the Septuagint and the Latin Vulgate the account of Susanna follows the last chapter of Daniel (which in Hebrew is ch. 12), and is numbered ch. 13. In the Greek text of Theodotion, however, as well as the Old Latin, Coptic, and Arabic versions the story of Susanna forms the introduction to the book of Daniel, being prefixed to ch. 1. It may be that this latter position was thought more appropriate because the addition describes Daniel as "a young lad" (v. 45).

Concerning date and original language, see the first part of the Introduction to the Prayer of Azariah and the Song of the Three Young Men.

THERE WAS A MAN LIVING IN BABYlon whose name was Joakim. ²And he took a wife named Susanna, the daughter of Hilkiah, a very beautiful woman and one who feared the Lord. ³Her parents were righteous, and had taught their daughter according to the law of Moses. ⁴Joakim was very rich, and had a spacious garden adjoining his house; and the Jews used to come to him because he was the most honored of them all.

5 In that year two elders from the people were appointed as judges. Concerning them the Lord had said: "Iniquity came forth from Babylon, from elders who were judges, who were supposed to govern the people." ⁶These men were frequently at Joakim's house, and all who had suits at law came to them.

7 When the people departed at noon, Susanna would go into her husband's garden to walk. ⁸The two elders used to see her every day, going in and walking about, and they began to desire her. ⁹And they perverted their minds and turned away their eyes from looking to Heaven or remembering righteous judgments. ¹⁰Both were overwhelmed with passion for her, but they did not tell each other of their distress, ¹¹for they were ashamed to disclose their lustful desire to possess her. ¹²And they watched eagerly, day after day, to see her.

13 They said to each other, "Let us go home, for it is mealtime." ¹⁴And when they went out, they parted from each other. But turning back, they met again; and when each pressed the other for the reason, they confessed their lust. And then together they arranged for a time when they could find her alone.

1–4: Introduction. The setting of the story is Babylon during the exile. **1:** The name *Joakim* means "the Lord will establish." **2:** The names *Susanna* and *Hilkiah* mean respectively "lily" and "the Lord is my portion." **4:** Some Jews prospered during the exile (Jer.29.5).

5–14: The two lustful elders. 5: *In that year*, apparently the year of Joakim's marriage (v. 2). The *two elders* are identified by Jewish tradition to be the two false prophets mentioned in Jer. 29.21–23. The quotation ("*Iniquity . . . people*") is either an unwritten prophetic saying or an allusion to Jer.23.14–15. **9:** *Heaven*, a metonym for God (see 1 Macc.3.18 n. and compare Lk.15.18).

[213]

15 Once, while they were watching for an opportune day, she went in as before with only two maids, and wished to bathe in the garden, for it was very hot. [16]And no one was there except the two elders, who had hid themselves and were watching her. [17]She said to her maids, "Bring me oil and ointments, and shut the garden doors so that I may bathe." [18]They did as she said, shut the garden doors, and went out by the side doors to bring what they had been commanded; and they did not see the elders, because they were hidden.

19 When the maids had gone out, the two elders rose and ran to her, and said: [20]"Look, the garden doors are shut, no one sees us, and we are in love with you; so give your consent, and lie with us. [21]If you refuse, we will testify against you that a young man was with you, and this was why you sent your maids away."

22 Susanna sighed deeply, and said, "I am hemmed in on every side. For if I do this thing, it is death for me; and if I do not, I shall not escape your hands. [23]I choose not to do it and to fall into your hands, rather than to sin in the sight of the Lord."

24 Then Susanna cried out with a loud voice, and the two elders shouted against her. [25]And one of them ran and opened the garden doors. [26]When the household servants heard the shouting in the garden, they rushed in at the side door to see what had happened to her. [27]And when the elders told their tale, the servants were greatly ashamed, for nothing like this had ever been said about Susanna.

28 The next day, when the people gathered at the house of her husband Joakim, the two elders came, full of their wicked plot to have Susanna put to death. [29]They said before the people, "Send for Susanna, the daughter of Hilkiah, who is the wife of Joakim." [30]So they sent for her. And she came, with her parents, her children, and all her kindred.

31 Now Susanna was a woman of great refinement, and beautiful in appearance. [32]As she was veiled, the wicked men ordered her to be unveiled, that they might feast upon her beauty. [33]But her family and friends and all who saw her wept.

34 Then the two elders stood up in the midst of the people, and laid their hands upon her head. [35]And she, weeping, looked up toward heaven, for her heart trusted in the Lord. [36]The elders said, "As we were walking in the garden alone, this woman came in with two maids, shut the garden doors, and dismissed the maids. [37]Then a young man, who had been hidden, came to her and lay with her. [38]We were in a corner of the garden, and when we saw this wickedness we ran to them. [39]We saw them embracing, but we could not hold the man, for he was too strong for us, and he opened the doors and dashed out. [40]So we seized this woman and asked her who the young man was, but she would not tell us. These things we testify."

41 The assembly believed them, because they were elders of the people and judges; and they condemned her to death.

42 Then Susanna cried out with a loud voice, and said, "O eternal God, who dost discern what is secret, who art aware of all things before they come to be, [43]thou knowest that these men have borne false witness against me. And now I am to die! Yet I have

---

15–27: The attempted seduction. 17: *Oil and* (perfumed) *ointments* were used after bathing. **22:** The Mosaic law prescribed *death* as punishment for the unfaithful wife (Lev.20.10; Dt.22.22). **23:** Compare Joseph's reply to his tempter (Gen.39.9).
   28–43: Susanna falsely accused and condemned to death. 34: The judges play the part of witnesses by laying their hands on the head of the accused (Lev.24.14). **35:** *She . . . looked up toward heaven,* appealing her cause to a higher tribunal (vv. 42–43). **41:** Since, according to Jewish law, a witness could not be the judge, the sentence of death is passed by the credulous *assembly.* **42:** *God, who dost discern what is secret,* Ps.33.13–15; Pr.15.11; Heb.4.13.

done none of the things that they have wickedly invented against me!"

44 The Lord heard her cry. ⁴⁵And as she was being led away to be put to death, God aroused the holy spirit of a young lad named Daniel; ⁴⁶and he cried with a loud voice, "I am innocent of the blood of this woman."

47 All the people turned to him, and said, "What is this that you have said?" ⁴⁸Taking his stand in the midst of them, he said, "Are you such fools, you sons of Israel? Have you condemned a daughter of Israel without examination and without learning the facts? ⁴⁹Return to the place of judgment. For these men have borne false witness against her."

50 Then all the people returned in haste. And the elders said to him, "Come, sit among us and inform us, for God has given you that right." ⁵¹And Daniel said to them, "Separate them far from each other, and I will examine them."

52 When they were separated from each other, he summoned one of them and said to him, "You old relic of wicked days, your sins have now come home, which you have committed in the past, ⁵³pronouncing unjust judgments, condemning the innocent and letting the guilty go free, though the Lord said, 'Do not put to death an innocent and righteous person.' ⁵⁴Now then, if you really saw her, tell me this: Under what tree did you see them being intimate with each other?" He answered, "Under a mastic tree."ᵃ ⁵⁵And Daniel said, "Very well! You have lied against your own head, for the angel of God has received the sen-

tence from God and will immediately cutᵃ you in two."

56 Then he put him aside, and commanded them to bring the other. And he said to him, "You offspring of Canaan and not of Judah, beauty has deceived you and lust has perverted your heart. ⁵⁷This is how you both have been dealing with the daughters of Israel, and they were intimate with you through fear; but a daughter of Judah would not endure your wickedness. ⁵⁸Now then, tell me: Under what tree did you catch them being intimate with each other?" He answered, "Under an evergreen oak."ᵇ ⁵⁹And Daniel said to him, "Very well! You also have lied against your own head, for the angel of God is waiting with his sword to sawᵇ you in two, that he may destroy you both."

60 Then all the assembly shouted loudly and blessed God, who saves those who hope in him. ⁶¹And they rose against the two elders, for out of their own mouths Daniel had convicted them of bearing false witness; ⁶²and they did to them as they had wickedly planned to do to their neighbor; acting in accordance with the law of Moses, they put them to death. Thus innocent blood was saved that day.

63 And Hilkiah and his wife praised God for their daughter Susanna, and so did Joakim her husband and all her kindred, because nothing shameful was found in her. ⁶⁴And from that day onward Daniel had a great reputation among the people.

---

a The Greek words for *mastic tree* and *cut* are so similar that the use of *cut* is ironic wordplay
b The Greek words for *evergreen oak* and *saw* are so similar that the use of *saw* is ironic wordplay

---

44–59: Susanna acquitted. 50: Here *the elders* are obviously not the two who had testified, but their colleagues on the bench. **53:** Ex.23.7. **54–59:** The wordplay of the original (see notes *a* and *b*) may be represented in English by the paraphrase, "Under a *clove* tree . . . the angel will *cleave* you"; "under a *yew* tree . . . the angel will *hew* you asunder."

60–62: The two elders condemned to death. 62: *The law of Moses*, concerning false witnesses (Dt.19.16–21).

BEL AND THE DRAGON

This addition to the Greek text of the book of Daniel comprises two popular tales, both designed to ridicule the folly of idolatry and to discredit heathen priestcraft. The first story tells of the great statue of Bel, the patron deity of Babylon, which every night devours huge quantities of food and drink and thus proves itself to be a living god. By clever detective work Daniel unmasks the chicanery of Bel's priests. The second story tells of Daniel's refusal to worship a monstrous dragon as a god, and his killing it with a ridiculous concoction of pitch, fat, and hair. The Babylonians, enraged by the death of their god, demand that Daniel be thrown into the lions' den. He is kept safe among the lions for six days, and is provided with food brought from Judea by the prophet Habakkuk. On the seventh day the king removes Daniel and throws into the den his enemies, who are immediately devoured.

The religious teaching of these stories, bizarre and fantastic as they appear to us today, is that those who worship the true and living God will be sustained in every kind of trial.

In the Greek manuscripts of Daniel the account of Bel and the Dragon is added at the close of ch. 12 of Daniel. In the Latin Vulgate it forms ch. 14, the story of Susanna being ch. 13. Concerning date and original language, see the first part of the Introduction to the Prayer of Azariah and the Song of the Three Young Men.

WHEN KING ASTYAGES WAS LAID with his fathers, Cyrus the Persian received his kingdom. ²And Daniel was a companion of the king, and was the most honored of his friends.

3 Now the Babylonians had an idol called Bel, and every day they spent on it twelve bushels of fine flour and forty sheep and fifty gallons of wine. ⁴The king revered it and went every day to worship it. But Daniel worshiped his own God.

5 And the king said to him, "Why do you not worship Bel?" He answered, "Because I do not revere man-made idols, but the living God, who created heaven and earth and has dominion over all flesh."

6 The king said to him, "Do you not think that Bel is a living God? Do you not see how much he eats and drinks every day?" ⁷Then Daniel laughed, and said, "Do not be deceived, O king; for this is but clay inside and brass outside, and it never ate or drank anything."

8 Then the king was angry, and he called his priests and said to them, "If you do not tell me who is eating these provisions, you shall die. ⁹But if you prove that Bel is eating them, Daniel shall die, because he blasphemed against Bel." And Daniel said to the king, "Let it be done as you have said."

10 Now there were seventy priests of Bel, besides their wives and children. And the king went with Daniel into the temple of Bel. ¹¹And the priests of Bel said, "Behold, we are going outside; you yourself, O king, shall set forth the food and mix and place the wine, and shut the door and seal it with your signet. ¹²And when you return in the morning, if you do not find that Bel has eaten it all, we will die; or else Daniel will, who is telling lies about us." ¹³They were unconcerned, for beneath the table they had made a hidden entrance, through which they used to go in regularly and consume the provisions. ¹⁴When they had gone out, the king

---

1-2: **Introduction.** 1: *Cyrus the Persian* (Dan.6.28) became king of Babylon in 538 B.C.

3-22: **The story of Bel.** 3: *Bel*, or Bel-Marduk (compare Merodach, Jer.50.2), was the chief god in the Babylonian pantheon. Several ancient sources testify to the enormous quantities of sacrifices presented to Marduk in the daily ritual. 7: Daniel ridicules the king's argument: clay and brass do not eat (Sir.30.19). 11: Dan.6.17. Archaeologists have found great numbers of Babylonian signets.

set forth the food for Bel. Then Daniel ordered his servants to bring ashes and they sifted them throughout the whole temple in the presence of the king alone. Then they went out, shut the door and sealed it with the king's signet, and departed. ¹⁵In the night the priests came with their wives and children, as they were accustomed to do, and ate and drank everything.

16 Early in the morning the king rose and came, and Daniel with him. ¹⁷And the king said, "Are the seals unbroken, Daniel?" He answered, "They are unbroken, O king." ¹⁸As soon as the doors were opened, the king looked at the table, and shouted in a loud voice, "You are great, O Bel; and with you there is no deceit, none at all."

19 Then Daniel laughed, and restrained the king from going in, and said, "Look at the floor, and notice whose footsteps these are." ²⁰The king said, "I see the footsteps of men and women and children."

21 Then the king was enraged, and he seized the priests and their wives and children; and they showed him the secret doors through which they were accustomed to enter and devour what was on the table. ²²Therefore the king put them to death, and gave Bel over to Daniel, who destroyed it and its temple.

23 There was also a great dragon, which the Babylonians revered. ²⁴And the king said to Daniel, "You cannot deny that this is a living god; so worship him." ²⁵Daniel said, "I will worship the Lord my God, for he is the living God. ²⁶But if you, O king, will give me permission, I will slay the dragon without sword or club." The king said, "I give you permission."

27 Then Daniel took pitch, fat, and hair, and boiled them together and made cakes, which he fed to the dragon. The dragon ate them, and burst open. And Daniel said, "See what you have been worshiping!"

28 When the Babylonians heard it, they were very indignant and conspired against the king, saying, "The king has become a Jew; he has destroyed Bel, and slain the dragon, and slaughtered the priests." ²⁹Going to the king, they said, "Hand Daniel over to us, or else we will kill you and your household." ³⁰The king saw that they were pressing him hard, and under compulsion he handed Daniel over to them.

31 They threw Daniel into the lions' den, and he was there for six days. ³²There were seven lions in the den, and every day they had been given two human bodies and two sheep; but these were not given to them now, so that they might devour Daniel.

33 Now the prophet Habakkuk was in Judea. He had boiled pottage and had broken bread into a bowl, and was going into the field to take it to the reapers. ³⁴But the angel of the Lord said to Habakkuk, "Take the dinner which you have to Babylon, to Daniel, in the lions' den." ³⁵Habakkuk said, "Sir, I have never seen Babylon, and I know nothing about the den." ³⁶Then the angel of the Lord took him by the crown of his head, and lifted him by his hair and set him down in Babylon, right over the den, with the rushing sound of the wind itself.

37 Then Habakkuk shouted,

16–22: The fraud detected (compare Dan.2.12; 6.24). **22:** According to ancient historians it was Xerxes who destroyed Bel's temple.

23–42: The story of the dragon. 23: *A great dragon,* that is, a live serpent worshiped as a god (compare Num.21.8–9; 2 Kg.18.4). **26:** *Permission* was granted because the king believed in the immortality of the serpent-god. **31–32:** The second time that Daniel is put in *the lions' den* (Dan.6.16–24).

33–39: The intervention of Habakkuk. 33: The author intends to identify this Habakkuk with the Minor Prophet of that name; chronologically, however, such an identification is impossible. **36:** *Hair,* Ezek.8.3. **37:** 1 Kg.17.4.

"Daniel! Daniel! Take the dinner which God has sent you." [38]And Daniel said, "Thou hast remembered me, O God, and hast not forsaken those who love thee." [39]So Daniel arose and ate. And the angel of God immediately returned Habakkuk to his own place.

40 On the seventh day the king came to mourn for Daniel. When he came to the den he looked in, and there sat Daniel. [41]And the king shouted with a loud voice, "Thou art great, O Lord God of Daniel, and there is no other besides thee." [42]And he pulled Daniel*a* out, and threw into the den the men who had attempted his destruction, and they were devoured immediately before his eyes.

a Gk *him*

40–42: Daniel's liberation. 41: Compare Dan.6.26–27.

THE PRAYER OF MANASSEH

One of the finest pieces in the Apocrypha is the little classic of penitential devotion known as the Prayer of Manasseh. Constructed in accord with the best liturgical forms and full without being protracted, this beautiful prayer breathes throughout a spirit of deep and genuine religious feeling.

According to 2 Chr.33.11–13, Manasseh, the wicked king of Judah, while in exile composed a prayer entreating divine forgiveness for his many sins. The Old Testament account also refers to two literary works that contained Manasseh's prayer (2 Chr.33.18–19). Since neither of these has survived, it is not surprising that some devout Jew undertook to remedy the loss by drawing up such a prayer as might have been used by the wicked though now repentant king. Henceforth the name Manasseh was associated in Jewish tradition not only with the grossest acts of idolatry (2 Chr.33.1–9), but also with the efficacy of genuine repentance in securing divine forgiveness. It may be that the unknown author also had in mind the practical use of the prayer in providing a suitable penitential devotion for those of his countrymen who, having fallen into idolatry, could be reclaimed from the error of their way.

The date of composition of the Prayer is difficult to determine. Though there is no positive evidence, many scholars place it sometime during the last two centuries B.C. Whether it was composed originally in Hebrew, Aramaic, or Greek is disputed; today it survives in Greek, Latin, Syriac, Armenian, and Ethiopic. The Latin translation of the Prayer in the Vulgate Bible (which since the Council of Trent has been put into an Appendix) is entirely different from the Old Latin translation, and is of much more recent origin.

O LORD ALMIGHTY,
   God of our fathers,
of Abraham and Isaac and Jacob
  and of their righteous posterity;
²thou who hast made heaven and
   earth
  with all their order;
³who hast shackled the sea by thy
   word of command,
  who hast confined the deep
  and sealed it with thy terrible
   and glorious name;
⁴at whom all things shudder,
  and tremble before thy power,
⁵for thy glorious splendor cannot be
   borne,
  and the wrath of thy threat to
   sinners is irresistible;
⁶yet immeasurable and unsearchable
  is thy promised mercy,
⁷ for thou art the Lord Most High,
of great compassion, long-suffering,
  and very merciful,

and repentest over the evils of
  men.
Thou, O Lord, according to thy
  great goodness
hast promised repentance and
  forgiveness
to those who have sinned against
  thee;
and in the multitude of thy
  mercies
thou hast appointed repentance
  for sinners,
that they may be saved.
⁸Therefore thou, O Lord, God of
  the righteous,
hast not appointed repentance
  for the righteous,
for Abraham and Isaac and
  Jacob, who did not sin against
  thee,
but thou hast appointed
  repentance for me, who am
  a sinner.

1–8: Invocation and ascription of praise to God, whose majesty is displayed in creation (vv. 1–4), and whose mercy grants repentance to sinners (vv. 6–8). **1:** *God of our fathers,* Ex.3.15–16; Dan.2.23; Acts 3.13. **2:** *All their order,* splendor and orderly array. **3:** *Shackled the sea,* Job 38.8–11. **7:** The second part of this verse (*Thou, O Lord . . . may be saved*) is preserved in the later Greek manuscripts and in the Latin and Syriac versions. **8:** *Not . . . for the righteous,* Lk.5.32. *For me . . . a sinner,* Lk.18.13.

⁹For the sins I have committed are
    more in number than the
    sand of the sea;
  my transgressions are multiplied,
    O Lord, they are multiplied!
  I am unworthy to look up and see
    the height of heaven
  because of the multitude of my
    iniquities.
¹⁰I am weighted down with many
    an iron fetter,
  so that I am rejected because of
    my sins,
  and I have no relief;
  for I have provoked thy wrath
  and have done what is evil in
    thy sight,
  setting up abominations and
    multiplying offenses.
¹¹And now I bend the knee of my
    heart,
  beseeching thee for thy
    kindness.

¹²I have sinned, O Lord, I have
    sinned,
  and I know my transgressions.
¹³I earnestly beseech thee,
  forgive me, O Lord, forgive me!
  Do not destroy me with my
    transgressions!
  Do not be angry with me for ever
    or lay up evil for me;
  do not condemn me to the
    depths of the earth.
  For thou, O Lord, art the God of
    those who repent,
¹⁴ and in me thou wilt manifest
    thy goodness;
  for, unworthy as I am, thou wilt
    save me in thy great mercy,
¹⁵ and I will praise thee continually
    all the days of my life.
  For all the host of heaven sings
    thy praise,
  and thine is the glory for ever.
    Amen.

9–10: Personal confession of sin. For the background see 2 Kg.21.1–18; 2 Chr.33.1–20.

11–15a: Supplication for pardon. 11: *Knee of my heart*, an expression indicating special depth of feeling. **12:** *I know my transgressions*, compare Ps.19.12. **13:** *The depths of the earth*, probably Sheol or Hades is meant (Ps.63.9).

15b: Concluding doxology. *Host of heaven*, multitude of angelic beings (2 Chr.18.18; Lk.2.13).

THE FIRST BOOK OF THE

MACCABEES

First Maccabees has come down to us in Greek, and also in Latin and several other versions derived from the Greek, the original Hebrew having been lost at an early time. The book was probably written shortly after the death of John Hyrcanus I (high priest 134–104 B.C.), since it refers to the chronicles of John's reign (16.23–24). Some scholars, however, think that chs. 14–16 are an addition made not long after A.D. 70, in which case the rest of the book may have been written about 140 B.C.

The author of 1 Maccabees was probably a Palestinian Jew who lived in Jerusalem. He modeled his work on the historical books of the Old Testament, particularly the books of Kings and Chronicles. After an introduction briefly sketching the conquests of Alexander the Great (336–323 B.C.), the division of his empire, and the origin of the Seleucid Empire (1.1–10), he recounts the principal events of Judea's history from the accession of Antiochus IV (175 B.C.) to the reign of John Hyrcanus I, which marked the period of the successful struggle for Jewish independence.

The style of 1 Maccabees is plain and straightforward and the book is generally an excellent historical source, though the order of events frequently differs from that in 2 Maccabees and it is not always certain which is to be preferred. Though the author (unlike the author of 2 Maccabees) records no miraculous interventions from heaven, he obviously sees the hand of God operative in the victories of Judas Maccabeus and his family. The letters of kings and others that are included are essential to the story, and, whether or not they are genuine copies of historical documents, they appear to be based on reliable information. The book also preserves portions of several contemporary poems (e.g. 1.24–28, 36–40; 2.7–13; 3.3–9, 45, 50–53; 14.4–15).

AFTER ALEXANDER SON OF PHILIP, the Macedonian, who came from the land of Kittim, had defeated*a* Darius, king of the Persians and the Medes, he succeeded him as king. (He had previously become king of Greece.) ²He fought many battles, conquered strongholds, and put to death the kings of the earth. ³He advanced to the ends of the earth, and plundered many nations. When the earth became quiet before him, he was exalted, and his heart was lifted up. ⁴He gathered a very strong army and ruled over countries, nations, and princes, and they became tributary to him.

5 After this he fell sick and per-ceived that he was dying. ⁶So he summoned his most honored officers, who had been brought up with him from youth, and divided his kingdom among them while he was still alive. ⁷And after Alexander had reigned twelve years, he died.

8 Then his officers began to rule, each in his own place. ⁹They all put on crowns after his death, and so did their sons after them for many years; and they caused many evils on the earth.

10 From them came forth a sinful root, Antiochus Epiphanes, son of Antiochus the king; he had been a hostage in Rome. He began to reign

a Greek adds and he defeated

1.1–10: Introduction. A summary of history from Alexander to Antiochus IV. 1: *Alexander* the Great (356–323 B.C.), son of Philip of Macedon, who had conquered *Kittim* (Greece), swept through Asia Minor, and *defeated Darius* III at Issus (333 B.C.) and at Gaugamela (331 B.C.). 3: After taking Egypt, Mesopotamia, and Persia he advanced to the *ends of the earth* (to Bactria and India). *He was exalted,* i.e. he accepted divine honors. 4: He planned a universal empire dominated by Greek culture. 5: *He fell sick* in Babylon. 8–9: By 275 B.C. three dynasties were established, the Antigonids of Macedonia, the Ptolemies of Egypt, and the Seleucids of Syria. 10: *Sinful root,* Is.11.10; Dan.11.7. *Antiochus IV,* who took the name

[221]

in the one hundred and thirty-seventh year of the kingdom of the Greeks.*[b]*

11 In those days lawless men came forth from Israel, and misled many, saying, "Let us go and make a covenant with the Gentiles round about us, for since we separated from them many evils have come upon us." ¹²This proposal pleased them, ¹³and some of the people eagerly went to the king. He authorized them to observe the ordinances of the Gentiles. ¹⁴So they built a gymnasium in Jerusalem, according to Gentile custom, ¹⁵and removed the marks of circumcision, and abandoned the holy covenant. They joined with the Gentiles and sold themselves to do evil.

16 When Antiochus saw that his kingdom was established, he determined to become king of the land of Egypt, that he might reign over both kingdoms. ¹⁷So he invaded Egypt with a strong force, with chariots and elephants and cavalry and with a large fleet. ¹⁸He engaged Ptolemy king of Egypt in battle, and Ptolemy turned and fled before him, and many were wounded and fell. ¹⁹And they captured the fortified cities in the land of Egypt, and he plundered the land of Egypt.

20 After subduing Egypt, Antiochus returned in the one hundred and forty-third year.*[c]* He went up against Israel and came to Jerusalem with a strong force. ²¹He arrogantly entered the sanctuary and took the golden altar, the lampstand for the light, and all its utensils. ²²He took also the table for the bread of the Presence, the cups for drink offerings, the bowls, the golden censers, the curtain, the crowns, and the gold decoration on the front of the temple; he stripped it all off. ²³He took the silver and the gold, and the costly vessels; he took also the hidden treasures which he found. ²⁴Taking them all, he departed to his own land.

He committed deeds of murder,
    and spoke with great arrogance.
²⁵Israel mourned deeply in every
    community,
²⁶   rulers and elders groaned,
maidens and young men became
    faint,
    the beauty of the women faded.
²⁷Every bridegroom took up the
    lament;
    she who sat in the bridal chamber
    was mourning.
²⁸Even the land shook for its
    inhabitants,
    and all the house of Jacob was
    clothed with shame.

29 Two years later the king sent to the cities of Judah a chief collector of tribute, and he came to Jerusalem with a large force. ³⁰Deceitfully he spoke peaceable words to them, and they believed him; but he suddenly fell upon the city, dealt it a severe blow, and

b 175 B.C.   *c* 169 B.C.

Epiphanes ("god manifest"), reigned 175–164 B.C.; he was *son of Antiochus* III the Great (223–187 B.C.), who had wrested Palestine from Egypt at the battle of Paneas in 198 B.C. but lost most of Asia Minor to Rome at Magnesia in 190 B.C. (compare Dan.11.18). Because of this defeat the son *had been a hostage in Rome. One hundred and thirty-seventh year* of the Seleucid era; reckoning of this era varied in different places; dates given in the margin (notes *b*, *c*, etc.) are approximate.

    1.11–15: The paganizing program. Greek culture had penetrated Palestine peacefully, but now enthusiasts introduced Greek religion (2 Macc.4.11–17). **11:** *Lawless men*, willing to abandon Judaism, led by Jason, whom Antiochus appointed in place of his brother Onias III (2 Macc.4.7). *Evils*, loss of business and prestige because relations with Syria were not close. **14:** *A gymnasium*, see 2 Macc.4.9–10 n.

    1.16–40: Antiochus invades Egypt and Palestine. Invasion of Egypt is followed by plundering of the temple in Jerusalem (2 Macc.5.1,11–26). **17:** The Syrian army had *elephants*, though the treaty of Apamea with Rome (188 B.C.) had forbidden this. **18:** *Ptolemy* VI Philometor reigned 180–145 B.C. **20:** *Antiochus returned* because the Roman envoy, Popilius Laenas, threatened him with war if he annexed Egypt. **24–28:** Fragment of a contemporary poem. **28:** *The house* destroyed many people of Israel. ³¹He plundered the city, burned it with fire, and tore down its houses and its surrounding walls. ³²And they took captive the women and children, and seized the cattle. ³³Then they fortified the city of David with a great strong wall and strong towers, and it became their citadel. ³⁴And they stationed there a sinful people, lawless men. These strengthened their position; ³⁵they stored up arms and food, and collecting the spoils of Jerusalem they stored them there, and became a great snare.

³⁶It became an ambush against the sanctuary,
an evil adversary of Israel continually.
³⁷On every side of the sanctuary they shed innocent blood;
they even defiled the sanctuary.
³⁸Because of them the residents of Jerusalem fled;
she became a dwelling of strangers;
she became strange to her offspring,
and her children forsook her.
³⁹Her sanctuary became desolate as a desert;
her feasts were turned into mourning,
her sabbaths into a reproach,
her honor into contempt.
⁴⁰Her dishonor now grew as great as her glory;
her exaltation was turned into mourning.

41 Then the king wrote to his whole kingdom that all should be one people, ⁴²and that each should give up his customs. ⁴³All the Gentiles accepted the command of the king. Many even from Israel gladly adopted his religion; they sacrificed to idols and profaned the sabbath. ⁴⁴And the king sent letters by messengers to Jerusalem and the cities of Judah; he directed them to follow customs strange to the land, ⁴⁵to forbid burnt offerings and sacrifices and drink offerings in the sanctuary, to profane sabbaths and feasts, ⁴⁶to defile the sanctuary and the priests, ⁴⁷to build altars and sacred precincts and shrines for idols, to sacrifice swine and unclean animals, ⁴⁸and to leave their sons uncircumcised. They were to make themselves abominable by everything unclean and profane, ⁴⁹so that they should forget the law and change all the ordinances. ⁵⁰"And whoever does not obey the command of the king shall die."

51 In such words he wrote to his whole kingdom. And he appointed inspectors over all the people and commanded the cities of Judah to offer sacrifice, city by city. ⁵²Many of the people, every one who forsook the law, joined them, and they did evil in the land; ⁵³they drove Israel into hiding in every place of refuge they had.

54 Now on the fifteenth day of Chislev, in the one hundred and forty-fifth year,ᵈ they erected a desolating sacrilege upon the altar of burnt offering. They also built altars in the surrounding cities of Judah, ⁵⁵and burned incense at the doors of the houses and in the streets. ⁵⁶The books of the law which they found they tore to pieces and burned with fire. ⁵⁷Where the book of the covenant was found in the possession of any one, or if any one adhered to the law, the decree of the king condemned him to death. ⁵⁸They kept using violence against Israel, against those found month after month

ᵈ 167 B.C.

---

of Jacob, Israel, the Jewish people. **33:** *City of David*, the Ophel hill south of the temple area (2 Sam.5.7). **34:** The *sinful people* were irreligious Jews. **36–40:** Poetic fragment (compare Pss.74; 79).

1.41–64: Desecration of the temple. The first outright religious persecution of the Jews, which is also reflected in the book of Daniel (compare 2 Macc. 6.1–11). **41–42:** *His whole kingdom*, Syria, Palestine, Mesopotamia, Persia, and parts of Asia Minor. *One people*, unified in language, religion, culture, and even dress; Judaism, with its revealed law and rejection of other gods, opposed this. **47:** Jews had no *idols* and regarded *swine* as *unclean*. **54:** *Chislev*, approximately December. The *desolating sacrilege* (Dan.11.31; 12.11; 2 Macc.6.2) was an altar to in the cities. ⁵⁹And on the twenty-fifth day of the month they offered sacrifice on the altar which was upon the altar of burnt offering. ⁶⁰According to the decree, they put to death the women who had their children circumcised, ⁶¹and their families and those who circumcised them; and they hung the infants from their mothers' necks.

62 But many in Israel stood firm and were resolved in their hearts not to eat unclean food. ⁶³They chose to die rather than to be defiled by food or to profane the holy covenant; and they did die. ⁶⁴And very great wrath came upon Israel.

2 In those days Mattathias the son of John, son of Simeon, a priest of the sons of Joarib, moved from Jerusalem and settled in Modein. ²He had five sons, John surnamed Gaddi, ³Simon called Thassi, ⁴Judas called Maccabeus, ⁵Eleazar called Avaran, and Jonathan called Apphus. ⁶He saw the blasphemies being committed in Judah and Jerusalem, ⁷and said,

"Alas! Why was I born to see this,
   the ruin of my people, the ruin
     of the holy city,
and to dwell there when it was
   given over to the enemy,
   the sanctuary given over to
     aliens?
⁸Her temple has become like a man
   without honor;ᵉ
⁹ her glorious vessels have been
   carried into captivity.
Her babes have been killed in her
   streets,

her youths by the sword of the
   foe.
¹⁰What nation has not inherited her
   palacesᶠ
and has not seized her spoils?
¹¹All her adornment has been taken
   away;
   no longer free, she has become
     a slave.
¹²And behold, our holy place, our
   beauty,
   and our glory have been laid
     waste;
the Gentiles have profaned it.
¹³ Why should we live any longer?"

14 And Mattathias and his sons rent their clothes, put on sackcloth, and mourned greatly.

15 Then the king's officers who were enforcing the apostasy came to the city of Modein to make them offer sacrifice. ¹⁶Many from Israel came to them; and Mattathias and his sons were assembled. ¹⁷Then the king's officers spoke to Mattathias as follows: "You are a leader, honored and great in this city, and supported by sons and brothers. ¹⁸Now be the first to come and do what the king commands, as all the Gentiles and the men of Judah and those that are left in Jerusalem have done. Then you and your sons will be numbered among the friends of the king, and you and your sons will be honored with silver and gold and many gifts."

19 But Mattathias answered and said in a loud voice: "Even if all the nations that live under the rule of the

e The text of this verse is uncertain
f Other authorities read has not had a part in her kingdom

Olympian Zeus and perhaps a statue of him. **59:** *Offered sacrifice*, probably of swine (2 Macc. 6.4–5). **60–64:** 2 Macc. chs. 6–7, and 4 Macc. contain stories of martyrdoms. *Chose to die rather than be defiled by food*, compare Dan.3.8–18. *Wrath came upon Israel*, as a punishment for sin (2 Macc.6.12–16).

    2.1–48: Revolt of Mattathias. 1: The family of *Mattathias* is known as Hasmoneans (see p. 295), from a traditional ancestor Hashmonia. *Joarib* was first in the list of divisions of priests (1 Chr.24.7; Neh.11.10). *Modein*, on the road to Beth-horon, about seventeen miles northwest of Jerusalem. **2–5:** *Simon*, third of the family to rule (chs. 13–16). *Maccabeus*, probably from a Hebrew word meaning "hammer." The other surnames are of uncertain derivation. *Jonathan*, successor of Judas (chs. 9–12). **7–13:** Poetic fragment; compare Pss.44; 74; 79; and the book of Lamentations. **14:** *Rent their clothes, put on sackcloth*, signs of mourning (Gen.37.34). **18:** *The friends of the king* were a special class of potentates and courtiers who wore distinctive dress king obey him, and have chosen to do his commandments, departing each one from the religion of his fathers, [20]yet I and my sons and my brothers will live by the covenant of our fathers. [21]Far be it from us to desert the law and the ordinances. [22]We will not obey the king's words by turning aside from our religion to the right hand or to the left."

23 When he had finished speaking these words, a Jew came forward in the sight of all to offer sacrifice upon the altar in Modein, according to the king's command. [24]When Mattathias saw it, he burned with zeal and his heart was stirred. He gave vent to righteous anger; he ran and killed him upon the altar. [25]At the same time he killed the king's officer who was forcing them to sacrifice, and he tore down the altar. [26]Thus he burned with zeal for the law, as Phinehas did against Zimri the son of Salu.

27 Then Mattathias cried out in the city with a loud voice, saying: "Let every one who is zealous for the law and supports the covenant come out with me!" [28]And he and his sons fled to the hills and left all that they had in the city.

29 Then many who were seeking righteousness and justice went down to the wilderness to dwell there, [30]they, their sons, their wives, and their cattle, because evils pressed heavily upon them. [31]And it was reported to the king's officers, and to the troops in Jerusalem the city of David, that men who had rejected the king's command had gone down to the hiding places in the wilderness. [32]Many pursued them, and overtook them; they encamped opposite them and prepared for battle against them on the sabbath day.

[33]And they said to them, "Enough of this! Come out and do what the king commands, and you will live." [34]But they said, "We will not come out, nor will we do what the king commands and so profane the sabbath day." [35]Then the enemy[g] hastened to attack them. [36]But they did not answer them or hurl a stone at them or block up their hiding places, [37]for they said, "Let us all die in our innocence; heaven and earth testify for us that you are killing us unjustly." [38]So they attacked them on the sabbath, and they died, with their wives and children and cattle, to the number of a thousand persons.

39 When Mattathias and his friends learned of it, they mourned for them deeply. [40]And each said to his neighbor: "If we all do as our brethren have done and refuse to fight with the Gentiles for our lives and our ordinances, they will quickly destroy us from the earth." [41]So they made this decision that day: "Let us fight against every man who comes to attack us on the sabbath day; let us not all die as our brethren died in their hiding places."

42 Then there united with them a company of Hasideans, mighty warriors of Israel, every one who offered himself willingly for the law. [43]And all who became fugitives to escape their troubles joined them and reinforced them. [44]They organized an army, and struck down sinners in their anger and lawless men in their wrath; the survivors fled to the Gentiles for safety. [45]And Mattathias and his friends went about and tore down the altars; [46]they forcibly circumcised all the uncircumcised boys that they found within the borders of Israel. [47]They hunted down

g Gk *they*

---

and insignia. **23:** Elsewhere in chs. 1–13, "man of Israel" is used instead of the term *Jew*, which here perhaps means "Judean." **24:** *His heart*, literally "his kidneys," which were considered the seat of deliberation. **26:** *As Phinehas did*, Num.25.6–15. **28:** 2 Macc.5.27. **29–30:** In *the wilderness* of Judea they found *hiding places* in grottoes and caves (Jg.20.47). **37:** 1.63. **41:** The earliest statement of the principle that one may profane one sabbath in order to keep all the others. **42:** *Hasideans*, "the pious," a group not concerned for Jewish nationalism but only for the religious law. At first they resisted passively (1.62–63; 2.37), but now turned to violent action.

the arrogant men, and the work prospered in their hands. ⁴⁸They rescued the law out of the hands of the Gentiles and kings, and they never let the sinner gain the upper hand.

49 Now the days drew near for Mattathias to die, and he said to his sons: "Arrogance and reproach have now become strong; it is a time of ruin and furious anger. ⁵⁰Now, my children, show zeal for the law, and give your lives for the covenant of our fathers.

51 "Remember the deeds of the fathers, which they did in their generations; and receive great honor and an everlasting name. ⁵²Was not Abraham found faithful when tested, and it was reckoned to him as righteousness? ⁵³Joseph in the time of his distress kept the commandment, and became lord of Egypt. ⁵⁴Phinehas our father, because he was deeply zealous, received the covenant of everlasting priesthood. ⁵⁵Joshua, because he fulfilled the command, became a judge in Israel. ⁵⁶Caleb, because he testified in the assembly, received an inheritance in the land. ⁵⁷David, because he was merciful, inherited the throne of the kingdom for ever. ⁵⁸Elijah because of great zeal for the law was taken up into heaven. ⁵⁹Hananiah, Azariah, and Mishael believed and were saved from the flame. ⁶⁰Daniel because of his innocence was delivered from the mouth of the lions.

61 "And so observe, from generation to generation, that none who put their trust in him will lack strength. ⁶²Do not fear the words of a sinner, for his splendor will turn into dung and worms. ⁶³Today he will be exalted, but tomorrow he will not be found, because he has returned to the dust, and his plans will perish. ⁶⁴My children, be courageous and grow strong in the law, for by it you will gain honor.

65 "Now behold, I know that Simeon your brother is wise in counsel; always listen to him; he shall be your father. ⁶⁶Judas Maccabeus has been a mighty warrior from his youth; he shall command the army for you and fight the battle against the peoples.ʰ ⁶⁷You shall rally about you all who observe the law, and avenge the wrong done to your people. ⁶⁸Pay back the Gentiles in full, and heed what the law commands."

69 Then he blessed them, and was gathered to his fathers. ⁷⁰He died in the one hundred and forty-sixth yearⁱ and was buried in the tomb of his fathers at Modein. And all Israel mourned for him with great lamentation.

3 Then Judas his son, who was called Maccabeus, took command in his place. ²All his brothers and all who had joined his father helped him; they gladly fought for Israel.
³He extended the glory of his people.
   Like a giant he put on his
      breastplate;
   he girded on his armor of war and
      waged battles,
   protecting the host by his sword.
⁴He was like a lion in his deeds,
   like a lion's cub roaring for
      prey.
⁵He searched out and pursued the
      lawless;
   he burned those who troubled
      his people.
⁶Lawless men shrank back for fear
      of him;
   all the evildoers were
      confounded;

h Or of the people
i 166 B.C.

2.49–70: Death of Mattathias. 52: *Faithful when tested,* Gen.22.15–18. *Reckoned to him,* Gen.15.6; Rom.4.3. **53:** *Joseph,* Gen. chs. 39–45. **54:** *Phinehas,* v. 26. **55–56:** *Joshua . . . Caleb,* Num.13.1–14.12; 26.65; Jos.1.1–9. **57:** *Merciful,* or perhaps "loyal" (2 Sam.7.16; Pss.89.35–37; 132.11–12). **58:** 2 Kg.2.9–12. **59–60:** Dan.3.8–30; 6.1–24. **63:** Ps.37.10, 35–36. **69:** *Gathered to his fathers,* buried with his ancestors (Jg.2.10).

   3.1–12: Defeat of Apollonius. 3–9: From a contemporary poem. **4:** *Like a lion,* Hos.5.14.

and deliverance prospered by his
hand.
⁷He embittered many kings,
　　but he made Jacob glad by his
　　　deeds,
　　and his memory is blessed for
　　　ever.
⁸He went through the cities of
　　　Judah;
　　he destroyed the ungodly out of
　　　the land;*ʲ*
　　thus he turned away wrath from
　　　Israel.
⁹He was renowned to the ends of the
　　　earth;
　　he gathered in those who were
　　　perishing.
10 But Apollonius gathered together
Gentiles and a large force from Samaria
to fight against Israel. ¹¹When Judas
learned of it, he went out to meet him,
and he defeated and killed him. Many
were wounded and fell, and the rest
fled. ¹²Then they seized their spoils;
and Judas took the sword of Apollonius, and used it in battle the rest of his
life.
13 Now when Seron, the commander
of the Syrian army, heard that Judas
had gathered a large company, including a body of faithful men who stayed
with him and went out to battle, ¹⁴he
said, "I will make a name for myself
and win honor in the kingdom. I will
make war on Judas and his companions, who scorn the king's command."
¹⁵And again a strong army of ungodly
men went up with him to help him,
to take vengeance on the sons of
Israel.
16 When he approached the ascent
of Beth-horon, Judas went out to meet
him with a small company. ¹⁷But when
they saw the army coming to meet

them, they said to Judas, "How can we,
few as we are, fight against so great and
strong a multitude? And we are faint,
for we have eaten nothing today."
¹⁸Judas replied, "It is easy for many
to be hemmed in by few, for in the
sight of Heaven there is no difference
between saving by many or by few.
¹⁹It is not on the size of the army that
victory in battle depends, but strength
comes from Heaven. ²⁰They come
against us in great pride and lawlessness
to destroy us and our wives and our
children, and to despoil us; ²¹but we
fight for our lives and our laws. ²²He
himself will crush them before us; as
for you, do not be afraid of them."
23 When he finished speaking, he
rushed suddenly against Seron and
his army, and they were crushed before him. ²⁴They pursued them*ᵏ* down
the descent of Beth-horon to the plain;
eight hundred of them fell, and the rest
fled into the land of the Philistines.
²⁵Then Judas and his brothers began
to be feared, and terror fell upon the
Gentiles round about them. ²⁶His fame
reached the king, and the Gentiles
talked of the battles of Judas.
27 When King Antiochus heard
these reports, he was greatly angered;
and he sent and gathered all the forces
of his kingdom, a very strong army.
²⁸And he opened his coffers and gave
a year's pay to his forces, and ordered
them to be ready for any need. ²⁹Then
he saw that the money in the treasury
was exhausted, and that the revenues
from the country were small because
of the dissension and disaster which he
had caused in the land by abolishing
the laws that had existed from the earli-

ʲ Gk *it*
ᵏ Other authorities read *him*

8: *He turned away wrath*, i.e. God's punishment, through his exploits (2 Macc.7.38). **10:** *Apollonius*, according to Josephus (*Antiquities*. xii. v. 5; vii.1), was governor of Samaria.
　3.13–26: Battle of Beth-horon. This was Judas' first great victory. **16:** *The ascent of Beth-
horon* was a route from the coastal plain to the Judean highlands. The town is about twelve
miles northwest of Jerusalem. **18:** The word *Heaven* was used to avoid pronouncing God's
name (compare "he himself," v. 22, and see Sus.9 n.). *By many or by few*, 1 Sam.14.6. **24:** *Land
of the Philistines*, the coastal plain.
　3.27–4.35: Campaigns of Lysias. Antiochus IV goes to Persia; Judas defeats Lysias at Emmaus and Beth-zur. **28:** *Any need* implies that Seleucid power was beginning to decline.

est days. ³⁰He feared that he might not have such funds as he had before for his expenses and for the gifts which he used to give more lavishly than preceding kings. ³¹He was greatly perplexed in mind, and determined to go to Persia and collect the revenues from those regions and raise a large fund.

32 He left Lysias, a distinguished man of royal lineage, in charge of the king's affairs from the river Euphrates to the borders of Egypt. ³³Lysias was also to take care of Antiochus his son until he returned. ³⁴And he turned over to Lysias*ˡ* half of his troops and the elephants, and gave him orders about all that he wanted done. As for the residents of Judea and Jerusalem, ³⁵Lysias was to send a force against them to wipe out and destroy the strength of Israel and the remnant of Jerusalem; he was to banish the memory of them from the place, ³⁶settle aliens in all their territory, and distribute their land. ³⁷Then the king took the remaining half of his troops and departed from Antioch his capital in the one hundred and forty-seventh year.*ᵐ* He crossed the Euphrates river and went through the upper provinces.

38 Lysias chose Ptolemy the son of Dorymenes, and Nicanor and Gorgias, mighty men among the friends of the king, ³⁹and sent with them forty thousand infantry and seven thousand cavalry to go into the land of Judah and destroy it, as the king had commanded. ⁴⁰So they departed with their entire force, and when they arrived they encamped near Emmaus in the plain. ⁴¹When the traders of the region heard what was said of them, they took silver and gold in immense amounts, and fet-

ters,*ⁿ* and went to the camp to get the sons of Israel for slaves. And forces from Syria and the land of the Philistines joined with them.

42 Now Judas and his brothers saw that misfortunes had increased and that the forces were encamped in their territory. They also learned what the king had commanded to do to the people to cause their final destruction. ⁴³But they said to one another, "Let us repair the destruction of our people, and fight for our people and the sanctuary." ⁴⁴And the congregation assembled to be ready for battle, and to pray and ask for mercy and compassion.

⁴⁵Jerusalem was uninhabited like a
    wilderness;
not one of her children went in
    or out.
The sanctuary was trampled down,
    and the sons of aliens held the
    citadel;
it was a lodging place for the
    Gentiles.
Joy was taken from Jacob;
    the flute and the harp ceased to
    play.

46 So they assembled and went to Mizpah, opposite Jerusalem, because Israel formerly had a place of prayer in Mizpah. ⁴⁷They fasted that day, put on sackcloth and sprinkled ashes on their heads, and rent their clothes. ⁴⁸And they opened the book of the law to inquire into those matters about which the Gentiles were consulting the images of their idols. ⁴⁹They also brought the garments of the priesthood and the first fruits and the tithes, and

l Gk *him*   *m* 165 B.C.
n Syr: Gk *slaves*

30: Antiochus was noted for his extravagance (see 2 Macc.4.30 n.). **33:** *Antiochus* V Eupator, *his son*, was only nine years old; he reigned 164–162 B.C. **36:** *Settle aliens*, as the Assyrians had done (2 Kg.17.24). **37:** *Antioch*, modern Antakya, was built by Seleucus I in 300 B.C. and expanded by Antiochus IV. *Upper provinces*, Persia. **38:** *Ptolemy*, known as Macron (2 Macc. 10.12). *Nicanor*, 2 Macc.8.9. *Gorgias*, 2 Macc.10.14. **40:** *Emmaus* (not the Emmaus of Lk.24.13), was about twenty-five miles west of Jerusalem. **41:** Some pro-Syrian Jews joined Antiochus' army. **45:** Compare Ps.74; Is.24.8. **46:** *Mizpah*, perhaps en-Nebi Samwil, seven miles northwest of Jerusalem, but sometimes identified with Tell en-Nasbeh, nine miles north of the city. **48:** They expected guidance from *the book of the law*, the Pentateuch, while the Greeks sought oracles from *their idols*. **49:** *Tithes* were brought to Jerusalem and there distributed (Neh.10.35–

they stirred up the Nazirites who had
completed their days; [50]and they cried
aloud to Heaven, saying,
"What shall we do with these?
    Where shall we take them?
[51]Thy sanctuary is trampled down
        and profaned,
    and thy priests mourn in
        humiliation.
[52]And behold, the Gentiles are
        assembled against us to
        destroy us;
    thou knowest what they plot
        against us.
[53]How will we be able to withstand
        them,
    if thou dost not help us?"
54 Then they sounded the trumpets
and gave a loud shout. [55]After this
Judas appointed leaders of the people,
in charge of thousands and hundreds
and fifties and tens. [56]And he said to
those who were building houses, or
were betrothed, or were planting vineyards, or were fainthearted, that each
should return to his home, according to
the law. [57]Then the army marched out
and encamped to the south of Emmaus.
58 And Judas said, "Gird yourselves
and be valiant. Be ready early in the
morning to fight with these Gentiles
who have assembled against us to
destroy us and our sanctuary. [59]It is
better for us to die in battle than to see
the misfortunes of our nation and of
the sanctuary. [60]But as his will in
heaven may be, so he will do."

4 Now Gorgias took five thousand
infantry and a thousand picked
cavalry, and this division moved out
by night [2]to fall upon the camp of the
Jews and attack them suddenly. Men
from the citadel were his guides. [3]But
Judas heard of it, and he and his
mighty men moved out to attack the
king's force in Emmaus [4]while the

division was still absent from the camp.
[5]When Gorgias entered the camp of
Judas by night, he found no one there,
so he looked for them in the hills, because he said, "These men are fleeing
from us."
6 At daybreak Judas appeared in the
plain with three thousand men, but
they did not have armor and swords
such as they desired. [7]And they saw
the camp of the Gentiles, strong and
fortified, with cavalry round about it;
and these men were trained in war.
[8]But Judas said to the men who were
with him, "Do not fear their numbers
or be afraid when they charge. [9]Re-
member how our fathers were saved at
the Red Sea, when Pharaoh with his
forces pursued them. [10]And now let
us cry to Heaven, to see whether he
will favor us and remember his
covenant with our fathers and crush
this army before us today. [11]Then all
the Gentiles will know that there is one
who redeems and saves Israel."
12 When the foreigners looked up
and saw them coming against them,
[13]they went forth from their camp to
battle. Then the men with Judas blew
their trumpets [14]and engaged in battle.
The Gentiles were crushed and fled into
the plain, [15]and all those in the rear fell
by the sword. They pursued them to
Gazara, and to the plains of Idumea,
and to Azotus and Jamnia; and three
thousand of them fell. [16]Then Judas
and his force turned back from pursuing them, [17]and he said to the people,
"Do not be greedy for plunder, for
there is a battle before us; [18]Gorgias
and his force are near us in the hills.
But stand now against our enemies
and fight them, and afterward seize
the plunder boldly."
19 Just as Judas was finishing this
speech, a detachment appeared, com-

---

38). *Nazirites*, Num.6.1–21. **50–53**: V. 45. **54**: *Trumpets*, to summon the army (Num.10.1–10).
55: In Moses' day such *leaders* assisted in civic administration (Ex.18.25); here, as in the
Essene *War Scroll* from Qumran, they have a military function (2 Macc.8.22–23). **56**: Dt.20.5–8.
4.2: *Men from the citadel*, Jewish refugees opposed to Judas. **9**: Ex.14.21–29. **15**: The pursuit
went in all directions. *Gazara*, or Gezer (Jos.21.21; 1 Kg.9.17), was five miles northwest of
Emmaus. *Idumea* was far to the south. *Azotus*, or Ashdod, and *Jamnia*, lay west and southwest.
17–18: Judas maintained discipline (2 Macc.8.26). **19**: *The hills*, the Judean highland.

ing out of the hills. ²⁰They saw that their army° had been put to flight, and that the Jews° were burning the camp, for the smoke that was seen showed what had happened. ²¹When they perceived this they were greatly frightened, and when they also saw the army of Judas drawn up in the plain for battle, ²²they all fled into the land of the Philistines. ²³Then Judas returned to plunder the camp, and they seized much gold and silver, and cloth dyed blue and sea purple, and great riches. ²⁴On their return they sang hymns and praises to Heaven, for he is good, for his mercy endures for ever. ²⁵Thus Israel had a great deliverance that day.

26 Those of the foreigners who escaped went and reported to Lysias all that had happened. ²⁷When he heard it, he was perplexed and discouraged, for things had not happened to Israel as he had intended, nor had they turned out as the king had commanded him. ²⁸But the next year he mustered sixty thousand picked infantrymen and five thousand cavalry to subdue them. ²⁹They came into Idumea and encamped at Beth-zur, and Judas met them with ten thousand men.

30 When he saw that the army was strong, he prayed, saying, "Blessed art thou, O Savior of Israel, who didst crush the attack of the mighty warrior by the hand of thy servant David, and didst give the camp of the Philistines into the hands of Jonathan, the son of Saul, and of the man who carried his armor. ³¹So do thou hem in this army by the hand of thy people Israel, and let them be ashamed of their troops and their cavalry. ³²Fill them with cowardice; melt the boldness of their strength; let them tremble in their destruction. ³³Strike them down with the sword of those who love thee, and let all who know thy name praise thee with hymns."

34 Then both sides attacked, and there fell of the army of Lysias five thousand men; they fell in action.ᵖ ³⁵And when Lysias saw the rout of his troops and observed the boldness which inspired those of Judas, and how ready they were either to live or to die nobly, he departed to Antioch and enlisted mercenaries, to invade Judea again with an even larger army.

36 Then said Judas and his brothers, "Behold, our enemies are crushed; let us go up to cleanse the sanctuary and dedicate it." ³⁷So all the army assembled and they went up to Mount Zion. ³⁸And they saw the sanctuary desolate, the altar profaned, and the gates burned. In the courts they saw bushes sprung up as in a thicket, or as on one of the mountains. They saw also the chambers of the priests in ruins. ³⁹Then they rent their clothes, and mourned with great lamentation, and sprinkled themselves with ashes. ⁴⁰They fell face down on the ground, and sounded the signal on the trumpets, and cried out to Heaven. ⁴¹Then Judas detailed men to fight against those in the citadel until he had cleansed the sanctuary.

42 He chose blameless priests devoted to the law, ⁴³and they cleansed the sanctuary and removed the defiled stones to an unclean place. ⁴⁴They deliberated what to do about the altar of burnt offering, which had been profaned. ⁴⁵And they thought it best to tear it down, lest it bring reproach upon them, for the Gentiles had defiled it.

o Gk *they*
p Or *and some fell on the opposite side*

24: *Heaven*, see 3.18 n. 26–35: The account in 2 Macc.11.1–12 puts the rout of Lysias after the death of Timothy. 28: *The next year*, perhaps as late as autumn, 164 B.C. 29: *Beth-zur*, about twenty miles south of Jerusalem on the road to Hebron. Lysias decided to attack Jerusalem from the south. 30–35: The account in 2 Macc.11.6–15 agrees that Judas won the battle, but states that there was a negotiated peace.

4.36–61: **Rededication of the temple. 38:** *Chambers of the priests* perhaps surrounded the sanctuary on three sides. 41: *The citadel* (1.33–35) was occupied by a Syrian garrison until the

So they tore down the altar, ⁴⁶and stored the stones in a convenient place on the temple hill until there should come a prophet to tell what to do with them. ⁴⁷Then they took unhewn*q* stones, as the law directs, and built a new altar like the former one. ⁴⁸They also rebuilt the sanctuary and the interior of the temple, and consecrated the courts. ⁴⁹They made new holy vessels, and brought the lampstand, the altar of incense, and the table into the temple. ⁵⁰Then they burned incense on the altar and lighted the lamps on the lampstand, and these gave light in the temple. ⁵¹They placed the bread on the table and hung up the curtains. Thus they finished all the work they had undertaken.

52 Early in the morning on the twenty-fifth day of the ninth month, which is the month of Chislev, in the one hundred and forty-eighth year,*r* ⁵³they rose and offered sacrifice, as the law directs, on the new altar of burnt offering which they had built. ⁵⁴At the very season and on the very day that the Gentiles had profaned it, it was dedicated with songs and harps and lutes and cymbals. ⁵⁵All the people fell on their faces and worshiped and blessed Heaven, who had prospered them. ⁵⁶So they celebrated the dedication of the altar for eight days, and offered burnt offerings with gladness; they offered a sacrifice of deliverance and praise. ⁵⁷They decorated the front of the temple with golden crowns and small shields; they restored the gates and the chambers for the priests, and furnished them with doors. ⁵⁸There

was very great gladness among the people, and the reproach of the Gentiles was removed.

59 Then Judas and his brothers and all the assembly of Israel determined that every year at that season the days of the dedication of the altar should be observed with gladness and joy for eight days, beginning with the twenty-fifth day of the month of Chislev.

60 At that time they fortified Mount Zion with high walls and strong towers round about, to keep the Gentiles from coming and trampling them down as they had done before. ⁶¹And he stationed a garrison there to hold it. He also*s* fortified Beth-zur, so that the people might have a stronghold that faced Idumea.

5 When the Gentiles round about heard that the altar had been built and the sanctuary dedicated as it was before, they became very angry, ²and they determined to destroy the descendants of Jacob who lived among them. So they began to kill and destroy among the people. ³But Judas made war on the sons of Esau in Idumea, at Akrabattene, because they kept lying in wait for Israel. He dealt them a heavy blow and humbled them and despoiled them. ⁴He also remembered the wickedness of the sons of Baean, who were a trap and a snare to the people and ambushed them on the highways. ⁵They were shut up by him in their towers; and he encamped against them, vowed their complete

q Gk *whole*
r 164 B.C.
s Gk adds *to hold it*

---

time of Simon (13.49–52). **46:** Malachi was regarded as the last *prophet;* though such men as John Hyrcanus I and John the Baptist were thought to have prophetic gifts, this was not universally recognized. **47:** Ex.20.25; Dt.27.5–6. **50:** *Burned incense . . . lighted the lamps,* Ex.30:7–8. **51:** *The bread,* of the Presence (Ex.25.30). **52–59:** Judas set the rededication of the temple exactly three years after its pollution (1.54) and three and a half years after Antiochus' capture of Jerusalem (Dan.7.25; but see 2 Macc.10.3). The Hanukkah festival, celebrated *for eight days* like Hezekiah's reconsecration (2 Chr.29.17), commemorates this event.
5.1–68: **Campaigns in all directions.** Judas now attacked Idumea in the south (vv. 3–5, 65), Ammon and Gilead east of the Jordan (vv. 6–13, 24–51), Galilee in the north (vv. 21–23), and the coastal plain. These events may have occurred after the death of Antiochus IV (6.16). **2:** *Descendants of Jacob,* Israelites or Jews. **3:** *Sons of Esau,* Edomites or Idumeans, south of the Dead Sea. *Akrabattene,* perhaps on the border between Idumea and Judea. **4:** *Baean,*

destruction, and burned with fire their[t] towers and all who were in them. [6]Then he crossed over to attack the Ammonites, where he found a strong band and many people with Timothy as their leader. [7]He engaged in many battles with them and they were crushed before him; he struck them down. [8]He also took Jazer and its villages; then he returned to Judea.

9 Now the Gentiles in Gilead gathered together against the Israelites who lived in their territory, and planned to destroy them. But they fled to the stronghold of Dathema, [10]and sent to Judas and his brothers a letter which said, "The Gentiles around us have gathered together against us to destroy us. [11]They are preparing to come and capture the stronghold to which we have fled, and Timothy is leading their forces. [12]Now then come and rescue us from their hands, for many of us have fallen, [13]and all our brethren who were in the land of Tob have been killed; the enemy[u] have captured their wives and children and goods, and have destroyed about a thousand men there."

14 While the letter was still being read, behold, other messengers, with their garments rent, came from Galilee and made a similar report; [15]they said that against them had gathered together men of Ptolemais and Tyre and Sidon, and all Galilee of the Gentiles,[v] "to annihilate us." [16]When Judas and the people heard these messages, a great assembly was called to determine what they should do for their brethren who were in distress and were being attacked by enemies.[w] [17]Then Judas said to Simon his brother, "Choose your men and go and rescue your brethren in Galilee; I and Jonathan my brother will go to Gilead." [18]But he left Joseph, the son of Zechariah, and Azariah, a leader of the people, with the rest of the forces, in Judea to guard it; [19]and he gave them this command, "Take charge of this people, but do not engage in battle with the Gentiles until we return." [20]Then three thousand men were assigned to Simon to go to Galilee, and eight thousand to Judas for Gilead.

21 So Simon went to Galilee and fought many battles against the Gentiles, and the Gentiles were crushed before him. [22]He pursued them to the gate of Ptolemais, and as many as three thousand of the Gentiles fell, and he despoiled them. [23]Then he took the Jews[x] of Galilee and Arbatta, with their wives and children, and all they possessed, and led them to Judea with great rejoicing.

24 Judas Maccabeus and Jonathan his brother crossed the Jordan and went three days' journey into the wilderness. [25]They encountered the Nabateans, who met them peaceably and told them all that had happened to their brethren in Gilead: [26]"Many of them have been shut up in Bozrah and Bosor, in Alema and Chaspho, Maked and Carnaim"—all these cities were strong and large—[27]"and some have been shut up in the other cities of Gilead; the enemy[y] are getting ready

t Gk *her*
u Gk *they*
v Gk *aliens*
w Gk *them*
x Gk *those*
y Gk *they*

---

probably in Transjordan (Num.32.3). **6:** *Ammonites*, a Semitic people east of the Jordan near the present Amman. **8:** *Jazer*, west of Amman, fifteen miles north of Heshbon (Num.32.3). **9:** *Gilead*, east of the Jordan between the Yarmuk and the Arnon (Jos.22.9). *Dathema*, possibly el-Hosn, in Gilead opposite Beisan; or Ramtha, now near the Syrian border. **13:** *Land of Tob*, possibly Hippos, twelve miles southeast of the Sea of Galilee (Jg.11.3; 2 Macc.12.17). **15:** *Ptolemais*, or Acco (Jg.1.31), now Acre, north of Haifa on the coast. *Tyre and Sidon*, farther north in Lebanon. As yet few Jews lived in *Galilee of the Gentiles* (Is.9.1; Mt.4.15). **23:** *Arbatta*, either near the Sea of Galilee, or the Arabah depression south of the Dead Sea (Dt.1.7; Jos. 11.16). **25:** *Nabateans*, or Nebaioth (Gen.25.13), an Aramaic-speaking people who occupied the desert east of Palestine as far north as Palmyra. **26:** *Bozrah*, southeast of Dera'a (Is.63.1; Jer.48.24). *Bosor*, Bezer in the desert (Dt.4.43). *Alema*, unidentified. *Chaspho* and *Maked*, cities to attack the strongholds tomorrow and take and destroy all these men in one day."

28 Then Judas and his army quickly turned back by the wilderness road to Bozrah; and he took the city, and killed every male by the edge of the sword; then he seized all its spoils and burned it with fire. ²⁹He departed from there at night, and they went all the way to the stronghold of Dathema.^z ³⁰At dawn they looked up, and behold, a large company, that could not be counted, carrying ladders and engines of war to capture the stronghold, and attacking the Jews within.^a ³¹So Judas saw that the battle had begun and that the cry of the city went up to Heaven with trumpets and loud shouts, ³²and he said to the men of his forces, "Fight today for your brethren!" ³³Then he came up behind them in three companies, who sounded their trumpets and cried aloud in prayer. ³⁴And when the army of Timothy realized that it was Maccabeus, they fled before him, and he dealt them a heavy blow. As many as eight thousand of them fell that day.

35 Next he turned aside to Alema,^b and fought against it and took it; and he killed every male in it, plundered it, and burned it with fire. ³⁶From there he marched on and took Chaspho, Maked, and Bosor, and the other cities of Gilead.

37 After these things Timothy gathered another army and encamped opposite Raphon, on the other side of the stream. ³⁸Judas sent men to spy out the camp, and they reported to him, "All the Gentiles around us have gathered to him; it is a very large force. ³⁹They also have hired Arabs to help them, and they are encamped across the stream, ready to come and fight

against you." And Judas went to meet them.

40 Now as Judas and his army drew near to the stream of water, Timothy said to the officers of his forces, "If he crosses over to us first, we will not be able to resist him, for he will surely defeat us. ⁴¹But if he shows fear and camps on the other side of the river, we will cross over to him and defeat him." ⁴²When Judas approached the stream of water, he stationed the scribes of the people at the stream and gave them this command, "Permit no man to encamp, but make them all enter the battle." ⁴³Then he crossed over against them first, and the whole army followed him. All the Gentiles were defeated before him, and they threw away their arms and fled into the sacred precincts at Carnaim. ⁴⁴But he took the city and burned the sacred precincts with fire, together with all who were in them. Thus Carnaim was conquered; they could stand before Judas no longer.

45 Then Judas gathered together all the Israelites in Gilead, the small and the great, with their wives and children and goods, a very large company, to go to the land of Judah. ⁴⁶So they came to Ephron. This was a large and very strong city on the road, and they could not go round it to the right or to the left; they had to go through it. ⁴⁷But the men of the city shut them out and blocked up the gates with stones. ⁴⁸And Judas sent them this friendly message, "Let us pass through your land to get to our land. No one will do you harm; we will simply pass by on foot." But they refused to open to him. ⁴⁹Then Judas ordered proclamation to be made to the army that each should

z Greek lacks *of Dathema.* See verse 9
a Gk *and they were attacking them*
b The name is uncertain

---

of Gilead (v. 36). *Carnaim*, Gen.14.5; Am.6.13; 2 Macc.12.21,26. **28:** *Killed every male*, Gen. 34.25. **37:** *The stream*, a tributary of the Yarmuk. **39:** *Arabs* were not usually hostile to the Jews but could be *hired* as mercenaries. **40–41:** Judas heard Timothy's order or decided to make a surprise attack (compare 1 Sam.14.7–10). **43:** *Sacred precincts*, of Atargatis, the Syrian fish goddess (2 Macc.12.26). **46:** *Ephron*, eight miles east of the Jordan, opposite Beth-shan (v. 52), and west of Irbid (Arbela). **48–51:** Num.21.21–24.

encamp where he was. ⁵⁰So the men of the forces encamped, and he fought against the city all that day and all the night, and the city was delivered into his hands. ⁵¹He destroyed every male by the edge of the sword, and razed and plundered the city. Then he passed through the city over the slain.

52 And they crossed the Jordan into the large plain before Beth-shan. ⁵³And Judas kept rallying the laggards and encouraging the people all the way till he came to the land of Judah. ⁵⁴So they went up to Mount Zion with gladness and joy, and offered burnt offerings, because not one of them had fallen before they returned in safety.

55 Now while Judas and Jonathan were in Gilead and Simon his brother was in Galilee before Ptolemais, ⁵⁶Joseph, the son of Zechariah, and Azariah, the commanders of the forces, heard of their brave deeds and of the heroic war they had fought. ⁵⁷So they said, "Let us also make a name for ourselves; let us go and make war on the Gentiles around us." ⁵⁸And they issued orders to the men of the forces that were with them, and they marched against Jamnia. ⁵⁹And Gorgias and his men came out of the city to meet them in battle. ⁶⁰Then Joseph and Azariah were routed, and were pursued to the borders of Judea; as many as two thousand of the people of Israel fell that day. ⁶¹Thus the people suffered a great rout because, thinking to do a brave deed, they did not listen to Judas and his brothers. ⁶²But they did not belong to the family of those men through whom deliverance was given to Israel.

63 The man Judas and his brothers were greatly honored in all Israel and among all the Gentiles, wherever their name was heard. ⁶⁴Men gathered to them and praised them.

65 Then Judas and his brothers went forth and fought the sons of Esau in the land to the south. He struck Hebron and its villages and tore down its strongholds and burned its towers round about. Then he marched off to go into the land of the Philistines, and passed through Marisa.ᶜ ⁶⁷On that day some priests, who wished to do a brave deed, fell in battle, for they went out to battle unwisely. ⁶⁸But Judas turned aside to Azotus in the land of the Philistines; he tore down their altars, and the graven images of their gods he burned with fire; he plundered the cities and returned to the land of Judah.

6 King Antiochus was going through the upper provinces when he heard that Elymais in Persia was a city famed for its wealth in silver and gold. ²Its temple was very rich, containing golden shields, breastplates, and weapons left there by Alexander, the son of Philip, the Macedonian king who first reigned over the Greeks. ³So he came and tried to take the city and plunder it, but he could not, because his plan became known to the men of the city ⁴and they withstood him in battle. So he fled and in great grief departed from there to return to Babylon.

5 Then some one came to him in Persia and reported that the armies which had gone into the land of Judah had been routed; ⁶that Lysias had gone first with a strong force, but had turned

c Other authorities read *Samaria*

52: *The large plain*, between the Jordan and Mt. Gilboa. *Beth-shan*, Beisan, about eighteen miles south of the Sea of Galilee (Jg.1.27; 1 Kg.4.12). **58:** *Jamnia*, 4.15. **62:** Only *the family* of the Hasmoneans is regarded as divinely chosen to save Israel. **65:** *Sons of Esau*, Edomites. *Hebron*, the old capital of David, twenty miles south of Jerusalem (Gen.23.2; 2 Sam.2.11). **66:** *Marisa*, or Mareshah (Jos.15.44), near Beit-Jibrin.

6.1–17: Death of Antiochus IV and accession of Antiochus V (2 Macc. ch. 9). **1:** *The upper provinces*, Persia and Mesopotamia (3.31–37). *Elymais*, biblical Elam or Susiana; but according to 2 Macc. 9.2 the incident occurred in Persepolis. **2:** *Its temple* was that of Nanea (2 Macc. 1.13–16), or Anahita, identified with Artemis. **5:** *In Persia*, perhaps at Ecbatana (2 Macc.9.3). According to Polybius (*History*, xxxi. 11) the king took sick and died at Tabae (perhaps Gabae, and fled before the Jews;[d] that the Jews[e] had grown strong from the arms, supplies, and abundant spoils which they had taken from the armies they had cut down; [7]that they had torn down the abomination which he had erected upon the altar in Jerusalem; and that they had surrounded the sanctuary with high walls as before, and also Beth-zur, his city.

8 When the king heard this news, he was astounded and badly shaken. He took to his bed and became sick from grief, because things had not turned out for him as he had planned. [9]He lay there for many days, because deep grief continually gripped him, and he concluded that he was dying. [10]So he called all his friends and said to them, "Sleep departs from my eyes and I am downhearted with worry. [11]I said to myself, 'To what distress I have come! And into what a great flood I now am plunged! For I was kind and beloved in my power.' [12]But now I remember the evils I did in Jerusalem. I seized all her vessels of silver and gold; and I sent to destroy the inhabitants of Judah without good reason. [13]I know that it is because of this that these evils have come upon me; and behold, I am perishing of deep grief in a strange land."

14 Then he called for Philip, one of his friends, and made him ruler over all his kingdom. [15]He gave him the crown and his robe and the signet, that he might guide Antiochus his son and bring him up to be king. [16]Thus Antiochus the king died there in the one hundred and forty-ninth year.[f] [17]And when Lysias learned that the king was dead, he set up Antiochus the king's[g] son to reign. Lysias[h] had brought him up as a boy, and he named him Eupator.

18 Now the men in the citadel kept hemming Israel in around the sanctuary. They were trying in every way to harm them and strengthen the Gentiles. [19]So Judas decided to destroy them, and assembled all the people to besiege them. [20]They gathered together and besieged the citadel[i] in the one hundred and fiftieth year;[j] and he built siege towers and other engines of war. [21]But some of the garrison escaped from the siege and some of the ungodly Israelites joined them. [22]They went to the king and said, "How long will you fail to do justice and to avenge our brethren? [23]We were happy to serve your father, to live by what he said and to follow his commands. [24]For this reason the sons of our people besieged the citadel[k] and became hostile to us; moreover, they have put to death as many of us as they have caught, and they have seized our inheritances. [25]And not against us alone have they stretched out their hands, but also against all the lands on their borders. [26]And behold, today they have encamped against the citadel in Jerusalem to take it; they have fortified both the sanctuary and Beth-zur; [27]and unless you quickly prevent them, they will do still greater things, and you will not be able to stop them."

28 The king was enraged when he heard this. He assembled all his friends, the commanders of his forces and those in authority.[l] [29]And mercenary forces came to him from other

d Gk *them*   *e* Gk *they*
f 163 B.C.   *g* Gk *his*
h Gk *he*   *i* Gk *it*   *j* 162 B.C.
k The Greek text underlying *the sons . . . the citadel* is uncertain
l Gk *those over the reins*

---

modern Isfahan). **7:** *The abomination*, statue of a pagan god. **8–9:** *Deep grief*, perhaps insanity; according to 2 Macc.9.5–12 he was stricken with a loathsome physical malady. **12:** *Her vessels*, Dan.5.2. **14–15:** *Philip . . . ruler*, Lysias, satrap in the west, had previously been given this commission (3.32). *The signet*, a symbol of transfer of authority to the regent. **16:** 2 Macc.11.33 implies that Antiochus IV had died before the restoration of the temple at Jerusalem. **17:** The word *Eupator* means "of a good father."

6.18–54: Attack on the citadel and second battle at Beth-zur. The citadel was equally important to the Syrians and to Judas, for without it the Seleucid monarchy could not maintain sovereignty in Palestine. **21:** *Ungodly*, i.e. pro-Greek. **28–30:** Lysias' second campaign is here kingdoms and from islands of the seas. 30 The number of his forces was a hundred thousand foot soldiers, twenty thousand horsemen, and thirty-two elephants accustomed to war. 31 They came through Idumea and encamped against Beth-zur, and for many days they fought and built engines of war; but the Jews*m* sallied out and burned these with fire, and fought manfully.

32 Then Judas marched away from the citadel and encamped at Beth-zechariah, opposite the camp of the king. 33 Early in the morning the king rose and took his army by a forced march along the road to Beth-zechariah, and his troops made ready for battle and sounded their trumpets. 34 They showed the elephants the juice of grapes and mulberries, to arouse them for battle. 35 And they distributed the beasts among the phalanxes; with each elephant they stationed a thousand men armed with coats of mail, and with brass helmets on their heads; and five hundred picked horsemen were assigned to each beast. 36 These took their position beforehand wherever the beast was; wherever it went they went with it, and they never left it. 37 And upon the elephants*n* were wooden towers, strong and covered; they were fastened upon each beast by special harness, and upon each were four*o* armed men who fought from there, and also its Indian driver. 38 The rest of the horsemen were stationed on either side, on the two flanks of the army, to harass the enemy while being themselves protected by the phalanxes. 39 When the sun shone upon the shields of gold and brass, the hills were ablaze with them and gleamed like flaming torches.

40 Now a part of the king's army was spread out on the high hills, and some troops were on the plain, and they advanced steadily and in good order. 41 All who heard the noise made by their multitude, by the marching of the multitude and the clanking of their arms, trembled, for the army was very large and strong. 42 But Judas and his army advanced to the battle, and six hundred men of the king's army fell. 43 And Eleazar, called Avaran, saw that one of the beasts was equipped with royal armor. It was taller than all the others, and he supposed that the king was upon it. 44 So he gave his life to save his people and to win for himself an everlasting name. 45 He courageously ran into the midst of the phalanx to reach it; he killed men right and left, and they parted before him on both sides. 46 He got under the elephant, stabbed it from beneath, and killed it; but it fell to the ground upon him and there he died. 47 And when the Jews*p* saw the royal might and the fierce attack of the forces, they turned away in flight.

48 The soldiers of the king's army went up to Jerusalem against them, and the king encamped in Judea and at Mount Zion. 49 He made peace with the men of Beth-zur, and they evacuated the city, because they had no provisions there to withstand a siege, since it was a sabbatical year for the land. 50 So the king took Beth-zur and stationed a guard there to hold it. 51 Then he encamped before the sanctuary for many days. He set up siege towers, engines of war to throw fire

m Gk *they*   *n* Gk *them*
o Cn: Some authorities read *thirty;* others *thirty-two*
p Gk *they*

---

dated 162 B.C. (v. 20), but in 2 Macc.13.1 a year earlier. **31:** Judas had won the first battle at *Beth-zur* (4.29–34) and had fortified it (4.61). **32:** *Beth-zechariah* was six miles from Beth-zur and ten miles southwest of Jerusalem. **34–35:** *The juice* may have been to simulate blood; but *elephants* were sometimes given wine to madden them. Here the animals were used to force an opening in the ranks. *Phalanxes,* the Greek infantry formation, eight to eighteen men deep, highly disciplined and mobile. The Seleucids could muster twenty thousand of such infantry. **43:** *Eleazar,* brother of Judas (2.5). **48:** *Mount Zion,* south of the temple (1.33). **49:** The garrison was promised immunity if it surrendered. Every seventh year the land had to lie fallow (Ex.23.11; Lev.25.3–7). This *sabbatical year* was apparently 162 B.C. (v. 20) or possibly a year earlier.

and stones, machines to shoot arrows, and catapults. ⁵²The Jews*�q* also made engines of war to match theirs, and fought for many days. ⁵³But they had no food in storage,*ʳ* because it was the seventh year; those who found safety in Judea from the Gentiles had consumed the last of the stores. ⁵⁴Few men were left in the sanctuary, because famine had prevailed over the rest and they had been scattered, each to his own place.

55 Then Lysias heard that Philip, whom King Antiochus while still living had appointed to bring up Antiochus his son to be king, ⁵⁶had returned from Persia and Media with the forces that had gone with the king, and that he was trying to seize control of the government. ⁵⁷So he quickly gave orders to depart, and said to the king, to the commanders of the forces, and to the men, "We daily grow weaker, our food supply is scant, the place against which we are fighting is strong, and the affairs of the kingdom press urgently upon us. ⁵⁸Now then let us come to terms with these men, and make peace with them and with all their nation, ⁵⁹and agree to let them live by their laws as they did before; for it was on account of their laws which we abolished that they became angry and did all these things."

60 The speech pleased the king and the commanders, and he sent to the Jews*ˢ* an offer of peace, and they accepted it. ⁶¹So the king and the commanders gave them their oath. On these conditions the Jews*ᵗ* evacuated the stronghold. ⁶²But when the king entered Mount Zion and saw what a strong fortress the place was, he broke the oath he had sworn and gave orders to tear down the wall all around. ⁶³Then he departed with haste and returned to Antioch. He found Philip in control of the city, but he fought against him, and took the city by force.

7 In the one hundred and fifty-first*ᵘ* year Demetrius the son of Seleucus set forth from Rome, sailed with a few men to a city by the sea, and there began to reign. ²As he was entering the royal palace of his fathers, the army seized Antiochus and Lysias to bring them to him. ³But when this act became known to him, he said, "Do not let me see their faces!" ⁴So the army killed them, and Demetrius took his seat upon the throne of his kingdom.

5 Then there came to him all the lawless and ungodly men of Israel; they were led by Alcimus, who wanted to be high priest. ⁶And they brought to the king this accusation against the people: "Judas and his brothers have destroyed all your friends, and have driven us out of our land. ⁷Now then send a man whom you trust; let him go and see all the ruin which Judas*ᵛ* has brought upon us and upon the land of the king, and let him punish them and all who help them."

q Gk *they*
r Other authorities read *in the sanctuary*
s Gk *them*   *t* Gk *they*
u 161 B.C.   *v* Gk *he*

6.55–63: Lysias makes peace. The return of Philip caused a diversion; Lysias abandoned the siege and restored Jewish religious rights. **55:** *Philip* had received the symbols of sovereignty (v. 15), though Antiochus IV had previously appointed Lysias. **59:** Judea had generally accepted Seleucid rule until Antiochus IV began his program of hellenization, though there was always a faction engaged in intrigue with Egypt. **62:** Judas had also built a citadel on *Mount Zion*; its wall was now destroyed.

7.1–4: Demetrius I becomes king (2 Macc.14.1–2). **1:** *Demetrius* I Soter (reigned 162–150 B.C.) was *son of Seleucus* IV Philopator, elder brother of Antiochus IV. When Rome demanded hostages (1.10), Antiochus IV was sent to Rome; later when Seleucus became king, his son Demetrius replaced Antiochus. On the latter's death, he vainly petitioned the senate to be released. Subsequently he escaped from Rome with a small group of men and landed in Tripolis, *a city by the sea* (2 Macc.14.1). **2:** *Antiochus*, that is, Antiochus V Eupator (6.17). **3:** *Do not let me see their faces*, a signal for the murder.

7.5–25: Alcimus as high priest. Legitimate high priests were descended from a particular

8 So the king chose Bacchides, one of the king's friends, governor of the province Beyond the River; he was a great man in the kingdom and was faithful to the king. ⁹And he sent him, and with him the ungodly Alcimus, whom he made high priest; and he commanded him to take vengeance on the sons of Israel. ¹⁰So they marched away and came with a large force into the land of Judah; and he sent messengers to Judas and his brothers with peaceable but treacherous words. ¹¹But they paid no attention to their words, for they saw that they had come with a large force.

12 Then a group of scribes appeared in a body before Alcimus and Bacchides to ask for just terms. ¹³The Hasideans were the first among the sons of Israel to seek peace from them, ¹⁴for they said, "A priest of the line of Aaron has come with the army, and he will not harm us." ¹⁵And he spoke peaceable words to them and swore this oath to them, "We will not seek to injure you or your friends." ¹⁶So they trusted him; but he seized sixty of them and killed them in one day, in accordance with the word which was written,
¹⁷"The flesh of thy saints and their
       blood
    they poured out round about
       Jerusalem,
    and there was none to bury them."
¹⁸Then the fear and dread of them fell upon all the people, for they said, "There is no truth or justice in them, for they have violated the agreement and the oath which they swore."

19 Then Bacchides departed from Jerusalem and encamped in Beth-zaith. And he sent and seized many of the men who had deserted to him,ʷ and some of the people, and killed them and threw them into the great pit. ²⁰He placed Alcimus in charge of the country and left with him a force to help him; then Bacchides went back to the king.

21 Alcimus strove for the high priesthood, ²²and all who were troubling their people joined him. They gained control of the land of Judah and did great damage in Israel. ²³And Judas saw all the evil that Alcimus and those with him had done among the sons of Israel; it was more than the Gentiles had done. ²⁴So Judasˣ went out into all the surrounding parts of Judea, and took vengeance on the men who had deserted, and prevented those in the cityʸ from going out into the country. ²⁵When Alcimus saw that Judas and those with him had grown strong, and realized that he could not withstand them, he returned to the king and brought wicked charges against them.

26 Then the king sent Nicanor, one of his honored princes, who hated and detested Israel, and he commanded him to destroy the people. ²⁷So Nicanor came to Jerusalem with a large force, and treacherously sent to Judas and his brothers this peaceable message, ²⁸"Let there be no fighting between me and you; I shall come with a few men to see you face to face in

w Or *many of his men who had deserted*
x Gk *he*
y Gk *they were prevented*

family. Antiochus IV appointed Jason in place of his brother Onias III (2 Macc.4.7); Jason was in turn supplanted by Menelaus (2 Macc.4.23–26), who was put to death about 162 B.C., after having officiated for ten years (2 Macc.13.1–8). Either Onias III or his son Onias IV, last legitimate claimant, fled to Egypt and established a temple at Heliopolis (Cairo). *Alcimus*, or Jakim (2 Macc.14.3), was not a member of the high-priestly family; he belonged to the hellenizing faction and was willing to further Demetrius' plans. **8:** *Beyond the River*, the province west of the Euphrates (Ezra 4.11). **12–14:** *The Hasideans* (2.42), probably the same as the *group of scribes*, had no political ambitions and were content to live under Syrian rule if they were permitted to keep the Mosaic law. **17:** Ps.79.2–3. All ancients regarded an unburied dead body with horror, and to leave foes unburied was the ultimate outrage. **19:** *Beth-zaith*, perhaps three miles north of Beth-zur; or Bezetha, north of the temple area in Jerusalem.

7.26–50: Defeat of Nicanor. The last of Judas' great victories (2 Macc.14.12–15.36). **26:** According to Josephus (*Antiquities*, XII. x. 4), *Nicanor* was one of the men who had escaped from peace." ²⁹So he came to Judas, and they greeted one another peaceably. But the enemy were ready to seize Judas. ³⁰It became known to Judas that Nicanor˟ had come to him with treacherous intent, and he was afraid of him and would not meet him again. ³¹When Nicanor learned that his plan had been disclosed, he went out to meet Judas in battle near Caphar-salama. ³²About five hundred men of the army of Nicanor fell, and the rest˟ fled into the city of David.

33 After these events Nicanor went up to Mount Zion. Some of the priests came out of the sanctuary, and some of the elders of the people, to greet him peaceably and to show him the burnt offering that was being offered for the king. ³⁴But he mocked them and derided them and defiled them and spoke arrogantly, ³⁵and in anger he swore this oath, "Unless Judas and his army are delivered into my hands this time, then if I return safely I will burn up this house." And he went out in great anger. ³⁶Then the priests went in and stood before the altar and the temple, and they wept and said,
³⁷"Thou didst choose this house to
    be called by thy name,
and to be for thy people a house
    of prayer and supplication.
³⁸Take vengeance on this man and
    on his army,
and let them fall by the sword;
remember their blasphemies,
and let them live no longer."
39 Now Nicanor went out from Jerusalem and encamped in Beth-horon, and the Syrian army joined him. ⁴⁰And Judas encamped in Adasa

with three thousand men. Then Judas prayed and said, ⁴¹"When the messengers from the king spoke blasphemy, thy angel went forth and struck down one hundred and eighty-five thousand of the Assyrians.ᵃ ⁴²So also crush this army before us today; let the rest learn that Nicanorᵇ has spoken wickedly against thy sanctuary, and judge him according to this wickedness." ⁴³So the armies met in battle on the thirteenth day of the month of Adar. The army of Nicanor was crushed, and he himself was the first to fall in the battle. ⁴⁴When his army saw that Nicanor had fallen, they threw down their arms and fled. ⁴⁵The Jewsᶜ pursued them a day's journey, from Adasa as far as Gazara, and as they followed kept sounding the battle call on the trumpets. ⁴⁶And men came out of all the villages of Judea round about, and they outflanked the enemyᵈ and drove them back to their pursuers,ᵉ so that they all fell by the sword; not even one of them was left. ⁴⁷Then the Jewsᶠ seized the spoils and the plunder, and they cut off Nicanor's head and the right hand which he had so arrogantly stretched out, and brought them and displayed them just outside Jerusalem. ⁴⁸The people rejoiced greatly and celebrated that day as a day of great gladness. ⁴⁹And they decreed that this day should be celebrated each year on the thirteenth day of Adar. ⁵⁰So the land of Judah had rest for a few days.

8 Now Judas heard of the fame of the Romans, that they were very

x Gk he
a Gk of them   b Gk he
d Gk them   e Gk these
z Gk they
c Gk they
f Gk they

Rome with Demetrius (see 7.1 n.). **30:** Judas never trusted the Syrians (vv. 10–11). **31:** *Caphar-salama*, perhaps Khirbet Deir Sellam, about five miles northeast of Jerusalem. **33:** The Jews customarily offered sacrifices to God for the welfare of their rulers. **37–38:** Compare 1 Kg.8.29,43; Pss.68.16; 87.1–2. **40:** *Adasa*, about seven miles from Beth-horon on the road to Jerusalem. **41:** 2 Kg.19.35. **43:** *Adar*, roughly March, in 161 B.C. (see 2 Macc.15.36 n.). **45:** *Gazara*, Gezer (4.15). **47:** *Head . . . right hand*, in punishment for blasphemy and for raising his hand against the temple (2 Macc.15.32). **49:** 2 Macc.15.36. This festival, which came to be called Nicanor Day, was one of the days on which the Jews prohibited mourning (compare 13.52).
8.1–32: Treaty with Rome. The author of 1 Maccabees emphasizes friendly relations between Rome and the Jews because the Romans checked the ambitions of the Seleucids. After 190 B.C. Rome steadily increased her influence in the Near East and Syrian power declined. **1:** *The*

[239]

strong and were well-disposed toward all who made an alliance with them, that they pledged friendship to those who came to them, [2]and that they were very strong. Men told him of their wars and of the brave deeds which they were doing among the Gauls, how they had defeated them and forced them to pay tribute, [3]and what they had done in the land of Spain to get control of the silver and gold mines there, [4]and how they had gained control of the whole region by their planning and patience, even though the place was far distant from them. They also subdued the kings who came against them from the ends of the earth, until they crushed them and inflicted great disaster upon them; the rest paid them tribute every year. [5]Philip, and Perseus king of the Macedonians,[g] and the others who rose up against them, they crushed in battle and conquered. [6]They also defeated Antiochus the Great, king of Asia, who went to fight against them with a hundred and twenty elephants and with cavalry and chariots and a very large army. He was crushed by them; [7]they took him alive and decreed that he and those who should reign after him should pay a heavy tribute and give hostages and surrender some of their best provinces, [8]the country of India and Media and Lydia. These they took from him and gave to Eumenes the king. [9]The Greeks planned to come and destroy them, [10]but this became known to them, and they sent a general against the Greeks[h]

and attacked them. Many of them were wounded and fell, and the Romans[i] took captive their wives and children; they plundered them, conquered the land, tore down their strongholds, and enslaved them to this day. [11]The remaining kingdoms and islands, as many as ever opposed them, they destroyed and enslaved; [12]but with their friends and those who rely on them they have kept friendship. They have subdued kings far and near, and as many as have heard of their fame have feared them. [13]Those whom they wish to help and to make kings, they make kings, and those whom they wish they depose; and they have been greatly exalted. [14]Yet for all this not one of them has put on a crown or worn purple as a mark of pride, [15]but they have built for themselves a senate chamber, and every day three hundred and twenty senators constantly deliberate concerning the people, to govern them well. [16]They trust one man each year to rule over them and to control all their land; they all heed the one man, and there is no envy or jealousy among them.

17 So Judas chose Eupolemus the son of John, son of Accos, and Jason the son of Eleazar, and sent them to Rome to establish friendship and alliance, [18]and to free themselves from the yoke; for they saw that the kingdom of the Greeks was completely enslaving Israel. [19]They went to Rome, a very long journey; and they entered the

g Or *Kittim*   h Gk *them*   i Gk *they*

Romans had made *an alliance* with kings in Asia Minor and Egypt. **2:** Two nations of *Gauls* were *defeated*, those of upper Italy in 190 B.C., and the Galatians of Asia Minor in 189 B.C. **3–4:** Rome conquered the Carthaginian colonies of *Spain*, not *the whole region*, in the Second Punic War. **5:** *Philip*, defeated at Cynoscephalae in 197 B.C.; *Perseus*, his son, last Macedonian king, beaten at Pydna in 168 B.C. **6–8:** *Antiochus* was not captured, but had to *give hostages* (7.1). *India* was not part of his domain; he kept *Media*, but he surrendered *Lydia* and other parts of Asia Minor. *Eumenes* II of Pergamum was given much of Seleucid Asia Minor. **9:** *The Greeks*, possibly the Macedonians (v. 5), or the Achaean league somewhat later. **12:** This is the estimate of a partisan; it is not true that they always *kept friendship*. **14:** *A crown*, Rome wanted no king, but magistrates, senators, and knights wore *purple* borders on their garments. **15:** *Every day*, actually senate meetings were held three times a month, and on the festivals. **16:** *One man*, in reality there were two consuls, and *envy and jealousy* were constant. The author of 1 Maccabees idealizes the Romans because their republican institutions were congenial to the Jews. **17:** *Eupolemus*, 2 Macc.4.11. *Accos*, a priestly family (Ezra 2.61).

senate chamber and spoke as follows:
²⁰"Judas, who is also called Maccabeus,
and his brothers and the people of the
Jews have sent us to you to establish
alliance and peace with you, that we
may be enrolled as your allies and
friends." ²¹The proposal pleased them,
²²and this is a copy of the letter which
they wrote in reply, on bronze tablets,
and sent to Jerusalem to remain with
them there as a memorial of peace and
alliance:

23 "May all go well with the Romans
and with the nation of the Jews at sea
and on land for ever, and may sword
and enemy be far from them. ²⁴If war
comes first to Rome or to any of their
allies in all their dominion, ²⁵the nation
of the Jews shall act as their allies
wholeheartedly, as the occasion may
indicate to them. ²⁶And to the enemy
who makes war they shall not give or
supply grain, arms, money, or ships, as
Rome has decided; and they shall keep
their obligations without receiving any
return. ²⁷In the same way, if war comes
first to the nation of the Jews, the
Romans shall willingly act as their
allies, as the occasion may indicate to
them. ²⁸And to the enemy allies shall
be given no grain, arms, money, or
ships, as Rome has decided; and they
shall keep these obligations and do so
without deceit. ²⁹Thus on these terms
the Romans make a treaty with the
Jewish people. ³⁰If after these terms
are in effect both parties shall determine to add or delete anything, they
shall do so at their discretion, and any
addition or deletion that they may
make shall be valid.

31 "And concerning the wrongs
which King Demetrius is doing to them
we have written to him as follows,
'Why have you made your yoke heavy
upon our friends and allies the Jews?
³²If now they appeal again for help
against you, we will defend their rights
and fight you on sea and on land.' "

9 When Demetrius heard that Nicanor and his army had fallen in
battle, he sent Bacchides and Alcimus
into the land of Judah a second time,
and with them the right wing of the
army. ²They went by the road which
leads to Gilgal and encamped against
Mesaloth in Arbela, and they took it
and killed many people. ³In the first
month of the one hundred and fifty-
second year*ʲ* they encamped against
Jerusalem; ⁴then they marched off and
went to Berea with twenty thousand
foot soldiers and two thousand cavalry.

5 Now Judas was encamped in
Elasa, and with him were three thousand picked men. ⁶When they saw the
huge number of the enemy forces, they
were greatly frightened, and many
slipped away from the camp, until no
more than eight hundred of them were
left.

7 When Judas saw that his army had
slipped away and the battle was imminent, he was crushed in spirit, for
he had no time to assemble them. ⁸He
became faint, but he said to those who
were left, "Let us rise and go up against
our enemies. We may be able to fight
them." ⁹But they tried to dissuade him,
saying, "We are not able. Let us rather

ʲ 160 B.C.

22: Important documents were often inscribed *on bronze tablets*. **23–30:** The treaty letter
begins with the conventional formula and is drawn up as though the two parties were equals,
and Judea a sovereign state. **31–32:** This postscript was not part of the treaty, and is correctly
omitted from it by Josephus (*Antiquities*, xii. x. 6); there is no evidence that the Romans
helped Judas against Demetrius.

9.1–22: Death of Judas. Continual Syrian pressure weakened Judas' forces, which were a
guerrilla band facing a highly organized army. Judas decided that it was better to fall in battle
than to withdraw. **1–2:** *Bacchides*, 7.8. *Alcimus*, see 7.5 n. Josephus (*Antiquities*, xii. xi. 1) says
that they started from Antioch, camped at Arbela in Galilee (not *Gilgal*), besieged refugees in
the caves, and went on toward Jerusalem. *Mesaloth*, perhaps the Hebrew word for "steps," i.e.
ascents to *Arbela*. **4:** *Berea*, perhaps el-Bireh, opposite Ramallah, ten miles north of Jerusalem.
5: *Elasa* has not been identified.

save our own lives now, and let us come back with our brethren and fight them; we are too few." ¹⁰But Judas said, "Far be it from us to do such a thing as to flee from them. If our time has come, let us die bravely for our brethren, and leave no cause to question our honor."

11 Then the army of Bacchides*ᵏ* marched out from the camp and took its stand for the encounter. The cavalry was divided into two companies, and the slingers and the archers went ahead of the army, as did all the chief warriors. ¹²Bacchides was on the right wing. Flanked by the two companies, the phalanx advanced to the sound of the trumpets; and the men with Judas also blew their trumpets. ¹³The earth was shaken by the noise of the armies, and the battle raged from morning till evening.

14 Judas saw that Bacchides and the strength of his army were on the right; then all the stouthearted men went with him, ¹⁵and they crushed the right wing, and he pursued them as far as Mount Azotus. ¹⁶When those on the left wing saw that the right wing was crushed, they turned and followed close behind Judas and his men. ¹⁷The battle became desperate, and many on both sides were wounded and fell. ¹⁸Judas also fell, and the rest fled.

19 Then Jonathan and Simon took Judas their brother and buried him in the tomb of their fathers at Modein, ²⁰and wept for him. And all Israel made great lamentation for him; they mourned many days and said, ²¹"How is the mighty fallen,
    the savior of Israel!"

²²Now the rest of the acts of Judas, and his wars and the brave deeds that he did, and his greatness, have not been recorded, for they were very many.

23 After the death of Judas, the lawless emerged in all parts of Israel; all the doers of injustice appeared. ²⁴In those days a very great famine occurred, and the country deserted with them to the enemy. ²⁵And Bacchides chose the ungodly and put them in charge of the country. ²⁶They sought and searched for the friends of Judas, and brought them to Bacchides, and he took vengeance on them and made sport of them. ²⁷Thus there was great distress in Israel, such as had not been since the time that prophets ceased to appear among them.

28 Then all the friends of Judas assembled and said to Jonathan, ²⁹"Since the death of your brother Judas there has been no one like him to go against our enemies and Bacchides, and to deal with those of our nation who hate us. ³⁰So now we have chosen you today to take his place as our ruler and leader, to fight our battle." ³¹And Jonathan at that time accepted the leadership and took the place of Judas his brother.

32 When Bacchides learned of this, he tried to kill him. ³³But Jonathan and Simon his brother and all who were with him heard of it, and they fled into the wilderness of Tekoa and camped by the water of the pool of Asphar. ³⁴Bacchides found this out on the sabbath day, and he with all his army crossed the Jordan.

k Gk *the army*

15: *Mount Azotus,* perhaps el-'Asur, six miles northeast of el-Bireh; Ashdod (4.15) is too far away. **19:** *Modein,* 2.1, 70; 13.27–30. **21:** 2 Sam.1.19. **22:** The expression *Now the rest of the acts* imitates the style of Hebrew chronicles (1 Kg.11.41).

9.23–73: Jonathan becomes leader and defeats Bacchides. 23: *The lawless,* i.e. the pro-Syrian element. **24:** *The country,* the majority of the nation, or perhaps the rural population; resistance now seemed futile. **25:** *The ungodly,* i.e. hellenized Jews. **27:** *Prophets ceased,* see 4.46 n. **31:** *We have chosen you,* Judas was self-appointed, but *Jonathan* was elected by his peers; he became leader about 160 or 159 B.C. and high priest in 152 (10.21). **33:** *Tekoa,* five miles southeast of Bethlehem (Am. 1.1); *the wilderness* reached from here to the Dead Sea. *The pool of Asphar* may be three miles south of Tekoa. **34:** *Bacchides* thought the Jews might be surprised *on the sabbath day.* He apparently came from Jerusalem, *crossed the Jordan,* and camped on the east

35 And Jonathan*l* sent his brother as leader of the multitude and begged the Nabateans, who were his friends, for permission to store with them the great amount of baggage which they had. ³⁶But the sons of Jambri from Medeba came out and seized John and all that he had, and departed with it.

37 After these things it was reported to Jonathan and Simon his brother, "The sons of Jambri are celebrating a great wedding, and are conducting the bride, a daughter of one of the great nobles of Canaan, from Nadabath with a large escort." ³⁸And they remembered the blood of John their brother, and went up and hid under cover of the mountain. ³⁹They raised their eyes and looked, and saw a tumultuous procession with much baggage; and the bridegroom came out with his friends and his brothers to meet them with tambourines and musicians and many weapons. ⁴⁰Then they rushed upon them from the ambush and began killing them. Many were wounded and fell, and the rest fled to the mountain; and they took all their goods. ⁴¹Thus the wedding was turned into mourning and the voice of their musicians into a funeral dirge. ⁴²And when they had fully avenged the blood of their brother, they returned to the marshes of the Jordan.

43 When Bacchides heard of this, he came with a large force on the sabbath day to the banks of the Jordan. ⁴⁴And Jonathan said to those with him, "Let us rise up now and fight for our lives, for today things are not as they were before. ⁴⁵For look! the battle is in front of us and behind us; the water of the Jordan is on this side and on that, with marsh and thicket; there is no place to turn. ⁴⁶Cry out now to Heaven that you may be delivered from the hands of our enemies." ⁴⁷So the battle began, and Jonathan stretched out his hand to strike Bacchides, but he eluded him and went to the rear. ⁴⁸Then Jonathan and the men with him leaped into the Jordan and swam across to the other side, and the enemy*m* did not cross the Jordan to attack them. ⁴⁹And about one thousand of Bacchides' men fell that day.

50 Bacchides*n* then returned to Jerusalem and built strong cities in Judea: the fortress in Jericho, and Emmaus, and Beth-horon, and Bethel, and Timnath, and*o* Pharathon, and Tephon, with high walls and gates and bars. ⁵¹And he placed garrisons in them to harass Israel. ⁵²He also fortified the city of Beth-zur, and Gazara, and the citadel, and in them he put troops and stores of food. ⁵³And he took the sons of the leading men of the land as hostages and put them under guard in the citadel at Jerusalem.

54 In the one hundred and fifty-third year,*p* in the second month, Alcimus gave orders to tear down the wall of the inner court of the sanctuary. He tore down the work of the prophets! ⁵⁵But he only began to tear it down, for at that time Alcimus was stricken and his work was hindered; his mouth was stopped and he was paralyzed, so that he could no longer say a word or give commands concerning his house.

l Gk *he*
m Gk *they*   *n* Gk *he*
o Some authorities omit *and*
p 159 B.C.

---

side. **35**: *His brother*, John (v. 36; 2.2). *The Nabateans*, see 5.25 n. **36**: *Sons of Jambri*, evidently a Nabatean tribe. *Medeba* or Madeba, twelve miles southeast of the north end of the Dead Sea. **37**: *Nadabath*, perhaps Nebo, a little north of Medeba (Num.33.47; Dt.32.49). **38**: *Blood of John*, the sequel to v. 36 was the murder of John and all his companions (Josephus, *Antiquities*, XIII. i. 2). **45**: The Jews were apparently on the east side of the Jordan, between the river and the Syrian forces. **50–53**: Bacchides established forces and garrisons to prevent guerrilla operations. *Emmaus*, see 3.40 n. *Beth-horon*, see 3.16 n. *Bethel*, now Beitin, about twelve miles north of Jerusalem. *Timnath*, perhaps twelve miles northwest of Bethel. *Pharathon*, six miles southwest of Shechem or Nablus. *Tephon*, Tappuah, twenty-five miles north of Jerusalem. *Beth-zur*, see 4.29 n. *Gazara*, see 4.15 n. **54**: *The wall of the inner court* separated this part from the rest of the temple mount, which was open to Gentiles. Pagans were now to have access to *the sanctuary*.

⁵⁶And Alcimus died at that time in great agony. ⁵⁷When Bacchides saw that Alcimus was dead, he returned to the king, and the land of Judah had rest for two years.

58 Then all the lawless plotted and said, "See! Jonathan and his men are living in quiet and confidence. So now let us bring Bacchides back, and he will capture them all in one night." ⁵⁹And they went and consulted with him. ⁶⁰He started to come with a large force, and secretly sent letters to all his allies in Judea, telling them to seize Jonathan and his men; but they were unable to do it, because their plan became known. ⁶¹And Jonathan's men*q* seized about fifty of the men of the country who were leaders in this treachery, and killed them.

62 Then Jonathan with his men, and Simon, withdrew to Bethbasi in the wilderness; he rebuilt the parts of it that had been demolished, and they fortified it. ⁶³When Bacchides learned of this, he assembled all his forces, and sent orders to the men of Judea. ⁶⁴Then he came and encamped against Bethbasi; he fought against it for many days and made machines of war.

65 But Jonathan left Simon his brother in the city, while he went out into the country; and he went with only a few men. ⁶⁶He struck down Odomera and his brothers and the sons of Phasiron in their tents. ⁶⁷Then he*r* began to attack and went into battle with his forces; and Simon and his men sallied out from the city and set fire to the machines of war. ⁶⁸They fought with Bacchides, and he was crushed by them. They distressed him greatly, for his plan and his expedition had been in vain. ⁶⁹So he was greatly enraged at the lawless men who had counseled him to come into the country, and he killed many of them. Then he decided to depart to his own land.

70 When Jonathan learned of this, he sent ambassadors to him to make peace with him and obtain release of the captives. ⁷¹He agreed, and did as he said; and he swore to Jonathan*s* that he would not try to harm him as long as he lived. ⁷²He restored to him the captives whom he had formerly taken from the land of Judah; then he turned and departed to his own land, and came no more into their territory. ⁷³Thus the sword ceased from Israel. And Jonathan dwelt in Michmash. And Jonathan began to judge the people, and he destroyed the ungodly out of Israel.

10 In the one hundred and sixtieth year*t* Alexander Epiphanes, the son of Antiochus, landed and occupied Ptolemais. They welcomed him, and there he began to reign. ²When Demetrius the king heard of it, he assembled a very large army and marched out to meet him in battle. ³And Demetrius sent Jonathan a letter in peaceable words to honor him; ⁴for he said, "Let us act first to make peace with him*u* before he makes peace with Alexander against us, ⁵for he will re-

q Gk *they*   *r* Other authorities read *they*
s Gk *him*   *t* 152 B.C.
u Gk *them*

The prophets, Haggai and Zechariah had built the second temple. **56:** *Alcimus* had been high priest for about two years (7.5). **57:** *He returned*, believing that with the fortresses garrisoned the situation was stable; his departure gave Jonathan a free hand. **61:** *Fifty . . . leaders*, probably the hellenizers (see v. 25 n.). **62:** *Bethbasi*, perhaps Khirbet Beit-Bassa, about three miles northeast of Tekoa. **66:** *Odomera . . . sons of Phasiron*, probably bedouin sheikhs. **68:** *He was crushed*, for Simon attacked by surprise and *Bacchides* had depended heavily on the war machines (v. 67). **72:** Josephus says that there was an exchange of prisoners (*Antiquities*, XIII. i. 6). **73:** *Thus the sword ceased*, for about seven years, until the events of 10.69. *Michmash*, now Mukhmas, eight miles northeast of Jerusalem (1 Sam.14.5–23). *To judge the people*, as a natural leader, like Samuel and those in the book of Judges.

10.1–21: Alexander Balas appoints Jonathan high priest. 1: *Alexander I Epiphanes*, who came from Ephesus and whose given name was Balas (or Ba'al), posed as *the son of Antiochus IV*. He claimed the kingship from 150 B.C. onward, and reigned until about 145. Attalus II of Pergamember all the wrongs which we did to him and to his brothers and his nation." [6]So Demetrius[v] gave him authority to recruit troops, to equip them with arms, and to become his ally; and he commanded that the hostages in the citadel should be released to him.

7 Then Jonathan came to Jerusalem and read the letter in the hearing of all the people and of the men in the citadel. [8]They were greatly alarmed when they heard that the king had given him authority to recruit troops. [9]But the men in the citadel released the hostages to Jonathan, and he returned them to their parents.

10 And Jonathan dwelt in Jerusalem and began to rebuild and restore the city. [11]He directed those who were doing the work to build the walls and encircle Mount Zion with squared stones, for better fortification; and they did so.

12 Then the foreigners who were in the strongholds that Bacchides had built fled; [13]each left his place and departed to his own land. [14]Only in Beth-zur did some remain who had forsaken the law and the commandments, for it served as a place of refuge.

15 Now Alexander the king heard of all the promises which Demetrius had sent to Jonathan, and men told him of the battles that Jonathan[w] and his brothers had fought, of the brave deeds that they had done, and of the troubles that they had endured. [16]So he said, "Shall we find another such man? Come now, we will make him our friend and ally." [17]And he wrote a letter and sent it to him, in the following words:

18 "King Alexander to his brother Jonathan, greeting. [19]We have heard about you, that you are a mighty warrior and worthy to be our friend. [20]And so we have appointed you today to be the high priest of your nation; you are to be called the king's friend" (and he sent him a purple robe and a golden crown) "and you are to take our side and keep friendship with us."

21 So Jonathan put on the holy garments in the seventh month of the one hundred and sixtieth year,[x] at the feast of tabernacles, and he recruited troops and equipped them with arms in abundance. [22]When Demetrius heard of these things he was grieved and said, [23]"What is this that we have done? Alexander has gotten ahead of us in forming a friendship with the Jews to strengthen himself. [24]I also will write them words of encouragement and promise them honor and gifts, that I may have their help." [25]So he sent a message to them in the following words:

"King Demetrius to the nation of the Jews, greeting. [26]Since you have kept your agreement with us and have continued your friendship with us, and have not sided with our enemies, we have heard of it and rejoiced. [27]And now continue still to keep faith with us, and we will repay you with good for what you do for us. [28]We will grant you many immunities and give you gifts.

v Gk *he*   *w* Gk *he*   *x* 152 B.C.

mum and Ptolemy VI persuaded the Roman senate to recognize him. **6:** *Gave him authority*, as a local prince or governor, but not independence. *The hostages*, 9.53. The Syrians held the citadel at Jerusalem. **10:** *Jonathan* now left Michmash. **11:** Lysias had ordered the wall of the Jewish fortress torn down (6.62). **14:** *Some*, i.e. hellenized Jews opposed to the Hasmoneans. **18–20:** *Alexander*, hearing of Demetrius' letter, decided to outbid him. Until the time of Antiochus IV, the hereditary high priest had been confirmed but not appointed by the ruler; now Alexander appointed Jonathan and made him one of his friends (see 2.18 n.); the Jews had not elected him. **21:** *The holy garments*, Ex.28.1–39; 39:1–26. *Tabernacles*, a seven day festival held in September (Lev.23.33–43), had come to be associated with the hope of victory over the Gentiles (Zech.14.16–19).

10.22–50: Demetrius' offer to the Jews; his defeat. 25: The letter was addressed *to the nation*, ignoring Jonathan. Demetrius thought that he could drive a wedge between leader and people.

29 "And now I free you and exempt all the Jews from payment of tribute and salt tax and crown levies, ³⁰and instead of collecting the third of the grain and the half of the fruit of the trees that I should receive, I release them from this day and henceforth. I will not collect them from the land of Judah or from the three districts added to it from Samaria and Galilee, from this day and for all time. ³¹And let Jerusalem and her environs, her tithes and her revenues, be holy and free from tax. ³²I release also my control of the citadel in Jerusalem and give it to the high priest, that he may station in it men of his own choice to guard it. ³³And every one of the Jews taken as a captive from the land of Judah into any part of my kingdom, I set free without payment; and let all officials cancel also the taxes on their cattle.

34 "And all the feasts and sabbaths and new moons and appointed days, and the three days before a feast and the three after a feast—let them all be days of immunity and release for all the Jews who are in my kingdom. ³⁵No one shall have authority to exact anything from them or annoy any of them about any matter.

36 "Let Jews be enrolled in the king's forces to the number of thirty thousand men, and let the maintenance be given them that is due to all the forces of the king. ³⁷Let some of them be stationed in the great strongholds of the king, and let some of them be put in positions of trust in the kingdom. Let their officers and leaders be of their own number, and let them live by their own laws, just as the king has commanded in the land of Judah.

38 "As for the three districts that have been added to Judea from the country of Samaria, let them be so annexed to Judea that they are considered to be under one ruler and obey no other authority but the high priest. ³⁹Ptolemais and the land adjoining it I have given as a gift to the sanctuary in Jerusalem, to meet the necessary expenses of the sanctuary. ⁴⁰I also grant fifteen thousand shekels of silver yearly out of the king's revenues from appropriate places. ⁴¹And all the additional funds which the government officials have not paid as they did in the first years,ʸ they shall give from now on for the service of the temple.ᶻ ⁴²Moreover, the five thousand shekels of silver which my officialsᵃ have received every year from the income of the services of the temple, this too is canceled, because it belongs to the priests who minister there. ⁴³And whoever takes refuge at the temple in Jerusalem, or in any of its precincts, because he owes money to the king or has any debt, let him be released and receive back all his property in my kingdom.

44 "Let the cost of rebuilding and restoring the structures of the sanctuary be paid from the revenues of the king. ⁴⁵And let the cost of rebuilding the walls of Jerusalem and fortifying it round about, and the cost of rebuilding the walls in Judea, also be paid from the revenues of the king."

46 When Jonathan and the people heard these words, they did not believe or accept them, because they remembered the great wrongs which

y The Greek text of this verse is uncertain
z Gk *house*   a Gk *they*

29–30: *All the Jews* in the Seleucid realm, not merely in Judea. *Tribute*, direct taxes proportionate to individual wealth. *Salt tax*, on salt from the marshes and the Dead Sea. *Crown levies*, fixed amounts of money. *The three districts* (11.34) that Alexander the Great had transferred from Samaria to Judea and Antiochus IV had reassigned to Samaria were now restored (v. 38). **32:** *Release* of *control of the citadel* would free Jerusalem from military domination. **34:** *Appointed days*, other public festivals. **36–37:** Opening the army and the civil service to Jews might strengthen their loyalty to the crown. **39:** *Ptolemais* was in the hands of Alexander (v. 1). This was an invitation to the Jews to help Demetrius recapture it. **41:** *The additional funds* were grants once made to the temple by Ptolemaic and Seleucid kings, but *not paid* since the time of Antiochus IV. **44–45:** Here Demetrius followed the custom of Persian kings (Ezra 6.8; 7.20).

[246]

Demetrius[b] had done in Israel and how he had greatly oppressed them. [47]They favored Alexander, because he had been the first to speak peaceable words to them, and they remained his allies all his days.

48 Now Alexander the king assembled large forces and encamped opposite Demetrius. [49]The two kings met in battle, and the army of Demetrius fled, and Alexander[c] pursued him and defeated them. [50]He pressed the battle strongly until the sun set, and Demetrius fell on that day.

51 Then Alexander sent ambassadors to Ptolemy king of Egypt with the following message: [52]"Since I have returned to my kingdom and have taken my seat on the throne of my fathers, and established my rule—for I crushed Demetrius and gained control of our country; [53]I met him in battle, and he and his army were crushed by us, and we have taken our seat on the throne of his kingdom— [54]now therefore let us establish friendship with one another; give me now your daughter as my wife, and I will become your son-in-law, and will make gifts to you and to her in keeping with your position."

55 Ptolemy the king replied and said, "Happy was the day on which you returned to the land of your fathers and took your seat on the throne of their kingdom. [56]And now I will do for you as you wrote, but meet me at Ptolemais, so that we may see one another, and I will become your father-in-law, as you have said."

57 So Ptolemy set out from Egypt, he and Cleopatra his daughter, and came to Ptolemais in the one hundred and sixty-second year.[d] [58]Alexander the king met him, and Ptolemy[e] gave him Cleopatra his daughter in marriage, and celebrated her wedding at Ptolemais with great pomp, as kings do.

59 Then Alexander the king wrote to Jonathan to come to meet him. [60]So he went with pomp to Ptolemais and met the two kings; he gave them and their friends silver and gold and many gifts, and found favor with them. [61]A group of pestilent men from Israel, lawless men, gathered together against him to accuse him; but the king paid no attention to them. [62]The king gave orders to take off Jonathan's garments and to clothe him in purple, and they did so. [63]The king also seated him at his side; and he said to his officers, "Go forth with him into the middle of the city and proclaim that no one is to bring charges against him about any matter, and let no one annoy him for any reason." [64]And when his accusers saw the honor that was paid him, in accordance with the proclamation, and saw him clothed in purple, they all fled. [65]Thus the king honored him and enrolled him among his chief friends, and made him general and governor of the province. [66]And Jonathan returned to Jerusalem in peace and gladness.

67 In the one hundred and sixty-fifth year[f] Demetrius the son of Demetrius came from Crete to the land of his fathers. [68]When Alexander the king heard of it, he was greatly grieved and returned to Antioch. [69]And Demetrius appointed Apollonius the governor of Coelesyria, and he

b Gk *he*
c Other authorities read *Alexander fled, and Demetrius*
d 150 B.C.   e Gk *he*   f 147 B.C.

47: *Alexander* was also recognized as king by the Jews' allies, the Romans. **50**: *Demetrius fell* probably in 150 B.C. (v. 57).

10.51–66: **Alexander's relations with Egypt and Judea. 51**: *Ptolemy* VI Philometor (1.18). **55**: *Ptolemy* recognized Alexander as legitimate (see 10.1–21 n.). **57**: *Cleopatra* III, who later married her uncle, Ptolemy VIII. **62**: A change of *garments* often signified honor or dishonor (Zech.3.3–5; Mt.22.11–14). **65**: *Chief friends*, see 2.18 n. *General and governor*, with military and civil authority.

10.67–89: **Victories of Jonathan. 67**: *Demetrius* II *the son of Demetrius* I disputed the throne with Alexander and later with Tryphon and Antiochus VI; in 138 B.C. he was taken captive by the Parthians. He reigned again from 129 till his death in 125 B.C. **69**: *Coelesyria*, meaning assembled a large force and encamped against Jamnia. Then he sent the following message to Jonathan the high priest: 70 "You are the only one to rise up against us, and I have become a laughingstock and reproach because of you. Why do you assume authority against us in the hill country? 71If you now have confidence in your forces, come down to the plain to meet us, and let us match strength with each other there, for I have with me the power of the cities. 72Ask and learn who I am and who the others are that are helping us. Men will tell you that you cannot stand before us, for your fathers were twice put to flight in their own land. 73And now you will not be able to withstand my cavalry and such an army in the plain, where there is no stone or pebble, or place to flee."

74 When Jonathan heard the words of Apollonius, his spirit was aroused. He chose ten thousand men and set out from Jerusalem, and Simon his brother met him to help him. 75He encamped before Joppa, but the men of the city closed its gates, for Apollonius had a garrison in Joppa. 76So they fought against it, and the men of the city became afraid and opened the gates, and Jonathan gained possession of Joppa.

77 When Apollonius heard of it, he mustered three thousand cavalry and a large army, and went to Azotus as though he were going farther. At the same time he advanced into the plain, for he had a large troop of cavalry and put confidence in it. 78Jonathang pursued him to Azotus, and the armies engaged in battle. 79Now Apollonius had secretly left a thousand cavalry behind them. 80Jonathan learned that there was an ambush behind him, for they surrounded his army and shot arrows at his men from early morning till late afternoon. 81But his men stood fast, as Jonathan commanded, and the enemy'sʰ horses grew tired.

82 Then Simon brought forward his force and engaged the phalanx in battle (for the cavalry was exhausted); they were overwhelmed by him and fled, 83and the cavalry was dispersed in the plain. They fled to Azotus and entered Beth-dagon, the temple of their idol, for safety. 84But Jonathan burned Azotus and the surrounding towns and plundered them; and the temple of Dagon, and those who had taken refuge in it he burned with fire. 85The number of those who fell by the sword, with those burned alive, came to eight thousand men.

86 Then Jonathan departed from there and encamped against Askalon, and the men of the city came out to meet him with great pomp. 87And Jonathan and those with him returned to Jerusalem with much booty. 88When Alexander the king heard of these things, he honored Jonathan still more; 89and he sent to him a golden buckle, such as it is the custom to give to the kinsmen of kings. He also gave him Ekron and all its environs as his possession.

||| Then the king of Egypt gathered great forces, like the sand by the seashore, and many ships; and he tried to get possession of Alexander's kingdom by trickery and add it to his

g Gk *he*   h Gk *their*

"hollow Syria," originally designated the country between the Lebanon and anti-Lebanon mountains; here it is Palestine and Transjordan, including the coast. *Jamnia*, 4.15. **72**: *Twice put to flight*, 6.54; 9.18. **74**: Jonathan now had forces for more than guerrilla engagements (v. 65); he had troops organized as phalanxes (v. 82). **75**: *Joppa*, now Jaffa, a seaport near Jamnia and forty miles from Jerusalem. **82**: *His force* had been held in reserve and was fresh. **83**: *Beth-dagon*, house of Dagon, the Philistine grain god (Jg.16.23). **86**: *Askalon*, about twelve miles north of Gaza. **89**: *Ekron*, northernmost of the Philistine cities, was given to Jonathan as a personal possession, and its taxes were assigned to him.

11.1–19: Invasion of Ptolemy VI and victory of Demetrius II. 1: Josephus says that Ptolemy came to aid Alexander, his son-in-law, but that the latter plotted against Ptolemy's life (*Antiq-*

own kingdom. ²He set out for Syria with peaceable words, and the people of the cities opened their gates to him and went to meet him, for Alexander the king had commanded them to meet him, since he was Alexander's[i] father-in-law. ³But when Ptolemy entered the cities he stationed forces as a garrison in each city.

4 When he[j] approached Azotus, they showed him the temple of Dagon burned down, and Azotus and its suburbs destroyed, and the corpses lying about, and the charred bodies of those whom Jonathan[k] had burned in the war, for they had piled them in heaps along his route. ⁵They also told the king what Jonathan had done, to throw blame on him; but the king kept silent. ⁶Jonathan met the king at Joppa with pomp, and they greeted one another and spent the night there. ⁷And Jonathan went with the king as far as the river called Eleutherus; then he returned to Jerusalem.

8 So King Ptolemy gained control of the coastal cities as far as Seleucia by the sea, and he kept devising evil designs against Alexander. ⁹He sent envoys to Demetrius the king, saying, "Come, let us make a covenant with each other, and I will give you in marriage my daughter who was Alexander's wife, and you shall reign over your father's kingdom. ¹⁰For I now regret that I gave him my daughter, for he has tried to kill me." ¹¹He threw blame on Alexander[l] because he coveted his kingdom. ¹²So he took his daughter away from him and gave her

to Demetrius. He was estranged from Alexander, and their enmity became manifest.

13 Then Ptolemy entered Antioch and put on the crown of Asia. Thus he put two crowns upon his head, the crown of Egypt and that of Asia. ¹⁴Now Alexander the king was in Cilicia at that time, because the people of that region were in revolt. ¹⁵And Alexander heard of it and came against him in battle. Ptolemy marched out and met him with a strong force, and put him to flight. ¹⁶So Alexander fled into Arabia to find protection there, and King Ptolemy was exalted. ¹⁷And Zabdiel the Arab cut off the head of Alexander and sent it to Ptolemy. ¹⁸But King Ptolemy died three days later, and his troops in the strongholds were killed by the inhabitants of the strongholds. ¹⁹So Demetrius became king in the one hundred and sixty-seventh year.[m]

20 In those days Jonathan assembled the men of Judea to attack the citadel in Jerusalem, and he built many engines of war to use against it. ²¹But certain lawless men who hated their nation went to the king and reported to him that Jonathan was besieging the citadel. ²²When he heard this he was angry, and as soon as he heard it he set out and came to Ptolemais; and he wrote Jonathan not to continue the siege, but to meet him for a conference at Ptolemais as quickly as possible.

i Gk *his*
j Other ancient authorities read *they*
k Gk *he*
l Gk *him*
m 145 B.C.

---

uities, XIII. iv. 5–6). **5:** *Kept silent*, he had not yet broken with Alexander, and was not ready to commit himself. **7:** *Eleutherus*, now Nahr el-Kebir, north of Tripoli. **8:** *Seleucia* in Pieria, the main port for Antioch, near the mouth of the Orontes. **9:** *My daughter*, Cleopatra III (10.57). **13:** According to Josephus, the army proclaimed *Ptolemy* as king, but he persuaded the people of Antioch to support Demetrius. **14:** *Cilicia*, on the south coast of Turkey, always closely related to Syria, and the only section of Asia Minor then part of the Seleucid Empire. **15:** *Ptolemy marched out*, according to Josephus (*Antiquities*, XIII. iv. 8) with his son-in-law, Demetrius, who had already married Cleopatra. **16:** *Arabia* here includes the country east of Aleppo and Damascus. **18:** *Ptolemy died* of wounds suffered in the victory over Alexander. **19:** *Demetrius* had claimed to be *king* since 150 B.C. (see 10.67 n.).

11.20–37: Agreement between Demetrius II and Jonathan. 20: Demetrius I had once promised to turn *the citadel* over to the high priest (10.32), but he refused to recognize Jonathan as such because the latter had supported Alexander. Now Jonathan resolved to attack the citadel and

23 When Jonathan heard this, he gave orders to continue the siege; and he chose some of the elders of Israel and some of the priests, and put himself in danger, [24]for he went to the king at Ptolemais, taking silver and gold and clothing and numerous other gifts. And he won his favor. [25]Although certain lawless men of his nation kept making complaints against him, [26]the king treated him as his predecessors had treated him; he exalted him in the presence of all his friends. [27]He confirmed him in the high priesthood and in as many other honors as he had formerly had, and made him to be regarded as one of his chief friends. [28]Then Jonathan asked the king to free Judea and the three districts of Samaria[n] from tribute, and promised him three hundred talents. [29]The king consented, and wrote a letter to Jonathan about all these things; its contents were as follows:

30 "King Demetrius to Jonathan his brother and to the nation of the Jews, greeting. [31]This copy of the letter which we wrote concerning you to Lasthenes our kinsman we have written to you also, so that you may know what it says. [32]'King Demetrius to Lasthenes his father, greeting. [33]To the nation of the Jews, who are our friends and fulfil their obligations to us, we have determined to do good, because of the good will they show toward us. [34]We have confirmed as their possession both the territory of Judea and the three districts of Aphairema and Lydda and Rathamin; the latter, with all the region bordering them, were added to Judea from Samaria. To all those who offer sacrifice in Jerusalem, we have granted release from[o] the royal taxes which the king formerly received from them each year, from the crops of the land and the fruit of the trees. [35]And the other payments henceforth due to us of the tithes, and the taxes due to us, and the salt pits and the crown taxes due to us—from all these we shall grant them release. [36]And not one of these grants shall be canceled from this time forth for ever. [37]Now therefore take care to make a copy of this, and let it be given to Jonathan and put up in a conspicuous place on the holy mountain.' "

38 Now when Demetrius the king saw that the land was quiet before him and that there was no opposition to him, he dismissed all his troops, each man to his own place, except the foreign troops which he had recruited from the islands of the nations. So all the troops who had served his fathers hated him. [39]Now Trypho had formerly been one of Alexander's supporters. He saw that all the troops were murmuring against Demetrius. So he went to Imalkue the Arab, who was bringing up Antiochus, the young son of Alexander, [40]and insistently urged him to hand Antiochus[p] over to him, to become king in place of his father. He also reported to Imalkue[p] what Demetrius had done and told of the hatred which the troops of Demetrius[p] had for him; and he stayed there many days.

41 Now Jonathan sent to Demetrius the king the request that he remove the troops of the citadel from Jerusalem, and the troops in the strongholds; for they kept fighting against Israel. [42]And Demetrius sent this message to

n Cn: Gk *the three districts and Samaria*
o Or *Samaria, for all those who offer sacrifice in Jerusalem, in place of*
p Gk *him*

---

make Judea independent. **23–24:** Jonathan decided to *continue the siege* so as to negotiate from strength, but his dangerous visit and gifts showed that he was willing to make terms. **27:** 10.20. **30–37:** The letter repeats earlier promises (10.25–45), but says nothing of the citadel. **31:** *Lasthenes*, probably governor of Coelesyria. **34:** *The three districts*, 10.30,38. *Aphairema*, probably et-Taiyibeh, four miles northeast of Bethel, the Ephraim of Jn.11.54. *Lydda*, or Lod, east of Jaffa. *Rathamin*, perhaps Ramathaim-zophim (1 Sam.1.1), the Arimathea of Mk.15.43.

11.38–52: Jonathan's aid to Demetrius. 38: *Demetrius* in overconfidence reduced his army, probably to save money. This made him unpopular. **42–43:** At last Demetrius seemed to agree

Jonathan, "Not only will I do these things for you and your nation, but I will confer great honor on you and your nation, if I find an opportunity. [43]Now then you will do well to send me men who will help me, for all my troops have revolted." [44]So Jonathan sent three thousand stalwart men to him at Antioch, and when they came to the king, the king rejoiced at their arrival.

[45] Then the men of the city assembled within the city, to the number of a hundred and twenty thousand, and they wanted to kill the king. [46]But the king fled into the palace. Then the men of the city seized the main streets of the city and began to fight. [47]So the king called the Jews to his aid, and they all rallied about him and then spread out through the city; and they killed on that day as many as a hundred thousand men. [48]They set fire to the city and seized much spoil on that day, and they saved the king. [49]When the men of the city saw that the Jews had gained control of the city as they pleased, their courage failed and they cried out to the king with this entreaty, [50]"Grant us peace, and make the Jews stop fighting against us and our city." [51]And they threw down their arms and made peace. So the Jews gained glory in the eyes of the king and of all the people in his kingdom, and they returned to Jerusalem with much spoil.

[52] So Demetrius the king sat on the throne of his kingdom, and the land was quiet before him. [53]But he broke his word about all that he had promised; and he became estranged from Jonathan and did not repay the favors which Jonathan[q] had done him, but oppressed him greatly.

[54] After this Trypho returned, and with him the young boy Antiochus, who began to reign and put on the crown. [55]All the troops that Demetrius had cast off gathered around him, and they fought against Demetrius,[r] and he fled and was routed. [56]And Trypho captured the elephants[s] and gained control of Antioch. [57]Then the young Antiochus wrote to Jonathan, saying, "I confirm you in the high priesthood and set you over the four districts and make you one of the friends of the king." [58]And he sent him gold plate and a table service, and granted him the right to drink from gold cups and dress in purple and wear a gold buckle. [59]Simon his brother he made governor from the Ladder of Tyre to the borders of Egypt.

[60] Then Jonathan set forth and traveled beyond the river and among the cities, and all the army of Syria gathered to him as allies. When he came to Askalon, the people of the city met him and paid him honor. [61]From there he departed to Gaza, but the men of Gaza shut him out. So he besieged it and burned its suburbs with fire and plundered them. [62]Then the people of Gaza pleaded with Jonathan, and he made peace with them, and took the sons of their rulers as hostages and sent them to Jerusalem. And he passed through the country as far as Damascus.

[63] Then Jonathan heard that the officers of Demetrius had come to

q Gk *he*　　*r* Gk *him*　　*s* Gk *beasts*

(compare v. 53) to evacuate the citadel and other fortresses. **45–47:** *Men of the city*, a mob, not an army. *Jews*, Judeans (see 2.23 n.).

　11.53–74: Estrangement of Demetrius and Jonathan. 53: Josephus says that Demetrius now demanded tribute as before (*Antiquities*, XIII. v. 3). **54:** *Antiochus* VI Epiphanes, son of Alexander Balas, reigned nominally from about 145 to 142 B.C. **55:** *All the troops*, v. 38. **57:** *The four districts*, the three of v. 34 and probably Ekron (10.89). **58:** *Gold cups*, Est.1.7. *Gold buckle*, sign of being a friend of the king (see 2.18 n.). **59:** *The Ladder of Tyre*, the coastline between Ptolemais and Tyre. *The borders of Egypt*, probably Wadi el-Arish. **60:** *The river*, Jordan. **61:** *Gaza*, southernmost of the Philistine cities, near the Egyptian border (Jg.16.1). **62:** *Damascus*, outside Jonathan's control, but his influence extended nearly that far. **63:** *Kadesh*, northwest of Lake Huleh or Merom (Jg.4.9).

Kadesh in Galilee with a large army, intending to remove him from office. [64]He went to meet them, but left his brother Simon in the country. [65]Simon encamped before Beth-zur and fought against it for many days and hemmed it in. [66]Then they asked him to grant them terms of peace, and he did so. He removed them from there, took possession of the city, and set a garrison over it.

[67] Jonathan and his army encamped by the waters of Gennesaret. Early in the morning they marched to the plain of Hazor, [68]and behold, the army of the foreigners met him in the plain; they had set an ambush against him in the mountains, but they themselves met him face to face. [69]Then the men in ambush emerged from their places and joined battle. [70]All the men with Jonathan fled; not one of them was left except Mattathias the son of Absalom and Judas the son of Chalphi, commanders of the forces of the army. [71]Jonathan rent his garments and put dust on his head, and prayed. [72]Then he turned back to the battle against the enemy[t] and routed them, and they fled. [73]When his men who were fleeing saw this, they returned to him and joined him in the pursuit as far as Kadesh, to their camp, and there they encamped. [74]As many as three thousand of the foreigners fell that day. And Jonathan returned to Jerusalem.

12 Now when Jonathan saw that the time was favorable for him, he chose men and sent them to Rome to confirm and renew the friendship with them. [2]He also sent letters to the same effect to the Spartans and to other places. [3]So they went to Rome and entered the senate chamber and said, "Jonathan the high priest and the Jewish nation have sent us to renew the former friendship and alliance with them." [4]And the Romans[u] gave them letters to the people in every place, asking them to provide for the envoys[v] safe conduct to the land of Judah.

[5] This is a copy of the letter which Jonathan wrote to the Spartans: [6]"Jonathan the high priest, the senate of the nation, the priests, and the rest of the Jewish people to their brethren the Spartans, greeting. [7]Already in time past a letter was sent to Onias the high priest from Arius,[w] who was king among you, stating that you are our brethren, as the appended copy shows. [8]Onias welcomed the envoy with honor, and received the letter, which contained a clear declaration of alliance and friendship. [9]Therefore, though we have no need of these things, since we have as encouragement the holy books which are in our hands, [10]we have undertaken to send to renew our brotherhood and friendship with you, so that we may not become estranged from you, for considerable time has passed since you sent your letter to us. [11]We therefore remember you constantly on every occasion, both in our feasts and on other appropriate days, at the sacrifices which we offer and in our prayers, as it is right and proper to remember brethren. [12]And we rejoice in your glory. [13]But as for ourselves, many afflictions and many wars have encircled us; the kings round about us have waged war against us. [14]We were unwilling to annoy you and our other allies and friends with these wars, [15]for we have the help which comes from Heaven for our aid; and we were delivered from our enemies and our enemies were humbled. [16]We there-

t Gk them
u Gk they
v Gk them
w Vg Compare verse 20: Gk Darius

67: *The waters of Gennesaret*, the Sea of Galilee. *Hazor*, southwest of Lake Huleh (Jos.11.1). 12.1–23: **Alliances with the Romans and Spartans** (compare ch. 8). 2: *The Spartans* had not joined the Achaean league against Rome. 4: *The Romans* continued the old alliance in order to keep Syria weak. 6: *The senate*, over which the high priest presided; it corresponds to the later council or Sanhedrin (Mk.14.55). 7: *Onias* I, high priest 320–290 B.C. *Arius*, king of Sparta fore have chosen Numenius the son of Antiochus and Antipater the son of Jason, and have sent them to Rome to renew our former friendship and alliance with them. [17]We have commanded them to go also to you and greet you and deliver to you this letter from us concerning the renewal of our brotherhood. [18]And now please send us a reply to this."

19 This is a copy of the letter which they sent to Onias: [20]"Arius, king of the Spartans, to Onias the high priest, greeting. [21]It has been found in writing concerning the Spartans and the Jews that they are brethren and are of the family of Abraham. [22]And now that we have learned this, please write us concerning your welfare; [23]we on our part write to you that your cattle and your property belong to us, and ours belong to you. We therefore command that our envoys[x] report to you accordingly."

24 Now Jonathan heard that the commanders of Demetrius had returned, with a larger force than before, to wage war against him. [25]So he marched away from Jerusalem and met them in the region of Hamath, for he gave them no opportunity to invade his own country. [26]He sent spies to their camp, and they returned and reported to him that the enemy[y] were being drawn up in formation to fall upon the Jews[z] by night. [27]So when the sun set, Jonathan commanded his men to be alert and to keep their arms at hand so as to be ready all night for battle, and he stationed outposts around the camp. [28]When the enemy heard that Jonathan and his men were prepared for battle, they were

afraid and were terrified at heart; so they kindled fires in their camp and withdrew.[a] [29]But Jonathan and his men did not know it until morning, for they saw the fires burning. [30]Then Jonathan pursued them, but he did not overtake them, for they had crossed the Eleutherus river. [31]So Jonathan turned aside against the Arabs who are called Zabadeans, and he crushed them and plundered them. [32]Then he broke camp and went to Damascus, and marched through all that region.

33 Simon also went forth and marched through the country as far as Askalon and the neighboring strongholds. He turned aside to Joppa and took it by surprise, [34]for he had heard that they were ready to hand over the stronghold to the men whom Demetrius had sent. And he stationed a garrison there to guard it.

35 When Jonathan returned he convened the elders of the people and planned with them to build strongholds in Judea, [36]to build the walls of Jerusalem still higher, and to erect a high barrier between the citadel and the city to separate it from the city, in order to isolate it so that its garrison[b] could neither buy nor sell. [37]So they gathered together to build up the city; part of the wall on the valley to the east had fallen, and he repaired the section called Chaphenatha. [38]And Simon built Adida in the Shephelah; he fortified it and installed gates with bolts.

39 Then Trypho attempted to become king of Asia and put on the crown, and to raise his hand against

x Gk *they*
y Gk *they*
z Gk *them*
a Other ancient authorities omit *and withdrew*
b Gk *they*

309–265 B.C. **21**: *Brethren . . . of the family of Abraham*, compare v. 7; such a tradition was evidently current in the East.
12.24–53: Jonathan captured by Trypho. 24–25: Jonathan met the Syrians at the border of Judea to prevent an invasion. *Hamath*, on the Orontes, modern Hama in Syria. **28**: *Kindled fires*, so that Jonathan would think they were still in camp. **30**: *The Eleutherus* is too far north (see 11.7 n.); perhaps the Orontes. **31**: *Zabadeans*, perhaps people northwest of Damascus. **36**: The purpose was to starve out the garrison. **37**: *The valley to the east*, the Kidron (1 Kg.2.37; Jn.18.1); here the slope was sometimes steep. The location of *Chaphenatha* is unknown. **38**: *Adida*, about three miles east of Lydda (Ezra 2.33; Neh.7.37). *Shephelah*, the foothill country

Antiochus the king. [40]He feared that Jonathan might not permit him to do so, but might make war on him, so he kept seeking to seize and kill him, and he marched forth and came to Beth-shan. [41]Jonathan went out to meet him with forty thousand picked fighting men, and he came to Beth-shan. [42]When Trypho saw that he had come with a large army, he was afraid to raise his hand against him. [43]So he received him with honor and commended him to all his friends, and he gave him gifts and commanded his friends and his troops to obey him as they would himself. [44]Then he said to Jonathan, "Why have you wearied all these people when we are not at war? [45]Dismiss them now to their homes and choose for yourself a few men to stay with you, and come with me to Ptolemais. I will hand it over to you as well as the other strongholds and the remaining troops and all the officials, and will turn round and go home. For that is why I am here."

46 Jonathan[c] trusted him and did as he said; he sent away the troops, and they returned to the land of Judah. [47]He kept with himself three thousand men, two thousand of whom he left in Galilee, while a thousand accompanied him. [48]But when Jonathan entered Ptolemais, the men of Ptolemais closed the gates and seized him, and all who had entered with him they killed with the sword.

49 Then Trypho sent troops and cavalry into Galilee and the Great Plain to destroy all Jonathan's soldiers. [50]But they realized that Jonathan[c] had been seized and had perished along with his men, and they encouraged one another and kept marching in close formation, ready for battle. [51]When their pursuers saw that they would fight for their lives, they turned back. [52]So they all reached the land of Judah safely, and they mourned for Jonathan and his companions and were in great fear; and all Israel mourned deeply. [53]And all the nations round about them tried to destroy them, for they said, "They have no leader or helper. Now therefore let us make war on them and blot out the memory of them from among men."

13 Simon heard that Trypho had assembled a large army to invade the land of Judah and destroy it, [2]and he saw that the people were trembling and fearful. So he went up to Jerusalem, and gathering the people together [3]he encouraged them, saying to them, "You yourselves know what great things I and my brothers and the house of my father have done for the laws and the sanctuary; you know also the wars and the difficulties which we have seen. [4]By reason of this all my brothers have perished for the sake of Israel, and I alone am left. [5]And now, far be it from me to spare my life in any time of distress, for I am not better than my brothers. [6]But I will avenge my nation and the sanctuary and your wives and children, for all the nations have gathered together out of hatred to destroy us."

7 The spirit of the people was rekindled when they heard these words, [8]and they answered in a loud voice, "You are our leader in place of Judas and Jonathan your brother. [9]Fight our battles, and all that you say to us we will do." [10]So he assembled all the warriors and hastened to complete the walls of Jerusalem, and he fortified it on every side. [11]He sent Jonathan the son of Absalom to Joppa, and with him

c Gk he

---

between the coastal plain and the central highlands. **40:** *Beth-shan*, see 5.52 n. **45:** *The other strongholds*, probably along the coast. **52:** *They mourned*, because of the supposition that Jonathan had been slain; but see 13.23.

    13.1–30: Simon becomes leader; death of Jonathan. 1: *Simon* (2.3) was governor of the coastal area (11.59). **4:** Eleazar, Judah, and John had died (6.46; 9.18,42), and Simon supposed that Jonathan had been slain. **7–8:** Jonathan had been chosen by his friends (9.28–30); *the people* now elected Simon *leader*, but not yet high priest (compare 14.41). **11:** *Jonathan the son of* a considerable army; he drove out its occupants and remained there.

12 Then Trypho departed from Ptolemais with a large army to invade the land of Judah, and Jonathan was with him under guard. ¹³And Simon encamped in Adida, facing the plain. ¹⁴Trypho learned that Simon had risen up in place of Jonathan his brother, and that he was about to join battle with him, so he sent envoys to him and said, ¹⁵"It is for the money that Jonathan your brother owed the royal treasury, in connection with the offices he held, that we are detaining him. ¹⁶Send now a hundred talents of silver and two of his sons as hostages, so that when released he will not revolt against us, and we will release him."

17 Simon knew that they were speaking deceitfully to him, but he sent to get the money and the sons, lest he arouse great hostility among the people, who might say, ¹⁸"Because Simon*ᵈ* did not send him the money and the sons, he perished." ¹⁹So he sent the sons and the hundred talents, but Trypho*ᵉ* broke his word and did not release Jonathan.

20 After this Trypho came to invade the country and destroy it, and he circled around by the way to Adora. But Simon and his army kept marching along opposite him to every place he went. ²¹Now the men in the citadel kept sending envoys to Trypho urging him to come to them by way of the wilderness and to send them food. ²²So Trypho got all his cavalry ready to go, but that night a very heavy snow fell, and he did not go because of the snow. He marched off and went into the land of Gilead. ²³When he approached Baskama, he killed Jonathan, and he

was buried there. ²⁴Then Trypho turned back and departed to his own land.

25 And Simon sent and took the bones of Jonathan his brother, and buried him in Modein, the city of his fathers. ²⁶All Israel bewailed him with great lamentation, and mourned for him many days. ²⁷And Simon built a monument over the tomb of his father and his brothers; he made it high that it might be seen, with polished stone at the front and back. ²⁸He also erected seven pyramids, opposite one another, for his father and mother and four brothers. ²⁹And for the pyramids*ᶠ* he devised an elaborate setting, erecting about them great columns, and upon the columns he put suits of armor for a permanent memorial, and beside the suits of armor carved ships, so that they could be seen by all who sail the sea. ³⁰This is the tomb which he built in Modein; it remains to this day.

31 Trypho dealt treacherously with the young king Antiochus; he killed him ³²and became king in his place, putting on the crown of Asia; and he brought great calamity upon the land. ³³But Simon built up the strongholds of Judea and walled them all around, with high towers and great walls and gates and bolts, and he stored food in the strongholds. ³⁴Simon also chose men and sent them to Demetrius the king with a request to grant relief to the country, for all that Trypho did was to plunder. ³⁵Demetrius the king sent him a favorable reply to this request, and wrote him a letter as follows, ³⁶"King Demetrius to Simon, the high

d Gk *I*   *e* Gk *he*
f Gk *for these*

Absalom, perhaps a brother of Mattathias (11.70). **15–16:** He regarded *Jonathan* as a vassal of Syria who had to pay for *the offices he held* (11.57). **20:** *Adora*, or Adoraim, now Dura, five miles southwest of Hebron (2 Chr.11.9). **22–23:** *He marched off*, south of the Dead Sea. *Baskama*, possibly northeast of the Sea of Galilee. *He killed Jonathan*, late in 143 or early in 142 B.C. **25:** *Modein*, 2.1; 9.19. **28:** *Pyramids*, following Egyptian fashion. **29:** *Carved ships*, symbols claiming domination of the sea, found also on coins of Herod and Archelaus.

   13.31–53: Simon makes Judea independent. 31–32: *He killed him*, probably in 142 B.C. *Antiochus* VI was about seven years old and had reigned since 145 (11.54). *Became king*, about 142 or 141 B.C. **34:** *Demetrius* II (see 10.67 n.) now disputed the throne with Trypho. **36–40:** The letter, addressed to *the elders and nation* and to *Simon* as head of a priestly state, recognizes priest and friend of kings, and to the elders and nation of the Jews, greeting. [37]We have received the gold crown and the palm branch which you[g] sent, and we are ready to make a general peace with you and to write to our officials to grant you release from tribute. [38]All the grants that we have made to you remain valid, and let the strongholds that you have built be your possession. [39]We pardon any errors and offenses committed to this day, and cancel the crown tax which you owe; and whatever other tax has been collected in Jerusalem shall be collected no longer. [40]And if any of you are qualified to be enrolled in our bodyguard,[h] let them be enrolled, and let there be peace between us."

41 In the one hundred and seventieth year[i] the yoke of the Gentiles was removed from Israel, [42]and the people began to write in their documents and contracts, "In the first year of Simon the great high priest and commander and leader of the Jews."

43 In those days Simon[j] encamped against Gazara[k] and surrounded it with troops. He made a siege engine, brought it up to the city, and battered and captured one tower. [44]The men in the siege engine leaped out into the city, and a great tumult arose in the city. [45]The men in the city, with their wives and children, went up on the wall with their clothes rent, and they cried out with a loud voice, asking Simon to make peace with them; [46]they said, "Do not treat us according to our wicked acts but according to your mercy." [47]So Simon reached an agreement with them and stopped fighting against them. But he expelled

them from the city and cleansed the houses in which the idols were, and then entered it with hymns and praise. [48]He cast out of it all uncleanness, and settled in it men who observed the law. He also strengthened its fortifications and built in it a house for himself.

49 The men in the citadel at Jerusalem were prevented from going out to the country and back to buy and sell. So they were very hungry, and many of them perished from famine. [50]Then they cried to Simon to make peace with them, and he did so. But he expelled them from there and cleansed the citadel from its pollutions. [51]On the twenty-third day of the second month, in the one hundred and seventy-first year,[l] the Jews[m] entered it with praise and palm branches, and with harps and cymbals and stringed instruments, and with hymns and songs, because a great enemy had been crushed and removed from Israel. [52]And Simon[n] decreed that every year they should celebrate this day with rejoicing. He strengthened the fortifications of the temple hill alongside the citadel, and he and his men dwelt there. [53]And Simon saw that John his son had reached manhood, so he made him commander of all the forces, and he dwelt in Gazara.

14 In the one hundred and seventy-second year[o] Demetrius the king assembled his forces and marched into Media to secure help, so that he could make war against Trypho.

g The word *you* in verses 37–40 is plural
h Or *court*
i 142 B.C.
j Gk *he*
k Cn: Gk *Gaza*
l 141 B.C.
m Gk *they*
n Gk *he*
o 140 B.C.

sovereignty (compare v. 42). The weakness of Demetrius II made possible a great diplomatic victory. **42:** The new era, replacing the Seleucid era, is a mark of sovereignty. It is debated whether Simon was the first of the Hasmoneans to strike coins. **43:** A Greek inscription hostile to Simon has been found at *Gazara*. **47–48:** The later Hasmoneans continued the policy of settling Jews in strategic places. **49–50:** *The men in the citadel*, probably Trypho's men, did not surrender until starved out. **51:** *The second month*, Iyyar or May. *Palm branches* symbolized victory (2 Macc.10.7). **52:** *Celebrate this day*, see 7.49 n. **53:** *John* Hyrcanus reigned as high priest 134–104 B.C.

14.1–24: Capture of Demetrius II. 1: Other historians date this invasion in 138 B.C., the year

²When Arsaces the king of Persia and Media heard that Demetrius had invaded his territory, he sent one of his commanders to take him alive. ³And he went and defeated the army of Demetrius, and seized him and took him to Arsaces, who put him under guard.

⁴The land*ᵖ* had rest all the days of
Simon.
He sought the good of his
nation;
his rule was pleasing to them,
as was the honor shown him, all
his days.
⁵To crown all his honors he took
Joppa for a harbor,
and opened a way to the isles of
the sea.
⁶He extended the borders of his
nation,
and gained full control of the
country.
⁷He gathered a host of captives;
he ruled over Gazara and
Beth-zur and the citadel,
and he removed its uncleanness
from it;
and there was none to oppose
him.
⁸They tilled their land in peace;
the ground gave its increase,
and the trees of the plains their
fruit.
⁹Old men sat in the streets;
they all talked together of good
things;
and the youths donned the
glories and garments of war.
¹⁰He supplied the cities with food,
and furnished them with the
means of defense,
till his renown spread to the ends
of the earth.

¹¹He established peace in the land,
and Israel rejoiced with great joy.
¹²Each man sat under his vine and
his fig tree,
and there was none to make
them afraid.
¹³No one was left in the land to fight
them,
and the kings were crushed in
those days.
¹⁴He strengthened all the humble of
his people;
he sought out the law,
and did away with every lawless
and wicked man.
¹⁵He made the sanctuary glorious,
and added to the vessels of the
sanctuary.

16 It was heard in Rome, and as far away as Sparta, that Jonathan had died, and they were deeply grieved. ¹⁷When they heard that Simon his brother had become high priest in his place, and that he was ruling over the country and the cities in it, ¹⁸they wrote to him on bronze tablets to renew with him the friendship and alliance which they had established with Judas and Jonathan his brothers. ¹⁹And these were read before the assembly in Jerusalem.

20 This is a copy of the letter which the Spartans sent: "The rulers and the city of the Spartans to Simon the high priest and to the elders and the priests and the rest of the Jewish people, our brethren, greeting. ²¹The envoys who were sent to our people have told us about your glory and honor, and we rejoiced at their coming. ²²And what they said we have recorded in our public decrees, as follows, 'Numenius the son of Antiochus and Antipater the

ᵖ Other authorities add *of Judah*

---

in which he was captured. *Media*, lying west of Tehran, was still claimed by the Seleucids. **2–3:** *Arsaces* VI Mithradates I (171–138 B.C.), founder of the Parthian Empire, treated Demetrius kindly and later married him to his sister.

14.4–15: A contemporary poem of rejoicing. **5–7:** 13.41–53. *A harbor*, important for trade connections with the sea (13.11). *The isles of the sea*, Cyprus, Rhodes, and Crete. **12:** 1 Kg.4.25; Mic.4.4.

14.16–24: Alliances with Rome and Sparta. Simon was perhaps the first high priest recognized by the Roman senate as ruler of the Jews. **19:** *The assembly*, the people as a whole. **22:** *Numenius* and *Antipater*, 12.16.

son of Jason, envoys of the Jews, have come to us to renew their friendship with us. ²³It has pleased our people to receive these men with honor and to put a copy of their words in the public archives, so that the people of the Spartans may have a record of them. And they have sent a copy of this to Simon the high priest.' "

24 After this Simon sent Numenius to Rome with a large gold shield weighing a thousand minas, to confirm the alliance with the Romans.�q

25 When the people heard these things they said, "How shall we thank Simon and his sons? ²⁶For he and his brothers and the house of his father have stood firm; they have fought and repulsed Israel's enemies and established its freedom." ²⁷So they made a record on bronze tablets and put it upon pillars on Mount Zion.

This is a copy of what they wrote: "On the eighteenth day of Elul, in the one hundred and seventy-second year,ʳ which is the third year of Simon the great high priest, ²⁸in Asaramel,ˢ in the great assembly of the priests and the people and the rulers of the nation and the elders of the country, the following was proclaimed to us:

29 "Since wars often occurred in the country, Simon the son of Matta-thias, a priest of the sonsᵗ of Joarib, and his brothers, exposed themselves to danger and resisted the enemies of their nation, in order that their sanctuary and the law might be preserved; and they brought great glory to their nation. ³⁰Jonathan rallied theᵘ nation, and became their high priest, and was gathered to his people. ³¹And when their enemies decided to invade their

country and lay hands on their sanctuary, ³²then Simon rose up and fought for his nation. He spent great sums of his own money; he armed the men of his nation's forces and paid them wages. ³³He fortified the cities of Judea, and Beth-zur on the borders of Judea, where formerly the arms of the enemy had been stored, and he placed there a garrison of Jews. ³⁴He also fortified Joppa, which is by the sea, and Gazara, which is on the borders of Azotus, where the enemy formerly dwelt. He settled Jews there, and provided in those citiesᵛ whatever was necessary for their restoration.

35 "The people saw Simon's faithfulnessʷ and the glory which he had resolved to win for his nation, and they made him their leader and high priest, because he had done all these things and because of the justice and loyalty which he had maintained toward his nation. He sought in every way to exalt his people. ³⁶And in his days things prospered in his hands, so that the Gentiles were put out of theˣ country, as were also the men in the city of David in Jerusalem, who had built themselves a citadel from which they used to sally forth and defile the environs of the sanctuary and do great damage to its purity. ³⁷He settled Jews in it, and fortified it for the safety of the country and of the city, and built the walls of Jerusalem higher.

38 "In view of these things King Demetrius confirmed him in the high priesthood, ³⁹and he made him one of

q Gk them   r 140 B.C.
s This word resembles the Hebrew words for *the court of the people of God* or *the prince of the people of God*
t The Greek text of this phrase is uncertain
u Gk *their*   v Gk *them*
w Other authorities read *conduct*   x Gk *their*

24: *Weighing a thousand minas*, an obvious exaggeration; a Greek mina is over 15 ounces (troy).
  14.25–49: **Simon elected high priest, military commander, and ruler.** The formal document of vv. 27–49 served as a constitution for the new state of Judea. 27–28: *Bronze tablets,* see 8.22 n. *Mount Zion,* 1.33; 4.37. *Elul,* August-September. *Third year,* see 13.42 n. *The great assembly,* or synagogue, represented all "states" or classes. In theory the high priest held his office by divine appointment, indicated by descent from a particular family. Since there was no legitimate claimant, Simon was legitimized by a democratic process (v. 41). 29: *Sons of Joarib,* see 2.1 n. 30: The decree recognizes in retrospect the office of *Jonathan,* first Hasmonean *high priest.* 32: Use of *his own money* had not been previously mentioned. 33–34: 13.43–48; 14.3–7. 35: The high priest must have moral responsibility along with his powers. 36–37: 1.34; 4.41,60;

the king's[y] friends and paid him high honors. [40]For he had heard that the Jews were addressed by the Romans as friends and allies and brethren, and that the Romans[z] had received the envoys of Simon with honor.

[41] "And[a] the Jews and their priests decided that Simon should be their leader and high priest for ever, until a trustworthy prophet should arise, [42]and that he should be governor over them and that he should take charge of the sanctuary and appoint men over its tasks and over the country and the weapons and the strongholds, and that he should take charge of the sanctuary, [43]and that he should be obeyed by all, and that all contracts in the country should be written in his name, and that he should be clothed in purple and wear gold.

[44] "And none of the people or priests shall be permitted to nullify any of these decisions or to oppose what he says, or to convene an assembly in the country without his permission, or to be clothed in purple or put on a gold buckle. [45]Whoever acts contrary to these decisions or nullifies any of them shall be liable to punishment."

[46] And all the people agreed to grant Simon the right to act in accord with these decisions. [47]So Simon accepted and agreed to be high priest, to be commander and ethnarch of the Jews and priests, and to be protector of them all.[b] [48]And they gave orders to inscribe this decree upon bronze tablets, to put them up in a conspicuous place in the precincts of the sanctuary, [49]and to deposit copies of them in the treasury, so that Simon and his sons might have them.

15 Antiochus, the son of Demetrius the king, sent a letter from the islands of the sea to Simon, the priest and ethnarch of the Jews, and to all the nation; [2]its contents were as follows: "King Antiochus to Simon the high priest and ethnarch and to the nation of the Jews, greeting. [3]Whereas certain pestilent men have gained control of the kingdom of our fathers, and I intend to lay claim to the kingdom so that I may restore it as it formerly was, and have recruited a host of mercenary troops and have equipped warships, [4]and intend to make a landing in the country so that I may proceed against those who have destroyed our country and those who have devastated many cities in my kingdom, [5]now therefore I confirm to you all the tax remissions that the kings before me have granted you, and release from all the other payments from which they have released you. [6]I permit you to mint your own coinage as money for your country, [7]and I grant freedom to Jerusalem and the sanctuary. All the weapons which you have prepared and the strongholds which you have built and now hold shall remain yours. [8]Every debt you owe to the royal treasury and any such future debts shall be canceled for you from henceforth and for all time. [9]When we gain control of our kingdom, we will bestow great honor upon you and your nation and the temple, so that your glory

y Gk *his*   *z* Gk *they*
a Gk *honor; and that*
b Or *to preside over them all*

6.18; 13.49–52. **41–43:** The office was to be hereditary in Simon's family, but since this was an act of the nation rather than of God, a *trustworthy prophet* might annul or confirm the decision (see 4.46 n.). *Clothed in purple and wear gold*, like a king or head of state. From Alexander Janneus onwards (103–76 B.C.), the Hasmoneans assumed the title of king. **46–47:** In this social contract, both the people and Simon accept the conditions. *Ethnarch*, civil magistrate. **49:** The *treasury* in the temple served as a national archive.

    15.1–14: Arrival of Antiochus VII. 1: *Antiochus* VII (known as Sidetes because reared at Side in Pamphylia), younger brother of Demetrius II, reigned 138–129 B.C. After his brother's capture he married Cleopatra III (10.57–58; 11.12). **5:** He reaffirms his brother's grants (13.39). **6:** *To mint your own coinage* was legal recognition of independence. When the Seleucids permitted subject cities to coin money, it bore the king's name. **7–8:** 13.38–39.

will become manifest in all the earth."

10 In the one hundred and seventy-fourth year[c] Antiochus set out and invaded the land of his fathers. All the troops rallied to him, so that there were few with Trypho. [11]Antiochus pursued him, and he came in his flight to Dor, which is by the sea; [12]for he knew that troubles had converged upon him, and his troops had deserted him. [13]So Antiochus encamped against Dor, and with him were a hundred and twenty thousand warriors and eight thousand cavalry. [14]He surrounded the city, and the ships joined battle from the sea; he pressed the city hard from land and sea, and permitted no one to leave or enter it.

15 Then Numenius and his companions arrived from Rome, with letters to the kings and countries, in which the following was written: [16]"Lucius, consul of the Romans, to King Ptolemy, greeting. [17]The envoys of the Jews have come to us as our friends and allies to renew our ancient friendship and alliance. They had been sent by Simon the high priest and by the people of the Jews, [18]and have brought a gold shield weighing a thousand minas. [19]We therefore have decided to write to the kings and countries that they should not seek their harm or make war against them and their cities and their country, or make alliance with those who war against them. [20]And it has seemed good to us to accept the shield from them. [21]Therefore if any pestilent men have fled to you from their country, hand them over to Simon the high priest, that he may punish them according to their law."

22 The consul[d] wrote the same thing to Demetrius the king and to Attalus and Ariarathes and Arsaces, [23]and to all the countries, and to Sampsames,[e] and to the Spartans, and to Delos, and to Myndos, and to Sicyon, and to Caria, and to Samos, and to Pamphylia, and to Lycia, and to Halicarnassus, and to Rhodes, and to Phaselis, and to Cos, and to Side, and to Aradus and Gortyna and Cnidus and Cyprus and Cyrene. [24]They also sent a copy of these things to Simon the high priest.

25 Antiochus the king besieged Dor anew,[f] continually throwing his forces against it and making engines of war; and he shut Trypho up and kept him from going out or in. [26]And Simon sent to Antiochus[g] two thousand picked men, to fight for him, and silver and gold and much military equipment. [27]But he refused to receive them, and he broke all the agreements he formerly had made with Simon,[g] and became estranged from him. [28]He sent to him Athenobius, one of his friends, to confer with him, saying, "You hold control of Joppa and Gazara and the citadel in Jerusalem; they are cities of my kingdom. [29]You have devastated their territory, you have done great damage in the land, and you have taken possession of many places in my kingdom. [30]Now then, hand over the cities which you have seized and the tribute money of the places which you have conquered outside the borders of Judea; [31]or else give me for them five hundred talents of silver, and for the destruction that you have caused and

c 138 B.C.   d Gk *He*
e The name is uncertain
f Or *on the second day*
g Gk *him*

10: He first landed in Seleucia (11.8), where Cleopatra was living.   **11:** *Dor,* about nine miles north of Caesarea (Jg.1.27).   **13:** The numbers are probably exaggerated.
  15.15–24: Renewal of alliance with Rome. 16: If the letter is genuine, this is *Lucius* Calpurnius Piso, consul 140–139 B.C. *Ptolemy* VII Physcon reigned 145–116 B.C. **18:** *Shield,* see 14.24 n.
22–23: *Demetrius* II was still a prisoner in Parthia; the Romans had not recognized Antiochus VII. *Attalus* II, king of Pergamum 159–138 B.C.; *Ariarathes* V, king of Cappadocia 162–130 B.C. *Delos* in the Cyclades and the other localities were free states in Greece, the Greek islands and Asia Minor. *Cyrene,* capital of Libya.
  15.25–16.10: War with Antiochus VII. 27: Josephus says that Antiochus accepted this aid (*Antiquities,* XIII. vii, 2). **28:** *Cities of my kingdom,* this contradicts v. 7. **30:** *Outside . . . Judea,*

the tribute money of the cities, five hundred talents more. Otherwise we will come and conquer you."

32 So Athenobius the friend of the king came to Jerusalem, and when he saw the splendor of Simon, and the sideboard with its gold and silver plate, and his great magnificence, he was amazed. He reported to him the words of the king, ³³but Simon gave him this reply: "We have neither taken foreign land nor seized foreign property, but only the inheritance of our fathers, which at one time had been unjustly taken by our enemies. ³⁴Now that we have the opportunity, we are firmly holding the inheritance of our fathers. ³⁵As for Joppa and Gazara, which you demand, they were causing great damage among the people and to our land; for them we will give a hundred talents." Athenobius^h did not answer him a word, ³⁶but returned in wrath to the king and reported to him these words and the splendor of Simon and all that he had seen. And the king was greatly angered.

37 Now Trypho embarked on a ship and escaped to Orthosia. ³⁸Then the king made Cendebeus commander-in-chief of the coastal country, and gave him troops of infantry and cavalry. ³⁹He commanded him to encamp against Judea, and commanded him to build up Kedron and fortify its gates, and to make war on the people; but the king pursued Trypho. ⁴⁰So Cendebeus came to Jamnia and began to provoke the people and invade Judea and take the people captive and kill them. ⁴¹He built up Kedron and stationed there horsemen and troops, so that they might go out and make raids along the highways of Judea, as the king had ordered him.

16 John went up from Gazara and reported to Simon his father what Cendebeus had done. ²And Simon called in his two older sons Judas and John, and said to them: "I and my brothers and the house of my father have fought the wars of Israel from our youth until this day, and things have prospered in our hands so that we have delivered Israel many times. ³But now I have grown old, and you by His mercy are mature in years. Take my place and my brother's, and go out and fight for our nation, and may the help which comes from Heaven be with you."

4 So John^i chose out of the country twenty thousand warriors and horsemen, and they marched against Cendebeus and camped for the night in Modein. ⁵Early in the morning they arose and marched into the plain, and behold, a large force of infantry and horsemen was coming to meet them; and a stream lay between them. ⁶Then he and his army lined up against them. And he saw that the soldiers were afraid to cross the stream, so he crossed over first; and when his men saw him, they crossed over after him. ⁷Then he divided the army and placed the horsemen in the midst of the infantry, for the cavalry of the enemy were very numerous. ⁸And they sounded the trumpets, and Cendebeus and his army were put to flight, and many of them were wounded and fell; the rest fled into the stronghold. ⁹At that time Judas the brother of John was wounded, but John pursued them until Cendebeus^j reached Kedron, which he had built. ¹⁰They also fled into the towers that were in the fields of Azotus,

h Gk *He*   *i* Other authorities read *he*
j Gk *he*

---

perhaps the districts of 11.34; but compare v. 8. **33**: The Hasmoneans claimed that all Palestine had always belonged by right to the Jews. **35**: *Joppa and Gazara*, 12.33; 13.43–48. **37**: *Orthosia*, a few miles north of Tripolis; from there Trypho went to Apamea, where he was besieged and slain. **39–40**: *Kedron*, perhaps Gedereth, southwest of Ekron (Jos.15.41). The plan was to control the coastal plain and recover Gazara and Joppa (13.53). **4**: *Horsemen* are now for the first time part of the Judean army. **7**: The cavalry were unseasoned, and he protected their flanks. **8**: *The stronghold*, Kedron (15.39). **10**: *Azotus*, destroyed by Jonathan (10.84).

and John[j] burned it with fire, and about two thousand of them fell. And he returned to Judea safely.

11 Now Ptolemy the son of Abubus had been appointed governor over the plain of Jericho, and he had much silver and gold, [12]for he was son-in-law of the high priest. [13]His heart was lifted up; he determined to get control of the country, and made treacherous plans against Simon and his sons, to do away with them. [14]Now Simon was visiting the cities of the country and attending to their needs, and he went down to Jericho with Mattathias and Judas his sons, in the one hundred and seventy-seventh year,[k] in the eleventh month, which is the month of Shebat. [15]The son of Abubus received them treacherously in the little stronghold called Dok, which he had built; he gave them a great banquet, and hid men there. [16]When Simon and his sons were drunk, Ptolemy and his men rose up, took their weapons, and rushed in against Simon in the banquet hall, and they killed him and his two sons and some of his servants. [17]So he committed an act of great treachery and returned evil for good.

18 Then Ptolemy wrote a report about these things and sent it to the king, asking him to send troops to aid him and to turn over to him the cities and the country. [19]He sent other men to Gazara to do away with John; he sent letters to the captains asking them to come to him so that he might give them silver and gold and gifts; [20]and he sent other men to take possession of Jerusalem and the temple hill. [21]But some one ran ahead and reported to John at Gazara that his father and brothers had perished, and that "he has sent men to kill you also." [22]When he heard this, he was greatly shocked; and he seized the men who came to destroy him and killed them, for he had found out that they were seeking to destroy him.

23 The rest of the acts of John and his wars and the brave deeds which he did, and the building of the walls which he built, and his achievements, [24]behold, they are written in the chronicles of his high priesthood, from the time that he became high priest after his father.

j Gk *he*
k 134 B.C.

16.11–24: Death of Simon and accession of John Hyrcanus I. 11: *Plain of Jericho*, the fertile region north of the Dead Sea. 12: *The high priest*, Simon. 14: *Shebat*, February-March. 15: *Dok*, 'Ain Duq, three miles northwest of Jericho. 18: *The king*, Antiochus VII. 23: *John* was high priest 134–104 B.C. When Antiochus later besieged Jerusalem, John was defeated but made peace and accompanied the king on an expedition to Parthia, where Antiochus was killed. Afterward he gained control of most of Palestine, and forced the Idumeans to adopt Judaism. Late in his reign the Pharisees turned against him and demanded that he give up the high priesthood. 24: *The chronicles* have been lost.

THE SECOND BOOK OF THE

MACCABEES

Second Maccabees is an epitome or abridgment (2.23–28) of a five volume history, now lost, written by a certain Jason of Cyrene. Both Jason's work and 2 Maccabees were evidently composed in Greek, in which language the latter has been preserved. Jason narrated the events of Jewish history from the time of the high priest Onias III and the Syrian king Seleucus IV to the defeat of Nicanor's army (from about 180 to 161 B.C.), thus paralleling 1 Macc.1.10–7.50.

The purpose of Jason was to interpret history theologically. One of his favorite themes is the sanctity of the temple. He is the first writer known to us who celebrates the deeds of the martyrs, though there is a foreshadowing of such an interest in the book of Daniel. He also seems to be the first to teach clearly that the world was created out of nothing (7.28). He believed that the saints in heaven interceded for men on earth (15.11–16), and that the living might pray and offer sacrifices for the dead (12.43–45). His book includes accounts of marvelous portents and the miraculous intervention of angels. Jason seems not to have been a Pharisee; he may reflect the ideas of Jews at Antioch or possibly Alexandria.

The epitomist added chs. 1–2, 15.37–39, and several pretentious comments elsewhere. Sometimes there are signs of careless abbreviation, and he may have rearranged some incidents. Jason's history was probably not written before 110 B.C., and 2 Maccabees, as we have it, may have been composed some time during the first century B.C. It often supplements the information contained in 1 Maccabees, but its historical veracity is, on the whole, less trustworthy than that of 1 Maccabees.

THE JEWISH BRETHREN IN JERUSALEM and those in the land of Judea, To their Jewish brethren in Egypt, Greeting, and good peace.

2 May God do good to you, and may he remember his covenant with Abraham and Isaac and Jacob, his faithful servants. ³May he give you all a heart to worship him and to do his will with a strong heart and a willing spirit. ⁴May he open your heart to his law and his commandments, and may he bring peace. ⁵May he hear your prayers and be reconciled to you, and may he not forsake you in time of evil. ⁶We are now praying for you here.

7 In the reign of Demetrius, in the one hundred and sixty-ninth year,ᵃ we Jews wrote to you, in the critical distress which came upon us in those years after Jason and his company revolted from the holy land and the kingdom ⁸and burned the gate and shed innocent blood. We besought the Lord and we were heard, and we offered sacrifice and cereal offering, and we lighted the lamps and we set out the loaves. ⁹And now see that you keep the feast of booths in the month of Chislev, in the one hundred and eighty-eighth year.ᵇ

a 143 B.C.
b 124 B.C.

1.1–9: Letter to the Jews in Egypt. The epitomist, who abridged the history of Jason of Cyrene (2.23), includes two letters urging that the new festival be kept (v. 9). The first is addressed to the large Jewish community that had lived in Egypt since Alexander the Great (1 Macc.1.1). **1:** Greek letters usually began with the word *greeting*, and Jewish ones with *peace* (Rom.1.7). **2:** Gen.15.18; 26.3; 35.12; Lev.26.27–45. **5:** To live outside Judea was thought of as divine punishment. **7:** The previous letter was in the reign of Demetrius II (see 1 Macc. 10.67 n.). *The critical distress* was the capture and murder of the high priest Jonathan (1 Macc. 12.48; see 13.23 n.). *Jason and his company*, 4.7–22. *The kingdom*, rule of the legitimate high priests. **8:** *Burned the gate*, 1 Macc.4.38. *Shed innocent blood*, 1 Macc.1.60–61. *We were heard*, i.e. by God, when Simon made Judea independent (1 Macc.13.1–42). **9:** *The feast of booths* would properly be kept in September (Lev.23.33–43). This refers to Hanukkah, celebrated on the 25th of *Chislev* (November-December), commemorating Judas Maccabeus' restoration of the temple (10.1–8; 1 Macc.4.59). Palestinian Jews now wished the Egyptian Jews to observe the feast in 124 B.C., when they wrote.

[263]

10 Those in Jerusalem and those in Judea and the senate and Judas,

To Aristobulus, who is of the family of the anointed priests, teacher of Ptolemy the king, and to the Jews in Egypt,

Greeting, and good health.

11 Having been saved by God out of grave dangers we thank him greatly for taking our side against the king.ᶜ ¹²For he drove out those who fought against the holy city. ¹³For when the leader reached Persia with a force that seemed irresistible, they were cut to pieces in the temple of Nanea by a deception employed by the priests of Nanea. ¹⁴For under pretext of intending to marry her, Antiochus came to the place together with his friends, to secure most of its treasures as a dowry. ¹⁵When the priests of the temple of Nanea had set out the treasures and Antiochus had come with a few men inside the wall of the sacred precinct, they closed the temple as soon as he entered it. ¹⁶Opening the secret door in the ceiling, they threw stones and struck down the leader and his men, and dismembered them and cut off their heads and threw them to the people outside. ¹⁷Blessed in every way be our God, who has brought judgment upon those who have behaved impiously.

18 Since on the twenty-fifth day of Chislev we shall celebrate the purification of the temple, we thought it necessary to notify you, in order that you also may celebrate the feast of booths and the feast of the fire given when Nehemiah, who built the temple and the altar, offered sacrifices.

19 For when our fathers were being led captive to Persia, the pious priests of that time took some of the fire of the altar and secretly hid it in the hollow of a dry cistern, where they took such precautions that the place was unknown to any one. ²⁰But after many years had passed, when it pleased God, Nehemiah, having been commissioned by the king of Persia, sent the descendants of the priests who had hidden the fire to get it. And when they reported to us that they had not found fire but thick liquid, he ordered them to dip it out and bring it. ²¹And when the materials for the sacrifices were presented, Nehemiah ordered the priests to sprinkle the liquid on the wood and what was laid upon it. ²²When this was done and some time had passed and the sun, which had been clouded over, shone out, a great fire blazed up, so that all marveled. ²³And while the sacrifice was being consumed, the priests offered prayer—the priests and every one. Jonathan led, and the rest responded, as did Nehemiah. ²⁴The prayer was to this effect:

"O Lord, Lord God, Creator of all things, who art awe-inspiring and strong and just and merciful, who alone art King and art kind, ²⁵who alone art bountiful, who alone art just and al-

c Cn: Gk *as those who array themselves against a king*

1.10–2.18: Letter to Aristobulus. The purpose of the letter is to show why the new eight day festival should be kept, though it had not been prescribed by the Mosaic law. Nehemiah's rededication of the temple was a precedent (1.18–36). **10:** *The senate,* see 1 Macc.12.6 n. *The anointed priests,* descendants of Zadok (2 Chr.31.10), from whom high priests were chosen. One branch of these came to Egypt with Ptolemy I. *The king,* Ptolemy VII Physcon, who reigned 145–116 B.C. **11:** *Grave dangers,* in the time of king Antiochus IV (4.7). **13:** *The leader,* Antiochus IV, died later; his forces *were cut to pieces* (9.1–4; 1 Macc.6.1–4). *Nanea,* a Syrian goddess equated with Artemis or Aphrodite and the Persian Anahita. **14:** *Marry her,* the goddess, so as to obtain a large *dowry* from the treasures at her temple (compare 9.2; 1 Macc.6.1–4). **18:** *The feast of booths,* compare 1 Macc.10.21; 1 Kg.8.2; Neh.8.13–18. *The feast of the fire,* vv. 19–36. Fire and light are associated with Hanukkah, which is celebrated with a nine-branched candlestick. A Talmudic tradition tells of a small amount of oil that burned miraculously for a long time till new oil could be consecrated. **19:** *Persia,* actually Babylonia (2 Kg.24.14), later part of the Persian empire. **20:** *Nehemiah . . . commissioned,* Neh.2.7–8; his book does not contain the legend of the fire. *Thick liquid,* naphtha or petroleum (v. 36). **22:** 1 Kg.18.33–38.

mighty and eternal, who dost rescue Israel from every evil, who didst choose the fathers and consecrate them, ²⁶accept this sacrifice on behalf of all thy people Israel and preserve thy portion and make it holy. ²⁷Gather together our scattered people, set free those who are slaves among the Gentiles, look upon those who are rejected and despised, and let the Gentiles know that thou art our God. ²⁸Afflict those who oppress and are insolent with pride. ²⁹Plant thy people in thy holy place, as Moses said."

30 Then the priests sang the hymns. ³¹And when the materials of the sacrifice were consumed, Nehemiah ordered that the liquid that was left should be poured upon large stones. ³²When this was done, a flame blazed up; but when the light from the altar shone back, it went out. ³³When this matter became known, and it was reported to the king of the Persians that, in the place where the exiled priests had hidden the fire, the liquid had appeared with which Nehemiah and his associates had burned the materials of the sacrifice, ³⁴the king investigated the matter, and enclosed the place and made it sacred. ³⁵And with those persons whom the king favored he exchanged many excellent gifts. ³⁶Nehemiah and his associates called this "nephthar," which means purification, but by most people it is called naphtha.[d]

2 One finds in the records that Jeremiah the prophet ordered those who were being deported to take some of the fire, as has been told, ²and that the prophet after giving them the law instructed those who were being de-

ported not to forget the commandments of the Lord, nor to be led astray in their thoughts upon seeing the gold and silver statues and their adornment. ³And with other similar words he exhorted them that the law should not depart from their hearts.

4 It was also in the writing that the prophet, having received an oracle, ordered that the tent and the ark should follow with him, and that he went out to the mountain where Moses had gone up and had seen the inheritance of God. ⁵And Jeremiah came and found a cave, and he brought there the tent and the ark and the altar of incense, and he sealed up the entrance. ⁶Some of those who followed him came up to mark the way, but could not find it. ⁷When Jeremiah learned of it, he rebuked them and declared: "The place shall be unknown until God gathers his people together again and shows his mercy. ⁸And then the Lord will disclose these things, and the glory of the Lord and the cloud will appear, as they were shown in the case of Moses, and as Solomon asked that the place should be specially consecrated."

9 It was also made clear that being possessed of wisdom Solomon[e] offered sacrifice for the dedication and completion of the temple. ¹⁰Just as Moses prayed to the Lord, and fire came down from heaven and devoured the sacrifices, so also Solomon prayed, and the fire came down and consumed the whole burnt offerings. ¹¹And Moses said, "They were consumed because the sin offering had not been eaten."

d Gk *nephthai*   *e* Gk *he*

25: *Who didst choose*, Gen.12.1–3; 22.15–18; Dt.14.2; Mal.1.2. **26:** *Thy portion*, Israel (Dt.32.9). *Holy*, Lev.19.2. **27:** *Gather together*, Ps.147.2; Jer.23.8; Sir.36.11; Bar.5.6. **28:** *Afflict . . . insolent*, 1 Sam.2.3–4; Lk.1.51–52. **29:** *As Moses said*, Dt.30.5. **34:** Localities where miracles occurred were *enclosed* as *sacred*. The Persians considered fire holy. **36:** *Nephthar* is an otherwise unknown word. **2.1:** No such *records* are known. *Jeremiah* remained in Judea after the exile (Jer.29.1–23; 40.1–42.7). **4:** Solomon brought the *tent* to Jerusalem with the ark (1 Kg.8.4). There is no further record in the Old Testament of the tent, but the ark was kept in the first temple; according to a later tradition Jeremiah concealed the ark after the temple was destroyed in 587–6 B.C. *The mountain*, Nebo (Dt.32.49). **8:** *The glory* and *the cloud* indicate God's direct presence (Ex.16.10; Mk.9.2–8). *Solomon*, 1 Kg.8.11. **9:** Solomon's *wisdom*, 1 Kg. 3.3–28; 4.29–34. *Offered sacrifice*, 1 Kg.8.62–64. **10:** *Moses prayed*, Lev.9.24. *Solomon*, 2 Chr.

¹²Likewise Solomon also kept the eight days.

13 The same things are reported in the records and in the memoirs of Nehemiah, and also that he founded a library and collected the books about the kings and prophets, and the writings of David, and letters of kings about votive offerings. ¹⁴In the same way Judas also collected all the books that had been lost on account of the war which had come upon us, and they are in our possession. ¹⁵So if you have need of them, send people to get them for you.

16 Since, therefore, we are about to celebrate the purification, we write to you. Will you therefore please keep the days? ¹⁷It is God who has saved all his people, and has returned the inheritance to all, and the kingship and priesthood and consecration, ¹⁸as he promised through the law. For we have hope in God that he will soon have mercy upon us and will gather us from everywhere under heaven into his holy place, for he has rescued us from great evils and has purified the place.

19 The story of Judas Maccabeus and his brothers, and the purification of the great temple, and the dedication of the altar, ²⁰and further the wars against Antiochus Epiphanes and his son Eupator, ²¹and the appearances which came from heaven to those who strove zealously on behalf of Judaism, so that though few in number they seized the whole land and pursued the barbarian hordes, ²²and recovered the temple famous throughout the world and freed the city and restored the laws that were about to be abolished, while the Lord with great kindness became gracious to them—²³all this, which has been set forth by Jason of Cyrene in five volumes, we shall attempt to condense into a single book. ²⁴For considering the flood of numbers involved and the difficulty there is for those who wish to enter upon the narratives of history because of the mass of material, ²⁵we have aimed to please those who wish to read, to make it easy for those who are inclined to memorize, and to profit all readers. ²⁶For us who have undertaken the toil of abbreviating, it is no light matter but calls for sweat and loss of sleep, ²⁷just as it is not easy for one who prepares a banquet and seeks the benefit of others. However, to secure the gratitude of many we will gladly endure the uncomfortable toil, ²⁸leaving the responsibility for exact details to the compiler, while devoting our effort to arriving at the outlines of the condensation. ²⁹For as the master builder of a new house must be concerned with the whole construction, while the one who undertakes its painting and decoration has to consider only what is suitable for its adornment, such in my judgment is the case with us. ³⁰It is the duty of the original historian to occupy the ground and to discuss matters from every side and to take trouble with details, ³¹but the one who

---

7.1. **11:** The meaning is obscure, but see Lev.10.16–19. **12:** *Eight days*, 1 Kg.8.65; 2 Chr.7.9. **13:** *The memoirs of Nehemiah*, Neh. ch. 8. There is no record that *he founded a library*, but the Pentateuch was canonized in his time, and part of *the books . . . and the writings of David* were perhaps collected then. *Votive offerings*, made to the temple (Ezra 7.15–20). **14:** *Judas* Maccabeus may have *collected all the books* remaining after the destruction in the time of Antiochus IV (1 Macc.1.56–57). **16:** 1.18. **17:** *The kingship*, independence; the Hasmoneans were not yet called kings. **18:** 1.27; Dt.30.3.

2.19–32: The epitomist's preface. This is like Polonius' long speech in *Hamlet:* "Since brevity is the soul of wit . . . I will be brief" (compare v. 31). He summarizes parts of the book (vv. 19–22): *wars against Antiochus* IV (4.7–10.9) and *his son* Antiochus V *Eupator* (10.10–13.26) and explains that he is condensing the work of *Jason* (vv. 23–24; see the Introduction to 2 Maccabees). **20–21:** *Appearances*, (Gr. *epiphaneiai*), true divine manifestations, in contrast to Antiochus' boastful title *Epiphanes*, "god manifest." *Judaism*, first known use of this term for the religion, in contrast to Hellenism (4.13).

recasts the narrative should be allowed to strive for brevity of expression and to forego exhaustive treatment. ³²At this point therefore let us begin our narrative, adding only so much to what has already been said; for it is foolish to lengthen the preface while cutting short the history itself.

3 While the holy city was inhabited in unbroken peace and the laws were very well observed because of the piety of the high priest Onias and his hatred of wickedness, ²it came about that the kings themselves honored the place and glorified the temple with the finest presents, ³so that even Seleucus, the king of Asia, defrayed from his own revenues all the expenses connected with the service of the sacrifices. ⁴But a man named Simon, of the tribe of Benjamin, who had been made captain of the temple, had a disagreement with the high priest about the administration of the city market; ⁵and when he could not prevail over Onias he went to Apollonius of Tarsus,ᶠ who at that time was governor of Coelesyria and Phoenicia. ⁶He reported to him that the treasury in Jerusalem was full of untold sums of money, so that the amount of the funds could not be reckoned, and that they did not belong to the account of the sacrifices, but that it was possible for them to fall under the control of the king. ⁷When Apollonius met the king, he told him of the money about which he had been informed. The kingᵍ chose

Heliodorus, who was in charge of his affairs, and sent him with commands to effect the removal of the aforesaid money. ⁸Heliodorus at once set out on his journey, ostensibly to make a tour of inspection of the cities of Coelesyria and Phoenicia, but in fact to carry out the king's purpose.

9 When he had arrived at Jerusalem and had been kindly welcomed by the high priest ofʰ the city, he told about the disclosure that had been made and stated why he had come, and he inquired whether this really was the situation. ¹⁰The high priest explained that there were some deposits belonging to widows and orphans, ¹¹and also some money of Hyrcanus, son of Tobias, a man of very prominent position, and that it totaled in all four hundred talents of silver and two hundred of gold. To such an extent the impious Simon had misrepresented the facts. ¹²And he said that it was utterly impossible that wrong should be done to those people who had trusted in the holiness of the place and in the sanctity and inviolability of the temple which is honored throughout the whole world. ¹³But Heliodorus, because of the king's commands which he had, said that this money must in any case be confiscated for the king's treasury. ¹⁴So he set a day and went in to direct the inspection of these funds.

There was no little distress through-

ᶠ Gk *Apollonius son of Tharseas*
ᵍ Gk *He*
ʰ Some authorities read *and*

3.1–4.6: Simon's plot against Onias. 1: Jerusalem was not *in unbroken peace*, though quieter than in later years. *The high priest Onias* III, son of Simon the Just (Sir.50.1–21), ruled before 175 B.C. He turned against Syria and collaborated with Egypt, while his cousins, the family of Tobias, to which Simon (v. 4) belonged, were pro-Syrian. **2:** *The kings,* i.e. the Ptolemies of Egypt and Antiochus III the Great (reigned 233–187 B.C.). **3:** *Seleucus* IV Philopator, son of Antiochus III, reigned 187–175 B.C. The events of 3.1–4.6 were in his reign. He was assassinated by Heliodorus (v. 7). **4:** *Simon* was a grandson of Tobias, who married a sister of Onias II. When Onias II refused to pay tribute to Egypt, Ptolemy III took away his civil authority and appointed Joseph, son of Tobias, *captain of the temple.* His son Simon succeeded him. **5:** *Tarsus,* capital of Cilicia (Acts 9.11), then part of the Seleucid empire. *Coelesyria,* see 1 Macc. 10.69 n. *Apollonius* was removed from office at the death of Seleucus IV in 175 B.C. **7:** *Heliodorus,* see v. 3 n. **9:** *The high priest,* Onias III. **11:** *Hyrcanus,* actually son of Joseph and half-brother of Simon (v. 4), was pro-Egyptian. He fled east of the Jordan after 198 B.C. and built the fortress of 'Araq el-Emir. He committed suicide on the accession of Antiochus IV in 175 B.C. *Simon had misrepresented the facts* only in part; Onias and Hyrcanus probably withheld tribute.

out the whole city. ¹⁵The priests prostrated themselves before the altar in their priestly garments and called toward heaven upon him who had given the law about deposits, that he should keep them safe for those who had deposited them. ¹⁶To see the appearance of the high priest was to be wounded at heart, for his face and the change in his color disclosed the anguish of his soul. ¹⁷For terror and bodily trembling had come over the man, which plainly showed to those who looked at him the pain lodged in his heart. ¹⁸People also hurried out of their houses in crowds to make a general supplication because the holy place was about to be brought into contempt. ¹⁹Women, girded with sackcloth under their breasts, thronged the streets. Some of the maidens who were kept indoors ran together to the gates, and some to the walls, while others peered out of the windows. ²⁰And holding up their hands to heaven, they all made entreaty. ²¹There was something pitiable in the prostration of the whole populace and the anxiety of the high priest in his great anguish.

22 While they were calling upon the Almighty Lord that he would keep what had been entrusted safe and secure for those who had entrusted it, ²³Heliodorus went on with what had been decided. ²⁴But when he arrived at the treasury with his bodyguard, then and there the Sovereign of spirits and of all authority caused so great a manifestation that all who had been so bold as to accompany him were astounded by the power of God, and became faint with terror. ²⁵For there appeared to them a magnificently caparisoned horse, with a rider of frightening mien, and it rushed furiously at Heliodorus and struck at him with its front hoofs. Its rider was seen to have armor and weapons of gold.

²⁶Two young men also appeared to him, remarkably strong, gloriously beautiful and splendidly dressed, who stood on each side of him and scourged him continuously, inflicting many blows on him. ²⁷When he suddenly fell to the ground and deep darkness came over him, his men took him up and put him on a stretcher ²⁸and carried him away, this man who had just entered the aforesaid treasury with a great retinue and all his bodyguard but was now unable to help himself; and they recognized clearly the sovereign power of God. ²⁹While he lay prostrate, speechless because of the divine intervention and deprived of any hope of recovery, ³⁰they praised the Lord who had acted marvelously for his own place. And the temple, which a little while before was full of fear and disturbance, was filled with joy and gladness, now that the Almighty Lord had appeared.

31 Quickly some of Heliodorus' friends asked Onias to call upon the Most High and to grant life to one who was lying quite at his last breath. ³²And the high priest, fearing that the king might get the notion that some foul play had been perpetrated by the Jews with regard to Heliodorus, offered sacrifice for the man's recovery. ³³While the high priest was making the offering of atonement, the same young men appeared again to Heliodorus, dressed in the same clothing, and they stood and said, "Be very grateful to Onias the high priest, since for his sake the Lord has granted you your life. ³⁴And see that you, who have been scourged by heaven, report to all men the majestic power of God." Having said this they vanished.

35 Then Heliodorus offered sacrifice to the Lord and made very great vows to the Savior of his life, and having bidden Onias farewell, he marched off

---

18: Temples, whether pagan or Jewish, were considered inviolate. **19:** *Sackcloth*, a sign of mourning and penitence. *Maidens* were usually *kept indoors* until their marriage. **20:** *Holding up their hands*, the ancient gesture of prayer (1 Kg.8.54; 1 Tim.2.8). **24:** *Manifestation*, see 2.21 n. **29:** *Speechless*, Lk.1.20. **31:** *The Most High* (Gen.14.18), a title often used by non-Jews with his forces to the king. ³⁶And he bore testimony to all men of the deeds of the supreme God, which he had seen with his own eyes. ³⁷When the king asked Heliodorus what sort of person would be suitable to send on another mission to Jerusalem, he replied, ³⁸"If you have any enemy or plotter against your government, send him there, for you will get him back thoroughly scourged, if he escapes at all, for there certainly is about the place some power of God. ³⁹For he who has his dwelling in heaven watches over that place himself and brings it aid, and he strikes and destroys those who come to do it injury." ⁴⁰This was the outcome of the episode of Heliodorus and the protection of the treasury.

4 The previously mentioned Simon, who had informed about the money against[i] his own country, slandered Onias, saying that it was he who had incited Heliodorus and had been the real cause of the misfortune. ²He dared to designate as a plotter against the government the man who was the benefactor of the city, the protector of his fellow countrymen, and a zealot for the laws. ³When his hatred progressed to such a degree that even murders were committed by one of Simon's approved agents, ⁴Onias recognized that the rivalry was serious and that Apollonius, the son of Menestheus[j] and governor of Coelesyria and Phoenicia, was intensifying the malice of Simon. ⁵So he betook himself to the king, not accusing his fellow citizens but having in view the welfare, both public and private, of all the people. ⁶For he saw that without the king's attention public affairs could not again reach a peaceful settlement, and that Simon would not stop his folly.

7 When Seleucus died and Antiochus who was called Epiphanes succeeded to the kingdom, Jason the brother of Onias obtained the high priesthood by corruption, ⁸promising the king at an interview[k] three hundred and sixty talents of silver and, from another source of revenue, eighty talents. ⁹In addition to this he promised to pay one hundred and fifty more if permission were given to establish by his authority a gymnasium and a body of youth for it, and to enrol the men of Jerusalem as citizens of Antioch. ¹⁰When the king assented and Jason[l] came to office, he at once shifted his countrymen over to the Greek way of life. ¹¹He set aside the existing royal concessions to the Jews, secured through John the father of Eupolemus, who went on the mission to establish friendship and alliance with the Romans; and he destroyed the lawful ways of living and introduced new customs contrary to the law. ¹²For with alacrity he founded a gymnasium right under the citadel, and he induced the noblest of the

i Gk *and*
j Vg Compare verse 21: Greek uncertain
k Or *by a petition*   *l* Gk *he*

(Dan.3.26; Mk.5.7). **4.1–6**: Intrigues concerning the high priesthood. *Simon* (see 3.4 n.) was disturbed because *Onias* and *Heliodorus* were now friends. The latter may already have planned to kill Seleucus IV and wanted the high priest's good will. *Apollonius*, in favor with Seleucus, continued to support Simon. **5**: Before Onias arrived in Antioch, Seleucus had already been assassinated by Heliodorus (175 B.C.). **4.7–22**: Jason as high priest. **7**: *Antiochus* IV *Epiphanes*, "god manifest," called Epimanes, "madman," by his enemies, was brother of Seleucus IV, and *succeeded to the kingdom* despite Heliodorus' attempt at revolution. He reigned 175–164 B.C. He had great ability but intense passion and pride (1 Macc.1.1–10). *Jason the brother of Onias* III (3.1), originally named Joshua, took a Greek name. **9–10**: Like Alexander the Great and his successors, Antiochus promoted *the Greek way of life* in order to strengthen his kingdom through cultural unity; this involved worship of other gods. *A gymnasium and a body of youth for it* were necessary *to enrol the men of Jerusalem as citizens of Antioch*, so that the city could coin money and have honors and commercial advantages. **11**: *Royal concessions*, granted by Antiochus III (3.2) The mission of *Eupolemus* (1 Macc.8.17) was later. *Destroyed*, 1 Macc.1.15,44–50. **12**: The broad-brimmed *Greek hat* was worn by the god Hermes; headgear has usually had national or

young men[m] to wear the Greek hat.
[13]There was such an extreme of Hellenization and increase in the adoption of
foreign ways because of the surpassing
wickedness of Jason, who was ungodly
and no high priest, [14]that the priests
were no longer intent upon their service at the altar. Despising the sanctuary and neglecting the sacrifices, they
hastened to take part in the unlawful
proceedings in the wrestling arena after
the call to the discus, [15]disdaining the
honors prized by their fathers and
putting the highest value upon Greek
forms of prestige. [16]For this reason
heavy disaster overtook them, and
those whose ways of living they admired and wished to imitate completely
became their enemies and punished
them. [17]For it is no light thing to show
irreverence to the divine laws—a fact
which later events will make clear.

18 When the quadrennial games
were being held at Tyre and the king
was present, [19]the vile Jason sent
envoys, chosen as being Antiochian
citizens from Jerusalem, to carry three
hundred silver drachmas for the sacrifice to Hercules. Those who carried
the money, however, thought best not
to use it for sacrifice, because that was
inappropriate, but to expend it for
another purpose. [20]So this money was
intended by the sender for the sacrifice
to Hercules, but by the decision of its
carriers it was applied to the construction of triremes.

21 When Apollonius the son of
Menestheus was sent to Egypt for the
coronation[n] of Philometor as king,
Antiochus learned that Philometor[o]

had become hostile to his government,
and he took measures for his own
security. Therefore upon arriving at
Joppa he proceeded to Jerusalem. [22]He
was welcomed magnificently by Jason
and the city, and ushered in with a
blaze of torches and with shouts. Then
he marched into Phoenicia.

23 After a period of three years
Jason sent Menelaus, the brother of
the previously mentioned Simon, to
carry the money to the king and to
complete the records of essential business. [24]But he, when presented to the
king, extolled him with an air of
authority, and secured the high priesthood for himself, outbidding Jason by
three hundred talents of silver. [25]After
receiving the king's orders he returned,
possessing no qualification for the high
priesthood, but having the hot temper
of a cruel tyrant and the rage of a
savage wild beast. [26]So Jason, who
after supplanting his own brother was
supplanted by another man, was driven
as a fugitive into the land of Ammon.
[27]And Menelaus held the office, but
he did not pay regularly any of the
money promised to the king. [28]When
Sostratus the captain of the citadel
kept requesting payment, for the collection of the revenue was his responsibility, the two of them were summoned
by the king on account of this issue.
[29]Menelaus left his own brother Lysimachus as deputy in the high priesthood,
while Sostratus left Crates, the commander of the Cyprian troops.

30 While such was the state of

m Some authorities add *subjecting them*
n The exact meaning of the Greek word is uncertain
o Gk *he*

---

religious significance in the East. **13**: *Hellenization*, Greek religion and culture (see vv. 9–10 n.).
No high priest, because he got the office by bribery and did not keep the Mosaic law. **18**: *Tyre*,
an important port north of Palestine (Jos.19.29; 1 Kg.7.13); *quadrennial games* had been held
there as early as the time of Alexander the Great. **19**: *Hercules*, the Greek name of the god
Melkart of Tyre. **20**: *Triremes*, war vessels manned by three benches of rowers. **21**: *Apollonius*,
v. 4. *The coronation* of Ptolemy VI *Philometor* occurred about 172 B.C., some time after the death
of his mother, Cleopatra I, and he ruled until 146 or 145 B.C. His advisers abandoned Cleopatra's
policy, became *hostile* to Syria, and claimed Palestine. *Joppa*, the port forty miles from Jerusalem. **22**: *Phoenicia*, the coastal plain.
    4.23–50: Menelaus as high priest. 23: *Menelaus* reigned from about 172 to 162 B.C., when
he was executed (13.3–8) and replaced by Alcimus (14.3–14). **26**: *Land of Ammon*, east of the
Jordan, near the present Amman. **29**: *The Cyprian troops* were mercenaries. **30**: *Mallus* was

affairs, it happened that the people of Tarsus and of Mallus revolted because their cities had been given as a present to Antiochis, the king's concubine. ³¹So the king went hastily to settle the trouble, leaving Andronicus, a man of high rank, to act as his deputy. ³²But Menelaus, thinking he had obtained a suitable opportunity, stole some of the gold vessels of the temple and gave them to Andronicus; other vessels, as it happened, he had sold to Tyre and the neighboring cities. ³³When Onias became fully aware of these acts he publicly exposed them, having first withdrawn to a place of sanctuary at Daphne near Antioch. ³⁴Therefore Menelaus, taking Andronicus aside, urged him to kill Onias. Andronicus*ᵖ* came to Onias, and resorting to treachery offered him sworn pledges and gave him his right hand, and in spite of his suspicion persuaded Onias*�q* to come out from the place of sanctuary; then, with no regard for justice, he immediately put him out of the way. ³⁵For this reason not only Jews, but many also of other nations, were grieved and displeased at the unjust murder of the man. ³⁶When the king returned from the region of Cilicia, the Jews in the city*ʳ* appealed to him with regard to the unreasonable murder of Onias, and the Greeks shared their hatred of the crime. ³⁷Therefore Antiochus was grieved at heart and filled with pity, and wept because of the moderation and good conduct of the deceased; ³⁸and inflamed with anger, he immediately stripped off the purple robe from Andronicus, tore off his garments, and led him about the whole city to that very place where he

had committed the outrage against Onias, and there he dispatched the bloodthirsty fellow. The Lord thus repaid him with the punishment he deserved.

39 When many acts of sacrilege had been committed in the city by Lysimachus with the connivance of Menelaus, and when report of them had spread abroad, the populace gathered against Lysimachus, because many of the gold vessels had already been stolen. ⁴⁰And since the crowds were becoming aroused and filled with anger, Lysimachus armed about three thousand men and launched an unjust attack, under the leadership of a certain Auranus, a man advanced in years and no less advanced in folly. ⁴¹But when the Jews*ˢ* became aware of Lysimachus' attack, some picked up stones, some blocks of wood, and others took handfuls of the ashes that were lying about, and threw them in wild confusion at Lysimachus and his men. ⁴²As a result, they wounded many of them, and killed some, and put them all to flight; and the temple robber himself they killed close by the treasury.

43 Charges were brought against Menelaus about this incident. ⁴⁴When the king came to Tyre, three men sent by the senate presented the case before him. ⁴⁵But Menelaus, already as good as beaten, promised a substantial bribe to Ptolemy son of Dorymenes to win over the king. ⁴⁶Therefore Ptolemy, taking the king aside into a colonnade as if for refreshment, induced the king to change his mind. ⁴⁷Menelaus, the

p Gk He   q Gk him
r Or in each city
s Gk they

---

on the Pyramus river east of *Tarsus* (3.5). Hellenistic kings often provided a wife or *concubine* with a regular income by giving her a city. Antiochus, being extravagant (see 1 Macc.3.30 n.), was often in need of money. **32:** *Gave them,* either to pay tribute or as a bribe. **33:** *Daphne,* about five miles from *Antioch,* had a *place of sanctuary* to Apollo and Artemis. **35:** *Unjust murder,* he had been lured from a place protected by the gods. **38:** *Stripped off the purple robe,* degrading him before execution. **39:** *The city,* Jerusalem. *Menelaus* was still in Antioch. **42:** *The temple robber,* Lysimachus. **44:** *The senate,* see 1 Macc.12.6 n. **45:** *Dorymenes* had fought for Ptolemy IV against Antiochus III; his son *Ptolemy* had been governor of Cyprus and deserted to Antiochus IV (see 10.12–13 n.). **47:** The *Scythians* (Col.3.11) lived in what is now southern Russia and were proverbial for their brutality.

cause of all the evil, he acquitted of the charges against him, while he sentenced to death those unfortunate men, who would have been freed uncondemned if they had pleaded even before Scythians. [48]And so those who had spoken for the city and the villages[t] and the holy vessels quickly suffered the unjust penalty. [49]Therefore even the Tyrians, showing their hatred of the crime, provided magnificently for their funeral. [50]But Menelaus, because of the cupidity of those in power, remained in office, growing in wickedness, having become the chief plotter against his fellow citizens.

5 About this time Antiochus made his second invasion of Egypt. [2]And it happened that over all the city, for almost forty days, there appeared golden-clad horsemen charging through the air, in companies fully armed with lances and drawn swords—[3]troops of horsemen drawn up, attacks and counterattacks made on this side and on that, brandishing of shields, massing of spears, hurling of missiles, the flash of golden trappings, and armor of all sorts. [4]Therefore all men prayed that the apparition might prove to have been a good omen.

[5]When a false rumor arose that Antiochus was dead, Jason took no less than a thousand men and suddenly made an assault upon the city. When the troops upon the wall had been forced back and at last the city was being taken, Menelaus took refuge in the citadel. [6]But Jason kept relentlessly slaughtering his fellow citizens,

not realizing that success at the cost of one's kindred is the greatest misfortune, but imagining that he was setting up trophies of victory over enemies and not over fellow countrymen. [7]He did not gain control of the government, however; and in the end got only disgrace from his conspiracy, and fled again into the country of the Ammonites. [8]Finally he met a miserable end. Accused[u] before Aretas the ruler of the Arabs, fleeing from city to city, pursued by all men, hated as a rebel against the laws, and abhorred as the executioner of his country and his fellow citizens, he was cast ashore in Egypt; [9]and he who had driven many from their own country into exile died in exile, having embarked to go to the Lacedaemonians in hope of finding protection because of their kinship. [10]He who had cast out many to lie unburied had no one to mourn for him; he had no funeral of any sort and no place in the tomb of his fathers.

[11]When news of what had happened reached the king, he took it to mean that Judea was in revolt. So, raging inwardly, he left Egypt and took the city by storm. [12]And he commanded his soldiers to cut down relentlessly every one they met and to slay those who went into the houses. [13]Then there was killing of young and old, destruction of boys, women, and children, and slaughter of virgins and infants. [14]Within the total of three days eighty thousand were destroyed, forty thousand in hand-to-hand fight-

t Other authorities read *the people*
u Cn: Gk *Imprisoned*

5.1–27: Antiochus IV desecrates the temple. 1: *Second invasion,* in 169 B.C.; perhaps the writer regards the coming of the Seleucid army into Palestine in 171 B.C. (4.21–22) as the first invasion. We would speak of them as the first and second phases of the invasion (compare 1 Macc.1.16–19). **2–4:** 3.25–26. *The city,* Jerusalem. **5–8:** *Jason* was an Oniad and pro-Egyptian (see 3.1 n.). Thinking *that Antiochus was dead,* he planned, with Egyptian help, to recover the high priesthood. He was opposed by *Menelaus* the Tobiad (4.23) and also by the Jews loyal to Judaism; he massacred people of both factions. *Ammonites,* 4.26. *Aretas,* king of Nabatean Arabia, south and east of Palestine; his capital was at Petra. **9–10:** Rejected in Egypt, Jason fled to Sparta (1 Macc.12.7). *Unburied,* see 1 Macc.7.17 n.; 1 Kg.13.22. **11–14:** So confused was the situation that Antiochus thought all *Judea was in revolt.* He was *raging inwardly* because the Romans had forced him out of Egypt (see 1 Macc.1.20 n.); both his foreign and his domestic programs were collapsing. **11:** *The city,* Jerusalem.

ing; and as many were sold into slavery as were slain.

15 Not content with this, Antiochus᎐ dared to enter the most holy temple in all the world, guided by Menelaus, who had become a traitor both to the laws and to his country. ¹⁶He took the holy vessels with his polluted hands, and swept away with profane hands the votive offerings which other kings had made to enhance the glory and honor of the place. ¹⁷Antiochus was elated in spirit, and did not perceive that the Lord was angered for a little while because of the sins of those who dwelt in the city, and that therefore he was disregarding the holy place. ¹⁸But if it had not happened that they were involved in many sins, this man would have been scourged and turned back from his rash act as soon as he came forward, just as Heliodorus was, whom Seleucus the king sent to inspect the treasury. ¹⁹But the Lord did not choose the nation for the sake of the holy place, but the place for the sake of the nation. ²⁰Therefore the place itself shared in the misfortunes that befell the nation and afterward participated in its benefits; and what was forsaken in the wrath of the Almighty was restored again in all its glory when the great Lord became reconciled.

21 So Antiochus carried off eighteen hundred talents from the temple, and hurried away to Antioch, thinking in his arrogance that he could sail on the land and walk on the sea, because his mind was elated. ²²And he left governors to afflict the people: at Jerusalem, Philip, by birth a Phrygian and in character more barbarous than the man who appointed him; ²³and at Gerizim, Andronicus; and besides these Menelaus, who lorded it over his fellow citizens worse than the others did. In his malice toward the Jewish citizens,ʷ ²⁴Antiochusˣ sent Apollonius, the captain of the Mysians, with an army of twenty-two thousand, and commanded him to slay all the grown men and to sell the women and boys as slaves. ²⁵When this man arrived in Jerusalem, he pretended to be peaceably disposed and waited until the holy sabbath day; then, finding the Jews not at work, he ordered his men to parade under arms. ²⁶He put to the sword all those who came out to see them, then rushed into the city with his armed men and killed great numbers of people.

27 But Judas Maccabeus, with about nine others, got away to the wilderness, and kept himself and his companions alive in the mountains as wild animals do; they continued to live on what grew wild, so that they might not share in the defilement.

6 Not long after this, the king sent an Athenianʸ senatorᶻ to compel the Jews to forsake the laws of their fathers and cease to live by the laws of God, ²and also to pollute the temple in Jerusalem and call it the temple of Olympian Zeus, and to call the one in Gerizim the temple of Zeus the Friend of Strangers, as did the people who dwelt in that place.

v Gk *he*
w Or *worse than the others did in his malice toward the Jewish citizens.*   x Gk *he*
y Some authorities read *Antiochian*
z Or *Geron an Athenian*

15–23a: The temple had been pillaged after the first Egyptian invasion (1 Macc.1.21–28). *Angered for a little while*, not permanently (compare 6.12–16). **21:** *His arrogance* was that of a god manifest (see 4.7 n.). **22–23:** *Philip*, probably not the later regent (9.29). *Andronicus* (4.31) was now made governor of Samaria. **24–26:** Antiochus sent *Apollonius* about two years after the events of vv. 15–23 (see 1 Macc.1.29). Loyal Jews did not yet fight on the *sabbath* (1 Macc.2.32–41). **27:** *Judas Maccabeus*, the third son of Mattathias, of the Hasmonean family (1 Macc.2.1–28). *The defilement*, 4.11; 1 Macc.1.48, 63.
6.1–6: Campaign against Judaism. What had been voluntary (4.9–17) was now enforced (see 1 Macc.1.41–64 n.). **2:** *Olympian Zeus* was now identified with the God of Israel and probably with Antiochus. *To pollute the temple*, they set up a statue or pagan altar (1 Macc.1.54). The Samaritans, descendants of the ten northern tribes and Assyrian settlers (2 Kg.17.6,24), had

3 Harsh and utterly grievous was the onslaught of evil. ⁴For the temple was filled with debauchery and reveling by the Gentiles, who dallied with harlots and had intercourse with women within the sacred precincts, and besides brought in things for sacrifice that were unfit. ⁵The altar was covered with abominable offerings which were forbidden by the laws. ⁶A man could neither keep the sabbath, nor observe the feasts of his fathers, nor so much as confess himself to be a Jew.

7 On the monthly celebration of the king's birthday, the Jews*ᵃ* were taken, under bitter constraint, to partake of the sacrifices; and when the feast of Dionysus came, they were compelled to walk in the procession in honor of Dionysus, wearing wreaths of ivy. ⁸At the suggestion of Ptolemy a decree was issued to the neighboring Greek cities, that they should adopt the same policy toward the Jews and make them partake of the sacrifices, ⁹and should slay those who did not choose to change over to Greek customs. One could see, therefore, the misery that had come upon them. ¹⁰For example, two women were brought in for having circumcised their children. These women they publicly paraded about the city, with their babies hung at their breasts, then hurled them down headlong from the wall. ¹¹Others who had assembled in the caves near by, to observe the seventh day secretly, were betrayed to Philip and were all burned together, because their piety kept them from defending themselves, in view of their regard for that most holy day.

12 Now I urge those who read this book not to be depressed by such calamities, but to recognize that these punishments were designed not to destroy but to discipline our people. ¹³In fact, not to let the impious alone for long, but to punish them immediately, is a sign of great kindness. ¹⁴For in the case of the other nations the Lord waits patiently to punish them until they have reached the full measure of their sins; but he does not deal in this way with us, ¹⁵in order that he may not take vengeance on us afterward when our sins have reached their height. ¹⁶Therefore he never withdraws his mercy from us. Though he disciplines us with calamities, he does not forsake his own people. ¹⁷Let what we have said serve as a reminder; we must go on briefly with the story.

18 Eleazar, one of the scribes in high position, a man now advanced in age and of noble presence, was being forced to open his mouth to eat swine's flesh. ¹⁹But he, welcoming death with honor rather than life with pollution, went up to the rack of his own accord, spitting out the flesh, ²⁰as men ought to go who have the courage to refuse things that it is not right to taste, even for the natural love of life.

21 Those who were in charge of that unlawful sacrifice took the man aside, because of their long acquaintance with him, and privately urged him to bring meat of his own providing, proper for him to use, and pretend that he was eating the flesh of the sacrificial meal which had been commanded by the king, ²²so that by doing this he might be saved from death, and be treated kindly on account of his old

a Gk *they*

---

built the temple on Mount *Gerizim*. 4: *Intercourse . . . sacred precincts*, as in Syrian fertility cults (see Let. Jer.6.11 n. and 6.43 n.). *Things unfit*, swine (Lev.11.7; 1 Macc.1.47). 6: 1 Macc. 1.45–51. *Jew*, originally "Judean"; here "one loyal to the religion" (Judaism, 2.21).
    6.7–17: The first martyrdoms. Chs. 6–7 are the earliest martyrologies, a type of writing popular subsequently in Christianity, designed to encourage the faithful when persecuted. **7**: *Dionysus*, god of wine and the grape harvest; *ivy* was one of his symbols. **8**: *Ptolemy*, see 4.45 n. *The same policy toward the Jews* outside Judea. **12–17**: The victories of Israel's enemies are explained as God's corrective punishment, always followed by mercy (compare Is.54.7–8).
    6.18–31: Martyrdom of Eleazar. The story is told more elaborately in 4 Maccabees. **18**: *Scribes*, scholars learned in the Mosaic law, not necessarily priests. **19**: *Of his own accord*, like

friendship with them. ²³But making a high resolve, worthy of his years and the dignity of his old age and the gray hairs which he had reached with distinction and his excellent life even from childhood, and moreover according to the holy God-given law, he declared himself quickly, telling them to send him to Hades.

24 "Such pretense is not worthy of our time of life," he said, "lest many of the young should suppose that Eleazar in his ninetieth year has gone over to an alien religion, ²⁵and through my pretense, for the sake of living a brief moment longer, they should be led astray because of me, while I defile and disgrace my old age. ²⁶For even if for the present I should avoid the punishment of men, yet whether I live or die I shall not escape the hands of the Almighty. ²⁷Therefore, by manfully giving up my life now, I will show myself worthy of my old age ²⁸and leave to the young a noble example of how to die a good death willingly and nobly for the revered and holy laws."

When he had said this, he went[b] at once to the rack. ²⁹And those who a little before had acted toward him with good will now changed to ill will, because the words he had uttered were in their opinion sheer madness.[c] ³⁰When he was about to die under the blows, he groaned aloud and said: "It is clear to the Lord in his holy knowledge that, though I might have been saved from death, I am enduring terrible sufferings in my body under this beating, but in my soul I am glad to suffer these things because I fear him."

31 So in this way he died, leaving in his death an example of nobility and a memorial of courage, not only to the young but to the great body of his nation.

7 It happened also that seven brothers and their mother were arrested and were being compelled by the king, under torture with whips and cords, to partake of unlawful swine's flesh. ²One of them, acting as their spokesman, said, "What do you intend to ask and learn from us? For we are ready to die rather than transgress the laws of our fathers."

3 The king fell into a rage, and gave orders that pans and caldrons be heated. ⁴These were heated immediately, and he commanded that the tongue of their spokesman be cut out and that they scalp him and cut off his hands and feet, while the rest of the brothers and the mother looked on. ⁵When he was utterly helpless, the king[d] ordered them to take him to the fire, still breathing, and to fry him in a pan. The smoke from the pan spread widely, but the brothers[e] and their mother encouraged one another to die nobly, saying, ⁶"The Lord God is watching over us and in truth has compassion on us, as Moses declared in his song which bore witness against the people to their faces, when he said, 'And he will have compassion on his servants.'"

7 After the first brother had died in this way, they brought forward the second for their sport. They tore off the skin of his head with the hair, and asked him, "Will you eat rather than have your body punished limb by limb?" ⁸He replied in the language of his fathers, and said to them, "No." Therefore he in turn underwent tortures as the first brother had done. ⁹And when he was at his last breath, he said, "You accursed wretch, you dismiss us from this present life, but the King of the universe will raise us

b Other authorities read *was dragged*
c The Greek text of this verse is uncertain
d Gk *he*　　*e* Gk *they*

---

many later martyrs. **29:** Pagans often regarded the martyrs as deluded fanatics. **30:** *Fear,* revere (Job 28.28; Ps.19.9).
　　7.1–42: Martyrdom of seven brothers and their mother. This story is the principal subject of 4 Maccabees. **2:** Dan.3.16–18. **6:** Dt.32.36. **7:** *Their sport,* Mk.15.17–20; Jn.19.2–3; Heb.11.36. **9:** God is often addressed in Jewish prayer as *King of the universe.* The doctrine of resurrection

up to an everlasting renewal of life, because we have died for his laws."

10 After him, the third was the victim of their sport. When it was demanded, he quickly put out his tongue and courageously stretched forth his hands, [11]and said nobly, "I got these from Heaven, and because of his laws I disdain them, and from him I hope to get them back again." [12]As a result the king himself and those with him were astonished at the young man's spirit, for he regarded his sufferings as nothing.

13 When he too had died, they maltreated and tortured the fourth in the same way. [14]And when he was near death, he said, "One cannot but choose to die at the hands of men and to cherish the hope that God gives of being raised again by him. But for you there will be no resurrection to life!"

15 Next they brought forward the fifth and maltreated him. [16]But he looked at the king,[f] and said, "Because you have authority among men, mortal though you are, you do what you please. But do not think that God has forsaken our people. [17]Keep on, and see how his mighty power will torture you and your descendants!"

18 After him they brought forward the sixth. And when he was about to die, he said, "Do not deceive yourself in vain. For we are suffering these things on our own account, because of our sins against our own God. Therefore[g] astounding things have happened. [19]But do not think that you will go unpunished for having tried to fight against God!"

20 The mother was especially admirable and worthy of honorable memory. Though she saw her seven sons perish within a single day, she bore it with good courage because of her hope in the Lord. [21]She encouraged each of them in the language of their fathers. Filled with a noble spirit, she fired her woman's reasoning with a man's courage, and said to them, [22]"I do not know how you came into being in my womb. It was not I who gave you life and breath, nor I who set in order the elements within each of you. [23]Therefore the Creator of the world, who shaped the beginning of man and devised the origin of all things, will in his mercy give life and breath back to you again, since you now forget yourselves for the sake of his laws."

24 Antiochus felt that he was being treated with contempt, and he was suspicious of her reproachful tone. The youngest brother being still alive, Antiochus[h] not only appealed to him in words, but promised with oaths that he would make him rich and enviable if he would turn from the ways of his fathers, and that he would take him for his friend and entrust him with public affairs. [25]Since the young man would not listen to him at all, the king called the mother to him and urged her to advise the youth to save himself. [26]After much urging on his part, she undertook to persuade her son. [27]But, leaning close to him, she spoke in their native tongue as follows, deriding the cruel tyrant: "My son, have pity on me. I carried you nine months in my womb, and nursed you for three years, and have reared you and brought you up to this point in your life, and have taken care of you.[i] [28]I beseech you, my child, to look at the heaven and the earth and see everything that is in them, and recognize that God did not make them out of things that existed.[j]

f Gk *him*
g Lat: other authorities omit *Therefore*
h Gk *he*
i Or *have borne the burden of your education*
j Or *God made them out of things that did not exist*

is now clearly stated (Dan.12.2; Mt.19.29; Lk.18.30). **11:** The whole body will be restored (Rom.8.23). **14:** The wicked will have *no resurrection to life* (Dan.12.2; Rev.20.14–15). **17:** Antiochus IV died in misery and his son was murdered (9.5–28). **18–19:** 6.12–16. **21:** *The language of their fathers*, Aramaic or possibly Hebrew. **22–23:** The hope of resurrection depends entirely on *the Creator* and his mercy. **27:** Children were often *nursed . . . for three years*. **28:** God made all things out of nothing, by his will and creative power, not from previously

Thus also mankind comes into being. [29]Do not fear this butcher, but prove worthy of your brothers. Accept death, so that in God's mercy I may get you back again with your brothers."

30 While she was still speaking, the young man said, "What are you[k] waiting for? I will not obey the king's command, but I obey the command of the law that was given to our fathers through Moses. [31]But you,[l] who have contrived all sorts of evil against the Hebrews, will certainly not escape the hands of God. [32]For we are suffering because of our own sins. [33]And if our living Lord is angry for a little while, to rebuke and discipline us, he will again be reconciled with his own servants. [34]But you, unholy wretch, you most defiled of all men, do not be elated in vain and puffed up by uncertain hopes, when you raise your hand against the children of heaven. [35]You have not yet escaped the judgment of the almighty, all-seeing God. [36]For our brothers after enduring a brief suffering have drunk[m] of everflowing life under God's covenant; but you, by the judgment of God, will receive just punishment for your arrogance. [37]I, like my brothers, give up body and life for the laws of our fathers, appealing to God to show mercy soon to our nation and by afflictions and plagues to make you confess that he alone is God, [38]and through me and my brothers to bring to an end the wrath of the Almighty which has justly fallen on our whole nation."

39 The king fell into a rage, and handled him worse than the others, being exasperated at his scorn. [40]So he died in his integrity, putting his whole trust in the Lord.

41 Last of all, the mother died, after her sons.

42 Let this be enough, then, about the eating of sacrifices and the extreme tortures.

8 But Judas, who was also called Maccabeus, and his companions secretly entered the villages and summoned their kinsmen and enlisted those who had continued in the Jewish faith, and so they gathered about six thousand men. [2]They besought the Lord to look upon the people who were oppressed by all, and to have pity on the temple which had been profaned by ungodly men, [3]and to have mercy on the city which was being destroyed and about to be leveled to the ground, and to hearken to the blood that cried out to him, [4]and to remember also the lawless destruction of the innocent babies and the blasphemies committed against his name, and to show his hatred of evil.

5 As soon as Maccabeus got his army organized, the Gentiles could not withstand him, for the wrath of the Lord had turned to mercy. [6]Coming without warning, he would set fire to towns and villages. He captured strategic positions and put to flight not a few of the enemy. [7]He found the nights most advantageous for such attacks. And talk of his valor spread everywhere.

8 When Philip saw that the man was gaining ground little by little, and that he was pushing ahead with more frequent successes, he wrote to Ptolemy, the governor of Coelesyria and Phoenicia, for aid to the king's government. [9]And Ptolemy[n] promptly ap-

k The Greek here for *you* is plural
l The Greek here for *you* is singular
m Cn: Gk *fallen*   n Gk *he*

---

existing matter (Heb.11.3). **31:** The Jews of Antioch called themselves *Hebrews*. **33:** 5.17; 6.12–16. **36:** The martyrs already enjoy *life*. *God's covenant* with Abraham (Gen.12.1–3; 15.5–6; 17.4–8) is believed to guarantee the resurrection of his descendants (compare Mk.12.26–27). **37:** Martyrs often prayed that their enemies would *confess that he alone is God* (compare 9.12).

8.1–7: Judas begins the revolt; after prayer (vv. 2–4) he begins guerrilla warfare (vv. 5–7).

8.8–29: First victory over Nicanor. Judas assembled his forces at Mizpah and attacked Gorgias' army at Emmaus (see 1 Macc.3.40 n.). **8:** *Philip*, see 5.22 n. *Ptolemy* (see 4.45 n.), appointed by Lysias after Antiochus had left for Persia (1 Macc.3.38). **9:** *Gorgias*, not Nicanor, pointed Nicanor the son of Patroclus, one of the king's chief friends, and sent him, in command of no fewer than twenty thousand Gentiles of all nations, to wipe out the whole race of Judea. He associated with him Gorgias, a general and a man of experience in military service. ¹⁰Nicanor determined to make up for the king the tribute due to the Romans, two thousand talents, by selling the captured Jews into slavery. ¹¹And he immediately sent to the cities on the seacoast, inviting them to buy Jewish slaves and promising to hand over ninety slaves for a talent, not expecting the judgment from the Almighty that was about to overtake him.

12 Word came to Judas concerning Nicanor's invasion; and when he told his companions of the arrival of the army, ¹³those who were cowardly and distrustful of God's justice ran off and got away. ¹⁴Others sold all their remaining property, and at the same time besought the Lord to rescue those who had been sold by the ungodly Nicanor before he ever met them, ¹⁵if not for their own sake, yet for the sake of the covenants made with their fathers, and because he had called them by his holy and glorious name. ¹⁶But Maccabeus gathered his men together, to the number of six thousand, and exhorted them not to be frightened by the enemy and not to fear the great multitude of Gentiles who were wickedly coming against them, but to fight nobly, ¹⁷keeping before their eyes the lawless outrage which the Gentiles*ᵒ* had committed against the holy place, and the torture of the derided city, and besides,

the overthrow of their ancestral way of life. ¹⁸"For they trust to arms and acts of daring," he said, "but we trust in the Almighty God, who is able with a single nod to strike down those who are coming against us and even the whole world."

19 Moreover, he told them of the times when help came to their ancestors; both the time of Sennacherib, when one hundred and eighty-five thousand perished, ²⁰and the time of the battle with the Galatians that took place in Babylonia, when eight thousand in all went into the affair, with four thousand Macedonians; and when the Macedonians were hard pressed, the eight thousand, by the help that came to them from heaven, destroyed one hundred and twenty thousand and took much booty.

21 With these words he filled them with good courage and made them ready to die for their laws and their country; then he divided his army into four parts. ²²He appointed his brothers also, Simon and Joseph and Jonathan, each to command a division, putting fifteen hundred men under each. ²³Besides, he appointed Eleazar to read aloud*ᵖ* from the holy book, and gave the watchword, "God's help"; then, leading the first division himself, he joined battle with Nicanor.

24 With the Almighty as their ally, they slew more than nine thousand of the enemy, and wounded and disabled most of Nicanor's army, and forced them all to flee. ²⁵They captured the money of those who had come to buy

o Gk *they*
p The Greek text of this clause is uncertain

---

is the principal figure in 1 Macc.3.38–4.25. **10:** Since the battle of Magnesia (see 1 Macc.1.10 n.) the Seleucids had been forced to pay *tribute;* perhaps the *two thousand talents* represented the last instalment. **11:** Slave traders accompanied the expedition (compare 8.34 and 1 Macc.3.41). **13:** Compare 1 Macc.3.56. **14:** They *sold . . . property* so as to escape and join Judas' army. **15:** *Covenants*, with the patriarchs and at Sinai (see 1.24–29 n.; Ex.19.5–6). *Called them by his . . . name*, as God's people (Dt.28.10). **17:** *Lawless outrage*, 5.15–16. *Ancestral way of life*, or government under true high priests. **19:** 2 Kg.19.35. **20:** *The Galatians* from Asia Minor often served as mercenaries. Jewish forces evidently aided Antiochus III and *the Macedonians*. **22:** *Simon*, high priest 142–134 B.C., and *Jonathan*, from 160 to 143 or 142 B.C. *Joseph*, called John in 1 Macc.2.2; 9.36. **23:** *Eleazar*, another brother, was killed at Beth-zechariah (1 Macc. 2.5; 6.43–46). The motto *"God's help"* is prescribed by the Qumran *War Scroll* for one of the them as slaves. After pursuing them for some distance, they were obliged to return because the hour was late. ²⁶For it was the day before the sabbath, and for that reason they did not continue their pursuit. ²⁷And when they had collected the arms of the enemy and stripped them of their spoils, they kept the sabbath, giving great praise and thanks to the Lord, who had preserved them for that day and allotted it to them as the beginning of mercy. ²⁸After the sabbath they gave some of the spoils to those who had been tortured and to the widows and orphans, and distributed the rest among themselves and their children. ²⁹When they had done this, they made common supplication and besought the merciful Lord to be wholly reconciled with his servants.

30 In encounters with the forces of Timothy and Bacchides they killed more than twenty thousand of them and got possession of some exceedingly high strongholds, and they divided very much plunder, giving to those who had been tortured and to the orphans and widows, and also to the aged, shares equal to their own. ³¹Collecting the arms of the enemy,*q* they stored them all carefully in strategic places, and carried the rest of the spoils to Jerusalem. ³²They killed the commander of Timothy's forces, a most unholy man, and one who had greatly troubled the Jews. ³³While they were celebrating the victory in the city of their fathers, they burned those who had set fire to the sacred gates, Callisthenes and some others, who had fled into one little

house; so these received the proper recompense for their impiety.*r*

34 The thrice-accursed Nicanor, who had brought the thousand merchants to buy the Jews, ³⁵having been humbled with the help of the Lord by opponents whom he regarded as of the least account, took off his splendid uniform and made his way alone like a runaway slave across the country till he reached Antioch, having succeeded chiefly in the destruction of his own army! ³⁶Thus he who had undertaken to secure tribute for the Romans by the capture of the people of Jerusalem proclaimed that the Jews had a Defender, and that therefore the Jews were invulnerable, because they followed the laws ordained by him.

9 About that time, as it happened, Antiochus had retreated in disorder from the region of Persia. ²For he had entered the city called Persepolis, and attempted to rob the temples and control the city. Therefore the people rushed to the rescue with arms, and Antiochus and his men were defeated,*s* with the result that Antiochus was put to flight by the inhabitants and beat a shameful retreat. ³While he was in Ecbatana, news came to him of what had happened to Nicanor and the forces of Timothy. ⁴Transported with rage, he conceived the idea of turning upon the Jews the injury done by those who had put him to flight; so he ordered his charioteer to drive without stopping until he com-

q Gk *their arms*
r The Greek text of this verse is uncertain
s Gk *they were defeated*

---

banners of the army returning from battle. **25**: *Slaves*, vv. 11, 34. **26**: Gorgias and his army were in the hills (1 Macc.4.16–18). **27–29**: The victory was a sign of God's favor, but the campaign had not yet been won (6.12–16; 1 Macc.4.19–25).

8.30–36: Other victories (1 Macc.5.37–44 tells of a battle against *Timothy* at Raphon). **30**: *Bacchides*, 1 Macc.7.8. **33**: *City of their fathers*, Jerusalem, with its *sacred gates*, Judas' ancestral home (1 Macc.2.1). **34**: *Thrice-accursed*, 15.3; Ad. Est.16.15.

9.1–12: Antiochus' illness (1 Macc.6.1–16). Here this story is placed before the purification of the temple (10.1–8; 1 Macc.4.36–61), Judas' southern campaigns (10.14–38; 1 Macc. ch. 5), and Lysias' first expedition (11.1–15; 1 Macc.4.26–35). **1**: *Antiochus* went to *Persia* to strengthen his authority there and to get funds. **2**: *Persepolis*, near Shiraz, the capital of Persia, founded by Darius I. **3**: Antiochus was on his way to Babylon (1 Macc.6.4) but went north by way of *Ecbatana*, Hamadan. **4**: 5.11; 7.3.

pleted the journey. But the judgment of heaven rode with him! For in his arrogance he said, "When I get there I will make Jerusalem a cemetery of Jews."

5 But the all-seeing Lord, the God of Israel, struck him an incurable and unseen blow. As soon as he ceased speaking he was seized with a pain in his bowels for which there was no relief and with sharp internal tortures —⁶and that very justly, for he had tortured the bowels of others with many and strange inflictions. ⁷Yet he did not in any way stop his insolence, but was even more filled with arrogance, breathing fire in his rage against the Jews, and giving orders to hasten the journey. And so it came about that he fell out of his chariot as it was rushing along, and the fall was so hard as to torture every limb of his body. ⁸Thus he who had just been thinking that he could command the waves of the sea, in his superhuman arrogance, and imagining that he could weigh the high mountains in a balance, was brought down to earth and carried in a litter, making the power of God manifest to all. ⁹And so the ungodly man's body swarmed with worms, and while he was still living in anguish and pain, his flesh rotted away, and because of his stench the whole army felt revulsion at his decay. ¹⁰Because of his intolerable stench no one was able to carry the man who a little while before had thought that he could touch the stars of heaven. ¹¹Then it was that, broken in spirit, he began to lose much of his arrogance and to come to his senses under the scourge of God, for he was tortured with pain every moment. ¹²And when he could not endure his own stench, he uttered these words: "It is right to be subject to God, and

no mortal should think that he is equal to God."ᵗ

13 Then the abominable fellow made a vow to the Lord, who would no longer have mercy on him, stating ¹⁴that the holy city, which he was hastening to level to the ground and to make a cemetery, he was now declaring to be free; ¹⁵and the Jews, whom he had not considered worth burying but had planned to throw out with their children to the beasts, for the birds to pick, he would make, all of them, equal to citizens of Athens; ¹⁶and the holy sanctuary, which he had formerly plundered, he would adorn with the finest offerings; and the holy vessels he would give back, all of them, many times over; and the expenses incurred for the sacrifices he would provide from his own revenues; ¹⁷and in addition to all this he also would become a Jew and would visit every inhabited place to proclaim the power of God. ¹⁸But when his sufferings did not in any way abate, for the judgment of God had justly come upon him, he gave up all hope for himself and wrote to the Jews the following letter, in the form of a supplication. This was its content:

19 "To his worthy Jewish citizens, Antiochus their king and general sends hearty greetings and good wishes for their health and prosperity. ²⁰If you and your children are well and your affairs are as you wish, I am glad. As my hope is in heaven, ²¹I remember with affection your esteem and good will. On my way back from the region of Persia I suffered an annoying illness, and I have deemed it necessary to take thought for the general security of all. ²²I do not despair of my condition, for I have good hope of recovering from my illness, ²³but I observed that my fa-

ᵗ Or *think thoughts proper only to God*

5: See 1 Macc.6.9 n. **8:** *Command the waves*, like Xerxes invading Greece. *Weigh the high mountains*, like God (see 5.21 n.; Is.40.12). **9:** *Worms*, Acts 12.23.
    9.13–29: Repentance and death of Antiochus. 15: *Citizens of Athens* were proud of their heritage, though the city no longer had actual power. **16:** 5.16. **17:** 7.37; Dan.4.31–35. **19–27:** The letter is no supplication (v. 18); it is addressed to Jews loyal to the king and bids them support his *son Antiochus* V (vv. 25–27). **23:** *My father*, Antiochus III (see 3.3 n.), who *appointed*

ther, on the occasions when he made expeditions into the upper country, appointed his successor, ²⁴so that, if anything unexpected happened or any unwelcome news came, the people throughout the realm would not be troubled, for they would know to whom the government was left. ²⁵Moreover, I understand how the princes along the borders and the neighbors to my kingdom keep watching for opportunities and waiting to see what will happen. So I have appointed my son Antiochus to be king, whom I have often entrusted and commended to most of you when I hastened off to the upper provinces; and I have written to him what is written here. ²⁶I therefore urge and beseech you to remember the public and private services rendered to you and to maintain your present good will, each of you, toward me and my son. ²⁷For I am sure that he will follow my policy and will treat you with moderation and kindness."

28 So the murderer and blasphemer, having endured the most intense suffering, such as he had inflicted on others, came to the end of his life by a most pitiable fate, among the mountains in a strange land. ²⁹And Philip, one of his courtiers, took his body home; then, fearing the son of Antiochus, he betook himself to Ptolemy Philometor in Egypt.

10 Now Maccabeus and his followers, the Lord leading them on, recovered the temple and the city; ²and they tore down the altars which had been built in the public square by the foreigners, and also destroyed the sacred precincts. ³They purified the sanctuary, and made another altar of sacrifice; then, striking fire out of flint, they offered sacrifices, after a lapse of two years, and they burned incense and lighted lamps and set out the bread of the Presence. ⁴And when they had done this, they fell prostrate and besought the Lord that they might never again fall into such misfortunes, but that, if they should ever sin, they might be disciplined by him with forbearance and not be handed over to blasphemous and barbarous nations. ⁵It happened that on the same day on which the sanctuary had been profaned by the foreigners, the purification of the sanctuary took place, that is, on the twenty-fifth day of the same month, which was Chislev. ⁶And they celebrated it for eight days with rejoicing, in the manner of the feast of booths, remembering how not long before, during the feast of booths, they had been wandering in the mountains and caves like wild animals. ⁷Therefore bearing ivy-wreathed wands and beautiful branches and also fronds of palm, they offered hymns of thanksgiving to him who had given success to the purifying of his own holy place. ⁸They decreed by public ordinance and vote that the whole nation of the Jews should observe these days every year.

Seleucus IV as *his successor. The upper country,* Babylonia and Persia (1 Macc.3.37). **28:** Antiochus IV *died among the mountains,* perhaps at Gabae or Isfahan (see 1 Macc.6.5 n.). **29:** *Philip* was perhaps Antiochus V's guardian (see 1 Macc.6.14–15 n.). *Fearing* Lysias, viceroy in the west, rather than *the son of Antiochus,* who was a child, he went over to Syria's enemy, *Ptolemy* VI (see 4.21 n.). Josephus says that Philip took over the Seleucid government and was later killed (*Antiquities,* xii. ix. 7).

10.1–9: Purification of the temple (compare 1 Macc.4.36–61). **1:** They *recovered the temple,* desecrated by Antiochus (6.2–4; 1 Macc.1.54), *and the city,* except for the citadel (1 Macc.4.60; 6.18). **2:** *The altars* had been used for pagan worship. **3:** They *purified the sanctuary* by removing the desecrated stones (1 Macc.1.44–46). The reference to *striking fire out of flint* ignores the legends of 1.19–2.1. *Two years,* according to 1 Macc.1.54 and 4.52 it was three years. The *incense, lamps,* and *bread of the Presence,* prescribed by Ex.30.7–8; 25.30. **4:** 5.17–20; 6.12–16. **5–6:** *Chislev,* December, 164 B.C. (see 1 Macc.4.52–59 n.). At the normal time of *the feast of booths,* in September, *they had been wandering* like their ancestors (Lev.23.43) and could not celebrate it. **7:** *Ivy-wreathed wands,* here in honor of God (compare 6.7). *Branches* were carried

9 Such then was the end of Antiochus, who was called Epiphanes.

10 Now we will tell what took place under Antiochus Eupator, who was the son of that ungodly man, and will give a brief summary of the principal calamities of the wars. [11]This man, when he succeeded to the kingdom, appointed one Lysias to have charge of the government and to be chief governor of Coelesyria and Phoenicia. [12]Ptolemy, who was called Macron, took the lead in showing justice to the Jews because of the wrong that had been done to them, and attempted to maintain peaceful relations with them. [13]As a result he was accused before Eupator by the king's friends. He heard himself called a traitor at every turn, because he had abandoned Cyprus, which Philometor had entrusted to him, and had gone over to Antiochus Epiphanes. Unable to command the respect due his office,*u* he took poison and ended his life.

14 When Gorgias became governor of the region, he maintained a force of mercenaries, and at every turn kept on warring against the Jews. [15]Besides this, the Idumeans, who had control of important strongholds, were harassing the Jews; they received those who were banished from Jerusalem, and endeavored to keep up the war. [16]But Maccabeus and his men, after making solemn supplication and beseeching God to fight on their side, rushed to the strongholds of the Idumeans. [17]Attacking them vigorously, they gained possession of the places, and beat off all who fought upon the wall, and slew those whom they encountered, killing no fewer than twenty thousand. [18]When no less than nine thousand took refuge in two very strong towers well equipped to withstand a siege, [19]Maccabeus left Simon and Joseph, and also Zacchaeus and his men, a force sufficient to besiege them; and he himself set off for places where he was more urgently needed. [20]But the men with Simon, who were money-hungry, were bribed by some of those who were in the towers, and on receiving seventy thousand drachmas let some of them slip away. [21]When word of what had happened came to Maccabeus, he gathered the leaders of the people, and accused these men of having sold their brethren for money by setting their enemies free to fight against them. [22]Then he slew these men who had turned traitor, and immediately captured the two towers. [23]Having success at arms in everything he undertook, he destroyed more than twenty thousand in the two strongholds.

24 Now Timothy, who had been defeated by the Jews before, gathered a tremendous force of mercenaries and collected the cavalry from Asia in no small number. He came on, intending to take Judea by storm. [25]As he drew near, Maccabeus and his men sprinkled dust upon their heads and girded their loins with sackcloth, in supplication to God. [26]Falling upon the steps before the altar, they besought him to be gracious to them and to be an enemy to their enemies and an adversary to their

u Cn: the Greek text here is uncertain

---

in procession at the feast of booths. *Fronds of palm* symbolize victory (1 Macc.13.51; Jn.12.13).
10.10–13: Antiochus V and Ptolemy Macron. 10–11: *Antiochus V Eupator* (9.25), son of Antiochus IV, reigned from 164 to 162 B.C., when he was murdered by order of Demetrius I. He was about nine years old; his father had *appointed . . . Lysias* as regent (1 Macc.3.32–33). **12–13:** *Ptolemy* had changed allegiance from Egypt to Syria (see 4.45 n.; 6.8); now he was friendly *to the Jews*.
10.14–23: Attacks on the Idumeans (1 Macc.5.1–3,9–54). **14:** *Gorgias* succeeded Ptolemy. **15:** *Idumeans*, or Edomites (see 1 Macc.5.3 n.); John Hyrcanus later forced them to adopt Judaism. *Those . . . banished*, supporters of Menelaus. **19:** *Urgently needed*, perhaps in Ammon and Gilead (1 Macc.5.6–13).
10.24–38: Victory over Timothy. 24: They met *Timothy* (8.30) *at dawn* (v. 28) at Dathema east of the Jordan (1 Macc.5.28–34). **26:** Ex.23.22.

adversaries, as the law declares. [27]And rising from their prayer they took up their arms and advanced a considerable distance from the city; and when they came near to the enemy they halted. [28]Just as dawn was breaking, the two armies joined battle, the one having as pledge of success and victory not only their valor but their reliance upon the Lord, while the other made rage their leader in the fight.

29 When the battle became fierce, there appeared to the enemy from heaven five resplendent men on horses with golden bridles, and they were leading the Jews. [30]Surrounding Maccabeus and protecting him with their own armor and weapons, they kept him from being wounded. And they showered arrows and thunderbolts upon the enemy, so that, confused and blinded, they were thrown into disorder and cut to pieces. [31]Twenty thousand five hundred were slaughtered, besides six hundred horsemen.

32 Timothy himself fled to a stronghold called Gazara, especially well garrisoned, where Chaereas was commander. [33]Then Maccabeus and his men were glad, and they besieged the fort for four days. [34]The men within, relying on the strength of the place, blasphemed terribly and hurled out wicked words. [35]But at dawn of the fifth day, twenty young men in the army of Maccabeus, fired with anger because of the blasphemies, bravely stormed the wall and with savage fury cut down every one they met. [36]Others who came up in the same way wheeled around against the defenders and set fire to the towers; they kindled fires and burned the blasphemers alive. Others broke open the gates and let in the rest of the force, and they occupied the city. [37]They killed Timothy, who was hidden in a cistern, and his brother Chaereas, and Apollophanes. [38]When they had accomplished these things, with hymns and thanksgivings they blessed the Lord who shows great kindness to Israel and gives them the victory.

11 Very soon after this, Lysias, the king's guardian and kinsman, who was in charge of the government, being vexed at what had happened, [2]gathered about eighty thousand men and all his cavalry and came against the Jews. He intended to make the city a home for Greeks, [3]and to levy tribute on the temple as he did on the sacred places of the other nations, and to put up the high priesthood for sale every year. [4]He took no account whatever of the power of God, but was elated with his ten thousands of infantry, and his thousands of cavalry, and his eighty elephants. [5]Invading Judea, he approached Beth-zur, which was a fortified place about five leagues*v* from Jerusalem, and pressed it hard.

6 When Maccabeus and his men got word that Lysias*w* was besieging the strongholds, they and all the people, with lamentations and tears, besought the Lord to send a good angel to save Israel. [7]Maccabeus himself was the first to take up arms, and he urged the others to risk their lives with him to aid their brethren. Then they eagerly rushed off together. [8]And there, while they were still near Jerusalem, a horseman appeared at their head, clothed in white and brandishing weapons of gold. [9]And they all together praised the

v About twenty miles. The text is uncertain here
w Gk *he*

29: 3.24–26. **31**: *Twenty thousand five hundred*, compare the number of fatalities mentioned in 8.30; 10.17,23. **32–38**: The fort of *Gazara* (1 Macc.4.15; 7.45) was well garrisoned; Simon captured it much later (1 Macc.13.43–48). **37**: *They killed Timothy;* but a Timothy reappears in 12.2, 18–25 (compare 1 Macc.5.11–40).

11.1–15: Victory over Lysias at Beth-zur. This probably occurred before the dedication of the temple (1 Macc.4.26–35). **1**: *Lysias,* see 10.10–13 n. **3**: In many Greek cults the *priesthood was for sale every year;* Antiochus IV had twice disposed of the Jewish high priesthood (4.7,24). **4**: *Elephants,* see 1 Macc.1.17 n.; 6.34–35 n. **5**: *Beth-zur,* about twenty miles south of Jerusalem on the road to Hebron. **6**: *Good angel,* Ex.23.20; Jos.5.13–15; Jg.6.11; 2 Kg.19.35.

merciful God, and were strengthened in heart, ready to assail not only men but the wildest beasts or walls of iron. [10]They advanced in battle order, having their heavenly ally, for the Lord had mercy on them. [11]They hurled themselves like lions against the enemy, and slew eleven thousand of them and sixteen hundred horsemen, and forced all the rest to flee. [12]Most of them got away stripped and wounded, and Lysias himself escaped by disgraceful flight. [13]And as he was not without intelligence, he pondered over the defeat which had befallen him, and realized that the Hebrews were invincible because the mighty God fought on their side. So he sent to them [14]and persuaded them to settle everything on just terms, promising that he would persuade the king, constraining him to be their friend.[x] [15]Maccabeus, having regard for the common good, agreed to all that Lysias urged. For the king granted every request in behalf of the Jews which Maccabeus delivered to Lysias in writing.

16 The letter written to the Jews by Lysias was to this effect:

"Lysias to the people of the Jews, greeting. [17]John and Absalom, who were sent by you, have delivered your signed communication and have asked about the matters indicated therein. [18]I have informed the king of everything that needed to be brought before him, and he has agreed to what was possible. [19]If you will maintain your good will toward the government, I will endeavor for the future to help promote your welfare. [20]And con-

cerning these matters and their details, I have ordered these men and my representatives to confer with you. [21]Farewell. The one hundred and forty-eighth year,[y] Dioscorinthius twenty-fourth."

22 The king's letter ran thus:

"King Antiochus to his brother Lysias, greeting. [23]Now that our father has gone on to the gods, we desire that the subjects of the kingdom be undisturbed in caring for their own affairs. [24]We have heard that the Jews do not consent to our father's change to Greek customs but prefer their own way of living and ask that their own customs be allowed them. [25]Accordingly, since we choose that this nation also be free from disturbance, our decision is that their temple be restored to them and that they live according to the customs of their ancestors. [26]You will do well, therefore, to send word to them and give them pledges of friendship, so that they may know our policy and be of good cheer and go on happily in the conduct of their own affairs."

27 To the nation the king's letter was as follows:

"King Antiochus to the senate of the Jews and to the other Jews, greeting. [28]If you are well, it is as we desire. We also are in good health. [29]Menelaus has informed us that you wish to return home and look after your own affairs. [30]Therefore those who go home by the thirtieth day of Xanthicus will have our pledge of friendship and full permission [31]for the Jews to enjoy

x The Greek text here is corrupt　　*y* 164 B.C.

13–15: According to 1 Macc.4.35 no peace was made, but Lysias returned to Antioch for reinforcements. He may have heard of Antiochus' death and hastened home to take control. **11.16–38: Letters of Lysias, Antiochus V, and the Romans.** If Lysias heard of Philip's plot (see 9.29 n.), he may have wished to gain time through friendly gestures to the Jews. **16:** He wrote *to the people;* he did not recognize Judas' authority. **19:** Part of the Jews had *good will toward the government.* **21:** The date is early December, 164 B.C., before Judas rededicated the temple (1 Macc.4.52). **23:** *Our father,* Antiochus IV, *has gone on to the gods;* in his lifetime he had been worshiped. **25:** 1 Macc.4.36–61 says nothing of this, but Lysias may have instructed the citadel garrison not to interfere with the temple. **27:** The letter *to the senate* (1.10) and people ignores Judas (compare vv. 16–21). **29:** *Menelaus* had gone to Antioch and advised the king to let the Jews *return* to Jerusalem. He was now sent back (v. 32), hoping to regain the high priesthood. **30:** *Xanthicus,* March-April. **31:** *Their own food and laws,* 1 Macc.1.47–49. The their own food and laws, just as formerly, and none of them shall be molested in any way for what he may have done in ignorance. ³²And I have also sent Menelaus to encourage you. ³³Farewell. The one hundred and forty-eighth year,ᶻ Xanthicus fifteenth."

34 The Romans also sent them a letter, which read thus:

"Quintus Memmius and Titus Manius, envoys of the Romans, to the people of the Jews, greeting. ³⁵With regard to what Lysias the kinsman of the king has granted you, we also give consent. ³⁶But as to the matters which he decided are to be referred to the king, as soon as you have considered them, send some one promptly, so that we may make proposals appropriate for you. For we are on our way to Antioch. ³⁷Therefore make haste and send some men, so that we may have your judgment. ³⁸Farewell. The one hundred and forty-eighth year,ᵃ Xanthicus fifteenth."

12 When this agreement had been reached, Lysias returned to the king, and the Jews went about their farming.

2 But some of the governors in various places, Timothy and Apollonius the son of Gennaeus, as well as Hieronymus and Demophon, and in addition to these Nicanor the governor of Cyprus, would not let them live quietly and in peace. ³And some men of Joppa did so ungodly a deed as this: they invited the Jews who lived among them to embark, with their wives and children, on boats which they had provided, as though there were no ill will to the Jews;ᵇ ⁴and this was done by public vote of

the city. And when they accepted, because they wished to live peaceably and suspected nothing, the men of Joppaᶜ took them out to sea and drowned them, not less than two hundred. ⁵When Judas heard of the cruelty visited on his countrymen, he gave orders to his men ⁶and, calling upon God the righteous Judge, attacked the murderers of his brethren. He set fire to the harbor by night, and burned the boats, and massacred those who had taken refuge there. ⁷Then, because the city's gates were closed, he withdrew, intending to come again and root out the whole community of Joppa. ⁸But learning that the men in Jamnia meant in the same way to wipe out the Jews who were living among them, ⁹he attacked the people of Jamnia by night and set fire to the harbor and the fleet, so that the glow of the light was seen in Jerusalem, thirty milesᵈ distant.

10 When they had gone more than a mileᵉ from there, on their march against Timothy, not less than five thousand Arabs with five hundred horsemen attacked them. ¹¹After a hard fight Judas and his men won the victory, by the help of God. The defeated nomads besought Judas to grant them pledges of friendship, promising to give him cattle and to help his peopleᶠ in all other ways. ¹²Judas, thinking that they might really be useful in many ways, agreed to make peace with them; and after receiving his pledges they departed to their tents.

13 He also attacked a certain city which was strongly fortified with

z 164 B.C.　　a 164 B.C.
b Gk *them*　　c Gk *they*
d Gk *two hundred and forty stadia*
e Gk *nine stadia*　　f Gk *them*

---

words *in ignorance* imply that the king still maintained his claims and merely granted pardon (1 Macc.13.39). **34–37:** The *envoys* acted as intermediaries in *matters . . . referred to the king* that were still under negotiation.

12.1–16: Attacks on Joppa, Jamnia, and Caspin (the section 11.1–12.1 is out of place, and 12.2 resumes the narrative of 10.31). **1:** Palestinian Jews lived by *farming.* **2:** *Timothy,* 8.30–33; 10.24–37. *Apollonius,* not the Apollonius of 4.21. *Nicanor* is called *governor of Cyprus;* it was under Egypt's rule till 58 B.C., but Syria may have claimed it after the defection of Ptolemy Macron (10.13). There may have been two Nicanors (see 14.12 n.). **8:** *Jamnia,* about twelve miles south of Joppa. **13:** *Caspin,* perhaps Chaspho (1 Macc.5.36). **15:** Jos.6.1–21.

[285]

earthworks[g] and walls, and inhabited by all sorts of Gentiles. Its name was Caspin. [14]And those who were within, relying on the strength of the walls and on their supply of provisions, behaved most insolently toward Judas and his men, railing at them and even blaspheming and saying unholy things. [15]But Judas and his men, calling upon the great Sovereign of the world, who without battering-rams or engines of war overthrew Jericho in the days of Joshua, rushed furiously upon the walls. [16]They took the city by the will of God, and slaughtered untold numbers, so that the adjoining lake, a quarter of a mile[h] wide, appeared to be running over with blood.

[17] When they had gone ninety-five miles[i] from there, they came to Charax, to the Jews who are called Toubiani. [18]They did not find Timothy in that region, for he had by then departed from the region without accomplishing anything, though in one place he had left a very strong garrison. [19]Dositheus and Sosipater, who were captains under Maccabeus, marched out and destroyed those whom Timothy had left in the stronghold, more than ten thousand men. [20]But Maccabeus arranged his army in divisions, set men[j] in command of the divisions, and hastened after Timothy, who had with him a hundred and twenty thousand infantry and two thousand five hundred cavalry. [21]When Timothy learned of the approach of Judas, he sent off the women and the children and also the baggage to a place called Carnaim; for that place was hard to besiege and difficult of access because of the narrowness of all the approaches. [22]But when Judas' first division appeared, terror and fear came over the enemy at the manifestation to them of him who sees all things; and they rushed off in flight and were swept on, this way and that, so that often they were injured by their own men and pierced by the points of their swords. [23]And Judas pressed the pursuit with the utmost vigor, putting ,the sinners to the sword, and destroyed as many as thirty thousand men.

[24] Timothy himself fell into the hands of Dositheus and Sosipater and their men. With great guile he besought them to let him go in safety, because he held the parents of most of them and the brothers of some and no consideration would be shown them. [25]And when with many words he had confirmed his solemn promise to restore them unharmed, they let him go, for the sake of saving their brethren.

[26] Then Judas[k] marched against Carnaim and the temple of Atargatis, and slaughtered twenty-five thousand people. [27]After the rout and destruction of these, he marched also against Ephron, a fortified city where Lysias dwelt with multitudes of people of all nationalities.[l] Stalwart young men took their stand before the walls and made a vigorous defense; and great stores of war engines and missiles were there. [28]But the Jews[m] called upon the Sovereign who with power shatters the might of his enemies, and they got the city into their hands, and killed as many as twenty-five thousand of those who were within it.

[29] Setting out from there, they hastened to Scythopolis, which is seventy-five miles[n] from Jerusalem. [30]But when the Jews who dwelt there bore witness to the good will which the people of Scythopolis had shown them and their kind treatment of them

g The Greek text here is uncertain
h Gk *two stadia*
i Gk *seven hundred and fifty stadia*
j Gk *them*   k Gk *he*
l The Greek text of this sentence is uncertain
m Gk *they*   n Gk *six hundred stadia*

12.17–31: Battles in the northeast (the account supplements 1 Macc.5.9–32). **17:** *Toubiani,* perhaps men of Tob (1 Macc.5.13). **18:** *One place,* perhaps Bozrah, southeast of Tob (1 Macc. 5.28). **21:** *Carnaim,* a little north of Dera'a in Syria (Gen.14.5; 1 Macc.5.26). **26:** *Atargatis,* the Syrian goddess to whom fish were sacred. **27:** He *marched* south *against Ephron,* eight miles east of the Jordan, opposite Scythopolis (v. 29; 1 Macc.5.46–51). **29:** *Scythopolis,* ancient in times of misfortune, ³¹they thanked them and exhorted them to be well disposed to their race in the future also. Then they went up to Jerusalem, as the feast of weeks was close at hand.

32 After the feast called Pentecost, they hastened against Gorgias, the governor of Idumea. ³³And he came out with three thousand infantry and four hundred cavalry. ³⁴When they joined battle, it happened that a few of the Jews fell. ³⁵But a certain Dositheus, one of Bacenor's men, who was on horseback and was a strong man, caught hold of Gorgias, and grasping his cloak was dragging him off by main strength, wishing to take the accursed man alive, when one of the Thracian horsemen bore down upon him and cut off his arm; so Gorgias escaped and reached Marisa.

36 As Esdris and his men had been fighting for a long time and were weary, Judas called upon the Lord to show himself their ally and leader in the battle. ³⁷In the language of their fathers he raised the battle cry, with hymns; then he charged against Gorgias' men when they were not expecting it, and put them to flight.

38 Then Judas assembled his army and went to the city of Adullam. As the seventh day was coming on, they purified themselves according to the custom, and they kept the sabbath there.

39 On the next day, as by that time it had become necessary, Judas and

his men went to take up the bodies of the fallen and to bring them back to lie with their kinsmen in the sepulchres of their fathers. ⁴⁰Then under the tunic of every one of the dead they found sacred tokens of the idols of Jamnia, which the law forbids the Jews to wear. And it became clear to all that this was why these men had fallen. ⁴¹So they all blessed the ways of the Lord, the righteous Judge, who reveals the things that are hidden; ⁴²and they turned to prayer, beseeching that the sin which had been committed might be wholly blotted out. And the noble Judas exhorted the people to keep themselves free from sin, for they had seen with their own eyes what had happened because of the sin of those who had fallen. ⁴³He also took up a collection, man by man, to the amount of two thousand drachmas of silver, and sent it to Jerusalem to provide for a sin offering. In doing this he acted very well and honorably, taking account of the resurrection. ⁴⁴For if he were not expecting that those who had fallen would rise again, it would have been superfluous and foolish to pray for the dead. ⁴⁵But if he was looking to the splendid reward that is laid up for those who fall asleep in godliness, it was a holy and pious thought. Therefore he made atonement for the dead, that they might be delivered from their sin.

13 In the one hundred and forty-ninth year^o word came to Judas

o 163 B.C.

Beth-shan, then and later an important city (see 1 Macc.5.52 n.). **31:** The *feast of weeks* or Pentecost was at the time of the wheat harvest, seven weeks after Passover, and was celebrated in Jerusalem (Ex.34.22–24; Dt.16.9–12).

　12.32–38: Battle with Gorgias. 35: *Marisa*, in the foothills southwest of Jerusalem near Beit-Jibrin (see 1 Macc.5.66 n.). **36:** *Esdris*, evidently a division leader (v. 20); the author of 2 Maccabees has abbreviated his source. **38:** *City of Adullam*, northeast of Marisa (Jos.12.15; 15.35). *They kept the sabbath*, when it was not necessary to fight (8.27; see 1 Macc.2.41 n.).

　12.39–45: Burial of the dead. The author believed that many had been killed because they wore *sacred tokens* of pagan gods *which the law forbids* (v. 40; Dt.7.25–26), but Josephus says (*Antiquities*, XII. viii. 6) this reverse befell them because they had disobeyed Judas' instructions not to join battle before his arrival. This is the first known statement of the doctrine that a *sin offering* and prayer make *atonement* for the sins of *the dead* (v. 45), and it is justified by the hope that *those who had fallen would rise again* (vv. 43–44; 7.11; 14.46). *Fall asleep*, die (1 Cor.15.20).

　13.1–8: Death of Menelaus. 1–2: *Antiochus* and *Lysias*, see 10.10–11 n. *Chariots armed with* and his men that Antiochus Eupator was coming with a great army against Judea, ²and with him Lysias, his guardian, who had charge of the government. Each of them had a Greek force of one hundred and ten thousand infantry, five thousand three hundred cavalry, twenty-two elephants, and three hundred chariots armed with scythes.

3 Menelaus also joined them and with utter hypocrisy urged Antiochus on, not for the sake of his country's welfare, but because he thought that he would be established in office. ⁴But the King of kings aroused the anger of Antiochus against the scoundrel; and when Lysias informed him that this man was to blame for all the trouble, he ordered them to take him to Beroea and to put him to death by the method which is the custom in that place. ⁵For there is a tower in that place, fifty cubits high, full of ashes, and it has a rim running around it which on all sides inclines precipitously into the ashes. ⁶There they all push to destruction any man guilty of sacrilege or notorious for other crimes. ⁷By such a fate it came about that Menelaus the lawbreaker died, without even burial in the earth. ⁸And this was eminently just; because he had committed many sins against the altar whose fire and ashes were holy, he met his death in ashes.

9 The king with barbarous arrogance was coming to show to the Jews things far worse than those that had been doneᵖ in his father's time. ¹⁰But when Judas heard of this, he ordered the people to call upon the Lord day and night, now if ever to help those who

were on the point of being deprived of the law and their country and the holy temple, ¹¹and not to let the people who had just begun to revive fall into the hands of the blasphemous Gentiles. ¹²When they had all joined in the same petition and had besought the merciful Lord with weeping and fasting and lying prostrate for three days without ceasing, Judas exhorted them and ordered them to stand ready.

13 After consulting privately with the elders, he determined to march out and decide the matter by the help of God before the king's army could enter Judea and get possession of the city. ¹⁴So, committing the decision to the Creator of the world and exhorting his men to fight nobly to the death for the laws, temple, city, country, and commonwealth, he pitched his camp near Modein. ¹⁵He gave his men the watchword, "God's victory," and with a picked force of the bravest young men, he attacked the king's pavilion at night and slew as many as two thousand men in the camp. He stabbed�q the leading elephant and its rider. ¹⁶In the end they filled the camp with terror and confusion and withdrew in triumph. ¹⁷This happened, just as day was dawning, because the Lord's help protected him.

18 The king, having had a taste of the daring of the Jews, tried strategy in attacking their positions. ¹⁹He advanced against Beth-zur, a strong fortress of the Jews, was turned back, attacked again,ʳ and was defeated. ²⁰Judas sent in to the garrison what-

p Or *the worst of the things that had been done*
q The Greek text here is uncertain
r Or *faltered*

scythes to cut down foot soldiers had been used since the days of the Persian Empire. 4: *The King of kings*, God (Rev.19.16). What *aroused* his *anger* is not known (but see 4.27). *Beroea*, now Aleppo in northern Syria. *The method* of execution (vv. 5–6) was Persian.
13.9–17: Preliminary skirmish. 12: Jews employed such acts of penitence particularly when there was danger of sacrilege (3.15; 10.4; 1 Macc.4.40). 14: The Syrian army had invaded Judea from the south, through Idumea (1 Macc.6.31). Judas first *pitched his camp near Modein* to watch the Syrian line along the coast. The first battle occurred at Beth-zechariah (1 Macc.6.32–47). 15: "*God's victory*," see 8.23 n. Eleazar *stabbed the leading elephant* (1 Macc.6.43–46). 16: According to 1 Macc.6.47 the Jews fled.
13.18–26: Attack on Beth-zur. 19: The Syrians were defeated in the first attempt (1 Macc.

ever was necessary. ²¹But Rhodocus, a man from the ranks of the Jews, gave secret information to the enemy; he was sought for, caught, and put in prison. ²²The king negotiated a second time with the people in Beth-zur, gave pledges, received theirs, withdrew, attacked Judas and his men, was defeated; ²³he got word that Philip, who had been left in charge of the government, had revolted in Antioch; he was dismayed, called in the Jews, yielded and swore to observe all their rights, settled with them and offered sacrifice, honored the sanctuary and showed generosity to the holy place. ²⁴He received Maccabeus, left Hegemonides as governor from Ptolemais to Gerar, ²⁵and went to Ptolemais. The people of Ptolemais were indignant over the treaty; in fact they were so angry that they wanted to annul its terms.ˢ ²⁶Lysias took the public platform, made the best possible defense, convinced them, appeased them, gained their good will, and set out for Antioch. This is how the king's attack and withdrawal turned out.

14 Three years later, word came to Judas and his men that Demetrius, the son of Seleucus, had sailed into the harbor of Tripolis with a strong army and a fleet, ²and had taken possession of the country, having made away with Antiochus and his guardian Lysias.

3 Now a certain Alcimus, who had formerly been high priest but had wilfully defiled himself in the times of separation, realized that there was no way for him to be safe or to have access

again to the holy altar, ⁴and went to King Demetrius in about the one hundred and fifty-first year,ᵗ presenting to him a crown of gold and a palm, and besides these some of the customary olive branches from the temple. During that day he kept quiet. ⁵But he found an opportunity that furthered his mad purpose when he was invited by Demetrius to a meeting of the council and was asked about the disposition and intentions of the Jews. He answered:

6 "Those of the Jews who are called Hasideans, whose leader is Judas Maccabeus, are keeping up war and stirring up sedition, and will not let the kingdom attain tranquillity. ⁷Therefore I have laid aside my ancestral glory—I mean the high priesthood—and have now come here, ⁸first because I am genuinely concerned for the interests of the king, and second because I have regard also for my fellow citizens. For through the folly of those whom I have mentioned our whole nation is now in no small misfortune. ⁹Since you are acquainted, O king, with the details of this matter, deign to take thought for our country and our hard-pressed nation with the gracious kindness which you show to all. ¹⁰For as long as Judas lives, it is impossible for the government to find peace."

11 When he had said this, the rest of the king's friends, who were hostile to Judas, quickly inflamed Demetrius still more. ¹²And he immediately chose Nicanor, who had been in command of

ˢ The Greek text of this clause is uncertain
ᵗ 161 B.C.

6.31). **21–22:** The garrison surrendered because of lack of food (1 Macc.6.49); possibly this was the *secret information*. **23:** *Philip*, see 9.29 n.; 1 Macc.6.14–15,55–56. **24:** *Gerar*, south of Gaza on the coastal plain. **26:** 1 Macc.6.63.

14.1–10: Accession of Demetrius I (1 Macc.7.1–7). **1:** *Three years later*, about 161 B.C. *Demetrius I Soter, the son of Seleucus* IV, reigned 162–150. *Tripolis*, see 1 Macc.7.1 n. **2:** *Antiochus . . . Lysias*, 1 Macc.7.3–4. **3:** *Alcimus* may not have *been high priest*. *Defiled*, 4.11–15. **4:** 1 Macc.7.5–7 may record an earlier visit. *Crown*, emblem of sovereignty; the *palm*, victory. **6:** *Hasideans*, see 1 Macc.2.42 n. **7:** *Ancestral glory*, he claimed legitimate succession. **8:** See 1 Macc.1.11 n.

14.11–14: Appointment of Nicanor and Alcimus. This story omits the expedition of Bacchides (1 Macc.7.8–25). Josephus says that *Nicanor* had escaped from Rome with Demetrius (*Antiqui-*

the elephants, appointed him governor of Judea, and sent him off [13]with orders to kill Judas and scatter his men, and to set up Alcimus as high priest of the greatest temple. [14]And the Gentiles throughout Judea, who had fled before[u] Judas, flocked to join Nicanor, thinking that the misfortunes and calamities of the Jews would mean prosperity for themselves.

15 When the Jews[v] heard of Nicanor's coming and the gathering of the Gentiles, they sprinkled dust upon their heads and prayed to him who established his own people for ever and always upholds his own heritage by manifesting himself. [16]At the command of the leader, they[w] set out from there immediately and engaged them in battle at a village called Dessau.[x] [17]Simon, the brother of Judas, had encountered Nicanor, but had been temporarily[y] checked because of the sudden consternation created by the enemy.

18 Nevertheless Nicanor, hearing of the valor of Judas and his men and their courage in battle for their country, shrank from deciding the issue by bloodshed. [19]Therefore he sent Posidonius and Theodotus and Mattathias to give and receive pledges of friendship. [20]When the terms had been fully considered, and the leader had informed the people, and it appeared that they were of one mind, they agreed to the covenant. [21]And the leaders[z] set a day on which to meet by themselves. A chariot came forward from each army; seats of honor were set in place; [22]Judas posted armed men in readiness at key places to prevent sudden treachery on the part of the enemy; they held the proper conference.

23 Nicanor stayed on in Jerusalem and did nothing out of the way, but dismissed the flocks of people that had gathered. [24]And he kept Judas always in his presence; he was warmly attached to the man. [25]And he urged him to marry and have children; so he married, settled down, and shared the common life.

26 But when Alcimus noticed their good will for one another, he took the covenant that had been made and went to Demetrius. He told him that Nicanor was disloyal to the government, for he had appointed that conspirator against the kingdom, Judas, to be his successor. [27]The king became excited and, provoked by the false accusations of that depraved man, wrote to Nicanor, stating that he was displeased with the covenant and commanding him to send Maccabeus to Antioch as a prisoner without delay.

28 When this message came to Nicanor, he was troubled and grieved that he had to annul their agreement when the man had done no wrong. [29]Since it was not possible to oppose the king, he watched for an opportunity to accomplish this by a stratagem. [30]But Maccabeus, noticing that Nicanor was more austere in his dealings with him and was meeting him more rudely than had been his custom, concluded that this austerity did not spring from the best motives. So he gathered not a few of his men, and went into hiding from Nicanor.

31 When the latter became aware that he had been cleverly outwitted by the man, he went to the great[a] and holy temple while the priests were offering the customary sacrifices, and com-

u The Greek text is uncertain
v Gk *they*
w Gk *he*
x The name is uncertain
y Other authorities read *slowly*
z Gk *they*
a Gk *greatest*

---

ties, xii. x. 4); if he is the person in 8.9–36 he must have gone from Syria to Rome to assist the escape.

14.15–36: Nicanor seeks friendship with Judas. **15**: *Sprinkled dust*, Jos.7.6. **16**: *The leader*, Judas, or possibly Nicanor. *Dessau*, perhaps Adasa (1 Macc.7.40–45). **20–21**: *The leader*, Nicanor. *The people*, his army. Afterward *the leaders*, Nicanor and Judas, met. **22**: 1 Macc.7.12–18. **24**: *Warmly attached* only so long as things went well (compare vv. 31–33). **26**: *Alcimus* failed to get civil power and feared that *Judas* would be made his *successor* as high priest.

[290]

manded them to hand the man over. [32]And when they declared on oath that they did not know where the man was whom he sought, [33]he stretched out his right hand toward the sanctuary, and swore this oath: "If you do not hand Judas over to me as a prisoner, I will level this precinct of God to the ground and tear down the altar, and I will build here a splendid temple to Dionysus."

34 Having said this, he went away. Then the priests stretched forth their hands toward heaven and called upon the constant Defender of our nation, in these words: [35]"O Lord of all, who hast need of nothing, thou wast pleased that there be a temple for thy habitation among us; [36]so now, O holy One, Lord of all holiness, keep undefiled for ever this house that has been so recently purified."

37 A certain Razis, one of the elders of Jerusalem, was denounced to Nicanor as a man who loved his fellow citizens and was very well thought of and for his good will was called father of the Jews. [38]For in former times, when there was no mingling with the Gentiles, he had been accused of Judaism, and for Judaism he had with all zeal risked body and life. [39]Nicanor, wishing to exhibit the enmity which he had for the Jews, sent more than five hundred soldiers to arrest him; [40]for he thought that by arresting[b] him he would do them an injury. [41]When the troops were about to capture the tower and were forcing the door of the courtyard, they ordered that fire be brought and the doors burned. Being surrounded, Razis[c] fell upon his own sword, [42]preferring to die nobly rather than to fall into the hands of sinners and suffer outrages unworthy of his noble birth. [43]But in the heat of the struggle he did not hit exactly, and the crowd was now rushing in through the doors. He bravely ran up on the wall, and manfully threw himself down into the crowd. [44]But as they quickly drew back, a space opened and he fell in the middle of the empty space. [45]Still alive and aflame with anger, he rose, and though his blood gushed forth and his wounds were severe he ran through the crowd; and standing upon a steep rock, [46]with his blood now completely drained from him, he tore out his entrails, took them with both hands and hurled them at the crowd, calling upon the Lord of life and spirit to give them back to him again. This was the manner of his death.

15 When Nicanor heard that Judas and his men were in the region of Samaria, he made plans to attack them with complete safety on the day of rest. [2]And when the Jews who were compelled to follow him said, "Do not destroy so savagely and barbarously, but show respect for the day which he who sees all things has honored and hallowed above other days," [3]the thrice-accursed wretch asked if there were a sovereign in heaven who had commanded the keeping of the sabbath day. [4]And when they declared, "It is the living Lord himself, the Sovereign in heaven, who ordered us to observe the seventh day," [5]he replied, "And I am a sovereign also, on earth, and I command you to take up arms and finish the king's business." Nevertheless, he did not succeed in carrying out his abominable design.

6 This Nicanor in his utter boastfulness and arrogance had determined to erect a public monument of victory

b The Greek text here is uncertain
c Gk *he*

33: *Stretched out his right hand . . . and swore,* 15.32–33. *Dionysus,* 6.7. **35–36:** 1 Kg.8.27–30. *Purified,* 10.1–8.

14.37–46: Death of Razis. A martyrology in the style of 6.18–7.42. **37:** *Elders,* 13.13. **46:** He expected his body to be restored in the resurrection (7.11).

15.1–36: Death of Nicanor (1 Macc.7.39–50). **1:** *Nicanor* camped at Beth-horon, and *Judas* was at Adasa, between Beth-horon and Jerusalem. **2:** *The Jews* in Nicanor's army wished to honor the sabbath. **3:** *Thrice-accursed,* 8.34. **4–5:** Ex.20.8–11; Dan.3.16–18.

over Judas and his men. ⁷But Maccabeus did not cease to trust with all confidence that he would get help from the Lord. ⁸And he exhorted his men not to fear the attack of the Gentiles, but to keep in mind the former times when help had come to them from heaven, and now to look for the victory which the Almighty would give them. ⁹Encouraging them from the law and the prophets, and reminding them also of the struggles they had won, he made them the more eager. ¹⁰And when he had aroused their courage, he gave his orders, at the same time pointing out the perfidy of the Gentiles and their violation of oaths. ¹¹He armed each of them not so much with confidence in shields and spears as with the inspiration of brave words, and he cheered them all by relating a dream, a sort of vision,*ᵈ* which was worthy of belief.

12 What he saw was this: Onias, who had been high priest, a noble and good man, of modest bearing and gentle manner, one who spoke fittingly and had been trained from childhood in all that belongs to excellence, was praying with outstretched hands for the whole body of the Jews. ¹³Then likewise a man appeared, distinguished by his gray hair and dignity, and of marvelous majesty and authority. ¹⁴And Onias spoke, saying, "This is a man who loves the brethren and prays much for the people and the holy city, Jeremiah, the prophet of God." ¹⁵Jeremiah stretched out his right hand and gave to Judas a golden sword, and as he gave it he addressed him thus: ¹⁶"Take this holy sword, a gift from God, with which you will strike down your adversaries."

17 Encouraged by the words of Judas, so noble and so effective in arousing valor and awaking manliness in the souls of the young, they determined not to carry on a campaign but to attack bravely, and to decide the matter, by fighting hand to hand with all courage, because the city and the sanctuary and the temple were in danger. ¹⁸Their concern for wives and children, and also for brethren and relatives, lay upon them less heavily; their greatest and first fear was for the consecrated sanctuary. ¹⁹And those who had to remain in the city were in no little distress, being anxious over the encounter in the open country.

20 When all were now looking forward to the coming decision, and the enemy was already close at hand with their army drawn up for battle, the elephants*ᵉ* strategically stationed and the cavalry deployed on the flanks, ²¹Maccabeus, perceiving the hosts that were before him and the varied supply of arms and the savagery of the elephants,*ᵉ* stretched out his hands toward heaven and called upon the Lord who works wonders; for he knew that it is not by arms, but as the Lord*ᶠ* decides, that he gains the victory for those who deserve it. ²²And he called upon him in these words: "O Lord, thou didst send thy angel in the time of Hezekiah king of Judea, and he slew fully a hundred and eighty-five thousand in the camp of Sennacherib. ²³So now, O Sovereign of the heavens, send a good angel to carry terror and trembling before us. ²⁴By the might of thy arm may these blasphemers who come against thy holy people be struck down." With these words he ended his prayer.

d The Greek text here is uncertain
e Gk *beasts*
f Gk *he*

8: 1 Macc.7.41. **9:** *The law and the prophets*, the first two major divisions of the Old Testament, were now regarded as scripture (compare the Prologue to Sirach; see 2 Esd.14.45 n.); not all the other books had been collected. **10:** *Violation of oaths*, 11.27–32; 14.20–28. **12:** *Onias*, 3.1–40. **14:** The writer believed that saints like *Jeremiah* were alive even before the resurrection. **15–16:** The *golden sword* was a sign that God approved the Jews' self-defense on the sabbath. **18:** *First fear*, compare 14.33. **20:** *Elephants*, to break through the Jewish infantry; the *cavalry* protected the *flanks* of the Syrian infantry. **22–23:** See 11.6 n.; 2 Kg.19.35.

25 Nicanor and his men advanced with trumpets and battle songs; ²⁶and Judas and his men met the enemy in battle with invocation to God and prayers. ²⁷So, fighting with their hands and praying to God in their hearts, they laid low no less than thirty-five thousand men, and were greatly gladdened by God's manifestation.

28 When the action was over and they were returning with joy, they recognized Nicanor, lying dead, in full armor. ²⁹Then there was shouting and tumult, and they blessed the Sovereign Lord in the language of their fathers. ³⁰And the man who was ever in body and soul the defender of his fellow citizens, the man who maintained his youthful good will toward his countrymen, ordered them to cut off Nicanor's head and arm and carry them to Jerusalem. ³¹And when he arrived there and had called his countrymen together and stationed the priests before the altar, he sent for those who were in the citadel. ³²He showed them the vile Nicanor's head and that profane man's arm, which had been boastfully stretched out against the holy house of the Almighty; ³³and he cut out the tongue of the ungodly Nicanor and

said that he would give it piecemeal to the birds and hang up these rewards of his folly opposite the sanctuary. ³⁴And they all, looking to heaven, blessed the Lord who had manifested himself, saying, "Blessed is he who has kept his own place undefiled." ³⁵And he hung Nicanor's head from the citadel, a clear and conspicuous sign to every one of the help of the Lord. ³⁶And they all decreed by public vote never to let this day go unobserved, but to celebrate the thirteenth day of the twelfth month—which is called Adar in the Syrian language—the day before Mordecai's day.

37 This, then, is how matters turned out with Nicanor. And from that time the city has been in the possession of the Hebrews. So I too will here end my story. ³⁸If it is well told and to the point, that is what I myself desired; if it is poorly done and mediocre, that was the best I could do. ³⁹For just as it is harmful to drink wine alone, or, again, to drink water alone, while wine mixed with water is sweet and delicious and enhances one's enjoyment, so also the style of the story delights the ears of those who read the work. And here will be the end.

***

25: *Battle songs*, such as Pss.68.1–3; 83. **29**: *Language of their fathers*, Hebrew or Aramaic. **31**: *The citadel* on the Ophel hill was held by Syrians (1 Macc.1.33; 6.18); but the Jews had built another fort (1 Macc.4.60). **32**: *Head ... arm*, 14.33. **35**: 1 Sam.31.9; Jdt.14.1; 1 Macc.7.47. **36**: The *twelfth month* (February-March) was *called Adar in the Syrian language* (that is, in Aramaic) and also in Hebrew. If there was but one month of Adar in this year (probably 161 B.C.), it was *the day before Mordecai's day*, but in some years a second month of Adar was intercalated to harmonize the calendar. Nicanor's day was observed up to A.D. 70 (see 1 Macc.7.49 n.).

    15.37–39: Conclusion. The epitomist wrote some time before the Jewish war (A.D. 66–70), when Jerusalem was still in Jewish hands. **37**: *Hebrews*, see 7.31 n. **39**: To *drink wine alone* was a mark of the drunkard or spendthrift. *Water alone* was the drink of the poor, or of certain Greek philosophers, or those who like the Rechabites were forbidden wine (Jer.35.5–10). *The style* will delight *the ears of those who read*, because in antiquity it was the custom to read literary works aloud, even to oneself.

THE THIRD BOOK OF THE

MACCABEES

The title of the book known as 3 Maccabees is a misnomer, for the contents deal not with the exploits of the Maccabean heroes, but with the struggles of Egyptian Jews who suffered under Ptolemy IV Philopator (221–203 B.C.), half a century prior to the Maccabean period and the persecution of Palestinian Jewry under Antiochus IV Epiphanes (175–164 B.C.). The book, which was written in Greek by an unknown Alexandrian Jew during the first century B.C., has been transmitted in manuscripts of the Greek Septuagint as well as of the Syriac Peshitta and in most manuscripts of the Armenian Bible. It is not, however, included in the Latin Vulgate. This may explain why the book has been accorded canonical status in Eastern Christendom, whereas in the Western Churches, both Roman and Reformed, it is regarded as apocryphal.

The author of 3 Maccabees describes the attempt made by Ptolemy IV Philopator to enter the holy of holies in the temple at Jerusalem, and his miraculous repulse (1.1–2.24). Having returned to Egypt, he determines to wreak his vengeance on the Jews of Egypt for his humiliation in Jerusalem. He alters not only their political status but also attempts to impose upon them the pagan cult of Dionysus (2.25–33). Unable to compel the great majority of the Jews to renounce their ancestral religion, he orders cruel and unusual punishments, and even death for all who refuse to apostatize (3.1–5.51). Finally, after Eleazar, an aged priest, prays earnestly for his people (6.1–25), through divine intervention the king repents and becomes the patron of the Jews, who return in safety and rejoicing to their homes (6.16–7.23).

The book was obviously written to console, exhort, and teach Egyptian Jews, who during the first century B.C. were several times threatened by efforts of the Roman administration to alter their civic status. The author intends to inspire faith in the providence of God (4.21) by recounting how the Jews had been delivered from similar tribulations in the past.

The style of the book is pseudoclassical, utilizing many uncommon and poetical words. Sentences are awkwardly constructed and full of repetitions. The author often exaggerates, and when in descriptions he attempts to introduce purple passages of rhetoric, he succeeds only in producing bombast and bathos.

Whether the events the author describes are fictional or real—and several names, places, and events can be corroborated in classical authors—3 Maccabees is significant for its religious message. The book represents the most orthodox type of Judaism, with its unswerving devotion to the Mosaic law and the temple cultus, as well as its emphasis upon the special position of the chosen people.

WHEN PHILOPATOR LEARNED FROM those who returned that the regions which he had controlled had been seized by Antiochus, he gave orders to all his forces, both infantry and cavalry, took with him his sister Arsinoë, and marched out to the region near Raphia, where Antiochus's supporters were encamped. ² But a certain Theodotus, determined to carry out the plot he had devised, took with him the best of the Ptolemaic arms that had been previously issued to him,[a] and crossed over by night to the tent of Ptolemy, intending single-handed to kill him and thereby end the war.

a Or the best of the Ptolemaic soldiers previously put under his command

1.1–7: The battle of Raphia (217 B.C.). The abruptness with which the book opens and the use of the Greek conjunctive particle de indicate that the introduction to 3 Macc. has not survived (see also 2.25 n.). 1: Ptolemy IV Philopator was king of Egypt 221–203 B.C. From those who returned, fugitives who had escaped. Antiochus III, later called the Great, was king of Syria 223–187 B.C. Raphia, a city of Palestine, three miles from Gaza and not far from the Egyptian frontier. Arsinoë, Ptolemy's sister, who became his wife, was later put to death at the instigation of her husband. 2: Theodotus had been chief commander of the Egyptian forces in Syria, but

³ But Dositheus, known as the son of Drimylus, a Jew by birth who later changed his religion and apostatized from the ancestral traditions, had led the king away and arranged that a certain insignificant man should sleep in the tent; and so it turned out that this man incurred the vengeance meant for the king.*ᵇ* ⁴ When a bitter fight resulted, and matters were turning out rather in favor of Antiochus, Arsinoë went to the troops with wailing and tears, her locks all disheveled, and exhorted them to defend themselves and their children and wives bravely, promising to give them each two minas of gold if they won the battle. ⁵ And so it came about that the enemy was routed in the action, and many captives also were taken. ⁶ Now that he had foiled the plot, Ptolemy*ᶜ* decided to visit the neighboring cities and encourage them. ⁷ By doing this, and by endowing their sacred enclosures with gifts, he strengthened the morale of his subjects.

8 Since the Jews had sent some of their council and elders to greet him, to bring him gifts of welcome, and to congratulate him on what had happened, he was all the more eager to visit them as soon as possible. ⁹ After he had arrived in Jerusalem, he offered sacrifice to the supreme God*ᵈ* and made thank-offerings and did what was fitting for the holy place.*ᵉ* Then, upon entering the place and being impressed by its excellence and its beauty, ¹⁰ he marveled at the good order of the temple, and conceived a desire to enter the holy of holies. ¹¹ When they said that this was not permitted, because not even members of their own nation were allowed to enter, nor even all of the priests, but only the high priest who was pre-eminent over all, and he only once a year, the king was by no means persuaded. ¹² Even after the law had been read to him, he did not cease to maintain that he ought to enter, saying, "Even if those men are deprived of this honor, I ought not to be." ¹³ And he inquired why, when he entered every other temple,*ᶠ* no one there had stopped him. ¹⁴ And someone heedlessly said that it was wrong to take this as a sign in itself. ¹⁵ "But since this has happened," the king*ᵍ* said, "why should not I at least enter, whether they wish it or not?"

16 Then the priests in all their vestments prostrated themselves and entreated the supreme God*ʰ* to aid in the present situation and to avert the violence of this evil design, and they filled the temple with cries and tears; ¹⁷ and those who remained behind in the city were agitated and hurried out, supposing that something mysterious was occurring. ¹⁸ The virgins who had been enclosed in their chambers rushed out with their mothers, sprinkled their hair with dust,*ⁱ* and filled the streets with groans and lamentations. ¹⁹ Those women who had recently been arrayed

b Gk that one   c Gk he   d Gk the greatest God
e Gk the place   f Or entered the temple precincts
g Gk he   h Gk the greatest God
i Other ancient authorities add and ashes

---

subsequently became disaffected and deserted to Antiochus III (so Polybius, v.40). **3**: A *Dositheus* is mentioned in Hibeh papyrus 90 as priest of Alexander in 222 B.C. **5**: According to Polybius (v.86.5–6) Antiochus lost nearly 10,000 infantry, 300 cavalry, and 4,000 prisoners; Ptolemy 1,500 infantry and 700 cavalry.

1.8–15: Ptolemy attempts to enter the sanctuary at Jerusalem. 9: Reference to *the supreme God*, Greek *megistos theos*, occurs frequently in 3 Macc. (1.9,16; 3.11; 4.16; 5.25; 7.22) as well as in 2 Macc. (3.36). That the pagan Ptolemy should have offered *sacrifice* to the God of the Jews was not an unusual practice in an age of religious syncretism. *The place*, a surrogate for "the temple" in 3 Macc. and other Jewish literature. **10:** Ptolemy's eagerness to inspect the interior of the temple may have been motivated by his curiosity concerning its architecture, for he considered himself a connoisseur of the arts. **11:** *High priest . . . once a year*, Ex.30.10; Lev.16.2, 11–12,15,34; Heb.9.7; Josephus, *Ant.* XII.iii.3.

1.16–28: Jewish reaction to Ptolemy's determination to enter the sanctuary. It is possible that because of religious superstition many regarded Ptolemy's desire as an evil omen of something calamitous that would befall them. **18:** *Virgins*, 2 Macc.3.19. **19:** *Bridal chambers*, Jl.2.16;

for marriage abandoned the bridal chambers prepared for wedded union, and, neglecting proper modesty, in a disorderly rush flocked together in the city. [20] Mothers and nurses abandoned even newborn children here and there, some in houses and some in the streets, and without a backward look they crowded together at the most high temple. [21] Various were the supplications of those gathered there because of what the king was profanely plotting. [22] In addition, the bolder of the citizens would not tolerate the completion of his plans or the fulfillment of his intended purpose. [23] They shouted to their fellows to take arms and die courageously for the ancestral law, and created a considerable disturbance in the holy place;[j] and being barely restrained by the old men and the elders,[k] they resorted to the same posture of supplication as the others. [24] Meanwhile the crowd, as before, was engaged in prayer, [25] while the elders near the king tried in various ways to change his arrogant mind from the plan that he had conceived. [26] But he, in his arrogance, took heed of nothing, and began now to approach, determined to bring the aforesaid plan to a conclusion. [27] When those who were around him observed this, they turned, together with our people, to call upon him who has all power to defend them in the present trouble and not to overlook this unlawful and haughty deed. [28] The continuous, vehement, and concerted cry of the crowds[l] resulted in an immense uproar; [29] for it seemed that not only the men but also the walls and the whole earth around echoed, be-

cause indeed all at that time[m] preferred death to the profanation of the place.

2 Then the high priest Simon, facing the sanctuary, bending his knees and extending his hands with calm dignity, prayed as follows:[n] [2] "Lord, Lord, king of the heavens, and sovereign of all creation, holy among the holy ones, the only ruler, almighty, give attention to us who are suffering grievously from an impious and profane man, puffed up in his audacity and power. [3] For you, the creator of all things and the governor of all, are a just Ruler, and you judge those who have done anything in insolence and arrogance. [4] You destroyed those who in the past committed injustice, among whom were even giants who trusted in their strength and boldness, whom you destroyed by bringing upon them a boundless flood. [5] You consumed with fire and sulphur the men of Sodom who acted arrogantly, who were notorious for their vices;[o] and you made them an example to those who should come afterward. [6] You made known your mighty power by inflicting many and varied punishments on the audacious Pharaoh who had enslaved your holy people Israel. [7] And when he pursued them with chariots and a mass of troops, you overwhelmed him in the depths of the sea, but carried through safely those who had put their confidence in you, the Ruler over the whole creation. [8] And when they had seen works of your hands, they praised

j Gk *the place*
k Other ancient authorities read *priests*
l Other ancient authorities read *vehement cry of the assembled crowds*
m Other ancient authorities omit *at that time*
n Other ancient authorities omit verse 1
o Other ancient authorities read *secret in their vices*

---

2 Esd.16.33,34; Bar.2.23. **21:** *Various* with respect to the persons offering prayer. **23:** *Die courageously for the ancestral law*, 1 Macc.2.40; 3.21; 13.3–4; 2 Macc.8.21.
    2.1–20: The prayer of Simon, the high priest. This was probably Simon II, son of Onias II and high priest about 219–196 B.C. (see Sir.50.1 n.). The prayer is in classic Jewish form which, like Eleazar's prayer in 6.1–15, follows the pattern of Pss.105 and 106 in addressing God in terms of his power, glory, and great works reflected in historical deliverances of Israel. **2:** *Holy among the holy ones*, Is.57.15 LXX. **3:** Ex.18.11; Ps.31.23. **4:** *Giants*, Jdt.16.7; Wis.14.6; Sir.16.7; Bar.3.26; 1 Enoch 7.2; 15.8. **5:** *Sodom*, Gen.19.24; Dt.29.23; Wis.10.7. *An example*, 2 Pet.2.6. **6:** *Power*, Ex.9.16; Rom.9.17. *Varied punishments*, Ex. chs. 5–12. **7:** *Overwhelmed him*, Ex. 14.21–28. **8:** *They praised*, Ex.15.1–21; Wis.19.8–9; 1 Macc.4.9. **9:** *Boundless and immeasurable*

you, the Almighty. ⁹ You, O King, when you had created the boundless and immeasurable earth, chose this city and sanctified this place for your name, though you have no need of anything; and when you had glorified it by your magnificent manifestation,ᵖ you made it a firm foundation for the glory of your great and honored name. ¹⁰ And because you love the house of Israel, you promised that if we should have reverses, and tribulation should overtake us, you would listen to our petition when we come to this place and pray. ¹¹ And indeed you are faithful and true. ¹² And because oftentimes when our fathers were oppressed you helped them in their humiliation, and rescued them from great evils, ¹³ see now, O holy King, that because of our many and great sins we are crushed with suffering, subjected to our enemies, and overtaken by helplessness. ¹⁴ In our downfall this audacious and profane man undertakes to violate the holy place on earth dedicated to your glorious name. ¹⁵ For your dwelling, the heaven of heavens, is unapproachable by man. ¹⁶ But because you graciously bestowed your glory upon your people Israel, you sanctified this place. ¹⁷ Do not punish us for the defilement committed by these men, or call us to account for this profanation, lest the transgressors boast in their wrath or exult in the arrogance of their tongue, saying, ¹⁸ 'We have trampled down the house of the sanctuary as offensive houses�q are trampled down.' ¹⁹ Wipe away our sins and disperse our errors, and reveal your mercy at this hour. ²⁰ Speedily let your mercies overtake us, and put praises in the mouth of those who are downcast and broken in spirit, and give us peace."

21 Thereupon God, who oversees all things, the first Father of all, holy among the holy ones, having heard the lawful supplication, scourged him who had exalted himself in insolence and audacity. ²² He shook him on this side and that as a reed is shaken by the wind, so that he lay helpless on the ground and, besides being paralyzed in his limbs, was unable even to speak, since he was smittenr by a righteous judgment. ²³ Then both friends and bodyguards, seeing the severe punishment that had overtaken him, and fearing lest he should lose his life, quickly dragged him out, panic-stricken in their exceedingly great fear. ²⁴ After a while he recovered, and though he had been punished, he by no means repented, but went away uttering bitter threats.

25 When he arrived in Egypt, he increased in his deeds of malice, abetted by the previously mentioned drinking companions and comrades, who were strangers to everything just. ²⁶ He was not content with his uncounted licentious deeds, but he also continued with such audacity that he framed evil reports in the various localities; and many of his friends, intently observing the king's purpose,

p Or *epiphany*
q Or *the houses of the abominations*
r Other ancient authorities read *pierced*

---

earth, Bar.3.24–25. *This city*, Jerusalem. *Place*, see 1.9 n.; 1 Kg.9.3. *No need of anything*, Acts 17.25; 2 Macc.14.35–36. **10:** *Promised . . . you would listen*, Dt.4.30; 30.1–6; 1 Kg.8.33–34, 48–50. **12:** *Our fathers . . . you . . . received*, 1 Sam.12.10–11; Ps.22.4–5; 106.43; Neh.9.28. **14:** *Glorious name*, Jdt.9.8. **15:** *The heaven of heavens*, 1 Kg.8.27; Is.66.1. *Unapproachable by man*, Pr.30.4; Is.57.15; Bar.3.29. **18:** *Trampled down*, Is.10.10–11; Dan.8.13. **19:** *Wipe away our sins*, Ps.51.2,9. **20:** *Mercies*, Ps.79.8,13.

2.21–24: The punishment of Ptolemy. 21: *Holy ones*, see Is.57.15 LXX. **22:** *Paralyzed*, compare the punishment of Heliodorus (2 Macc.3.22–30) and of Antiochus (2 Macc.9.4–7). **23:** *Friends*, the higher officers and courtiers of the king (see 4 Macc.8.5 n.). *Lose his life*, 2 Macc.3.31. **24:** *By no means repented*, 2 Macc.9.7.

2.25–33: Hostile measures against the Jews of Alexandria. 25: Inasmuch as these *companions* have not, in fact, been *previously mentioned* in the present text of 3 Macc., we have additional evidence that the opening section has been lost (see 1.1–7 n.). **26:** *Friends*, see v.23 n.

themselves also followed his will. [27] He proposed to inflict public disgrace upon the Jewish community,[s] and he set up a stone[t] on the tower in the courtyard with this inscription: [28] "None of those who do not sacrifice shall enter their sanctuaries, and all Jews shall be subjected to a registration involving poll tax and to the status of slaves. Those who object to this are to be taken by force and put to death; [29] those who are registered are also to be branded on their bodies by fire with the ivy-leaf symbol of Dionysus, and they shall also be reduced to their former limited status." [30] In order that he might not appear to be an enemy to all, he inscribed below: "But if any of them prefer to join those who have been initiated into the mysteries, they shall have equal citizenship with the Alexandrians."

31 Now some, however, with an obvious abhorrence of the price to be exacted for maintaining the religion of their city,[u] readily gave themselves up, since they expected to enhance their reputation by their future association with the king. [32] But the majority acted firmly with a courageous spirit and did not depart from their religion; and by paying money in exchange for life they confidently attempted to save themselves from the registration. [33] They remained resolutely hopeful of obtaining help, and they abhorred those who separated themselves from them, considering them to be enemies of the Jewish nation,[v] and depriving them of common fellowship and mutual help.

3 When the impious king comprehended this situation, he became so infuriated that not only was he enraged against those Jews who lived in Alexandria, but was still more bitterly hostile toward those in the countryside; and he ordered that all should promptly be gathered into one place, and put to death by the most cruel means. [2] While these matters were being arranged, a hostile rumor was circulated against the Jewish nation[v] by men who conspired to do them ill, a pretext being given by a report that they hindered others[w] from the observance of their customs. [3] The Jews, however, continued to maintain good will and unswerving loyalty toward the dynasty; [4] but because they worshiped God and conducted themselves by his law, they kept their separateness with respect to foods. For this reason they appeared hateful to some; [5] but since they adorned their style of life with the good deeds of upright people, they were established in good repute among all men. [6] Nevertheless those of other races paid no heed to their good service to their nation, which was common talk among all; [7] instead they gossiped about the differences in worship and foods, alleging that these people were loyal neither to the king nor to his authorities, but were hostile and greatly opposed to his government. So they attached no ordinary reproach to them.

8 The Greeks in the city, though wronged in no way, when they saw an

s Gk *the nation*   t Gk *stele*
u The Greek text of this clause is uncertain
v Gk *the nation*   w Gk *them*

28: *Registration*, a rare Greek word (*laographia*), which has been found in Greek papyri from Egypt, refers to a list of all people of the lower classes and of the slaves. **29:** Such branding in honor of a deity was not uncommon in ancient times (compare Rev.7.3; 13.16–17). According to 2 Macc.6.7 Antiochus introduced the worship of Dionysus into Jerusalem. **32:** *Paying money*, as bribes. **33:** *Depriving them of . . . fellowship*, 2 Jn.10–11.

   3.1–10: The Jews and their neighbors. 1: The distinction between Jews in *Alexandria* and those in the *country* is made also in 4.11–12. **2:** The *rumor* (Est.3.8) maliciously represents the Jews as hostile to the best interests of the state. **4:** *Separateness with respect to foods*, for a defense of the observance of Jewish dietary rules, see the *Letter of Aristeas*, §§128–166. **5:** Dt.4.5; Col.4.5; 1 Th.4.12. **7:** For similar charges see Est.3.8; Ad. Est.13.4–5. **8:** *The Greeks*, the nobler, cultivated class, in distinction from "those of other races" (v.6).

unexpected tumult around these people and the crowds that suddenly were forming, were not strong enough to help them, for they lived under tyranny. They did try to console them, being grieved at the situation, and expected that matters would change; [9] for such a great community ought not be left to its fate when it had committed no offense. [10] And already some of their neighbors and friends and business associates had taken some of them aside privately and were pledging to protect them and to exert more earnest efforts for their assistance.

11 Then the king, boastful of his present good fortune, and not considering the might of the supreme God,[x] but assuming that he would persevere constantly in his same purpose, wrote this letter against them: [12] "King Ptolemy Philopator to his generals and soldiers in Egypt and all its districts, greetings and good health. [13] I myself and our government are faring well. [14] When our expedition took place in Asia, as you yourselves know, it was brought to conclusion, according to plan, by the gods' deliberate alliance with us in battle, [15] and we considered that we should not rule the nations inhabiting Coele-Syria and Phoenicia by the power of the spear but should cherish them with clemency and great benevolence, gladly treating them well. [16] And when we had granted very great revenues to the temples in the cities, we came on to Jerusalem also, and went up to honor the temple of those wicked people, who never cease from their folly. [17] They accepted our presence by word, but insincerely by deed, because when we proposed to enter their inner temple and honor it with magnificent and most beautiful offerings, [18] they were carried away by their traditional conceit, and excluded us from entering; but they were spared the exercise of our power because of the benevolence which we have toward all. [19] By maintaining their manifest ill-will toward us, they become the only people among all nations who hold their heads high in defiance of kings and their own benefactors, and are unwilling to regard any action as sincere.

20 "But we, when we arrived in Egypt victorious, accommodated ourselves to their folly and did as was proper, since we treat all nations with benevolence. [21] Among other things, we made known to all our amnesty toward their compatriots here, both because of their alliance with us and the myriad affairs liberally entrusted to them from the beginning; and we ventured to make a change, by deciding both to deem them worthy of Alexandrian citizenship and to make them participants in our regular religious rites.[y] [22] But in their innate malice they took this in a contrary spirit, and disdained what is good. Since they incline constantly to evil, [23] they not only spurn the priceless citizenship, but also both by speech and by silence they abominate those few among them who are sincerely disposed toward us; in every situation, in accordance with their infamous way of life, they secretly suspect that we may soon alter our policy. [24] Therefore, fully convinced by these indications that they are ill-disposed toward us in every way, we have taken precautions lest, if a sudden disorder should later arise against us, we should have these impious people behind our backs as traitors and barbarous enemies. [25] Therefore we have given orders that, as soon as this letter shall arrive, you are to send to

x Gk *the greatest God*
y Other ancient authorities read *partners of our regular priests*

3.11–30: Ptolemy orders the arrest of all Jews in his kingdom. 11: *Assuming that he would persevere*, a reference to the calamity that came upon him by which he forgot his own previous commands (5.27–28). **15:** *Benevolence*, Greek *philanthropia* (see vv.18,20), was regarded as a major political virtue during the Hellenistic (and Byzantine) period. **18:** *Excluded*, 1.10–12. **21:** For the confidence reposed in Jews, see 6.25 and Josephus, *Ant.* XIX.v.2. **24:** *Behind our* us those who live among you, together with their wives and children, with insulting and harsh treatment, and bound securely with iron fetters, to suffer the sure and shameful death that befits enemies. 26 For when these all have been punished, we are sure that for the remaining time the government will be established for ourselves in good order and in the best state. 27 But whoever shelters any of the Jews, old people or children or even infants, will be tortured to death with the most hateful torments, together with his family. 28 Any one willing to give information will receive the property of the one who incurs the punishment, and also two thousand drachmas from the royal treasury, and will be awarded his freedom.z 29 Every place detected sheltering a Jew is to be made unapproachable and burned with fire, and shall become useless for all time to any mortal creature." 30 The letter was written in the above form.

4 In every place, then, where this decree arrived, a feast at public expense was arranged for the Gentiles with shouts and gladness, for the inveterate enmity which had long ago been in their minds was now made evident and outspoken. 2 But among the Jews there was incessant mourning, lamentation, and tearful cries; everywhere their hearts were burning, and they groaned because of the unexpected destruction that had suddenly been decreed for them. 3 What district or city, or what habitable place at all, or what streets were not filled with mourning and wailing for them? 4 For with such a harsh and ruthless spirit were they being sent off, all together, by the generals in the several cities, that at the sight of their unusual punish-

ments, even some of their enemies, perceiving the common object of pity before their eyes, reflected upon the uncertainty of life and shed tears at the most miserable expulsion of these people. 5 For a multitude of gray-headed old men, sluggish and bent with age, was being led away, forced to march at a swift pace by the violence with which they were driven in such a shameful manner. 6 And young women who had just entered the bridal chamber to share married life exchanged joy for wailing, their myrrh-perfumed hair sprinkled with ashes, and were carried away unveiled, all together raising a lament instead of a wedding song, as they were torn by the harsh treatment of the heathen.a 7 In bonds and in public view they were violently dragged along as far as the place of embarkation. 8 Their husbands, in the prime of youth, their necks encircled with ropes instead of garlands, spent the remaining days of their marriage festival in lamentations instead of good cheer and youthful revelry, seeing death immediately before them.b 9 They were brought on board like wild animals, driven under the constraint of iron bonds; some were fastened by the neck to the benches of the boats, others had their feet secured by unbreakable fetters, 10 and in addition they were confined under a solid deck, so that with their eyes in total darkness, they should undergo treatment befitting traitors during the whole voyage.

11 When these men had been brought to the place called Schedia, and the voyage was concluded as the king had decreed, he commanded that they

z Gk *crowned with freedom*
a One ancient authority reads *as though torn by heathen whelps*
b Gk *seeing Hades already lying at their feet*

---

backs, Ex.1.10. **28**: *Awarded his freedom*, another rendering is "crowned at the Eleutheria" (a festival of Dionysus; see 2.29 n.). **29**: *Useless for all time*, Ad. Est.16.24.
4.1–21: The Jews brought to Alexandria and imprisoned. 1: *Enmity* on the part of native-born Egyptians for the Jews is assumed in 3 Macc.; contrast 3.8. **2**: *Mourning, lamentation, and tearful cries*, Est.4.3. **4**: *Unusual punishments*, 2 Macc.9.6. **6**: *Young women*, 1 Macc.1.26–27. **11**: *Schedia*, a promontory about three miles from Alexandria. *The hippodrome* was situated at the east or Canobic gate of Alexandria; according to Strabo (xvii.1.10, 16) a canal joined Schedia and the Canobic gate. *Inside . . . the city*, implies that Jews living in Alexandria (see

should be enclosed in the hippodrome which had been built with a monstrous perimeter wall in front of the city, and which was well suited to make them an obvious spectacle to all coming back into the city and to those from the city*c* going out into the country, so that they could neither communicate with the king's forces nor in any way claim to be inside the circuit of the city.*d* 12 And when this had happened, the king, hearing that the Jews' compatriots from the city frequently went out in secret to lament bitterly the ignoble misfortune of their brothers, 13 ordered in his rage that these men be dealt with in precisely the same fashion as the others, not omitting any detail of their punishment. 14 The entire race was to be registered individually, not for the hard labor that has been briefly mentioned before, but to be tortured with the outrages that he had ordered, and at the end to be destroyed in the space of a single day. 15 The registration of these people was therefore conducted with bitter haste and zealous intentness from the rising of the sun till its setting, and though uncompleted it stopped after forty days.

16 The king was greatly and continually filled with joy, organizing feasts in honor of all his idols, with a mind alienated from truth and with a profane mouth, praising speechless things that are not able even to communicate or to come to one's help, and uttering improper words against the supreme God.*e* 17 But after the previously mentioned interval of time the scribes declared to the king that they were no longer able to take the census of the Jews because of their innumerable multitude, 18 although most of them were still in the country, some still residing in their homes, and some at the place;*f* the task was impossible for all the generals in Egypt. 19 After he had threatened them severely, charging that they had been bribed to contrive a means of escape, he was clearly convinced about the matter 20 when they said and proved that both the paper*g* and the pens they used for writing had already given out. 21 But this was an act of the invincible providence of him who was aiding the Jews from heaven.

5 Then the king, completely inflexible, was filled with overpowering anger and wrath; so he summoned Hermon, keeper of the elephants, 2 and ordered him on the following day to drug all the elephants – five hundred in number – with large handfuls of frankincense and plenty of unmixed wine, and to drive them in, maddened by the lavish abundance of liquor, so that the Jews might meet their doom. 3 When he had given these orders he returned to his feasting, together with those of his friends and of the army who were especially hostile toward the Jews. 4 And Hermon, keeper of the elephants, proceeded faithfully to carry out the orders. 5 The servants in charge of the Jews*h* went out in the evening and bound the hands of the wretched people and arranged for their continued custody through the night, convinced that the whole nation would experience its final destruction. 6 For to the Gentiles it appeared that the Jews were left

c Gk *those of them*
d Or *claim protection of the walls;* Greek obscure
e Gk *the greatest God*
f Other ancient authorities read *on the way*
g Or *paper factory* h Gk *them*

v.12, *compatriots from the city*) had been thus far unmolested (yet compare 3.1). **14:** *Mentioned before*, see 2.28. **15:** *Forty days*, see 2 Macc.5.2. **16:** *Feasts*, Dan.5.4. *Supreme God*, see 1.9 n. **17:** *Their innumerable multitude*, an obvious hyperbole. **19:** *Bribed*, see 2.32. **21:** *Was aiding*, the author prepares his readers to expect that a vigilant Providence will provide further help *from heaven*.

5.1–51: Ptolemy orders the execution of the Jews, but is twice thwarted (vv.12,27–28). **2:** *Five hundred elephants* is an exaggeration; Ptolemy had seventy-three elephants at the battle of Raphia. **3:** *Returned to his feasting*, 4.16. **5:** *Bound the hands*, according to 3.25 they had already been bound securely, but perhaps their hands had been loosened when the Jews were enclosed without any aid, [7] because in their bonds they were forcibly confined on every side. But with tears and a voice hard to silence they all called upon the Almighty Lord and Ruler of all power, their merciful God and Father, praying [8] that he avert with vengeance the evil plot against them and in a glorious manifestation rescue them from the fate now prepared for them. [9] So their entreaty ascended fervently to heaven.

10 Hermon, however, when he had drugged the pitiless elephants until they had been filled with a great abundance of wine and satiated with frankincense, presented himself at the courtyard early in the morning to report to the king about these preparations. [11] But the Lord[i] sent upon the king a portion of sleep, that beneficence which from the beginning, night and day, is bestowed by him who grants it to whomever he wishes. [12] And by the action of the Lord he was overcome by so pleasant and deep a sleep[j] that he quite failed in his lawless purpose and was completely frustrated in his inflexible plan. [13] Then the Jews, since they had escaped the appointed hour, praised their holy God and again begged him who is easily reconciled to show the might of his all-powerful hand to the arrogant Gentiles.

14 But now, since it was nearly the middle of the tenth hour, the person who was in charge of the invitations, seeing that the guests were assembled, approached the king and nudged him. [15] And when he had with difficulty roused him, he pointed out that the hour of the banquet was already slipping by, and he gave him an account of the situation. [16] The king, after considering this, returned to his drinking, and ordered those present for the banquet to recline opposite him. [17] When this was done he urged them to give themselves over to revelry and to make the present[k] portion of the banquet joyful by celebrating all the more. [18] After the party had been going on for some time, the king summoned Hermon and with sharp threats demanded to know why the Jews had been allowed to remain alive through the present day. [19] But when he, with the corroboration of his friends, pointed out that while it was still night he had carried out completely the order given him, [20] the king,[l] possessed by a savagery worse than that of Phalaris, said that the Jews[m] were benefited by today's sleep, "but," he added, "tomorrow without delay prepare the elephants in the same way for the destruction of the lawless Jews!" [21] When the king had spoken, all those present readily and joyfully with one accord gave their approval, and each departed to his own home. [22] But they did not so much employ the duration of the night in sleep as in devising all sorts of insults for those they thought to be doomed.

23 Then, as soon as the cock had crowed in the early morning, Hermon, having equipped[n] the beasts, began to move them along in the great colonnade. [24] The crowds of the city had been assembled for this most pitiful spectacle and they were eagerly waiting for daybreak. [25] But the Jews, at their last gasp, since the time had run out, stretched their hands toward heaven and with most tearful supplication and mournful dirges implored the supreme God[o] to help them again at once. [26] The rays of the sun were not yet shed abroad, and while the king was receiving his friends, Hermon arrived and invited him to come out,

i Gk *he*
j Other ancient authorities add *from evening to the ninth hour*
k Other ancient authorities read *delayed* (Gk *untimely*)
l Gk *he*   m Gk *they*   n Or *armed*
o Gk *the greatest God*

within the hippodrome (see 5.49 n.). **7:** The title *Father* is also given to God in Tob.13.4; Wis.11.10. **8:** *Glorious manifestation*, 2 Macc.2.21. **11:** The divine gift of *sleep* is extolled in the Latin poets (Seneca, *Hercules Furens* 1066 ff.; Statius, *Silvae* v.4) compare Ps.127.2. **14:** *Middle of the tenth hour*, 3:30 p.m. **19:** *Friends*, see 2.23 n. **20:** *Phalaris*, tyrant of Agrigentum (c. 570–554 B.C.) whose cruelty was proverbial (Polybius XII.25). **23:** *The great colonnade* was no indicating that what the king desired was ready for action. ²⁷ But he, upon receiving the report and being struck by the unusual invitation to come out – since he had been completely overcome by incomprehension – inquired what the matter was for which this had been so zealously completed for him. ²⁸ This was the act of God who rules over all things, for he had implanted in the king's mind a forgetfulness of the things he had previously devised. ²⁹ Then Hermon and all the king's friends pointed out that the beasts and the armed forces were ready, "O king, according to your eager purpose."^p ³⁰ But at these words he was filled with an overpowering wrath, because by the providence of God his whole mind had been deranged in regard to these matters; and with a threatening look he said, ³¹ "Were your parents or children present, I would have prepared them to be a rich feast for the savage beasts instead of the Jews, who give me no ground for complaint and have exhibited to an extraordinary degree a full and firm loyalty to my ancestors. ³² In fact you would have been deprived of life instead of these, were it not for an affection arising from our nurture in common and your usefulness." ³³ So Hermon suffered an unexpected and dangerous threat, and his eyes wavered and his face fell. ³⁴ The king's friends one by one sullenly slipped away and dismissed^q the assembled people, each to his own occupation. ³⁵ Then the Jews, upon hearing what the king had said, praised the manifest Lord God, King of kings, since this also was his aid which they had received.

36 The king, however, reconvened the party in the same manner and urged the guests to return to their celebrating. ³⁷ After summoning Hermon he said in a threatening tone, "How many times, you poor wretch, must I give you orders about these things? ³⁸ Equip^r the elephants now once more for the destruction of the Jews tomorrow!" ³⁹ But the officials who were at table with him, wondering at his instability of mind, remonstrated as follows: ⁴⁰ "O king, how long will you try us, as though we are idiots, ordering now for a third time that they be destroyed, and again revoking your decree in the matter?^s ⁴¹ As a result the city is in a tumult because of its expectation; it is crowded with masses of people, and also in constant danger of being plundered." ⁴² Upon this the king, a Phalaris in everything and filled with madness, took no account of the changes of mind which had come about within him for the protection of the Jews, and he firmly swore an irrevocable oath that he would send them to death^t without delay, mangled by the knees and feet of the beasts, ⁴³ and would also march against Judea and rapidly level it to the ground with fire and spear, and by burning to the ground the temple inaccessible to him^u would quickly render it forever empty of those who offered sacrifices there. ⁴⁴ Then the friends and officers departed with great joy, and they confidently posted the armed forces at the places in the city most favorable for keeping guard. ⁴⁵ Now when the beasts had been brought virtually to a state of madness, so to speak, by the very fragrant draughts of wine mixed with frankincense and had been equipped with frightful devices, the elephant keeper ⁴⁶ entered at about dawn into the courtyard – the city now being filled with countless masses of people

p Other ancient authorities read *pointed to the beasts and the armed forces, saying, "They are ready, O king, according to your eager purpose."*
q Other ancient authorities read *he dismissed*
r Or *Arm*
s Other ancient authorities read *when the matter is in hand*
t Gk *Hades*   u Gk *us*

---

doubt some well-known place in Alexandria. **28:** *The act of God,* Pr.21.1. **29:** An interpolation in several Greek manuscripts indicates that though Ptolemy was moved by compassion and determined to release the Jews, Hermon influenced him to proceed with his plans to destroy them. **41:** The revolutionary character of the Alexandrians in ancient times is well known. **42:** *Phalaris,* see v. 20 n. **45:** The *frightful devices* were probably scythes, knives, and other

crowding their way into the hippodrome – and urged the king on to the
matter at hand. [47] So he, when he had
filled his impious mind with a deep
rage, rushed out in full force along with
the beasts, wishing to witness, with
invulnerable heart and with his own
eyes, the grievous and pitiful destruction of the aforementioned people.
[48] And when the Jews saw the dust
raised by the elephants going out at
the gate and by the following armed
forces, as well as by the trampling of
the crowd, and heard the loud and
tumultuous noise, [49] they thought that
this was their last moment of life, the
end of their most miserable suspense,
and giving way to lamentation and
groans they kissed each other, embracing relatives and falling into one
another's arms[v] – parents and children,
mothers and daughters, and others
with babies at their breasts who were
drawing their last milk. [50] Not only
this, but when they considered the
help which they had received before
from heaven they prostrated themselves
with one accord on the ground, removing the babies from their breasts,
[51] and cried out in a very loud voice,
imploring the Ruler over every power
to manifest himself and be merciful
to them, as they stood now at the
gates of death.[w]

6 Then a certain Eleazar, famous
among the priests of the country,
who had attained a ripe old age and
throughout his life had been adorned
with every virtue, directed the elders
around him to cease calling upon the
holy God and prayed as follows:
[2] "King of great power, Almighty

God Most High, governing all creation
with mercy, [3] look upon the descendants of Abraham, O Father, upon the
children of the sainted Jacob, a people
of your consecrated portion who are
perishing as foreigners in a foreign
land. [4] Pharaoh with his abundance of
chariots, the former ruler of this
Egypt, exalted with lawless insolence
and boastful tongue, you destroyed
together with his arrogant army by
drowning them in the sea, manifesting
the light of your mercy upon the nation
of Israel. [5] Sennacherib exulting in
his countless forces, oppressive king
of the Assyrians, who had already
gained control of the whole world by
the spear and was lifted up against
your holy city, speaking grievous words
with boasting and insolence, you, O
Lord, broke in pieces, showing your
power to many nations. [6] The three
companions in Babylon who had
voluntarily surrendered their lives to
the flames so as not to serve vain
things, you rescued unharmed, even
to a hair, moistening the fiery furnace
with dew and turning the flame against
all their enemies. [7] Daniel, who through
envious slanders was cast down into
the ground to lions as food for wild
beasts, you brought up to the light
unharmed. [8] And Jonah, wasting away
in the belly of a huge, sea-born monster,
you, Father, watched over and restored[x]
unharmed to all his family. [9] And now,
you who hate insolence, all-merciful
and protector of all, reveal yourself
quickly to those of the nation of

v Gk *falling upon their necks*   w Gk *Hades*
x Other ancient authorities read *rescued and restored;*
others, *recognized and restored;* others, *mercifully
restored*

---

military equipment attached to the different parts of the bodies of the elephants. **49:** *Embracing*,
but according to 6.27 they are still bound. **50–51:** The author continues to build up his thesis
that God was the only resort for the captives, and that their hope would not be frustrated. **51:**
Gates of death, Ps.9.13; 107.18.

6.1–15: The Prayer of Eleazar. Like Simon's prayer in 2.1–20, it is plainly Jewish in form and
style, containing doxology, thanksgiving for God's earlier interventions in Israel's history, and
petition for a new miracle. The emphasis is on the exclusiveness and separate standing of Israel
before God (v.3). Eleazar expects God's intervention, not on account of Israel's virtues or merits,
but because of divine mercy. **1:** *Eleazar*, a favorite name for a Jewish hero (2 Macc.6.18).
Priests, perhaps those of the Jewish temple at Leontopolis. **4:** *Pharaoh*, Ex.14.28. **5:** Sennacherib,
2 Kg.18.13; 19.35–37. **6:** *Three companions in Babylon*, Dan.3.22,27; S. of 3 Y.22–27. **7:** *Daniel*,
Dan.6.22. **8:** *Jonah*, Jon.2.10. **11:** Ps.115.2. **15:** *As you have said*, Lev.26.44.

Israel[y] – who are being outrageously treated by the abominable and lawless Gentiles. [10] Even if our lives have become entangled in impieties in our exile, rescue us from the hand of the enemy, and destroy us, Lord, by whatever fate you choose. [11] Let not the vain-minded praise their vanities[z] at the destruction of your beloved people, saying, 'Not even their god has rescued them.' [12] But you, O Eternal One, who have all might and all power, watch over us now and have mercy upon us who by the senseless insolence of the lawless are being deprived of life in the manner of traitors. [13] And let the Gentiles cower today in fear of your invincible might, O honored One, who have power to save the nation of Jacob. [14] The whole throng of infants and their parents entreat you with tears. [15] Let it be shown to all the Gentiles that you are with us, O Lord, and have not turned your face from us; but just as you have said, 'Not even when they were in the land of their enemies did I neglect them,' so accomplish it, O Lord."

16 Just as Eleazar was ending his prayer, the king arrived at the hippodrome with the beasts and all the arrogance of his forces. [17] And when the Jews observed this they raised great cries to heaven so that even the nearby valleys resounded with them and brought an uncontrollable terror upon the army. [18] Then the most glorious, almighty, and true God revealed his holy face and opened the heavenly gates, from which two glorious angels of fearful aspect descended, visible to all but the Jews. [19] They opposed the forces of the enemy and filled them with confusion and terror, binding them with immovable shackles. [20] Even the king began to shudder bodily, and

he forgot his sullen insolence. [21] The beasts turned back upon the armed forces following them and began trampling and destroying them. [22] Then the king's anger was turned to pity and tears because of the things that he had devised beforehand. [23] For when he heard the shouting and saw them all fallen headlong to destruction, he wept and angrily threatened his friends, saying, [24] "You are committing treason and surpassing tyrants in cruelty; and even me, your benefactor, you are now attempting to deprive of dominion and life by secretly devising acts of no advantage to the kingdom. [25] Who is it that has taken each man from his home and senselessly gathered here those who faithfully have held the fortresses of our country? [26] Who is it that has so lawlessly encompassed with outrageous treatment those who from the beginning differed from[a] all nations in their goodwill toward us and often have accepted willingly the worst of human dangers? [27] Loose and untie their unjust bonds! Send them back to their homes in peace, begging pardon for your former actions![b] [28] Release the sons of the almighty and living God of heaven, who from the time of our ancestors until now has granted an unimpeded and notable stability to our government." [29] These then were the things he said; and the Jews, immediately released, praised their holy God and Savior, since they now had escaped death.

30 Then the king, when he had returned to the city, summoned the official in charge of the revenues and ordered him to provide to the Jews both wines and everything else needed

y Other ancient authorities read *to the saints of Israel*
z Or *bless their vain gods*   a Or *excelled above*
b Other ancient authorities read *revoking your former commands*

6.16–29: The Jews are delivered, and the king now favors them. 18: *Most glorious*, Greek *megalodoxos*, compare 1 Enoch 14.20 and Testament of Levi 3.4, where God is called "the Great Glory." *Angels of fearful aspect*, for similar terror-inspiring apparitions, see Wis.17.3,15; 18.17; 2 Macc.3.25–29; 10.29. *Visible to all but the Jews*, Dan.10.7; Acts 9.7; 22.6–9. **21:** *The beasts turned* upon the king's own *forces*, a detail found also in Josephus's account (*Against Apion*, ii.5), compare Ps.7.15–16; 9.15–16; 35.8; 57.6. **25:** *Faithfully*, contrast the king's language in 3.24. **28:** *Sons of . . . God*, Wis.18.13.

for a festival of seven days, deciding that they should celebrate their rescue with all joyfulness in that same place in which they had expected to meet their destruction. [31] Accordingly those disgracefully treated and near to death,[c] or rather, who stood at its gates, arranged for a banquet of deliverance instead of a bitter and lamentable death, and full of joy they apportioned to celebrants the place which had been prepared for their destruction and burial. [32] They ceased their chanting of dirges and took up the song of their fathers, praising God, their Savior and worker of wonders.[d] Putting an end to all mourning and wailing, they formed choruses[e] as a sign of peaceful joy. [33] Likewise also the king, after convening a great banquet to celebrate these events, gave thanks to heaven unceasingly and lavishly for the unexpected rescue which he[f] had experienced. [34] And those who had previously believed that the Jews would be destroyed and become food for birds, and had joyfully registered them, groaned as they themselves were overcome by disgrace, and their fire-breathing boldness was ignominiously[g] quenched. [35] But the Jews, when they had arranged the aforementioned choral group, as we have said before, passed the time in feasting to the accompaniment of joyous thanksgiving and psalms. [36] And when they had ordained a public rite for these things in their whole community and for their descendants, they instituted the observance of the aforesaid days as a festival, not for drinking and gluttony, but because of the deliverance that had come to them through God. [37] Then they petitioned the king, asking for dismissal to their homes. [38] So their registration was carried out from the twenty-fifth of Pachon to the fourth of Epeiph,[h] for forty days; and their destruction was set for the fifth to the seventh of Epeiph,[i] the three days [39] on which the Lord of all most gloriously revealed his mercy and rescued them all together and unharmed. [40] Then they feasted, provided with everything by the king, until the fourteenth day,[j] on which also they made the petition for their dismissal. [41] The king granted their request at once and wrote the following letter for them to the generals in the cities, magnanimously expressing his concern:

7 "King Ptolemy Philopator to the generals in Egypt and all in authority in his government, greetings and good health. [2] We ourselves and our children are faring well, the great God guiding our affairs according to our desire. [3] Certain of our friends, frequently urging us with malicious intent, persuaded us to gather together the Jews of the kingdom in a body and to punish them with barbarous penalties as traitors; [4] for they declared that our government would never be firmly established until this was accomplished, because of the ill-will which these people had toward all nations. [5] They also led them out with harsh treatment as slaves, or rather as traitors, and, girding themselves with

c Gk *Hades*
d Other ancient authorities read *praising Israel and the wonder-working God;* or *praising Israel's Savior, the wonder-working God*
e Or *choral groups*
f Other ancient authorities read *they*
g Other ancient authorities read *completely*
h May 20–June 28   i June 29–July 1   j July 8

6.30–41: The Jews celebrate their deliverance. 32: *The song of their fathers,* perhaps Ps.136, which was used earlier as a hymn of thanksgiving (1 Chr.16.41; 2 Chr.5.13; 7.3; Ezra 3.11). **34:** *Food for birds,* Gen.40.19; Ezek.39.4; 2 Macc.9.15. **36:** The institution of Jewish festivals is a common feature at this period (compare Est.9.15; 1 Macc.4.56; 7.49; 13.51; 2 Macc.10.6; 15.36). **38:** *Epeiph,* or Epiphi.

7.1–9: Ptolemy's letter on behalf of the Jews. 2: *Children,* Philopator had only one legitimate son, born in 209–8, who reigned later as Ptolemy V Epiphanes (203–181 B.C.). Either the author had no knowledge of Philopator's family life, or the king referred in general terms to include all members of his court. **3:** The king seeks to exonerate himself, blaming others. **4:** *Ill-will,* 3.2,7; Est.3.8; Ad. Est.13.4–5. **5:** *Scythian custom,* see 2 Macc.4.47 n.; 4 Macc.10.7 n.

a cruelty more savage than that of Scythian custom, they tried without any inquiry or examination to put them to death. ⁶ But we very severely threatened them for these acts, and in accordance with the clemency which we have toward all men we barely spared their lives. Since we have come to realize that the God of heaven surely defends the Jews, always taking their part as a father does for his children, ⁷ and since we have taken into account the friendly and firm goodwill which they had toward us and our ancestors, we justly have acquitted them of every charge of whatever kind. ⁸ We also have ordered each and every one to return to his own home, with no one in any place*ᵏ* doing them harm at all or reproaching them for the irrational things that have happened. ⁹ For you should know that if we devise any evil against them or cause them any grief at all, we always shall have not man but the Ruler over every power, the Most High God, in everything and inescapably as an antagonist to avenge such acts. Farewell."

10 Upon receiving this letter the Jews did not immediately hurry to make their departure, but they requested of the king that at their own hands those of the Jewish nation who had willfully transgressed against the holy God and the law of God should receive the punishment they deserved. ¹¹ For they declared that those who for the belly's sake had transgressed the divine commandments would never be favorably disposed toward the king's government. ¹² The king*ˡ* then, admitting and approving the truth of what they said, granted them a general license so that freely and without royal authority or supervision they might destroy those everywhere in his kingdom who had transgressed the law of God. ¹³ When they had applauded him in fitting manner, their priests and the whole multitude shouted the Hallelujah and joyfully departed. ¹⁴ And so on their way they punished and put to a public and shameful death any whom they met of their fellow-countrymen who had become defiled. ¹⁵ In that day they put to death more than three hundred men; and they kept the day as a joyful festival, since they had destroyed the profaners. ¹⁶ But those who had held fast to God even to death and had received the full enjoyment of deliverance began their departure from the city, crowned with all sorts of very fragrant flowers, joyfully and loudly giving thanks to the one God of their fathers, the eternal Savior*ᵐ* of Israel, in words of praise and all kinds of melodious songs.

17 When they had arrived at Ptolemais, called "rose-bearing" because of a characteristic of the place, the fleet waited for them, in accord with the common desire, for seven days. ¹⁸ There they celebrated their deliverance,*ⁿ* for the king had generously provided all things to them for their journey, to each as far as his own house. ¹⁹ And when they had landed in peace with appropriate thanksgiving, there too in like manner they decided to observe these days as a joyous festival during the time of their stay. ²⁰ Then, after inscribing them as holy on a pillar and dedicating a place of

k Other ancient authorities read *way*   *l* Gk *He*
m Other ancient authorities read *the holy Savior;* others, *the holy One*
n Gk *they made a cup of deliverance*

6: *Threatened them,* that is, the enemies of the Jews. *Father,* 5.7 n.; Ps.103.13. **8:** *In any place* through which the Jews might pass on their return.

7.10–23: The Jews punish the renegades and return home. 10: *They requested of the king,* in the later periods of their history the Jews were obliged to seek permission from their foreign rulers to execute their own laws pertaining to capital punishment (Dt.13.6–18; Est.8.8–11; Jn.18.31. **13:** *Hallelujah,* Tob.13.18. **16:** Bar.5.6,8. **17:** This *Ptolemais* was probably not the city of this name near Thebes in Upper Egypt, but "Ptolemais at the harbor" in the Arsinoite nome, about twelve miles from present-day Cairo. *Rose-bearing* is not elsewhere applied to Ptolemais. **20:** *And sea,* there was no sea to cross in Egypt.

prayer at the site of the festival, they departed unharmed, free, and over-joyed, since at the king's command they had been brought safely by land and sea and river each to his own place. ²¹ They also possessed greater prestige among their enemies, being held in honor and awe; and they were not subject at all to confiscation of their belongings by any one. ²² Besides

they all recovered all of their property, in accordance with the registration, so that those who held any restored it to them with extreme fear.º So the supreme God perfectly performed great deeds for their deliverance. ²³ Blessed be the Deliverer of Israel through all times! Amen.

o Other ancient authorities read *a very large supplement*

THE FOURTH BOOK OF THE

MACCABEES

The book known as 4 Maccabees is included in important manuscripts of the Greek Bible, and was early translated into Syriac. Although never canonized, it has deeply influenced the preaching and piety of the Eastern Churches.

At one time 4 Maccabees was attributed to Josephus and given the title *On the Supremacy of Reason.* This describes it well, for it is a diatribe or lecture, or perhaps a panegyric, on religious reason, as exemplified by the story of the martyrdoms of Eleazar, the seven brothers, and their mother. Its traditional title was no doubt adopted because the account is an expansion of 2 Macc.6.12–7.42, and the story belongs to the Maccabean period.

The book is a classic example of the interpretation of Judaism in terms of Greek philosophy. The ideas are Stoic (with some significant differences), and so is the terminology. The treatise was written originally in Greek, and in the florid Asiatic style. Possibly it was first delivered as an oration at a festival commemorating the Maccabean martyrs or at the Feast of Dedication (1.10; 3.19; 14.9; compare Jn.10.22).

The author's theology is genuinely Jewish but with two special characteristics. The martyrdoms are a substitutionary atonement that expiates the nation's sin and purifies the land (1.11; 17.21; 18.4). The martyrs are immediately immortal, received by the patriarchs and living in God (7.19; 16.25).

The book was evidently written in the period A.D. 20–54, when Cilicia was joined to Syria and Phoenicia as a single province (4.2), and it is tempting to date it to the reign of Caligula (A.D. 37–41), who proposed to violate the Jerusalem temple (compare 4.5–14).

Alexandria has been proposed as the place of composition, and Jerusalem cannot be excluded. Antioch, however, has the best claim, for the martyrs might have been brought to the royal capital (5.1), and in Antioch the Jews were called "Hebrews," as in this book.

THE SUBJECT THAT I AM ABOUT TO discuss is most philosophical, that is, whether devout reason is sovereign over the emotions. So it is right for me to advise you to pay earnest attention to philosophy. ² For the subject is essential to everyone who is seeking knowledge, and in addition it includes the praise of the highest virtue – I mean, of course, rational judgment. ³ If, then, it is evident that reason rules over those emotions that hinder self-control, namely, gluttony and lust, ⁴ it is also clear that it masters the emotions that hinder one from justice, such as malice, and those that stand in the way of courage, namely, anger, fear, and pain. ⁵ Some

might perhaps ask, "If reason rules the emotions, why is it not sovereign over forgetfulness and ignorance?" Their attempt at argument is ridiculous!*ᵃ* ⁶ For reason does not rule its own emotions, but those that are opposed to justice, courage, and self-control;*ᵇ* and it is not for the purpose of destroying them, but so that one may not give way to them.

7 I could prove to you from many and various examples that reason*ᶜ* is dominant over the emotions, ⁸ but I can demonstrate it best from the noble bravery of those who died for the sake

a Or *They are attempting to make my argument ridiculous!*
b Other ancient authorities add *and rational judgment*
c Other ancient authorities read *devout reason*

1.1–3.18: Philosophical introduction. The principal thesis is stated in vv.3–12, which concludes with a short doxology, and is developed further in 1.13–3.18. **1**: *Devout,* Greek *eusebēs,* religious or pious; compare 5.7,31. **2–4**: *Rational judgment . . . self-control . . . justice . . . courage,* the four cardinal virtues of the Platonic and Stoic traditions. **5**: The objection is dealt with in 2.24–3.1. **8**: *Eleazar,* 2 Macc.6.18; 3 Macc.6.1. **10**: Compare 3.19 and see Introduction.

of virtue, Eleazar and the seven brothers and their mother. ⁹ All of these, by despising sufferings that bring death, demonstrated that reason controls the emotions. ¹⁰ On this anniversary*d* it is fitting for me to praise for their virtues those who, with their mother, died for the sake of nobility and goodness, but I would also call them blessed for the honor in which they are held. ¹¹ For all people, even their torturers, marveled at their courage and endurance, and they became the cause of the downfall of tyranny over their nation. By their endurance they conquered the tyrant, and thus their native land was purified through them. ¹² I shall shortly have an opportunity to speak of this; but, as my custom is, I shall begin by stating my main principle, and then I shall turn to their story, giving glory to the all-wise God.

13 Our inquiry, accordingly, is whether reason is sovereign over the emotions. ¹⁴ We shall decide just what reason is and what emotion is, how many kinds of emotions there are, and whether reason rules over all these. ¹⁵ Now reason is the mind that with sound logic prefers the life of wisdom. ¹⁶ Wisdom, next, is the knowledge of divine and human matters and the causes of these. ¹⁷ This, in turn, is education in the law, by which we learn divine matters reverently and human affairs to our advantage. ¹⁸ Now the kinds of wisdom are rational judgment, justice, courage, and self-control. ¹⁹ Rational judgment is supreme over all of these, since by means of it reason rules over the emotions. ²⁰ The two most comprehensive types*e* of the emotions are pleasure and pain; and each of these is by nature concerned with both body and soul. ²¹ The emotions of both pleasure and pain have many consequences. ²² Thus desire precedes pleasure and delight follows it. ²³ Fear precedes pain and sorrow comes after. ²⁴ Anger, as a man will see if he reflects on this experience, is an emotion embracing pleasure and pain. ²⁵ In pleasure there exists even a malevolent tendency, which is the most complex of all the emotions. ²⁶ In the soul it is boastfulness, covetousness, thirst for honor, rivalry, and malice; ²⁷ in the body, indiscriminate eating, gluttony, and solitary gormandizing.

28 Just as pleasure and pain are two plants growing from the body and the soul, so there are many offshoots of these plants,*f* ²⁹ each of which the master cultivator, reason, weeds and prunes and ties up and waters and thoroughly irrigates, and so tames the jungle of habits and emotions. ³⁰ For reason is the guide of the virtues, but over the emotions it is sovereign.

Observe now first of all that rational judgment is sovereign over the emotions by virtue of the restraining power of self-control. ³¹ Self-control, then, is dominance over the desires. ³² Some desires are mental, others are physical, and reason obviously rules over both. ³³ Otherwise how is it that when we are attracted to forbidden foods we abstain from the pleasure to be had from them? Is it not because reason is able to rule over appetites? I for one think so. ³⁴ Therefore when we crave seafood and fowl and animals and all sorts of foods that are forbidden to us by the law, we abstain because of domination by reason. ³⁵ For the

d Gk *At this time*   *e* Or *sources*
f Other ancient authorities read *these emotions*

11: *Tyranny*, the attempt of Antiochus IV (4.15) to impose pagan worship on the Jewish *nation*; see 5.1 n. *Purified*, the idea of expiation is developed further in 6.28–29; 17.21. **17:** *Education in the law*, Jews regarded the Mosaic law as philosophical and the highest form of education (see 11.21 n.; 18.6–19 n.). *We learn . . . to our advantage*, compare the Stoic definition of wisdom in Cicero's *Tusculan Disputations* iv.25.57. **18:** The four *kinds* are found also in Wis.8.7. **24:** *As a man . . . experience*, the Greek is obscure. **27:** Job 31.17. **33:** *Reason is able to rule over appetites*, in Judaism, desires are not to be extirpated, as Stoics taught, but are to be controlled; compare v.6; Mishnah *P. Aboth* 4.1. **34:** *Seafood*, Lev.11.1–31; Dt.14.3–21; Acts 10.10–14.

emotions of the appetites are restrained, checked by the temperate mind, and all the impulses of the body are bridled by reason.

2 And why is it amazing that the desires of the mind for the enjoyment of beauty are rendered powerless? ² It is for this reason, certainly, that the temperate Joseph is praised, because by mental effort*ᵍ* he overcame sexual desire. ³ For when he was young and in his prime for intercourse, by his reason he nullified the frenzy*ʰ* of the passions. ⁴ Not only is reason proved to rule over the frenzied urge of sexual desire, but also over every desire.*ⁱ* ⁵ Thus the law says, "You shall not covet your neighbor's wife . . . or anything that is your neighbor's." ⁶ In fact, since the law has told us not to covet, I could prove to you all the more that reason is able to control desires.

Just so it is with the emotions that hinder one from justice. ⁷ Otherwise how could it be that someone who is habitually a solitary gormandizer, a glutton, or even a drunkard can learn a better way, unless reason is clearly lord of the emotions? ⁸ Thus, as soon as a man adopts a way of life in accordance with the law, even though he is a lover of money, he is forced to act contrary to his natural ways and to lend without interest to the needy and to cancel the debt when the seventh year arrives. ⁹ If one is greedy, he is ruled by the law through his reason so that he neither gleans his harvest nor gathers the last grapes from the vineyard.

In all other matters we can recognize that reason rules the emotions. ¹⁰ For the law prevails even over affection for parents, so that virtue is not abandoned for their sakes.

¹¹ It is superior to love for one's wife, so that one rebukes her when she breaks the law. ¹² It takes precedence over love for children, so that one punishes them for misdeeds. ¹³ It is sovereign over the relationship of friends, so that one rebukes friends when they act wickedly. ¹⁴ Do not consider it paradoxical when reason, through the law, can prevail even over enmity. The fruit trees of the enemy are not cut down, but one preserves the property of enemies from the destroyers and helps raise up what has fallen.*ʲ*

15 It is evident that reason rules even*ᵏ* the more violent emotions: lust for power, vainglory, boasting, arrogance, and malice. ¹⁶ For the temperate mind repels all these malicious emotions, just as it repels anger – for it is sovereign over even this. ¹⁷ When Moses was angry with Dathan and Abiram he did nothing against them in anger, but controlled his anger by reason. ¹⁸ For, as I have said, the temperate mind is able to get the better of the emotions, to correct some, and to render others powerless. ¹⁹ Why else did Jacob, our most wise father, censure the households of Simeon and Levi for their irrational slaughter of the entire tribe of the Shechemites, saying, "Cursed be their anger"? ²⁰ For if reason could not control anger, he would not have spoken thus. ²¹ Now when God fashioned man, he planted in him emotions and inclinations, ²² but at the same time he enthroned the mind among the senses as a sacred governor over them all. ²³ To the mind he gave the law; and one who lives subject to this

g Other ancient authorities add *in reasoning*
h Or *gadfly*
i Or *all covetousness*
j Or *the beasts that have fallen* (Ex 23.4–5 LXX)
k Other ancient authorities read *through*

2.1: *Enjoyment of beauty* refers to sexual desire but also suggests the concept of *eros* in Plato's *Symposium.* **2:** *Joseph*, Gen.39.7–12. **8:** *Lend without interest*, to other Jews, Ex.22.25. *Seventh year*, Dt.15.1–3. **9:** Lev.19.9–10; Dt.20.19–20. **11–12:** Mt.10.37; Lk.14.26. **14:** Dt.20.19–20; Ex.23.4–5; Josephus, *Against Apion* ii.211–212. **17:** *Dathan and Abiram*, Num.16.1–35; Sir.45.18. **19:** Gen.49.7. **21:** According to rabbinic Judaism, God *planted* the good and the evil *inclinations* in man; the latter is to be controlled, and in itself is not essentially evil. **23:** *Will rule a kingdom*, according to the Stoics and Philo, the wise man is a king. Compare the different concept of the will rule a kingdom that is temperate, just, good, and courageous.

24 How is it then, one might say, that if reason is master of the emotions, it does not control forgetfulness and ignorance? 3 ¹ This notion is entirely ridiculous; for it is evident that reason rules not over its own emotions, but over those of the body. ² No one of us can eradicate that kind of desire, but reason can provide a way for us not to be enslaved by desire. ³ No one of us*ˡ* can eradicate anger from the mind, but reason can help to deal with anger. ⁴ No one of us can eradicate malice, but reason can fight at our side so that we are not overcome by malice. ⁵ For reason does not uproot the emotions but is their antagonist.

6 Now this can be explained more clearly by the story of King David's thirst. ⁷ David had been attacking the Philistines all day long, and together with the soldiers of his nation had slain many of them. ⁸ Then when evening fell, he*ᵐ* came, sweating and quite exhausted, to the royal tent, around which the whole army of our ancestors had encamped. ⁹ Now all the rest were at supper, ¹⁰ but the king was extremely thirsty, and although springs were plentiful there, he could not satisfy his thirst from them. ¹¹ But a certain irrational desire for the water in the enemy's territory tormented and inflamed him, undid and consumed him. ¹² When his guards complained bitterly because of the king's craving, two staunch young soldiers, respecting*ⁿ*

the king's desire, armed themselves fully, and taking a pitcher climbed over the enemy's ramparts. ¹³ Eluding the sentinels at the gates, they went searching throughout the enemy camp ¹⁴ and found the spring, and from it boldly brought the king a drink. ¹⁵ But David,*ᵒ* although he was burning with thirst, considered it an altogether fearful danger to his soul to drink what was regarded as equivalent to blood. ¹⁶ Therefore, opposing reason to desire, he poured out the drink as an offering to God. ¹⁷ For the temperate mind can conquer the drives of the emotions and quench the flames of frenzied desires; ¹⁸ it can overthrow bodily agonies even when they are extreme, and by nobility of reason spurn all domination by the emotions.

19 The present occasion now invites us to a narrative demonstration of temperate reason.

20 At a time when our fathers were enjoying profound peace because of their observance of the law and were prospering, so that even Seleucus Nicanor, king of Asia, had both appropriated money to them for the temple service and recognized their commonwealth – ²¹ just at that time certain men attempted a revolution against the public harmony and caused many and various disasters.

4 Now there was a certain Simon, a political opponent of the noble and good man, Onias, who then held

l Gk *you*
m Other ancient authorities read *he hurried and*
n Or *embarrassed because of*   *o* Gk *he*

---

reign of the saints in 1 Cor.4.8; 6.2–3; 1 Pet.2.9. **3.1:** *Those of the body*, but the emotions of vv. 2–4 are those of the mind; thus 1.6 would fit better here.

3.6–18: King David's thirst. Some details are different in 2 Sam.23.13–17; 1 Chr.11.15–19. **7:** *Philistines*, literally "foreigners"; in the Greek Bible this word usually translates the Hebrew word "Philistines". **15:** *Equivalent to blood*, 2 Sam.23.17, "Shall I drink the blood . . .?" **17:** *Frenzied desires*, in Greek mythology the *oistros* was the gadfly that tormented Io, and it became a symbol of uncontrolled sexual desire.

3.19–4.14: Attempt on the temple treasury. Compare 2 Macc.3.1–40. **19:** *The present occasion*, perhaps when 4 Macc. was first read publicly (see Introduction). **20:** *Profound peace*, see 2 Macc.3.1 n. *Seleucus Nicanor*, the author is confused. Seleucus I Nicator ruled 305/304–281/280 B.C.; the king who is meant here is Seleucus IV Philopator, 187–175 B.C. (see 2 Macc.3.3 n.). **4.1:** *Simon*, 2 Macc.3.4 n. *Onias* III, 2 Macc.3.1 n. Life tenure of *the high priesthood* was the regular rule until the first century A.D. when the Roman procurators disregarded it, Jn.18.13 n.;

the high priesthood for life. When despite all manner of slander he was unable to injure Onias in the eyes of the nation, he fled the country with the purpose of betraying it. [2] So he came to Apollonius, governor of Syria, Phoenicia, and Cilicia, and said, [3] "I have come here because I am loyal to the king's government, to report that in the Jerusalem treasuries there are deposited tens of thousands in private funds, which are not the property of the temple but belong to King Seleucus." [4] When Apollonius learned the details of these things, he praised Simon for his service to the king and went up to Seleucus to inform him of the rich treasure. [5] On receiving authority to deal with this matter, he proceeded quickly to our country accompanied by the accursed Simon and a very strong military force. [6] He said that he had come with the king's authority to seize the private funds in the treasury. [7] The people indignantly protested his words, considering it outrageous that those who had committed deposits to the sacred treasury should be deprived of them, and did all that they could to prevent it. [8] But, uttering threats, Apollonius went on to the temple. [9] While the priests together with women and children were imploring God in the temple to shield the holy place that was being treated so contemptuously, [10] and while Apollonius was going up with his armed forces to seize the money, angels on horseback with lightning flashing from their weapons appeared from heaven, instilling in them great fear and trembling. [11] Then Apollonius fell down half dead in the temple area

that was open to all, stretched out his hands toward heaven, and with tears besought the Hebrews to pray for him and propitiate the wrath of the heavenly army. [12] For he said that he had committed a sin deserving of death, and that if he were delivered he would praise the blessedness of the holy place before all people. [13] Moved by these words, Onias the high priest, although otherwise he had scruples about doing so, prayed for him lest King Seleucus suppose that Apollonius had been overcome by human treachery and not by divine justice. [14] So Apollonius, having been preserved beyond all expectations, went away to report to the king what had happened to him.

15 When King Seleucus died, his son Antiochus Epiphanes succeeded to the throne, an arrogant and terrible man, [16] who removed Onias from the priesthood and appointed Onias's[p] brother Jason as high priest. [17] Jason[q] agreed that if the office were conferred upon him he would pay the king three thousand six hundred and sixty talents annually. [18] So the king appointed him high priest and ruler of the nation. [19] Jason[q] changed the nation's way of life and altered its form of government in complete violation of the law, [20] so that not only was a gymnasium constructed at the very citadel[r] of our native land, but also the temple service was abolished. [21] The divine justice was angered by these acts and caused Antiochus himself to make war on them. [22] For when he was warring against Ptolemy in Egypt, he heard that a rumor of his death had spread

p Gk *his*　　*q* Gk *He*　　*r* Or *high place*

Josephus, *Ant*.xviii.ii.2; xx.10. **2**: *Cilicia* was joined to Syria and Phoenicia as one province only in A.D. 20–54; 2 Macc.3.5 is more accurate. **3**: *Private funds* were often deposited in temples, as in a bank. **5**: *Authority*, but according to 2 Macc. 3.7–8, Heliodorus was put in command. **6**: *Private funds* in the Jerusalem temple, see Josephus, *B.J.*i.xiii.9; vi.v.2. **10**: Compare 3 Macc. 2.21–24; 6.18.
4.15–25: **Antiochus's persecution of the Jews.** Compare 1 Macc.1.20–64; 2 Macc.5.11–6.11. **15**: *Antiochus* IV *Epiphanes* was the brother of *Seleucus* IV, and son of Antiochus III; see 1 Macc.1.10 n. **16**: *Jason*, 2 Macc.4.7 n. **20**: *At the very citadel*, more probably "under the citadel," as in 2 Macc.4.12. **21**: *The divine justice*, a theological interpretation of 2 Macc.4.16–17. **22**: *Ptolemy* VI Philometor (180–145 B.C.), 1 Macc.1.16–19.

and that the people of Jerusalem had rejoiced greatly. He speedily marched against them, ²³ and after he had plundered them he issued a decree that if any of them should be found observing the ancestral law they should die. ²⁴ When, by means of his decrees, he had not been able in any way to put an end to the people's observance of the law, but saw that all his threats and punishments were being disregarded, ²⁵ even to the point that women, because they had circumcised their sons, were thrown headlong from heights along with their infants, though they had known beforehand that they would suffer this – ²⁶ when, then, his decrees were despised by the people, he himself, through torture, tried to compel everyone in the nation to eat defiling foods and to renounce Judaism.

5 The tyrant Antiochus, sitting in state with his counselors on a certain high place, and with his armed soldiers standing about him, ² ordered the guards to seize each and every Hebrew and to compel them to eat pork and food sacrificed to idols. ³ If any were not willing to eat defiling food, they were to be broken on the wheel and killed. ⁴ And when many persons had been rounded up, one man, Eleazar by name, leader of the flock, was brought*ˢ* before the king. He was a man of priestly family, learned in the law, advanced in age, and known to many in the tyrant's court because of his philosophy.*ᵗ*

⁵ When Antiochus saw him he said, ⁶ "Before I begin to torture you, old man, I would advise you to save yourself by eating pork, ⁷ for I respect your age and your gray hairs. Although you have had them for so long a time, it does not seem to me that you are a philosopher when you observe the religion of the Jews. ⁸ Why, when nature has granted it to us, should you abhor eating the very excellent meat of this animal? ⁹ It is senseless not to enjoy delicious things that are not shameful, and wrong to spurn the gifts of nature. ¹⁰ It seems to me that you will do something even more senseless if, by holding a vain opinion concerning the truth, you continue to despise me to your own hurt. ¹¹ Will you not awaken from your foolish philosophy, dispel your futile reasonings, adopt a mind appropriate to your years, philosophize according to the truth of what is beneficial, ¹² and have compassion on your old age by honoring my humane advice? ¹³ For consider this, that if there is some power watching over this religion of yours, it will excuse you from any transgression that arises out of compulsion."

14 When the tyrant urged him in this fashion to eat meat unlawfully, Eleazar asked to have a word. ¹⁵ When he had received permission to speak, he began to address the people as follows: ¹⁶ "We, O Antiochus, who have been persuaded to govern our lives by the divine law, think that there is no compulsion more powerful than our obedience to the law. ¹⁷ Therefore

ˢ Or *was the first of the flock to be brought*
ᵗ Other authorities read *his advanced age*

5.1–7.23: Martyrdom of Eleazar. Compare 2 Macc.6.18–31. **1:** *Tyrant*, in Greek usually with a bad connotation, denoting not a legitimate monarch but one who rules by force. *Sitting in state*, perhaps in Jerusalem; but early Christian tradition located this in Antioch, and a church was erected there in honor of the martyrs. **2:** Jews regarded the eating of *pork and food sacrificed to idols* as idolatry and profanation of the divine name because it was a public defiance of God's law; compare 1 Cor.10.6–22. **3:** *Defiling*, the Greek word, peculiar to 4 Macc., implies that forbidden foods were polluted and particularly odious. **4:** *Eleazar* may mean "God has helped"; it is the same name as Lazarus (Lk.16.20; Jn.11.1) and serves as a symbol for a man of great piety; compare 3 Macc.6.1; 2 Macc.8.23 n. **7–8:** A Stoic *philosopher* regarded the distinctions of national religions and laws, such as those of Judaism, as unimportant, whereas Jews considered the Mosaic law to be the highest philosophy; compare 1.17 n. Stoics also taught that one should live according to *nature*. **7:** *Religion*, Greek *thrēskeia*, religious practice or cult; compare v. 31. **13:** *Some power watching over*, a Greek philosophical expression; compare we consider that we should not transgress it in any respect. [18] Even if, as you suppose, our law were not truly divine and we had wrongly held it to be divine, not even so would it be right for us to invalidate our reputation for piety. [19] Therefore do not suppose that it would be a petty sin if we were to eat defiling food; [20] to transgress the law in matters either small or great is of equal seriousness, [21] for in either case the law is equally despised. [22] You scoff at our philosophy as though living by it were irrational, [23] but it teaches us self-control, so that we master all pleasures and desires, and it also trains us in courage, so that we endure any suffering willingly; [24] it instructs us in justice, so that in all our dealings we act impartially,[u] and it teaches us piety, so that with proper reverence we worship the only real God.

25 "Therefore we do not eat defiling food; for since we believe that the law was established by God, we know that in the nature of things the Creator of the world in giving us the law has shown sympathy toward us. [26] He has permitted us to eat what will be most suitable for our lives,[v] but he has forbidden us to eat meats that would be contrary to this. [27] It would be tyrannical for you to compel us not only to transgress the law, but also to eat in such a way that you may deride us for eating defiling foods, which are most hateful to us. [28] But you shall have no such occasion to laugh at me, [29] nor will I transgress the sacred oaths of my ancestors concerning the keeping of the law, [30] not even if you gouge out my eyes and burn my entrails. [31] I am not so old and cowardly as not to be young in reason on behalf of piety. [32] Therefore get your torture wheels ready and fan the fire more vehemently! [33] I do not so pity my old age as to break the ancestral law by my own act. [34] I will not play false to you, O law that trained me, nor will I renounce you, beloved self-control. [35] I will not put you to shame, philosophical reason, nor will I reject you, honored priesthood and knowledge of the law. [36] You, O king, shall[w] not stain the honorable mouth of my old age, nor my long life lived lawfully. [37] The fathers will receive me as pure, as one who does not fear your violence even to death. [38] You may tyrannize the ungodly, but you shall not dominate my religious principles either by word or by deed."

6 When Eleazar in this manner had made eloquent response to the exhortations of the tyrant, the guards who were standing by dragged him violently to the instruments of torture. [2] First they stripped the old man, who remained adorned with the gracefulness of his piety. [3] And after they had tied his arms on each side they scourged him, [4] while a herald opposite him cried out, "Obey the king's commands!" [5] But the courageous and noble man, as a true Eleazar, was unmoved, as though being tortured in a dream; [6] yet while the old man's eyes were raised to heaven, his flesh was being torn by scourges, his blood flowing, and his sides were being cut to pieces. [7] And though he fell to the ground because his body could not endure the agonies, he kept his reason upright and unswerving. [8] One of the cruel guards rushed at him and began to kick him in the side to make him get up again after he fell. [9] But he

u Or *so that we hold in balance all our habitual inclinations*
v Or *souls*   *w* Gk *You shall*

---

2 Macc.7.35; 9.5; 3 Macc.2.21. **23–24:** *Self-control . . . courage . . . justice,* cardinal virtues (see 1.2–4 n.). In Xenophon's *Memorabilia,* and sometimes in Philo, *piety* or religion is the fourth virtue. **27:** *Deride us,* because this would bring discredit on the Jewish people, the Mosaic law, and the God who gave it. God's name must be hallowed (Mt.6.9). **31:** *Piety,* Greek *eusebeia,* proper reverence toward God (see v. 7 n.; 1.1 n.). No single Greek word corresponds to the English word "religion." **37:** 13.17; 17.12; Mk.12.26–27. Immortality of the martyrs is implied in 9.22; 2 Macc.7.36. **6.5:** *True Eleazar,* see 5.4 n. **6:** *Eyes . . . to heaven,* a natural gesture in prayer, particularly that of a martyr. Compare v. 26 and Stephen's supplication in Acts 7.55.

bore the pains and scorned the punishment, and endured the tortures. [10] And like a noble athlete the old man, while being beaten, was victorious over his torturers; [11] in fact, with his face bathed in sweat, and gasping heavily for breath, he amazed even his torturers by his courageous spirit.

12 At that point, partly out of pity for his old age, [13] partly out of sympathy from their acquaintance with him, partly out of admiration for his endurance, some of the king's retinue came to him and said, [14] "Eleazar, why are you so irrationally destroying yourself through these evil things? [15] We will set before you some cooked meat; save yourself by pretending to eat pork."

16 But Eleazar, as though more bitterly tormented by this counsel, cried out: [17] "May we, the children of Abraham,[x] never think so basely that out of cowardice we feign a role unbecoming to us! [18] For it would be irrational if we, who have lived in accordance with truth to old age and have maintained in accordance with law the reputation of such a life, should now change our course [19] and ourselves become a pattern of impiety to the young, in becoming an example of the eating of defiling food. [20] It would be shameful if we should survive for a little while and during that time be a laughing stock to all for our cowardice, [21] and if we should be despised by the tyrant as unmanly, and not protect our divine law even to death. [22] Therefore, O children of Abraham, die nobly for your religion! [23] And you, guards of the tyrant, why do you delay?"

24 When they saw that he was so courageous in the face of the afflictions, and that he had not been changed by their compassion, the guards brought him to the fire. [25] There they burned him with maliciously contrived instruments, threw him down, and poured stinking liquids into his nostrils. [26] When he was now burned to his very bones and about to expire, he lifted up his eyes to God and said, [27] "You know, O God, that though I might have saved myself, I am dying in burning torments for the sake of the law. [28] Be merciful to your people, and let our punishment suffice for them. [29] Make my blood their purification, and take my life in exchange for theirs." [30] And after he said this, the holy man died nobly in his tortures, and by reason he resisted even to the very tortures of death for the sake of the law.

31 Admittedly, then, devout reason is sovereign over the emotions. [32] For if the emotions had prevailed over reason, we would have testified to their domination. [33] But now that reason has conquered the emotions, we properly attribute to it the power to govern. [34] And it is right for us to acknowledge the dominance of reason when it masters even external agonies. It would be ridiculous to deny it.[y] [35] And I have proved not only that reason has mastered agonies, but also that it masters pleasures and in no respect yields to them.

7 For like a most skilful pilot, the reason of our father Eleazar steered the ship of religion over the sea of the emotions, [2] and though buffeted by the stormings of the tyrant and overwhelmed by the mighty waves of tortures, [3] in no way did he turn the rudder of religion until he sailed into the haven of immortal victory. [4] No

x Or *O children of Abraham*
y Syr: Greek obscure

10: *Noble athlete,* 1 Cor.9.24–27; Heb.12.1. **17–21:** See 5.27 n. **23:** *Why do you delay?* Compare 9.1; 2 Macc.7.30. **29:** *In exchange,* Greek *antipsychon,* a word used by the martyr Ignatius of Antioch in his letters. Compare 1.11; 9.24; 12.17; 17.21–22; 18.4; Mk.10.45. The idea of expiation derives ultimately from Is.53.5–12 and is also found in the Qumran *Manual of Discipline.* **31:** The transition from religious language in vv. 27–29 to the philosophical note of *devout reason* is abrupt; but for this author the two are one. **7.1–3:** The metaphor of the *pilot* and *the ship,* common in Greek literature, recurs in 13.6–7 and in 15.31–32 as a reference to city besieged with many ingenious war machines has ever held out as did that most holy man. Although his sacred life was consumed by tortures and racks, he conquered the besiegers with the shield of his devout reason. [5] For in setting his mind firm like a jutting cliff, our father Eleazar broke the maddening waves of the emotions. [6] O priest, worthy of the priesthood, you neither defiled your sacred teeth nor profaned your stomach, which had room only for reverence and purity, by eating defiling foods. [7] O man in harmony with the law and philosopher of divine life! [8] Such should be those who are administrators of the law, shielding it with their own blood and noble sweat in sufferings even to death. [9] You, father, strengthened our loyalty to the law through your glorious endurance, and you did not abandon the holiness which you praised, but by your deeds you made your words of divine[z] philosophy credible. [10] O aged man, more powerful than tortures; O elder, fiercer than fire; O supreme king over the passions, Eleazar! [11] For just as our father Aaron, armed with the censer, ran through the multitude of the people and conquered the fiery[a] angel, [12] so the descendant of Aaron, Eleazar, though being consumed by the fire, remained unmoved in his reason. [13] Most amazing, indeed, though he was an old man, his body no longer tense and firm,[b] his muscles flabby, his sinews feeble, he became young again [14] in spirit through reason; and by reason like that of Isaac he rendered the many-headed rack ineffective. [15] O man of blessed age and of venerable gray hair and of law-abiding life,

whom the faithful seal of death has perfected!

16 If, therefore, because of piety an aged man despised tortures even to death, most certainly devout reason is governor of the emotions. [17] Some perhaps might say, "Not every one has full command of his emotions, because not every one has prudent reason." [18] But as many as attend to religion with a whole heart, these alone are able to control the passions of the flesh, [19] since they believe that they, like our patriarchs Abraham and Isaac and Jacob, do not die to God, but live in God.[c] [20] No contradiction therefore arises when some persons appear to be dominated by their emotions because of the weakness of their reason. [21] What person who lives as a philosopher by the whole rule of philosophy, and trusts in God, [22] and knows that it is blessed to endure any suffering for the sake of virtue, would not be able to overcome the emotions through godliness? [23] For only the wise and courageous man is lord of his emotions.

8 For this is why even the very young, by following a philosophy in accordance with devout reason, have prevailed over the most painful instruments of torture. [2] For when the tyrant was conspicuously defeated in his first attempt, being unable to compel an aged man to eat defiling foods, then in violent rage he commanded that others of the Hebrew captives be brought, and that any who ate defiling food should be freed after eating, but if any were to refuse, these should be tortured even more cruelly.

z Other ancient authorities omit *divine*
a Other ancient authorities omit *fiery*
b Gk *the tautness of the body already loosed*
c Or *to God*

Noah's ark; compare 1 Pet.3.20. **6**: *Defiled . . . profaned*, the Jewish concept was realistic, as though a physical infection were incurred (see 2 Macc. 6.20); contrast Mk.7.15; Acts 10.13–15. **8**: *Administrators*, literally "those who make (or create) something"; the Greek is obscure. A rabbi or priest was responsible for maintenance of the law in the community (Mal.2.7). **9**: *Credible*, in both Judaism and Stoicism, the ultimate test is the conformity of one's deeds to one's profession. **10**: *Eleazar*, see 5.4 n. **11**: Num.16.46–50. **14**: Compare 2 Cor.4.7–18. *Isaac*, Gen.22.1–14. **19**: *Abraham and Isaac and Jacob* are living (Mk.12.26). *Live in God*, or "to God," a similar expression is found in Lk.20.38; Rom.6.10; 14.8; Gal.2.19. Compare 16.25.

3 When the tyrant had given these orders, seven brothers – handsome, modest, noble, and accomplished in every way – were brought before him along with their aged mother. ⁴ When the tyrant saw them, grouped about their mother as if in a chorus, he was pleased with them. And struck by their appearance and nobility, he smiled at them, and summoned them nearer and said, ⁵ "Young men, I admire each and every one of you in a kindly manner, and greatly respect the beauty and the number of such brothers. Not only do I advise you not to display the same madness as that of the old man who has just been tortured, but I also exhort you to yield to me and enjoy my friendship. ⁶ Just as I am able to punish those who disobey my orders, so I can be a benefactor to those who obey me. ⁷ Trust me, then, and you will have positions of authority in my government if you will renounce the ancestral tradition of your national life. ⁸ And enjoy your youth by adopting the Greek way of life and by changing your manner of living. ⁹ But if by disobedience you rouse my anger, you will compel me to destroy each and every one of you with dreadful punishments through tortures. ¹⁰ Therefore take pity on yourselves. Even I, your enemy, have compassion for your youth and handsome appearance. ¹¹ Will you not consider this, that if you disobey, nothing remains for you but to die on the rack?"

12 When he had said these things, he ordered the instruments of torture to be brought forward so as to persuade them out of fear to eat the defiling food. ¹³ And when the guards had placed before them wheels and joint-dislocators, rack and hooks*ᵈ* and catapults*ᵉ* and caldrons, braziers and thumbscrews and iron claws and wedges and bellows, the tyrant resumed speaking: ¹⁴ "Be afraid, young fellows, and whatever justice you revere will be merciful to you when you transgress under compulsion."

15 But when they had heard the inducements and saw the dreadful devices, not only were they not afraid, but they also opposed the tyrant with their own philosophy, and by their right reasoning nullified his tyranny. ¹⁶ Let us consider, on the other hand, what arguments might have been used if some of them had been cowardly and unmanly. Would they not have been these? ¹⁷ "O wretches that we are and so senseless! Since the king has summoned and exhorted us to accept kind treatment if we obey him, ¹⁸ why do we take pleasure in vain resolves and venture upon a disobedience that brings death? ¹⁹ O men and brothers, should we not fear the instruments of torture and consider the threats of torments, and give up this vain opinion and this arrogance that threatens to destroy us? ²⁰ Let us take pity on our youth and have compassion on our mother's age; ²¹ and let us seriously consider that if we disobey we are dead! ²² Also, divine justice will excuse us for fearing the king when we are under compulsion. ²³ Why do we banish ourselves from this most pleasant life and deprive

d Greek obscure
e Here and elsewhere in 4 Macc. an instrument of torture

8.1–9.9: The seven brothers defy the tyrant. This account is an amplification of 2 Macc.7.1–2. **3**: *Accomplished*, or graceful, the Greek ideal of physical beauty joined to perfect education. **4**: A Greek *chorus* was a company of dancers, who often moved in a circle and spoke lines in unison; compare 14.7. **5**: *Beauty*, see 2.1 n. *Friendship*, almost a technical term, because the "friends" of a Hellenistic king were employed in the government; see v.7 and 3 Macc.2.23 n. **6**: *Benefactor*, a title often adopted by Hellenistic monarchs; in Lk.22.25 it seems ironical, as here. **8**: *Adopting the Greek way of life*, Antiochus could have believed sincerely that this was the highest civilization and that Judaism was "superstition." Thus it is a tragic conflict between two points of view. **13**: *Hooks*, these and some of the other instruments of torture cannot be described precisely; compare 11.10. **14**: *Justice*, a philosophical way of speaking of God. **15**: *Nullified his tyranny*, Epictetus the Stoic taught that, while the tyrant might chain a man's leg or cut off his head, he could neither chain nor cut off his moral purpose (*Discourses* i.18.17).

ourselves of this delightful world? [24] Let us not struggle against compulsion[f] nor take hollow pride in being put to the rack. [25] Not even the law itself would arbitrarily slay us for fearing the instruments of torture. [26] Why does such contentiousness excite us and such a fatal stubbornness please us, when we can live in peace if we obey the king?"

27 But the youths, though about to be tortured, neither said any of these things nor even seriously considered them. [28] For they were contemptuous of the emotions and sovereign over agonies, [29] so that as soon as the tyrant had ceased counseling them to eat defiling food, all with one voice together, as from one mind, said:

9 "Why do you delay, O tyrant? For we are ready to die rather than transgress our ancestral commandments; [2] we are obviously putting our forefathers to shame unless we should practice ready obedience to the law and to Moses[g] our counselor. [3] Tyrant and counselor of lawlessness, in your hatred for us do not pity us more than we pity ourselves.[h] [4] For we consider this pity of yours which insures our safety through transgression of the law to be more grievous than death itself. [5] You are trying to terrify us by threatening us with death by torture, as though a short time ago you learned nothing from Eleazar. [6] And if the aged men of the Hebrews because of their religion lived piously[i] while enduring torture, it would be even more fitting that we young men should die despising your coercive tortures, which our aged instructor also overcame. [7] Therefore, tyrant, put us to the test; and if you take our lives because of our religion, do not suppose

that you can injure us by torturing us. [8] For we, through this severe suffering and endurance, shall have the prize of virtue and shall be with God, for whom we suffer; [9] but you, because of your bloodthirstiness toward us, will deservedly undergo from the divine justice eternal torment by fire."

10 When they had said these things the tyrant not only was angry, as at those who are disobedient, but also was enraged, as at those who are ungrateful. [11] Then at his command the guards brought forward the eldest, and having torn off his tunic, they bound his hands and arms with thongs on each side. [12] When they had worn themselves out beating him with scourges, without accomplishing anything, they placed him upon the wheel. [13] When the noble youth was stretched out around this, his limbs were dislocated, [14] and though broken in every member he denounced the tyrant, saying, [15] "Most abominable tyrant, enemy of heavenly justice, savage of mind, you are mangling me in this manner, not because I am a murderer, or as one who acts impiously, but because I protect the divine law." [16] And when the guards said, "Agree to eat so that you may be released from the tortures," [17] he replied, "You abominable lackeys, your wheel is not so powerful as to strangle my reason. Cut my limbs, burn my flesh, and twist my joints. [18] Through all these tortures I will convince you that sons of the Hebrews alone are invincible where virtue is concerned." [19] While he was saying these things, they spread fire under him, and while

f Or *fate*
g Other ancient authorities read *knowledge*
h Greek obscure
i One manuscript reads *died*

25: *The law* would not condemn them for *fearing*; but a Jew could not be excused for committing idolatry, even under duress (see 5.2 n.). 29: *With one voice*, as if they were a chorus (see 8.4 n.). 9.6: *Aged men*, the plural may refer to Hebrew prophets such as Isaiah, who, according to Jewish tradition, were also martyred; compare Heb.11.35–37. 7: *Do not suppose that you can injure us*, a Stoic principle; suffering cannot affect the wise man's essential nature. 8: *Prize of virtue*, an athletic metaphor; compare 6.10; Wis.10.12; 1 Cor.9.24.

9.10–25: **Martyrdom of the eldest.** The details do not agree with the earlier account in 2 Macc.7.3–6; here the author allows himself the freedom of an historical novelist. 17: See v.7 n.

fanning the flames[j] they tightened the wheel further. [20] The wheel was completely smeared with blood, and the heap of coals was being quenched by the drippings of gore, and pieces of flesh were falling off the axles of the machine. [21] Although the ligaments joining his bones were already severed, the courageous youth, worthy[k] of Abraham, did not groan, [22] but as though transformed by fire into immortality he nobly endured the rackings. [23] "Imitate me, brothers," he said. "Do not leave your post in my struggle[l] or renounce our courageous brotherhood. [24] Fight the sacred and noble battle for religion. Thereby the just Providence of our ancestors may become merciful to our nation and take vengeance on the accursed tyrant." [25] When he had said this, the saintly youth broke the thread of life.

26 While all were marveling at his courageous spirit, the guards brought in the next eldest, and after fitting themselves with iron gauntlets having sharp hooks, they bound him to the torture machine and catapult. [27] Before torturing him, they inquired if he were willing to eat, and they heard his noble decision.[m] [28] These leopard-like beasts tore out his sinews with the iron hands, flayed all his flesh up to his chin, and tore away his scalp. But he steadfastly endured this agony and said, [29] "How sweet is any kind of death for the religion of our fathers!" [30] To the tyrant he said, "Do you not think, you most savage tyrant, that

you are being tortured more than I, as you see the arrogant design of your tyranny being defeated by our endurance for the sake of religion? [31] I lighten my pain by the joys that come from virtue, [32] but you suffer torture by the threats that come from impiety. You will not escape, most abominable tyrant, the judgments of the divine wrath."

10 When he too had endured a glorious death, the third was led in, and many repeatedly urged him to save himself by tasting the meat. [2] But he shouted, "Do you not know that the same father begot me and those who died, and the same mother bore me, and that I was brought up on the same teachings? [3] I do not renounce the noble kinship that binds me to my brothers."[n] [5] Enraged by the man's boldness, they disjointed his hands and feet with their instruments, dismembering him by prying his limbs from their sockets, [6] and breaking his fingers and arms and legs and elbows. [7] Since they were not able in any way to break his spirit,[o] they abandoned the instruments[p] and scalped him with their fingernails in Scythian fashion. [8] They immediately brought him to the wheel, and while his vertebrae were being dislocated upon it he saw his

j Greek obscure   k Other authorities read *a son*
l Other authorities read *post for ever*
m Other ancient authorities read *having heard his noble decision they tore him to shreds*
n Some ancient authorities add verse 4: *So if you have any instrument of torture, apply it to my body; for you cannot touch my soul, even if you wish.*
o Gk *strangle him*
p Other ancient authorities read *they tore off his skin*

22: *Transformed*, the same Greek verb is used in Phil.3.21; synonymous verbs in 1 Cor.15.51–52; 2 Cor.3.18. *Immortality*, literally "incorruption," "that which is imperishable," as in 17.12; 1 Cor.15.53. Here the author comes close to the Greek doctrine that the soul is by nature immortal, but his emphasis is on reward and punishment after this life, compare Lk.16.19–31; 23.43. This is in contrast to the doctrine of the resurrection expressed in 2 Macc.12.44–45. 23: *Brotherhood*, referring to the immediate family, but kinship with the whole Jewish nation may be implied. 24: *Fight*, compare 2 Tim.4.7. *Accursed*, Greek *alastōr*, a word from the Greek tragedies.
    9.26–12.19: Martyrdom of the other brothers. These stories follow 2 Macc.7.7–40 in general, but are made more vivid and sensational. 28: *Beasts*, 1 Cor.15.32. 29: *How sweet*, compare 2 Macc.6.30. One may compare the letter to the Romans by the Christian martyr Ignatius and also the Latin saying, *Dulce et decorum est pro patria mori.* **10.4:** *You cannot touch my soul*, see 9.7 n. and compare Mt.10.28; Lk.12.4–5. 5: *Boldness*, Acts 4.13; 2 Cor.3.12. Freedom of speech was one of the ideals of Greek democracy. 7: *Scythian fashion*, the Scythians were

own flesh torn all around and drops of blood flowing from his entrails. [9] When he was about to die, he said, [10] "We, most abominable tyrant, are suffering because of our godly training and virtue, [11] but you, because of your impiety and bloodthirstiness, will undergo unceasing torments."

[12] When he also had died in a manner worthy of his brothers, they dragged in the fourth, saying, [13] "As for you, do not give way to the same insanity as your brothers, but obey the king and save yourself." [14] But he said to them, "You do not have a fire hot enough to make me play the coward. [15] No, by the blessed death of my brothers, by the eternal destruction of the tyrant, and by the everlasting life of the pious, I will not renounce our noble brotherhood. [16] Contrive tortures, tyrant, so that you may learn from them that I am a brother to those who have just been tortured." [17] When he heard this, the bloodthirsty, murderous, and utterly abominable Antiochus gave orders to cut out his tongue. [18] But he said, "Even if you remove my organ of speech, God hears also those who are mute. [19] See, here is my tongue; cut it off, for in spite of this you will not make our reason speechless. [20] Gladly, for the sake of God, we let our bodily members be mutilated. [21] God will visit you swiftly, for you are cutting out a tongue that has been melodious with divine hymns."

|| When this one died also, after being cruelly tortured, the fifth leaped up, saying, [2] "I will not refuse, tyrant, to be tortured for the sake of virtue. [3] I have come of my own accord, so that by murdering me you will incur punishment from the heavenly justice for even more crimes. [4] Hater of virtue, hater of mankind, for what act of ours are you destroying us in this way? [5] Is it because[q] we revere the Creator of all things and live according to his virtuous law? [6] But these deeds deserve honors, not tortures."[r]

[9] While he was saying these things, the guards bound him and dragged him to the catapult; [10] they tied him to it on his knees, and fitting iron clamps on them, they twisted his back[s] around the wedge on the wheel,[t] so that he was completely curled back like a scorpion, and all his members were disjointed. [11] In this condition, gasping for breath and in anguish of body, [12] he said, "Tyrant, they are splendid favors that you grant us against your will, because through these noble sufferings you give us an opportunity to show our endurance for the law."

[13] After he too had died, the sixth, a mere boy, was led in. When the tyrant inquired whether he was willing to eat and be released, he said, [14] "I am younger in age than my brothers, but I am their equal in mind. [15] Since to this end we were born and bred, we ought likewise to die for the same principles. [16] So if you intend to torture me for not eating defiling foods, go on torturing!" [17] When he had said this, they led him to the wheel. [18] He was carefully stretched tight upon it, his back was broken, and he was roasted[u] from underneath. [19] To his back they applied sharp spits that had been heated in the fire, and pierced his ribs so that his entrails were burned through. [20] While being tortured he said, "O contest befitting holiness, in which so many of us brothers have been summoned to an arena of suffer-

q Other ancient authorities read *Or does it seem evil to you that*
r Other authorities add verses 7 and 8: [7] *If of course you had human feelings and had hope of salvation from God—*[8] *but, as it is, you are a stranger to God and persecute those who serve him.*"
s Gk *loins*   t Greek obscure
u Other ancient authorities add *by fire*

---

notorious for their barbarous cruelty (2 Macc.4.47; 3 Macc.7.5). **15:** *Everlasting life*, or glorious life; see 9.22 n. *Brotherhood*, see 9.23; the seven brothers and their mother represent the entire Jewish nation. **19:** 2 Macc.7.10. **11.3:** A new idea; he welcomes torture so that the tyrant may be punished the more. **7:** *Human feelings*, ironical because the compassion expressed in 12.2 was genuine but did not go far enough. **10:** *Wedge on the wheel*, it is not certain how the wheel was constructed. **13–27:** 2 Macc.7.18–19. **20:** *Contest*, compare 6.10. *Arena*, literally "gymnasium."

ings for religion, and in which we have not been defeated! [21] For the religious knowledge, O tyrant, is invincible. [22] I also, equipped with nobility, will die with my brothers, [23] and I myself will bring a great avenger upon you, you inventor of tortures and enemy of those who are truly devout. [24] We six boys have paralyzed your tyranny! [25] Since you have not been able to persuade us to change our mind or to force us to eat defiling foods, is not this your downfall? [26] Your fire is cold to us, and the catapults painless, and your violence powerless. [27] For it is not the guards of the tyrant but those of the divine law that are set over us; therefore, unconquered, we hold fast to reason."

12 When he also, thrown into the caldron, had died a blessed death, the seventh and youngest of all came forward. [2] Even though the tyrant had been fearfully reproached by the brothers, he felt strong compassion for this child when he saw that he was already in fetters. He summoned him to come nearer and tried to console him, saying, [3] "You see the result of your brothers' stupidity, for they died in torments because of their disobedience. [4] You too, if you do not obey, will be miserably tortured and die before your time, [5] but if you yield to persuasion you will be my friend and a leader in the government of the kingdom." [6] When he had so pleaded, he sent for the boy's mother to show compassion on her who had been bereaved of so many sons and to influence her to persuade the surviving son to obey and save himself. [7] But

when his mother had exhorted him in the Hebrew language, as we shall tell a little later, [8] he said, "Let me loose, let me speak to the king and to all his friends that are with him." [9] Extremely pleased by the boy's declaration, they freed him at once. [10] Running to the nearest of the braziers, [11] he said, "You profane tyrant, most impious of all the wicked, since you have received good things and also your kingdom from God, were you not ashamed to murder his servants and torture on the wheel those who practice religion? [12] Because of this, justice has laid up for you intense and eternal fire and tortures, and these throughout all time[v] will never let you go. [13] As a man, were you not ashamed, you most savage beast, to cut out the tongues of men who have feelings like yours and are made of the same elements as you, and to maltreat and torture them in this way? [14] Surely they by dying nobly fulfilled their service to God, but you will wail bitterly for having slain without cause the contestants for virtue." [15] Then because he too was about to die, he said, [16] "I do not desert the excellent example[w] of my brothers, [17] and I call on the God of our fathers to be merciful to our nation;[x] [18] but on you he will take vengeance both in this present life and when you are dead." [19] After he had uttered these imprecations, he flung himself into the braziers and so ended his life.[y]

v Gk *throughout the whole age*
w Other ancient authorities read *the witness*
x Other ancient authorities read *my race*
y Gk *and so gave up;* other ancient authorities read *gave up his spirit* or *his soul*

21: *Religious knowledge,* or science. In Greek thought true knowledge almost always leads to virtue; in Judaism, knowledge of the Mosaic law at least predisposes one toward it; see 1.17 n.; 18.6–19 n. **25:** *Downfall,* see 8.15 n. **26:** *Painless,* compare Heb.12.2, "despising the shame." **12.2:** *The tyrant* could feel *strong compassion;* see 8.10. **5:** *Friend,* see 8.5 n. **7:** *Hebrew language,* or perhaps Aramaic, as in Acts 21.40; compare 2 Macc.7.21,27. Many Palestinians, and certainly the author's first readers, spoke Greek. *A little later,* for dramatic effect, the author postpones the speech to 16.16–23. **11:** *Those who practice,* Greek *askētas,* almost "the athletes of religion"; compare v.14 and Philo, *On Dreams* i.59. **13:** *Feelings like yours,* a Stoic idea, found also in Wis.7.1–6; Acts 14.15. **14:** *Contestants,* see 11.20 n. **19:** *Flung himself,* as the mother does in 17.1. The remaining defenders of Masada at the end of the Jewish War of A.D. 66–73 killed one another. Jews, like Stoics, approved of suicide in certain circumstances.

13 Since, then, the seven brothers despised sufferings even unto death, everyone must concede that devout reason is sovereign over the emotions. [2] For if they had been slaves to their emotions and had eaten defiling food, we would say that they had been conquered by these emotions. [3] But in fact it was not so. Instead, by reason, which is praised before God, they prevailed over their emotions. [4] The supremacy of the mind over these cannot be overlooked, for the brothers[z] mastered both emotions and pains. [5] How then can one fail to confess the sovereignty of right reason over emotion in those who were not turned back by fiery agonies? [6] For just as towers jutting out over harbors hold back the threatening waves and make it calm for those who sail into the inner basin, [7] so the seven-towered right reason of the youths, by fortifying the harbor of religion, conquered the tempest of the emotions. [8] For they constituted a holy chorus of religion and encouraged one another, saying, [9] "Brothers, let us die like brothers for the sake of the law; let us imitate the three youths in Assyria who despised the same ordeal of the furnace. [10] Let us not be cowardly in the demonstration of our piety." [11] While one said, "Courage, brother," another said, "Bear up nobly," [12] and another reminded them, "Remember whence you came, and the father by whose hand Isaac would have submitted to being slain for the sake of religion." [13] Each of them and all of them together looking at one another, cheerful and undaunted, said, "Let us with all our hearts consecrate ourselves to God, who gave us our lives,[a] and let us use our bodies as a bulwark for the law. [14] Let us not fear him who thinks he is killing us, [15] for great is the struggle of the soul and the danger of eternal torment lying before those who transgress the commandment of God. [16] Therefore let us put on the full armor of self-control, which is divine reason. [17] For if we so die,[b] Abraham and Isaac and Jacob will welcome us, and all the fathers will praise us." [18] Those who were left behind said to each of the brothers who were being dragged away, "Do not put us to shame, brother, or betray the brothers who have died before us."

19 You are not ignorant of the affection of brotherhood, which the divine and all-wise Providence has bequeathed through the fathers to their descendants and which was implanted in the mother's womb. [20] There each of the brothers dwelt the same length of time and was shaped during the same period of time; and growing from the same blood and through the same life, they were brought to the light of day. [21] When they were born after an equal time of gestation, they drank milk from the same fountains. For such embraces brotherly-loving souls are nourished; [22] and they grow stronger from this common nurture and daily companionship, and from both general education and our discipline in the law of God.

23 Therefore, when sympathy and brotherly affection had been so established, the brothers were the more sympathetic to one another. [24] Since they had been educated by the same law and trained in the same virtues and brought up in right living, they loved one another all the more. [25] A common zeal for nobility expanded their goodwill and harmony toward one another, [26] because, with the aid of their religion, they rendered their brotherly love more fervent. [27] But although nature and companionship

z Gk *they*   a Or *souls*
b Other ancient authorities read *suffer*

13.1–14.10: Philosophical interpretation. Compare 6.31–35. **13.8:** *Chorus*, see 8.4 n.; 14.7. **9:** Dan. ch. 3. **12:** *Remember whence you came*, Is.51.1–2. *The father and Isaac*, 15.28; Gen.22.1–19; Wis.10.5. Their story became a favorite theme for Christians (Heb.11.17–19). **13:** *Each of them and all of them together*, as in a Greek chorus (see 8.4 n.). **14:** Mt.10.28; Lk.12.4. **17:** 5.37 n.; compare Lk.16.22. **19:** *Affection*, Greek *philtra*, a magical charm believed to produce love.

and virtuous habits had augmented the affection of brotherhood, those who were left endured for the sake of religion, while watching their brothers being maltreated and tortured to

14 death. [1] Furthermore, they encouraged them to face the torture, so that they not only despised their agonies, but also mastered the emotions of brotherly love.

2 O reason,[c] more royal than kings and freer than the free! [3] O sacred and harmonious concord of the seven brothers on behalf of religion! [4] None of the seven youths proved coward or shrank from death, [5] but all of them, as though running the course toward immortality, hastened to death by torture. [6] Just as the hands and feet are moved in harmony with the guidance of the mind, so those holy youths, as though moved by an immortal spirit of devotion, agreed to go to death for its sake. [7] O most holy seven, brothers in harmony! For just as the seven days of creation move in choral dance around religion, [8] so these youths, forming a chorus, encircled the sevenfold fear of tortures and dissolved it. [9] Even now, we ourselves shudder as we hear of the tribulations of these young men; they not only saw what was happening, yes, not only heard the direct word of threat, but also bore the sufferings patiently, and in agonies of fire at that. [10] What could be more excruciatingly painful than this? For the power of fire is intense and swift, and it consumed their bodies quickly.

11 Do not consider it amazing that reason had full command over these men in their tortures, since the mind of woman despised even more diverse agonies, [12] for the mother of the seven young men bore up under the rackings of each one of her children.

13 Observe how complex is a mother's love for her children, which draws everything toward an emotion felt in her inmost parts. [14] Even unreasoning animals, like mankind, have a sympathy and parental love for their offspring. [15] For example, among birds, the ones that are tame protect their young by building on the housetops, [16] and the others, by building in precipitous chasms and in holes and tops of trees, hatch the nestlings and ward off the intruder. [17] If they are not able to keep him away, they do what they can to help their young by flying in circles around them in the anguish of love, and warning them in with their own calls. [18] And why is it necessary to demonstrate sympathy for children by the example of unreasoning animals, [19] since even bees at the time for making honeycombs defend themselves against intruders and as though with an iron dart sting those who approach their hive and defend it even to the death? [20] But sympathy for her children did not sway the mother of the young men; she was of the same mind as Abraham.

15 O reason of the children, tyrant over the emotions! O religion, more desirable to the mother than her children! [2] Two courses were open to this mother, that of religion, and that of preserving her seven sons for a time, as the tyrant had promised. [3] She loved religion more, religion that preserves them for eternal life according to God's promise. [4] In what manner might I express the emotions of parents who love their children? We impress upon the character of a small child a wondrous likeness both of mind and of form. Especially is this true of mothers, who because of their birthpangs have a deeper sympathy toward

c Or *O minds*

14.5: 9.8 n.; Heb.12.1. **8:** *Sevenfold fear*, the Greek here is obscure. **9:** *Even now*, see 3.19 n.   **14.11–17.1: The mother of the seven.** Her death is merely mentioned in 2 Macc.7.41; here it is made the climax of the oration. **14.14:** The analogy between *unreasoning animals* and *mankind* (vv. 14–19) was a theme of popular Greek philosophy. **20:** *Did not sway*, the mother's constancy is the supreme proof of the dominance of religious reason. *Abraham* had offered Isaac; see 13.12 n. **15.2:** *Two courses*, the two ways of Jer.21.8 became a pattern of Jewish thought.

their offspring than do the fathers.
⁵ Considering that mothers are the
weaker sex and give birth to many,
they are the more devoted to their
children.*ᵈ* ⁶ The mother of the seven
boys, more than any other mother,
loved her children. In seven pregnancies
she had implanted in herself tender love
toward them, ⁷ and because of the
many pains she suffered with each of
them she had sympathy for them;
⁸ yet because of the fear of God she
disdained the temporary safety of her
children. ⁹ Not only so, but also
because of the nobility of her sons and
their ready obedience to the law she
felt a greater tenderness toward them.
¹⁰ For they were righteous and self-
controlled and brave and magnan-
imous, and loved their brothers and
their mother, so that they obeyed
her even to death in keeping the
ordinances. ¹¹ Nevertheless, though so
many factors influenced the mother to
suffer with them out of love for her
children, in the case of none of them
were the various tortures strong enough
to pervert her reason. ¹² Instead, the
mother urged them on, each child
singly and all together, to death for
the sake of religion. ¹³ O sacred nature
and affection of parental love, yearning
of parents toward offspring, nurture,
and indomitable suffering by mothers!
¹⁴ This mother, who saw them tortured
and burned one by one, because of
religion did not change her attitude.
¹⁵ She watched the flesh of her children
consumed by fire, their toes and
fingers scattered*ᵉ* on the ground, and
the flesh of the head to the chin exposed like masks. ¹⁶ O mother, tried
now by more bitter pains than even the
birth-pangs you suffered for them!
¹⁷ O woman, who alone gave birth to
such complete devotion! ¹⁸ When the
first-born breathed his last it did not
turn you aside, nor when the second
in torments looked at you piteously,

nor when the third expired; ¹⁹ nor
did you weep when you looked at the
eyes of each one in his tortures gazing
boldly at the same agonies, and saw
in their nostrils signs of the approach
of death. ²⁰ When you saw the flesh
of children burned upon the flesh of
other children, severed hands upon
hands, scalped heads upon heads, and
corpses fallen on other corpses and
when you saw the place filled with
many spectators of the torturings, you
did not shed tears. ²¹ Neither the
melodies of sirens nor the songs of
swans attract the attention of their
hearers as did the voices of the children
in torture calling to their mother.
²² How great and how many torments
the mother then suffered as her sons
were tortured on the wheel and with
the hot irons! ²³ But devout reason,
giving her heart a man's courage in the
very midst of her emotions, strengthened her to disregard her temporal
love for her children.

24 Although she witnessed the destruction of seven children and the
ingenious and various rackings, this
noble mother disregarded all these*ᶠ*
because of faith in God. ²⁵ For as in
the council chamber of her own soul
she saw mighty advocates – nature,
family, parental love, and the rackings
of her children – ²⁶ this mother held
two ballots, one bearing death and the
other deliverance for her children.
²⁷ She did not approve the deliverance
which would preserve the seven sons
for a short time, ²⁸ but as the daughter
of God-fearing Abraham she remembered his fortitude.

29 O mother of the nation, vindicator
of the law and champion of religion,
who carried away the prize of the contest in your heart! ³⁰ O more noble

d Or *For to the degree that mothers are weaker and the
more children they bear, the more they are devoted to
their children.*
e Or *quivering*
f Other ancient authorities read *having bidden them
farewell surrendered them*

Religion, 5.31 n. **4:** *Of mind and of form,* a Stoic idea. **13:** *Indomitable suffering,* actually it is
the mother who is *indomitable* in spite of her *love* and *suffering.* **17:** *Gave birth,* includes the idea
of spiritual birth; compare 16.13 n.; 17.6; Gal.4.19. **25–26:** *Ballots,* as though she were in the
council chamber of a Greek city. **28:** See 13.12 n. **31:** *Noah's ark,* see 7.1–3 n.; also Wis.14.6.

than males in steadfastness, and more manly than men in endurance! [31] Just as Noah's ark, carrying the world in the universal flood, stoutly endured the waves, [32] so you, O guardian of the law, overwhelmed from every side by the flood of your emotions and the violent winds, the torture of your sons, endured nobly and withstood the wintry storms that assail religion.

16 If, then, a woman, advanced in years and mother of seven sons, endured seeing her children tortured to death, it must be admitted that devout reason is sovereign over the emotions. [2] Thus I have demonstrated not only that men have ruled over the emotions, but also that a woman has despised the fiercest tortures. [3] The lions surrounding Daniel were not so savage, nor was the raging fiery furnace of Mishael so intensely hot, as was her innate parental love, inflamed as she saw her seven sons tortured in such varied ways. [4] But the mother quenched so many and such great emotions by devout reason.

5 Consider this also. If this woman, though a mother, had been faint-hearted, she would have mourned over them and perhaps have spoken as follows: [6] "O how wretched am I and many times unhappy! After bearing seven children, I am now the mother of none! [7] O seven childbirths all in vain, seven profitless pregnancies, fruitless nurturings and wretched nursings! [8] In vain, my sons, I endured many birth-pangs for you, and the more grievous anxieties of your upbringing. [9] Alas for my children, some unmarried, others married and without offspring.[g] I shall not see your children or have the happiness of being called grandmother. [10] Alas, I who had so many and beautiful children am a widow and alone, with many sorrows.[h] [11] Nor when I die, shall I have any of my sons to bury me."

12 Yet the sacred and God-fearing mother did not wail with such a lament for any of them, nor did she dissuade any of them from dying, nor did she grieve as they were dying, [13] but, as though having a mind like adamant and giving rebirth for immortality to the whole number of her sons, she implored them and urged them on to death for the sake of religion. [14] O mother, soldier of God in the cause of religion, elder and woman! By steadfastness you have conquered even a tyrant, and in word and deed you have proved more powerful than a man. [15] For when you and your sons were arrested together, you stood and watched Eleazar being tortured, and said to your sons in the Hebrew language, [16] "My sons, noble is the contest to which you are called to bear witness for the nation. Fight zealously for our ancestral law. [17] For it would be shameful if, while an aged man endures such agonies for the sake of religion, you young men were to be terrified by tortures. [18] Remember that it is through God that you have had a share in the world and have enjoyed life, [19] and therefore you ought to endure any suffering for the sake of God. [20] For his sake also our father Abraham was zealous to sacrifice his son Isaac, the ancestor of our nation; and when Isaac saw his father's hand wielding a sword and descending upon him, he did not cower. [21] And Daniel the righteous was thrown to the lions, and Hananiah, Azariah, and Mishael were hurled into the fiery furnace and endured it for the sake of God. [22] You too must have the same faith in God and not be grieved. [23] It is unreasonable for people who have religious knowledge not to withstand pain."

24 By these words the mother of the seven encouraged and persuaded each of her sons to die rather than violate

g Gk *without benefit*   h Or *much to be pitied*

16.3: *Daniel*, Dan.6.1–24. *Mishael*, Dan.1.7; 3.19–30. 11: *Any . . . sons to bury me*, for both Jews and Greeks a supreme calamity. 13: *Giving rebirth for immortality*, see 15.17 n.; Jn.3.5. 15: *Hebrew language*, see 12.7 n. 16–23: Compare this more rhetorical speech with 2 Macc.7.27–29. 16: *Contest*, 6.10; 11.20. 20: *Isaac*, see 13.12 n. 21: *Daniel*, v. 3. *Hananiah, Azariah, and Mishael*,

God's commandment. [25] They knew also that those who die for the sake of God live in God,[i] as do Abraham and Isaac and Jacob and all the patriarchs.

17 Some of the guards said that when she also was about to be seized and put to death she threw herself into the flames so that no one might touch her body.

2 O mother, who with your seven sons nullified the violence of the tyrant, frustrated his evil designs, and showed the courage of your faith! [3] Nobly set like a roof on the pillars of your sons, you held firm and unswerving against the earthquake of the tortures. [4] Take courage, therefore, O holy-minded mother, maintaining firm an enduring hope in God. [5] The moon in heaven, with the stars, does not stand so august as you, who, after lighting the way of your star-like seven sons to piety, stand in honor before God and are firmly set in heaven with them. [6] For your children were true descendants of father Abraham.[j]

7 If it were possible for us to paint the history of your piety as an artist might, would not those who first beheld it have shuddered as they saw the mother of the seven children enduring their varied tortures to death for the sake of religion? [8] Indeed it would be proper to inscribe upon their tomb these words as a reminder to the people of our nation:[k]

9 "Here lie buried an aged priest and an aged woman and seven sons, because of the violence of the tyrant who wished to destroy the way of

life of the Hebrews. [10] They vindicated their nation, looking to God and enduring torture even to death."

11 Truly the contest in which they were engaged was divine, [12] for on that day virtue gave the awards and tested them for their endurance. The prize was immortality in endless life. [13] Eleazar was the first contestant, the mother of the seven sons entered the competition, and the brothers contended. [14] The tyrant was the antagonist, and the world and the human race were the spectators. [15] Reverence for God was victor and gave the crown to its own athletes. [16] Who did not admire the athletes of the divine[l] legislation? Who were not amazed?

17 The tyrant himself and all his council marveled at their[m] endurance, [18] because of which they now stand before the divine throne and live through blessed eternity. [19] For Moses says, "All who are consecrated are under your hands." [20] These, then, who have been consecrated for the sake of God,[n] are honored, not only with this honor, but also by the fact that because of them our enemies did not rule over our nation, [21] the tyrant was punished, and the homeland purified – they having become, as it were, a ransom for the sin of our nation. [22] And through the blood of

i Or *to God*
j Gk *For your childbearing was from Abraham the father;* other authorities read *For . . . Abraham the servant*
k Or *as a memorial to the heroes of our people*
l Other authorities read *true*
m Other ancient authorities add *virtue and*
n Other ancient authorities omit *for the sake of God*

Dan. ch. 3. **25:** *Live in God,* see 7.19 n. **17.1:** *Threw herself,* compare 12.19; 2 Macc.7.41. *Touch her body,* this would be a violation of her chastity.
   17.2–18.5: Panegyric on the mother. The author has already pronounced encomiums on Eleazar (7.1–15), the brothers (14.2–10), and the mother (ch. 15), sometimes addressing them directly. The oration now comes to its climax. **3:** *Roof . . . pillars . . . earthquake,* metaphors appropriate to Antioch, where there were frequent earthquakes, but applicable also to Palestine. **5:** Stoics regarded *the stars* as living beings; for Jews the language was metaphorical. *Lighting the way,* mystical language; compare Jn.12.35–36,46. **6:** *True descendants,* compare 15.28; 13.12 n.; the giving of new birth is like Isaac's return from impending death; compare Heb. 11.17–19. **7:** *Possible,* or "permitted." At this time the Jews may have taken the commandment of Ex.20.4 strictly. **9:** *Way of life,* Greek *politeia,* "commonwealth." **11–12:** *Contest . . . awards . . . prize,* 6.10; 11.20. **21:** *Ransom,* see 6.29 n. **22:** *Through the blood,* Rom.3.25; *expiation,*

those devout ones and their death as an expiation, divine Providence preserved Israel that previously had been afflicted.

23 For the tyrant Antiochus, when he saw the courage of their virtue and their endurance under the tortures, proclaimed them to his soldiers as an example for their own endurance, [24] and this made them brave and courageous for infantry battle and siege, and he ravaged and conquered all his enemies.

18 O Israelite children, offspring of the seed of Abraham, obey this law and exercise piety in every way, [2] knowing that devout reason is master of all emotions, not only of sufferings from within, but also of those from without.

3 Therefore those who gave over their bodies in suffering for the sake of religion were not only admired by men, but also were deemed worthy to share in a divine inheritance. [4] Because of them the nation gained peace, and by reviving observance of the law in the homeland they ravaged the enemy. [5] The tyrant Antiochus was both punished on earth and is being chastised after his death. Since in no way whatever was he able to compel the Israelites to become pagans and to abandon their ancestral customs, he left Jerusalem and marched against the Persians.

6 The mother of the seven sons expressed also these principles to her children: [7] "I was a pure virgin and did not go outside my father's house; but I guarded the rib from which woman was made.[o] [8] No seducer corrupted me on a desert plain, nor did the destroyer, the deceitful serpent, defile the purity of my virginity. [9] In the time of my maturity I remained with my husband, and when these sons had grown up their father died. A happy man was he, who lived out his life with good children, and did not have the grief of bereavement. [10] While he was still with you, he taught you the law and the prophets. [11] He read to you about Abel slain by Cain, and Isaac who was offered as a burnt offering, and of Joseph in prison. [12] He told you of the zeal of Phineas, and he taught you about Hananiah, Azariah, and Mishael in the fire. [13] He praised Daniel in the den of the lions and blessed him. [14] He reminded you of the scripture of Isaiah, which says, 'Even though you go through the fire, the flame shall not consume you.' [15] He sang to you songs of the psalmist David, who said, 'Many are the afflictions of the righteous.' [16] He recounted to you Solomon's proverb, 'There is a tree of life for those who do his will.' [17] He confirmed the saying of Ezekiel, 'Shall these dry bones live?' [18] For he did not forget to teach you the song that Moses taught, which says, [19] 'I kill and I make alive: this is your life and the length of your days.'"

20 O bitter was that day–and yet not bitter – when that bitter tyrant of the Greeks quenched fire with fire

o Gk *the rib that was built* (Gen 2.22 LXX)

Greek *hilastērion*, as in Rom.3.25; compare Heb.9.11–15; 1 Pet.1.19; 1 Jn.1.7. **24**: *Ravaged and conquered*, but Antiochus was not successful, and died in Babylon (1 Macc.6.1–16). **18.1–5**: The exhortation seems repetitious after 17.7–24, but it is the author's method to employ recurrent themes. **5**: *Marched against the Persians*, 17.24 n. The second sentence in this verse does not fit well with the first.

18.6–19: The mother's last words. Compare 2 Macc.7.22–29. The mother is the supreme heroine of the story. This is a quiet passage after the highly emotional parts, designed to move the reader to reflection. Jewish education began in the home, and the mother's influence was always important. **7**: *Rib*, Gen.2.22. **8**: *Desert plain*, Dt.22.25–27. In such places women were in danger from men and also from demons, who were believed to inhabit the wilderness. **11**: *Abel*, Gen.4.2–15. *Isaac*, Gen.22.1–19. *Joseph*, Gen.39.1–23. **12**: *Phineas*, Num.25.1–9. *Hananiah*, 16.21. **13**: *Daniel*, Dan.6.1–24. **14**: Is.43.2. **15**: Ps.34.19. **16**: Pr.3.18, modified slightly. **17**: Ezek. 37.2–3. **19**: Dt.32.39; 30.20.

18.20–24: Conclusion. This peroration sums up many previous themes set forth in 4 Macc.

in his cruel caldrons, and in his burning rage brought those seven sons of the daughter of Abraham to the catapult and back again to more[p] tortures, [21] pierced the pupils of their eyes and cut out their tongues, and put them to death with various tortures. [22] For these crimes divine justice pursued and will pursue the accursed tyrant. [23] But the sons of Abraham with their victorious mother are gathered together into the chorus of the fathers, and have received pure and immortal[q] souls from God, [24] to whom be glory for ever and ever. Amen.

p Other ancient authorities read *to all his*
q Other ancient authorities read *victorious*

23: *Abraham*, 13.12 n. *Chorus*, see 8.4 n. *Immortal*, see 9.22 n. **24:** Compare Rom.11.36; 16.27; 2 Tim.4.18; Heb.13.21.

PSALM 151

Besides the 150 psalms comprising the Book of Psalms in the Masoretic text of the Hebrew Bible, a supernumerary psalm ascribed to David is included in manuscripts of the Greek Septuagint. The scribe of codex Sinaiticus regarded it as part of the Psalter, for his subscription reads "The 151 Psalms of David." On the other hand, in codex Alexandrinus and most other manuscripts of the Septuagint the psalm is excluded from the Psalter proper by the title which identifies the psalm to be "outside the number [of the 150 psalms]." Besides being in the Greek Bible, the psalm is current also in several other ancient versions, including the Old Latin, Syriac, Armenian, Ethiopic, and Arabic.

In 1956 a fragmentary leather scroll from Qumran Cave XI was found which contains portions of the Hebrew text of about thirty-five canonical psalms (not all in the traditional sequence) along with several non-canonical psalms. One of these latter is a somewhat enlarged form of what has been known as Ps.151. A translation of the Hebrew text, made by J. A. Sanders, the original editor of the scroll, in *Discoveries in the Judaean Desert of Jordan*, Vol. IV (Oxford, 1965), is given here for purposes of comparison with the Septuagint form of the psalm. It should be mentioned that the Hebrew script presents several palaeographical and philological uncertainties not yet satisfactorily resolved by scholars.

A Hallelujah of David the Son of Jesse.

1 Smaller was I than my brothers
    and the youngest of the sons of my father,
So he made me shepherd of his flock
    and ruler over his kids.

2 My hands have made an instrument
    and my fingers a lyre;
And [so] have I rendered glory to the Lord,
    thought I, within my soul.

3 The mountains do not witness to him,
    nor do the hills proclaim;
The trees have cherished my words
    and the flock my works.

4 For who can proclaim and who can bespeak
    and who can recount the deeds of the Lord?
Everything has God seen,
    everything has he heard and he has heeded.

5 He sent his prophet to anoint me,
    Samuel to make me great;
My brothers went out to meet him,
    handsome of figure and appearance.

6 Though they were tall of stature
    and handsome by their hair,
The Lord God chose
    them not.

7 But he sent and took me from behind the flock
    and anointed me with holy oil,
And he made me leader of his people
    and ruler over the sons of his covenant.

In the line following the Hebrew text of this psalm another psalm (with its heading) begins, of which only two poorly preserved lines remain. Apparently they celebrate David's victory over Goliath; Sanders's translation is as follows:

> At the beginning of David's power after
> the prophet of God had anointed him.

> ¹ Then I [saw] a Philistine
> uttering defiances from the r[anks of the Philistines].

It thus appears that the Greek text of Ps.151 is a condensed recension of what was originally two separate psalms in Hebrew.

PSALM 151

This psalm is ascribed to David as his own composition (though it is outside the number*ᵃ*), after he had fought in single combat with Goliath.

I WAS SMALL AMONG MY BROTHERS,
and youngest in my father's house;
I tended my father's sheep.

² My hands made a harp,
my fingers fashioned a lyre.

³ And who will declare it to my
Lord?
The Lord himself; it is he who
hears.*ᵇ*

⁴ It was he who sent his messenger*ᶜ*

and took me from my father's
sheep,
and anointed me with his
anointing oil.

⁵ My brothers were handsome and
tall,
but the Lord was not pleased
with them.

⁶ I went out to meet the Philistine,*ᵈ*
and he cursed me by his idols.

⁷ But I drew his own sword;
I beheaded him, and removed
reproach from the people of
Israel.

a Other authorities add *of the one hundred fifty* (psalms)
b Some witnesses add *everything;* others add *me;* others
read *who will hear me*
c Or *angel*
d Or *foreigner*

1: *Small . . . youngest*, 1 Sam.16.7 and 11. *Tended . . . sheep*, 1 Sam.16.11. One form of the Syriac version continues, "and I met a lion and also a wolf, and I killed them and tore them in pieces" (compare 1 Sam.17.34–36). **2**: *My hands made a harp*, 2 Chr.29.26. **4**: *Anointed me*, 1 Sam.16.13; Ps.89.20. *Took me from my father's sheep*, Ps.78.70. **5**: *The Lord was not pleased with them*, 1 Sam.16.7–10. **6**: *He cursed . . . by his idols*, 1 Sam.17.43. Certain manuscripts of the Old Latin, Arabic, and Ethiopic versions continue, with minor deviations: "And I slung three stones at him in the middle of his forehead, and laid him low by the might of the Lord." According to 1 Sam.17.49–50 David felled Goliath with only one stone. **7**: *His own sword*, 1 Sam.17.51.

CHRONOLOGICAL TABLES OF RULERS

THE SELEUCID DYNASTY

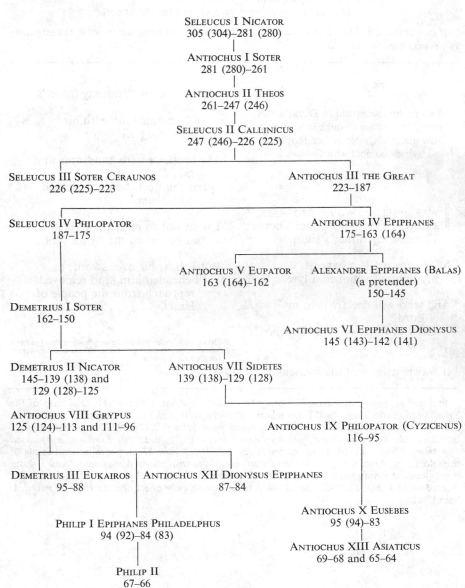

SELEUCUS I NICATOR
305 (304)–281 (280)

ANTIOCHUS I SOTER
281 (280)–261

ANTIOCHUS II THEOS
261–247 (246)

SELEUCUS II CALLINICUS
247 (246)–226 (225)

SELEUCUS III SOTER CERAUNOS
226 (225)–223

ANTIOCHUS III THE GREAT
223–187

SELEUCUS IV PHILOPATOR
187–175

ANTIOCHUS IV EPIPHANES
175–163 (164)

ANTIOCHUS V EUPATOR
163 (164)–162

ALEXANDER EPIPHANES (BALAS)
(a pretender)
150–145

DEMETRIUS I SOTER
162–150

ANTIOCHUS VI EPIPHANES DIONYSUS
145 (143)–142 (141)

DEMETRIUS II NICATOR
145–139 (138) and
129 (128)–125

ANTIOCHUS VII SIDETES
139 (138)–129 (128)

ANTIOCHUS VIII GRYPUS
125 (124)–113 and 111–96

ANTIOCHUS IX PHILOPATOR (CYZICENUS)
116–95

DEMETRIUS III EUKAIROS
95–88

ANTIOCHUS XII DIONYSUS EPIPHANES
87–84

ANTIOCHUS X EUSEBES
95 (94)–83

PHILIP I EPIPHANES PHILADELPHUS
94 (92)–84 (83)

ANTIOCHUS XIII ASIATICUS
69–68 and 65–64

PHILIP II
67–66

THE HOUSE OF THE MACCABEES (HASMONEANS)

These two family trees include the names of the more important rulers. The presence of short parallel lines between two names indicates marriage. The date of an individual's death or the dates of his rule are in some cases disputed, and alternative possibilities are given within parentheses. All the dates are B.C. Besides the standard works on the chronology of the inter-testamental period, special mention should be made of F. M. Heichelheim's "Chronological Table from 323–30 B.C." in *Proceedings of the IX International Congress of Papyrology*, Oslo, 1958, pp. 163–182 (also published separately by the Norwegian Universities Press). Seleucus I became king in the seventh year of the Seleucid era; see A. J. Sachs and D. J. Wiseman, "A Babylonian King List of the Hellenistic Period," *Iraq*, xvi (1954), p. 205. Syria became a Roman province in 64 B.C., and Pompey conquered Jerusalem in 63 B.C.

TITLES GIVEN TO BOOKS ASSOCIATED WITH EZRA AND NEHEMIAH IN SELECTED VERSIONS

Version \ Document	Old Testament Book of Ezra	Old Testament Book of Nehemiah	Paraphrase of 2 Chronicles chs. 35–36; the whole Book of Ezra; Nehemiah 7.38–8.12; plus a tale about Darius's bodyguards	A Latin Apocalypse
Greek Bible (Septuagint)	II Esdras		I Esdras	
Latin Vulgate Bible	I Esdras	II Esdras	III Esdras	IV Esdras
Many later Latin Manuscripts	I Esdras		III Esdras	II Esdras = chs. 1–2 · IV Esdras = chs. 3–14 · V Esdras = chs. 15–16
Douay English Version (1609–1610)	I Esdras	II Esdras	III Esdras	IV Esdras
Russian Bible, Moscow Patriarchate (1956)	I Esdras	Nehemiah	II Esdras	III Esdras
King James and Revised Standard Versions	The Book of Ezra	The Book of Nehemiah	I Esdras	II Esdras

INDEX TO THE ANNOTATIONS

Index to the Annotations

The following index lists important persons, places, and ideas which are mentioned in the general introduction and the annotations. In order to gain the fullest information, the verse (or verses) of the passage of the Apocrypha as well as the annotation itself should be read, and all cross references should be consulted.

Aaron, Sir.45.6–22
Abbot, George, p. xviii
Abel, 4 Macc.18.11
Abiram, 4 Macc.2.17
Abraham, Sir.44.19–23; S. of 3 Y.12; 4 Macc. 7.19; 13.12; 14.20
Achior, Jdt.5.5–21
Adam, creation of, 2 Esd.3.4–5
Ahikar, Tob.1.21; 11.18; 14.10
Alcimus, 1 Macc.7.5–25
Alexander Balas, 1 Macc.10.1
Alexander the Great, 1 Macc.1.1
Alexander Janneus, 1 Macc.14.41–43
Alexandria, 3 Macc.4.11; p. 300
Alexandrian pseudepigrapha, p. xxii
Almsgiving, Tob.4.7–11; Sir.3.30
Almsgiving atones for sin, Sir.3.30; 7.10
Almsgiving, discretion in, Sir.12.1–7
Almsgiving, right spirit in, Sir.18.15–18
Angels, 2 Esd.6.41; Tob.12.12–15; Man.15b; 2 Macc.11.6
Anglo-Saxon poem of Judith, Jdt.10.21; 11.17; 12.14
Anointed, Ps.151.6
Antioch, p. 309
Antiochus III the Great, 1 Macc.1.10; 3 Macc.1.1–2
Antiochus IV Epiphanes, 1 Macc.1.10; 3.30; 2 Macc.4.7; p. 294; 4 Macc.1.11; 4.15–26; 17.24
Antiochus V Eupator, 1 Macc.3.33; 2 Macc. 10.10–11
Antiochus VII Sidetes, 1 Macc.15.1
Anti-Semitism, Ad.Est.10.4–11.1
Apocalyptic literature, p. xiv
Apocrypha, meaning of the word, p. xi
Apollonius, governor of Samaria, 1 Macc.3.10
Arrogance, Sir.10.6–18
Arsinoë, 3 Macc.1.1
Art and the Apocrypha, p. xx
Artaxerxes I, 1 Esd.2.16–30
Artaxerxes II, 2 Esd.1.3
Asmodeus, Tob.3.8
Atargatis, 2 Macc.12.26
Athlete, 4 Macc.6.10; 9.8; 11.20; 12.11,14; 16.16; 17.11–12
Atonement, almsgiving and, Sir.3.30
Attharates, 1 Esd.9.49
Authority, 4 Macc.4.5
Azareth, 2 Esd.13.45
Azariah, Prayer of, p. 209; 4 Macc.16.21

Bagoas, Jdt.12.11
Baruch, book of, p. 198
Beccau, p. xx
Behemoth, 2 Esd.6.49–52
Bel and the Dragon, p. 216
Belshazzar, Bar.1.11
Beltethmus, 1 Esd.2.16
Bethulia, Jdt.4.6
Book of Common Prayer, p. xvii

Book of life, 2 Esd.6.20
Bridal chambers, 3 Macc.1.19
Brotherhood, 4 Macc.9.23; 10.15

Caligula, p. 309
Cambyses, 1 Esd.2.16–30
Canon of the Old Testament, the Hebrew, pp. xii, xiv, 2 Esd.14.45; Sir.39.1
Canon of the Old Testament, the Protestant, pp. xii, xvi
Canon of the Old Testament, the Roman Catholic, pp. xv, xvii
Canon, the Hebrew, p. xii, 2 Esd.14.45; Sir. 39.1
Carlstadt, p. xvi
Carmonians, 2 Esd.15.30
Carthage, p. xv
Children, on bringing up, Sir.30.1–13
Chorus, 4 Macc.8.4; 13.8,13
Church of England, p. xvii
Church Fathers and the Apocrypha, pp. xiv–xv
Cilicia, p. 309; 4 Macc.4.2
Coelesyria, 1 Macc.10.69
Columbus, Christopher, pp. xviii, xx
Confessio Esdrae, 2 Esd.8.19b–36
Confession of sin, Bar.1.15–3.8
Contentment, Sir.29.21–28
Coverdale and the Apocrypha, p. x
Craftiness contrasted with wisdom, Sir.19.20–30
Cyrus of Persia, 1 Esd.2.1–15; Bel 1

Dagon, 1 Macc.10.82
Damascus, Jdt.2.27
Damasus, Pope, p. xii
Daniel, 3 Macc.6.7; 4 Macc.16.3,21; 18.13
Daphne, 2 Macc.4.33
Darius I, 1 Esd.2.16–30; 3.2
Dathan, 4 Macc.2.17
David and Goliath, p. xxi, Ps.151
David, Sir.47.1–11; 4 Macc.3.6–18
Dead Sea Scrolls, pp. xxi–xxii, 128, 205, 1 Macc.3.55; 2 Macc.8.23, 4 Macc.6.29, p. 330
De Canonicis Scripturis Libellus, p. xvi
Decretum Gelasianum, p. xv
Defilement, 4 Macc.5.2–3; 7.6
Demetrius I Soter, 1 Macc.7.1; 2 Macc.14.1–10
Demetrius II, 1 Macc.10.67
Demons, Bar.4.7, 35
Deuterocanonical, meaning of, pp. xii–xiii
Dionysus, 2 Macc.6.7; p. 294; 3 Macc.2.29; 3.28
Dositheus, 3 Macc.1.3
Dreams, Sir.34.1–8
Dutch Bible, p. xvi
Duties toward the poor, Sir.4.1–10

Eastern Orthodox Churches, p. xiii
Ecbatana, 1 Esd.6.23

Ptolemy VI Philometor, 1 Macc.1.18; 2 Macc.4.21; 4 Macc.4.22
Ptolemy VII Physcon, 2 Macc.1.10
Punishment for sin, Sir.16.6–23; 3 Macc.2.6, 21–22
Purgatory, disputes over doctrines of, p. xvi
Puritans and the Apocrypha, p. xvii
Purvey, John, p. xv

Qumran, pp. xxi–xxii, 128, 205, 1 Macc.3.55; 2 Macc.8.23; 4 Macc.6.29; p. 330

Raguel, Tob.8.9b–21
Ransom, 4 Macc.6.29; 17.21
Raphael, Tob.3.16–17
Raphia, battle of, 3 Macc.1.1–7
Razis, death of, 2 Macc.14.37–46
Rehum, 1 Esd.2.16
Resurrection, doctrine of the, 2 Macc.7.9 ff.
Retribution, Sir.3.26–31
Return from exile, the, 1 Esd.2.1–15; Bar.5.1–9
Rewards of wisdom, Sir.4.11–18
Roman Catholic Church, pp. xii–xiii, xv, xvii
Rulers, pp. 332–333
Russian Orthodox Church, p. xiii

Sadducees, pp. xxi–xxii
Sacrifices, acceptable and unacceptable, Sir. 3.4.18–35.11
Salathiel, 2 Esd.3.1
Salvadori, p. xx
Samuel, Sir.46.13–20
Sanhedrin, Jdt.11.14
Sapor I, 2 Esd.15.28–63
Savoy Conference, p. xvii
Schedia, 3 Macc.4.11
Schroeder, Father H. J., p. xvii
Scribes, Sir.38.24–39.11
Scythians, 2 Macc.4.47; 3 Macc.7.5; 4 Macc. 10.7
Self-control, Sir.6.2–4; 18.30–19.3; 22.27–23.6
Seleucid era, 1 Macc.1.10, p. 332
Seleucus I Nicanor, 4 Macc.3.20
Seleucus IV Philopator, 2 Macc.3.3; 4 Macc. 3.20
Senate, the Jewish, Jdt.11.14; 1 Macc.12.6
Sennacherib, 3 Macc.6.5
Septuagint, p. xii
Seven brothers, pp. xxii, 309, 4 Macc.8.1–9.9
Shakespeare and the Apocrypha, pp. xviii–xix
Shalmaneser, Tob.1.2; 1.15
Shame, true and false, Sir.41.14–42.14
Simon, son of Mattathias, 1 Macc.13.1–30
Simon, son of Onias, Sir.50.1–24; 3 Macc.2.1–20
Sin, characteristics of, Sir.21.2–3
Sin, confession of, Bar.1.15–3.8
Sins of the flesh, Sir.23.16–27
Sirach, Wisdom of Jesus the Son of, p. 128
Sisinnes, 1 Esd.6.3
Sixtus of Sienna, p. xii
Slander, Sir.28.13–26
Slaves, treatment of, Sir.34.24–31
Slavonic Bibles, p. xiii
Sodom, 3 Macc.2.5

Solomon, Sir.47.12–22
Solomon, Psalms of, p. xxi
Solomon, Wisdom of, p. 102
Son of Man, p. xxii
Song of the Three Young Men, p. 209
Sorites, Wis.6.17–20
Soul, pre-existence of the, 2 Esd.8.4–5; Wis. 8.19
Spartans, 1 Macc.12.1–23
Stoicism, p. 309; 4 Macc.5.7–8; 8.15; 9.7; 12.13,19; 15.4; 17.5
Stones, Ps.151.6
Suffering, 4 Macc.15.13
Suretyship, Sir.29.14–20
Susanna, book of, p. 213
Swiss–German Bible, p. xvi
Swiss Reformers, p. xvii
Synod of Jerusalem, p. xv
Syria, p. 309; 4 Macc.4.2

Tabernacles, feast of, 1 Macc.10.21
Temperance, Sir.31.12–30; 37.27–31
Temple, attempt on the treasury of the, 4 Macc.3.19–4.14
Temple, desecration of the, 1 Macc.1.41–64; 2 Macc.5.1–27
Temple, rededication of the, 1 Macc.4.36–61; 2 Macc.10.1–9
Theodotus, 3 Macc.1.2
Theras, 1 Esd.8.41
Thirty-nine Articles, the, and the Apocrypha, p. x
Timothy, victory over, 2 Macc.10.24–38
Tobit, book of, p. 63
Tongue, the, Sir.20.1–26; 23.7–15
Transformation, 4 Macc.9.22
Trent, the Council of, pp. ix, xii, xvii
Tyranny, 4 Macc.1.11; 8.15

Uriel, 2 Esd.4.1
Urim and Thummim, 1 Esd.5.40

Vengeance, Sir.22.30–28.7
Virgins, 3 Macc.1.18
Virtues, the four cardinal, Wis.8.7

Weeks, feast of, 2 Macc.12.31
Westminster Confession of Faith, the, and the Apocrypha, p. x
Wife, the wicked and the good, Sir.26.5–18
Wisdom, divine, Sir.1.1–10 ff.
Wisdom, given to Israel, Bar.3.9–4.4
Wisdom of Solomon, p. 102
Wisdom, twenty-one attributes of, Wis. 7.22b–23
Women, Sir.25.13–26; 42.12–14
Wyclif, John, p. xv

Yeṣer, the evil, 2 Esd.4.30; 7.[48], [92]; Sir. 15.14

Zerubbabel, 1 Esd.4.13–32
Zeus, Olympian, 1 Macc.1.54
Zurich Bible, p. xvi

35 M-177-RT

NOTES

NOTES

NOTES

NOTES